THE HUNDRED THOUSAND
SONGS OF *Milarepa*

The life-story and teaching of the greatest Poet-Saint ever to appear in the history of Buddhism.

SHAMBHALA   *Boston & London*   1999

THE HUNDRED THOUSAND

SONGS OF *Milarepa*

TRANSLATED AND ANNOTATED

BY *Garma C. C. Chang*

Shambhala Publications, Inc.
Horticultural Hall
300 Massachusetts Avenue
Boston, Massachusetts 02115
www.shambhala.com

Published by arrangement with Carol Publishing Group, Inc.,
Secaucus, NJ © 1962 Oriental Studies Foundation

14   13   12   11   10   9   8   7

Printed in the United States of America

♾ This edition is printed on acid-free paper that meets the
American National Standards Institute Z39.48 Standard.

♻ This book is printed on 30% postconsumer recycled paper.
For more information please visit www.shambhala.com.

Distributed in the United States by Penguin Random House LLC
and in Canada by Random House of Canada Ltd

Library of Congress Cataloging-in-Publication Data
Mi-la-ras-pa, 1040–1123.
[Songs. English]
The hundred thousand songs of Milarepa
p.   cm.
ISBN 978-1-57062-476-6 (cloth)
1. Mi-la-ras-pa, 1040–1123.   2. Lamas—China—Tibet—
Biography—Early works to 1800.   3. Spiritual life—
Buddhism—Early works to 1800.
BQ7950.M5571999
294.3'923'092—dc21
[B]   98-43692
CIP

To the memory of

My Guru

His Holiness, Lama Kong Ka

To my wife

Hsiang-hsiang

and

To my Brother-in-the-Dharma

Peter Gruber

without whom the publication of this

book would not have been possible

FOREWORD

M Y FIRST meeting with the translator of this book goes back to the year 1947. We met in Darjeeling, a resort town in the foothills of the Himalaya Mountains. He had just come from Tibet, a distance which, though not far from Darjeeling, has to be measured in the number of days' travel by horses and yaks. Tibet was then a great mystery and source of curiosity to most people; the country was still closed to foreigners and only a few Europeans had been there. The barrier, however, was less stringent on the Chinese side. With this advantage, Mr. Chang had left China for Tibet in the late 1930's to search for Dharma and Enlightenment. He traveled extensively in the Kham region of Tibet and studied Buddhism in various monasteries for more than eight years. His fascinating and inspiring adventures in this "innermost part of Tibet" are a matter for another book. Because of his long years of study and practice in Tibet, his personal devotion and committment to Buddhism, and his first-hand experience of the lives of the Tibetan people, he is best qualified to translate this great Tibetan classic, *The Hundred Thousand Songs of Milarepa,* which, up to the present, has not appeared in complete translation in any Western language.

But what contribution has this book to make to a modern man, with no time to read, who has already been swamped in a *flood* of books? To answer this question, some relevant facts should first be reviewed.

If the average modern man is asked what he is living for, and what is the aim of his striving, he will probably tell you, with some embarrassment, that he lives "to enjoy life," "to support his family," "to have fun," "to make money," or "to achieve something meaningful and worthwhile." But in reality, we are all aware that no one seems to know exactly *what* he is living for. If he broods over the things surrounding him and the kind of world he is living in, he will soon become skeptical about the relevance of raising these questions. He cannot help but ask honestly, "Can we really know the right answers, do we have any choice over these matters, and after all, what difference will it make?"

In spite of the unavoidable resignation and bewilderment that the modern man feels, sooner or later he finds himself compelled to choose between two alternatives: he can either turn to religion with blind faith and hope, or turn to the world and "make the best of it." It is certain that men choose the former, not always because they are convinced of the truth of religion, but rather because doubt and despair have made their lives unbearable. On the other hand, they choose the latter, not because they have proved the untruth of religion, but because, in all likelihood, their spirits are deadened by pessimism and indifference. One fact, however, remains clear: in both cases the choice is made under the coercion of pain, sorrow, or despair.

It is common knowledge that an awareness of impending peril stirs men to act and to strive, that an awakening to man's limitations and helplessness in the face of the Universe, inspires him to pursue the "beyond" and the eternal. Thus both heaven and earth, Nirvāṇa and Saṃsāra, owe their births to human sufferings and despair. A thoughtful man must ask: "Is it really advantageous to lead a life without any suffering? Are not misfortune and grief prerequisites for spiritual awakening? From the ultimate viewpoint, are we, the sophisticated 'men-of-abundant-knowledge-and-possessions,' truly better off than the 'men-of-ignorance-and-scarcity' of olden times?" Let us think twice before we give an affirmative answer to these questions. Let us also ponder on some further ones: "Is it not true that science and technology, at their best, can alleviate but not eliminate the sufferings of men? Can plastic surgery, or the 'face-lift,' really make a miserable old woman happy? Does it really matter much whether or not we can defer our entrance into the grave for ten or fifteen years beyond schedule?" Many ingenious devices have been invented to conceal the unpleasant facts of life, and many gadgets have been created to gratify men's insatiable desires; but in the final analysis, what else have these contrivances brought us save their contributions to a fool's paradise for men to live in? Science, as some wise man has said, "makes major contributions to minor needs." Religion, whether or not it comes up with anything, at least is at work on the things that are truly important.

Deluded by material achievements and comforts, the majority of modern men are deprived of the opportunity and privileges of leading a rich spiritual life as their forefathers once did. In just reading a few stories of this great Tibetan classic, *The Hundred Thousand Songs of Milarepa*, we can readily find evidence that it was immeasurably easier for the "backward" Tibetans to contact the spiritual verities and to lead devotional lives than for their more "advanced" contemporaries. The reason for this is apparent: *They had much simpler minds and they led much simpler lives.* Being closer to the sheer *facts* of life uncloaked by camouflage and disguises, they had more opportunity to observe its sufferings and transiency; and in closer contact with Gurus and Saints they could draw more inspiration from them as witnesses of the concrete results and rewards of a devotional life. But the majority of modern men are deprived of these privileges, for they are living in a civilization which a keen observer has wisely defined as "one vast conspiracy against the spiritual life." And so the wave of Karma keeps on rolling, and one is swept along by it regardless of his unwillingness and dismay. No one is foolish enough to think that the world will reverse itself and return to "the good old days"; what is gone is gone. All one can do, perhaps, is to make use of the best that the past has bequeathed us and apply it to the future and to the "here and now." Any person, message, or action that may spark a spiritual inspiration for men who must live in this age of spiritual un-dernourishment should, therefore, be of great value to all concerned, because they are what we need most, and what so rarely appear in our time.

With this view in mind, Mr. Chang has spent many years in pre-paring the English translation of this great spiritual classic of Tibet, the *Mila Grubum*, or *The Hundred Thousand Songs of Milarepa*, in the hope of making it available to the people of the West.

What kind of a book is the *Mila Grubum?* An adequate answer to this question is extremely difficult to make. Beyond doubt, it is one of the greatest religious classics, ranking with the *Mahābhārata, the Ava-taṃsaka Sūtra*, the Old and New Testaments, and the like. But at the same time, it is far more — a different kind of book in its *own* right, and no real parallel can be found in the literary field. Because of its unique style, unusual setting, and comprehensive content, the *Mila Grubum* is a book hard to introduce and to appraise in the ordinary sense. Therefore, the best answer to the question, "What kind of a book is this *Mila Grubum?*" should be given by the individual reader himself through his own understanding and appreciation.

I can perhaps speak now for myself as to why, among the many great religious classics, the *Mila Grubum* is a personal favorite. To name just a few, I may say first of all that I found this book to be an inexhaustible fountainhead of inspiration, an immense treasury of spiritual teachings, a repository of yogic instructions, a guide on the Bodhi-Path, and above all, an unfailing friend of the sincere devotee. Secondly, it provides inside information on the religious life of the Tibetan people — laymen, yogis, and monks alike — presenting a vivid picture of their spiritual problems, strivings, and accomplishments. In this book the profoundest ideas and teachings of Buddhism are re-vealed in sixty-one fascinating stories presented in simple language. The reading, therefore, is extremely pleasant and interesting. Since each story is an account of Milarepa's personal experience in a specific situation, the messages and instructions given therein carry, inherently, an unusual persuasive power and charm which truly move one to greater conviction, wider consolation, and deeper insight. In addition, the *Grubum* contains clear descriptions and unequivocal evaluations of critical yogic experiences, including those of the most advanced stages, hitherto unrevealed in other scriptures.

If to evaluate the *Mila Grubum* is difficult, to praise it is even more so. Words, after all, may not be a good means of praise for a book of this kind. My sincere hope is that the readers may share with me, in silence and joy, a most rewarding experience in reading this beloved book of Tibet as millions of Tibetans once did, in the recent past and long ago.

PETER GRUBER

Oriental Studies Foundation
New York
September, 1962

A WORD FROM
THE TRANSLATOR

My Commentary, to be found in the Appendix under the title of "The 'Hundred Thousand Songs of Milarepa' — Its Origin, Background, Function, and Translation," was originally designed to serve as an Introduction to this book. But in order to encourage the general reader's direct contact with the text itself, I have transferred my comments to the Appendix — together with other material of particular interest to serious students and scholars. For them, it is strongly recommended that this Commentary be read first.

For readers who are not acquainted with the Tibetan literature, the actual sequence of the stories may not be the best way in which to read them. They follow each other in an interconnection which will be apparent enough to persons familiar with Tibetan literature; but the sequence may be more difficult to new readers. For them, I have starred certain representative stories in the Table of Contents, and recommend that they be read first. These will provide a cross-section of the three Parts into which the text is divided: Part One, stories concerned principally with Milarepa's subjugation and conversion of demons; Part Two, Milarepa's relationships with and instructions to his human disciples; and Part Three, miscellaneous stories that fall into no specific category.

The stories in this book cover a wide range of spiritual problems and their solutions in the light of Buddhist doctrine and of mystic and yogic experiences. For information on Milarepa's life and the central Teaching of Tibetan Tantrism, please see my Commentary in the Appendix.

Tibetan terms in the explanatory Notes are enclosed in parentheses and preceded by the letters "T.T.", denoting that these are Tibetan transcriptions as rendered in the English alphabet.

I wish to express my sincerest gratitude to the Bollingen Foundation for its generous grant, which has made possible the completion of this work; to Mrs. Dorothy C. Donath and Mr. Gerald Yorke for their most helpful editorial suggestions and assistance; to Miss Toni Schmid of the Statens Ethnografiska Museum, Stockholm, Sweden, for her kind permission to use an illustration from her beautiful book, *The*

Cotton-clad Mila, as our frontispiece; to Dr. W. Y. Evans-Wentz, Miss Natasha Rambova, Mr. Peter Gruber, and Miss Gwendolyn Winser, for their constant encouragement and aid; and to my wife, Hsiang-hsiang, for the typing of the entire manuscript and for her unfailing help and interest throughout the translation of this book.

GARMA C. C. CHANG

CONTENTS

VOLUME I

PART THREE. Miscellaneous Stories

APPENDIX

*It is recommended that these stories be read first. See "A Word from the Translator," p. xiii.

PART ONE

MILAREPA'S SUBJUGATION AND CONVERSION OF DEMONS

THE TALE OF RED ROCK
JEWEL VALLEY

Obeisance to all Gurus

Once the great Yogi Milarepa was staying at the Eagle Castle of [Red Rock] Jewel Valley,[1] absorbing himself in the practice of the Mahāmudrā meditation.[2] Feeling hungry, he decided to prepare some food, but after looking about he found there was nothing left in the cave, neither water nor fuel, let alone salt, oil, or flour. "It seems that I have neglected things too much!" he said, "I must go out and collect some wood."

He went out. But when he had gathered a handful of twigs, a sudden storm arose, and the wind was strong enough to blow away the wood and tear his ragged robe. When he tried to hold the robe together, the wood blew away. When he tried to clutch the wood, the robe blew apart. [Frustrated], Milarepa thought, "Although I have been practicing the Dharma[3] and living in solitude for such a long time, I am still not rid of ego-clinging! What is the use of practicing Dharma if one cannot subdue ego-clinging? Let the wind blow my wood away if it likes. Let the wind blow my robe off if it wishes!" Thinking thus, he ceased resisting. But, due to weakness from lack of food, with the next gust of wind he could no longer withstand the storm, and fell down in a faint.

When he came to, the storm was over. High up on the branch of a tree he saw a shred of his clothing swaying in the gentle breeze. The utter futility of this world and all its affairs struck Milarepa, and a strong feeling of renunciation overwhelmed him. Sitting down upon a rock, he meditated once more.

Soon, a cluster of white clouds rose from Dro Wo Valley[4] far away to the East. "Below this bank of clouds lies the temple of my Guru, the great Translator Marpa,"[5] mused Milarepa, "At this very

1

moment He and His wife must be preaching the doctrines of Tantra, giving initiation and instruction to my brothers. Yes, my Guru is there. If I could go there now, I should be able to see Him." An immeasurable, unbearable longing for his teacher arose in his heart as he thought despairingly of his Guru. His eyes filled with tears, and he began to sing a song, "Thoughts of My Guru":

> In thoughts of you, Father Marpa, my
>   suffering is relieved;
> I, the mendicant, now sing you a fervent song.

> Above Red Rock Jewel Valley, in the East,
> Floats a cluster of white clouds;
> Beneath them, like a rearing elephant, a
>   huge mountain towers;
> Beside it, like a lion leaping, looms another peak.

> In the temple of Dro Wo Valley rests a great
>   seat of stone;
> Who is now enthroned there?
> Is it Marpa the Translator?
> If it were you, I would be joyful and happy.
> Though limited in reverence, I wish to see you;
> Though weak in faith, I wish to join you.
> The more I meditate, the more I long for my Guru.

> Does your wife, Dagmema, still dwell with you?
> To her I am more grateful than to my mother.
> If she is there I will be joyful and happy.
> Though long the journey, I wish to see her,
> Though perilous the road, I wish to join her.
> The more I contemplate, the more I think of you;
> The more I meditate, the more I think of my Guru.

> How happy I would be could I join the gathering,
> At which you may be preaching the Hevajra Tantra.[6]
> Though of simple mind, I wish to learn.
> Though ignorant, I long to recite.
> The more I contemplate, the more I think of you;
> The more I meditate, the more I think of my Guru.

> You may now be giving the Four Symbolic
>   Initiations[7] of the Oral Transmission;[8]

If I could join the gathering, I would be
　　joyful and happy.
Though lacking merit, I wish to be initiated—
Though too poor to offer much, I desire it.
The more I contemplate, the more I think of you;
The more I meditate, the more I think of my Guru.

You may now be teaching the Six Yogas
　　of Nāropa;[9]
If I could be there, I would be joyful and happy.
Though short my diligence, I have need for
　　learning;
Though poor my perseverance, I wish to practice.
The more I contemplate, the more I think of you;
The more I meditate, the more I think of my Guru.

The brothers from Weu and Tsang may be there.
If so, I would be joyful and happy.
Though inferior my Experience and Realization,
I wish to compare mine with theirs.
Though in my deepest faith and veneration
I have never been apart from you,
I am now tortured by my need to see you.
This fervent longing agonizes me,
This great torment suffocates me.
Pray, my gracious Guru, relieve me from this
　　torment.

No sooner had Milarepa finished than the Revered One, the Jet-sun[10] Marpa, appeared on a cluster of rainbow clouds resembling a robe of five colors. With an ever-increasing [celestial] radiance suffusing his countenance, and riding a lion with rich trappings, he approached Milarepa.

"Great Sorcerer,[11] my son, why with such deep emotion," he asked, "did you call to me so desperately? Why do you struggle so? Have you not an abiding faith in your Guru and Patron Buddha? Does the outer world attract you with disturbing thoughts?[12] Do the Eight Worldly Winds[13] howl in your cave? Do fear and longing sap your strength? Have you not continuously offered service to the Guru and to the Three Precious Ones[14] above? Have you not dedicated your merits to sentient beings[15] in the Six Realms?[16] Have not you yourself reached that state of grace in which you can purify your sins and achieve merits? No matter what the cause, you may be certain that we will never part. Thus, for the sake of the Dharma and the welfare of sentient beings, continue your meditation."

Inspired by this sublimely joyous vision, Milarepa sang in reply:

When I see my Guru's countenance and hear his words,
I, the mendicant, am stirred by the Prāṇa in
        my heart.[17]
In remembrance of the teachings of my Guru,
Respect and reverence arise in my heart.
His compassionate blessings enter me;
All destructive thoughts[18] are banished.

My earnest song, called "Thoughts of my Guru,"
Must surely have been heard by you, my teacher;
Yet am I still in darkness.
Pray, pity me and grant me your protection!

Indomitable perseverance
Is the highest offering to my Guru.
The best way to please Him
Is to endure the hardship of meditation!
Abiding in this cave, alone,
Is the noblest service to the Ḍākinīs![19]
To devote myself to the Holy Dharma
Is the best service to Buddhism—
To devote my life to meditation, thus
To aid my helpless, sentient fellow beings!
To love death and sickness is a blessing
Through which to cleanse one's sins;
To refuse forbidden food helps one to attain
Realization and Enlightenment;
To repay my Father Guru's bounties
I meditate, and meditate again.

Guru mine, pray grant me your protection!
Help this mendicant to stay ever in his hermitage.

Exalted, Milarepa adjusted his robe and carried a handful of wood back to his cave. Inside, he was startled to find five Indian demons with eyes as large as saucers. One was sitting on his bed and preaching, two were listening to the sermon, another was preparing and offering food, and the last was studying Milarepa's books.

Following his initial shock, Milarepa thought, "These must be magical apparitions of the local deities who dislike me. Although I have been living here a long time, I have never given them any offering or compliment." He then began to sing a "Complimentary Song to the Deities of Red Rock Jewel Valley":

> This lonely spot where stands my hut
> Is a place pleasing to the Buddhas,
> A place where accomplished beings dwell,
> A refuge where I dwell alone.
>
> Above Red Rock Jewel Valley
> White clouds are gliding;
> Below, the Tsang River gently flows;
> Wild vultures wheel between.
>
> Bees are humming among the flowers,
> Intoxicated by their fragrance;
> In the trees birds swoop and dart,
> Filling the air with their song.
>
> In Red Rock Jewel Valley
> Young sparrows learn to fly,
> Monkeys love to leap and swing,
> And beasts to run and race,
> While I practice the Two Bodhi-Minds[20]
>   and love to meditate.
>
> Ye local demons,[21] ghosts,[22] and gods,
> All friends of Milarepa,
> Drink the nectar of kindness and compassion,
> Then return to your abodes.

But the Indian demons did not vanish, and stared balefully at Milarepa. Two of them advanced, one grimacing and biting his lower lip, and the other grinding his teeth horribly. A third, coming up behind, gave a violent, malicious laugh and shouted loudly, as they all tried to frighten Milarepa with fearful grimaces and gestures.

Milarepa, knowing their evil motives, began the Wrathful Buddha Meditation and recited forcefully a powerful incantation.[23] Still the demons would not leave. Then, with great compassion, he preached the Dharma to them; yet they still remained.

Milarepa finally declared, "Through the mercy of Marpa, *I have already fully realized that all beings and all phenomena are of one's own mind. The mind itself is a transparency of Voidness.*[24] *What,*

therefore, is the use of all this, and how foolish I am to try to dispel
these manifestations physically!"[25]

Then Milarepa, in a dauntless mood, sang "The Song of Realization":

Father Guru, who conquered the Four Demons,[26]
I bow to you, Marpa the Translator.

I, whom you see, the man with a name,
Son of Darsen Gharmo,[27]
Was nurtured in my mother's womb,
Completing the Three Veins.[28]
A baby, I slept in my cradle;
A youth, I watched the door;
A man, I lived on the high mountain.

Though the storm on the snow peak is awesome,
I have no fear.
Though the precipice is steep and perilous,
I am not afraid!

I, whom you see, the man with a name,
Am a son of the Golden Eagle;[29]
I grew wings and feathers in the egg.
A child, I slept in my cradle;
A youth, I watched the door;
A man, I flew in the sky.
Though the sky is high and wide, I do not fear;
Though the way is steep and narrow, I am not afraid.

I, whom you see, the man with a name,
Am a son of Nya Chen Yor Mo,[30] the King of fishes.
In my mother's womb, I rolled my golden eyes;
A child, I slept in my cradle;
A youth, I learned to swim;
A man, I swam in the great ocean.
Though thundering waves are frightening,
    I do not fear;
Though fishing hooks abound, I am not afraid.

I, whom you see, the man with a name,
Am a son of Ghagyu Lamas.
Faith grew in my mother's womb.
A baby, I entered the door of Dharma;

A youth, I studied Buddha's teaching;
A man, I lived alone in caves.
Though demons, ghosts, and devils multiply,
    I am not afraid.

The snow-lion's paws are never frozen,
Or of what use would it be
To call the lion "King"—
He who has the Three Perfect Powers.[31]

The eagle never falls down from the sky;
If so, would that not be absurd?
An iron block cannot be cracked by a stone;
If so, why refine the iron ore?
I, Milarepa, fear neither demons nor evils;
If they frightened Milarepa, to what avail
Would be his Realization and Enlightenment?

Ye ghosts and demons, enemies of the Dharma,
    I welcome you today!
It is my pleasure to receive you!
I pray you, stay; do not hasten to leave;
We will discourse and play together.
Although you would be gone, stay the night;
We will pit the Black against the White Dharma,[32]
And see who plays the best.

Before you came, you vowed to afflict me.
Shame and disgrace would follow
If you returned with this vow unfulfilled.

Milarepa arose with confidence and rushed straight at the demons in his cave. Frightened, they shrank back, rolling their eyes in despair and trembling violently. Then, swirling together like a whirlpool, they all merged into one and vanished.

"This was the Demon King, Vināyaka[33] the Obstacle-Maker, who came searching for evil opportunities," thought Milarepa. "The storm, too, was undoubtedly his creation. By the mercy of my Guru he had no chance to harm me."

After this, Milarepa gained immeasurable spiritual progress.

This story relates the attack of the Demon King Vināyaka; it has three different meanings, and hence may be called either "The Six Ways of Thinking of My Guru," "The Tale of Red Rock Jewel Valley," or "The Story of Milarepa Collecting Wood."

NOTES

1 The Eagle Castle of Red Rock Jewel Valley (T.T.: mChoñ.Luñ. Khyuñ. Gi.rDsoñ.). Although "mChoñ" usually means to leap or jump, here it seems better to translate it as "Gem," or "Jewel" — the other meaning of the word.

2 Mahāmudrā (T.T.: Phyag.rGya.Chen.Po.), meaning the "Great Symbol," is the practical teaching of Śūnyatā (Voidness). Śūnyatā is the principle that stresses the non-existence of the "substance" of all beings, which is the most important doctrine of Mahāyāna Buddhism as well as of Tibetan Tantrism. According to some Tibetan scholars, the Mādhyamika (Middle Way Doctrine), is a teaching of Śūnyatā in its general form, while Mahāmudrā is a teaching of Śūnyatā by which one can actually put the Mādhyamika principles into practice. Mādhyamika is often referred to as the "Theory of Voidness," and Mahāmudrā, "The Practice of Voidness."

At this point a few words on "Voidness" may be helpful. When we say "That house is empty," we mean that it contains no occupants; but Buddhist "Voidness" *does not mean absence.* When we say, "That whole block is now empty," we mean there were houses in the block before, but none exist now; but Buddhist "Voidness" *does not mean extinction.* Voidness is difficult to define and describe. We can say a great deal about what Voidness is *not,* but very little about what it *is.* Voidness denotes the relative, flowing, undefinable, and ungraspable nature of all things. Philosophically it represents the illusory and dream-like nature of phenomena; psychologically it signifies a total liberation from all bondage.

The Whispered Transmission School (Ghagyuba, T.T.: bKah.rGyud.Pa.) and the Old School (Ningmaba, T.T.: rÑiñ.Ma.Pa.) in Tibet, regard Mahāmudrā as the highest and most important of all the teachings of Buddhism. But the Yellow School (Gelugba, T.T.: dGe.Lugs.Pa.) does not entirely agree with this view.

Mahāmudrā is, in many ways, very similar to Chinese Ch'an (Zen.) See the translator's "Yogic Commentary" in "Tibetan Yoga and Secret Doctrines," 2nd ed., W. Y. Evans-Wentz, Ed., Oxford University Press, London, 1958.

3 Dharma: This term, most frequently employed in Buddhist literature, has two common usages: to denote the teaching of Buddha, sometimes translated as the Law or Doctrine; and to denote being or objects. Here it is used in the former sense.

4 Dro Wo Valley: the location of Marpa's temple.

5 Marpa the Translator was Milarepa's teacher. He was a great scholar as well as a great yogi, who founded the Oral, or Whispered Transmission School (Ghagyuba) of Tibet.

6 Hevajra: a Sanskrit name; its Tibetan equivalent is dGyes.Pa.rDor.rJe. To help readers who are not familiar with the Tibetan words, many equivalent Sanskrit names and terms are also used in the translation and Notes.

7 The Four Symbolic Initiations (T.T.: dWañ.bShi.): The first initiation is called "The Initiation of the Vase." The person who has taken it is allowed to practice Mantra Yoga. The second is called "The Secret Initiation," and gives the initiate the privilege of practicing Prāna Yoga. The third is called "The Wisdom Initiation," and allows the initiate to practice advanced Prāna Yoga. The fourth is called "The Symbolic Initiation," and confers the privilege of practicing Mahāmudrā Yoga. These four initiations embrace almost all the major teachings of Tibetan Tantrism.

8 The Oral Transmission (T.T.: bKah.rGyud.Pa.), is translated in this book

in several different ways: Whispered, or Oral Succession, Transmission, or Lineage. This School (the Ghagyuba) in its early period, stressed the Yoga practice and tradition — including secrecy by transmitting the teachings orally. Later, when it grew into a large monastic Order, this tradition was partially lost.

9 Naro Chu Dru (T.T.: Naro.Chos.Drug.): The Six Yogas of Nāropa are as follows: (1) Heat Yoga, (2) Dream Yoga, (3) Illusory Body Yoga, (4) Bardo Yoga, (5) Yoga of Transformation, and (6) Yoga of Light.

10 Jetsun (T.T.: rJe.bTsun.): A Tibetan term of reverence and respect given to religious leaders, saints, and great teachers.

11 Great Sorcerer: Milarepa's nickname. See Milarepa's Biography. "Tibet's Great Yogi, Milarepa," W. Y. Evans-Wentz, Ed., Oxford University Press, London, 1951.

12 Disturbing thoughts, Nhamdog (T.T.: rNam.rTog.) is a very frequently used term in Buddhist literature as well as in this book. Nhamdog has many meanings, the most common one being "disturbing thoughts" or "flowing thoughts." This constant flow of thoughts never stops, though men may not be aware of its existence. To curb and halt this unceasing thought-flow is a prerequisite for the attainment of Samādhi. Nhamdog also means wild thoughts, wrong judgements, fantasy, whims, imagination, impulse, and so forth.

13 Eight Worldly Winds or Dharmas (T.T.: Chos.brGyad.): the eight "winds," or influences, which fan the passions, i.e., gain, loss; defamation, eulogy; praise, ridicule; sorrow, joy. This term is also translated in this book as "Eight Worldly Desires."

14 The Three Precious Ones, or the Three Gems: the Buddha; the Dharma; and the Saṅgha. Buddha is He who has attained Perfect Enlightenment, Dharma is His teachings, Saṅgha the enlightened Buddhist sages.

15 Sentient beings: a term for mankind and all living beings, for whose benefit Dharmic training is undertaken and to whom all merits are dedicated.

16 Six Realms, or Six Lokas: the six Realms in Saṃsāra, i.e., the Realms of Hell, of Hungry Ghosts, of Animals, of Asuras or Non-men, of Mankind, and of the Heavenly Beings.

17 Heart-Prāṇa or Heart-Wind (T.T.: sÑiñ.Rluñ.; pron.: Nin Lung): It is believed that most visions seen and emotions felt in meditation are caused by Prāṇa from the Heart Center.

18 Destructive thoughts: non-Dharmic thoughts, or thoughts which are against the Buddhist teachings.

19 Ḍākinīs (T.T.: mKhah.hGro.Ma.): female sky-travelers, or goddesses. Ḍākinīs are female deities who play very important roles in performing various Tantric acts.

20 The Two Bodhi-Minds (T.T.: Byañ.Chub.Sems.gÑis.): These are the Mundane and the Transcendental Bodhi-Minds (T.T.: Kun.rDsob. [and] Don.Dam. Byañ.Chub.Gyi.Sems.); or the Bodhi-Mind-as-a-Wish (sMon.Pa.Byañ.Chub.Gyi. Sems.) and the Bodhi-Mind-as-a-Practice (sPyod.Pa.Byañ.Chub.Gyi.Sems.). Bodhi-Mind is perhaps the most important term which symbolizes and represents the central spirit, idea, and principle of Mahāyāna Buddhism. Because of its manifold meanings and usages, Bodhi-Mind (Skt: Bodhicitta; T.T.: Byañ.Chub.Sems.) is extremely difficult to translate. Bodhi-Mind can perhaps be roughly described as the wish, vow, aspiration, and realization of the noble idea of bringing oneself and all sentient beings to the state of great perfection — Buddhahood. The following are a few examples of the variance of this term in denoting the different aspects of the Bodhi-Mind:

(1) Bodhi-Mind-as-a-Wish: the wish, vow, or aspiration to deliver all

sentient beings from all suffering, and to bring them to the state of Buddhahood.

(2) Bodhi-Mind-as-Practice: the aspiration, determination, and practice of all meritorious deeds in the light of Dharma, which include the Six Pāramitās, and other Bodhisattvic practices.

(3) Mundane Bodhi-Mind: the Bodhi-Mind of a person who has not yet realized the truth of Sūnyatā (Voidness).

(4) Transcendental Bodhi-Mind: the Bodhi-Mind of a person who has realized the truth of Sūnyatā (Voidness).

(5) Bodhi-Mind, as "borrowed" by Tantrism, is used to denote the essence of the positive and negative energy, i.e., seed or semen (T.T.: Tig.Le.)

Bodhi-Mind is sometimes translated in different contexts as Bodhi-Heart, Heart-for-Bodhi, Enlightened Mind, and the Great Compassionate Mind.

21 Lit.: Jung Bo (T.T.: hByuñ.Po.): a type of Tibetan demon.

22 Lit.: Non-men (T.T.: Mi.Ma.Yin.): the general term for demons, ghosts, Asuras, or heavenly beings.

23 Powerful incantation (T.T.: Drag.sÑags.): a potent Mantra or spell to dispel demons and obstacles. It includes mantras, mudrās, visualization, and other ritualistic practices.

24 According to Mahāmudrā, the nature of mind can best be described as being the Illumination-of-Voidness, or the Illuminating-Void (T.T.: gSal.sToñ.). It teaches that the primordial nature of mind is not only "void" in its essence, but is also an illuminating self-awareness embodied in the Void.

25 Lit.: " . . . how foolish I am to try to dispel these demons and troublemakers outwardly."

26 Four Demons: the four major hindrances that impede one's spiritual progress are figuratively called "The Four Demons." They are: the demons of illness, of interruption, of death, and of desires and passions.

27 Darsen Gharmo: the name of the snow lioness. See first song of Story 4.

28 Lit.: Completing the Three Nādis. These are the three mystic Channels in the human body — the Right, the Left, and the Center. The Right Channel (T.T.: Ro.Ma.rTsa.; Skt.: Pingalā Nādi), is said to correspond to the solar system; the Left (T.T.: rKyañ.Ma.rTsa.; Skt.: Idā Nādi) to the lunar system; the Center Channel (T.T.: dBu.Ma.rTsa.; Skt.: Susumnā Nādi) to Unity. Tibetan scholars have given many differing opinions and explanations regarding these three mystical Channels. A single clear-cut dèfinition or description of them is very difficult.

29 Lit.: The King-bird Eagle (T.T.: Bya.rGyal.Khyañ.) or the Gāruda bird.

30 Nya Chen Yor Mo (T.T.: Ña.Chen.Yor.Mo.): the King of all fish, according to Tibetan legend.

31 The translator is not certain as to what these three legendary "perfect powers of the lion" found in Tibetan folklore may be. However, they do imply three superior qualities of this animal.

32 The Black Dharma is black magic; the white Dharma, the teaching of Buddha.

33 Vināyaka (T.T.: Bi.Na.Ya.Ga.): A particular class of demon. According to some sources, it is another name for "Ganêsa" or for "Gāruda."

2

THE JOURNEY TO LASHI

Obeisance to all Gurus

ONCE, when the great Master of Yoga, Jetsun[1] Milarepa, was staying in the Jewel Valley hermitage, he thought, "I should obey my Guru's order to go to Lashi Snow Mountain and practice meditation there," and set out for that place.

Milarepa approached Nya Non Tsar Ma, the gateway to Lashi Snow Mountain, where the people of Tsar Ma were holding a drinking party. In their talk, someone asked, "Do you know that at the present time there lives a great yogi called Milarepa? He always dwells alone in the snow mountains, in remote and uninhabited places, observing an ascetic discipline which none except the perfect Buddhist can attain. Have you ever heard of him?" While they were thus praising the Jetsun, Milarepa arrived at the door. A beautiful girl named Lesebum, decked with rich ornaments, greeted him there, asking, "Who are you and where do you come from?" "Dear hostess," Milarepa replied, "I am the Yogi Milarepa, who always dwells in unknown places in the mountains. I came here to beg food." "I will gladly give you some," said the girl, "but are you really Milarepa?" He replied, "There is no reason why I should lie to you." The girl, delighted, immediately rushed back into the house to spread the news. She called all the revelers, saying, "You were talking about that celebrated yogi who lives so far away. He is now standing at the door."

Everyone rushed to the door, some making obeisance to the Jetsun, others asking him various questions. All became aware that he was the actual Milarepa. Then they invited him in, paid him great respect and reverence, and gave him food.

The hostess, a rich young girl named Shindormo, extended her hospitality to the Jetsun, and asked, "Revered one, may I ask where you are going?" Milarepa replied, "I am on my way to Lashi Snow Mountain to practice meditation." The girl then said, "We hope you will grant us the boon of staying in Dreloon Joomoo and blessing this place. We will provide all the food you need without any effort on your part."

Among the guests was a teacher called Shaja Guna, who said to Milarepa, "If you would be kind enough to remain here in Dreloon Joomoo, the valley of ghosts, it would help you and would also help us. I shall try my best to serve you." A layman exclaimed, "How wonderful it would be if we could have the great Yogi staying with us! I have a fine cattle farm, but the demons and ghosts are becoming so bold that they actually appear [even in the daytime]! They are so vicious that even I do not dare to go near the place any more. I beseech you, in your kindness and grace, to vist my farm very soon." All the guests then made obeisance to the Jetsun, begging him to go to the farm.

Milarepa replied, "I will go there at once—not because of your farm and cattle, but in obedience to my Guru."

"We are satisfied as long as you have promised to go," they declared. "Now, let us prepare the best food and arrange for your departure."

Milarepa then said, "I am accustomed to solitude . . . I dwell in a hermitage and need neither companionship nor good food. But please accept my gratitude for your thoughtfulness in offering it. First, I should like to go to the farm alone. Afterwards, you may come and see what has been done."

When Milarepa arrived at the foot of the mountain, the Non-men created frightful hallucinations to harass him. The path to the top of the peak, which seemed to reach to the sky, quaked and tossed. Angry thunder rolled, jagged lightning struck all around, and the mountains on both sides trembled and shifted. The river suddenly became a raging torrent and burst its banks, turning the valley into a vast lake, in later years called Demon Lake. Milarepa arose and made a gesture, and the flood at once subsided. He went on to the lower part of the valley. The demons shattered the mountains on both sides, and showers of tumbling rocks fell like heavy rain. Then the Hill Goddess created for the Jetsun a path like a running snake along the range, a track later called Hill Goddess Path [or Ḍākinī's Ridge]. This subdued all the lesser demons, but the greater and more powerful demons, angered by their failure, gathered round the end of Hill Goddess Path to unleash a new attack. Milarepa concentrated his mind, and made another mystic gesture to subdue them. Suddenly all the evil visions disappeared. A footprint was impressed in the rock where Milarepa had stood.[2] He had gone only a few steps when the whole sky cleared. In an exalted mood, he then sat down at the top of the hill; he entered the Samādhi of Mercy,[3] and an immeasurable compassion toward all sentient beings arose in his heart. Because of this, Milarepa experienced great spiritual growth and inspiration. Later, the place where he sat was called the Hill of Mercy.

Milarepa then went to the bank of the river [lit.: Good River], where he practiced the Flowing-River Yoga [Samādhi].⁴

On the tenth day of the autumn moon of the Fire Tiger Year, a demon from Nepal called Bha Ro, leading a vast demonic army which filled the earth and sky in the valley of Good River, came to challenge Milarepa. The demons shifted the mountains and threw them down upon the Jetsun, and attacked him with thunderbolts and a rain of weapons. They screamed at him, abusing him with threats: "We'll kill you! We'll tie you up and chop you into pieces!" and on and on. They also appeared in hideous and dreadful shapes to frighten him.

Sensing the evil purpose of the demon army, Milarepa sang "The Truth of Karma":

> I take refuge in all gracious Gurus,
> And pay homage to them.
>
> Through mirages and illusions,
> You pernicious male and female devils
> Can create these fantastic terrors.
>
> You pitiable Ah Tsa Ma demons,⁵ hungry ghosts,
> You can never harm me.
>
> Because your sinful Karma in the past
> Has fully ripened,⁶ you have received
> Demonic bodies for this life.
> With minds and bodies so deformed,
> You wander in the sky forever.
>
> Driven by the fiery Kleśas,⁷
> Your minds are filled with hostile and
>   vicious thoughts.
> Your deeds and words are malignant and destructive.
> You screamed, "Kill him! Chop him! Beat him!
>   Cut him up!"
>
> I am a yogi who is devoid of thoughts,⁸
> Knowing that there is no such thing as mind.
>
> Walking valiant as a lion,
> Actions fearless as the brave,

My body merges with the body of Buddha,
My words are like the true words of the Tathāgata,
My mind is absorbed in the Realm of Great Light.[9]
I see clearly the void nature of the Six
         Groups.[10]
A yogi, such as I, ignores the abuse of
         hungry ghosts!

If the Law of Cause and Effect is valid,
And one commits the deeds deserving of it,
The force of Ripened Karma[11] will drive him down
Into the miserable Path
Of suffering and grief.

It is distressing and woeful that you
         ghosts and demons
Should not understand the Truth![12]
I, the plain-looking Milarepa,
Now preach to you the song of Dharma.

All sentient beings who live by nourishment
Are my fathers and my mothers!
To afflict those to whom we owe gratitude
Is indeed senseless and foolish!

Would it not be a happy and a joyous act
If you were to renounce your vicious thoughts?
Would it not be a blessed and joyful thing
If you were to practice the Ten Virtues?[13]
Remember this and ponder its meaning,
Exert yourselves and carefully consider it.

The demons then scoffed at Milarepa: "Your rambling talk will
not deceive us. We refuse to cease our magic and set you free." They
then multiplied their supernatural weapons and increased the force of
their demonic army to afflict him. Milarepa pondered awhile and then
said, "Hearken to me, you army of demons! By the grace of my Guru
I have become a yogi who has fully realized the Ultimate Truth. To
me, the afflictions and obstructions caused by demons are the glories
of a yogi's mind. The greater such affliction, the more I gain in the
Path of Bodhi.[14] Now listen to my song of 'The Seven Adornments' ":

I pay homage to Marpa the Translator,

I, who see the ultimate essence of being,
Sing the song of [Seven] Adornments.

You mischievous demons here assembled,
Lend your ears and listen closely to my song.

By the side of Sumeru,[15] the central mountain,
The sky shines blue o'er the Southern Continent;[16]
The firmament is the beauty of the earth,
The blue of heaven its adornment.

High above the Great Tree of Sumeru[17]
Shine radiant beams from sun and moon,
Lighting the Four Continents.
With love and compassion, the Nāga King[18]
    wields his miraculous power:
From the immense sky, he lets fall the rain.
Of the earth, this is the adornment.

From the great ocean vapors rise,
Reaching the vast sky.
They form great clouds;
A causal law governs the transformations
    of the elements.

In midsummer, rainbows appear above the plain,
Gently resting upon the hills.
Of the plains and mountains,
The rainbow is the beauty and adornment.

In the West, when rain falls in the cold ocean,
Bushes and trees flourish on the earth.
To all creatures on the Continent,
These are the beauty and adornment.

I, the Yogi who desires to remain in solitude,
Meditate on the Voidness of Mind.
Awed by the power of my concentration,
You jealous demons are forced to practice magic.
Of the yogi, demonic conjurations
Are the beauty and adornment.

You Non-men, listen closely and hearken to me!

Do you know who I am?
I am the Yogi Milarepa;
From my heart emerges
The flower of Mind—Enlightenment.
With a clear voice[19] I sing this allegory to you,
With sincere words I preach the Dharma for you,
With a gracious heart I give you this advice.
If in your hearts the Will-for-Bodhi[20] sprouts,
Though you may not be of help to others,
By renouncing the Ten Evils,[21]
Know that you will win joy and liberation.
If you follow my teachings,
Your accomplishments will increase greatly;
If you practice the Dharma now,
Everlasting joy will at last enfold you.

Most of the demons were converted by the song, becoming faithful and respectful to Milarepa, and the evil conjurations ceased. They said, "You are indeed a great yogi of marvelous powers. Without your explanation of the Truth, and the revelation of your miraculous powers, we would never have understood. Henceforth, we will not trouble you. We are also most grateful for your preaching of the truth of Karma. In all frankness, we are of limited intelligence and limitless ignorance. Our minds are steeped in a morass of stubborn habitual thoughts.[22] Pray, therefore, teach us a lesson profound in meaning, great in profit, and simple in comprehension and observation."

Milarepa then sang "The Song of the Seven Truths":

I make obeisance to you, Marpa the Translator.
I pray that you grant me increase of Bodhi-Mind.

However beautiful a song's words may be,
It is but a tune to those
Who grasp not the words of Truth.

If a parable agrees not with Buddha's teaching,
However eloquent it may sound,
'Tis but a booming echo.

If one does not practice Dharma,
However learned in the Doctrines one may claim to be,
One is only self-deceived.

Living in solitude is self-imprisonment,
If one practice not the instruction of the
    Oral Transmission.
Labor on the farm is but self-punishment,
If one neglects the teaching of the Buddha.

For those who do not guard their morals,
Prayers are but wishful thinking.
For those who do not practice what they preach,
Oratory is but faithless lying.

Wrong-doing shunned, sins of themselves diminish;
Good deeds done, merit will be gained.
Remain in solitude, and meditate alone;
Much talking is of no avail.
Follow what I sing, and practice Dharma!

Faith in Milarepa was further aroused in his listeners, and they paid him great respect. They made obeisances and circumambulated[23] him many times. Most of them then returned to their homes. But the leader of the demons, Bha Ro, and some of his followers still would not depart. Once again they conjured dreadful visions to frighten Milarepa, but he countered them with the song in which the truth of good and evil is told:

I bow at the feet of gracious Marpa.

Are you pernicious demons still in an angry mood?
Your bodies through the sky can fly with ease,
But your minds are filled with sinful habitual thoughts.
You bare your deadly fangs to frighten others,
But you may be sure, when you afflict them,
You are only bringing trouble on yourselves.

The Law of Karma never fails to function;
No one escapes from its ripening.[24]
You are only bringing trouble on yourselves,
You hungry ghosts, confused and sinful!
I feel only sorrow and pity for you.

Since you are ever sinning,
To be vicious is natural to you.
Since the Karma of killing binds you,

You relish meat and blood for food.
By taking the lives of others,
You are born as hungry ghosts.

Your sinful deeds led you
To the depths of the lower Path.
Turn back, my friends, from this ensnaring Karma,
And try to attain true happiness which is
Beyond all hope and fear!

The demons scoffed: "Your skillful impersonation of a preacher who knows the Doctrine thoroughly is most impressive, but what conviction have you gained from the practice of Dharma?"

Milarepa replied with "The Song of Perfect Assurance":

Obeisance to the perfect Marpa.

I am the Yogi who perceives the Ultimate Truth.
In the Origin of the Unborn, I first gain assurance;
On the Path of Non-extinction, slowly
     I perfect my power;
With meaningful symbols and words
Flowing from my great compassion,
I now sing this song
From the absolute realm of Dharma Essence.

Because your sinful Karma has created
Dense blindness and impenetrable obstruction,
You cannot understand the meaning
Of Ultimate Truth.
Listen, therefore, to the Expedient Truth.[25]

In their spotless, ancient Sūtras,
All the Buddhas in the past, repeatedly
Admonished with the eternal Truth of Karma—
That every sentient being is one's kinsman.
This is eternal Truth which never fails.
Listen closely to the teaching of Compassion.

I, the Yogi who developed by his practices,
Know that outer hindrances are but a shadow-show,
And the phantasmal world
A magic play of mind unborn.

By looking inward into the mind is seen
Mind-nature—without substance, intrinsically void.
Through meditation in solitude, the grace
Of the Succession Gurus and the teaching
Of the great Nāropa[26] are attained.
The inner truth of the Buddha
Should be the object of meditation.

By the gracious instruction of my Guru,
Is the abstruse inner meaning of Tantra understood.
Through the practice of Arising and
    Perfecting Yoga,[27]
Is the Vital Power engendered
And the inner reason for the microcosm realized.
Thus in the outer world I do not fear
The illusory obstacles.

To the Great Divine Lineage I belong,
With innumerable yogis great as all Space.

When in one's own mind one ponders
On the original state of Mind,
Illusory thoughts of themselves dissolve
Into the Realm of Dharmadhātu.[28]
Neither afflicter nor afflicted can be seen.
Exhaustive study of the Sūtras
Teaches us no more than this.

The chief and subordinate demons then offered their skulls[29] to
Milarepa, made obeisance, and circumambulated him many times.
They promised to bring him a month's supply of food, and vanished
like a rainbow in the sky.

The next morning at sunrise the demon Bha Ro brought from Mon
many richly clad female ghosts and a numerous retinue. They carried
jeweled cups filled with wine, and brass plates heaped with many different foods, including rice and meat, which they offered to the Jetsun.
Promising henceforward to serve and obey him, they bowed to him
many times and disappeared. One of the demons, called Jarbo Ton
Drem, was the leader of many Devas.

Through this experience, Milarepa gained great yogic improvement.
He remained there for a month, spirited and joyous, and without the
pangs of hunger.

One day, [when the month had passed,] Milarepa recalled a place in Lashi renowned for its good water, and decided to go there. On the way, he came to a plain dotted with flourishing tamarisks. In the middle of the plain rose a large rock with a projecting ledge above it. Milarepa sat upon the rock for a time; many goddesses appeared, bowed to him, and served him with desirable offerings. One of the goddesses also left two footprints on the rock, and then disappeared like a rainbow.

As Milarepa proceeded on his way, a host of demons assembled and conjured visions of huge female organs on the road to shock him. Then the Jetsun concentrated his mind and exposed his erected male organ with a gesture. He went farther, and passing an apparition of nine female organs, reached a place with a rock shaped like a vagina standing in its center—the quintessence of the region. He inserted a phallic-shaped stone into the hollow of the rock, [a symbolic act][30] which dispersed the lascivious images created by the demons. The place was later called Làdgu Lungu.

When Milarepa reached the middle of the plain, the demon Bha Ro returned to welcome him. He prepared a preaching seat for the Jetsun, gave offerings and service, and asked him for the Buddhist teachings. Milarepa lectured him comprehensively on Karma, and the demon then melted into a huge rock in front of the seat.

Milarepa, in a very joyous state, remained on the central plain for a month, and then journeyed to Nya Non Tsar Ma. He told the people there that the plain had indeed been infamous until he had conquered its demons and transformed it to a place suitable for the practice of Dharma. He also told them he wanted to return there to mediate as soon as possible. After this, the people of Nya Non had deep faith in Milarepa.

This is the story of "The Journey to Lashi."

NOTES

1 Meaning the "Revered One." See Story 1, Note 10.

2 Tibetans believe that spiritually enlightened beings should be able to perform out-of-the-ordinary, or miraculous, deeds. To leave a footprint or handprint in hard material, such as rock, was considered a proof of a yogi's occult powers, and accomplishments. Much evidence of this belief can be found in Tibet.

3 Samādhi of Mercy: According to Buddhism, Samādhi is merely a mental state of deep concentration. It can be applied or utilized for any religious purpose. How-

ever, the power of Samādhi enables the yogi to accomplish almost all the spiritual wishes he may have. Here Samādhi is applied to the expansion and perfection of love or mercy. In other words, the Samādhi of Mercy is a deep and pure conscious state in which the purest love is brought to consummation.

4 Flowing-River Yoga [Samādhi] (T.T.: Chu.Wo.rGyun.Gyi.rNal.hByor): In this Samādhi the yogi experiences his identity with the flow of the Universe, yet he transcends it. He never withdraws from the flow, nor does he intend to ignore it; he is in it, but not bound by it. This Samādhi is the active or dynamic aspect of Mahāmudrā Yoga.

5 Ah Tsa Ma Demons (T.T.: A.Tsa.Ma.): a Tibetan name for Indian demons.

6 Ripened Karma (T.T.: rNam.sMin.Gyi.Las.; Skt.: Vipāka Karma) may be translated as "fully ripened Karma," or "the Karmic force that ripens in different lives." The Law of Karma says that usually a deed brings not merely one, but many, effects. For example, if a man commits murder, he will be punished by his conscience, by the law, by the ruin of his reputation and life, and so on. But this is not all. The force of Karma has not yet been exhausted. In a future incarnation, or incarnations, the murderer will be subjected by this mysterious Karmic force to shorter lives and much sickness; or he will be prone to rebirths in times and lands where there are frequent wars and perils. This force, the Karma that ripens in different lives, seems to be the most fundamental and mysterious aspect of the Buddhist doctrine.

7 Fiery Kleśas: These are the strong desires and passions that cause all the pains and distresses of Saṃsāric life.

8 Devoid of thoughts: An accomplished yogi should have freed himself from *all* thoughts or conceptualizations, be they simple or complex, good or evil, monistic or dualistic . . . , then he is said to have acquired the Wisdom of Equality or Non-discrimination.

9 The Realm of Great Light is the realm of primordial Buddhahood. The term "Light" should not be treated in its literal sense as denoting luminosity. It is actually beyond description and attribution. Free and universal clarity, devoid of the slightest clinging or attachment, perhaps can best be described in words as "Great Light."

10 Six Groups (T.T.: Tsogs.Drug.): the Six Consciousnesses and the Six Sense Objects. The Six Consciousnesses are: consciousness of eye, ear, nose, tongue, body, and discernment (mind). The Six Sense Objects are: color or form, sound, smell, taste, touch, and dharma (being).

11 See Note 6.

12 This sentence could also be translated " . . . should not understand the Immanent Truth."

13 The Ten Virtues: These are the antitheses of the Ten Evils. See Note 21.

14 Path of Bodhi: the Path that leads to Buddhahood. This is the practice of the Bodhisattva, as taught in Mahāyāna Buddhism.

15 Sumeru: The legendary center of the Universe, an idea borrowed by the Buddhists from the Hindus, and believed by some modern scholars to represent a place in the Himālaya Mountains.

16 Southern Continent: In Buddhist legends, the earth on which we live is the Southern Continent. There are four continents in this universe, floating in a sea: Northern, Eastern, Southern, and Western. In the center of these four continents stands the great mountain, Sumeru.

17 The Great Tree of Sumeru: This refers to another Buddhist legend: From the bottom of the ocean grows a tree which reaches to the top of Heaven. The

Asuras, who live in the ocean, quarreled and fought with the beings in Heaven over the ownership of this tree.

18 The Nāga King is the Dragon who controls rainfall.

19 Milarepa is said to have had a very fine singing voice. See his Biography, "Tibet's Great Yogi, Milarepa," edited by W. Y. Evans-Wentz, Oxford University Press, 1951.

20 Or, Mind-for-Bodhi, Heart-for-Bodhi, or Bodhi-Mind (Skt.: Bodhicitta; T.T.: Byan.Chub.Sems.): "Bodhi" refers to the state of the realization of Buddhahood. "Mind-for-Bodhi" is the desire to attain such realization; but usually, this term implies more than just the wish; it also implies the vow to serve and save all sentient beings through meritorious deeds and spiritual practices, including the Six Pāramitās. "Bodhicitta" is a term of many connotations. It not only refers to the wish or "heart" for Buddhahood and the practices that lead toward it, but in many cases it refers to the intuitive wisdom with which the Ultimate Truth — the Dharmakāya — is realized. "Bodhicitta," therefore, can be translated as Bodhi-Mind, Mind-for-Bodhi, Heart-for-Bodhi, or, THE MIND OF BODHI, depending on how it is used in different contexts. See Story 1, Note 20.

21 The Ten Evils: killing, stealing, adultery, cheating, double-talk, coarse language, talking nonsense, covetousness, anger, and perverted views.

22 Habitual thinking or thought (T.T.: Bag.Chags.): the force driving sentient beings in Saṃsāra. See Story 4, Note 11.

23 Circumambulation: In paying homage to the Buddha, the Dharma, the Guru, or any revered monk, Buddhist disciples were in the habit of circling or walking around the person or object of veneration three times in a clockwise direction and then making obeisance. This custom, however, has died out in many Buddhist countries today.

24 Karma-Ripening or in some cases, Ripened Karma (T.T.: rNam.sMin.): See Note 6.

25 Expedient Truth (T.T.: Draṅ.Don.): Because individuals and groups differ in their dispositions and capacities, it is not advisable to give the highest teaching to all. Expedient teachings that lead one *toward* the Final Truth are needed for the majority. These expedient teachings, however, are in principle in accord with, and in practice conducive to, the Final Truth. Thus they are also known as "Expedient *Truths.*" It is in this light that the Mahāyāna Buddhist evaluates the various teachings from different schools and religions.

26 Nāropa: Marpa's teacher.

27 Arising and Perfecting Yoga (T.T.: sKyed.Rim.Daṅ.rDsogs.Rim.): In the Anuttara Tantra (the Highest Division of Tantra) there are two main practices:

> (1) The teaching of the "Successive Steps toward Creation" (T.T.: sKyes. Rim.), which may be translated as the "Arising, or Growing Yoga." It is a teaching and practice of identifying oneself with Tantric Creation.
>
> (2) The teaching of the "Successive Steps of Completion, or Perfection" (T.T.: rDsogs.Rim.), may be translated as the "Perfecting Yoga." This is the advanced type of Yoga practice in which one identifies oneself with the Ultimate Perfection, or the great Nirvāṇa.

28 Dharmadhātu: The Absolute Universality, or the Truth of Totality.

29 Offered their skulls: According to Tantric tradition, offering his skull is the most solemn pledge that a demon or ghost can make. It symbolizes the complete surrender of his body and soul to whomsoever his oath has been made.

30 The meaning of this passage in the text is esoteric and therefore obscure; it may thus be subject to different interpretations. This is a free translation.

3

THE SONG
OF THE SNOW RANGES

Obeisance to all Gurus

J ETSUN Milarepa's reputation for conquering malignant demons and
ghosts grew as a result of his visit to the region of Lashi Snow Mountain. All the people of Nya Non village became his patrons and rendered him service and offerings. Among them was a lady named Wurmo, who with deep faith earnestly sought the teachings of the Dharma.
She had a young son called Joupuva, whom she decided to offer to
Milarepa as a servant when the boy grew up.

Milarepa was invited to stay at Nya Non Tsar Ma by the villagers,
and while there was attended by his patroness, Shindormo. The Jetsun
stayed in the village for some time, but soon became severely depressed
by the worldliness of everyone. Indicating his unhappiness, he told the
villagers that he wanted to return to Lashi Snow Mountain.

The villagers then cried, "Revered One! It is simply for our own
sake and not for the welfare of other sentient beings that we ask you
to remain in our village this winter and teach us. You can conquer
evil demons at any time. Next spring everything will be ready for
your journey." Venerable Dunba[1] Shajaguna [a priest] and Shindormo were especially earnest in their petitions: "The winter is coming,
and you will meet too much difficulty and hardship on the snow
mountain. Please postpone your departure until later."

Disregarding their repeated supplications, Milarepa made up his
mind to go. "I am a son of the Nāropa Succession," he said. "I do
not fear hardships and raging storms on the snow mountain. For me
to remain permanently in a village would be far worse than death.
My Guru Marpa also commanded me to avoid worldly distractions
and to remain in solitude to pursue my devotions."

Then the villagers of Tsar Ma quickly prepared provisions for him;

23

before leaving, he promised to see those who would come to him for instruction in the Dharma during the winter. Dunba Shajaguna, Shindormo, and four others, monks and laymen, carrying drink for the farewell party, accompanied the Jetsun. They crossed a hill and came to a small plateau.

Taking with him flour, rice, a piece of meat, and a cut of butter, Milarepa set out alone for the Great Cave of Conquering Demons, where he intended to reside.

On their way home, the six disciples encountered a terrible storm on the far side of the mountain, so blinding they could hardly find their way. They had to summon all their strength to struggle against it, and only reached the village after everyone had retired for the night.

The snow fell for eighteen days and nights, cutting off communication between Drin and Nya Non for six months. All of Milarepa's disciples assumed that their Guru must have died in the storm and, in his memory, held a sacramental feast.

In the Month of Saga [part of March and April], the disciples, carrying axes and other tools, went to search for the Jetsun's corpse. Just short of their destination, they sat down to take a long rest. In the distance they saw a snow-leopard yawning and stretching as it climbed up on a big rock. They watched it for a long while, until it finally disappeared. They were quite sure they would not find the Jetsun's corpse, as they firmly believed the leopard had killed him and eaten his body. They murmured, "Is it still possible to obtain some remnants of his clothes, or hair?" The very thought of this made them cry out in agonized grief. Then they noticed many human footprints beside the leopard's tracks. Afterward, the narrow path where the vision of the leopard [or tiger] had appeared became known as "The Tiger and Leopard Path." [Having seen this phantasm of the leopard], the villagers were very mystified. They thought, "Could this be a conjuration of a Deva or ghost?" In bewilderment, they approached the Cave of Conquering Demons, and, hearing Milarepa singing, they asked themselves, "Is it possible that passing hunters have offered food to the Jetsun, or that he has acquired some left-over prey, so that he did not die?"

When they reached the cave, Milarepa chided them: "You laggards, you reached the other side of the mountain quite a while ago. Why did it take you so long to get here? The food has been prepared for a long time and must be cold. Hasten yourselves and enter!" The disciples were overjoyed, and cried and danced happily. Swiftly they rushed up to the Jetsun, bowing down before him. Milarepa said, "Now is not the time to discuss this; now it is time to eat." But they first made obeisance to him, greeting him and asking after his health. Then they looked round the cave and saw that the flour which they had given him earlier was still not used up. A dish of barley, rice, and meat stood ready. Dunba Shajaguna exclaimed to the Jetsun, "Indeed, it is dinner-time for us, but surely you must have known that we were coming." Milarepa replied, "When I was sitting on the rock, I saw you all resting on the other side of the pass." "We saw a leopard sitting there," said Dunba Shajaguna, "but we did not see you. Where were you then?" "I was the leopard," Milarepa answered. "To a yogi who has completely mastered Prāna-Mind,[2] the essence of the Four Elements is perfectly controlled. He can transform himself into whatever bodily form he chooses. I have shown you my occult powers of performing supernormal acts because you are all gifted and advanced disciples. However, you should never speak of this to anyone."

Shindormo said, "Jetsun, your face and body seem to glow with even more health than last year. The paths on both sides of the mountain were blocked by snow, and no one could get through to bring you food. Were you fed by divinities, or did you find some animal killed by wild beasts? What is the secret?"

Milarepa replied, "Most of the time, I was in the state of Samādhi, and hence required no food. On feast days, many Dākinīs[3] offered me food in their Tantric festival gatherings. Occasionally, I ate a little dry flour on the tip of a spoon, as I did yesterday and several days ago. At the end of the Month of the Horse, I had a vision that all of you, my disciples, surrounded me and offered me so much to drink and eat that for many days afterward I felt no hunger at all. By the way, what were you doing at the end of the Month of the Horse?" The disciples counted back and found that it was the date on which they had held the sacramental feast for the Jetsun in the belief that he had passed away. Milarepa commented, "When worldly men make charitable offerings, it is surely helpful to their Bardo[4] state. However, it is still better and more useful to realize the Bardo of Here-and-Now."[5]

The disciples earnestly besought Milarepa to come down to Nya Non, but he refused, saying, "I am enjoying my stay here very much; my Samādhi also shows improvement. I want to remain, so return without me!" But the disciples countered, "If the honored Jetsun does not come down with us this time, the people of Nya Non will blame us for leaving him alone to go to his grave. Then abuse and curses will be heaped upon us." Wurmo cried, "If you do not come, we will either carry you down or sit here until death overtakes us." Milarepa could not resist their insistent appeals and, forced to yield, agreed to go with them.

The disciples then said, "Maybe the Dākinīs do not need you, but the disciples in your Succession certainly do. Now let us show the Dākinīs how we can conquer the snow without snowshoes."

The next morning they all left the cave and set out for Nya Non. Shindormo went ahead to bring the villagers the good tidings that the Jetsun was still alive and was returning to them.

[As they neared the village] Milarepa and his disciples came to a huge flat rock shaped like a platform, upon which the farmers threshed their wheat. By then the news of his arrival had spread. Men and women, adults and children, old and young, all flocked to the Jetsun, gazing at him, embracing him, crying with great emotion, asking after his well-being, greeting him reverently, and making obeisance to him. In reply to them, Milarepa, with the snowshoes still on his feet and resting his chin on a headstick sang:

> You and I—patrons, patronesses, and old Milarepa,
> Under the blessed canopy of this auspicious sky,
> Meet once more before our worldly lives
>   have passed away.
> I sing in answer to your questions on my welfare.
> Listen closely, and pay heed to my song!
>
> At the end of the Tiger Year
> Before the Rabbit Year began,
> On the sixth day of Wa Jal,
> A sense of renunciation grew within me.
> To the remote Lashi Snow Mountain
> Came Milarepa, the anchorite, who
>   clings to solitide.
> It seems that sky and earth agreed; between,
> A wind which tears the skin was sent;
> The rivers ran and torrents surged;
> Black clouds swept in from all directions;
> The sun and moon were shut in darkness;
> And the Twenty-eight Constellations[6]
>   were fixed.
> The Milky Way was pegged,
> And the Eight Planets[7] were tied by an
>   iron chain.
> The firmament was wrapped in fog;
> In the mist, snow fell for nine days and nights.
> Then more and more for a further eighteen
>   nights and days.

The snow fell, big as bags of wool,
Fell like birds flying in the sky,
Fell like a whirling swarm of bees.
Flakes fell small as a spindle's wheel,
Fell as tiny as bean seed,
Fell like tufts of cotton.

The snowfall was beyond all measure.
Snow covered all the mountain and even
     touched the sky,
Falling through the bushes and weighing down the trees.
Black mountains became white,
All the lakes were frozen.
Clear water congealed beneath the rocks;
The world became a flat, white plain;
Hills and valleys were leveled.
The snow was such that even evil-doers
     could not venture out.[8]
Wild beasts starved and farmyard creatures, too,
Abandoned by the people in the mountains,
Pitiful, hungry, and enfeebled.
In the tree-mists famine struck the birds,
While rats and mice hid underground.

In this great disaster I remained in utter
     solitude.
The falling snow in the year's-end blizzard
Fought me, the cotton-clad, high on Snow Mountain,
I fought it as it fell upon me
Until it turned to drizzle.
I conquered the raging winds—
Subduing them to silent rest.
The cotton cloth[9] I wore was like a burning
     brand.

The struggle was of life and death,
As when giants wrestle and sabers clash.
I, the competent Yogi, was victorious—
I set a model for all Buddhists,
An example for all great yogis.

My power over the Vital Heat[10] and the
     Two Channels was thus shown.

By observing carefully the Four Ills[11]
        caused by meditation,
And keeping to the inward practice,
The cold and warm Prānas became the Essence.
This was why the raging wind grew tame,
And the storm, subdued, lost all its power;
Not even the Devas' army could compete
With me. This battle I, the Yogi, won.

A faithful son of Dharma in a tiger skin,
I have never worn a coat of fox-fur.
Son of a giant, I have never
From the wrathful run.
Son of a lion—of all beasts the king—
I have ever lived in the snow mountains.
To make a task of life is but a joke to me.

If you believe what this old man tells
Hearken to his prophecy:

The teaching of the Practiced Succession[12]
        will grow and spread afar;
A few accomplished beings will then appear on earth;
The fame of Milarepa will spread throughout the world.
You, disciples, in the memory of man
Will abound with faith;
Fame and praise of us
Will be heard in aftertimes.

To answer your concern for my health,
I, the Yogi Milarepa, am very well indeed.
And how are you, dear patrons? Are you all
        well and happy?

The Jetsun's happy song so inspired the villagers that they danced
and sang for joy, and Milarepa, in a merry mood, joined in. The
great stone platform on which the dance was held became impressed
with his foot- and hand-prints, as if they had been carved in it. The
center of the platform sank, forming a small basin with irregular
steps; thenceforth the platform, formerly called "White-Stepped Rock,"
became known as "Snowshoe Rock."

Then the villagers escorted Milarepa to the village of Nya Non
Tsar Ma, and gave service and offerings to him. The patroness Lese-

bum said, "Revered One, nothing could give us greater joy than to learn that you are alive and have returned safely to our village. Your countenance is more radiant than ever, and you are energetic and spirited. Is this because the goddesses made offerings to you when you were in solitude?"

In answer, Milarepa sang:

> I bow down at the feet of my Guru Marpa.
>
> The gift of blessing is bestowed by the Ḍākinīs;
> The nectar of Samaya[13] is abundant nourishment;
> Through faithful devotion the organs of sense are fed.
> Propitious merits are thus garnered by my disciples.
>
> The immediate Mind has no substance;
> It is void, less than a smallest atom.
> When seer and seen are both eliminated,
> The "View" is truly realized.
>
> As for the "Practice" — in the Stream of Illumination,
> No stages can be found.
> Perseverence in Practice is confirmed
> When actor and acting are both annulled.
>
> In the Realm of Illumination,
> Where subject and object are one,
> I see no cause, for all is Void.
> When acting and actor disappear,
> All actions become correct.
>
> The finite thoughts[14] dissolve in Dharmadhātu;
> The Eight Worldly Winds bring neither hope nor fear.
> When the precept and the precept-keeper disappear,
> The disciplines are best observed.
>
> By knowing that the Self-mind is Dharmakāya[15] —
> Buddha's Body absolute —
> By an earnest, altruistic vow,
> The deed and doer disappear.
> Thus the glorious Dharma triumphs.
>
> In answer to his disciples' questioning,
> This is the happy song the old man sings!

The falling snow enclosed
My house of meditation;[16]
Goddesses gave me food and sustenance;
The water of Snow Mountain was the purest draught.
All was done without effort;
There is no need to farm when there's no
      demand [for food].
My store is full without preparation or hoarding.
By observing my own mind, all things are seen;
By sitting in a lowly place, the royal throne
      is reached.
Perfection is attained through the Guru's grace;
This bounty is repaid by Dharma practice.
Followers and patrons here assembled,
Give your services with faith.
Be happy, all, and gay.

Dunbar Shajaguna made obeisance to Milarepa, saying, "It is indeed wondrous and pleasing to learn that so much snow did not harm the Jetsun, and that we, your disciples, were able to return with you safely to the village. What a joy that all the disciples could see their Guru! We will be deeply grateful and happy if you preach the Dharma on your meditative experiences this winter, as an arrival-gift to us."

Milarepa, in answer to Shajaguna's request and as an arrival-gift to the disciples of Nya Non, sang the song of "The Six Essences of Meditative Experience":

Obeisance to my Guru with the Three Perfections.

This evening, at the request
Of my disciples Shajaguna and the Patron Dormos,
I, Milarepa, tell what I experienced when meditating,
I who ever dwell in the remote fastnesses.

The pure vow made this congregation possible;
The pure precept of Dharma united me and my patrons.
My sons! What you have asked, will I,
The father, present as my arrival-gift.

I renounce the world, and have lamented for it.
I, Milarepa, came to Lashi Snow Mountain
To occupy alone the Cave of Conquering Demons.

For six full months, the experiences of meditation
    grew;
I now disclose them in this, the song of the
    Six Essences.

First come the Six Parables of Outer Appearance;
Second, the Six Inner Misconducts,
Which one should carefully consider;
Third, the Six Ropes which bind us in Saṃsāra;
Fourth, the Six Ways through which Liberation
    is achieved;
Fifth, the Six Essences of Knowledge
Through which one attains confidence;
Sixth, the Six Blissful Experiences of Meditation.

If one does not commit this song to memory,
No impression is left upon the mind.
Heed carefully, then, my explanations.

If there be obstacles,
It cannot be called space;
If there be numbers,
It cannot be called stars.
One cannot say "This is a mountain,"
If it moves and shakes.
It cannot be an ocean
Should it grow or shrink.
One cannot be called a swimmer
If he needs a bridge.
It is not a rainbow
If it can be grasped.
These are the Six Outer Parables.

The limits of the definite
Limit understanding.
Drowsiness and distractions
Are not meditation.
Acceptance and rejection
Are not acts of will.
A constant flow of thought
Is not Yoga.
If there be East and West,[17]
It is not Wisdom;

If birth and death,
It is not Buddha.
These are the Six Inner Faults.

Denizens of Hell are bound by hate,
Hungry ghosts by misery,
And beasts by blindness.
Men by lust are bound,
By jealousy, Asuras,
And Devas in Heaven by pride.
These Six Fetters are the Obstacles to Liberation.

Great faith, reliance
On a wise and strict Guru,
Good discipline,
Solitude in a hermitage,
Determined, persevering
Practice, and meditation—
These are the Six Ways that lead to Liberation.

The Original Inborn Wisdom[18] is
The sphere of primordial [depth].
Without "exterior" or "interior" is the sphere
        of Awareness;
Without brightness or darkness is the sphere
        of Insight;
Omnipresent and all-embracing is the sphere
        of Dharma;
Without mutation or transition is the sphere
        of Tig Le;[19]
Without interruption is the sphere of Experience.[20]
These are the Six Unshakable Realms of Essence.

Bliss rises when the Vital Heat is fanned,
When air from the Nāḍīs[21] flows in the
        Central Channel,
When the Bodhi-Mind[22] flows from above,
When it is purified below,
When white and red meet in the middle,
And the joy of leakless body satiates one,
These are the Six Blissful Experiences of Yoga.
To please you, my sons and followers,
I sing this song of the Six Essences,

Of my experiences last winter when meditating.
May all at this delightful meeting
Drink the heavenly nectar of my song.
May everyone be gay and full of joy.
May your pure wishes be fulfilled.

This is the silly song sung by this old man;
Do not belittle it, this gift of Dharma,
But with joyous hearts stride forward
On the Path of the Blessed Doctrine!

Shindormo cried, "Jetsun! Most Precious One! You are like unto the Buddhas of the past, present, and future. The opportunity to serve you and to learn from you is a rare privilege. Those who do not have faith in you are indeed more foolish than the animals."

Milarepa replied, "It may not be so very important for a person to have faith in me. It does not matter much either way. But if you have a precious human body and have been born at a time and place in which the Buddhist religion prevails, it is very foolish indeed not to practice the Dharma." Milarepa thus sang:

At the feet of the Translator Marpa, I
     prostrate myself,
And sing to you, my faithful patrons.

How stupid it is to sin with recklessness
While the pure Dharma spreads all about you.
How foolish to spend your lifetime without meaning,
When a precious human body is so rare a gift.
How ridiculous to cling to prison-like
     cities and remain there.
How laughable to fight and quarrel with your
     wives and relatives,
Who do but visit you.
How senseless to cherish sweet and tender words
Which are but empty echoes in a dream.
How silly to disregard one's life by fighting foes
Who are but frail flowers.

How foolish it is when dying to torment
     oneself with thoughts of family,
Which bind one to Māyā's[23] mansion.
How stupid to stint on property and money,

Which are a debt on loan from others.
How ridiculous it is to beautify and deck the body,
Which is a vessel full of filth.
How silly to strain each nerve for wealth and goods,
And neglect the nectar of the inner teachings!

In a crowd of fools, the clever and sensible
Should practice the Dharma, as do I.

The people in the assembly said to Milarepa, "We are deeply grateful for your songs of wisdom. But we can never emulate your industry and intelligence. We can only try to avoid the foolish things you have cited. Our only wish is for the privilege of your continued presence, that the living may give their service and obtain instruction from you, and that the dead, too, may be saved through your grace."

Milarepa replied, "In obedience to the order of my Guru, I have been meditating on Lashi Snow Mountain. I may stay here for a time, but I can never stay here as you worldly people do. Disrespect, and not goodwill, would result if I were to remain among you. He then sang:

Obeisance to Marpa the Translator.

May all my patrons and patronesses here assembled
Have immutable faith, and pray to me with
        sincerity unfeigned.

If one stays too long with friends,
They will soon tire of him;
Living in such closeness leads to dislike and hate.
It is but human to expect and demand too much
When one dwells too long in companionship.

The belligerence in human nature leads to
        broken precepts;
Bad company destroys good deeds;
Honest words bring evil when spoken in a crowd;
To argue the right and wrong only makes more foes.

To cling to sectarian bigotry and dogma
Makes one vicious and more sinful.

An obligatory response to the offerings of
        the faithful ever causes evil thoughts.

To enjoy the Food of the Dead[24] is sinful
 and dangerous.
The offerings of worldly beings are low and worthless.

Companionship itself causes contempt;
From contempt hate and aversion grow.

The more houses one owns, the more one
 suffers at the time of death.
These sufferings and lamentations are indeed
 intolerable,
Especially to yogis who dwell in solitude.

I, Milarepa, am going to a quiet hermitage,
 to live alone.
Faithful patrons, your endeavor to amass
 merits is wonderful;
My patrons and patronesses, it is good
To make offerings and to serve your Guru.
I confirm my wish to meet you soon,
And see you many times.

The patrons all said to Milarepa, "We never tire of hearing your instruction and preaching; it may be that you have tired of us. No matter how warmly we entreat you to remain here, we know it will be in vain. We only hope that from time to time you will come to visit us from Lashi."

The villagers then offered Milarepa many provisions and other goods, but he did not take them. All the people were inspired with veneration and paid him deep respect. In a mood of great delight and happiness, the villagers strongly confirmed their unshakable faith in the Jetsun.

This is the Song of the Snow Ranges.

NOTES

1 Dunba (T.T.: sTon.Pa.): a high priest who is versed in Buddhist scriptures and proficient in giving spiritual instructions to Buddhist followers.

2 Prāṇa-Mind: According to Tantric teaching, mind and Prāṇa manifest as

two aspects of a unity. Mind is that which is aware; Prāṇa is the active energy which gives support to the awareness. He who masters the mind automatically masters the Prāṇa, and vice versa. The aim of any system of meditation is to control or master the Prāṇa-Mind. An accomplished yogi is one who has mastered his Prāṇa-Mind.

3 See story 1, Note 19.

4 Bardo (T.T.: Bar.Do.): the intermediate state of existence between death and rebirth. According to Tibetan Buddhism, this very important state is like a crossroad, the fate and fortune of one's rebirth depending much upon it.

5 The Bardo of Here-and-Now: From the viewpoint of Tantric teachings, the state of Bardo is not confined to the state after death. This very life itself is a state of Bardo. The person in physical existence, as we know it, goes through the same experiences as in Bardo, only in more "substantial fashion." To a Bardo-dweller, it is the person in physical existence who seems to be in Bardo, whereas the two states of life and death are actually correlative and similar.

6 The Twenty-eight Constellations (T.T.: rGyu.sKar.Ñer.brGyad.; lit.: the twenty-eight running stars): They are the constellations through which the moon passes in her revolution round the heavens.

7 The Eight Planets (T.T.: gZah.brGyad.) refer to the Sun, Moon, Mars, Mercury, Venus, Jupiter, Saturn, and Rāhu (see Story 4, Note 1).

8 The snowfall is sometimes so heavy in Tibet that all activity stops. Thus, even if one wants to do evil things, one is prevented.

9 Cotton cloth: The Tantric yogi who practices Heat Yoga is not supposed to wear furs — he wears only simple cotton clothing even in a cold country like Tibet.

10 Vital Heat, Dumo (T.T.: gTum.Mo.): the "mystic" heat produced from the Navel Center in Tantric meditations. It is one of the most important practices of Tibetan Tantrism. See "The Six Yogas of Nāropa," in Evans-Wentz' "Tibetan Yoga and Secret Doctrines," 2nd ed., Oxford University Press, 1958. See also the translator's "Teachings of Tibetan Yoga."

11 The Four Ills: the sicknesses that are caused by the unbalancing strength and activity of the Four Elements — earth, water, fire, and air — in the yogi's body.

12 The Practiced Succession (T.T.: sGrub.brGyud.): another name for Ghagyuba, the School of Marpa and Milarepa. The reason for this nomenclature is due to the spirit and tradition of this School which emphasizes Yoga practice and actual experience, rather than scholastic investigation. This tradition differs sharply from the traditions of the Yellow (Gelugba) and Gray (Sajyaba) Schools of Tibet.

13 Nectar of Samaya: Samaya implies the Tantric precepts. He who observes these precepts receives grace and blessings, a necessary nourishment for spiritual growth.

14 This can also be rendered as: "thoughts of a limitative pattern" (T.T.: Phyogs.Chahi.rTog.Pa.). The patterns of thought of sentient beings are of a limited or finite nature. When one realizes the truth of Voidness (Śūnyatā), the limitative patterns of thought are fundamentally transformed. Using Buddhist terminology, they "dissolve" into the Dharmadhātu — the absolute, universal, and inter-penetrating state of all the different aspects of existence in the light of the Void.

15 Dharmakāya: the "Body of Truth," which is ultimate, formless, omnipresent, and yet without any attributes.

16 When a yogi is preparing to meditate over a long period, he will mark lines on the ground around his dwelling, outside of which he will not go. In this case Milarepa did not have to make any marks, as the snow itself was deep and heavy enough to confine him.

17 East and West: If the very idea of *direction* still exists, then there is no Wisdom, because direction implies a limitation and differentiation, while Wisdom transcends both.

18 T.T.: lHan.Cig.sKyes.Pahi.Ye.Çes. This term is translated in this book as the Original Inborn Wisdom, or as Innate, or Inborn Wisdom. Its literal translation should perhaps be the Coemergent, or Simultaneously Born Wisdom, implying that it is within one at all times. However, for convenience sake, Innate, or Inborn Wisdom is used.

19 Tig Le (T.T.: Thig.Le.; Skt.: Bindu): This term has many meanings, such as "the dot," "the solid one," "the essence," etc. It is also used to signify male semen or female "blood," which represent the Life-Essence of physical bodies. Here Tig Le implies the essence or immutability of Absolute Truth.

20 Sphere of Experience: The yogi, in all activities of daily life, whether walking, eating, sleeping, talking, or the like, never loses the feeling or "sensation," of his yogic experience.

21 The Nāḍis (Roma and Junma): the mystical left and right Channels (see Story 1, Note 28).

22 Bodhi-Mind (or Bodhi-Heart) here means Tig Le.

23 Māyā means delusion or illusion. The phenomenal world is considered by Buddhism to be a dream, a phantasm, a magic shadow play, a reflection — in short it has only an illusory existence and not a real one.

24 Food of the Dead: The Tibetan Lamas believe that to accept offerings from relatives of the deceased person on his behalf incurs a great responsibility. Once the "Food of the Dead" is taken, the Lama is responsible for liberating the "soul" from sufferings and dangers. Therefore, in Tibet, to receive the offering for the dead is considered a very serious matter.

4

CHALLENGE FROM A WISE DEMONESS

Obeisance to all Gurus

ONCE Milarepa stayed in Nya Non [for a short period]. The people there besought him to remain but he would not consent, and, in compliance with his Guru's order, went to Riwo Balnbar and practiced meditation in a cave near Linba. To the right of his seat there was a cleft in the rock. Late one night, Milarepa heard a cracking sound from the crevice. He got up from his seat and looked around. But as he saw nothing, he thought it must be an illusion, and so returned to his bed-seat. Suddenly, a great beam of light shone out from the crevice. In the midst of the light appeared a red man on a black deer led by a beautiful woman. The man gave Milarepa a blow with his elbow accompanied by a suffocating wind, and then disappared. The woman became a red bitch, who immediately caught Milarepa by the foot. Milarepa realized that this was an apparition conjured by [the she-demon] Draug Srin Mo, so he sang the following song to her:

I make obeisance to Marpa, the gracious one.

You, malignant Draug Srin Mo of Linba Draug,
    you sinful female ghost
Appearing in a vicious conjured form,
In your contempt you come looking for a
    chance [to harm me].
I do not deceive in tuneful song:
I sing only honest words and truth.

In the midst of the blue sky,
The blessing of moon and sun brings affluence.

38

From the marvelous Palace of Heaven
    shines the ray of light
By which all sentient beings are illumined and seen.
[I pray] the planet Chamju[1] will not rival
The sun and moon as they circle the Four
    Continents.[2]

In the Eastern Quarter, on the top of Snow Mountain,
Darsen Gharmo, the snow lioness, brings prosperity;
She is the queen of beasts,
And never eats spoiled meat.
When she appears on the horizon
Do not afflict her with a storm!

In the South, amid the forest trees,
The mountain tigress, Dagmo Ridra, brings prosperity;
She is the champion of all wild beasts,
    gallant and invincible.
When she walks on a narrow and dangerous path,
Do not ambush her in a hunter's trap!

In the West, in the Ma Päm ocean, blue and vast,
The Dogar Nya [White-bellied Fish] brings
    prosperity;
She is the supreme dancer of the water-element,
In a marvelous way she rolls her eyes.
When she seeks delicious food,
Do not harm her with a fish-hook!

In the North, above the wide Red Rock,
Shajageubo, the great vulture brings prosperity;
She is the queen of birds.
Wondrous indeed, she never takes the
    lives of others.
When she seeks food on the top of the
    three mountains,
Do not trap her in a net!

In the cave of Linba where the vultures live,
I, Milarepa, bring prosperity.
I aim at my own and others' welfare,
Renouncing a worldly life.
With an enlightened mind,[3]

I strive for Buddhahood in one lifetime.
Diligent and undistracted I practice Dharma.
Draug Srin Mo, pray do not afflict me!
Pray hearken to this song with five
        parables and six meanings,
The song with rhythm, the song like a golden string.

Pitiable Draug Srin Mo! Do you understand me?
To commit evil Karma is a heavy sin.
Should you not take heed of this sinful Karma?
Should you not control your harmful thoughts
        and vicious heart?
If you do not realize that all things are
        merely of the mind,
The endless apparitions of Nhamdog⁴ will
        never cease.
If one realizes not that the Mind-Essence is void,
How can one dispel the spirit of evil?
You sinful demon hag! Do not afflict me!
Harm me not, and return to your own abode!

Instantaneously she disappeared. However, still holding his foot, she
replied to Milarepa:

Oh, you gifted son of the Dharma,
The one alone who has courage and fortitude,
The yogi who treads the Path of the Cemetery,⁵
The saintly Buddhist who follows the ascetic way,
Your song is the Buddha's teaching,
More precious than gold.
To exchange gold for brass is shameful.
Should I not atone for the sins I have committed,
All that I have ever said will be a lie.

For an answer to the Song of Karma
Which you have just sung to me,
Hearken closely to my allegories.

In the midst of the blue sky,
Shines the light of sun and moon
Through which prosperity to earth is brought.

As you have just said,

Rays from the Measureless Palace[6] of the Gods
Dispel the darkness in the Four Continents,
While moon and sun circle the Islands Four,
With ease they give out beams of light;
Were they not dazzled by their glowing rays,
How could Rāhu afflict[7] them?

In the East, where towers the crystal snow mountain,
Darsen Gharmo brings prosperity;
She is the queen of beasts;
She commands them as her servants.
When she appeared on the horizon,
The hurricanes and storms would not have
        afflicted her
Had she not become too proud and arrogant.

In the South, amid the dense forest trees,
The mountain tigress brings prosperity;
Champion is she of all the beasts.
With pride she boasts of conquests with her claws;
When she comes close to a narrow and dangerous path,
She shows off her pride with great hauteur.
Were she not flaunting her delusive stripes
        and smiles,
The hunter's trap would never catch her.

In the Western Quarter, in the depth of the
        blue ocean,
The White-bellied Fish brings prosperity;
She is the dancer in the water element.
She claims to be the seer of great gods.
Because of her gluttony, she searches for
        delicious food.
Had she not used her illusive body
To search for human food,
How could the fish-hook harm her?

In the North, above the wide Red Rock,
The vulture, queen of birds, brings prosperity.
She is the Deva[8] of birds, who dwells among
        the trees.
She proudly claims that she disposes of all the birds.
When she searches for blood and flesh to eat,

She flies over the three mountains.
If she swooped not at her prey,
How could the bird net catch her?

In the vulture-dwelling Rock, you,
    Milarepa, bring prosperity.
You claim that you are doing good, both
    for yourself and others.[9]
With the flowering of the perfect Bodhi-Heart,
    attentively you meditate;
Your ambition is, in one life, to become Buddha.
Your hope is to save sentient beings in the
    Six Realms.[10]
When you were engrossed in the practice of
    meditation,
The powerful force of your habitual-thoughts
    arose,[11]
It stirred your Self-mind and aroused delusory
    discriminations.
If in your mind the discriminating thought,
    "Enemy," had ne'er arisen,
How could I, Draug Srin Mo, afflict you?

You should know that from one's mind alone
Comes the evil of habitual-thinking.
What is the use of my following your guidance
If you have not realized the Mind of Suchness?[12]
You had better go your own way, while I go mine.

He who does not realize the mind's voidness,
Can never be exempted from the influence of evil.
If one knows the Self-mind by oneself,
All obstacles and difficulties become one's aids.
Even I, Draug Srin Mo, will then gladly be
    his servant.
You, Milarepa, still have wrong ideas,
You have yet to pierce into the Self-mind's nature,
You have yet to penetrate to illusion's root.

When Draug Srin Mo finished her singing, Milarepa was much impressed with her cleverness. He appeared to be very pleased [and somewhat surprised] to hear such expressions from a demoness, and, in answer to her, replied with a song, "The Eight Parables of Thinking":

Yes! Yes! What you have said is true, true indeed.
Oh! You vicious Draug Srin Mo,
It is hard to find words truer than these.
Although I have traveled far and wide,
Never have I heard a song so beautiful.
Even should one hundred great scholars assemble here,
No better illustration could they give.
You, a specter, have sung good words;
They are like a rod of gold,
Which strikes into my very heart.
Thus the Heart-air,[13] the Dharma-clinging[14]
    are dispelled;
The darkness of my ignorant blindness is
    thus illumined;
The white lotus of wisdom blossoms thus;
The lamp which brightens self-awareness[15]
    is lit;
And mindfulness of awareness is fully liberated.

[In observing that] this mindfulness is liberated
I stare upward at the great blue sky,
I realize completely the empty nature of being;
Of palpable existence,
No anxiety or fear have I.

When I look at the sun and moon
I realize their nakedness, the radiance of
    Mind-Essence;
Of distraction and drowsiness,[16] no fear have I.

When I gaze at the top of the mountains,
I clearly realize the immutable Samādhi;
Of change and flow I have no fear.

When I look down at the flowing river,
I fully realize the running nature of all flux;
Of the wrong view of Non-cause, I have no
    fear or misgiving.

When I contemplate the rainbow-like [illusions
    of existence]
I clearly realize the identity of Form and
    Voidness;

Of the nihilistic and realistic wrong-views[17]
    I have no fear.

When I see the shadows and the moon-in-water,
I fully realize the self-radiance of Non-clinging;
Of subjective and objective thoughts,[18]
    I have no fear.

When I look inwardly to the self-aware mind,
I clearly see the light of the inner lamp;
Of ignorant blindness, I have no fear.

When I hear what you, sinful spirit, have sung,
I fully realize the nature of self-awareness;
Of the obstacles and difficulties, I have no fear.

You, specter, are indeed eloquent in speech!
Do you really understand the nature of mind
    as you have said?
Look at the ugly birth of a hag-specter which
    you have merited!
You do nothing but vicious and evil deeds.
This is caused by your Dharma-ignorance and
    disregard of morality.
You should heed more diligently
The evils and sufferings of Saṃsāra.
You should thoroughly renounce the Ten
    Evil Actions![19]
A yogi, lion-like, I have neither fear nor panic.
You, sinful demon, should not think my
    joking words are true.[20]
I was only making fun of you.
Oh spirit! You have mocked me this evening!
But may we follow the legend of the Buddha
    and the Five Demons,[21]
And may the perfect Bodhi-Mind arise in you!
With your pure vow, combined with my compassion,
May you become one of my disciples in the
    future life.

Moved by his reply, a full faith in the Jetsun blossomed in Draug Srin Mo's heart. She released Milarepa's foot and sang with a sweet voice:

It is by virtue of the stock of Merits[22]
That you, oh gifted Yogi,
Are able to practice the Dharma
And remain alone within this mountain solitude!
Your merciful eyes keep watch o'er all beings
      in compassion!

I follow the Lineage of Bedma Tutrin[23]
And have heard the rosary of precious
      words in the holy Dharma.
Though I have listened to much preaching,
And attended great congregations,
Still my craving and clinging are excessive.

I lead to goodness those who observe the Dharma;
I show the right Path to gifted Buddhists.

Although my intention is friendly and my
      motive good,
Food must be sought to support this depraved body.

I roam the earth in this evil form,
Desiring blood and flesh for food.

I enter into the soul of whomsoever I encounter;
I incite the hearts of maidens, pretty and
      charming;
I madden with lust the blood of young men,
      strong and handsome.
With my eyes, I amuse myself watching all
      the dramas;
With my mind, I instigate cravings in all nations;
With my body I incite people to excitement
      and restlessness.

My home is at Linba,
My residence is in the Rock.

These are the things I do,
This is my sincere reply and honest
      self-confession.
These are the words of greeting for our meeting,

This is the evidence of my faith in you,
    and of my offerings.
Singing this song of honesty,
Let us be inspired and happy.

Milarepa thought, "This demon's earnest inquiry must be well answered, and her pride subdued." He then sang:

Hearken, hearken closely, you depraved hag.
The Guru is good, but the disciple is bad.
Those who have only heard and read the
    teaching of the Dharma,
Merely grasp at words.
They do not understand the real Dharma.
Eloquent and convincing as their words may sound,
There is neither use nor value in them.

Deceitful sayings and empty talk help not
In cleansing the defilements of one's mind.

Because of your evil *habit-propensities*
    formed in the past,
And your vicious doings in the present,
You have violated the Precepts and your Vows.[24]
By force of these transgressions,
You were born as a lower form of woman.
Your body wanders in the wretched haunts
    of cannibals;
Your talk is self-cheating and deceiving;
Your mind is saturated with thoughts of
    afflicting others.

It was because of your disregard of the
    Law of Karma,
That an ugly body in an inferior birth was taken,
Should you think now upon the vices of Saṃsāra,
You would confess your guilt, and promise to
    do good.

Like a lion, I do not fear;
Like an elephant, I have no anxiety;
Like a madman, I have no pretension and no hope.
I tell you the honest truth.

To make trouble and afflict me
Will only bring more sorrow on yourself.

Make a vow toward the pure Dharma.
Make a wish to be my disciple in the future.
Oh, you confused, depraved hag,
Think on these words with care!

Draug Srin Mo now appeared visibly as before, and with honesty she sang:

Of the Holy Buddhas of the Three Times,[25]
The Buddha Vajradhara is the chief;
He also is the Lord of the wondrous Doctrine.
The arising of Bodhi-Mind is indeed remarkable.

You may call me a depraved hag, but I do
      have great Merits.
True understanding arose when I heard your
      warning.
At first I swore to obey my Guru's instructions,
I studied and learned the holy Dharma.
But then I indulged myself, committing evil deeds.
With vicious passions[26] burning wildly,
      unbearably in my heart,
I was born in the ugly form of a she-demon.
I meant to help all sentient beings,
But again and again the results were evil.

You came, great Yogi, at the beginning of last year;
Staying alone in the cave, you meditated in
      solitude.
Sometimes I like you, but sometimes I do not!
It is because I like you that I came tonight;
It is because I do not, that I seized your foot.
I now repent this evil deed.

Hereafter, this wretched hag will renounce
      her wrong-doings;
With all her heart she will practice the Dharma;
She will serve Buddhism as best she can.
From now on, with the cool shade of the
      tree of grace,

Please protect her from the Five Poisonous
     Cravings.[27]

I, the depraved woman with ugly form,
     take refuge in you,
And rely on the instructions you have given.
I herewith renounce my malicious intentions.
From now until the time I achieve Buddhahood,
I swear to protect the yogis, and befriend
     all who meditate.
I will serve and assist the followers
Of the Doctrine, the observers of the Precepts.
To advanced yogis and the Dharma, I shall be
     an honest servant.

Thereupon, Draug Srin Mo swore before Milarepa that in the future
she would never harm anyone. She also took an oath to protect all
who meditate. In order to guide Draug Srin Mo, Milarepa then sang:

I am the venerable one who has renounced Saṃsāra;
I am the noble son of my Guru;
In me are stored the precious teachings;
A Buddhist with great sincerity and devotion am I.

I am the yogi who perceives the essence of being;
I am like a mother to all sentient beings;
I am a man who has courage and perseverance,
The holder of the spirit of Gautama Buddha,
The master of the Heart-aspiring-to-Bodhi.

I am the one who always adheres to kindness;
With great compassion I have subdued all
     evil thoughts.
I am the one who stays in the cave of Linba,
Who practices meditation without distraction.

Do you think you are happy now? You confused,
     wretched hag!
If you have not found happiness, it is your
     own fault.
Beware! Your clinging-to-Ego[28] is greater
     than yourself;

Pay heed! Your emotions are stronger
    than yourself.
Oh, specter, your vicious will is far
    wickeder than yourself;
Your habitual-thought is more characteristic
    than yourself;
Your ceaseless mental activity[29] is more
    frantic than yourself!

To maintain the existence of a ghost,
Only brings about mischief;
To understand the non-existence of a ghost
Is the way of Buddha;
To know that ghost and Reality are one
Is the way to Liberation.
Knowing that the ghosts are all one's parents
Is the right understanding;
Realizing that the ghost itself is Self-mind
Is glory supreme.

You will be emancipated from all fetters
If you realize the truth that I have stated;
This is my instruction to you, demoness!

To become my disciple you must observe the
    precepts.
Violate not the rules of Vajrayāna,[30]
Debase not the great Compassion,
Afflict not the body, word, and mind of Buddhists.
If you ever violate these rules.
You can be assured of plummeting to
    the Vajra Hell![31]
Recite these important rules three times;
Remember their meaning and practice them.

Let us now make a wish, and may the boon
    come quickly to you!
With the peerless Bodhi-Heart, inconceivably
    great, may you have great happiness.
In your future life,
May you then become my chief disciple,
Oh, woman of Dorje Semba.[32]

After Draug Srin Mo had taken the oath before the Jetsun, she made obeisances to him and also circumambulated him many times. She swore that thereafter she would obey all his orders. Then she disappeared like a rainbow, vanishing into the sky.

In the meantime, the day was dawning, and the sun shone. After a while Draug Srin Mo returned, bringing with her brothers, sisters, and a retinue, all with handsome faces and dressed in their best, to see the Jetsun. They made many offerings to him.

Draug Srin Mo said to Milarepa, "I am a sinful ghost. Forced by evil Karma, I was caught in a low form of birth; driven by evil habitual-thoughts, I influenced others, also, to become evil. I pray you to forgive me. Evil intention made me do you mischief. I entreat you to forgive me for what I have done. Hereafter I will obey your orders strictly and try to be your honest servant. Be gracious, and tell us of the supreme Truth that you have realized." In making this request Draug Srin Mo sang:

> Oh, thou! Thou [great one]! The son of
>   great heroes!
> Having amassed numerous merits,
> You have become a gifted person;
> Belonging to a distinguished Succession,[33]
> You are endowed with Waves of Grace.[34]
>
> You are the one who meditates with great perseverance,
> Who with endurance stays alone,
> Who industriously practices the deep teachings.
> To you there are no devils and no obstacles!
>
> Through realizing the microcosm of the
>   inner Channels and Prāṇas,
> You can work great miracles.
>
> We and you are in harmonious relationship.
> Our pure wishes in previous lives brought
>   about our meeting.
> Though I have met numerous accomplished saints,
> Only through you have I received grace and guidance.
> I, a hag-specter, speak with sincerity!
>
> The expedient truth of Hīnayāna[35] may
>   be illusive;

It is indeed hard to subdue the passions
    due to Karma!
One may talk eloquently about the Dharma,
But talk is of no avail when suffering
    and misery come.
That kind of Guru who strays from the Dharma,
Will not help himself, and merely incurs hatred.

You! The Incarnation Body of Buddha[36]
    in the Three Times,
Realize the immutable truth of Dharmata.[37]
With the inner teaching, you practice the
    quintessence of Dharma.
In this blessed place where grew the Ultimate
    Enlightenment,
We, Draug Srin Mo and her retinue,
Pray you to elucidate for us the teaching
    of the Innermost Secret.
Pray! Grant us the secret words of Vajrayāna,
    the truth of the Ultimate;
Pray! Teach us the great illuminating Wisdom,
Pray! Grant us the radiance of the Light!

By hearing the immutable Truth, the profound
    Secret Doctrine,
One will not fall into the lower path.
By practicing the teaching of the Secret Doctrine,
One will not wander in Saṃsāra's paths.
Without hiding and concealment,
We pray you to unfold to us the Truth complete.

Milarepa then said, "From what I can see now, not all of you
are able to practice the highest teaching of the immutable Truth. If
you insist on learning the Inner Teaching you must swear with your
life and pledge a solemn oath."

Thereupon, Draug Srin Mo swore an oath that henceforth she would
follow all the orders of the Jetsun, and that she would serve and assist all Buddhists. In answer to her questions, Milarepa sang a song,
"The Immutable and Real Dharma on the Twenty-seven Vanishments":

To the secret Buddha with a human body,
To the incomprable Translator, Marpa,
    my father Guru,

At your feet I bow, oh Gracious One!

I am not a singer who wishes to display his art,
But you, specter, entreat me to sing and sing again.
Today I will sing to you of the Ultimate Truth.

Thunder, lightning, and the clouds,
Arising as they do out of the sky,
Vanish and recede back into it.

The rainbow, fog, and mist,
Arising as they do from the firmament,
Vanish and recede back into it.

Honey, fruit, and crops grow out of the earth;
All vanish and recede back into it.

Flowers, leaves, and forests,
Arising as they do out of the earth,
Vanish and return back into it once more.

The ripple, tide, and flux,
Arising as they do from the great ocean,
Also vanish and into it return.

Habitual-thinking, clingings, and desires,
Arising as they do from the Alaya Consciousness,[38]
All vanish and return to the Alaya.

Self-awareness, self-illumination, and self-liberation,
Arising as they do from the Mind-Essence,
All vanish and dissolve back into the mind.

Non-arising, Non-extinction, and Non-description,
Arise from the Dharmata
And all return to it again.

Phantasms, hallucinations, and visions of demons,
All are produced from Yoga,
And all go back and vanish into it again.

Should one cling to the reality of visions,[39]
He would be confused in his meditation.

If he knew not that all obstacles
Reveal the Void, the manifestation of Mind,
He would be misled in his meditation.
The very root of all confusion
Also comes out of the mind.
He who realizes the nature of that mind,
Sees the great Illumination without coming
    and going.
Observing the nature of all outer forms,
He realizes that they are but illusory visions
    of mind.
He sees also the identity of the Void and Form.

Moreover, to meditate is an illusory thought;
Not to meditate is illusory, too.
It is the same whether or not you meditate.

Discrimination of "the two"[40] is the
    source of all wrong views.
From the ultimate viewpoint there is no
    view whatsoever.
This is the nature[41] of Mind.
The teaching of observation of
The Dharma-nature is illustrated through
    the simile of space.
You, Draug Srin Mo, should look into the
    meaning of beyond-thoughts;
You should enter the non-distracted realm
    in meditation;
You should act naturally and spontaneously,
Ever conscious of the Essence.

Beyond words is the Accomplishment, free
    from hope and fear.
I have no time to sing for fun, chatting with
    empty words.
Oh, spirit! Think of the auspicious Dharma.
Ask little, do not raise so many questions;
But be relaxed and sit at ease!

I sing as you requested;
These are my mad words.[42]
If you can practice them,

You will eat the food of Great Bliss[43]
    when hungry,
And drink the Nectar[44] when thirsty.
Then you can help yogis by your actions.

Whereupon Draug Srin Mo and her retinue were overwhelmed with devotion for the Jetsun, making obeisances and circumambulating him many times. They cried, "Revered One, we are indeed deeply grateful to you!" and disappeared like a rainbow, vanishing into the sky. From then on, they obeyed the orders of Milarepa; they served yogis, never afflicting them, and became their good friends.

This is the story of [Milarepa's meeting with] Draug Srin Mo at the cave of Linba.

NOTES

1 The Planet Chamju (or Rāhu) (T.T.: Khyab.hJug.): a legendary planet which was supposed to be malignant to the destinies of mankind, and was known for continually wreaking vengence on the sun and the moon.

2 Four Continents: See Story 2, Notes 15, 16, and 17.

3 An enlightened mind — the Bodhi-Heart, or Bodhi-Mind (Skt.: Bodhicitta; T.T.: Byan.Chub.Sems.): This most important and frequently used term in Mahāyāna Buddhism signifies the fundamental spirit, doctrine, and philosophy of the Mahāyāna. Among the meanings and applications of this term, two are most significant: first, the vow and action of liberating all sentient beings from suffering and bringing them to Buddhahood; and second, the direct realization of the Ultimate Truth. To signify these different aspects of Bodhicitta, Bodhi-Heart, Bodhi-Mind, enlightened heart or mind, etc., are alternatively used in this book. See Story 1, Note 20.

4 Nhamdog (T.T.: rNam.rTog.): This is also a very frequently used term in Buddhist texts. It has many meanings, such as the incessant flow of thoughts; illusory conceptions; uncontrollable and wild notions; and wrong ideas. See Story 1, Note 12.

5 Treading the Path of the Cemetery: Tantric yogis are urged to practice meditation in a cemetery, such surroundings being considered extremely helpful in furthering one's progress.

6 Measureless Palace (T.T.: gShal.Yas.Khan.): the heavenly "dwelling" of the Buddha in the "Pure Land," which transcends the limitation of space, and is immeasurable.

7 This implies an eclipse. See Note 1.

8 Deva (T.T.: lHa.): In Tibetan scriptures, all Buddhas, Bodhisattvas, heavenly beings, gods, and goddesses are called "Lha," but here it is used in a figurative sense.

9 Mahāyāna Buddhism teaches that all religious practices and spiritual efforts should be dedicated to the welfare and emancipation of all sentient beings.

10 Six Realms: the Six Worlds, or Lokas, in which different kinds of sentient beings live under different conditions. Devas, men, and asuras live in the upper three Lokas; animals, hungry ghosts, and denizens of hell, in the lower three.

11 Habitual thoughts, (T.T.: Bag.Chags.; Skt.: Vāsanā): According to Mahāyāna Buddhism, especially Yogācāra, sentient beings' consciousnesses are brought into play by the force of habitual thoughts. Reason and affect are all made up of the accumulated "psychic contents" that have been well-preserved in the Ālaya or Store Consciousness.

12 Suchness (T.T.: De.bShin.Ñid; Skt.: Tathatā), is also translated as "Thatness," implying that Absolute Reality is essentially indescribable; it is *as such* all the time.

13 Heart-air: See Story 1, Note 17.

14 Dharma-clinging (T.T.: Chos.hDsin.): According to Buddhism. there are two forms of clinging: (1) The Clinging-to-Ego (see Note 28), and (2) the Clinging-to-Dharma. The Clinging-to-Dharma implies an innate tendency to hold becomings and manifestations to be real and subsistent. The very conception of "being," declares Mahāyāna Buddhism, is a product of the Clinging-to-Dharma.

15 Self-awareness (T.T.: Rañ.Rig.): the self-aware or self-witnessing faculty of the consciousness which is, according to Yogācāra, the mind per se. The function of self-awareness is to be aware of the awareness itself; it is a pure awareness without any subject-content. To cultivate this pure awareness is the pinnacle practice of Mahāmudrā.

16 Distraction and drowsiness: These two hindrances are experienced by all who practice meditation — the two major enemies of the yogi.

17 The human mind is inclined either to cling to the "View of existence-and-permanency" (T.T.: rTag.lTa.), or to the "View of annihiliation-and-non-existence" (T.T.: Chad.lTa.). The former holds to the eternal existence of true being, and the latter to the ultimate annihiliation of all existence. The remedy for both of these extremes or "wrong views" is the Middle Way Doctrine upheld by Buddhism.

18 Or, subjectivity and objectivity: All Saṃsāric conceptions and emotions are characterized by a subjective objective pattern — the knower and the known, the lover and the one loved, etc. This dualistic pattern of thought is the fundamental cause of Saṃsāra. Enlightenment is but the transformation and emancipation from the *two grasping jaws of the pincers* of dualism.

19 See Story 2, Note 21.

20 Joking words: Milarepa here alludes to his remarks in praise of the demoness Draug Srin Mo, made in the beginning of the first song, as merely ridicule.

21 Buddha and the Five Demons: On the eve of His enlightenment, Guatama Buddha conquered the demons of the Five Desires who came to afflict Him.

22 The stock, or accumulation of merits (T.T.: Tshogs.bSags.): another frequently used phrase in Buddhism. This term implies a rather complicated doctrine of Buddhist ethics. In brief, all the "states of well-being," worldly or religious, material or spiritual, Saṃsāric or Nirvāṇic, are brought into being through deeds-of-merit. Buddhahood is viewed as the consummation of all merits.

23 Bedma Tutrin (T.T.: Pat.Ma.Thod.Phreñ.): This is another name of Padma Saṃbhava, the great Indian Yogi, who founded the Ningmaba School of Tibet.

24 Violating the Precepts and one's Vows: This demoness once swore before Padma Saṃbhava to protect the Dharma and to observe the Precepts.

25 Three Times: Past, present, and future.

26 Passions (Skt.: Kleśas; T.T.: Ñon.Moñs.Pa.): This word is very difficult to translate into English accurately because of its various meanings. Usually it signifies the burning passions and desires, such as lust, hate, anger, blindness, distractions, and the like. Both the innate and the acquired desires which hinder the way to Nirvāṇa, are Kleśas.

27 Five Poisonous Cravings, or Five Klesas: Lust, hate, blindness, pride, and jealousy.

28 Clinging-to-Ego (Skt.: Ātma-grāha; T.T.: bDag.hDsin.): the delusion of a permanent, unconditioned Ego, which causes the continuation of Saṃsāric existence. The Clinging to Ego manifests itself in two forms, (1) the Innate or Inborn Ego, the fundamental notion of "self"; and (2) the acquired Ego, which is developed through experience and education.

29 Ceaseless mental activity or constant-flow-of-thought: Men's thoughts never stop, with or without their awareness. They continue to flow on unceasingly, like a waterfall.

30 The rules of Vajrayāna: Tantric or Samaya precepts.

31 Vajra Hell: The purgatory where all violators of Tantric precepts go.

32 Dorje Semba, (Skt.: Vajrasattva): Among the five "Maṇḍala" Buddhas, this is the one who sits in the center, sometimes also called Dorje-Chang, (Skt.: Vajradhara) from whom all the teachings of Tantra originated.

33 Succession: A transmission of Tantric teachings.

34 Waves-of-Grace: The blessing power that emanates from Gurus of a Succession. This blessing power, or grace-wave, is considered to be one of the determining factors of a yogi's success in his devotion. The speed of his accomplishment is said to depend largely on the intensity and amount of the grace-waves that he is capable of receiving from his Guru.

35 Hīnayāna, meaning the Small Vehicle, denotes the original form of Buddhism that developed after Śākyamuni's death. Hīnayāna Buddhism now prevails in Ceylon, Burma, and Siam, and is therefore also known as Southern Buddhism in contrast to Mahāyāna, meaning the Great Vehicle, now prevailing in Tibet, China, Korea, and Japan.

36 For the sake of respect and reverence, Draug Srin Mo called Milarepa "Trolgu," the Incarnation, or Transformation Body of Buddha (T.T.: sPrul.sKu.). However, Milarepa himself never claimed to be an incarnation of Buddha or a gifted, superior being. He asserted that he was an ordinary man.

37 Dharmata (T.T.: Chos.Ñid.), meaning the nature or truth of being.

38 Ālaya Consciousness or Store Consciousness (T.T.: Kun.gShi.rNam.Çes.): the Eighth Consciousness. This consciousness has more than ten different names, which appear in the different Buddhist texts, each indicating one of its aspects or characteristics. The philosophy of Yogācāra puts its main stress on the study of this Consciousness. "Kun.gShi.rNam.Çes." may be translated as "Universal or Primordial Consciousness," the "All-sources Consciousness," the "Conciousness of Ripening Karma," etc. A fair study of this Consciousness is necessary for a better understanding of the teachings of Mahāyāna and of Tantric Buddhism. See Story 10, Note 1.

39 The literal translation should be "the visions of ghosts." Milarepa referred to the conjurations of Draug Srin Mo.

40 The conception of "Yes and No," affirmation and negation.

41 Lit.: Form-nature (T.T.: mTshan.Ñid.). This word originally means defi-

nition, reason, essence, nature, etc. Here Milarepa used it in a very loose sense, implying something quite different from the above ordinary usage of this term.

42 Enlightened yogis always have a good sense of humor. Being fully aware of the limitation of words and the absurdity of human conceptions, they sometimes ridicule their own words, which also cannot escape the dilemma and predicament inherent in the human way of thinking and expression.

43 Great Bliss (T.T.: bDe.Chen.) implies the great ecstasy the yogi experiences in meditation.

44 Nectar: The literal translation should be, "The Nectar of Non-outflowing" (T.T.: Zag.Med.). Using yogic Power, the yogi may increase the secretion of the salivary glands to quench his feeling of thirst.

5

MILAREPA IN RAGMA

Obeisance to all Gurus

W HEN the Jetsun Milarepa decided to go to Riwo Balnbar from Linba Draug to practice meditation, he notified his patrons in Ragma. They said, "Near Riwo Balnbar there is a temple in a very delightful place. We recommend that you stay there. As to Riwo Balnbar, we do not know very much about it. Revered One, you may remain in the temple at first; meantime, we will send out people to survey the region for you."

Milarepa thought to himself, "First I shall go to the temple for awhile, then I shall proceed to Riwo Balnbar." He then said to them, "I do not need your guide; I can find the way myself." When the patrons asked, "Do you have a guide?" Milarepa replied, "Yes, I have." "Who is he? Tell us more about him."

In answer Milarepa sang:

> The glorious and accomplished Guru
> Who dispels the darkness, is the guide.
>
> Away from cold and warmth, these cotton
> clothes,[1]
> By which I renounce fur-craving, are the guide.
>
> The Invocation, Identification, and
> Transformation Yogas[2]
> Which crush the delusion of Bardo, are
> the guide.
>
> That which shows you the way in all journeys
> through all lands—
> The complete mastery of Prāṇa-Mind[3]
> is the guide.

58

To give up one's body as a good-offering[4] —
The teaching of Subduing-the-Ego — is the guide.

To remain in solitude and practice meditation,
Leading one to Enlightenment, is the guide.

Led by these six guides, and abiding in
　　Jaung Chub Tsong,[5]
All will be well with me.

Thereupon Milarepa went to the upper part of Ragma, which from that time on was called Jaung Chub Tsong. He then absorbed himself in the Samādhi of the Flowing River.[6]

One midnight, he heard a great noise and clamor, horns roaring in the air as if an army in battle were approaching. Milarepa thought, "Is there fighting in this country?" He then absorbed himself in the Samādhi of Great Compassion. But the sound came closer and closer. Both Heaven and earth seemed bathed in red light. Milarepa wondered what was happening. He looked about and saw that the whole plain was burning, that nothing was left on earth or in Heaven. A band of the [demon] army was busily engaged in lighting fires, tossing water, and throwing down mountains. Through innumerable conjurations, the demons threatened Milarepa with many types of weapons, tearing down the rocks and the cave, and also heaping him with abuse. Milarepa became aware that demons were assembling to afflict him. He thought, "What a pity, from time immemorial until now these sinful Ah Tsa Ma Demons[7] have practiced evil deeds in the Six Realms, thus becoming hungry specters flying in the sky. With vicious thoughts and evil intentions they have harmed so many sentient beings, that with this black Karma they have no choice but to go to a hell in their future life." With great compassion, therefore, Milarepa sang:

I pay homage to you, Marpa the Translator.
In the immense sky of your compassion
Are gathered from all sides the clouds of mercy
From which fell the productive rain of grace.
Thus the harvest of your disciples was increased.
To immeasurable sentient beings as infinite
　　as space,
Pray grant your grace-waves for the attainment
　　of Enlightenment.

You assembled Non-men and demons,
You who fly and travel in the sky
Perpetually longing for food,
You hungry specters!
Driven by the force of Full-ripening Karma,[8]
In th·· life you were born as hungry ghosts;
Also by the Karma of evil-doing,
Through harming others,
You shall fall into a hell in your future life.
I sing of the truths of Karma.
Think closely on these beneficent words.

I am the son of Ghagyu Gurus;
With faith arising in my heart,
I am learning the Dharma.
Knowing the Law of Cause and of Effect,
I practice austere living;
Diligent and persevering,
I see the true nature of Mind.

I realize that all forms are but illusions [Māyā].
I thus free myself from the illness of ego-clinging,
I thus cut off the Subject-Object Fetter[9]
     of Saṃsāra,
And reach the Buddha's realm, the immutable Dharmakāya.

I am a yogi who has gone beyond the [human] mind;
How can you afflict me, you troublemakers?
Your vicious deeds and mischievous intentions,
Weary you, but do me no harm.

Again, you must know that mind is the
     source of hatred.
Though from the depths of the eighteen
     hells below
To the Heaven of Brahmā above,
You collect all the forces therein to
     throw against me,
It can hardly ripple my all-embracing Wisdom,
For in my mind no fear can arise.

You assembled demons and Non-men,
With all your spells and magic weapons,

You cannot hurt me;
All you have done is useless.
What a waste and pity if you return
　　without harming me!
Show your power and do your worst, you
　　pitiable demons.

Whereupon Milarepa became absorbed in the Samādhi of Suchness. [Awed and overpowered by his greatness], all the demons repented before him and became faithful to him. They made obeisance and circumambulated him many times, saying: "We were indeed blind, not knowing that you are such an accomplished yogi. Pray forgive us for what we have done to you. From now on we will follow whatever instructions you may give. Pray grant us the teachings, so a relationship in Dharma may thus be established between us."

Milarepa replied, "Very well. In that case I shall give you this teaching":

Refrain from sin,
Practice virtue!

All the demons cried, "Yes, we will obey!" Then they offered him their lives and hearts, and also promised the Jetsun to obey his orders. Following this, they all went back to their own realm.

Among them was one called Seyi Lhamo, from Mang, and others were local deities from Riwo Balnbar. Milarepa felt that, since the demons of Riwo Balnbar had already been subdued, it would not be necessary to go there to meditate any more. He decided to remain at the Bodhi-Place for a few days. In a very elated mood he sang:

Here in the home of Enlightenment,
I, the Bodhi-Path [practitioner], Milarepa,
Who has mastered the Mind-of-Bodhi,
Practice the Yoga of Bodhi-Heart.
I will soon obtain the great Bodhi,
And bring the innumerable mother-like beings[10]
To the sanctuary of Perfect Enlightenment.

One day, a patron came to Milarepa's hut bringing with him a load of wood and a half-measure of flour. The visitor did not wear enough clothes and felt very cold. He said, "Ragma is the coldest region in the South and this is the coldest place in Ragma. I would like, Lama, to offer you a fur coat if you would accept it."

Milarepa asked, "My dear patron, what is your name?" and the man replied, "Labar Shawa." Milarepa then said, "You have a very good name, indeed. Although I do not need your flour and fur coat, I thank you very much. I'll take the flour, if you wish, but as to the fur coat, I really do not need it." And he sang:

As a child who loses his way home,
The confused mind wanders in the Six
    delusive Realms.
By the force of illusory Karma,
One sees a myriad visions and feels
    endless emotions.

Sometimes I have illusory feelings of hunger,
Therefore I prepare my food and dinner.
Sometimes I exert myself to build a house;[11]
At others I endure the hardship of eating
    stones.[12]
Sometimes I eat the food of Śūnyatā [Voidness];
Or I change my ways and do not eat at all.[13]

At times when I feel thirsty, I drink pure
    blue water;
At others, I rely on my own secretions.
Frequently, I drink the flow from the
    Fountain of Compassion;
Quite often, I sip enchanting nectar of goddesses.

Sometimes I feel cold, so I wear the clothes
    of the Two Channels;[14]
At others, Heat Yoga gives burning bliss
    and warmness.

Occasionally, I change my ascetic way of life;
At times when I feel like having friends
    around me;
I live with the Wisdom of Awareness as my companion.

I practice the white deeds of the Ten Virtues;
I contemplate the true knowledge of Reality,
And know for certain the self-radiant mind.

Adorned with the precious gem of true knowledge,

I am the Yogi Milarepa — a lion among men.

Proficient and victorious, I am skilled in
     meditation.
On the snow mountain I practice in solitude.
I am the yogi who obtains the fruits of merit,
I am the Yogi Milarepa, a tiger among men.

I have thrice animated the Bodhi-Mind,[15]
I smile with joy at the Non-distinction of
     Means and Wisdom;[16]
I dwell in the woods of the Radiant Valley
     of Remedy;[17]
And produce the fruits of the welfare of
     sentient beings.

I am the Yogi Milarepa—an eagle among men.
I have a pair of mighty wings of the clear-
     sighted Arising Yoga;[18]
I possess two flying wings of the stable
     Perfecting Yoga.[19]
I soar to the sky of Two-in-One Suchness;[20]
I sleep in the cave of transcendental Truth;
I attain the fruits of self and others' benefit.
I am the Yogi Milarepa—a man among men.

I am the one who sees the face of form,
I am he who gives good counsel.
I am a yogi without attributes.

I am a man who cares not what may happen.
I am an almsbeggar who has no food,
A nude hermit without clothes,
A beggar without jewels.
I have no place to lay my head;
I am the one who never thinks of external
     objects—
The master of all yogic action.

Like a madman, I am happy if death comes:
I have nothing and want nought.

If one desires to acquire property,

It only leads to jealousy and anger;
It merely causes trouble to the patrons
And leads them into erring ways of life.

To a yogi, all is fine and splendid!
With a benevolent heart and accompanying blessings,
Almsgiving should ever be your practice.

I wish you all happiness and prosperity;
I wish you good health, leisure, and long life.
May you, in the next life, be born in the Pure
        Land of Buddha,
There to practice [joyfully] the Dharma.
May you then be able without ceasing
To devote yourself to the welfare of all men.

Thereupon, great faith in the Jetsun was aroused in this man. He said, "Because you are the accomplished Yogi Milarepa, you can do without these things. It is only for the sake of benefiting us sinful people that you remain here. Pray pity me and take my offerings."

Thereafter, while Milarepa stayed at the Bodhi-Place, this man always brought bountiful food and provisions to him. Imbued with great joy, Milarepa remained there for some time.

One day, some villagers from Ragma came to see the Jetsun. They asked him, "Do you like this place? Do you feel happy in remaining here?" He replied, "Yes, I am very happy indeed. I am also greatly pleased with my progress." They asked "Why do you like this place so much? Why is it that you are so happy here? Pray tell us what you think of all these things!" In answer, Milarepa sang:

Here is the Bodhi-Place, quiet and peaceful.
The snow mountain, the dwelling place of
        deities, stands high above;
Below, far from here in the village, my
        faithful patrons live;
Surrounding it are mountains nestling in
        white snow.

In the foreground stand the wish-granting trees;
In the valley lie vast meadows, blooming wild.
Around the pleasant, sweet-scented lotus,
        insects hum;
Along the banks of the stream

And in the middle of the lake,
Cranes bend their necks, enjoy the scene,
    and are content.

On the branches of the trees, the wild birds sing;
When the wind blows gently, slow dances
    the weeping willow;
In the treetops monkeys bound and leap with joy;
In the wild green pastures graze the scattered herds,
And merry shepherds, gay and free from worry,
Sing cheerful songs and play upon their reeds.
The people of the world, with burning desires
    and craving,
Distracted by affairs, become the slaves of earth.

From the top of the Resplendent Gem Rock,
I, the Yogi, see these things.
Observing them, I know that they are fleeting
    and transient;
Contemplating them, I realize that comforts
    and pleasures
Are merely mirages and water-reflections.

I see this life as a conjuration and a dream.
Great compassion rises in my heart
For those without a knowledge of this truth.

The food I eat is the Space-Void;
My meditation is Dhyāna—beyond distraction.

Myriad visions and various feelings all
    appear before me—
Strange indeed are Saṃsāric phenomena!
Truly amusing are the dharmas in the
    Three Worlds,[21]
Oh, what a wonder, what a marvel!
Void is their nature, yet everything is manifested.

The villagers were [delighted with this song], and, with their faith also strengthened, they all returned home [in a very joyful mood].

This is the first part of the story of Milarepa's stay at Ragma.

NOTES

1 The yogi who practices Heat Yoga is supposed to wear only cotton clothing, no fur being allowed. The purpose of this rigid practice is twofold: to renounce the procurement of fur and the craving for it, and to train himself for doing without furs in an extremely cold region such as Tibet, thus stimulating the production of more inner heat.

2 The Yogas (lit.: Instructions) of Invocation, Identification, and Transformation (T.T.: bSre.hPho.sKor.gSum.): In the Bardo plane (the intermediate stage between death and rebirth) the deceased sees numerous visions and images which are actually manifestations of his own mind. But, because of habitual-thinking and the Clinging-to-Ego, the uninitiated one cannot identify these visions and see into their true nature. Tantric Yoga not only serves the purpose of enabling one to realize the innate Buddhahood in this life, but also is a preparation for the stage of Bardo. When a proficient yogi sees the various manifestations of the Bardo, he can immediately identify the sound which he hears with the Mantra (or invocation) of his patron Buddha, and the images he sees with figures of the same. Through the practice of the Yogas of Invocation, Identification, and Transformation in this lifetime, the yogi is able to dispel the fear of Bardo. These three Yogas may be described as follows:

        (1) Invocation Yoga: By praying, and reciting the Mantra of a special patron Buddha, the yogi invokes the protection of that tutelary.

        (2) Identification Yoga: In Yoga practice, the yogi identifies or unites himself with the tutelary. Thus in the stage of Bardo, when wrathful and peaceful deities appear, the yogi may identify himself with them. (See W. Y. Evans-Wentz' "Tibetan Book of the Dead," Oxford University Press, London, 1957.)

        (3) Transformation Yoga: Through the practice of this Yoga the visions of the Bardo may be transformed at will.

3 Prāṇa-Mind or Energy-Mind (T.T.: Rluṅ. Sems.): This is an important term in Tantrism. It is said that a yogi who has mastered the Mind-energy, or Energy-mind, is capable of performing supernormal feats, one of them being to fly wherever he chooses. (See also Story 3, Note 2.)

4 A special Tibetan Yoga called "gCod," devised for destroying one's Ego-clinging. In practicing this Yoga, the yogi offers his own body to sentient beings through special visualizations.

5 Jaung Chub Tsong: The Castle of Bodhi (T.T.: Byan.Chub.rDson.).

6 Samādhi of the Flowing River: This refers to a mental state experienced by the yogi in Mahāmudrā practice, in which he feels he is free from attachment to all phenomena. Although immersed in phenomenal existence, he is not affected by it; he encompasses the flux of things, he watches the flux of becoming flow by. Though he is aware of the identity of himself and the flux, he knows that he is the master, and enjoys a liberated spirit within the great flow. (See also Story 2, Note 4.)

7 Ah Tsa Ma demons: See Story 2, Note 5.

8 Full-ripening Karma: See Story 2, Note 6.

9 Subject-Object Fetter: The doer, and that which is done; the seer, and that which is seen; etc. This dualistic pattern of thought is considered to be the basic cause of Saṃsāra.

10 Since in every incarnation one has a mother, from beginningless time one must have had innumerable mothers. In fact, according to Mahāyāna Buddhism,

all sentient beings have had, more than once, a parental relationship between one another. This calls forth the great compassion of a Bodhisattva.

11 This refers to Milarepa's labors for his Master, Marpa, in the trial period of his discipleship. (See Milarepa's Biography, "Tibet's Great Yogi, Milarepa," 2nd ed., edited by W. Y. Evans-Wentz, Oxford University Press, London, 1951.)

12 Eating stones: To avoid involvement in the world, a technique for eating stones in place of food is provided for determined Tantric yogis.

13 Through the power of Samādhi, the yogi is able to live without eating for a long time.

14 Two Channels (T.T.: rTsa.gÑis.): the mystical right and left Channels in the human body through which yogic heat powers are engendered. See also Story 1, Note 28.

15 The meaning of this sentence is not very clear. The translator believes that "thrice animated the Bodhi-Mind" signifies the complete unfoldment of the so-called three-fold Bodhi-Mind: (1) the Bodhisattva's Vow, (2) the Transcendental Bodhi-Mind, or the Non-distinction Wisdom, and (3) the "Occult" Bodhi-Mind, that is, according to Tantrism, the essence (semen), or the source-energy of the physical body.

16 Non-distinction of Means and Wisdom, or, rendered in a different way, the Two-in-One Means-Wisdom: The Bodhisattva's activity includes two main facets, (1) the cultivation of Wisdom, i.e., the practice and realization of the Prajñāpāramitā (Perfect Wisdom); and (2) the practice of Means or Virtue, i.e., the first five Pāramitās, namely, charity, discipline, patience, diligence, and meditation. Only advanced yogis are capable of realizing the Non-distinction or Non-differentiation of these two practices.

17 "Radiant" denotes the self-radiant or self-illuminating nature of Mind; "Valley of Remedy" denotes the realization of the Self-mind as being the cure or remedy for all evils.

18 Arising Yoga (T.T.: sKyed.Rim.): In the Anuttara Tantra, the Supreme Tantra, there are two major practices: one is the Arising Yoga, the other is the Perfecting Yoga. The former is the preparation for the latter — it places emphasis on concentration and visualization exercises, and through them the Dhyāna or Samādhi state is reached. Unless the yogi has reached a stage of advanced Dhyāna or Samādhi, he is not capable of practicing the latter.

19 Perfecting Yoga (T.T.: rDsogs.Rim.): the advanced Yoga of Tibetan Tantrism. It is a practice of uniting mind and Prāna. (See W. Y. Evans-Wentz' "Tibetan Yoga and Secret Doctrines," 2nd ed., Oxford University Press, London, 1958.)

20 Two-in-One Suchness: This term may also be rendered as "Non-dualistic Suchness." In the realm of Samsāra, different views and interpretations on a thing are formed from different levels and positions. To the average person, a glass of water is merely a means of quenching thirst; to a physicist. it is a combination of elements in motion; and to a philosopher, it is a series of relationships. These different views or understandings, arising from different levels and realms of thinking, are thus the distinctive characteristic of Samsāric thought, whereas in the Two-in-One or Many-in-One State, these different views do not exist as such.

21 The Three Worlds, or the Three Realms (T.T.: Khams.gSum.): According to Buddhism, these are the World of Desire, the World of Form, and the World of Non-form. They are believed to include all sentient beings in the various realms of Samsāric existence.

၅ဥ၅၊၊

6

MILAREPA AT JUNPAN NANKA TSANG

Obeisance to all Gurus

Fʀᴏᴍ Ragma, Milarepa went to Junpan Nanka Tsang[1] and remained there for some time.

One day a monkey came to Milarepa's hut riding on a rabbit, wearing mushroom armor and carrying a bow and arrow made from stalks. [His appearance was so ludicrous that] Milarepa could not help laughing. The demon said to the Jetsun, "You came here through fear.[2] If you are no longer afraid, you can go away." Milarepa replied, "I realize fully that manifestation is Mind itself; also, I see that Mind-Essence is identical with the Dharmakāya. You pitiable wraith! Whatever apparitions you may conjure, they are a mere laughing matter to me." Thereupon, the demon made his offering and took an oath before Milarepa. Then, like a rainbow, he disappeared into the sky. He was the demon king of Dro Tang.

One day, Milarepa's patrons from Dro Tang came to visit him. They aaked him what benefits Junpan Nanka Tsang had to offer. In reply, Milarepa sang:

> I pray to my Guru, the Holy One.
> Listen, my patrons, and I will tell you
>   the merits of this place.
>
> In the goodly quiet of this Sky Castle of Junpan
> High above, dark clouds gather;
> Deep blue and far below flows the River Tsang.
>
> At my back the Red Rock of Heaven rises;
> At my feet, wild flowers bloom, vibrant
>   and profuse;

At my cave's edge [wild] beasts roam, roar,
    and grunt;
In the sky vultures and eagles circle freely,
While from heaven drifts the drizzling rain.

Bees hum and buzz with their chanting;
Mares and foals gambol and gallop wildly;
The brook chatters past pebbles and rocks;
Through the trees monkeys leap and swing;
And larks carol in sweet song.

The timely sounds I hear are all my fellows.
The merits of this place are inconceivable—
I now relate them to you in this song.

Oh, good patrons,
Pray follow my Path and my example;
Abandon evil, and practice good deeds.
Spontaneously from my heart
I give you this instruction.

There was a Tantric yogi among the patrons who said to Milarepa, "We would be deeply grateful if you would graciously give us the essential instructions on the View, Meditation, and Action,[3] as a greeting or a gift of welcome."

Milarepa sang in reply:

The grace of my Guru enters my heart;
Pray help me to realize the truth of the Void!

In answer to my faithful patrons,
I sing to please the Deities and Buddhas:

Manifestation, the Void, and Non-differentiation,
These three are the quintessence of the View.

Illumination, Non-thought, and Non-distraction
Are the quintessence of the Meditation.

Non-clinging, Non-attachment, and complete
    Indifference
Are the quintessence of the Action.

No Hope, no Fear, and no Confusion
Are the quintessence of Accomplishment.

Non-attempt, Non-hiding, and Non-discrimination,
These three are the quintessence of the Precept.

Having heard Milarepa's song, the patrons all returned home. A few days later, many disciples came again to visit the Jetsun, asking after his health and welfare, and giving their best wishes. Milarepa sang in response:

I bow down at the feet of my Guru.

Deep in the forest by man untrod,
I, Milarepa, happily practice meditation.

With no attachment and no clinging,
Walking and tranquility are both pleasing.

Free from sickness and disorder, I willingly
    sustain this body of illusion;
Never sleeping, I sit in the comfort of quietude.

Abiding in the Samādhi of Non-permanence,[4]
    I taste enjoyment.
Continuance in Heat-Yoga without cold is
    indeed felicitous.

With no cowardliness or dismay,
Joyfully I follow the Tantric practice;
With no effort I perfect the cultivation;
With no distraction whatsoever,
Remaining in solitude, I am truly happy.
These are the pleasures of the body.

Happy is the path of both Wisdom and Means![5]
Happy the Yoga of Arising and Perfecting;
    the meditation of the Two-in-One.
Happy the Prajñā; the awareness of no-
    coming-and-going!
Happy the absence of talk; no friends and
    no chatting!
These are the pleasures of words.

Happy is the understanding of Non-grasping;
Happy the meditation without interruption;
Happy the accomplishment without hope or fear;
Happy the action done without defilement.
These are the pleasures of Mind.

Happy is the illumination with no thought
    and no mutation!
Happy the great bliss in the purity of
    Dharmadhātu![6]
Happy the Non-ceasing Realm of Form!

This little song of great happiness
That flows freely from my heart,
Is inspired by meditation,
By the merging of act and knowledge.
Those who aim at the fruit of Bodhi
May follow this way of yogic practice.

The disciples said to Milarepa, "Wonderful indeed are the joys of Body, Word, and Mind, as you have just said. Pray tell us, how were they brought about?" Milarepa replied, "By the *realization* of Mind." The disciples then said, "Although we shall never be able to acquire such happiness and pleasures as you have enjoyed, we hope that we can win a small portion; we beg you, therefore, to give us a clear teaching, easy to understand and simple to practice, by which we may realize the Essence of Mind." Whereupon the Jetsun sang "The Twelve Meanings of Mind":

I bow down at the feet of my Guru.

Oh good patrons! If you wish to realize
    the Essence of Mind,
You should practice the following teachings:
Faith, knowledge, and discipline,
These three are the Life-Tree[7] of Mind.
This is the tree you should plant and foster.

Non-attachment, non-clinging, and non-blindness,
These three are the shields of Mind;
They are light to wear, strong for defense,
And the shields you should seek.

Meditation, diligence, and perseverance,
These three are the horses of Mind;
They run fast and quickly flee!
If you look for horses, these are the right ones.

Self-awareness, self-illumination, and
    self-rapture,[8]
These three are the fruits of Mind;
Sow the seeds, ripen the fruit,
Refine the fluid, and the essence emerges.
If you look for fruit, these are the fruit
    you should seek.

Sprung from yogic intuition,
This song of the Twelve Meanings of Mind is sung.
Inspired by your faith, continue with your
    practice, my good patrons!

Henceforth, the patrons placed even more faith in Milarepa, and brought him excellent offerings. Milarepa then decided to go to Yolmo Snow Range.

This is the story of Milarepa at Junpan Nanka Tsang [The Sky Castle of Junpan].

NOTES

1 Junpan Nanka Tsan (T.T.: rKan.Phan.Nam.mKhah.rDson.): a place near the Himalaya Mountains, meaning "The Sky Castle of Junpan."

2 Fear: the fear of suffering in Saṃsāra, that motivates the yogi's striving for emancipation.

3 View, Meditation, and Action; or View, Practice, and Action (T.T.: lTa., sGom., sPyod.): "View" is the knowledge or principle upon which all meditations are based and religious activities conducted. "Practice" refers to the yogic exercise of the View; "Action" to a state in which the yogi is absorbed in the View while carrying out his daily activities. The following example illustrates these terms: In the case of the Mahāmudrā teaching, the View is the understanding of the void nature of Mind; the Practice is the contemplation on this understanding; and the Action is the mindfulness of this View in daily activities, meaning that the yogi is able to remember his meditation experience even during all the vicissitudes of his daily existence.

4 Non-permanence: The realization of higher Samādhis should transcend both transitoriness and permanence.

5 Wisdom and Means (Skt.: Prajñā [and] Upāya; T.T.: Thabs. [and] Çes. Rab.): Wisdom is the understanding, or the View, or the "eye" of the yogi, while Means are the methods, the techniques, or the "legs."

6 Dharmadhātu (T.T.: Chos.dWyin.): This term has several different meanings. Here it means the Universal, Infinity, Totality, and the like.

7 Life-Tree (T.T.: Srog.Çiñ.): a symbolic term used to denote the life force upon which the existence of one's life depends. It also refers to the spine. Sometimes it denotes the center pillar in Buddhist stūpas.

8 Self-awareness, self-illumination, self-rapture (T.T.: Rañ.Ri., Rañ.gSal., Rañ bDe.): Despite the fact that the nature of Mind is indescribable, it can be apprehended through an illustration of its three main characteristics, i.e., self-awareness, self-illumination, and self-rapture, of which, though existing all the time, the un-initiated are not aware. Being conscious of consciousness (or self-awareness) is to approach the threshold of Enlightenment; the self-illuminating and self-rapturous aspects of mind were claimed by Buddhist sages, who found, in their mystical experiences, that the mind was itself illuminating and blissful.

7

THE SONG
OF A YOGI'S JOY

Obeisance to all Gurus

THE Master of Yoga, the Jetsun Milarepa, in obedience to his Guru's orders, went from Junpan to Yolmo Snow Range, where he dwelt at the Tiger Cave of Senge Tson[1] in the woods of Singalin. The local goddess of Yolmo appeared in a gracious form, obeying the Jetsun's orders and rendering her best service to him. Milarepa remained there for some time in a deeply inspired mood.

One day, five young nuns came from Mon to visit him. They addressed him thus: "It is said that this place is full of terror, and an ideal place in which to attain great improvement in meditation. Can this be true? Have you found it so?" Milarepa then sang in praise of the place:

> Obeisance to you, my Guru!
> I met you through having accumulated great merits,
> And now stay at the place you prophesied.[2]
>
> This is a delightful place, a place of hills
>   and forests.
> In the mountain-meadows, flowers bloom;
> In the woods dance the swaying trees!
> For monkeys it is a playground.
> Birds sing tunefully,
> Bees fly and buzz,
> And from day until night the rainbows come and go.
> In summer and winter falls the sweet rain,
> And mist and fog roll up in fall and spring.
> At such a pleasant place, in solitude,

I, Milarepa, happily abide,
Meditating upon the void-illuminating Mind.

Oh, happy are the myriad manifestations!
The more ups-and-downs, the more joy I feel.
Happy is the body with no sinful Karma,
Happy indeed are the countless confusions!
The greater the fear, the greater the
     happiness I feel.[3]
Oh, happy is the death of sensations and passions!

The greater the distress and passions,
The more can one be blithe and gay!
What happiness to feel no ailment or illness;
What happiness to feel that joy and suffering
     are one;
What happiness to play in bodily movement
With the power aroused by Yoga.
To jump and run, to dance and leap, is
     more joyful still.

What happiness to sing the victorious song,
What happiness to chant and hum,
More joyful still to talk and loudly sing!
Happy is the mind, powerful and confident,
Steeped in the realm of Totality.

The most extreme happiness
Is the self-emanation of self-power;
Happy are the myriad forms, the myriad revelations.
As a welcoming gift to my faithful pupils,
I sing of yogic happiness.

Thereupon, Milarepa initiated the five young nun-novices and gave
them the verbal instructions. After practicing these teachings for some
time, the light of inner Realization was born within them. Milarepa
was overjoyed and sang the "Nectar of Instruction":

Oh, my Guru, he who shows
The unmistakable path to Liberation,
The Perfect Savior, the great Compassionate One,
Pray, never leave me, ever remain
Above my head[4] as my crest-jewel!

Hearken, followers of the Dharma,
Ye meditators seated here,
Though the teachings of Buddha are most numerous,
He who can practice this Profound Path[5]
Is gifted indeed!

If you wish to become a Buddha in one lifetime,
You should not crave the things of this life,
Nor intensify your self-longing,
Else you will be entangled between good and evil,
And you may fall into the realm of misery.

When you give service to your Guru,
Refrain from thinking, "I am the one who works,
He is the one who enjoys."
Should you have this kind of feeling,
Quarrel and discord will surely follow,
And your wish can never be fulfilled.

When you observe the Tantric Precepts,
Cease association with the vicious,
Else you will be contaminated by evil influences,
And you may risk breaking the Precepts.

When you engage in study and learning,
Do not attach yourself to words with pride,
Else the dormant fire of the Five
    Poisonous Passions[6] will blaze,
And virtuous thoughts and deeds will be consumed.

When you meditate with friends in retreat,
Do not attempt too many things,
Else your virtuous deeds will cease,
And your devotion will be distracted.

When you practice the Path with Form[7]
    of the Whispered Transmission,[8]
Do not exorcise demons, nor curse ghosts for others,
Lest demons rise within your mind
And a longing for worldly aims will blaze.

When you have acquired Experience and
    Realization,[9]

Do not display your miraculous powers, nor prophesy,
Lest the secret words and symbols slip away
And merits and spiritual insight will diminish.

Beware of these pitfalls and avoid them.
Commit not evil deeds. Eat not beguiling food.
Take not the burden of the corpse.[10]
Utter not sweet words to please others.
Be humble and modest, and you will find your way.

The nuns then asked Milarepa how they might find their own way, beseeching him for further instruction. In reply, Milarepa sang:

I pay homage to my Guru, the gracious one.
I pray you to vouchsafe me your grace-waves.
Pray help me, the mendicant, happily to meditate.

Though you children of the new generation
Dwell in towns infested with deceitful Karma,
The link of Dharma still remains.
Because you have heard the Buddha's teaching
You now come to me,
And thus avoid going astray.

By constant practice of the Accumulation-
        of-Merits[11]
You will foster an aptitude for devotion.
The grace-waves will then enter you,
While the corresponding and actual
        Realization[12] will grow.

But even if you do all this, it will help
        but little
If you cannot reach full mastery.
Having pity on you, I now give you this instruction.
Listen closely, my young friends!

When you remain in solitude,
Think not of the amusements in the town,
Else the evil one will rise up in your heart;
Turn inward your mind,
And you will find your way.

When you meditate with perseverance and
    determination,
You should think upon the evils of Saṃsāra
And the uncertainty of death.
Shun the craving for worldly pleasures;
Courage and patience then will grow in you,
And you will find your way.

When you solicit the deep teachings of
    the Practice,
Do not long for learning, nor to become a scholar,
Else worldly actions and desires will dominate;
Then this very life will be thrown away.
Be humble and modest,
And you will find your way.

When the various experiences come to you
    in meditation,
Do not be proud and anxious to tell people,
Else you will disturb the Goddesses and Mothers.[18]
Meditate without distractions,
And you will find your way.

When you accompany your Guru,
Do not look upon his merits or demerits,
Else you will find mountains of faults.
Only with faith and loyalty
Will you find your way.

When you attend holy meetings
With brothers and sisters in the Dharma,
Do not think of heading the row,
Else you will arouse both hate and craving,
And offend against the Precepts.
Adjust yourselves, understand each other,
And you will find your way.

When you beg for alms in the village,
Do not use the Dharma for deceit and exploitation,
Else you will force yourself down to the lower Path.
Be honest and sincere,
And you will find your way.

Beyond all else remember, at all times and places,
Never be overweening, nor of yourself be proud,
Else you will be overbearing in your self-esteem
And overloaded with hypocrisy.
If you abandon deceit and pretense,
You will find your way.

The person who has found the way
Can pass on the gracious teachings to others;
Thus he aids himself and helps the others, too.
To give is then the only thought
Remaining in his heart.

The disciples were all greatly inspired with the determination to practice diligently and to renounce the world. An unalterable faith in the Jetsun was established in them. They said, "We want to offer you a golden Maṇḍala.[14] Pray accept it, and give us the practical teaching of the View, Practice, and Action."

Milarepa replied, "I do not need the gold; you may use it to maintain your meditation. As for the teaching of the View, Practice, and Action, I shall tell you. Pray hearken to my song":

Oh, my Guru! The Exemplar of the View,
      Practice, and Action,
Pray vouchsafe me your grace, and enable me
To be absorbed in the realm of Self-nature!

For the View, Practice, Action, and Accomplishment
There are three Key-points you should know:

All the manifestation, the Universe itself,
      is contained in the mind;
The nature of Mind is the realm of illumination
Which can neither be conceived nor touched.
These are the Key-points of the View.

Errant thoughts are liberated in the Dharmakāya;
The awareness, the illumination, is always
      blissful;
Meditate in a manner of non-doing and non-effort.
These are the Key-points of Practice.

In the action of naturalness

The Ten Virtues spontaneously grow;
All the Ten Vices are thus purified.
By corrections or remedies
The Illuminating Void is ne'er disturbed.[15]
These are the Key-points of Action.

There is no Nirvāṇa to attain beyond;
There is no Saṃsāra here to renounce;
Truly to know the Self-mind
It is to be the Buddha Himself.
These are the Key-points of Accomplishment.

Reduce inwardly the Three Key-points to One.
This One is the Void Nature of Being,
Which only a wondrous Guru
Can clearly illustrate.

Much activity is of no avail;
If one sees the Simultaneously Born[16] Wisdom,
He reaches his goal.

For all practitioners of Dharma
This preaching is a precious gem;
It is my direct experience from yogic meditation.
Think carefully and bear it in your minds,
Oh, my children and disciples.

The disciples then asked Milarepa, "As we understood you, the un-mistakable guide along the Path of Practice is to pray to one's Guru with great earnestness. Is there anything else beyond this?" Milarepa smiled and answered, "The Tree of Guidance has also many branches." In explaining this to them, he sang:

The Guru, the disciple, and the secret teachings;
Endurance, perseverance, and the faith;
Wisdom, compassion, and the human form;
All these are ever guides upon the Path.

Solitude with no commotion and disturbance
Is the guide protecting meditation.
The accomplished Guru, the Jetsun,
Is the guide dispelling ignorance and darkness.
Faith without sorrow and weariness

Is the guide which leads you safely to happiness.

The sensations of the five organs
Are the guides which lead you to freedom
        from "contact."[17]
The verbal teachings of the Lineage Gurus
Are the guides which illustrate the Three
        Bodies of Buddha.
The protectors, the Three Precious Ones,
Are the guides with no faults or mistakes.
Led by these six guides,
One will reach the happy plane of Yoga—
Abiding in the realm of Non-differentiation
In which all views and sophisms[18] are no more.

Remaining in the realm of self-knowledge
        and self-liberation
Is indeed happy and joyful;
Abiding in the valley where no men dwell,
With confidence and knowledge, one lives
        in his own way.
With a thundering voice,
He sings the happy song of Yoga.
Falling in the Ten Directions is the rain of fame;
Brought to blooming are the flowers and
        leaves of Compassion.
The enterprise of Bodhi encompasses the Universe;
The pure fruit of the Bodhi-Heart thus
        attains perfection.

The disciples thought, "It makes no difference now to the Jetsun where he stays. We will invite him to our village." Thereupon they said to Milarepa, "Revered One, since your mind no longer changes, there is no need for you to practice meditation. Therefore, for the sake of sentient beings please come to our village and preach the Dharma for us." Milarepa replied, "Practicing meditation in solitude is, in itself, a service to the people. Although my mind no longer changes, it is still a good tradition for a great yogi to remain in solitude." He then sang:

Through the practice [of meditation] I
        show gratitude to my Guru.
Pray grant me your grace, ripen and liberate me.

You, gifted disciples, the followers of Dharma,
Heed carefully, with all attention
While I sing of the profound Essential Teaching.

The great lioness in the upper snow mountain
Poses proudly on the summit of the peak;
She is not afraid—
Proudly dwelling on the mountain
Is the snow lion's way.

The queen vulture on Red Rock
Stretches her wings in the wide sky;
She is not afraid of falling—
Flying through the sky is the vulture's way.

In the depths of the great ocean
Darts the Queen of fish, glittering;
She is not afraid—
Swimming is the fish's way.

On the branches of the oak trees,
Agile monkeys swing and leap;
They are not afraid of falling—
Such is the wild monkey's way.

Under the leafy canopy of the dense wood,
The striped tiger roams and swiftly runs,
Not because of fear or worry—
This shows her haughty pride,
And is the mighty tiger's way.

In the wood on Singa Mountain,
I, Milarepa, meditate on Voidness,
Not because I fear to lose my understanding—
Constant meditation is the yogi's way.

Without distraction, the yogi meditates absorbed
Upon the pure Maṇḍala of Dharmadhātu,
Not because he fears to go astray—
But to hold to Self-quintessence is the yogi's way.

When he works on the Nādis, Prāṇa, and Bindu[19]
He avoids hindrances and errors,

Not that the teaching has faults in itself —
But it is a good way to improve true Realization.

With natural and spontaneous behavior
One surely meets with countless ups-and-downs,[20]
Not because there is discrimination and
　　　dualistic thought —
But because to manifest all, is causation's nature.

When he develops other beings by
　　　demonstrating the power of Karma,
Though seemingly he sees as real both good and evil,
It is not because he has gone astray in his
　　　practice,[21]
But because, to explain the truth to different
　　　people,
He must use appropriate illustrations.

Those great yogis who have mastered the Practice,
Never desire anything in this world.
It is not because they want fame that
　　　they remain in solitude;
It is the natural sign springing from their hearts—
The true feeling of non-attachment and renunciation.

Yogis who practice the teaching of the
　　　Path Profound,
Dwell always in caves and mountains;
Not that they are cynical or pompous,
But to concentrate on meditation is their
　　　self-willing.

I, the cotton-clad,[22] have sung many songs,
Not to amuse myself by singing sophistries,
But for your sake, faithful followers who
　　　assemble here,
From my heart I have spoken words helpful
　　　and profound.

The disciples then said to Milarepa, "One may live alone in solitude, but it is necessary to have food and a suitable dwelling in which he can meditate properly." The Jetsun replied, "I have my own food and dwelling which I will illustrate to you."

I bow down at the feet of the wish-fulfilling Guru.
Pray vouchsafe me your grace in bestowing
        beneficial food,
Pray make me realize my own body as the
        house of Buddha,
Pray grant me this sure knowledge.

I built the house[23] through fear,
The house of Sūnyatā, the void nature of being;
Now I have no fear of its collapsing.
I, the Yogi with the wish-fulfilling gem,
Feel happiness and joy where'er I stay.

Because of the fear of cold, I sought for clothes;
The clothing I found is the Ah Shea Vital Heat.[24]
Now I have no fear of coldness.

Because of the fear of poverty, I sought for riches;
The riches I found are the inexhaustible
        Seven Holy Jewels.[25]
Now I have no fear of poverty.

Because of the fear of hunger, I sought for food;
The food I found is the Samādhi of Suchness.
Now I have no fear of hunger.

Because of the fear of thirst, I sought for drink;
The heavenly drink I found is the wine
        of mindfulness.[26]
Now I have no fear of thirst.

Because of the fear of loneliness, I searched
        for a friend;
The friend I found is the bliss of
        perpetual Sūnyatā.[27]
Now I have no fear of loneliness.

Because of the fear of going astray,
I sought for the right path to follow.
The wide path I found is the Path of
        Two-in-One.[28]
Now I do not fear to lose my way.

I am a yogi with all desirable possessions,
A man always happy where'er he stays.

Here at Yolmo Tagpu Senge Tson,
The tigress howling with a pathetic, trembling cry,
Reminds me that her helpless cubs are
      innocently playing.
I cannot help but feel a great compassion for them,
I cannot help but practice more diligently,
I cannot help but augment thus my Bodhi-Mind.

The touching cry of the monkey,
So impressive and so moving,
Cannot help but raise in me deep pity.
The little monkey's chattering is amusing
      and pathetic;
As I hear it, I cannot but think of it with
      compassion.

The voice of the cuckoo is so moving,
And so tuneful is the lark's sweet singing,
That when I hear them I cannot help but listen—
When I listen to them,
I cannot help but shed my tears.

The varied cries and cawing of the crow,
Are a good and helpful friend unto the yogi.
Even without a single friend,
To remain here is a pleasure.
With joy flowing from my heart, I sing this happy song;
May the dark shadow of all men's sorrows
Be dispelled by my joyful singing.

The disciples were all deeply moved, and a feeling of weariness
with Saṃsāra overwhelmed them. They swore to Milarepa that they
would never leave the mountain. Afterwards, through the practice of
meditation, they all reached the state of perfection.

One day, Milarepa's patron Buddha[29] told him the time had come
for him to go to Tibet proper and there meditate in solitude to help
sentient beings. The patron Buddha also prophesied the success of his
career in helping people and in spreading the Dharma. Hence, about
this time, Milarepa decided to go to Tibet.

This is the story of Yolmo Snow Mountain.

NOTES

1 T.T.: sTag.Pug.Sen.Ge.rDson. — the Tiger Cave at Lion Place.

2 Marpa, Milarepa's Guru, admonished Milarepa to remain in solitude for most of his life. He also prophesied as to those places wherein Milarepa should practice meditation.

3 The one who practices Mahāmudrā should know that, from the ultimate viewpoint, Saṃsāra is Nirvāna, evil is good, Kleśas are Bodhi. The up-and-down feelings, or the vicissitudinous emotions occurring in meditation, do not in their ultimate sense differ from Mind-Essence. To an advanced yogi, the greater the Kleśas that arise in his mind, the brighter, deeper, and better his illumination as to Reality.

4 According to Tantrism the Guru is even more important than Buddha. To be blessed by one's Guru is of the utmost importance. According to Tibetan tradition, in the beginning of any type of meditation, the yogi always visualizes the Guru sitting above his head, and prays to him.

5 Here Milarepa implies the teaching of advanced Tantrism.

6 The Five Poisonous Passions or Desires (the Five Kleśas) are lust, hate, blindness, pride, and jealousy.

7 Path with Form: the Arising Yoga and the Perfecting Yoga of Tantrism (see the translator's comments in the Appendix, and Story 5, Notes 18 and 19).

8 Whispered Transmission (T.T.: sÑan.brGyud.): (1) We are told that in olden days the hidden teachings of Tantra were given to the disciples in a most secret manner, i.e., through whispering; (2) this term is used as another name for the Ghagyuba School, the School of Marpa and Milarepa.

9 Experience (T.T.: Ñams.) and Realization (T.T.: rTogs.): These two words, Ñams. and rTogs., are difficult to translate into adequate English. Ñams is the indirect, incomplete, imperfect, and "half-opaque" experience and understanding that the yogi attains in meditation; while rTogs (Realization) is the direct, complete, clear, and perfect experience. The former is *similar* to Enlightenment, while the latter is the *real Enlightenment*. Ñams is like the experience of a traveler approaching a city who sees the city as a whole, but has not yet reached it; nevertheless, he gets an over-all picture and impression. However, Realization (rTogs.) of the city comes when he is *in* the city and knows what it really is at first hand.

10 This means, "Do not unscrupulously take the offerings of the relatives of a deceased person."

11 "Accumulation of Merits" (T.T.: Tshogs.bSags.) is a frequently used Buddhist term that can be explained in a variety of ways. Generally it means all the virtuous and spiritual practices. Specifically, in Mahāyāna Buddhism, it denotes the first five Pāramitās of the Bodhisattva, i.e., charity, discipline, patience, diligence, and meditation. See Story 9, Note 8.

12 Corresponding and actual Realization (T.T.: Ñams.rTogs.): Realization or Englightenment brought about in meditation usually follows a sequence: the corresponding, or resembling Realization comes first; the actual Realization follows: See Note 9.

13 Mothers: Here this term seems to imply the Mother-Divinities such as Tārā, Dorje Paumo, Lhamo, and others.

14 Maṇḍala, in this case, signifies a Tantric utensil for sacramental offerings.

The original meaning of the word "Maṇḍala" is "circle" or "center"; it is a complex design of a picture that symbolizes the phenomenal world of Tantric Buddhas.

15 "Corrections and remedies" here imply all the conscious efforts toward preventing or remedying "wrong-doings," which are, in reality, not against the Illuminating Void, but rather identical with it. Illumination and Voidness are the two immanent characteristics of Mind for which no corrections or remedies are needed.

16 Simultaneously Born Wisdom (T.T.: Lhan.Cig.sKyes.Pahi.Ye.Çes.): When one is born the Wisdom of Buddhahood is also born with him, implying that the Buddha-nature is innate and exists all the time. See Story 3, Note 18.

17 "Contact": All the sensations and perceptions are produced through contact of the consciousness with objects.

18 Lit.: Beyond empty words or sophisms, away-from-playwords, or away-from-nonsense (T.T.: sPros.Bral.). All ideas, such as monism, dualism, being or non-being, existence or non-existence, etc. — all these conceptual notions — are equal to empty words, playwords, or nonsense to enlightened beings.

19 Nāḍis, Prāna, and Bindu (T.T.: rTsa.rLuñ. [and] Thig.Le.): The Path-with-Form of Tantrism emphasizes the physical practice as well as the mental practice. In order to build up a favorable condition in which the realization of transcendental Truth may easily be achieved, Tantrism provides exercises to purify the nervous, breathing, and excretory systems.

20 "Ups-and-downs" here signifies the fluctuating actions and emotions in daily activity.

21 To those who have not reached the state of the Perfect Mutual-containing, or the Non-discriminating Whole, the antithetical aspect of being, which originates from dualistic ideas, becomes the paramount obstacle that debars them from realizing the non-differentiated Totality. Also, it produces a belief in the incompatibility of opposites, i.e., of being and non-being, existence and non-existence, etc. — in this case, Voidness and moral values. In certain aspects, the yogi who realizes the teaching of Voidness should not even see the existence of good and evil in his practice.

22 Cotton-clad (T.T.: Ras.Pa.): The yogi who is able to produce bodily heat through Yoga, thus wearing only cotton clothes in severe cold weather, is called Repa (Ras.Pa.).

23 This house is, of course, symbolic; but Milarepa did build many houses for Marpa before he was accepted by him.

24 Ah Shea (T.T.: A.Çad.) Vital Heat: the heat produced in Tantric meditation. See "The Six Yogas of Nāropa," in "Tibetan Yoga and Secret Doctrines," edited by W. Y. Evans-Wentz.

25 The Seven Holy Jewels are: gold, silver, crystal, ruby, coral, agate, and carnelian. Here Milarepa spoke of them in a figurative sense.

26 The text is not clear here. The translator presumes that it implies the voluntary springing forth of secretion through self-suggestion, by the yogic power.

27 Perpetual Sūnyatā: the eternal Voidness.

28 Path of Two-in-One (T.T.: Lam.Zuñ.hJug.): A very widely used phrase in Tibetan Buddhism. It means the unification of antitheses, the joining of opposing forces, the merging of differentiations, and the like.

29 Patron Buddha (T.T.: Yi.Dam.): Every Tantric yogi has a chosen patron Buddha, who is his protector, to whom he prays, and upon whom he relies.

8

MILAREPA
AND THE PIGEON

Obeisance to all Gurus

IN ACCORDANCE with the prophecy [of his Patron Buddha], Milrepa went to Tibet proper from Yolmo. He arrived at Gu Tang and lived in a cave, absorbing himself in the Meditation of the Great Illumination.

One day a pigeon wearing golden ornaments came to Milarepa. The bird nodded, bowed, and circled him many times. Then it flew away in the direction of the Immaculate Rock. Milarepa understood that this must be a spell of the Non-men to make him welcome. So he followed the pigeon and went up to the hill, where he found a heap of white rice. The bird pecked the rice with its bill and brought some to Milarepa as if showing him hospitality and welcome. Milarepa, [surprised and delighted], broke into song:

> Oh! My gracious Guru, Marpa Lho Draug Wa,
> From the depth of my heart I think of you.
> In deepest earnestness I meditate on you.
> That I never be separated from you, is my prayer.
>
> Merging the Self-mind with the Guru is indeed
>   a happy thing.
> Manifestation itself is the essence of Reality.
> Through the realization of this unborn Dharmakāya,
> I merge myself in the Realm of Non-effort.[1]
> To both the high and low Views[2] am I indifferent.
> In the mind of Non-effort I feel happiness and joy.
>
> The nature of Mind is the Light and the Void.

By realizing the awareness of Light-Void,
I merge myself in the original state of Non-effort.
To good and bad experiences am I indifferent.
With a mind of Non-effort, I feel happiness and joy.

The Six Senses and Sense Objects[3] of themselves
    dissolve [into the Dharmadhātu].
Where the Non-differentiation of subject
    and object is realized.
I merge happiness and sorrow into one;
I enter the original state of Non-effort.
To right and wrong actions, am I indifferent.
Happy indeed is the Non-effort mind.

The very nature of the Dharmakāya
Is identified through its myriad forms;
The myriad forms are the Nirmānakāya of Buddha.
With this understanding in mind,
Whatever circumstance I may encounter,
I am free in the happy realm of Liberation!
To return to the home of Buddha
I have no longing!
Happy indeed is this mind of Non-effort.

Whereupon the pigeon, with seven companions, came nearer to
Milarepa. They all bowed to him and circled him many times, as the
first bird had done before. Milarepa thought, "These pigeons must
be Non-men. I shall ask them and see whether they will tell the
truth." So he said, "Who are you, and why do you come here?" The
pigeons then broke the spell and displayed their real forms as female
Devas. Their leader said, "We are the angel-maidens of Heaven. Because we have great faith in you, we come here to learn the Dharma
from you. We beseech you to give us the instructions."
In response, Milarepa sang:

Oh! The wondrous Transformation Body of my Guru!
Pray, kindly grant me your grace-wave.

You eight charming maidens of Heaven,
Who appeared just now in pigeon form,
Your spell was fine, and in conformity
    with the Dharma!
If you, the eight beautiful maidens of Heaven,

Wish to practice the white Dharma of Buddha,
Pray remember the meaning of this song.

Though worldly happiness and pleasure
Seem delightful and pleasing,
They soon will pass away.

Though high-ranking ladies are proud and exultant
In their lofty dignity,
What refuge and shelter do they have?

To dwell in the fiery home of Saṃsāra
Sometimes seems pleasant, but is mostly misery.

If a well-endowed and well-loved son
Has no self-respect and makes no self-effort,
His father will meet nothing but distress.

If a disciple commits evil deeds,
He must fall into Saṃsāra,
No matter how superb his Guru may be.

You maidens of Heaven, the conjurers of
          the pigeons!
It is easy for you to ask for Dharma,
But hard to have deep faith in it.
You should remind yourselves
Of the inevitable misfortunes
Connected with worldly joys.
The pains and miseries of this life,
You should regard as friends leading
          you toward Nirvāṇa.
As for me, I am very grateful for
The misfortunes I have met.
Oh, my friends, bear this in mind, and do the same!

The Devas smiled at Milarepa and said, "We shall do so." Then
they made obeisance and circumambulated him many times. The Jetsun then asked the angels, "Why did you come here in pigeon form?"
They replied, "You are a yogi who has not the slightest attachment
to yourself, nor any desire for this worldly life. It is only for the
sake of Bodhi and the welfare of sentient beings that you have remained in solitude and meditated without distraction. With our heav-

enly eyes, we have been able to see you; and with respect and faith we now come to you for Dharma. But in order to [conceal our real form from] sinful beings, we have transformed ourselves into pigeons. We pray that your Reverence will now be kind enough to go up into Heaven with us to preach the righteous Dharma for us." But Milarepa replied, "As long as life lasts, I shall remain in this world to benefit sentient beings here. You must know that *Heaven is far from dependable; it is not eternal, and one should not rely on it. To be born in Heaven is not necessarily a wonderful thing.* You should pay heed and follow these instructions":

I bow down at the feet of Marpa Lho Draug.
Oh, Father Guru! Pray grant me your
    grace-wave and accomplishment.

You, eight beauties of the Deva-realm,
Have offered me white rice, the wondrous
    fruit of Dhyāna.
Eating it my body is strengthened, and my
    mind enlivened.
As a token of my gratitude, I sing this
    song of Dharma to you.
Now, lift up your ears, and listen to me carefully.

Even though one reaches the highest Heaven
    of the White Devas,[4]
It has no permanent value and meaning!
Lovable and touching are those flowers of
    youth in Heaven.
But however pleasant it may seem to be,
In the end comes separation.

Although the bliss in Heaven seems to be very great,
It is merely a deceitful mirage, a
    bewildering hallucination;
In fact, it is the very cause of the
    return to suffering!

Thinking of the miseries of the Six Realms in Saṃsāra,
I cannot help but have a feeling of disgust
    and aversion —
A feeling of anguish and distressed emotion!

Should you intend to practice the teaching of Buddha,
You must take refuge in the Three Precious
        Ones and pray to them.

Sentient beings in the Six Realms
You should consider as your parents.

Give to the poor, and offer to the Guru!
For the benefit of all, dedicate your merits.
Always remember that death may come at any moment.

Identify your body with Buddha's body!
Identify your own voice with Buddha's Mantra.
Contemplate the Śūnyatā of self-awakening Wisdom,
And always try to be master of your mind!

The Devas of Heaven said, "In ignorant beings like us, the Kleśas always follow the mind. Pray give us a teaching with which we can correct this fault, so we may depend upon it and practice it frequently."

In response to their request, Milarepa sang:

Obeisance to Marpa, the gracious one!
Pray grant me the blessing of virtuous remedy.

Should you, oh faithful lady Devas, intend
        to practice the Dharma often,
Inwardly you should practice concentration
        and contemplation.
The renunciation of external affairs is
        your adornment.

Oh, bear in mind this remedy for external
        involvement!
With self-composure and mindfulness, you
        should remain serene.
Glory is the equainimity of mind and speech!
Glory is the resignation from many actions!

Should you meet disagreeable conditions,
Disturbing to your mind,
Keep watch upon yourself and be alert;
Keep warning yourself:

"The danger of anger is on its way."
When you meet with enticing wealth,
Keep watch upon yourself and be alert;
Keep a check upon yourself:
"The danger of craving is on its way."

Should hurtful, insulting words come to your ears,
Keep watch upon yourself and be alert,
And so remind yourself:
"Hurtful sounds are but delusions of the ear."

When you associate with your friends,
Watch carefully and warn yourself:
"Let not jealousy in my heart arise."

When you are plied with services and offerings,
Be alert and warn yourself:
"Let me beware, lest pride should spring up
        in my heart."

At all times, in every way, keep watch upon
        yourself.
At all times try to conquer the evil thoughts
        within you!
Whatever you may meet in your daily doings,[5]
You should contemplate its void and
        illusory nature.

Were even one hundred saints and scholars
        gathered here,
More than this they could not say.
May you all be happy and prosperous!
May you all, with joyful hearts,
Devote yourselves to the practice of the Dharma!

The maidens of Heaven were all very happy, and in their delight and satisfaction they again turned their bodies into pigeons, and flew up toward Heaven. Milarepa then ate the offered rice, and set out for the Gray Rock Vajra Enclosure.

This is the story of the angel-maidens [in pigeon form] and their offerings.

All the preceding stories have dealt with the accounts of Milarepa's subjugation and conversion of demons.

NOTES

1 Non-effort (T.T.: rTsol.Med.), or no action, no disturbance, no doing, and the like: The Non-effort or Non-doing technique of meditation is the most important teaching of Mahāmudrā.

2 The high and low Views: Since the different Schools hold different views on Buddhist doctrine, they classify Buddhism into different groups of teaching — the high, the low, the expedient, the Ultimate, and so forth. For instance. the Yogācāra School holds that the "Mind-only" doctrine is the high view and the "Void" doctrine of the Middle Way (Mādhymika) School is the low view; the Middle Way School says just the opposite. This dissension also exists in other Buddhist Schools and Sects.

3 Six Senses and Sense Objects (T.T.: Tsogs.Drug.): Literally, this term should be translated as the Six Groups; e.g., eyes and form comprise one group, ears and sound another, and so on.

4 The Heaven of the White Devas: According to Buddhism, there are many different levels of heavens, some with form and some without. The Devas in the "highest" Heaven are supposedly without form or desires. However, Buddhism claims that even these heavenly beings are still in Saṃsāra.

5 Lit.: four kinds of daily activity — walking, standing, sitting, and lying down.

PART TWO
MILAREPA
AND HIS HUMAN
DISCIPLES

THE GRAY ROCK
VAJRA ENCLOSURE

Obeisance to all Gurus

THE Jetsun Milarepa, having arrived at the Gray Rock Vajra Enclosure, stayed in a state of inspiration at the Saddle Cave.

Now there was a Tantric yogi at Gu Tang who had heard the
preaching of the Jetsun, and became imbued with a deep faith in him.
[Coming] to Milarepa, he said, "Revered One, although I have practiced meditation for some time, I have not had the experiences or
earned the merits [that should have resulted]. This is probably due
to my ignorance of the proper way to practice. Pray, be kind enough
to grant me the appropriate teachings!" Milarepa replied, "In that
case, it is necessary that you should know all the essential points."
Therefore he sang for him a song, "The Six Essentials":

> The manifestations of mind outnumber the
>   myriads of dust-motes
> In the infinite rays of sunlight;
> The lord-like Yogi knows
> The self-nature of these manifestations.
>
> The reality of the true nature of beings
> Is neither produced by cause nor by conditions;
> The lord-like Yogi knows
> The sole truth precisely and positively.
>
> Even when he is faced with the threat
>   of a hundred spears,
> His thorough-knowing View will not be shaken;
> Thus the lord-like Yogi naturally subdues
>   all attachments.

The ever-moving mind is hard to tame
Even when shut up in an iron box;
The lord-like Yogi knows
That all these emanations are illusions.

The disciple then asked, "Are experiences such as you have just mentioned brought about gradually, or instantaneously?" Milarepa replied, "Well-endowed people will attain Enlightenment instantaneously; average and inferior people will gradually attain their Realizations. I shall describe to you the signs of real Enlightenment, and also the signs of those experiences *resembling* Enlightenment, but which are wrongly considered by some people to be the real ones."

Thereupon he sang the following song to explain the different experiences, both real and false, of the four stages of Mahāmudrā,[1]

I bow down at the feet of the supreme Guru.

To cling to the actuality of mind is the
        cause of Saṃsāra;
To realize that non-clinging and illuminating
        Self-awareness
Is unborn and immanent,
Is the consummation sign of the
        Stage of One-Pointedness.

If one talks about the Two-In-One
But still meditates on form,
If one acknowledges the truth of Karma
But still commits wrong-doing,
He is actually meditating with blindness
        and passion!
Things, as such, are never found
In the true Stage of One-Pointedness.

In realizing that the non-clinging and
        illuminating mind,
Is embodied in bliss and transcends all playwords,[2]
One sees his mind's nature as clearly as
        great Space.
This is the sign of the consummation
Of the Stage of Away-from-Playwords.

Though one talks about the Stage of

        Away-from-Playwords,
Still he is declaring this and that;
In spite of illustrating what is beyond
        all words,
Still he is but piling words on words.
He then, is the ignorant one,
Who with self-clinging meditates.
In the Stage of Away-from-Playwords,
There is no such thing as this.

The non-diffferentiation of manifestation
        and Voidness
Is the Dharmakāya,
In which Saṃsāra and Nirvāṇa are felt to be the same.
It is a complete merging of Buddha and
        sentient beings.
These are the signs of the Stage of One-Taste,
As many have declared.

He who says that "all is one,"
Is still discriminating;
In the Stage of One-Taste,
There is no such blindness.

A wandering thought is itself the essence
        of Wisdom—
Immanent and intrinsic.
Cause and effect are both the same.
This is a realization of Buddha's Three Bodies[3]
Existing within oneself.
These are the consummation signs
Of the Stage of Non-Practice.

When one talks about Non-Practice,
His mind is still active;
He talks about illumination,
But in fact is blind.
In the Stage of Non-Practice,
There is no such thing!

The disciple cried, "These instructions are indeed extraordinary! To help ignorant men like us, pray now, instruct us on the practice of the Six Pāramitās." Milarepa sang in reply:

I bow down at the feet of the perfect Jetsun Gurus.

Property and wealth are like dew on grass;
Knowing this, gladly should one give them away.

It is most precious to be born a worthy and
    leisured human being;[4]
Knowing this, one should with care observe
    the precepts
As if protecting his own eyes.

Anger is the cause of falling to the Realms Below;
Knowing this, one should refrain from wrath,
Even at the risk of life.

Benefit to oneself and to others
Can never be achieved through sloth;
Strive, therefore, to do good deeds.

A perturbed, wandering mind never sees the
    truth of Mahāyāna;
Practice, therefore, concentration.

Buddha cannot be found through searching;
So contemplate your own mind.[5]

Until the autumn mists dissolve into the sky,
Strive on with faith and determination.

Having heard this song, a great admiration and faith toward the Jetsun arose in the heart of the disciple, and he returned home. Several days later, he and many other patrons came to entertain Milarepa, and brought copious offerings. They had all heard the Jetsun's life story, and with great faith, they came this time to learn the Dharma. They asked Milarepa how he had managed to undergo the trials of probationship[6] and had exerted himself in ascetic practice, and to recount the way through which he had finally obtained his Enlightenment. Milarepa answered with "The Six Resolutions":

When one has lost interest in this world,
His faith and longing for the Dharma is confirmed.

To relinquish one's home ties is very hard;

Only by leaving one's native land
Can one be immune from anger.

It is hard to conquer burning passions
Toward relatives and close friends;
The best way to quench them
Is to break all associations.

One never feels that he is rich enough;
Contented, he should wear humble, cotton clothes.
He may thus conquer much desire and craving.

It is hard to avoid worldly attractions;
By adhering to humbleness,
Longing for vainglory is subdued.

It is hard to conquer pride and egotism;
So, like the animals, live in the mountains!

My dear and faithful patrons!
Such is the real understanding
That stems from perseverance.
I wish you all to practice deeds that
        are meaningful,[7]
And amass all merits![8]

Like space, the Dharmakāya pervades
        all sentient beings,
Yet [Karmic] blindness drives them into Saṃsāra.

Easy it is to glimpse the Dharmakāya,
But hard to stabilize its realization.
Hence, one is still beset by the Five Poisons.[9]

If the realization [of Śūnyatā] is stable,
The organs and senses[10] move freely but do not cling.
One then forever merges with the Trikāya.
This is the conviction of Enlightenment.

The Main and the Ensuing Samādhis[11]
Are two states only for beginners.
In stabilized minds they are as one.

In the Yoga of Non-wandering,[12]
The Six non-attached Senses e'er arise,
Yet I remain steadfast in the inseparable Trikāya.
Unattached, I walk with power;
Free from clinging, I gain
The wish-fulfilling merits.[13]

A wise man knows how to practice
The space-like meditation.
In all he does by day
He attaches himself to nothing.
With a liberated spirit,
He desires nor wealth nor beauty.

One should see that all appearance
Is like mist and fog;
Though one has vowed to liberate all
      sentient beings,
He should know that all manifestations
Are like reflections of the moon in water.

Without attachment, he knows
That the human body is but a magic spell.
So from all bindings he gains freedom.
Like the immaculate lotus growing out of mud,
He attains the conviction of Practice.

The mind is omnipresent like space;
It illumines all manifestations as the Dharmakāya;
It knows all and lightens all.
I see it clearly like a crystal
In my palm!

In the beginning, nothing comes;
In the middle, nothing stays;
At the end, nothing goes.
Of the mind there is no arising and extinction!
Thus, one remains in the Equality of past,
      present, and future.

Immanent, the mind, like the sky, is pure.
The red and white clouds[14] vanish of themselves;
No trace of the Four Elements[15] can be found.

The omnipresent mind resembles Space:
It never separates from the Realm of the Unborn,
It cuts the path of the Three Worlds of Saṃsāra.
This is the conviction of Enlightenment.

If a yogi realizes this,
When he leaves his mortal body
And enters into the [momentous] Bardo,[16]
He may then perfect all merits.

With an understanding of the profound instruction.
One makes the Mother and Son Minds[17] meet;
If he then fails to unite them,
Through the teaching of the Simultaneously Born
He can still transform the phantom Bardo form
Into the Pure Body of Bliss!

If he knows that even the Sambhogakāya is
     unreal, like a shadow,
How can he ever go astray?
This is infallibly my own—
The yogi's sure conviction about Bardo!

The people of Gu Tang were all strongly confirmed in their faith, and thereafter often brought offerings to Milarepa.

One day, in the very early morning, Milarepa, in a state of Illumination, saw the Vajra Ḍākinī appear before him. She prophesied: "Milarepa! You will have one sun-like, one moon-like, twenty-three star-like, and twenty-five accomplished human disciples; one hundred enlightened beings who never fall back; one hundred and eight great men who will attain the initial Realization of the Path;[18] and one thousand male and female yogis who will enter the Path. Those who, with you, have the affinity of Dharma and thus forever escape the lower path of Saṃsāra, are beyond number. In the upper part of Gung Tang there is a destined man, who will be your moon-like disciple. Go there for his sake." And so Milarepa set his mind upon going to the Upper Gung Tang.

This is the first of the series of stories of the Gray Rock Vajra Enclosure.[19]

NOTES

1 The four stages of Mahāmudrā are:
  (1) The stage of One-Pointedness (T.T.: rTse.gCig.),
  (2) The stage of Away-from-Playwords (T.T.: sProd.Bral.),
  (3) The stage of One-Taste (T.T.: Ro.gCig.),
  (4) The stage of Non-Practice (T.T.: sGom.Med.).
In the *first* stage the meditator experiences the tranquility of Mind-Essence. However, he still has not eradicated the dualistic view, nor has he actually realized in full the uncreated voidness of the mind.

In the *second* stage the meditator sees clearly the "original state of mind." In virtue of this direct experience with Mind-Essence, he rids himself once and for all of Saṃsāric views — the views of "playwords," such as "one and many," "good and bad," "yes and no," "finite and infinite," etc. This stage is considered by Tibetan sages to be that of initial Enlightenment.

In the *third* stage the meditator is completely free from all obstacles or hindrances. It is therefore called the Stage of One-Taste (the Realm of Universal Totality, or the Realm of the Identity of Saṃsāra and Nirvāṇa). However, this experience should by no means be regarded as a realization of any form of monism — a major "false view," that has been refuted by many Buddhist scholars, notably those of the Mādhyamika School. (See Story 18, Note 9.)

In the *fourth* stage the meditator has already reached the Ultimate Realm. He has nothing more to look for or to learn: he has reached the State of Buddhahood.

These four stages represent the complete process through which a Buddhist yogi proceeds to Ultimate Enlightenment.

2 Playwords: All Saṃsāric conceptions and ideas which have to be expressed through words and symbols are meaningless sophistries from the viewpoint of an enlightened being. The term "Playwords" (T.T.: sPros.Pa.) also implies that all Saṃsāric conceptualizations and verbalizations are on a par with children's prattle — little more than nonsense. Realization of this is considered the initial stage of Enlightenment.

3 Three Bodies: the Trikāya, or Three Bodies of Buddha, i.e., the Dharmakāya, the Sambhogakāya, and the Nirmāṇakāya.

4 The human body is considered to be a precious possession, without which no spiritual development is possible.

5 This sentence is extremely important as representing the essence of the teaching of Mahāmudrā. In general Buddhism one is taught to search for Enlightenment and to attain Buddhahood, while in Mahāmudrā the Guru points out to the disciple that one's own mind is Buddha Himself, and therefore, to search for anything, even Buddhahood, is a waste of time.

6 This refers to the trials imposed on Milarepa by his Guru, Marpa, before he was accepted for initiation. (See Milarepa's Biography, edited by W. Y. Evans-Wentz.)

7 Meaningful deeds: the virtuous deeds that lead one to Enlightenment.

8 "Amass merits": This phrase is often used by Buddhists to denote all virtuous deeds. (See Story 4, Note 22; and Story 7, Note 11.)

9 Five Poisons: the Five Kleśas, the basic causes of all miseries of Saṃsāra. They are lust, hate, blindness, pride, and envy.

10 Lit.: Six Groups: a general term denoting the six outer objects, six organs, and six senses.

11 Main Samādhi and Ensuing Samādhi (T.T.: mÑam.bShag. [and] rJes.Tob.): mÑam.bShag. may be otherwise translated as the "Actual-Meditation-State," and rJes.Tob. as the "After-Meditation-State."

12 Yoga of Non-wandering: The state of concentration in which the mind is fixed and does not wander.

13 If the yogi can free himself from all clinging, he will gain all the miraculous powers, which in turn will enable him to grant all sentient beings' wishes.

14 "Red-and-White" denotes the positive and negative elements in the body.

15 The text is very obscure here and the meaning is not certain.

16 The Bardo stage, or the stage between death and rebirth, is a critical stage wherein one can either attain liberation easily, or fall back into Saṃsāric existence. (See Story 3, Note 4).

17 The Mother and Son Minds: The Mother Mind, or more correctly, Mother Light (T.T.: Mahi.Hod.Zer.) exists all the time, but is not yet unfolded. The Son Mind (T.T.: Buhi.Hod.Zer.), or Son Light, is the enlightened mind, or the Enlightenment of the Path.

18 Initial Realization of the Path: This is the first stage of Enlightenment. (See Note 1.)

19 This is a literal translation of the original text. The latter part of the series seems to be missing.

10

MILAREPA'S FIRST MEETING WITH RECHUNGPA

Obeisance to all Gurus

As prophesied by [Marpa], Milarepa went to the upper part of Gung Tang. When he arrived at the Castle there, he found that many people were building a house and asked them for some food. They replied, "We are working on this building. You can see that we are very busy and have no time for that sort of thing. It looks as though you have plenty of time to spare, so why don't you join us in the work?"

Milarepa said, "Yes, I now have plenty of leisure, but I have earned it by finishing the construction of my 'house' in my own way. Even if you do not give me any food, I will never work on a worldly building, which I would most certainly abandon." The men asked him, "How did you build your house, and why do you spurn our work so strongly?"

Milarepa sang in reply:

> Faith is the firm foundation of my house,
> Diligence forms the high walls,
> Meditation makes the huge bricks,
> And Wisdom is the great cornerstone.
> With these four things I built my castle,
> And it will last as long as the Truth eternal!
> Your worldly houses are delusions,
> Mere prisons for the demons,
> And so I would abandon and desert them.

The workers said, "What you have sung is most enlightening. Please also tell us whether, in your way of life, you have anything like our farms, properties, relatives, companions, wives, and children? It seems to us that these things are worth more than you have suggested. Please tell us what possessions you have that are so much better than ours? Why do you look upon our way of life as worthless?"

Milarepa answered:

> The Alaya Consciousness[1] is the good earth,
> The inner teaching is the seed that is sowed,
> Achievement in meditation is the sprout,
> And the Three Bodies of Buddha are the
>   ripened crop.
> These are the four lasting mainstays of
>   heavenly farming.
> Your worldly farming, delusive and deceiving,
> Is merely the slave-labor of the hungry;
> Without hesitation I discard it!
>
> The fine warehouse of Śūnyatā,
> The Supramundane Jewels,[2]
> The service and action of the Ten Virtues,
> And the great happiness of Non-outflow[3] —
> These four jewels are the lasting proper-
>   ties of Heaven.
> Your worldly jewels and possessions are
>   deceiving and delusive;
> Like deceptive magic spells, they lead you astray.
> Without any hesitation, I discard them.
>
> The Father and Mother Buddha are my parents,
> The immaculate Dharma is my face,
> The assembly of Saṅgha are my cousins and nephews,
> And the guardians of Dharma are my friends.
> These four are my lasting, heavenly kinsmen.
> Your worldly kinsmen are deceitful and delusive;
> Without hesitation I throw all ephemeral
>   associates away!
>
> The Blissful Passing[4] is like my father,
> The Blissful Illumination in well-done
>   work is [my background],
> The Two-in-One is my glossy, lustrous skin,
> The Experiences and Realization[5] are my
>   glorious clothing.

These four are my heavenly and lasting wives.
Delusive and deceiving are your worldly companions,
They are but temporary friends, inclined to quarrel;
Without hesitation, I throw them all away.

Mind-Awareness is my new-born babe,
Experience of Meditation is my infant,
Understanding-and-Realization is my child,
And the grown youth who can keep the
        Doctrine is my young companion.
These four are my lasting, heavenly sons.
Your worldly offspring are delusive and deceitful;
Without hesitation I throw them all away.

I wish sincerely that I and you, the good
        folk of Gung Tang,
Through the Karma-affinity of this conversation,
May meet once more in the Pure Land of Oujen.[6]

The villagers, strongly moved with faith, then made obeisance and offerings to Milarepa. Later, they all became his sincere disciples.

After this, Milarepa went to the upper part of Goat Hill (Ra La) where he found Silk Cave (Zhaoo Pug). Now, there was at Goat Hill a youth, who in his early infancy had lost his father. He was a fine, intelligent boy, whom his mother and uncle jointly supported. Having an excellent memory, he could recite a great many stories and sermons from the Buddhist Sūtras. Thus he always received many gifts from the people.[7] One day, while herding oxen on his donkey in the upper part of the valley, he came upon the cave where Milarepa was meditating. Thinking that he heard someone singing, he got off the donkey, left the oxen, and approached the cave. As soon as he saw Milarepa, an ineffable experience of Samādhi arose within him, and for a moment he stood transfixed in ecstasy. (Afterwards, he became a Heart-Son of Milarepa—the renowned Rechung Dorje Dragpa.)

Awakened thus from Karma, an immutable faith toward the Jetsun arose within the boy. He offered Milarepa all the gifts that he had acquired for his services. Then he stayed with him to learn the Dharma, completely forgetting his mother and uncle. Because of this, he naturally received no income, and his mother and uncle thought, "what has happened? [Where is he?] Have people stopped paying him?" With misgivings they began asking the patrons whether they had duly paid Rechungpa. Everybody said that he had been paid. It then dawned upon the uncle and mother [where the boy must be, and] that all the gifts must have been offered to Milarepa. They tried in every way to stop Rechungpa from continuing in this course, but to no avail. The young lad remained with Milarepa and learned the Dharma from him. Before long, the Experience and Realization of meditation grew within him. By virtue of mastering the art of Heat Yoga he was able to wear merely a single piece of cotton clothing, and thus earned the name of Rechungpa.[8]

Meanwhile, Rechungpa's mother and uncle became very angry. They sent him a pot on which a curse had been placed.[9] As a result, Rechungpa contracted leprosy.[10] Hoping to be cured, he confined himself [in the hermitage] for meditation.

One day, five Indian yogis arrived, to whom Rechungpa offered some roasted barley which had been sent by his mother and uncle. While the Indians were eating they exclaimed, "What a deadly disease! What a deadly disease!" They knew that Rechungpa had caught leprosy. Rechungpa then asked them whether there was any cure. One of the yogis said, "You are indeed a pitiful person deserving of sympathy, and I feel for you. I have a Guru called Wala Tsandra who may be able to relieve you. As he will not be coming to Tibet, you will have to go to India." And so Rechungpa asked the Jetsun for permission to go. Milarepa agreed and sang as a parting gift:

> I pray my Guru to whom I owe immense gratitude,
> I pray you to protect and bless my son, Rechungpa.
>
> Son, you should renounce the world,
> And work hard at the Dharma.
> To the Guru, Patron Buddha,[11] and the Three
>   Precious Ones,
> You should pray with sincere heart and not
>   just words.
> Bear this in mind when you travel in India.
>
> By taking the food of Perseverance in Samādhi,
> By wearing the clothes of Ah Tung,[12]
> And by riding the horse of the magic
>   Prāna-Mind,[13]
> Thus, my son, should you travel in India.
>
> You should always keep the non-defiled mind clean;
> You should always remember the silver-bright
>   mirror of the Tantric Precept,

And observe it without vexation.
Bear this in mind, my son, as you travel in India.

If you are followed and captured by bandits,
You should remind yourself how worthless
    are the Eight Worldly Claims.[14]
Conceal your powers and merits.
With a humble and merry mind travel in India.

My son, with my sincere prayer and blessing,
May you recover from your illness and enjoy long life.

Milarepa then resumed his meditation in the cave. Rechungpa
closed the cave's mouth with clay, and set out for India with the
yogis. [Upon arriving] there, he met Lama Wala Tsandra, who [con-
sented to give] him the complete teachings of the Wrathful Thunderbolt-Holder with Eagle Wings.[15] By practicing this for some time
Rechungpa was cured.

When he returned to Tibet and reached Happy Valley, he inquired
of the whereabouts of the Jetsun from a native of that valley who
said, "Some time ago, I heard that there was a yogi called Mila, but
I have heard nothing about him recently." Hearing this, Rechungpa
became very disturbed. He thought, "Is my Guru dead?", and in great
distress he proceeded to Silk Cave. He saw that the clay wall with
which he had blocked the entrance was still there. Thinking, "I wonder if the Jetsun is dead inside," he tore down the wall and entered.
Seeing Milarepa sitting upright in meditation, he felt extremely happy
and relieved. He asked the Jetsun about his health and welfare. In
answer Milarepa [arose from meditation and] sang:

I bow down at the feet of Marpa, the Gracious One.

Because I have left my kinsmen, I am happy;
Because I have abandoned attachment to my
    country, I am happy;
Since I disregard this place, I am happy;
As I do not wear the lofty garb of priesthood,
    I am happy;
Because I cling not to house and family, I am happy;
I need not this or that, so I am happy.
Because I possess the great wealth of Dharma,
    I am happy;

Because I worry not about property,
    I am happy;
Because I have no fear of losing anything,
    I am happy;
Since I never dread exhaustion, I am happy;
Having fully realized Mind-Essence,
    I am happy;
As I need not force myself to please my patrons,
    I am happy;
Having no fatigue nor weariness, I am happy;
As I need prepare for nothing, I am happy;
Since all I do complies with Dharma,
    I am happy;
Never desiring to move, I am happy.
As the thought of death brings me no fear,
    I am happy;
Bandits, thieves, and robbers ne'er molest me,
So at all times I am happy!
Having won the best conditions for Dharma
    practice, I am happy;
Having ceased from evil deeds and left off
    sinning, I am happy;
Treading the Path of Merits, I am happy;
Divorced from hate and injury, I am happy;
Having lost all pride and jealousy,
    I am happy;
Understanding the wrongness of the Eight
    Worldly Winds,[16] I am happy;
Absorbed in quiet and evenmindedness, I am happy;
Using the mind to watch the mind, I am happy;
Without hope or fear, I am ever happy.
In the sphere of non-clinging Illumination,
    I am happy;
The Non-distinguishing Wisdom of Dharmadhātu
    itself is happy;
Poised in the natural realm of Immanence,
    I am happy;
In letting the Six Groups of Consciousness go by
To return to their original nature,
    I am happy.
The five radiant gates of sense all make me happy;
To stop a mind that comes and goes is happy;
Oh, I have so much of happiness and joy!

This is a song of gaiety I sing,
This is a song of gratitude to my Guru and
the Three Precious Ones—
I want no other happiness.

Through the grace of Buddhas and the Gurus,
Food and clothes are provided by my patrons.
With no bad deeds and sins, I shall be
joyful when I die;
With all good deeds and virtues, I am happy
while alive.
Enjoying Yoga, I am indeed most happy.
But how are you Rechungpa? Is your wish
fulfilled?

Rechungpa said to Milarepa, "I am well again. I have obtained what I wanted. From now on I would like to remain in solitude and stay near you. Please be so kind as to grant me further inner teachings." Milarepa then imparted to Rechungpa additional instructions, and stayed with him in the Silk Cave. Through the continued practice of meditation Rechungpa attained the perfect Experiences and Realization.

This is the story of Milarepa meeting his Heart-Son Rechungpa in the Cave of Zhaoo.

NOTES

1 Alaya means store or reservoir. The main function of this consciousness is to preserve the "seeds" of mental impressions. Without it, memory and learning would become impossible. Alaya consciousness is also called the primordial consciousness, or the "Fruit-bearing Consciousness." In some aspects, it is quite similar to Jung's "Collective Unconscious."

2 Supramundane Jewels: a symbolic term which denotes the transcendental merits and virtues of Buddha.

3 Non-outflow (T.T.: Zag.Med.) means non-desire. The term usually denotes the realm of transcendency.

4 The Blissful Passing: This may be otherwise rendered as "The Blissful Manifestation or Becoming." When one reaches a higher level of consciousness, even the contacts with outer manifestations become blissful.

5 See Story 7, Notes 9 and 12.

6 Oujen (T.T.: Ao.rGyan.): the name of the Pure Land of Padma Samb-hava.

7 Tibetans are very generous in offering Lamas and story-tellers gifts for their services in reciting Buddhist Sūtras and relating Buddhist legends.

8 Rechungpa: the chief and closest disciple of Milarepa, who served and lived with Milarepa for most of his life. Since he was the youngest disciple, he was called Rechungpa, meaning the little Repa.

9 A pot cursed by a malignant spell.

10 Lit.: the disease of the Earth Lord, or the disease of the Dragon. Tibetans believe that leprosy is a disease caused by malignant, metamorphic dragons.

11 Yidham (T.T.: Yi.Dam.): See Story 7, Note 29.

12 Ah Tung (T.T.: A.Thuñ.): the small seed-syllable "Ah" which is visualized at the navel center in the Heat-Yoga practice. See "The Six Yogas of Nāropa," in Evans-Wentz' "Tibetan Yoga and Secret Doctrines," and the translator's "Teachings of Tibetan Yoga."

13 Prāna-Mind: See Story 3, Note 2.

14 Eight Worldly Claims, or Eight Worldly Winds or Desires: See Story 1, Note 13.

15 The Wrathful Thunderbolt-Holder with Eagle Wings (T.T.: Phyag.rDor. gTum.Po.Khyuñ.gÇog.Can.).

16 See Note 14.

11

ADMONISHMENT ON THE "RARE OPPORTUNITY OF PRACTICING DHARMA"

Obeisance to all Gurus

FROM Zhaoo, the Jetsun Milarepa went to the Light Cave of Runpu and remained there for some time. One day, some young men from his native country came to visit him. They said, "In the past you destroyed all your enemies for revenge, and now you are practicing the Dharma in such an outstanding way. This is indeed marvelous and extraordinary! When we are near you we cannot help but feel like devoting ourselves to religion; but when we return home, we again become preoccupied with worldly affairs. How can we correct this?" Milarepa replied, "If one is really determined to free himself from the sufferings of Saṃsāra, such as birth, old age, illness, death, and so on, he will have peace of mind all the time and will not need to make any effort. Otherwise he should bear in mind that the sufferings in a future life could be much more durable and long-lasting than those in this life; and the burden could also be much heavier. It is therefore of paramount importance to take steps to prepare for the next life.

"Please hearken, and I will sing a song for you."

> We sentient beings moving in the world
> Float down the flowing stream
> Of the Four sufferings.[1]
> Compared to this, how much more formidable
> Are the unceasing future lives in Saṃsāra.
> Why not, then, prepare a boat for the "crossing"?

The state of our future lives is far more fearful
And deserving of far more concern
Than are the dreadful demons, ghosts, and Yama.
So why not prepare for yourself a guide?

Even the dread passions—craving, hatred and blindness—
Are not so fearful as the state of our
    [unknown] future,
So why not prepare for yourself an antidote?

Great is the kingdom of the Three Realms
    of Saṃsāra,
But greater is the endless road of birth-and-death,
So why not prepare for yourself provisions?
It will be better that you practice Dharma
If you have no assurance in yourselves.

The young men said, "Your admonishment is very helpful. We will come and practice the Dharma with you. However, as it makes no sense to punish oneself by practicing the extreme ascetic way of living, we beg you, for the sake of protecting the resources of your patrons and disciples, to keep for yourself a tiny share of belongings as a token. Also, we do not quite understand what you have just said in your song. Please make it clearer."

In reply Milarepa sang:

Reliance on a qualified Guru is the
    guide to Saṃsāra and Nirvāṇa;
Unsparing charity provides for the journey;
As the rising moon shines brightly in the darkness,
The real experiences in meditation
    [enlighten one's mind].
This is the companionship
One should search for as a guide.

To give accumulated wealth for the cause of Dharma
Prepares one's boat for Saṃsāra's stream.
Holding the View without sectarian bigotry,
One can meditate without distraction.
If action accords with Buddhist teaching
Precept is clear, and the Guru pleased.
The reward is to die without regret.

Kinsmen, patrons, and disciples
Mean nought to me, the Yogi;
Only you worldly beings need them.

Fame, grandeur, and honor
Mean nought to me, the Yogi.
Pursuers of the Eight Desires need them.

Property, goods, and social life
Mean nought to me, the Yogi.
Pursuers of fame require them.

Tidiness, washing, and sanitation,
Mean nought to me, the Yogi.
Never do I want them.
They are what you young men need.
These twelve things do not concern me.

[I know well] that it is not everyone
Who can practice all these things;
But you young men assembled here,
Remember the "boastful talk" of this old man!
If you want happiness in life
Practice, then, the Dharma,
Renounce distractions, and remain in solitude.
Cling to the hermitage with perseverance.
Yearn for Buddhahood and your fortitude will grow.
You will then vanquish the Four Demons.

Among the youths was a well-gifted, most intelligent, hard-working, and compassionate young man. He said to Milarepa, "My Guru, it is solely because we have been attached to the affairs of this life that we have neglected to look after our destiny in future lives. Please accept us as your servants. We shall renounce this life and devote ourselves to the preparation for our future lives. [In this light] please be kind enough to give us some further instructions."

"A human body, free and opportune, is as precious as a jewel," replied Milarepa, "and to have a chance to practice the Dharma is likewise very rare. Also, to find one serious Buddhist in a hundred is difficult! Considering the difficulties of meeting the right Gurus, and other necessary favorable conditions for practicing Buddhism, you should deem yourselves very fortunate that you have now met all these requirements. Do not, therefore, [waste them], but practice the Dharma."

Milarepa then sang:

> To escape from the Eight Non-Freedoms[2] is hard,
> As it is to gain the human form, free and opportune.
>
> To realize the sorrows of Saṃsāra
> And to seek Nirvāṇa is difficult!
>
> Out of one hundred seekers of Bodhi, it is
>   hard to find
> One who may attain the pure and favorable conditions!
>
> To renounce the pleasures of this life is hard,
> As it is to make full use of the gem-like human body.
>
> Slight is the chance to meet a compassionate Guru
> Who knows the traditional and expedient[3]
>   inner Teachings.
>
> A sincere and faithful disciple
> With ability to practice Dharma, is most rare.
>
> To find a temple without fear
> And commotion is most hard.
>
> To find a congenial companion, whose Views
> Practice, and School agree with you, is rare.
>
> To attain a body without pain and sickness,
> Able to endure hard practice, is difficult!
>
> Even when you have fulfilled all these conditions,
> It is still hard to concentrate on meditation!
>
> These are the nine hard conditions;
> However formidable and exacting they may be,
> With determination and practice one can
>   conquer them.

Having heard this admonishment, the young man could not but develop a very strong faith in the Jetsun. He devoted himself to serve

Milarepa, who gave him the Initations and Instructions. Later he became a well-accomplished yogi and attained Liberation. He was known as Milarepa's intimate son-disciple, Tsapu Repa.

This is the story of Tsapu Repa meeting Milarepa in the Great Light Cave.

NOTES

1 Four Sufferings: those of birth, of age, of sickness, and of death.

2 The Eight Non-Freedoms (T.T.: Mi.Khom.brGyad.) are the eight conditions in which it is difficult to receive and practice Dharma: in the hells; as hungry ghosts or animals; in Uttarakuru (the legendary "Northern Continent" where all is pleasant); in the heavens (where life is long and easy); as deaf, blind, and dumb; as a worldly philosopher; and in the intermediate period between a Buddha and his successor.

3 A qualified Guru should be able to give not only the traditional teachings of the Dharma, but also the appropriate or expedient teachings for the individual disciple. But literally, this line should be translated as: "Who knows the essential instructions of Sūtra and of Reasoning" (T.T.: Luñ. [and] Rig.Pa.).

12

THE SHEPHERD'S SEARCH FOR MIND

Obeisance to all Gurus

O NE day, Jetsun Milarepa descended from the Great Light Cave to the Happy Village of Mang Yul for food and alms. Seeing many people in the center of the village, he said to them, "Dear patrons, please give me some food this morning." They asked, "Are you the much-talked-about yogi who formerly resided at Ragma?" He replied, "Yes, I am." Then a great respect for him arose within them and they cried, "Oh, here comes the wonderful yogi!"

Among them was a married couple who had no children. Inviting Milarepa to their house, they served him and said, "Dear Lama, where are your home and relatives?" Milarepa replied, "I am a poor beggar who has disavowed his relatives and native land and has also been forsaken by them." Then the couple cried, "In that case we would like to adopt you into our family! We have a good strip of land which we can give you; you can then marry an attractive woman, and soon you will have relatives." Milarepa replied, "I have no need of these things, and will tell you why":

> Home and land at first seem pleasant;
> But they are like a rasp filing away one's
> body, word, and mind!
> How toilsome ploughing and digging can become!
> And when the seeds you planted never
> sprout, you have worked for nought!
> In the end it becomes a land of misery—
> desolate and unprotected—
> A place of Hungry Spirits, and of haunting ghosts!
> When I think of the warehouse
> For storing sinful deeds,

119

It gnaws at my heart;
In such a prison of transciency I will not stay,
I have no wish to join your family!

The married couple said, "Please do not talk like that! We will find
you a fine girl from a prominent family, who is fit to be your bride
and who will suit your taste. Please consider this." Milarepa sang:

At first, the lady is like a heavenly angel;
The more you look at her, the more you want to gaze.
Middle-aged, she becomes a demon with a
          corpse's eyes;
You say one word to her and she shouts back two.
She pulls your hair and hits your knee,
You strike her with your staff, but back
          she throws a ladle.
At life's end, she becomes an old cow with
          no teeth.
Her angry eyes burn with a devilish fire
Penetrating deep into your heart!
I keep away from women to avoid fights and
          quarrels.
For the young bride you mentioned, I have
          no appetite.

The husband then said, "Dear Lama, it is true that when one
grows old and close to death he has not the same capacity for enjoying life or for being pleasant as when he was young. But if I have
no son, my grief and disappointment will be unbearable. How about
you? Don't you need a son at all?" Milarepa sang in reply:

In youth, a son is like the Prince of Heaven;
You love him so much that the passion is
          hard to bear.
In middle age, he becomes a ruthless creditor
To whom you give all, but he still wants more.
Driven from the house are his own parents,
Invited in is his beloved, charming lady.
His father calls, but he will not answer;
His mother cries out, but he will not listen.
Then the neighbors take advantage, spreading
          lies and rumors.

Thus I learned that one's child oft becomes
　　one's enemy.
Bearing this in mind, I renounce the
　　fetters of Saṃsāra.
For sons and nephews I have no appetite.

Both husband and wife agreed with him, replying, "What you have said is indeed true. Sometimes one's own son becomes an enemy. Perhaps it would be better to have a daughter. What do you think?"
In answer Milarepa sang:

In youth, a daughter is like a smiling,
　　heavenly angel;
She is more attractive and precious than are jewels.
In middle age, she is good for nothing.
Before her father, she openly carries things away;
She pilfers secretly behind her mother's back.
If her parents do not praise her and satisfy
　　her wants,
They will suffer from her bitterness and temper.
In the end, she becomes red-faced and wields
　　a sword.
At her best, she may serve and devote herself
　　to others;
At her worst, she will bring mishaps and disaster.
Woman is always a trouble-maker;
Bearing this in mind, one should avoid
　　irretrievable misfortunes.
For women, the primary source of suffering,
　　I have no appetite.

The husband and wife then said, "One may not need sons and daughters, but without relatives, life would be too miserable and help-less. Is that not so?"
Milarepa again sang:

At first, when a man greets his relatives,
He is happy and joyful; with enthusiasm
He serves, entertains, and talks to them.
Later, they share his meat and wine.
He offers something to them once, they may
　　reciprocate.

In the end, they cause anger, craving, and
    bitterness;
They are a fountain of regret and unhappiness.
With this in mind, I renounce pleasant and
    sociable friends;
For kinsmen and neighbors, I have no appetite.

The couple then said, "Indeed, you may not need kinsmen. However, since we own a great deal of property, would you like to have and take care of it?" Milarepa replied, "As the sun and moon never stop to brighten one small place, so I devote myself to the welfare of *all* sentient beings. I cannot, therefore, become a member of your family. By merely beholding me, both of you will be benefited in this and future lives. I will also make a wish that we may meet in the Pure Land of Oujen."

Milarepa then burst into another song:

Wealth, at first, leads to self-enjoyment,
Making other people envious.
However much one has, one never feels it is enough,
Until one is bound by the miser's demon;
It is then hard to spend it on virtuous deeds.

Wealth provokes enemies and stirs up ghosts.
One works hard to gather riches which others
    will spend;
In the end, one struggles for life and death.
To amass wealth and money invites enemies;
So I renounce the delusions of Saṃsāra.
To become the victim of deceitful devils,
I have no appetite.

These songs gave the couple unshakable faith in Milarepa and they gave away all their possessions for the sake of the Dharma. They began to practice the Jetsun's teachings and were forever released from falling into the three lower Realms. When they died, they entered the Path [of Bodhi] and step by step approached Buddhahood.

After this, the Jetsun returned to the Bodhi Cave of Ragma. His former patrons gave their services and offerings to him, and he remained there in an inspired mood.

One day, two young shepherds came to him. The younger one asked, "Dear Lama, have you a companion?"

Milarepa replied, "Yes, I have."

"Who is he?"

"His name is 'Friend Bodhi-Heart'."

"Where is he now?"

"In the House of the Universal Seed Consciousness."[1]

"What do you mean by that?"

"My own body."

The elder boy then said, "Lama, we had better go, as you cannot guide us." But the younger one said, "Do you mean this Consciousness is mind itself, and that the physical body is the house of the mind?"

"Yes, that is correct."

The boy continued, "We know that although a house usually belongs only to one person, many people can enter it, so we always find a number of people living in one house. In the same way, is there only one mind in the body, or are there many? If there are many, how do they live together?"

"Well, as to whether there is only one mind in the body or many, you had better find that out by yourself."

"Revered One, I will try."

At this point, the boys took their leave and went home. Next morning, the younger boy returned and said to Milarepa, "Dear Lama, last night I tried to find out what my mind is and how it works. I observed it carefully and found that I have only one mind. Even though one wants to, one cannot kill this mind. However much one wishes to dismiss it, it will not go away. If one tries to catch it, it cannot be grasped; nor can it be held by pressing it. If you want it to remain, it will not stay; if you release it, it will not go. You try to gather it; it cannot be picked up. You try to see it; it cannot be seen. You try to understand it; it cannot be known. If you think it is an existing entity and cast it off, it will not leave you. If you think that it is non-existent, you feel it running on. It is something illuminating, aware, wide-awake, yet incomprehensible. In short, it is hard to say what the mind really is. Please be kind enough to explain the meaning of the mind."

In response, Milarepa sang:

> Listen to me, dear shepherd, the protector
>   [of sheep]!
> By merely hearing about sugar's taste,
> Sweetness cannot be experienced;
> Though one's mind may understand
> What sweetness is,
> It cannot experience directly;
> Only the tongue can know it.

> In the same way one cannot see in full
>   the nature of mind,
> Though he may have a glimpse of it
> If it has been pointed out by others.[2]
> If one relies not on this one glimpse,
> But continues searching for the nature of mind,
> He will see it fully in the end.
> Dear shepherd, in this way you should observe
>   your mind.

The boy then said, "In that case, please give me the Pointing-out-Instruction,[3] and this evening I will look into it. I shall return tomorrow and tell you the result." Milarepa replied, "Very well. When you get home, try to find out the color of the mind. Is it white, red, or what? What is its shape? Is it oblong, round, or what? Also, try to locate where in your body it dwells."

The next morning when the sun rose, the shepherd drove the sheep before him, and came to Milarepa, who asked, "Did you try last night to find out what the mind is like?" The boy replied, "Yes, I did."

"What does it look like?"

"Well, it is limpid, lucid, moving, unpredictable, and ungraspable; it has no color or shape. When it associates with the eyes, it sees; when with the ear, it hears; when with the nose, it smells; when with the tongue, it tastes and talks; and when with the feet it walks. If the body is agitated, the mind, too, is stirred. Normally the mind directs the body; when the body is in good condition, the mind can command it at will, but when the body becomes old, decayed, or bereft, the mind will leave it behind without a thought as one throws away a stone after cleaning oneself. The mind is very realistic and adaptable. On the other hand, the body does not remain quiet or submissive, but frequently gives trouble to the mind. It causes suffering and pain until the mind loses its self-control. At night in the state of sleep the mind goes away; it is indeed very busy and hard-working. It is clear to me that all my sufferings are caused by it [the mind]."

The Jetsun then sang:

> Listen to me, young shepherd.
> The body is between the conscious and
>   unconscious state,
> While the mind is the crucial and decisive factor!
> He who feels sufferings in the lower Realms,
> Is the prisoner of Saṃsāra,
> Yet it is the mind that can free you from Saṃsāra.

Surely you want to reach the other shore?
Surely you long for the City of Well-Being
and Liberation?
If you desire to go, dear child, I can show
The way to you and give you the instructions.

The shepherd replied, "Certainly, dear Lama, I have made up my mind to seek it." Milarepa then asked, "What is your name?"

"Sangje Jhap."

"How old are you?"

"Sixteen."

Thereupon the Jetsun gave him the teaching of "Taking Refuge,"[4] explaining briefly its benefits and significance. He then said, "When you get back home this evening, do not stop reciting the Prayer; and in the meantime try to find out which takes refuge, the mind or the body. Tell me the result tomorrow."

The next morning the shepherd came and said to Milarepa. "Dear Lama, last night I tried to find out which of these two takes refuge, the body or the mind. I found that it is neither of them. [I observed the body first.] Each part, from the head down to the toes, has a name. I asked myself, 'Is it the body as a whole which takes refuge?' It cannot be so, for when the mind leaves the body, the latter no longer exists. People then call it a 'corpse,' and certainly it cannot be called a 'refuge-seeker.' Furthermore, when it disintegrates, it ceases to be a corpse; therefore, it cannot be the body which takes refuge in Buddha. I then asked myself, 'Is it the mind that takes refuge?' But the refuge-seeker cannot be the mind, as the latter is only the mind and nothing else. If one says that the present mind is the [real] mind, and the succeeding one is the one which takes refuge, there will be two minds; and names for both, such as the 'present mind,' and the 'future mind' should then be given them. Besides, when the act of 'Refuge-seeking' takes place, both the present and succeeding minds have passed away! If one says both take refuge, then the mind will [become something immutable] which never [grows] or ceases to be. If that is so, then in all the lives of the past and future in the Six Realms of Saṃsāra, we need nothing but this 'Refuge-seeker.' But I cannot remember anything in my past life; nor do I know what will take place in my future one. The mind of last year and yesterday are gone; that of tomorrow has not yet come; the present flowing one does not stay. Pray, my teacher, please give me an explanation! I submit everything to you; you know everything, you know what I need!"

In answer to his request, Milarepa sang:

I sincerely pray to my Guru
Who realized the truth of Non-ego,
I pray with body, words, and mind;
I pray with great faith and sincerity.
Pray bless me and my disciples,
Enable us to realize the Truth of Non-ego!
Pity us and deliver us from the plight of
        ego-clinging!

Listen carefully, dear shepherd.
Clinging to the notion of ego is
        characteristic of this consciousness.
If one looks into this consciousness itself,
He sees no ego; of it nothing is seen!

If one can practice the teaching of Mahāmudrā
And knows how to see nothing, something will
        be seen.

To practice the teaching of Mahāmudrā
One needs great faith, humility, and zeal
        as the Foundation.[5]
One should understand the truth of Karma
        and Causation as the Path.[6]
In order to achieve the Accomplishment,[7]
        one should depend upon a Guru
For the Initiation, Instruction, and Inner Teaching.

It requires a disciple possessing merit[8]
        to receive the teaching;
It requires a man who disregards discomfort
        and suffering;
It requires the courage of fearlessness,
        the defiance of death!
Dear shepherd, can you do these things?
If so, you are well-destined;
If not, it is better not to talk about the subject.
This ask yourself, and think carefully.

When you sought the "I" [last night] you
        could not find it.
This is the practice of Non-ego of Personality.
If you want to practice the Non-ego of Existence,[9]

Follow my example and for twelve years meditate.
Then you will understand the nature of Mind.
Think well on this, dear boy!

The shepherd said, "I offer you my body and my head. Please make me understand my own mind definitely and clearly.". The Jetsun thought, "I shall see whether this child can really practice," and then he said, "First pray to the Three Precious Ones, then visualize an image of Buddha in front of your nose." Thus Milarepa gave the shepherd the instruction of concentration and sent him away.

There was no sign of the boy for seven days. On the seventh day, his father came to Milarepa, saying, "Dear Lama, my son has not come home for a week. This is very unusual. Wondering whether he was lost, I inquired of the other shepherds who had been with him. They all said that he had come to you for the Dharma, and thought he had then gone home. But where is he?" "He was here," replied Milarepa, "but has not come back now for seven days."

The father was deeply grieved and wept bitterly as he left Milarepa. Many people were then sent out to search for the boy. Finally, they found him in a clay pit sitting upright with his eyes wide open staring straight in front. They asked him, "What are you doing here?" He replied, "I am practicing the meditation my Guru taught me." "Then why have you not returned home for seven days?" "I have only been meditating a little while, you must be joking!" As he said this, he looked at the sun and found that it was earlier than the time he had started to meditate. In his bewilderment he asked, "What has happened?"

From that day on, the boy's family had great difficulty with him, because he had almost completely lost the notion of time. What appeared to him to have been only one day, was the passing of four or five days to others. Many times his parents sent people out to search for him. Thus both he and his family began to feel miserable. At this juncture they asked him whether he wanted to live with Milarepa for good. He said that he would like nothing better. So they provided him with food and sent him to the Teacher.

Milarepa first gave him the Precepts of Five Virtues,[10] preached the doctrine of Dharma, and then granted him the teaching of the Innate-born Wisdom.[11] Through practice, the boy gradually attained good meditation experience and Milarepa was very pleased. [In order, however, to clarify the boy's misapprehension on the nature of true Realization], he sang:

I bow down at the feet of Marpa,
He who received grace from Nāropa and Medripa.

Those who practice the Dharma with their mouths
Talk much and seem to know much teaching,
But when the time comes for the perceiver to
    leave the deadened body,
The mouth-bound preacher into space is thrown.

When the Clear Light[12] shines, it is cloaked
    by blindness;
The chance to see the Dharmakāya at the time
    of death
Is lost through fear and confusion.

Even though one spends his life in studying
    the Canon,
It helps not at the moment of the mind's departure.

Alas! Those proficient yogis who long
    have practiced meditation
Mistake the psychic experience of illumination
For Transcendental Wisdom,
And are happy with this form of self-deception.[13]
Therefore when at death the Transcendental
    Wisdom of the Dharmakāya shines,
These yogis cannot unify the Light of
    Mother-and-Son.[14]
Since meditation cannot help them as they die,
They are still in danger of rebirth in
    lower Realms.[15]

My dear son, best of laymen, listen to me carefully!

When your body is rightly posed, and your
    mind absorbed deep in meditation,
You may feel that thought and mind both disappear;
Yet this is but the surface experience of Dhyāna.
By constant practice and mindfulness thereon,
One feels radiant Self-awareness shining like
    a brilliant lamp.
It is pure and bright as a flower,
It is like the feeling of staring
Into the vast and empty sky.
The Awareness of Voidness is limpid and
    transparent, yet vivid.

This Non-thought, this radiant and transparent
     experience
Is but the feeling of Dhyāna.
With this good foundation
One should further pray to the Three Precious Ones,
And penetrate to Reality by deep thinking
     and contemplation.[16]
He thus can tie the Non-ego Wisdom
With the beneficial life-rope of deep Dhyāna.
With the power of kindness and compassion,
And with the altruistic vow of the Bodhi-Heart,
He can see direct and clear
The truth of the Enlightened Path,
Of which nothing can be seen, yet all is
     clearly visioned.
He sees how wrong were the fears and hopes
     of his own mind.
Without arrival, he reaches the place of Buddha;
Without seeing, he visions the Dharmakāya;
Without effort, he does all things naturally.
Dear son, the Virtue-seeker, bear this in-
     struction in your mind.

Milarepa then gave the boy the complete Initiation and verbal instructions. After practicing them, the boy attained superlative Experience and Realization. He was known as one of the "Heart-Sons" of
the Jetsun, Repa Sangje Jhap.

This is the story of Milarepa's second visit to Ragma, and of his
meeting with Repa Sangje Jhap.

NOTES

1 This is another name for the Ālaya Consciousness. See Story 4, Note 38.

2 Lit.: "Through the 'Pointing-out-Instruction' one may glimpse it." The
Pointing-out-Instruction (T.T.: Ño.sProd.) is an essential practice of Mahāmudrā. The main concern of Mahāmudrā is the unfoldment of the essence of one's
mind. To accomplish this, the disciple is given by his Guru the "Pointing-out"
demonstration. This can be done in different ways with different gestures — a
smile, a blow, a push, a remark, etc. This is strikingly similar to the tradition of Zen,
though the style and process appear somewhat different.

3 See Note 2.

4 "Taking Refuge" (T.T.: sKyabs.hGro.): This is the basic and universal prayer of all Buddhists. It reads: "I take refuge in the Buddha, I take refuge in the Dharma, I take refuge in the Saṅgha."

5, 6, 7 Foundation, Path, and Accomplishment (T.T.: gShi, Lam, hBres.Bu.): These three terms are frequently used in Buddhist Tantric texts. They have various meanings and uses. Generally speaking, the "Foundation" (gShi.) implies the basic principles of Buddhism; the "Path" (Lam.) is the practice, or way of action which is in conformity with the principles of the "Foundation"; and the "Accomplishment" (hBres.Bu.), otherwise translated as "Fruit," is the full realization of the principles of the Foundation. For example, the Foundation of the teaching of Mahāmudrā is the view that the innate Buddha-nature is within all sentient beings, without which no sentient being could possibly become Buddha regardless of how hard he attempted to practice the Dharma. "Foundation" is, therefore, the cause, the seed, the potentiality, or the original innate Suchness that exists in all beings at all times. The Path of Mahāmudrā is the practice that one follows within the framework of the basic Mahāmudrā Doctrine. The Accomplishment of Mahāmudrā is the full realization of the original, endowed Buddha-nature — the Foundation — within oneself. These three terms, in addition to their special and specific connotations, are used here, as well as in many other places throughout the book, in a very general sense to denote religious faith, practice, and achievement.

8 A merit-possessor is a good vessel for Dharma, a well-destined person. According to Buddhism, a person becomes a good vessel for Dharma in this life partly because he has performed meritorious deeds in his past lives.

9 Non-ego of existence (T.T.: Chos.Kyi.bDag.Med.): the truth of Non-being or Voidness.

10 The Precepts of Five Virtues: These are the basic precepts for all Buddhists, including monks and laymen. They are: One should not (1) kill, (2) steal, (3) commit adultery, (4) lie, or (5) take intoxicants.

11 Innate-born Wisdom: From the Tantric viewpoint, the realization of this inborn and ubiquitous Wisdom is the realization of Buddhahood itself, and so is the core of Tantric teachings.

12 At the time of death, the Clear Light of the Dharmakāya will shine for a short while, but because of ignorance and habitual clinging men cannot recognize it, thus they miss the chance of Liberation. See "The Tibetan Book of the Dead," edited by W. Y. Evans-Wentz, Oxford University Press, 1957.

13 Milarepa gave this very important warning to yogis, pointing out that there are many different *kinds and degrees* of illumination. Some are mundane, some are transcendental, some are psychic phenomena, and some are the real illuminations of Transcendental Wisdom.

14 Mother-and-Son Light: See Story 9, Note 17.

15 Buddhism claims that faith and meditation alone cannot liberate one from Saṃsāra. Without the complete destruction of ego-clinging, or the absolute annihilation of the habitual-thinking seeds in the Store Consciousness (Ālaya-vijñāna), a real Liberation is impossible. Various teachings are given by different Buddhist Schools to attain this Liberation, such as the Prajñāpāramitā of Mādhyamika; the Contemplation-on-Away-from-Subjective-Objective-Ideas of Yogācāra; the Sameness of Saṃsāra and Nirvāṇa of general Tantrism; and the Unification of the Mother-and-Son Light of Mahāmudrā.

16 Faith, good will, compassion, and Samādhi cannot bring one to Enlightenment without the Prajñā insight. Deep contemplation on Śūnyatā, or Voidness, is therefore absolutely necessary.

ཨོཾ༎

13

THE SONG OF
REALIZATION

Obeisance to all Gurus

THE Jetsun Milarepa returned to Nya Non from the Happy Town of
Mang Yul. His former patrons were all delighted [to see him again]
and begged him to stay in Nya Non permanently. At the foot of a
huge tree stood a belly-shaped rock, beneath which there was a cave,
and Milarepa took up his abode there. Then the Venerable Shaja
Guna and a number of patrons of Nya Non came and asked him what
progress and Realization he had attained during his sojourn in other
places. In answer he sang:

> I make obeisance to Marpa, the Translator.

> During my stay elsewhere
> I realized that nothing is;
> I freed myself from the duality of
>   past and future;
> I apprehended that the Six Realms do not exist.
> I was delivered once and for all from
>   life and death,
> And understood that all things are equal.
> I shall cling no more to happiness or sorrow.
> I realized as illusion all that I perceive,
> And was freed from taking and from leaving.
> I realized the truth of Non-difference,
> And was freed from both Saṃsāra and Nirvāṇa.
> I also realized as illusions the Practice,
>   Steps, and Stages.
> My mind is thus devoid of hope and fear.

The patrons again asked Milarepa, "What else did you understand?"
Milarepa replied, "Well, to please you, I will sing an appropriate,
helpful song":

> One's parents provide the outer cause
>   and conditions;
> One's Universal Seed Consciousness[1]
>   is within;
> The acquired pure human body is between these two.
> With these three endowments one stands apart
> From the Three Miserable Realms.
> By observing the wearisome process of
>   birth in the outer world,
> The longing for renunciation and the
>   faith for Dharma will grow from within.
> In addition, one should e'er remember the
>   teaching of Buddha;
> Thus will one be freed from worldly kinsmen
>   and enemies.
>
> The Father-Guru provides help from without;
> Self-discrimination arises from the effort within;
> Between these two grows confidence and conviction.
> Thus is one freed from all doubt and confusion.
>
> One thinks of sentient beings in the Six
>   Realms without,
> While unbounded love shines from the mind within.
> Between the two come the experiences of
>   meditation.
> Thus one is freed from all partial compassion.[2]
>
> Outwardly, the Three Kingdoms are self-liberated;
> Inwardly, self-present Wisdom[3] brightly shines;
> Between the two, faith in Realization stands firm.
> Thus fade anxiety and fear.
>
> The Five Desires manifest without;
> Non-clinging Wisdom shines within;
> A feeling of [the two] tasting as one[4]
> Is experienced in between.
> Thus one is freed from the distinction of
>   weal and woe.
>
> The absence of act and deed appears without,
> The departure of fear and hope is seen within;

Between the two, and from you apart,
Is the sickness that comes from effort.
Thus one is freed from choosing
    between good and evil.

The Venerable Shaja Guna said to Milarepa, "My dear Jetsun, your mind has long been absorbed in Purity, yet though I was with you before, I never received a definitive and convincing teaching from you. Now, please give me the Initiations and instructions." The Jetsun complied with his request, and made him start practicing.

After some time, Shaja Guna had an experience, and came to Milarepa, saying, "If Saṃsāra and manifestations do not exist, there is no need to practice Dharma; if the mind is non-existent, there is no need for the Guru; but if there is no Guru, how can one learn the practice? Please explain the nature of these things and enlighten me upon the Essence of Mind."

Milarepa then sang:

Manifestation is not [something] coming
    into being;
If one sees something happen, it is merely clinging.
The nature of Saṃsāra is the absence of substance;
If one sees substance therein, it is merely
    an illusion.

The nature of mind is two-in-one;
If one discriminates or sees opposites,
It is one's attachment and affection.

The qualified Guru is the Lineage-possessor;
It is then folly to create one's own Guru.

The Essence of Mind is like the sky;
Sometimes it is shadowed by the clouds
    of Thought-flow.
Then the wind of the Guru's inner teaching
Blows away the drifting clouds;
Yet the Thought-flow itself is the illumination.
The Experience is as natural as sun- and moon-light;
Yet it is beyond both space and time.

It is beyond all words and description.
But assurance grows in one's heart, like
    many stars a'shining;
Whenever it so shines, great ecstasy arises.

Beyond all playwords lies the nature of
    the Dharmakāya;
Of the action of the Six Groups, it is
    utterly devoid.
It is transcendant, effortless, and natural,
Beyond the grasp of self and non-self.
Dwelling forever in it is the Wisdom of
    Non-clinging.
Wondrous is the Trikāya, Three in One.

He then told Shaja Guna not to become attached to pleasure, fame, and the world, but to devote himself to the practice of the Dharma all his life and urge others to do likewise.

Then Milarepa sang:

Hear me, you well-gifted man!
Is not this life uncertain and delusive?
Are not its pleasures and enjoyments like a mirage?
Is there any peace here in Saṃsāra?
Is not its false felicity as unreal as a dream?
Are not both praise and blame empty as an echo?
Are not all forms the same as the Mind-nature?
Are not Self-mind and the Buddha identical?
Is not the Buddha the same as the Dharmakāya?
Is not the Dharmakāya identical with Truth?

The enlightened one knows that all things are mental;
Therefore one should observe one's mind by
    day and night.
If you watch it, you can still see nothing.
Fix then your mind in this non-seeing state.

There is no self-entity in Milarepa's mind;
I, myself, am the Mahāmudrā;
Because there is no difference between Static
    and Active Meditation,
I have no need for the different stages in the Path.
Whatever they may manifest, their essence
    is Voidness;
There is neither mindfulness nor non-
    mindfulness in my contemplation.

I have tasted the flavor of Non-existence;

Compared to other teachings, this is the highest.
The Yoga-practice of the Nāḍīs, Prāṇa, and Bindu,⁵
The teaching of Karma Mudrā⁶ and of Mantra Yoga,
The practice of visualizing Buddha and the
    Four Pure Positions,
These are only the first steps in Mahāyāna.
To practice them uproots not lust and hate.

Bear what I now sing firmly in your minds;
All things are of the Self-mind, which is void.
He who ne'er departs from the Experience and
    Realization [of the Void],
Without effort has accomplished all practices
    of worship and discipline.
In this are found all merits and marvels!

Thus Milarepa sang, and the teacher, Shaja Guna, devoted himself to practicing meditation. He attained an extraordinary understanding and became one of the intimate Son-Disciples of the Jetsun.

This is the story of Milarepa's ripening the priest, Shaja Guna of Nya Non, in the Belly Cave.

NOTES

1 Universal Seed Consciousness: Store Consciousness (Ālaya-vijñāna). See Story 4, Note 38.

2 Partial compassion: An enlightened being should have an unlimited and indiscriminative compassion in contrast to the limitative and favoring love of ordinary men. This ever-present infinite compassion is brought about by the Mahāmudrā Practice. It is said an infinite compassion will flow naturally from the Inborn-Buddha-Mind when one reaches the advanced stage of Mahāmudrā.

3 Self-present Wisdom: An enlightened being never feels that he *attains* the Wisdom of Buddha, he merely *discovers* it — the ever-present Wisdom.

4 Tasting as one, or One-taste (T.T.: Ro.gCig.): When one is freed from discriminitive thoughts, he then reaches the realm of "One-taste," whence he sees the non-differentiation of beings and becomes one with the "Universal Harmony" and the "Interpenetrating Totality." (See the "Avataṁsaka Sūtra"; and D. T. Suzuki's "The Essence of Buddhism," The Buddhist Society, London, 1957.)

5 Nāḍīs, Prāṇa, and Bindu: See Story 7, Note 19.

6 Karma Mudrā: an advanced Perfecting Yoga through which the sexual energy is sublimated.

14

A WOMAN'S ROLE IN
THE DHARMA

Obeisance to all Gurus

Oncе Jetsun Milarepa intended to go to North Horse Gate snow mountain to practice meditation. [On the way], he came to Gebha Lesum in the district of Jung. It was autumn, and the villagers were busy harvesting. In a large field a very beautiful girl, about fifteen years of age, was leading a group of laborers. She seemed to have all the qualifications of an Angel of Wisdom (Ḍākinī). Milarepa approached her and said, "Dear Patroness, please give me alms." "Dear Yogi, please go to my house," the girl replied, "It is over there. Wait for me at the door. I will come directly."

Accordingly, Milarepa went to her home, pushed the door open with his staff, and entered. Immediately, an ugly old woman with a handful of ashes rushed at him, shouting, "You miserable yogi-beggars! I never see you in one place! In the summer you all show up begging for milk and butter! In the winter you all come for grain! I'll wager you wanted to sneak in to steal my daughter's and daughter-in-law's jewelry!" Grumbling and trembling with rage, she was about to throw the ashes at Milarepa, when he said, "Wait a minute, Grandmother! Please listen to me!" He then sang a song with nine meanings:

> Above is the auspicious Heaven,
> Below are the Three Paths of misery,
> In between, are those who are not free to
> choose their birth.[1]
> These three all converge on you.
> Grandmother, you are an angry woman;
> And dislike the Dharma!

Question your own thoughts and your mind examine.
You should practice the Buddha's teaching,
You need a qualified and dependable Guru.
Think carefully, dear lady;
When you were first sent here,
Did you dream you would become an old nanny-goat?

In the morning you get up from bed,
In the evening you go to sleep,
In between, you do the endless housework;
You are engrossed in these three things.
Grandmother, you are the unpaid maid.
Question your own thought and your mind examine.
You should practice Buddha's teaching,
You need a qualified and dependable Guru,
And then things may be different for you.

The head of the family is the most important one,
Income and earnings are the next most longed-for
      things,
Then sons and nephews are wanted most.
By these three you are bound.
Grandmother, for yourself you have no share.
Question your own thought and your mind examine.
You should practice Buddha's teaching,
You need a qualified and dependable Guru,
And then things may be different for you.

Attaining what you want even though you steal,
Getting what you desire even though you rob,
Fighting your foe without regard for death
      and wounds,
To these three things you are subjected.
Grandmother, you are burned up with fury
When you come upon your foe.
Question your own thought and your mind examine.
You should practice Buddha's teaching,
You need a qualified and dependable Guru,
And then things may be different for you.

Gossip about other women and their manners
Is what interests you;
To the affairs of your own son and nephew

You pay attention;
To talk of widows and relatives is your delight.
These three things enchant you.
Grandmother, are you so gentle when you gossip?
Question your own thought and your mind examine.
You should practice Buddha's teaching,
You need a qualified and dependable Guru,
And then things may be different for you.

To lift you from a chair is like pulling out a peg;
With feeble legs
You waddle like a thieving goose;
Earth and stone seem to shatter
When you drop into a seat;
Senile and clumsy is your body.
Grandmother, you have no choice but to obey.
Question your own thought and your mind examine.
You should practice the Buddha's teaching,
What you require is a qualified and dependable Guru,
And from that you may find out how you have changed.

Your skin is creased with wrinkles;
Your bones stand out sharply from your shrunken flesh;
You are deaf, dumb, imbecile, eccentric, and
          tottering;
You are thrice deformed.
Grandmother, your ugly face is wrapped in wrinkles.
Question your own thought and your mind examine.
You should practice Buddha's teaching,
You need a qualified and dependable Guru,
And then things may be different for you.

Your food and drink are cold and foul,
Your coat is heavy and in rags,
Your bed so rough it tears the skin;[2]
These three are your constant companions.
Grandmother, you are now a wretch,
          half woman and half bitch!
Question your own thought and your mind examine!
You should practice Buddha's teaching,
What you need is a qualified and dependable Guru,
And then things may be different for you.

To attain a higher birth and Liberation
Is harder than to see a star in daytime;
To fall into Samsāra's wretched path
Is easy and happens often.
Now, with fear and grief at heart,
You watch the time of death draw nigh.
Grandmother, can you face death with confidence?
Question your own thought and your mind examine!
What you need is to practice the teaching of Buddha,
What you need is a qualified and dependable Guru.

Upon hearing this profound, yet melodious song, the old woman was so moved that she could not but develop a deep faith in the Jetsun. Unconsciously her fists loosened, and the ashes slipped through her fingers to the floor. She regretted what she had done to the Jetsun, and touched by his compassion and words, she could not help shedding tears.

Meantime the girl in the field [whose name was Bardarbom] was just entering the house. Seeing the old woman in tears she turned to Milarepa and cried, "What is the matter? Did you, a follower of Buddha, strike a poor old woman?" The grandmother quickly intervened, "No, no, please do not wrongly accuse him! He never said anything unkind to me. It was I who treated him wrongly. He gave me such a proper and much-needed lesson that it moved me very deeply. It also awakened me to my neglect of religion. I was touched with such great remorse that it compelled me to shed tears. Oh, you are young and different from me; you have faith as well as wealth, and it is very fortunate for you to meet such a teacher as Milarepa. You should give him offerings and service, and ask him to bestow upon you the teachings and instructions."

The girl replied, "Both of you are very wonderful! Are you the great Yogi, Milarepa? By merely meeting you I shall have accumulated a great deal of merit. If you would kindly tell us your Lineage, it will inspire us and also your other disciples. It will certainly change our hearts. So, please do relate it for me."

Milarepa thought, "This is a well-gifted woman; she will become a good disciple of mine." And so he sang:

The omnipresent Dharmakāya is Buddha
     Samantabhadra;
The majestic Sambhogakāya is Buddha
     the Thunderbolt-Holder;

> The Savior of sentient beings, the
>   Nirmāṇakāya, is Gautama Buddha.
> One may find [the teachings] of all
>   three Buddhas in my Lineage.
> Such is the Lineage of this yogi; will you
>   entrust yourself to it?

"Your Lineage is indeed superb," said Bardarbom, "it is what the snow mountain is to rivers—the original source of all [merits]. I have heard people say that you, the followers of Dharma, have a so-called 'Outer Pointing Guru'; and that by relying on him, one will be able to observe and see inwardly the so-called Uncreated Dharmakāya. What kind of Guru do you have? Who is your primary Guru?"

Milarepa replied, "I will sing a short song to explain the qualifications of a genuine Guru."

> The Guru who indicates the true knowledge
>   from without,
> Is your Outer Guru;
> The Guru who elucidates the Awareness of
>   Mind within,
> Is your Inner Guru;
> The Guru who illuminates the nature of your mind,
> Is your real Guru.
> I am a yogi who has all three Gurus,
> Is there a disciple here who wishes to
>   be faithful to them?"

"These Gurus are extraordinary!" exclaimed the girl, "It is just like a string of gems on a golden chain. But before we beseech the teachings from them, what kind of Initiations are required?" Milarepa then sang:

> The Vase placed on your head
> Is the Outer Initiation;
> The proof of the identity of self-body
>   and the Body of Buddha
> Is the Inner Initiation;
> The Illumination of the self-recognition
>   of Mind-Essence
> Is the real Initiation.
> I am a yogi who has attained all three.
> Is there a disciple here who wishes to attain them?

Bardarbom cried out, "These Initiations are indeed profound! It is just like the majesty of the lion, which overawes all other animals. I have also heard that after the Initiation there is an absolute teaching called 'Leading Awareness into the Path.' What is that? Please be kind enough to explain it to me."

In answer to her question, Milarepa sang:

> The Outer Teaching is hearing, thinking,
>   and practicing;
> The Inner Teaching is the clearest
>   elucidation of Awareness;
> The Absolute Teaching is the non-gathering
>   or separation of Experience and Realization.[3]
> I am a yogi who has all three Teachings.
> Is there a disciple here who wishes to attain them?

Bardarbom declared, "These teachings are indeed like a rustless mirror, which reflects images flawlessly." Milarepa replied, "Having attained these teachings, one should go to a hermitage and practice." The girl then asked, "Will you tell me about these practices?" Milarepa sang in answer:

> Living in a rugged, deserted, and solitary hut
> Is the Outer Practice;
> Complete disregard of the self-body
> Is the Inner Practice;
> Knowing the sole Absolute, through and through,
> Is the Absolute Practice.
> I am a yogi who knows all three.
> Is there a disciple here who wishes to learn them?

After hearing this, the girl said, "The Practice you have mentioned is like a great eagle flying in the sky. Its splendor overshadows all other birds!" She continued, "I have heard people say that some yogis know a teaching called 'Pai Practice,'[4] which is very helpful in improving meditation. Could you tell me about it?" Milarepa then sang:

> By applying the Outer "Pai Teaching" to
>   the distracted thought-flow,
> The mind is collected;
> By applying the Inner "Pai Teaching" to awareness,
> The mind is awakened from drowsiness.
> To rest [the mind] on the innate nature,

Is the Absolute "*Pai* Teaching."
I am the Yogi who knows all three.
Is there a disciple here who wishes to know them?

"This *Pai* Teaching of yours is indeed wonderful!" exclaimed Bardarbom, "It is just like the order or summons of the Emperor; it quickens and intensifies one's accomplishments. But if one practices it, what experiences will one have?" Milarepa sang in reply:

> One will experience the great and
>   omnipresent Non-effort Root;
> One will experience the Non-effort
>   Path, the great transparency;
> One will experience the Non-effort
>   Fruit,[5] great Mahāmudrā.
> I am a yogi who has experienced them all.
> Is there a disciple here who wishes to do likewise?

Bardarbom then said, "These three experiences are like the bright sun shining from a cloudless sky, outlining everything on the earth clearly and distinctly. They are indeed wonderful! But what assurance have you gained through them?" Milarepa sang again:

> No Heaven and no Hell, is the assurance
>   of Knowledge,[6]
> No meditation and no distraction is the
>   assurance of Practice,
> No hope and no fear is the assurance of Accomplishment.
> I am a yogi with these three assurances.
> Is there a disciple here who wishes to attain them?

Thereupon, the girl became very faithful to the Jetsun. She bowed down at his feet, and with great veneration she invited him to the inner [chamber], and gave him perfect service and offerings. Then she said "Dear Guru, so far, I have been hindered by ignorance, and so have not been able to think of the real Teachings. Now, through your great compassion, please take me as your servant and disciple." Thus the girl fully realized her past faults of self-conceit. She then sang:

> Oh! You peerless Teacher!
> You most perfect of men, the incarnation of Buddha!
> How stupid, blind, and ignorant am I.

How wrong and sinful is this world!
The heat of summer was so great that it
    scattered the cool clouds,
And I found no shelter in the shade. ·
The cold of winter was so severe
That though flowers still grew, I
    never found them.
The influence of my evil habitual-thinking
    was so strong
That I never saw you as an accomplished being.

Let me tell you my story:
Because of my sinful Karma I was given
    this inferior [female] body.
Through the evil-hindrance of this world,
I never realized the identity of self and Buddha.
Lacking the necessary diligence,
I seldom thought of Buddha's teaching.
Though I desired the Dharma,
Lazy and inert, I frittered time away.

To a woman, a prosperous birth means
    bondage and non-freedom.
To a woman, a wretched birth means the
    loss of companionship.
To our husbands we sometimes talk of suicide;
We set aside and leave our gracious parents;
Great is our ambition, but our perseverance small.
We are experts in slander, ingenious to blame,
The source of news and gossip.
We are those who must be kept away from the betrothed,
For though to all we give food and money,
We are ever slandered as stingy and ill-tempered.
Seldom do we think of impermanence and death.
The sinful hindrances always follow us like shadows.
Now, with deep sincerity, I look forward to
    the Dharma.
Pray, give me a teaching easy to practice
    and understand!

This pleased Milarepa very much and he sang in reply:

Happy and fortunate girl,

Should I praise your story or disparage it?
If I praise it, you will be proud;
If I disparage it, you will be angry;
If I tell the truth, it will expose your
        hidden faults.

Now, listen to the song of an old man:
If you sincerely wish to practice Dharma,
Wash the dirt from off your face,
And sweep away the filth from your heart.

Sincerity and earnestness are good,
But humility and modesty are better.
Even though you may give away your son and husband,
It is better to rely on a qualified Guru.
Though you may abandon worldly life,
To strive for future Enlightenment[7] is better.
Though one may renounce parsimony and avarice,
It is better still to give without sparing.
It is wise to know these things.

With high spirits,
You play and sport as shrewdly as a rat.
You may be very eloquent,
But have no Dharma in your heart.
Like a wild peahen you play—
Of coquetry you know too much,
But too little of devotion.
My dear, you are full of cunning and deceit
Like a merchant in the market-place.
It is hard for you to practice Dharma.

If you want to practice Buddha's teaching rightly,
You should follow me and my Path,
Meditating without distraction in a remote
        mountain.

Bardarbom then sang:

You are the Jetsun, the precious Yogi!
One surely will gain benefits by associating with you.
In the daytime I am busy working;
Drowsy, I go to bed at night.

A slave of household work am I.
Where can I find the time to practice Dharma?

Milarepa replied, "If you seriously want to practice the Dharma,
you must learn that worldly affairs are your enemies and renounce
them." And he sang a song called "The Four Renunciations":

> Listen, you fortunate girl,
> You who have wealth and faith!
>
> Future lives last longer than this life—
> Do you know how to make provision?
> Giving with a niggardly heart
> As if feeding a strange watchdog,
> Only brings more harm than good—
> Bringing nothing in return but a vicious bite.
> Renounce parsimony, now that you know its evil.
>
> Listen, you fortunate girl!
> We know less of this life than the next one.
> Have you prepared and lit your lamp?
> Should it not be ready,
> Meditate on the "Great Light."
>
> If you choose to help an ungrateful foe,
> You will gain not a friend, but damage.
> Beware of acting blindly;
> Beware of this evil and discard it.
>
> Listen, you fortunate girl.
> Future lives are worse than this life—
> Have you a guide or escort for your journey?
> If you have not the right companion,
> Rely on the holy Dharma.
> Beware of relatives and kinsmen;
> They hinder and oppose [the Dharma].
> They never help, but only harm one.
> Did you know that your kinsmen are your foes?
> If this be true, surely you should leave them.
>
> Listen, you fortunate girl.
> The journey in the future life is more
>   hazardous than this one—

> Have you prepared a fine horse of
>   perseverance for it?
> If not, you should strive hard and work
>   with diligence.
> The excitement of the start will soon diminish;
> Beware the foe, "Inertness," which makes
>   one go astray.
> Of no avail are hurry and excitement, which
>   only harm one.
> Do you yet know that your enemies are
>   laziness and caprice?
> If you understand my words, you should
>   cast them both away.

Bardarbom then said, "Dear Lama, I have not yet made any preparation for the next life, but will now begin to do so. Please be kind enough to teach me the Practice." Thus with great sincerity she besought him. Milarepa was delighted, and replied, "I am glad that you are really earnest in devoting yourself to religion. In the tradition of my Lineage, it is not necessary to change one's name or to cut off one's hair.[8] One may reach Buddhahood either as a layman, or as a monk. Without changing one's status, one may still become a good Buddhist." Then he sang for her a song called "The Four Parables and Five Meanings," giving the instruction of Mind-Practice:

> Listen, you fortunate girl,
> You who have wealth and faith!
> Thinking of the magnitude of the sky,
> Meditate on the Vastness with no center
>   and no edge.
>
> Thinking of the sun and moon,
> Meditate upon their light
> Without darkness or obscurity.
>
> Resembling the unchanging, solid mountain
>   before you,
> You should meditate with steadiness and solidity.
>
> Like the ocean, infinitely great and un-
>   fathomably deep,
> Absorb yourself in deepest contemplation.
> Thus meditate on your Self-mind;

Thus, with no doubt and error, practice.

Then Milarepa instructed her in the physical and mental practices, and sent her to meditate. Later on the girl, having had some experiences, and in order to dispel her doubts and break down her hindrances, came and sang to him:

> Oh You, the Jetsun, the precious Guru,
> You man of consummation, the Transformation
> Body of Buddha!
>
> It was fine, when I contemplated on the sky!
> But I felt uneasy when I thought of clouds.
> How should I meditate on them?
>
> It was good, when I contemplated on the sun and moon!
> But I felt uneasy when I thought of stars
> and planets.
> How should I meditate on them?
>
> It was fine, when I contemplated the solid mountain!
> But I felt uneasy when I thought of trees and bushes.
> How should I meditate on them?
>
> It was good, when I contemplated the great ocean!
> But I felt uneasy when I thought of waves.
> How should I meditate on them?
>
> It was fine, when I contemplated the nature
> of Self-mind,
> But I felt uneasy when I encountered ever-
> flowing thoughts![9]
> How should I meditate on them?

After hearing her song, Milarepa was greatly pleased. He knew that she really had had the Experiences in meditation. Thus, in order to clear her doubts and further her understanding, he sang:

> Listen, you fortunate girl,
> You who have wealth and faith!
>
> If you felt fine in meditating on the
> sky, so be it with the clouds.

Clouds are but manifestations of the sky;
Therefore, rest *right in the sphere of the sky!*

The stars are but reflections of the sun and moon;
If you can meditate on *them*, then why not
        on the stars?
Therefore, absorb yourself *in the light of
        the sun and moon!*

Bushes and trees are but manifestations of
        a mountain;
If you can meditate well on that, so be it with the trees!
Therefore, *abide in the steadfastness of the mountain!*

Waves are but the movement of the ocean;
If you can meditate well on that, why not
        on the waves?
Therefore, dissolve yourself *right in the ocean!*

The disturbing Thought-flow manifests the mind;
If you can meditate well on that, so be it
        with the Thought-flow!
Therefore, dissolve yourself into the very
        Essence of Mind!

From then on, Bardarbom strove to contemplate on the real nature of the mind, and eventually she achieved perfect Realization in one life. At her death she flew to the Ḍākinī's Pure Land in her human body. People all heard the sound of the small drum that she was carrying at the time.

This is the story of Milarepa meeting his woman disciple, Bardarbom, one of his four female heirs, at the place of Gebha Lesum of Jung.

NOTES

1 Driven by the force of Karma, Saṃsāric beings are not able to choose their own birth when they reincarnate.

2 This is a free translation.

3 Experience and Realization: See Story 7, Notes 9 and 12.

4 "*Pai* Practice," or the Teaching of *Pai* (T.T.: Phat): The Tibetan word "Phat," pronounced "Pai," is common in Tantric incantations. It is used as a means of cutting distracting thoughts and to arouse the consciousness from drowsiness occurring in meditation. In applying the *Pai* teaching, the yogi first concentrates on the thought-flow, drowsiness, apparitions, or whatever hindrances appear, and then suddenly shouts "Pai!" with all his strength. By doing this the hindrances are eventually eliminated.

5 The Non-effort Root, Path, and Fruit: "Root" means the basic principle, the nature of Buddhahood. "Path" refers to the practice of this basic principle. "Fruit" is the resulting accomplishment or realization of the basic principle. (See Story 12, Notes 5, 6, and 7.)

6 Knowldege, (T.T.: lTa.Wa.), or the "View" of the absolute non-existence of being

7 Lit.: "to strive for the Great Affair."

8 To cut off the hair: This refers to the shaving of a monk's head during the ceremony of ordination.

9 Ever-flowing thoughts: Only through actual meditation practice can one experience the ungovernable and ever-running errant thoughts that constantly arise in one's own mind.

15

THE SONG AT THE INN

Obeisance to all Gurus

Having meditated at Jundhagho [North Horse Gate], the Jetsun Milarepa went to Shri Ri to meditate; on his way, he lodged in an inn at Yei Ru Jang. A scholar named Yaugru Tangbha, with many monk disciples, and a merchant called Dhawa Norbu [the Moon Jewel], with a great retinue, were also stopping there. Milarepa begged alms from the merchant, who said, "You yogis are accustomed to taking the belongings of others to enjoy yourselves; why don't you try to earn your own living? It would be much better to be self-supporting!" Milarepa replied, "It is true that by following your way one may have more immediate happiness and enjoyment, but this very enjoyment will cause more suffering in the future. This is the important point you have neglected. Now listen to my song, 'The Eight Reminders' ":

> Castles and crowded cities are the places
> Where now you love to stay;
> But remember that they will fall in ruins
> After you have departed from this earth.
>
> Pride and vainglory are the lure
> Which now you love to follow;
> But remember, when you are about to die
> They offer you no shelter and no refuge!
>
> Kinsmen and relatives are the people
> With whom now you love to live!
> But remember that you must leave them all behind
> When from this world you pass away!
>
> Servants, wealth, and children

Are things that you love to hold;
But remember, at the moment of your death
Your empty hands can take nothing with you!

Vigor and health are dearest to you now;
But remember that at the moment of your death
Your corpse will be bundled up[1] and borne away!

Now your organs are clear, your blood and
    flesh are strong and vigorous;
But remember, at the moment of your death
They will no longer be at your disposal!

Sweet and delicious foods are things
That now you love to eat;
But remember, at the moment of your death
Your mouth will let the spittle flow!

When of all this I think, I cannot help
But seek the Buddha's teachings!
The enjoyments and pleasures of this world,
For me have no attraction.

I, Milarepa, sing of the Eight Reminders,
At the Guest House of Garakhache of Tsang.
With these clear words I give this helpful warning;
I urge you to observe and practice them!

Thus he sang, and his song roused in the merchant, Dhawa Norbu, such a deep faith that he exclaimed, "Dear Lama, what you have sung is indeed very true and clear and has made me think of the Dharma. Pray, instruct me how to practice the teaching of Buddha." In answer, Milarepa sang:

The rugged hermitage is the place of virtue,
The Guru with knowledge and practice is the
    precious jewel
To whom one should pray with sincerity and reverence.
Without errors the teachings should be practiced.

He who feels his mind run wild,
Should apply his View[2] [of Voidness] for the cure.
The attachments of his mind are thus freed.

How wonderful this is!

He whose mind feels sick,
Should beg the alms of Non-discrimination.[3]
He will then experience the self-liberation
     of the places to which [he travels].
How wonderful this is!

He who dislikes his meditation experiences,
Should compare and discuss them with
          proficient Gurus.
To talk and live with these experienced yogis,
Surely will help his mind!

If sometimes doubts arise, and skepticism,
One should read the holy sayings of the Buddha.
With conviction in the true words of the Dharma,
Confidence and faith in one's heart will grow!

He who feels uneasy and unwell,
Should pray to his Father Guru
With all earnestness;
Thus will he be blessed and his mind made tranquil.

Again, one should think of those faithless men
Who lay their bodies down on Saṃsāra's bed,
Who lay their heads upon the pillows of the Five Poisons
And fling the dung of their passions to the Ten
          Directions.
One should search for [the physician who
     can] cure them.
With the devotion of the Three Gates[4]
     one should make the diagnosis;
Through the Six Merits of the Guru-Doctor
     one should give the medicine.
Thus one is assured that the Three Bodies
     will be attained,
And the Five Poisonous Passions cured!

In order to beg pardon and forgiveness
One should give offerings sincerely.

Upon hearing this song the merchant was confirmed with the deepest faith toward the Jetsun. From that time on, as a layman, he followed the Jetsun's instruction in Dharma practice and became a very good yogi.

At the same time in the inn, while Milarepa was appearing as an ascetic, the scholar-doctor, Yaugru Tangbha was preaching the Dharma. His monk-disciples busily recited prayers in the evening, and sat in a crouching posture practicing Samādhi in the daytime. They even held religious ceremonies and started their sermons before daybreak.

One day, Milarepa went to the congregation during the midday meal to beg a little food.[5] Several monks said, "What a pitiful sight this man is! He acts and dresses like a yogi, but does not practice or learn any teaching of the Dharma; without any knowledge or desire for meditation, he fails even to recite a single prayer; and he even asks alms from the priests! What a pity! What a pity!" And they all felt great pity and sorrow for him. Milarepa then said to them, "My mind is always at ease and happy, because I can practice simultaneously the various devotions, such as reciting Mantras and visualizing Devas' bodies, while learning and carrying out the teachings of the Buddha. Please listen to my song":

> The Three Precious Ones, supporting all
> In the realm of Non-doing Awareness —
> I realize them all!
> Why then should I pray to them?
> Happy is the practice of Yoga
> Without Mantra and muttering!
>
> The bestower of the two Siddhis[6] is
>   the protecting Buddha.
> In the realm of Great Illumination,
> I have completely realized the Buddha
>   of Non-existence,
> And so I need not practice the Arising Yoga!
> Happy is the experience
> Of identifying the Self-body with the Buddha!
>
> The Ḍākinīs sweep all obstacles away and
>   destroy misfortunes;
> In the realm of Self-essence, the plane of origin,
> I have completely realized them.
> And so I have no need to make the ritual offering!
> Happy is the Yoga

In which the six sense-organs relax at ease!

Apprehensions are the source of hindrances.
In the realm of Dharma-Essence,
I identify demon-seeing with the Perfection;
Therefore, I need do no exorcising.
Happy is the Yoga
In which I identify the Dharmakāya with apprehensions!

The words and writing, the dogmas
And the logic I absorb
In the Realm of Illuminating Consciousness.
For me, there is no need of learning.
Happy is the experience of Yoga,
The source of all the Sūtras.

Whereupon the Doctor, Yaugru, said to Milarepa, "Dear Yogi, your experience and understanding are indeed marvelous. However, according to the principles of Buddhism, an object or teaching must be given from which beginners may learn; also it is desirable and helpful to encourage people to follow the Yellow-robed [monks] in the practice of virtuous deeds. Is that not so?" Milarepa replied, "This may be the teaching of your School, and you may do what you like. But my teaching is a little different. In it, if one feels he has nothing to be ashamed of, that will be sufficient! From what I can see, your way of devotion is like this—judge for yourself and see whether what I am going to say is true":

I take refuge in the Three Precious Ones;
May my compassionate Guru ever protect and bless me.

You scholar-doctor of the Eight Worldly Engagements,
How can you clear away ignorance and distraction
      for others,
When you cannot conquer your own mind?

Under the white canopy, stands a lovely peacock;
But he vanishes as quickly as the lightning!
Think, my dear Doctor! Is that not true?

The kitchen of the monastery behind the village
Is a symbol of misery and cheating;
Think, my dear Doctor! Is that not so?

Attending a boisterous public meeting
Is like being driven round in a circle of fierce foes!
Think, my dear Doctor! Is that not true?

Accumulating horses, sheep, and jewels
Is like dew upon the grass
Under the warm breath of the wind.
Think, my dear Doctor! Are they not alike?

The illusory human body with its mass of passions
Is like a corpse that has been gilded!
Think, my dear Doctor! Are they not alike?

Leading women practicers, without inner experience,
Is a travesty of dignity, and a disgrace.
Think, my dear Doctor! Is that not so?

The food and offerings in the sacrificial circle
Are like the tax collections of an arrogant inspector.
Think, my dear Doctor! Are they not alike?

Divination, Astrology, and Bon⁷ rituals —
These three Dharmas-of-the-town are like
        swindler's tricks.
Think, my dear Doctor! Are they not alike?

The tuneful hymns which enchant disciples
Are like the malicious invocation of the Dragon Demon.
Think, my dear Doctor! Are they not alike?

Country, home, and fields are not true possessions
But delusive, and tantalizing like rainbows
        to the young!
Think, my dear Doctor! Is that not so?

To sway and dominate disciples by fraud and hypocrisy
Is like a lackey serving many masters.
Think, my dear Doctor! Is that not true?

To preach without the Essence
Is a lie and fraud!
Think, my dear Doctor! Is that not so?

If you cannot help yourself
How can you help others?

After hearing this song, Doctor Yaugru took a very reverent attitude toward the Jetsun. Rising from his seat he bowed, with his eyes
full of tears, and said, "What you say is very true. Please teach me
the Dharma and allow me to become your disciple."

Among the disciples of Doctor Yaugru there was a young monk
called Sevan Dunchon Shawa who followed the Jetsun and obtained
from him the Initiations and instructions. Having devoted himself
to meditation, he attained the highest accomplishment. He was one
of the heart-sons of the Jetsun, known as Sevan Repa from Dodra.

This is the story of how Milarepa met his disciple Sevan Repa at
the Garakhache Guest House of Yei Ru Jang in Tsang.

NOTES

1 In Tibet the corpse is usually loaded on a horse, like a folded bundle, and
so carried away to the cemetery by the relatives.

2 View: the basic understanding of the Voidness. If distracting thoughts run
wildly during meditation, the yogi should identify them with the Void. They can
thus be tranquilized and transformed.

3 Non-discrimination: Whether his patrons are rich or poor, high or low, the
yogi should beg alms without discrimination. At the same time he should remember
that the giver, the receiver, and the alms are all non-existent, or illusory.

4 Three Gates: body, mouth, and mind.

5 The food remaining from the sacrament.

6 The two Siddhis are the mundane and transcendental "accomplishments,"
or powers.

7 Bon: the pre-Buddhist, native religion of Tibet.

THE BANDIT-DISCIPLE

Obeisance to all Gurus

ONE day when the Jetsun Milarepa was meditating in Shri Ri of Deut Jal, several bandits came to his hermitage. When they could not find any food or clothes, and learned how he lived and made his devotions, they could not help but have deep faith in him. They said, "Dear Lama, this place is very bad. Because of the unfavorable conditions, it must be very hard to get food. Please come to our country, and we will supply you properly."

Milarepa replied, "It is true that conditions here may not be favorable, but I have everything I need to further my devotion. Though your place may be better, I do not want to go there. Instead, I would like you, on my behalf, to send to your country for well-endowed devotees to come here for meditation." And he sang a song called "Welcome to Meditate in Shri Ri":

Shri Ri, that wondrous place in Jal,
Is far to circle, but near to approach.
Come here, you faithful and destined devotees
And all who would renounce this world and life.

Here is the wonderland, Shri Ri,
Far indeed from towns,
But close to meditation and accomplishment!
Come to Shri Ri, you faithful and destined devotees
And all who would renounce this world and life!

Though the water here is scarce, the
        goddesses are many.
Come to Shri Ri, you faithful and well-
        gifted devotees!

Come to Shri Ri of Jal, you disavowers of
this world and life.

Here is the wonderland, Shri Ri of Jal.
It is a place of blessing, the palace of Dem Chog,
He who bestows accomplishments and Siddhis!
Come to Shri Ri, you faithful and well-gifted
devotees,
All you who disavow this world and life!

This is the land of wonder, Shri Ri of Jal,
Where the marvelous Guardian-brothers dwell,
They who destroy your obstacles and difficulties!
Come to Shri Ri, you faithful and destined devotees,
And you who disavow this world and life.

Having heard this song, the leader of the bandits was deeply moved
with faith. He bowed down at Milarepa's feet and told him that he
would come back to see him soon. Some time later, when he returned, he brought with him a large turquoise, but could not decide
whether to offer it to Milarepa. Having a small present with him as
well, he gave this to the Jetsun first.

Milarepa smiled and said, "Do not hesitate! You may offer me
that turquoise, although I have little use for jewels. I will accept it to
perfect your merits." The bandit leader realized that Milarepa possessed the perfect miraculous power of knowing others' thoughts. He
then offered him the turquoise. After accepting it, Milarepa said, "I
now give you back this jewel, hoping that you will use it to sustain
your devotion."

The leader thought: "How wonderful! He has not the slightest desire for money!" And his faith in the Jetsun was confirmed. Milarepa
then gave him the Initiations and instructions. After practicing them,
he eventually attained superlative Experiences and Realization. Later
on, he was known as Drigom Linkawa, and became one of the heart-
sons of Milarepa.

This is the story of how Milarepa met Drigom Repa in Shri Ri of Jal.

17

THE MEETING
AT SILVER SPRING

Obeisance to all Gurus

ONE summer, the great Yogi, Jetsun Milarepa, was meditating at North Shri Ri. When autumn came and the harvest was ready, he went out for alms, but fell asleep in Upper Gog Tang. He dreamed that he saw a green girl with golden hair and shining eyebrows, leading a youth about twenty years old. She said, "Milarepa, you will have eight petals from [the lotus of] your heart. This is one of them. Please bless him and bring him up!" She then disappeared.

Upon awakening from his sleep, Milarepa thought over the meaning of his dream. He decided that the girl must have been a Ḍākinī and that the "eight petals" must imply that he would have eight superlative, destined, heart-like disciples. "Today, I shall probably meet a Karma-exhausted disciple, and I will try my best to help him." With this in mind, he climbed the road leading to Bong. When he reached a brook which flowed like silver, he paused for another nap. After a while, a young man riding on a black horse approached and asked, "Why, dear Yogi, do you sleep here?" Milarepa parried the question by another one: "My dear patron, where are you going?"

"I am going to cross this brook to Din Ri."

Milarepa then explained, "Because of my age, I find it very difficult to wade through water. Could you give me a ride?"

The young man replied, "As I am going to play with some youths over there, I am in a very great hurry and will not be able to take you with me. Besides, it would strain my horse too much, and he might be hurt."

After saying this he went on ahead, alone, without even looking back.

Thereupon Milarepa, with sincere concentration, entered the

Samādhi of Guru-Union.[1] Holding his breath he walked softly on the water, gliding smoothly across the stream to the other bank. He looked back and saw that the young man and the horse were floundering in midstream, making a big splash. In the meantime, the boy had noticed Milarepa walk past him on the water without sinking. Although he had seen it with his own eyes, he still could not accept it. He muttered to himself, "What's the matter with me? Am I having an hallucination? [If not,] this man must have been born to float!"

When he reached the other bank, he approached Milarepa and observed his feet carefully, discovering that not even his soles were wet; whereupon, a deep faith toward the Jetsun arose within the youth. He cried out, "I did not realize that you were an accomplished Lama. I regret very much that I did not allow you to mount my horse. Please forgive me and accept my apology." Saying this, he bowed to Milarepa many times. With great sincerity and faith, he asked, "Lama, from whence do you come? To what Order do you belong? Who is your Guru? Where is your temple? What meditation do you practice? Where did you come from this morning? Where will you stay tonight?" In answer, the Jetsun sang:

> Ah! My good young friend!
> Listen to me, young playboy!
>
> Do you know who I am? I am the Yogi Milarepa;
> Gung Tang is whence I came.
> My feet have trod all over Weu and Tsang,[2]
> While learning the orders and decrees.
>
> From the gracious Guru Ngomi to Lama Rondonlaga,
> I have studied with ten Gurus and learned the
>   Tantras five,
> The views, and the philosophies of Dharma.
>
> From my teacher, Lhaje Nu Chon, I learned
> The fierce exorcism of the Black and Red Planets.
> Though he was very expert,
> He could never clear my doubts.
>
> Then I heard people say there was a wondrous teacher
> Dwelling in the South, in the river-circled Valley.
> He was blessed by the Lords Nāropa and Medripa,
> And had experienced the mother-like Essence of Mind.
> Having mastered the control of his body,

He dwelt alongside the South River.
He, whose fame had spread afar
Was the father Guru, Marpa the Translator.

Just to hear his name caused my skin to
      tingle and my hair to rise.
Despite the hardships of the journey, I made
      my way to him.
Just by glancing at his face, my heart was changed.
In my life, he is the only Guru,
The peerless one, the gracious Lho Draug Wa.[3]

No money or wealth had I to offer him,
So I reduced my body to powder in his service.
From him, I learned the profound Hevajra Tantra
And the teachings of Nāropa's Skillful Path.[4]
I took the vows and won the Four Initiations
      of the blessed Dem Chog.

When I realized the essence of Mahāmudrā,
I saw plainly the real nature of the mind;
I realized in full the ultimate "Beyond-all-Playwords."

In the Four River-like Teachings[5] of the
      Whispered Succession
I practiced the profound doctrine of the
      Nine Essentials.
Having practiced the art of manipulating
      the Nāḍīs, Prāṇa, and Bindu,
I completely mastered both the mind and Prāṇa.[6]

I am a yogi [who can] dwell in the sky;
Having united the Four Elements,
I have no fear of water.

For your information,
My temple is at Shri Ri.
This morning I came from Upper Gog Tang;
Where I shall go this evening, I am not certain,
For mine is the yogi's way of life.

Have you heard what I have sung,
My happy boy who seeks nought but pleasure?

After hearing this song, an unalterable faith in the Jetsun was established in the young man. His tears fell incessantly. He then handed the reins of his black horse to Milarepa, and sang:

> You are the Sage unrecognized, a man of
>   the beyond!
> You are the Buddha whom one meets so rarely.
> Your instructions are the preaching of Nirmāṇakāya.
>
> It seems that I have heard your name before,
> But yet I am not sure.
> It seems that I may have seen you before,
> But again, I am not sure.
>
> Whether the obeisance that I made you
> Was sincere enough, I do not know.
> If my questions were improper, my mien irreverent,
> I beg for your forgiveness, for I did not know you.
>
> This black horse of mine runs like the wind.
> On his neck hangs a wondrous bell;
> On his back of well-known pedigree
> Is a saddle cloth, most warm and smooth;
> On it rests a strong wooden saddle.
> The girth is fashioned of steel from Mon.
> A dainty knot adorns his reddish crupper;
> Close to the headstall of reddish-gray
> His forelock curls like a tiger's smile,
> Shining brightly like a mirrored star.
>
> Whip in hand, give your command;
> Shake the rein, he will obey and run.
> When he sees the flag before him
> He will win the race!
> When you cry "Run fast!" he'll gallop
>   at full speed.
> To a man of the world, a good horse is his pride.
> I give you this fine horse as an offering,
> Praying that you may keep me from the hell
> Into which I else would fall.

Having ended his song, the young man offered Milarepa his horse, but the Jetsun would not accept it, and told him that he had another, even better one. And he sang:

> Listen to me, dear patron!
> A horse of Prāna-Mind have I;
> I adorn him with the silk scarf of Dhyāna.
> His skin is the magic Ensuing Dhyāna Stage,[7]
> His saddle, illuminating Self-Awareness.
> My spurs are the Three Visualizations,[8]
> His crupper the secret teaching of the Two Gates.[9]
>
> His headstall is the Prāna of Vital-force;[10]
> His forelock curl is Three-pointed Time.[11]
> Tranquillity within is his adornment,
> Bodily movement is his rein,
> And ever-flowing inspiration is his bridle.
>
> He gallops wildly along the Spine's Central Path.
> He is a yogi's horse, this steed of mine.
> By riding him, one escapes Saṃsāra's mud,
> By following him one reaches the safe land of Bodhi.
>
> My dear patron, I have no need of your black horse.
> Go your way, young man, and look for pleasure!

The youth thought, "Though he does not want my horse, his feet are bare. He must need a pair of shoes!" So thinking, he offered his own to Milarepa, singing:

> Revered Yogi, jewel-like accomplished Saint,
> Because there is no attachment in your heart,
> You wander aimless from place to place.
> Sometimes you meet dogs with sharp teeth;
> At others, you walk through brambles and defiles;
> And so your bare feet may be hurt.
>
> Walking without shoes is painful;
> These blue boots shall be your faithful servants.
> With brass spurs on their heels
> And silk-embroidered, they are costly;
> A skillful craftsman made them
> With the skins of elk, wild yak, and crocodile.

These boots are my mark, the mark of the young man,
Which I now offer you.
Pray, grant me your compassionate blessing.

Thus he sang; but the Jetsun would not accept the gift. He told
the boy that he had a better pair of boots, singing:

Listen, you faithful young man.
This land of darkness and blind views
Is part of the Three Kingdoms of Saṃsāra.

Full of mud is Craving Meadow,
Full of thorns is Jealous Swamp.
Savage and malignant is the furious dog of Hate,
Dangerous and steep the hill of Pride.

But I have crossed the Rivers Four[12]
And reached the shore of the Pure Land.
I cut my boots from the hide of the
         renunciation of Saṃsāra
And with the leather of awakening from
         transciency and delusion.
I made my boots with the craftsmanship
         of deep faith in Karma,
With the dye of Non-clinging to the Myriad Forms,
And with the thread and rope of Devotion;
While the clasps are the Teachings of
         the Three Bindings.[13]

These are my boots, the boots of a yogi;
I have no desire for yours.
My dear patron, you may now leave for home.

Then the young man said, "Revered One, though you will not
take my boots, I still would like to offer you my reddish-green jacket
which is good to sleep in, for I see you have only a thin cloth with
which to cover your body. You must feel cold all the time. *Please*
accept this jacket!" In pleading with Milarepa to take it, the young
man sang:

Precious and accomplished Guru,
Freed from Ego-clinging,
You wander with no bourne in mind.

Sometimes you climb the summit of a mountain;
Sometimes you sleep soundly in a city street.
To wear a thin cloth sheet is the same as starving;
It must be still worse unclad to suffer cold.

This is my best tailored jacket
Made of the reddish-green Mandari cloth.
The front is silk,
The lining of best quality.
It is trimmed with lynx fur.
A collar of otter-skin matches the hem,
The shoulder pads are well embroidered.
It is light to wear and grand to see.
In it one does not fear a biting wind,
For it is a noble's jacket.
Please accept it, Reverend Father;
Please bless me, and grant your grace.

But Milarepa would not take the coat, and replied, "I have a jacket which excels even yours!" He then sang:

Listen, you eloquent youth!
O'er the cities of the Six Realms in Saṃsāra,
With fury blows the evil, Karmic wind.
Driven by the senses and deprived of freedom,
One wanders between life and death, roving in Bardo!

Sometimes one climbs the summit of the mountain
In the dream-like state between life and death.
Sometimes one sleeps in the street
In the Bardo city of Saṃsāra.

For my part, I aspire to the Realm of Reality,
And adorn the cloth of pure mind and heart
With the embroidery of immaculate discipline.

Mindfulness is the tailor cutting
My clothes into the shape of the Three Yogas.
My coat lining is the art
Of uniting the Three Key Points.[14]
I brighten the shoulder padding
With the Great Light [which shines at the
        time] of death.

> I cut the hem of Bardo Enlightenment
> To the "measurement" of pure Magic-Bodies.[15]

> This is my coat, the coat of a yogi;
> I have no wish for yours.
> Go then, young patron, and be cheerful!

Said the young man, "Revered One, since you will not accept my jacket though your clothes are still too thin, please, then, take this short coat." And he sang in persuasion:

> Precious Guru, supreme being,
> In the summer, in bright sunshine
> When the cuckoo's song is heard,
> One may go naked and not feel the cold.
> But in the winter, when the cold moon brightly shines
> And the blinding storm rages [in the hills],
> Cotton clothes than silk are thinner,
> And the piercing cold stings like an arrow!

> Father Jetsun, this ordeal
> Is too much for you.
> Here is a gray-green woolen coat
> With maroon fur hemmed
> And gay in colored silk of five colors;
> The cloth is of fine quality.
> I now offer it to you.
> *Please* accept it and grant me your blessing.

But Milarepa would not take it, saying that he had a better coat still. And he sang:

> Gracious patron, listen closely to me.
> With blindness as a guide
> I wandered down perilous paths;
> Buffeted by Passionate Winds,[16] now hot, now cold,
> I was drenched in the rain of Retribution-Karma.
> Worn out by these ordeals,
> I longed for Freedom City.

> With the cloth of Ah Shea Vital Heat[17]
> Is the lapel of Four Cakras[18] made.
> My tailor is the inner Prāna-Mind

Who warms Tig Le[19] and makes it flow;
The merged Bliss-Void experience
Is the needle used for sewing;
The cloth is Inborn Vital Heat.
Now summer and winter are for me the same!

Though your woolen clothes are pretty,
My cotton shirt is lighter and gives more comfort.
Dear patron, I do not want your clothes;
You should now go home.

The young man replied, "Although you will not accept my coat,
you must be wearied by your long practice of meditation. Please be
kind enough to accept my turban, which you can trade for some meat
to sustain and nourish your body." And he sang:

Precious Yogi, supreme one,
Disgusted with Saṃsāra, you look forward
To liberation from the wheel of life-and-death.
You meditate at length
And practice your devotions.

Thus you must sometimes feel the cold.
My magnificent headgear
Is the wonder of India!
Its frame of precious metal was made by
    a skilled craftsman.
'Tis covered with the skin of crocodile and vulture,
And decked with the feathers of lovely birds.
Its price equals the cost of a big Yak.
I now offer it to you—the Nirmāṇakāya Buddha.
You can trade it for much meat
For your health and nourishment.
In summer and in winter,
I will follow and pay homage to you!

But Milarepa did not accept this offer either. Instead, he sang:

My dear young man,
Do not lose your head!
I follow the Great Nāropa's Lineage,
He who has completely mastered the art of
    cosmic causations.

The master of deep practice,
I fear not the element of air within,
Nor do I depend on falcon's flesh.
I feel gay and joyous in a biting wind.

On the crown of my head[20]
Is a jewel splendid as the sun and moon,
On which sits my Guru, Marpa the Translator,
Adorned with ornaments of human bone.
He is the Wish-Fulfilling Gem, Buddha's
    Transformation Body.
If you see him with the eye of veneration,
You will find he is the Buddha Dorje-Chang!
He will forever guard you like a son.
This rare turban is my secret adornment.

The sublime Guru on my head is very beautiful.
Dear boy, I do not want a turban.
Ride off with cheerful heart!

The young man thought, "This revered Lama does not accept anything I have offered him. Perhaps he considers my gifts too small." And so he untied the string of his neck-jewel, which was a very fine piece of jade, and sang:

Precious Guru, supreme being,
You strive for devotion with no attachment
    in your heart.
To you, all material things are but delusions!
You have no wish for goods or wealth.
A deep faith in you has risen of itself in me.

'Tis shameful to begrudge one's father's hoardings;
People would despise one from their hearts:
One might well become a miser-ghost.
Therefore, I pray your Reverence,
Do not refuse this jade.
This white translucent six-edged jade
Gleams brightly like a sparkling light.
The supple deer skin, and red poppy,
Make the setting yet more graceful.
With this jade you never can be poor.
I offer it as a neck-ornament.

> Pray, grant me your grace
> And bestow the Buddha's teaching.

The boy then offered the jade to the Jetsun, but Milarepa still would not take it, saying, "I do not need your jade; I have a jewel which is far more precious. Listen to my song":

> Listen, my dear patron,
> You with a good father.
> In all countries, far and wide,
> I, the Yogi, roam.
> In streets, at doors, I beg for food.
> I am not greedy for good meals,
> I long not for possessions.
>
> There is no end to human greed.
> Even with hoarded wealth head-high,
> One cannot reach contentment.
> I do not envy you your wealth and goods.
>
> The greatest treasure is contentment in my heart;
> The teaching of the Whispered Lineage is
>   my wealth;
> My devotion to the Dharma is my ornament.
> I deck myself with Retaining Mindfulness;[21]
> The Yogas of Four Periods are my entertainment;
> The great and small Mind-Awarenesses are my
>   adorations.
> I have no need for your neck-jade.
> Dear boy, be of good cheer and go your way.

The young man thought, "Is it because I am too great a sinner that His Reverence will not be gracious to me?" He said to Milarepa, "It is natural for a supreme being like you not to want these illusory possessions. I now offer you my Three Companions.[22] From now on I will never carry a weapon or kill sentient beings. I beg you to grant me the Ordination. I pray you to protect me with your compassionate grace!" Saying this, he untied his carrying pouch[23] and sang:

> Oh supreme and compassionate Lama,
> I have always seen an enemy as such,
> And never lost sight of my foes.

From the right, I untie my wooden quiver;
From the left, I take my ornate bow,
And the sharp sword at my waist
Which disillusioned all my foes!

With these three things at my side,
I was like a ruthless bandit.
When I appeared before my enemies
Their hearts trembled and their bodies quivered.
Like frightened yaks, they fled away!

Thinking of them and my misdeeds
I feel regret and sorrow.
Today I offer you my Three Companions.
I will observe the precepts strictly
And follow you where'er you go.

But Milarepa was still adamant. He said, "I do not think that
you can keep your oath. Nor do I need your Three Companions,
because mine are better. Now, hearken to my song":

Listen to me, dauntless fighter.
The Five Hostile Poisons[24] run wild
In the land of evil thoughts.
He who does not renounce the "all-important" combat,
Will be imprisoned and lose his chance for freedom!
Battles and armies are not for the yogi.

The world without is my quiver,
The Non-clinging Self-Illumination within
Is my sheath of leopard skin,
My weapon is the sword of Great Wisdom.

The Two-in-One Path is my rope,
My thumb-guard is the merit of meditation.
These are my hidden inner meanings.

Upon the bow-string of Ultimate Unborn Voidness
I set steady the notch of Bodhi-Heart;
I shoot the arrow of the Four Infinities[25]
At the army of the Five Poisons.
There is no doubt that I shall win the battle;
I will destroy the hostile enemies of desire.

That is *my* way, the yogi's way of conquering.
I have no interest in your gifts.
Young patron, be of good cheer and go.

The young man said, "Revered Sir! Though you do not accept my offer of the Three Companions, I must receive your Blessing. Please, therefore, accept my belt[26] and knife." And he sang:

You Yogi, who are the living Buddha,
Although many know the Dharma,
Few can practice it.
One in hundreds is hard to find
Who can give proof of his accomplishment.
I would not ask the teaching from another,
E'en though he knew a world of Dharma;
Only from you, the living Buddha, the Father Repa.
Your teachings spring from much hard work,
And so I dare not ask without paying first.

In the center of Nepal, an angry river flows,
With clouds like pillars standing round.
At the lion-head of this raging torrent
Was made this sheath with silver ornaments,
Slung on my belt with gold and silver cord.
When I wear it, my whole body brightens!
I now offer you this knife and belt.
Later, I will ask you for the Teachings.

The youth then gave his belt and knife to Milarepa. The Jetsun said, "At present, I cannot give you the Teachings and instruction; neither do I want your offerings. I have a better belt than yours. Listen to my song":

Listen to me, ingenuous young man!
From my hut's roof in the snow mountain
Flows the quintessence of milk and nectar.
Though it is not made of gold or jewels,
I would not pour it into earthenware.

Around this waist of mine, the poor man
    of strong will,
Is tied to a cotton belt of fanatic devotion!
The absence of pretence and hypocrisy

Is the pattern of my belt.
Bright wisdom is my knife,
Its sheath, the confidence of the Three
        Measurements.[27]
Faith and diligence in Dharma is my gold-and-
        silver cord.
The beauty of the Dharma is the glory over all.

Lest goddesses punish me,
I have never asked for wealth or money
When teaching in the past,
Nor shall I do so now.
Dear boy, you may go home;
I do not want your gifts.

The young man again said to Milarepa, "Revered Sir! Indeed you
have not the slightest desire for wealth or goods. Therefore, I think
that you may not object to my offering you a temple in a quiet
place wherein you may dwell." Saying this he sang:

You are a real yogi, an ascetic worker,
Disgusted with mundane things
And indifferent to the world.
You renounced your native land and went away!
Without a bourne in mind, you wandered everywhere.

Although one thing to you is as another,
A permanent home may help your inspiration.

Let us find a good place in the hills to
        build a temple,
Let us make the pillars immaculate and tall!

Hanging above the pillars, the sun and moon
        will shine.
On the broad floor of the temple
We will draw a Mandal[28] with stone-made colors.
We will plant flowers all about
And dig a deep ditch round.
The Ka Be ornaments[29] will be of wood,
And a pagoda with eight adornments will
        make the place more beautiful.

> There will be a shrine for worship and
>   great reverence.
> Pray, accept it as your dwelling.
> Then at ease, you may stay in comfort there!

But Milarepa still would not accept this offer. He said, "I will not stay in any temple and make it my home. Nor do I know anything about how to please people. Now, listen":

> My confused young lad!
> Do you not know that this world is transient
>   and unreal?
> When you come before the King of the Dead
> Your rich man's money is of no avail.
> There your wealth can never buy you off;
> There you will find no place to swing a
>   strong man's sword,
> No place to dance or strut about the stage.
> Your flesh will be as dust.
>
> Because I fear these things may happen to me,
> I bind myself in a place of strict austerity.
>
> The temple wherein I dwell in the inner unborn Mind;
> The Ka Be ornament is unwavering Prāṇa;
> I erect the pillars of the Real
> On the foundation of immutability.
> The sun and moon are the Arising and Perfecting Yoga.
>
> On the ground of the Dhyānic Warmth[30]
> I draw a Mandal of Clear Observation.[31]
> The experiences of Bliss, Illumination, and
>   Non-thought
> Are the lovely flowers in my garden!
> Encircling the pagoda of Ten Virtues
> Is my strong ditch of Voidness.
>
> This is mine, the Yogi's temple;
> I have no need of yours.
> My young patron, be of good cheer and go!

The young man said to Milarepa, "Revered Sir, though you do not want the temple, this feeble human body is liable to sickness.

I have a very capable sister, who has great faith in the Dharma. I would like to offer her to you as a Jomo[32] servant. Pray do not disdain, but please accept this offer." And he sang:

> Revered Yogi, who clings to the hermitage,
> Though you have fully realized the faults of women,
> And have no lustful wish,
> This fragile human body is liable to sickness
> And so one always needs a solicitous companion.
>
> I offer you my only sister,
> Dearly beloved of her three brothers.
> She is sprung from an outstanding line—
> Her father and mother are of noble stock;
> She is heiress to a royal tradition.
> Do not mistakenly regard her as of common stock;
> She is the heart-taker among the crowds,
> Radiant as a rainbow, she is more beautiful
>   than angels.
> Cotton clothes on her,
> Look lovelier than silk.
> Jewelry and gold adorn her head;
> Sparkling jewels and pearl necklaces
> Cannot match her radiant beauty;
> Her grace and charm are hard to paint.
> Her suitors have been many,
> But to none have we given our consent.
> Today, I offer her to you, the Nirmāṇakāya of Buddha.
> Pray do not disdain my offer.

But Milarepa still would not accept it. He said "Do not talk like a fool. I have already renounced family ties. I am not interested in an ego-clinging woman. The so-called faith of the common people is most unstable and liable to change. I am an old beggar with no family and no relatives. People will laugh at you, if you give her to me. Afterwards, you will regret what you have done. I have no desire to become your brother-in-law. I have a consort who is much better than your sister. Listen":

> On the whole, young lord,
> Women are the cause of lust and attachment.
> A qualified Illumination-Woman[33] is indeed
>   most rare.

To have angelic company on the Bodhi-Path
Is a wonder and a marvel;
Yet you a little have exaggerated.
This is why the Mudrā Practice[34] is so very hard.

My wonder woman is the lust-free Śūnyatā.
There is compassion on her face,
And kindness in her smile.
The Red and White Elements[35] are her clothing,
The Two-in-One Unity, her silk ornaments.
Indiscriminating action is her girdle
And the Four Blisses[36] her adornments.
Her necklace makes all things Taste-as-One.
She is such a charming witch—
The realization of Truth is her origin!
This is my wife, the yogi's mate.
I have no interest in your Saṃsāric women.
Young patron, it is time for you to go!

Knowing that Milarepa would not accept this offer, the young man said, "Although to your enlightened mind, there is no such thing as shame or disgrace, to be human and to prevent possible scandal among the people, I now sincerely offer you a pair of trousers. *Please* accept them." And he sang:

You Yogi, you who have nothing left to hide,
But follow the Tantric path,
Living naked in the mountains—
Your jewel-like penis, exposed so openly,
Can be seen by all at any time.

Though you are free from all ideas of disgrace
        and shame,
We worldly men are shamed by indecent exposure.
Even the perfect Buddha, the fully enlightened
        Being,
Discreetly follows worldly customs.

This pair of trousers are for my own wear;
They are made of the finest wool
Which my mother and sister spun.
My noble wife wove it into woolen cloth,
A neighbor's daughter dyed it for me;

And my kind uncle tailored it.

With such clothes we cover the shameful part.
To you, this pair of trousers I now offer.
Please say not again, "I need it not!"

Milarepa replied, "Dear boy, it seems that you know nothing about
shame! My organ hangs there very naturally. There is nothing funny
about it, so why do you laugh? In the beginning, I came from my
mother's belly stark naked. When death comes, I shall leave the body·
without any covering. And so I shall do nothing about it now. Nor
do I care to know about this self-made "shame" of yours, as you call it.
Now listen":

Why, my good lad, do you take
Things without shame to be shameful?
That is merely the nature-born male organ;
I cannot understand this so-called "shame" of yours.
Of the really shameful things, you are most ignorant.

Look at sinful, evil, and meaningless deeds;
You are *not* ashamed of them.
Let me tell you how I keep my self-respect:

My fine wool is the Heart-for-Bodhi
With which I spin the thread of Four Initiations;[87]
The cloth I weave is the liberation Path of Samādhi;
The dye I use is made of virtues and good-wishes;
My tailor uncle is the sense of con-
    scientious discretion
By whom the trousers of self-respect are made.

These are my dignified and altruistic trousers,
And so of yours I have no need!
Dear patron, you may now go home!

The youth thought, "This great man will not accept anything I
offer. I had better find out where he lives and where he is going.
I will try by all possible means to persuade him to visit my country."
So he said: "Though you have not accepted anything I have offered
you, please come to my country; also, please tell me where you are
going now. There must be a destination in your mind, or you would

not choose this particular road. Pray do not conceal your intention, but please tell me the truth."

Milarepa replied, "Son, I have nothing to hide from you. In the harvest I go to Din Ri to beg for alms. When the crops are threshed, I go to Nya Non. In the winter I remain at some remote place where only birds and marmots dwell." The young man thought, "After a few days, I shall invite him to my house to preach for us. I wonder if he will accept." And he sang:

> Peerless Guru, the Transformation Body of Buddha,
> You said that you are going to Din Ri to beg
>   for alms.
> But that is a place of the damned, and has no merit.
> Though vast sky hangs above,
> The virtue of the people there
> Is as small as mustard-seed;
> Their hands are tighter than the barred
>   doors of the congregation hall![38]
> The flour costs more than gold.
> A hundred pleas for alms are wasted time;
> Poverty and famine stalk the place.
>
> The land of Nya Non is full of fear,
> A paradise for bandits and murderers.
> Lepers are there in crowds,
> While burial grounds and cemeteries abound.
> So fearful is that country, one dares
> Not travel without a hundred friends,
> Or take three steps without a guide.
> That cursed place, Nya Non, is of the worst repute.
>
> The Nepalese-Tibetan border is cold and high—
> A land of snow where blizzards rage.
> Its people are as dumb as mules!
> Its rivers flow south to Nepal,
> Where the lower valleys steam with heat
> And dangerous rope bridges sway high above
>   the rocks.
> In Nepal heat and disease endanger life,
> While people in the South speak a different tongue,
> And the trees are stiff like corpses.
> With all my heart, I wish you would not go there,
> So please postpone your journey.

Although you would not take my gifts,
I beg that you will grant my boon
And visit my country for a fortnight.

Milarepa replied, "On the whole, I cannot tolerate arrogant patrons.
I am not interested in going to your country. As for Nya Non and
Din Ri, I know them better than you. Hearken to my song":

You arrogant young man with strong desires,
Listen to my song with faith.
It is hard to meet an immaculate man of merit,
Hard to find a place where men of virtue live,
For times have changed.

I am a yogi who thinks and says whate'er he likes,
But I have never caused malicious gossip.

Though the flour be very dear in Din Ri,
It is not hard for me to get it.
Yet I prefer the taste of the Five Nectars,
And never gorge myself with tasty morsels.

I am an abandoned yogi, who eats for food
The inner Samādhi of Non-discernment.
Thus the desire for tasty meals has no appeal.
Cheerful and comfortable am I in times of famine.

Though the paths are perilous and dreadful,
My prayer to the Gracious One will never fail me.
The Three Precious Ones are my safest shelter
        and refuge;
The goddesses in the Three Places will always
        be my guides.
My inseparable companion is the Bodhi-Mind;
My protectors are the Guards of the Eight Divisions.

Since I have no possessions, I have no enemy.
Cheerful and at ease I meet the bandits.
Though Nya Non may be of bad repute,
The people there are candid and ingenuous.

As in days of old, they are straightforward
        and outspoken.

Easy-going and carefree,
They eat and drink without pretension;
They keep things as they are,
And groves and forests flourish.

As for me, I take no interest in worldly wealth,
Nor am I attached to food and drink.
Contented, I care not for loitering and amusement.
When, therefore, I meditate, my Samādhi deepens.

This is why I go to Nya Non.
Having mastered the art of Dumo's Fire,[39]
I have no fear of cold or heat;
Cheerful and in comfort I meet the falling snow.

Today I see no reason to delay my journey,
But I shall not go to your country;
Proud and haughty patrons are distasteful to me.
How can I ingratiate myself with those I do not know ?
Mount your horse, as it is growing late.
My dear, contented youth, it is time for you to go.
May your health be good and your life long.

Upon hearing this song of rejection, the young man was overcome with dejection and disappointment. He said, "Revered Sir, whatever I have offered you, you would not accept. Whatever instruction I have applied for, you would not grant. I realize that I am too sinful. I now swear that I will not go anywhere, but will kill myself here in your sight." So saying, he drew his razor-sharp knife, and, pressing the point against his heart, sang:

Listen to me, Revered Yogi,
On this auspicious morning, while riding on my way,
I saw a naked man, lying beside a silver spring.

I said, "Is he a mad yogi,
Or just a foolish joker?
Exposing his naked body without shame,
He must be a fool out of his mind!"

And so, not faith, but contempt arose within me.
I rejected any thought of your companionship
        and went on alone.

Of this, you, Revered One, were clearly well aware.
As if wounded badly, I now repent in pain.

When you were crossing the blue river
To reach the seat of the other shore,
I saw you fly over the water
Like an eagle in the sky.
Soaring like wind in space,
I saw you flying.
Displaying your miraculous powers,
I saw you glide over the Tsang River
And reach the other shore.

I was bewildered and overjoyed
To see such an accomplished being.
Proud and happy as I was, conceit arose
      within me;
I thought that I was a well-gifted person,
Who had few hindrances and habit-forming thoughts.
I thought that I must be a good vessel
      for the Dharma;
I thought that I must be a virtuous and
      destined person,
Who had great merits and pure wishes.[40]

Since the day that I was born,
I have never been so happy as today.
In the wealth, property, and comfort that I offered
You have not the slightest interest.
I have never heard of a yogi like you in Tibet;
I have never met such a perfect Buddhist,
One so marvelous and unusual.

On this auspicious day in my pilgrimage,
I made offerings and besought you in all ways!
Marvelous and unusual as you are,
You have paid no heed to what I said.
I feel that I am most ignorant and pitiful.
I realize that I am stupid and lack merit;
I am utterly confused and most disheartened.
With a feeling of frustration, I have lost my way.
I am beginning to believe I have no capacity
      for Dharma!

What then would be the use and meaning
Should one chance to meet a Buddha,
If from Him one does not receive a discourse?
How can one face, and what can one tell one's
　　countrymen?
Rather than return in shame
I will end my life before you!
All are bound to die in time;
'Tis better for me now to die,
To die before such an accomplished saint,
When my heart is full of Dharma.
Oh, all-compassionate, revered Jetsun!
After hearing such a sorry tale from this poor lad,
With your omniscient mind, you know what
　　should be said.

Having heard his sincere prayer, Milarepa thought: "He has indeed great earnestness and sincerity. There must be a mutual vow[41] between us. The prophecy given by the goddess in my dream seems to point to him. I must, therefore, accept him." And so he sang:

Listen to me, dear young patron!
You have a zealous aspiration for virtuous deeds.
You must be a man with little sin or evil Karma.

Since you have intense longing to solicit
　　Dharma [from me]
Your pride and self-conceit must be small indeed!

Diligent and enthusiastic,
You cannot be lazy.

Since you made generous offerings,
You cannot be close or greedy.

Your intelligence and sympathy are good,
So you have little ignorance or hate.

Since you pay respect and homage to me,
You must have been closely associated
With Dharma in your previous lives!

On this auspicious morning, I, the
　　vagabond from Gung Tang,

And you, the young man from lower Jhal Khrum
Met on this blue river bank.
It seems our hopes in bygone lives arranged
        the meeting;
It was our destiny to meet before the Silver Spring.
You must be one whose Karma is unstained,
Who has awakened from the habitual-thought
        of the Store-Consciousness.

Young patron, I sing this auspicious song for you.
Since you have heard authentic teaching,
Will you now be keen to practice Dharma?

If faith has risen from your heart,
If you take no heed of worldly gain,
If you really want to follow me,
Know that kinsmen are the devil-planned
        hindrances of Dharma;
Think not of them as real, but quench your
        craving for them.

Money and dainties are the devil's envoys;
Association with them is pernicious.
Renounce them and all other things that bind you.

Delight in pleasures is the devil's rope;
Think, then, of death to conquer your desires.
Young companions are the tempting devil's snare;
Knowing they are delusive, watch them carefully.

One's native land is the dungeon of the devil;
Imprisoned therein 'tis hard
To win liberation.
Try then to escape at once;
Put all aside and strive for Dharma.
Only by instant action can you succeed!

In time your body of illusion will decay.
'Tis better to associate with Dharma now.

The darting bird of mind will fly up anyway;
'Tis better now to wing your way to Heaven!

If you believe and follow what I have said,
You will be a worthy vessel for the Dharma.
You will be given benediction and instruction;
The profound teachings of the Whispered Lineage
Will also be imparted.

My son! This is the start of your journey
   on the Bodhi-Path.
Even I, the Yogi, rejoice at your success.
You too, young man, should be glad and joyful!

The youth was indescribably happy when he heard this song. With great exhilaration, he bowed down at the Jetsun's feet, made many obeisances, and circumambulated him many times. Then he made a vow [to return], and departed.

Four months later, when Milarepa was staying at Manlun Chubar of Drin, the young man came with his nephew to visit him. The uncle offered a piece of immaculate white jade, and the nephew half an ounce of gold, but the Jetsun would not accept the gifts.

At that time, the Translator Bhari was building a stūpa of the Tsudor Namjhal Buddha at Drin, so Milarepa said to them, "It is not necessary for me to take your offerings; you may offer them to Bhari, the Translator, and ask him to initiate you. As for the Pith-Instructions,[42] I shall give them to you myself."

Accordingly, they went to Bhari, the Translator, and asked him to impart to them the complete initiation of Dem Chog. Whereupon, Bhari bestowed upon them the Outer Teachings of Tsudor Namjhal, the Me Ru Sinha practice for prolonging life, and the teachings of the Buddha of Performance. He also gave them the Inner Teachings of Dem Chog, that is, the Practice of Seven Words, the instructions of the Guru Symbol Goddess, and the meditation practice of the Goddess Kurukullā. After that they accompanied him to Sajya Monastery.[43]

Then the lad returned to Milarepa and lived with him for five years. From the Jetsun, he obtained the teaching of the renowned Six Yogas of Nāropa, and the teaching of the Mahāmudrā transmitted from the Great Master Medripa. Because he practiced these teachings diligently, Milarepa also imparted to him all the Pith-Instructions. Formerly, the young man had been called Dharma Wonshu;[44] later, Milarepa gave him another name, Repa Shiwa Aui [the Cotton-clad Light of Peace]. Before turning to religion, he was a great sensualist; afterwards, for the sake of his devotion, he utterly renounced the world. He took an oath before Milarepa that for the rest of his life, he would never wear leather shoes, or more than one piece of cotton clothing, and that he would not return to his native land, or secure provisions for more than two days' consumption. With the greatest diligence he absorbed himself in his devotions and eventually attained good experiences. Milarepa was delighted with his improvement and sang:

> I bow down to all Gurus. Great is the blessing
> From the compassionate Gurus of the
>   Practice Lineage;[45]
> Great and powerful are the Key-Instructions
>   of Marpa and Mila!
> You, Shiwa Aui, are industrious and hard-working.
> Through the grace of the Ḍākinīs you have
>   attained good understanding.

> Dear son, if you want to consummate your meditation,
> Restrain yourself from bigotry and empty talk;
> Think not of the noble glories of the past;
> Stay in the valley to which no men come;
> Keep from bad companions, and yourself examine;
> Yearn not to become a Guru;
> Be humble and practice diligently;
> Never hope quickly to attain Enlightenment,
> But meditate until you die.
> Forgetting words and studies,
> Practice the Key-Instructions.
> If you would benefit yourself,
> Renounce talk and words;
> Concentrate on your devotions.

Shiwa Aui replied, "You have just said that he who learns a great deal without actual practice is liable to go astray. Please elaborate this a little."

Milarepa answered, "By that, I mean there is a danger of clinging to the worldly affairs of this life without completely renouncing them. Another danger is that this person is liable to miss the key-point of the practice. In the teaching of Marpa's Line, we do not have such errors or dangers, for we never pay attention to words and talk. What we emphasize is the actual practice. Hearken to my 'Song of Dangers and Fallacies' ":

Obeisance to the holy Gurus.

Listen to those high-flown words, and pompous talk;
Look at those charlatans, madly engaged
    in fervent argument.

In talk they seem intent to frighten you;
In sleep, they slumber, pompous men;
They walk like haughty Mongols.
Dangers and obstacles encompass them.

The Three Kingdoms and Six Realms are jeopardized
By desires forever leading sentient beings
    into danger.

There are seven dangers you should watch:
Falling into the blissful Hīnayāna peace;[46]
Using your Buddhist knowledge to get food;
Inflating yourself with pride of priesthood;
Falling into yogic-madness;[47]
Indulging in empty speeches;
Falling into the trap of nothingness.
Thus, ignorance is the cause of fallacies and dangers.

The teaching of the Whispered Lineage
    is the Ḍākinīs' breath.
Never doubt this truth, but if you do,
Remember that this doubt occurred
Through the devil's influence.

Shiwa Aui, how can you ever go astray
Since you are near me, the great Cotton-clad One?

Lay down your doubts and meditate.
He who relies on the true Teachings will
    never go astray.

Think not, my son, of meaningless word-knowledge
But concentrate on your devotions.
Then you will soon attain the great Accomplishment.

Whereupon, Shiwa Aui abandoned his search for word-knowledge

and concentrated on his devotions with never a thought for clothing
and food.

One day a friend called on Shiwa Aui. Seeing his body emaciated
from lack of food and clothing, the friend misunderstood, and feeling
pity for him, said, "Dharma Wonshu, you were a gay spark from a
rich family. But now you look old and poor, with no clothes or food.
How sad! How sad!" Shiwa Aui sang in reply:

> Oh My Father Guru, the Jetsun, the real Buddha,
> The Field-of-Offering[48] for my parents!
>
> Brothers, sisters, and all [relatives] give
>   rise to Saṃsāra;
> But I have now renounced them.
> The Jetsun is my sole companion and comrade
>   in the Dharma,
> Alone he is my source for the Buddha's Teaching;
> With him, the real Buddha, I remain in solitude.
>
> A group of three or four leads but to empty talk,
> To avoid which I stay in solitude.
>
> *Books and commentaries bring one nought but
>   pride,*
> *But the authentic Buddha gives*
> *The one-sentence Pith-Instruction.*
> I thus renounce all books and commentaries,
> Relying on the clear-cut Pith-Instruction.
>
> The hermit-temple is a place near Buddha
> Wherein I practice virtuous deeds and gather merits.
>
> The more one has, the more one craves.
> So I forsake my home and renounce my native land.
>
> The country with no boundary-posts is the
>   place near Buddha
> Wherein the faithful one can practice virtuous deeds.
>
> Associates and servants cause more anxiety
>   and craving,
> So I renounce them for all time.

A deep faith arose within the man after he had listened to this song of his former friend, whereupon he offered him many good things. Milarepa was very much pleased by this incident.

From that time on, Shiwa Aui served Milarepa until the day of his Guru's entering into Nirvāṇa. During the course of his life, he learned the complete teachings from Milarepa, and thus was kept from going astray in his meditation experience and understanding.

The nephew, known as the foolish and powerful Sang Jye Jhab, did not act as a good Repa. He held a small temple near the edge of Nya Non. The Jetsun was slightly displeased with him.

After the Nirvāṇa of Milarepa, Shiwa Aui went to the cave of Man Chu in the Goh Valley of Padru to practice meditation. Eventually he attained the Perfect Enlightenment and merits of the Path. He achieved the Accomplishment-of-Freedom-from-Obstacles[49] and so was able to pass through the rocks of the cave and mount to the Pure Land of Goddesses in his lifetime.

This is the story of Milarepa meeting his disciple, the Cotton-clad Shiwa Aui, at Silver Spring.

NOTES

1 Samādhi of Guru-Union (T.T.: bLa.Mahi.rNal.hByor.): A Samādhi of uni-fying one's mind with those of the Gurus.

2 Weu and Tsang (T.T.:dWus.gTsan): Weu is a region in Central Tibet, Tsang is a region in southwestern Tibet.

3 Lho Draug Wa was another of Marpa's names.

4 Skillful Path: the Yoga with Form (T.T.: Thabs.Lam.) See the transla-tor's comments in the Appendix.

5 The Four River-like Teachings are probably: (1) the Teaching of the Arising Yoga, (2) the Teaching of the Six Yogas, (3) the Teaching of the advanced Perfecting Yoga, and (4) the Teaching of Mahāmudrā. "River-like" implies that these teachings convey continual grace-waves.

6 See Story 3, Note 2.

7 Ensuing Dhyāna Stage: Every Dhyāna has two stages: the Main, and the Ensuing Stage. In the Main Dhyāna Stage, the mind of the yogi is wholly absorbed in concentration. In the Ensuing Dhyāna Stage, while the yogi continues his daily activities, his mind is still held somewhat in contemplation, i.e., not complete-ly departing from the meditation experience.

8 Three Visualizations: This probably implies the following practices: the vis-

ualization (1) of the Patron Buddha, (2) of the Maṇḍala, and (3) of the inner Cakras.

9 Two Gates: Yoga with Form and Yoga without Form.

10 Prāṇa of Vital-force, or Life Prāṇa (T.T.: Srog.Rluṅ): This is the chief Prāṇa which supports one's life and which also, according to Tibetan Tantra, is the energy-source of the Ālaya (Store) Consciousness.

11 This phrase is not clear to the translator. It probably implies the three favorable times for practicing meditation.

12 Four Rivers: a symbolic term denoting the four stages of Saṃsāric becomings: production, remaining, decaying, and termination.

13 Three Bindings: the term for the teachings directed toward taming the body, word, and mind.

14 Three Key Points: to unite the mind with the Manifestation-Void (T.T.: sNaṅ.sToṅ.), with the Bliss-Void (T.T.: bDe.sToṅ.), and with the Illuminating-Void (T.T.: Rig.sToṅ.).

15 The Sambhogakāya and the Nirmāṇakāya.

16 Passionate Winds: a figurative term to denote the changeable emotions of men.

17 See Story 7, Note 24.

18 Four Cakras: the psychic centers of the head, throat, heart, and navel.

19 Tig Le (Bindu): male semen and female "blood."

20 An important psychic center situated at the top of the head.

21 Retaining Mindfulness: the remembering of meditation-experience during daily activities.

22 Three Companions: Bow, arrow, and sword were the three companions (safeguards) of Tibetan travelers in ancient times.

23 Carrying pouch: The scabbard and quiver were fastened to the belt, along with a pouch in which miscellaneous articles were carried.

24 See Story 7, Note 6.

25 The Four Infinities, or the Four Unlimited Good Wills, i.e., Unlimited Friendliness, Compassion, Sympathetic Joy, and Evenmindness.

26 See Note 23.

27 This probably implies the three standards by which the yogi judges his experience in meditation, i.e., whether the experience is in accord with the Sūtras, whether it enhances or weakens his compassion toward sentient beings, and whether it enlarges his understanding of Śūnyatā.

28. Mandal: The translator presumes that "Mandal," pronounced as "Mandral" by the Tibetans, is a corruption of the Sanskrit word "Maṇḍala." See Story 7, Note 14.

29 Ka Be (T.T.: Kha.Bad.): an architectural ornament of Tibetan houses placed forward by the projecting ends of the beams which support the roof.

30 Dhyānic Warmth: the heat produced in meditation practice.

31 Clear observation (T.T.: lHag.mThoṅ.): deep contemplation on the truth of Prajñāpāramitā.

32 Jomo: the wife of a lay preacher.

33 Illumination-Woman (Tib.: Rig.Ma.): a woman who is well-gifted in understanding and in practicing Tantrism.

34 Mudrā Practice: an advanced form of Heat Yoga.

35 Red and White Elements: the positive and negative energies.

36 Four Blisses: When the Tig Le, the essence of energy, comes down from the Head Center, it successively produces four blisses, namely, the First Bliss, the Superlative Bliss, the Beyond-Reach Bliss, and the Innate-Born Bliss. See the translator's book, "Teachings of Tibetan Yoga."

37 Four Initiations: the Vase, the Secret, the Wisdom, and the Symbolic Initiations. See Story 1, Note 7.

38 The doors of the congregation hall in Tibetan monasteries are kept closed and locked most of the time.

39 Dumo's Fire: the "mystic" fire or heat produced in the Navel Center.

40 The pure wishes for Dharma made in one's previous existence.

41 If two person have made a mutual vow in their previous lives, the force of this vow, or the Karma-of-Wishes will bring its fulfillment in a future life.

42 Pith-Instructions (T.T.: Man.Ñag. or gDams.Ñag.): This may also be rendered as Key-Instructions, which consist of the essence of the Tantric teaching conveyed from Guru to disciple, usually in a very simple, precise, yet practical form, and therefore termed "Pith-Instructions."

43 Sajya (T.T.: Sa.sKya.) Monastery: the main monastery of Sajyaba (the Gray School).

44 Lit. (T.T.): Shu.Yas.Dar.Ma.dWañ.Phyug.

45 Practice Lineage (T.T.: sGrub.brGyud.): This is another name for the Ghagyuba School because this School stresses meditation practice.

46 According to Mahāyāna Buddhism, the Hīnayāna's version of Nirvāṇa and Samādhi is shallow, insufficient, limitative, and negative, in contrast to that of Mahāyāna, which is positive and dynamic. To cling to the blissful serenity of Samādhi is a great danger that may lead one to fall into the Hīnayāna Path.

47 Yogic madness: There is a recognized "stage of insanity" which all yogis should overcome before final or complete Enlightenment. This reference is to the danger of falling into this so-called "spiritual insanity" of advanced yogis.

48 Field of Offering: a term which denotes the qualified receiver of offerings, such as the Guru, Buddha, or the enlightened sages. These offerings will ripen into the giver's merits as seeds sown in good soil.

49 Freedom-from-Obstacles (T.T.: Zan.Thal.): Advanced yogis who have perfectly mastered their Prāṇa-Mind are supposed to be able to pass through all concrete, material obstacles without difficulty. This accomplishment is called Zañ.Thal.

THE SONG OF THE STAFF

Obeisance to all Gurus

Having renounced all worldly belongings and material things, the Jetsun Milarepa's only possession was a cane staff. One day, carrying his staff, Milarepa and his disciple Sevan Repa went to Jen Valley for alms. They came to a barred house, which was near the bank of the river. Except for an old woman, not a living soul was there. Milarepa asked her for alms. She said, "I am a pennyless old woman; but across the field there is a rich man called Shangchub Bar, who is working on his farm. Go there and ask him, and your wish will be granted."

When they arrived at the rich man's house, they saw that he was sorting seeds for sowing. Milarepa said, "My dear patron, we were told that you are a rich man, so we come here to you for alms." The man replied, "It is pleasant to offer you alms; but, if you are a real yogi, you should understand the symbolic meaning of things and be able to preach an exemplary sermon. Now, please use my farming as a parable, and sing me a preaching song." Thereupon, the Jetsun and Sevan sang together:

> Oh, my proud and arrogant patron,
> Listen to me, you rich man of Ngan Tson.
>
> In this month of spring the peasants
> Of Tibet are busy on their farms.
> I, the Yogi, also farm.
>
> Upon the bad field of desires,
> I spread the fertilizer of the Preparatory Practice;[1]
> I wet the field with manure of the Five Nectars;[2]
> I plant the seeds of the Non-confusing Mind,
> Farming with discriminative thought.

I plow with Non-dualistic oxen
Harnessed to the Wisdom-Plow,
With Observation of Precepts as the nose-rope,
And Non-distraction Effort as the girth.
Diligence is my whip, and skill my bridle.
With these tools and efforts, the bud of Bodhi sprouts;
In due season ripe will be my fruit.

You are a farmer who grows annual crops;
For eternity I cultivate.
At harvest you are proud and joyful.
Which of us will be happier in the end?

In allegory I have phrased this song of farming.
Though proud and arrogant, be now gay and joyful.
By making many offerings, accumulate
Merits for your own good.

The man countered, "Dear Yogi, I see you have a staff in your hand. What does it mean? Is it for amusement like a child's toy, or is it for lunatics to hold? Please tell me, what is it for?" Milarepa sang in answer:

Listen, my dear, inquisitive patron!
Do you know who I am?
I am the Yogi, Milarepa,
Who follows the ascetic way;
I am a yogi, great in strength and perseverance,
Who has no limitations.

The staff in my hand
Grew on a huge rock.
It was cut by a sickle and became
A companion of wild stags.

It came from Nepal, in the South;
From it I hung the Mahāyāna Sūtras;
I take it with me to the marketplace;
It was offered to me by a faithful follower.
This is the story of my walking-staff.
If you do not understand my meaning,
Listen then with great care:

The stout end, cut from near the root,
Symbolizes being "cut off" from Saṃsāra.
The thin end, cut from near the top,
Symbolizes the "cutting off" of all doubts and
    confusions.
It is two cubits[3] long and represents
The twin qualities of a Buddhist.[4]

Of good quality and pliant, it is like
The original Mind-Essence—good and sound.
The varnish, of a pleasant brown, is like
The great harmony of the "Original Mind Nature."

Straight and supple, it symbolizes
Unmistaken practice and devotion.

The tiny grooves you see, represent
The perfection of the Bodhi-Path,
The four joints in the cane
Are the Four Infinite Wishes,[5]
The three knots symbolize
The Three Bodies of the Buddha.

It never changes color. This represents
The immutable reality of the Root Principle.[6]
Its head, curved and covered, displays
The "beyond-playwords" nature of reality;
Its white and glittering appearance shows
The Dharmakāya—immaculate and pure.

The hollows symbolize the void nature of all beings,
The spots are a symbol of the sole Tig Le.
The scattered black marks indicate
That Tibetan yogis and Repas
Have few disturbing thoughts.

This cane most excellent represents
My devotion and practice in compliance with the Dharma.
Its elegance and loveliness displays
My disciples' sincerity and faith.

The iron ferrule on the tip conveys
The perseverance of yogis in the hermitage.

The handle, wrapped with copper, represents
The mastery and attraction of Ḍākinīs.

The nail attached to the tip displays
The bravery and diligence of yogis;
The hanging brass ring represents
The increase of inner merits.

The ornament of Sha Bran [?] hanging down
Is the flexible understanding of the yogi.
The thong of two twisted ropes represents
The entering of the Two-in-One Path;
The Mother-and-Son thongs intermingling,
The meeting with the Mother of the Three Bodies.

The bone-ornaments hanging on the staff
Mean many travels for the yogi.
The flint and bellows signify
That all he sees and meets
Are the yogi's friends.

The white shell hanging on the staff
Means that I shall turn the Wheel of Dharma.
The rag of leather symbolizes
The yogi's attitude, without fear or shame.

The mirror hanging on the staff
Is the Enlightenment that shines within.
The sharp knife indicates
That the pain of passions will be cut.
The stone-crystal symbolizes
The purifying of defiled habitual thoughts.

The ivory chain hanging on the staff
Is the Chain-of-Regard between Guru and disciple.
The set of bells symbolizes
My widespread reputation;
The woolen cords of red and white,
That my disciples will be numerous.

The handsome staff that now I hold
Is the means and symbol of the conquest over evil
     beings.

Patron, you ask me for the meaning of this staff;
This proves you have sincerity and faith.
This present meeting witnesses
Our pure wishes in a former life.

For mankind and Devas, conceivers of all symbols,
I have sung this "Song of the White Staff."
Revere then and appreciate its Dharma teaching.
Dear patron, I hope you practice Dharma and win
      happiness supreme.

Great faith was engendered in the heart of this rich man. Bowing
down at Milarepa's feet, he said, "Dear Lama, from now until the
day of my death, I shall serve you. Please come and live permanently
in my house." But the Jetsun and Sevan Repa would not promise
to stay more than seven days, saying, "We have no wish to accept
your worldly offerings."

At the end of their sojourn, as they started to take leave, the
patron cried: "Since you have made up your minds to depart, before
you go, please tell us your Experiences and Realizations during meditation." In answer, the Jetsun and his disciple sang together:

Listen to me, faithful patron,
Who are rich but imprudent!
Easy is it to talk of Dharma,
But 'tis hard to practice it.

Oh you confused and worldly beings,
You always waste your leisure, letting time slip by.
Though your mind is ever saying, "I must practice
      Dharma,"
Your life is wasted as the hours slip by.
You should now determine to start practice:

Cool mountain water
Heals the bladder's ills,
But only grouse and mountain birds can reach it;
Beasts of the valley have no chance to drink it.

The Sword of Heavenly Iron[7] falling when it thunders
Is the weapon with which to destroy the foe,
But only the Elephant-Earth-Protector
Can grasp and use it effectively;

Small elephants have not the strength.

The Nectar of Heaven is the essence of long life
Ever keeping the quintessence of body strong,
But only the Holy Guru, Nāgārjuna, could use it—
Not all who practice Dharma.

The golden chest, that gives enjoyment
Is a treasure which cures poverty,
But only "Prince Moonlight" can possess it—
Not the common people.

The wondrous gem beneath the ocean
Is a marvel granting all desires,
But it belongs to the Dragon of Happiness;
Men on the earth cannot obtain it.

Grand scenery, indeed, has the Palace of Joyous
    Heaven,
But only Guru Asaṅga can enjoy it;
Not all human beings can reach or see it.

The medicine of Six Merits
Can cure colds and fever.
'Tis made from Tsan Dan wood,
And not from other trees.

The Ten White Virtues from causation's law
Enable one to roam the higher Realms,
But only those with faith can practice them—
Great sinners are not free.

The Pith-Instructions of the
    Gurus
Enable one to win highest Enlightenment,
But only he with Karma can learn and practice them;
Without capacity or Karma one seldom has the opportunity.

The precious Pith-Instruction of the Oral
    Succession
Enables one, without fail, to become Buddha,
But only determined men can follow it;
Not pleasure-seekers, like yourself.

Poverty is cured by food and wealth
Which the generous and clever soon amass,
But these the miserly can ne'er enjoy.

Generosity is a merit of which one can be proud.
You, the rich man of Ngan Tson, have it;
But not all the wealthy are so generous.

I, Milarepa, and the disciple Se Ston Repa,[8]
Due to wishes made in former lives have stayed
With you, the rich man of Jenlun Ngan Tson,
For seven delightful days. Now we must go.
Health and long life to you and yours!

Milarepa then said, "You offered me food and lodging, and I preached for you. This [relationship] is important. He who reveres and rejoices in the Dharma and has faith in it at all times, is planting the Seed-of-Dharma from which the Innate-born Wisdom will grow in his future lives. He who has rightly made a good wish, does not have to learn many teachings. Nor must he associate [with his Guru] for a long time. If the outer conditions and the inner seeds in one's own mind meet together, though temporarily one may go astray, the power of the seeds-of-the-wish will eventually bring one to the right path. Furthermore, faith and earnestness are most important. Nowadays, because people do not accumulate merits [by practicing virtuous deeds], they seldom see the inner merits of others, but only their outer faults, even though these faults are small and insignificant. If you have faith in me, whether I live near or far from you will make no difference. If we live too close and our relationship becomes too intimate, it will only cause discord and trouble between us. I think it would be too difficult for you, at the present time, to be a perfect practitioner of the Dharma. You must try to understand your own habitual-thinking. In any case, I shall make a good wish for you, and you should also try to pray to, and have faith in me. If you now practice virtuous deeds and put your faith [in the Dharma], you will be reborn in a special, favorable country, with perfect conditions and means [to practice the Dharma]. It is not necessary for a real follower of Dharma to go to many places. Again, he who sees many faults in other people, is liable to be an ignorant person himself. To you worldly beings, your native land is always the best; also, you like grand religious ceremonies. But in fact, if you have goodwill and give provisions often and unsparingly to a single beggar, this would be quite sufficient. There is no such thing as 'this teaching is good' and 'that teaching is bad'; you should never be sectarian. It is hard for you to imitate me. The fox can never go where the lion leaps; he would break his back if he tried to copy the lion. It is indeed very difficult for most lovers of the Dharma to follow my way of practicing. I hope that you, the aristocrat, will never lose faith in Dharma."

Having said this to the rich man, Milarepa and his disciple traveled on again for alms, [and soon] came to a town where they met a yogi who appeared to be, and was dressed like, a Tantra-follower. This Tantric yogi said to Milarepa, "Dear Yogi, where have you come from? Judging by your appearance, it seems that you are a person having the Pure View, Pure Practice, and Equal Action.[9] Have you anything to say which may help to further my progress?" Milarepa replied, "Do you have a real understanding of the View, Practice, and Action? If not, I may tell you about mine, but you might not quite appreciate it. It may be better this morning just to establish an auspicious and beneficial Karma-relationship between us." "Never mind," said the yogi, "I shall give you alms. I am a teacher of Tantrism myself, and so have some understanding of these things According to my School, the View, Practice, and Action are like this ...." And he expounded the teachings at length. Then he asked Milarepa, "Does your School agree with mine?" Milarepa replied, "He who does not fear Saṃsāra, renounce the world, and follow the instruction of a qualified Guru, with a very strong desire to attain Buddhahood immediately — driven by his craving and evil instincts is liable to become a mere babbler. Although he talks a great deal about the View, Practice, and Action, he is most likely to go astray." And the Jetsun sang:

> Hearken, you great teacher!
> It is hard to help others
> If one does not renounce this world.
>
> If you do not *realize* Saṃsāra and Nirvāṇa are one,
> And hold a faint idea but dimly in your mind,
> In indulgence you will freely gratify [your senses],
> And be carried away by the torrent of Eight
>   Desires.
>
> [You should carefully observe and ask yourself]:
> "Have I realized the truth of Two-in-One which
>   is beyond extremes,[10]
> Or have I thrown myself over the Four Edges?[11]

Is my practice free of 'mind effort'?
Am I haunted by the ghost of 'form and substance'?
Is my blissful and rapturous Samādhi
A delusive state defiled by 'grasping-craving'?
Have I been shackled by the laws of form
Without grace and blessing?
When I meditate on the identity of manifestation
        and Guru[12]
Does my Awareness wander?
When I illustrate the truth through Tantric symbols,
Have I taught the Truth beyond all symbols?
Have I polluted with 'intentional effort,' and distorted,
The originally pure Self-mind?
Have I done that which I willed
In a way that righteous Lamas ne'er behave?
Did I ever ask myself: 'Am I aware
That wordly prosperity and achievements
Are but the hindrances set up by devils?' "

If you do not understand or practice
The teaching of a Lineage with grace,
The devils will mislead you with their art.
Then you will never free yourself
From the realms of misery and Saṃsāra.
Rely then on a genuine Lineage, and practice
Your devotion without craving and self-indulgence.

Having heard this song, the teacher turned to Milarepa in faith
and reliance, crying, "This is indeed marvelous!" He bowed down at
the feet of the Jetsun and invited him into his house, giving perfect
offerings and service to him. He then asked Milarepa to accept him
as his disciple. The Jetsun knew that he was a destined person, and
granted his request. Thereupon, all three returned to Lashi Snow
Mountain. Having received the Initiation and Pith-instructions from
Milarepa, the teacher later acquired the Accomplishments and reached
the state of Emancipation. He was destined eventually to become
one of the heart-sons of Milarepa, and was known as Shangchub
Jarbo—the Teacher of Ngan Tson.

This is the story of Milarepa singing the "Song of the Staff" at
Jen Valley, and of his meeting with the teacher of Ngan Tson.

NOTES

1 Preparatory Practice (T.T.: sÑon.hGro.): Before engaging in the main meditation practices such as the Arising Yoga, the Perfecting Yoga, and Mahāmudrā, the yogi should first complete all the preparatory practices. The four most common ones are (1) 100,000 prostrations before the symbols of the Three Precious Ones; (2) 100,000 prayers to one's Guru and Patron Buddha; (3) 100,000 prayers of penitence, together with 100,000 Mantras of Vajrasattva; and (4) offering 100,000 "Maṇḍalas."

2 Five Nectars: Five different secretions of the human body.

3 Two Cubits or Two Troos: The Tibetan word "Troo" (T.T.: Khru) denotes a local unit of measure. Its length is from the elbow to the tip of the middle finger.

4 Twin Qualities: probably the merits of Wisdom and of Compassion.

5 Four Infinite Wishes: (1) that all sentient beings may sow the seeds of happiness and attain it; (2) that all sentient beings may avoid suffering and the cause of suffering; (3) that all sentient beings may attain "pure happiness"; (4) that all sentient beings may reach the state of tranquillity. See also Story 17, Note 25.

6 Root Principle: See Story 12, Notes 5, 6, and 7.

7 Heavenly Iron (T.T.: gNam.lCags.): According to Tibetan legends, the weapons made of meteoric metal are extremely strong and valuable.

8 Probably a misprint for "Sevan Repa."

9 Equal Action: Absorbed in the Realm of the "Equality of Saṃsāra-Nirvāṇa," the enlightened being acts fearlessly and indifferently at all times.

10 Lit.: "beyond the Four Edges." See Note 11.

11 The Four Edges or Four Ends (T.T.: mThah.bShi.), are the four basic patterns along which one settles his opinion on reality. They are that reality is (1) positive, or being; (2) negative, or non-being; (3) a combination of both being and non-being; or (4) a state beyond being and non-being. If one clings to any of these four "ends" or "extremes" he is said, according to Buddhism, to have missed the point.

12 A Tantric yogi should know that all manifestations are representations of Absolute Truth, and that the "real Guru" — the embodiment of the Absolute — is his own mind. Thus, to meditate on one's own mind is to realize the identity of the manifestations and Gurus.

19

THE TWENTY-ONE
EXHORTATIONS

Obeisance to all Gurus

ONE night while meditating on Lashi Snow Mountain, Milarepa dreamt that a most beautiful young girl, adorned with jewels and bone ornaments, came to him and said, "Yogi Milarepa, you should follow your Guru's instruction, go to Di Se Snow Mountain and meditate *there*. On your way, you will meet a well-gifted and destined person whom you should influence and guide according to his need." After saying this she disappeared. When Milarepa awoke, he thought to himself, "This message is sent by the Patron Buddha and Ḍākinī to enable me to repay my Guru's bounty. I must comply with her request and go at once."

On his way from Lashi to Di Se Snow Mountain, he met an inhabitant of Nya Non called Dhamba Jhaupu.

This man invited Milarepa to his house, made great offerings, and gave an elaborate feast in his honor. [At the feast], he said to the Jetsun, "For the sake of the disciples now assembled here, please be kind enough to preach for us the Dharma which blossoms within you. Please put this preaching into a song and sing it for us."

And so Milarepa sang "The Twenty-One Exhortations for Mind":

> Great is the Skillful Path of Tantra
> And the Guru's Pith-Instruction,
> So, too, are perseverance and resolution;
> These are the "Three Greatnesses."

> Put the Life-active Prāṇa at the key point,
> The Mind-Essence in its Natural State,

200

And consciousness under self-examination;
These are the "Three Enterings."

To fulfill the commandments of my Guru,
Achieve the wishes of my heart,
And be altruistic without effort;
These are the "Three Accomplishments."

Outer hindrances and demons disappear,
Inner desires and passions are extinguished,
Disorder and illness of body cease to be;
These are the "Three Absences."

My skill and my resourcefulness in speech,
My eloquence in answering all questions,
My knowledge of the nature and aspects of Mind;
These are the "Three Proficiencies."

I see clearly that bliss is void of substance,
I see all things manifest without discriminating,
I see clearly That which is beyond all words;
These are the "Three Sights."

When men in crowds assemble,
Means and enjoyments are gathered there
And Ḍākinīs congregate;
These are the "Three Gatherings."

These one-and-twenty Exhortations for the Mind
Are fruit of my experience in meditation;
All Dharma seekers should value them,
Especially my followers and sons.

Too much instruction hinders Liberation.
Follow then and practice the precious words
That I have sung to this assembly.

Thereupon Dhamba Jhaupu served Milarepa, who gave him the Initiation and Key Instructions. Having practiced these teachings for some time he attained the Experiences and Realization, and later on became one of the "intimate sons" of the Jetsun.

This is the story of Milarepa's meeting with Dhamba Jhaupu.

20

MILAREPA'S MEETING WITH KAR CHON REPA

Obeisance to all Gurus

As predicted in Marpa's prophecy, the Jetsun Milarepa set out for Di Se Snow Mountain with several of his disciples. When they reached Lowo Lake, one of the disciples pretended to be ill and would go no farther, so the journey was interrupted. Milarepa then stayed at the Upper Lowo that summer and preached the Dharma there.

When the autumn came and Milarepa was about to go to Di Se Snow Mountain, the disciples and patrons gave him a farewell party. They all circled round and made offerings and obeisance to him. The patrons then besought him for instructions because they all realized that no one could tell when they would meet again. In response, Milarepa sang "The Right Yoga Practice":

> I, Milarepa, the man, the Yogi of Tibet,
> Have little learning, yet are my instructions great.
> I take little sleep, though persevering at my
>   meditation,
> Humble am I in heart, but great is my persistence.
>
> Knowing one thing, I know all;
> Knowing all, I know that they are one.
> I am an expert in Absolute Truth.
>
> My bed is small, yet I am free to stretch my legs.
> My clothes are thin, yet is my body warm.
> I eat but little, yet am satisfied.
>
> I am the one whom all yogis venerate,

To whom all faithful come, a guide
On the dread path of life and death.
Unattached to any home,
I have no fixed dwelling;
Disregarding all, I do my will.

I crave for no possessions. Between clean
And unclean food I do not discriminate.
I suffer little pain from passion's sting.

With little self-importance, I have few desires;
I crave not for objective and subjective things;
Thus can I untie Nirvāṇa's knots.

I console old people when they grieve;
Loving fun, to the young I am a friend.
A yogi, I rove about all regions, wishing
Devas and human beings to live in happiness.

After hearing this song, they said to Milarepa, "To be sure, Revered One, this is your life and practice; but please tell us what *we* should do. Be kind enough to give us, your disciples, some instructions and advice." The Jetsun then emphasized the transiency of all beings, admonishing them to practice Dharma earnestly. And he sang "The Song of Transience with Eight Similes":

Faithful disciples here assembled [ask yourselves]:
"Have I practiced Dharma with great earnestness?
Has the deepest faith arisen in my heart?"
He who wants to practice Dharma and gain non-regressive
     faith,
Should listen to this explanation of the Mundane
     Truths
And ponder well their meaning.
Listen to these parables and metaphors:

A painting in gold,
Flowers of turquoise blue,
Floods in the vale above,
Rice in the vale below,
Abundance of silk,
A jewel of value,
The crescent moon,

And a precious son—
These are the eight similes.

No one has sung before
Such casual words [on this].
No one can understand their meaning
If he heeds not the whole song.

The gold painting fades when it is completed—
This shows the illusory nature of all beings,
This proves the transient nature of all things.
Think, then, you will practice Dharma.

The lovely flowers of turquoise-blue
Are destroyed in time by frost—
This shows the illusory nature of all beings,
This proves the transient nature of all things.
Think, then, you will practice Dharma.

The flood sweeps strongly down the vale above,
Soon becoming weak and tame in the plain below—
This shows the illusory nature of all beings,
This proves the transient nature of all things.
Think, then, you will practice Dharma.

Rice grows in the vale below;
Soon with a sickle it is reaped —
This shows the illusory nature of all beings,
This proves the transient nature of all things.
Think, then, you will practice Dharma.

Elegant silken cloth
Soon with a knife is cut—
This shows the illusory nature of all beings,
This proves the transient nature of all things.
Think, then, you will practice Dharma.

The precious jewel that you cherish
Soon will belong to others—
This shows the illusory nature of all beings,
This proves the transient nature of all things.
Think, then, you will practice Dharma.

The pale moonbeams
Soon will fade and vanish—
This shows the illusory nature of all beings,
This proves the transient nature of all things.
Think, then, you will practice Dharma.

A precious son is born;
Soon he is lost and gone —
This shows the illusory nature of all beings,
This proves the transient nature of all things.
Think, then, you will practice Dharma.

These are the eight similes I sing.
I hope you will remember and practice them.

Affairs and business will drag on forever,
So lay them down and practice now the Dharma.
If you think tomorrow is the time to practice,
Suddenly you find that life has slipped away.
Who can tell when death will come?

Ever think of this. Devote
Yourselves to Dharma practice.

Hearing this song, all the patrons fell prostrate before Milarepa in
their deep faith. Feeling a strong conviction of the truth contained in
his admonishments, tears gushed from their eyes like the waters of a
spring. Three young men among them asked Milarepa to take them as
his disciple-servants. Thereupon, the Jetsun sang of "The Ten Difficulties":

If a Buddhist be without benevolence,
How can he subdue and convert evil people?

If spiritual longing be not awakened,
How can the merits grow within one?

If a "great yogi" has no perseverance,
How can the Experiences and Realization come?

If a monk keeps not the priestly rules,
How can he receive gifts, service, or respect?

If a Tantric yogi violates the Precepts of Samaya,
How can he gain powers or grace?

If a patron be mean and parsimonious,
He can never be of pood repute.

If a yogi jokes and talks of nonsense,
He will never be respected.

He who pays no heed to Karma or to virtue,
Will never understand the truth of Voidness.

If a trusted Lama grows tired of religion,
He finds it hard to readjust to life.

Though faith arises now within you, happy young men,
Self-control will still be hard. Though now you feel
Pressing and urgent need to practice Dharma,
If you go too far, my sons,
Later you will be regretful.

Let us now wish that we meet again—
The power of Karma will bring this to pass.
Till we meet once more, will I, the Yogi,
By my own words steadfastly abide.

All happiness and good fortune,
I wish for you, dear patrons,
Health and freedom from all sickness,
A long life free from injuries,
And may sons and fathers meet again.

I, the Yogi, will wander where I please.
You, young men, so spoiled and happy,
Return now to your homes.

Upon hearing this song, they all surrounded the Jetsun, grasped his clothing, and embraced his body, weeping, bowing down at his feet, and making their wishes.

Among them there was a young man who was extremely sincere. He pleaded again and again with Milarepa in great earnestness; eventually the Jetsun relented and accepted him as a disciple. He then brought the young man back to De Si Snow Mountain, where he gave him the Initiation and Instructions. Later, this young man attained emancipation and became known as Kar Chon Repa, one of Milarepa's "intimate sons."

This is the story of Milarepa's meeting with Kar Chon Repa.

ADMONISHMENTS TO DHARMA WONSHU

Obeisance to all Gurus

ONCE in the early part of the last month of autumn, Milarepa and his disciples went to Bushen Chitang for alms. Many people were gathered there. Milarepa said to them, "Patrons, please give me the alms for which I have come." Now among them was a young, well-dressed girl, who said, "Dear Yogi, who are you? Who are your father and mother, your brother and sister?" Whereupon, the Jetsun sang:

> I bow down to all Holy Gurus!
> Pray grant me your grace and blessings!
>
> My father is Gungtuzunpo,[1] the All-Perfect One;
> My mother, Drowazunpo, the Worthy-Woman.
> My brother is called King-of-Knowledge,
> My aunt, Lamp-of-Illumination,
> And my sister, Dazzling-Faith.
> My friend is called Natural-Wisdom,
> And my child, Son-of-Illumination.
> My book is Foundation-of-the-Universe-and-Manifestation,
> My horse, Mount-of-Consciousness-Prāna,
> And my patrons are the Four-Regions-of-Weu-and-Tsang,[2]
> As for me, I am a small white Buddha Stūpa.
> I have never practiced singing,
> Yet will I sing clearly for you:
>
> My father, the All-Perfect One,
> Earns the wages of Knowledge and Practice;

Never do worldly thoughts arise in him.
My mother, Worthy-Woman, always feeds me
The milk of Pith-Instruction from her breast.
Imbibing the Practice-Teachings, I have ne'er felt
      hungry.
My brother, King-of-Knowledge, holds within his hand
The knife of Skill-and-Wisdom,[3]
And with it kills wrong views both coarse and fine.
My aunt, Lamp-of-Illumination, displays her Mirror
      of Self-Mind
Unsullied by the rust of habitual-thought.
My sister, Dazzling-Faith,
Has long been free from meanness.
In her practice of devotion,
She has goods but does not hold them;
What she has, she never hoards.

I and my comrade, Natural-Wisdom,
Like one man live together
And never raise our voice in strife.

My only child, Son-of-Illumination,
Is heir and holder of the Buddha's Line;
I have never raised a child
Who needed washing or change of diapers.

My book, Foundation-of-Universe-and-Manifestation,
Illustrates for me the Principles and Meanings;
Never have I read books with printed words.

My horse, Mount-of-Consciousness-Prāṇa,
Carries me swiftly where e'er I want to go.
I never need a horse of flesh and blood.

My patrons in the Four Regions of Weu and Tsang,
Offer me provisions when I ask for them.
I never weigh or press my bag of flour.
When I offer, it is to the Precious Ones;
When I rely, it is upon my own Guru.

I say that I am white, because I practice deeds of
      whiteness.
I say that I am small, for few are my desires.

Therefore, I say that I'm a Stūpa, small and white.

"These sayings are indeed very wonderful," remarked the girl. "But do you also have any Samsāric companions, sons, and belongings?"
Milarepa then sang in reply:

> At first my experiences in Saṃsāra
> Seemed most pleasant and delightful;
> Later, I learned about its lessons;
> In the end, I found a Devil's Prison.
> These are my thoughts and feelings on Saṃsāra.
> So I made my mind up to renounce it.
>
> At first, one's friend is like a smiling angel;
> Later, she turns into a fierce, exasperated woman;
> But in the end a demoness is she.
> These are my thoughts and feelings on companions.
> So I made my mind up to renounce a friend.
>
> At first, the sweet boy smiles, a Babe of Heaven;
> Later, he makes trouble with the neighbors;
> In the end, he is my creditor and foe.
> These are my thoughts and feelings about children.
> So I renounced both sons and nephews.
>
> At first, money is like the Wish-fulfilling Gem;
> Later, one cannot do without it;
> In the end, one feels a pennyless beggar.
> These are my thoughts and feelings about money.
> So I renounced both wealth and goods.
>
> When I think of these experiences,
> I cannot help but practice Dharma;
> When I think of Dharma,
> I cannot help but offer it to others.
> When death approaches,
> I shall then have no regret.

Hearing the Jetsun's song, the light of faith was aroused in the girl. She invited Milarepa and his disciples to her house, and gave them perfect service and offerings. She was then given the Instruction, and entered the Path.

Milarepa and his disciples then went together to Dre Tze Snow Mountain. One day, many patrons came to visit him. Among them there was a well-gifted, aristocratic young man — a descendant of the Jowo family, who had the greatest faith in Milarepa. He said "Dear Lama, all your doings are inconceivably marvelous! Please grant us a teaching which we can always practice."

In response to his request, Milarepa sang:

> Listen, all you faithful patrons.
> When you walk, identify your perceptions with Mind-
> Essence;[4]
> This is self-liberation when you walk.
>
> When you sit, relax and be at ease;
> This is the Heart-Teaching of how to sit.
>
> When you sleep, sleep in the Realm of Equality;
> This is the way to sleep in the Great Light.
>
> When you eat, eat in the Realm of Voidness;
> This is the way to eat without dichotomy.
>
> When you drink, drink the water of Skill and Wisdom;
> This is the way to drink without cessation.
>
> When you walk, sit, or sleep, always look at your mind;
> This is a worthy practice without pause or interruption.

"We are incompetent people and do not know how to practice this profound teaching," exclaimed the patrons, "Oh, those who know how to do so are fortunate indeed!" Milarepa replied, "When you say you do not know how to practice this teaching, that only means you want to shun it; this is also the very sign of incapability for devotion. If you *determine* to practice it, you will know how to do it and really understand it. Now, listen to the profit of this teaching in my song":

> My gifted patrons, in the transient,
> Flask-like human body dwells
> An innate-born Buddha Kāya.[5]
> If one can display the lamp of Great Light,
> The outer and inner Dharmakāya will shine brightly!
>
> In the Saṃsāric house of Complex-Thought

Dwells a baby eagle—the Bodhi-Mind,
If once she flaps her wings of Wisdom-Skill,
Surely she will fly up to the Sky of All-Knowing!

In the Victorious Snow Mountain of Self-Body
Dwells a baby lion of consciousness.
He who can practice [Dharma] without clinging
To the Six-Consciousnesses-Group,
Surely will conquer both Saṃsāra and Nirvāṇa!

On the blind ocean of Saṃsāra float
The seagoing merchants of the Six Realms.
He who never parts from the Trikāya,[6]
Surely will conquer the raging seas!

In the illusive house of the Five Poisons
Dwells a group of bandits to prevent one's liberation.
He who can hold secure the Rope of Skill, will
Surely overcome these dreadful outlaws.

The Absolute Body, Dharmakāya, is like the firmament;
The Wish-fulfilling Gem may there be found.
He who can meditate on it without distraction,
Surely will attain the Trikāya of Buddhahood.

In the cities of the Three Kingdoms of Saṃsāra
Lie the iron chains that bind us in the Six Realms.
He who can untie them through the Guru's teachings,
Surely will tread the Path of Liberation.

From the gem-like, precious Guru
Springs the fountain of the Pith-Instruction.
He who quaffs it with unshaken faith
Surely will be freed from sinful thirsting.

Thus he sang; and the patrons were all confirmed in their belief, and departed. But the young aristocrat determined to devote himself to the pursuit of Dharma, thinking: "One day I must come to this Lama and offer myself as his servant-disciple." Meanwhile, the Jetsun and his disciples decided to remain at that place, enjoying the offerings and services from both human and non-human beings. They worked on furthering their patron's progress until the end of spring.

When they were about to return to Di Se Snow Mountain, the patron gave them a grand festival. Arising from the assembly, the young aristocrat, who had the utmost faith toward Milarepa, said, "Dear Lama, I have heard that you, the Dharma practitioner, have the teaching called the 'View, Practice, Action, and Fruit.' Would you please be kind enough to tell us your own experience of them?"

In answer, Milarepa sang:

> Because I see the self-face of the View,
> The thought of contrast by itself dissolves;
> How then can I have the Idea-of-Two—
>   the self and others?
> The View is void of limit and discrimination.
>
> When in the Practice I become absorbed,
> Good and evil are reduced to self-liberation;
> How then can I have the Idea-of-Two—
>   happiness and suffering?
> The Practice is devoid of limitary feelings and
>   experience.
>
> When I adhere to the self-continuance of Action,
> Dislike is reduced to self-liberation;
> How then can I have the Impulse-of-Two—
>   craving and aversion?
> The Action is free from limitary attachment.
>
> Since self-liberation is the Fruit,
> Both Nirvāṇa and Saṃsāra are reduced to it.
> How then can I have the Idea-of-Two—
>   getting and abandoning?
>
> Absence of fear and hope is
> The Fruit of this great Practice.

The young aristocrat then said to Milarepa, "Dear Lama, I have made up my mind to devote myself to the practice of Dharma. But I do not dare to start without the permission of my parents and relatives. Although I will have to ask their permission first, please be kind enough to accept me as your disciple-servant and take me with you." Milarepa replied, "He who wants to practice the Dharma, should think of the miseries of Saṃsāra. Then, if he still cannot make up his mind and, instead, looks for permission or recommendation from others, he will never succeed. Listen to my song":

If a pious person, who wants to practice Dharma,
Cannot cut off the tie of influence,
How can he break through others' domination?

If one cannot live on the alms of Non-attachment,
How can he free himself from the bonds of
         honor and pride?

If, knowing the transiency of all being,
He has no sense of contentment,
How can he be content with his amassed wealth?

How can one understand the truth beyond words,
By talking and discussing without first-hand
         experience?
How can he who does not realize
The truth beyond all symbols,
Describe It with a darkened mind?

How can he who shuns not the evils of bad partnership
Avoid the painful consequences?

If one cannot utilize this suffering
To further his spiritual growth,
How can he overcome all griefs and blind striving?

If one knows not that disturbing thoughts themselves
         are Dharmakāya,
How can he reduce them
By corrective measures?

If one renounces not all concerns and undertakings,
How in moderation can he practice his devotion?

How can he who does not resign from all activities
And cut off all attachments, achieve success
In Dharma by doing this and that, or by mere thinking?

How can he who renounces not all ties,
Practice meditation without worldly thoughts in mind?

If he does not renounce at once,
How can he hope to do so later?

If he thinks he need not strive for improvement now,
But can do so later, he must fail.

If he does not strengthen now his will,
Success from hope and expectation will not spring.

Upon hearing Milarepa's song, the young aristocrat was deeply moved and convinced of the truth contained in it. He decided at once to practice the Dharma, and his parents also gave their permission. After serving his apprenticeship with Milarepa, he was given the Initiation and Pith-Instructions, and eventually attained success and Liberation. He was known as Ngogom Repa Dharma Wonshu Shawa, one of the "close sons" of Milarepa.

This is the story of Milarepa meeting his disciple Repa Dharma Wonshu at Bu Shen.

NOTES

1 Gungtuzunpo (T.T.: Kun.Du.bZañ.Po.; Skt.: Samantabhadra): The "Ādi Buddha," or "Primordial Buddha," which, according to most Tibetan scholars, is a symbolic name to denote the Primordial Buddha-nature within all sentient beings, but not a name to denote a person or deity whose existence is prior to all beings.

2 Weu and Tsang: Central and Southwestern Tibet.

3 Skillfulness and Wisdom (T.T.: Thabs.Dañ.Çes.Rab.; Skt.: Upāya [and] Prajñā): Upāya means the skillful or ingenious methods and conduct with which a Bodhisattva applies his altruistic deeds to benefit sentient beings. Prajñā means the transcendental Wisdom shared only by enlightened beings. Upāya in its most general application denotes the first five Pāramitās, i.e., Charity, Discipline, Patience, Diligence, and Meditation; Prajñā denotes the last Pāramitā, i.e., the Prajñāpāramitā, the Perfection of Wisdom.

4 Lit.: "Bring all manifestation to the Path."

5 Kāya: meaning Body.

6 Trikāya: the three Bodies of Buddha, i.e., the Body of Truth (Dharmakāya); the Body of Divinity or Reward (Sambhogakāya); and the Body of Manifestation (Nirmāṇakāya).

THE MIRACLE CONTEST
ON DI SE SNOW MOUNTAIN

Obeisance to all Gurus

O NCE when the Jetsun with many of his disciples were on their way to Di Se Snow Mountain from Bu Shen, the local deities of Di Se and Ma Päm came out with a great retinue to welcome them. They bowed down to Milarepa, and made offerings to him on a grand scale. They welcomed him sincerely and pointed out the local meditation hermitages, all of which were places distinguished in history and legend. They also swore to protect his followers, and then returned to their own abodes.

When Milarepa and his disciples reached the banks of Lake Ma Päm, there came a Bon[1] Priest called Naro Bhun Chon. This man, having heard a great deal about Milarepa, and having learned that he was coming to Di Se, went with his brothers and sisters to Lake Ma Päm to meet the Jetsun and his disciples. Pretending that he did not know who they were, the Bon priest asked, "From whence have you come and where might you be going?" Milarepa replied, "We are going to Di Se Snow Mountain to practice meditation. Our destination is a hermitage there." The priest then asked, "Who are you, and what is your name?"

"My name is Milarepa."

"Oh, in that case," replied the priest, "you are just like Ma Päm—it has a great reputation in far-away places, but when one reaches it one finds it not really so wonderful as reputed. Perhaps the lake *is* quite marvelous, but it and the encircling mountains nearby are all dominated by us, followers of Bon. If you want to stay here, you must follow our teachings and sow your seeds [in Bon]."

Milarepa replied, "Generally speaking, this mountain was prophesied by Buddha Himself to be a place of the Doctrine-holders. For me, in particular, it has great significance, for it was spoken of by my Guru Marpa. You Bonists, who have been staying here so far, are indeed very fortunate! If you want to remain here in future, you should follow the teachings of *my* religion; otherwise, you had better go elsewhere."

"It seems to me that you have a dual personality," said the Bon priest. "From a far distance I heard that you were indeed great; but when one comes close to you, you look small and insignificant. If you are really the remarkable person that people say, you should not mind having a contest with me. We will *see* whose miraculous powers are superior. The one who wins shall remain here and be considered as the legitimate owner of the place, and the one who loses shall leave." Saying this, the priest straddled the Ma Päm lake and sang:

> The Di Se Snow Mountain [of the Himalayas] is
>   most famous,
> But its summit is covered deep in snow!
>
> The lake of Ma Päm is indeed well-known,
> But the power of water breaks through it!
>
> Milarepa's reputation is indeed most great,
> Yet he is an old eccentric who sleeps naked.
> From his mouth he chants melodious songs,
> But he holds in his hands a metal staff.[2]
> There is nothing great about him!
>
> In our Bon religion,
> The Immutable One is the Swastika-Body[3] —
> The Lord Ye Shin Dsu Pud, and other heavenly beings.
> The fierce blood-drinking Deity with gaping mouth
> Has nine heads, eighteen arms, and many miraculous
>   powers.
> Yes, His Transformation Body has nine heads!
>
> His sister is the World-Conquering Mother.
> I, the Bon novice, am her disciple.
> Look at me! See how I demonstrate miraculous power!

In reply, Milarepa seated himself above the lake and, without his body growing any bigger or the lake any smaller, he appeared to cover it all. He sang:

Listen to me, you heavenly and human beings here
    assembled.

On the summit of the Eagle Mountain
Upon the Seat of Eight Non-Fears[4]
Sits the Victorious One, Buddha Śākyamuni.

In the Dharma Palace of the Heaven of Og Men[5]
Abides the Sixth Buddha, Great Dorje-Chang, the
    Wisdom Body of Not-Two.

The great Mother, the Goddess, is Dagmema;
The Transformation Body of the Inborn is the great
    Tilopa;
The Teacher, the Door-Protector,[6] is the great Nāropa;
The Buddha-like Translator is the great Marpa.
From these four Deities, I receive grace and blessings.

I, Milarepa, the renowned and celebrated one,
Following the order of my Guru, Marpa,
For the welfare of all men
Meditate on Di Se Snow Mountain.

To you, the wrong-view-holder Bonist,
I now give answer with this song:

The famous Di Se Mountain blanketed with snow
Symbolizes the pure, white Buddhist doctrine.
The streams flowing into the famous Blue Lake of
    Ma Päm
Symbolize one's deliverance to the Realm of
    the Absolute.

I, the famous Milarepa, the old man who sleeps naked,
Am he who now transcends the dualistic realm!

The little songs springing from my mouth
Are but the natural outflow of my heart;
They tell of, and describe the Sūtras of the Buddha.

The staff held in my hand
Symbolizes the crossing of the ocean of Saṃsāra.
I have mastered both the mind and forms;

Unaided by worldly deities
I can perform all miracles.

Di Se, where dwell worldly Devas with crude bodies,[7]
Is the king of all snow mountains on this earth.
This place belongs to Buddhists,
To the followers of Milarepa.

If you, Bon priests and heretics, will now practice
    the Dharma,
You, too, will soon be able to benefit all;
If not, you should depart and go elsewhere,
Because my powers of magic are greater far than yours.
Watch closely now and see what I can do!

At this, Milarepa performed another miracle by putting the whole
Ma Päm Lake on his finger-tip, without doing the slightest harm to the
living beings in it. The Bon priest said, "In this first contest, your miracle was better than mine. But I came here first. We must have another
contest to see which of us is the more powerful." Milarepa replied, "I
shall not emulate you, the magician who smears drugs on his body in
order to deceive others by conjuring up delusive visions. I will not enter
into any contest with such a person. If you do not wish to follow the
teachings of the Buddha, you may go elsewhere." The Bon priest countered, "I will not renounce the teaching of the Swastica-Bon. If you
win the contest, I will give up and go away. Otherwise, I will never
leave here. According to the Buddhist precepts, you may not kill or
harm me. Is this not so? Now let us fight with our supernatural powers."
    Thereupon, the Bon priest started to circle Di Se Snow Mountain
from right to left,. while Milarepa and his followers circled it clockwise.
They met on a big rock in the northeastern valley of Di Se. The Bonist said to Milarepa, "It is very good that you [pay homage to this holy
place] by circumambulating it. Now, you should follow the Bon way
of circling the mountain." Saying this, he took Milarepa by the hand
and dragged him in his direction. The Jetsun retorted, "I will not follow
your wrong path and reverse the Buddhist tradition. I think it better
that you follow me and adopt the Buddhist way of making the circle."
Saying this, Milarepa in turn grabbed the Bon priest's hand and dragged
him in *his* direction. Pulling each other back and forth on the rock,
both the Jetsun and the Bon priest left many of their footprints there.
But because the power of Milarepa was much greater than that of the
priest, he was forced to follow Milarepa's direction.
    When they reached the north side of Di Se, the priest said, "Later,

we should follow the Bon way, go in the opposite direction, and make another circle." "Well, that will depend on how great your power is," replied Milarepa. The priest then said, "It seems that your power is greater than mine this time. But we should still try our strength further." Saying this, he lifted up a huge rock, as big as a yak, in front of the hill. Then Milarepa came forward and lifted up the priest as well as the rock. The priest then said, "This time you win again. But to win once or twice means nothing. We should continue our contest." Milarepa replied, "The stars may try to emulate the light of the moon and sun, but the darkness covering the Four Continents will be dispelled only by the sun and moon. You may try to emulate me, but you can never match me. Now, Di Se Mountain belongs to me. It was to please you that I revealed my miraculous power. Everyone can now see that the Buddhist practice is superior."

Thereupon, the Jetsun sat in the Lotus Cave on the western side of Castle Valley, while the Bon priest sat in a cave on the eastern side. Milarepa stretched his leg from the west side of the valley and reached right in front of the cave where the priest was sitting. He then called, "Now, you do the same thing!" The priest also stretched out his leg, but it did not even reach the brook! Whereupon, the Non-men spectators in the sky all laughed heartily at him.

Although the priest was now a little ashamed and embarrassed, he cried out, "I still want to fight on!" Saying this, he again started circling the mountain in the Bon way. The Jetsun also resumed the circling in the Buddhist way. This time they met on the south side of Di Se. When it began to rain, Milarepa said, "We need a shelter to protect us. Let us now build a house. Would you like to lay the foundation stone and floor, or do you prefer to put on the roof?" The priest said, "I prefer to put on the roof. You do the foundation work." Milarepa agreed. Then he pointed to a rock as big as three persons standing up together, and said, "Let us go over there." When they reached it, the Jetsun began to lay the foundation. He saw that the Bon priest had split a giant rock, as big as the body of an eight-year-old child. Whereupon, Milarepa made a sign, a mudrā of Conquering, and the rock held by the priest split down the middle and broke in half. Milarepa then said, "Now, you can bring the roof here." "But you have already broken it!" cried the priest. "Well, it was because of our contest of miracle-working that I did it," replied Milarepa, "but this time I shall let you prepare another rock and will not repeat the gesture of breaking. This time you may bring me the prepared rock." Accordingly, the priest split another rock and was about to lift it up, when Milarepa immediately made a gesture of pressing-down. The priest was surprised, as he tried to lift the rock, to find that it had become extremely heavy. So he stopped trying and made an excuse, saying, "I have already prepared the rock-roof. Now it is your turn to carry it to the other side." Milarepa replied, "My job is to lay the foundation; yours is to put on the roof. Now try to lift it up and bring it here." So the Bon priest tried again. He used all his strength, struggling with distended eyes to lift the rock, but he could not move it an inch. Seeing this, Milarepa said, "I am a yogi who has attained both the Common and Ultimate Accomplishments. My miraculous powers are different from yours. Though you have achieved the miraculous power of the Common Accomplishment, it can never emulate mine. If I make another subduing-gesture, you will not even be able to split the rock any more. The reason that I did not do so in the beginning was simply because I wanted to amuse the spectators. Now look at me and see how I lift it up!" So saying, Milarepa merely used one hand to pick up the giant rock and put it on his shoulder. Thereby, his handprint was found impressed in the rock. Then he stood on it and left his footprints. Finally he put the rock on his head and left his headprint and [more] handprints upon it. Later on, this cave was called the Cave of Miracle-Working and became very famous. It was then that the Bon priest admitted his defeat.

The Jetsun had many other contests with Naro Bhun Chon. His performances were far superior to, and much more wonderful, than the priest's. Finally, Naro Bhun Chon said, "You said that I am a magician; but from what I can see, you are the magician. I am not convinced by your miracle-working. Now, on the fifteen of this month, we shall have a race to see who can first reach the summit of Di Se Mountain. The winner will be recognized as the host of the mountain. This will also decide, beyond dispute, the one who has really attained the Ultimate Accomplishment." "Very well," replied Milarepa, "we will do as you wish. But what a pity that you Bon priests think your little bit of mystical inner experience is the Ultimate Accomplishment! To attain the Ultimate Accomplishment one has to behold the nature of his own mind. If one wants to realize this, he should follow and meditate on the teachings of my School — the Practice Succession." The Bon priest replied, "What difference is there between your mind and mine? Is yours good and mine bad? What difference is there between Bonism and Buddhism? Although your practice and mine are alike, you may be more proficient in the art of delusive magic. Therefore, so far, it looks as if you are superior. Anway, the race to Di Se will settle everything once and for all." Milarepa replied, "All right! Very good! That will settle everything."

Whereupon, Naro Bhun Chon concentrated his mind to pray to his god diligently and undistractedly, while Milarepa just carried on naturally. When it came to the fifteenth day, in the very early morning, Naro Bhun Chon, wearing a green cloak and playing a Bon musical instrument, flew through the sky on a drum towards Di Se. Milarepa's disciples all saw this, but Milarepa was still sound asleep. Thereupon, Rechungpa called out: "Dear Jetsun, wake up! Look! Though it is still so early in the morning, Naro Bhun Chon is flying on a drum to Di Se! He has reached the waist of the mountain now!"

The Jetsun still lay there as if nothing had happened, and finally said slowly, "Has our Bon friend arrived there already?" Then all the disciples pressed Milarepa to take immediate action. He said, "Very well. Look!", and he made a gesture toward the Bon priest. When the disciples looked at the priest again, they found that despite all his efforts to mount higher, he could only circle round and round the mountain.

When the day broke, and the sun appeared, Milarepa snapped his fingers, donned a cloak for wings, and flew over toward Di Se. In a second he arrived at the summit of the mountain, reaching it just at the time when the sunlight also shone upon it. There the Jetsun beheld the Gurus of the Transmission, and the tutelary deities. Buddha Dem Chog and his retinues all appeared, rejoicing before him. Although he knew that in essence all are equal — that the nature of Equality is imbued in all — Milarepa was nevertheless very pleased at his victory.

Meanwhile Naro Bhun Chon had reached the neck of the mountain. When he saw the Jetsun, lofty and compassionate, sitting at ease on the summit, he was dumbfounded and fell down from the heights, his riding-drum rolling down the southern slope of Di Se. As his pride and arrogance were now utterly subdued, he humbly cried to Milarepa, "Your power and miracle-working are indeed superior to mine! Now you are the master of Di Se. I will leave, but go to a place from where I can still see Di Se Snow Mountain."

Milarepa then said, "Although you are blessed by the worldly gods and have attained a smattering of Common Accomplishment, I, on the other hand, am a person who has fully realized the Innate Wisdom and attained the Ultimate Accomplishment. How can you possibly emulate me? The summit of Di Se Snow Mountain is the Mystic Vajra garden wherein the Wisdom Buddha, Korlo Dompa [Saṃvara], dwells. You have no merit to reach there. For the sake of the Buddhists who are assembled here, I asked permission of the deities, and showed it to all. Because I wanted to suppress your pride, I made you fall down from the mountain and lose your drum. From now on, even if you want to reach the foot of Di Se, you will have to rely on my power to get there. I will now tell you why I possess such power:

I bow down to my Guru, the gracious Marpa!

Through His mercy and the compassion of all Buddhas

I heard the wondrous Lord Buddha Śākyamuni,
He who subdued the heretics and followers of the
    Six Schools[8]
With the rightful teaching of Dharma.
The doctrine of Buddhism has thus been spread over
    the world.

On the Mountain, the Snow Di Se,
I, the Yogi of Tibet, with the Dharma conquer Bon,
And make the Buddha's Practice Lineage illuminate
    Tibet.

My miraculous powers come from superstrength,
Which I have many reasons to possess:
Belonging to a Lineage with great blessing and grace
Is one of the sources of this strength.

The primordial Buddha, Dorje-Chang, is a strength;
The compassionate Guru, the Master of all Pith-
    Instructions, is another;
From the Translator Marpa comes a third.

The Mind-Beyond, with its boundless knowledge, is a
    strength;
The Originally Pure[9] is another;
So is the unwavering meditation practice of
    Non-discrimination,
And so also is the Great Light.

If, when relaxed completely,[10] one observes what
    happens,
This very act in itself produces strength.

The All-flowing, All-abundant, and All-embracing,
And the self-face of the Being-Nature all bring
    strength.

The self-liberation of all forms is a strength.
If one follows the orders of his Guru,
The observation of precepts becomes a
    strength.

To be without sinful deeds and transgression is a
    strength.
If one can meditate in all one does,
This very practice will bring strength.
When all manifestations become your friends,[11]
A Great Strength will emerge;
Strong perseverance and determination do the same.

This is my strength, the strength of Milarepa.
With it have I now conquered heretics.
Hereafter I shall be the master of Di Se Snow Mountain,
Whence I shall propagate the Buddha's teachings.
To you, oh Wisdom-Deities, I give worship, and pray.

So went his song. "I am now fully convinced of your miraculous strength and powers." said the Bon priest, "They are indeed superior and marvelous. I sincerely beg you to allow me to stay where I can still see Di Se Snow Mountain." Milarepa replied, "In that case, you might live on the mountain over there." Saying which, he grasped a handful of snow and threw it to the top of a mountain to the east. Since that time a lump of snow has always been seen on the top of that mountain. Then, by Milarepa's power, both he and the Bon priest came to the neck of Di Se. The priest said: "In future I would like to circumambulate Di Se to pay my homage, but I will need a place to stay during my pilgrimage." "You may stop over there — the mountain opposite Di Se," replied the Jetsun. Afterwards, the Bonists built a stūpa in a cave there, and used it as a dwelling place during their pilgrimages to Di Se. Thus the followers in Milarepa's Lineage controlled all the region of the three lakes in the snow mountains.

This is the story of how Milarepa subdued Naro Bhun Chon at Di Se Snow Mountain.

NOTES

1 The aboriginal religion of Tibet.

2 Milarepa's staff was made of cane, but certain parts were probably covered by metal.

3 Swastika-Body; Swastica-Bon: The Swastika sign is a holy symbol of the Bon religion.

4 The Seat of Eight Non-Fears: This perhaps implies liberation from the Eight Worldly Desires.

5 Og Men (T.T.: Hog.Min.) Heaven: the central Heaven where Buddha Dorje-Chang resides.

6 Nāropa, the Door-Protector: Because Nāropa was one of the six famous professors of Vikramasila Monastery, in charge of one section (the North Section) of the School, he was so named.

7 The crude bodies of Devas: Though the heavenly bodies of Devas are illuminating and magnificent, in comparison with the splendor of the "Reward-Body of Buddha" (Sambhogakāya) they are crude and vulgar.

8 This implies the six main Schools of Hinduism: (1) Nyāya, (2) Vaisesika, (3) Sāṁkhya, (4) Yoga, (5) Mīmāṁsā, and (6) Vedānta.

9 The "Originally Pure": This is another term denoting the innate and pure Buddha-nature.

10 The most important Key-Instruction of Mahāmudrā is relaxation. Only through complete relaxation of mind may the Mind-Essence be seen.

11 The enlightened being feels that all becomings are conducive, and not obstructive, to his spiritual growth.

THE ENLIGHTENMENT
OF RECHUNGPA

Obeisance to all Gurus

Having circled Di Se Snow Mountain, Milarepa and his disciples returned to the Gray Cave of Dorje Tson of Gu Tang. The former patrons all came to visit the Jetsun, and asked him about his welfare and health. He told them that he felt extremely well and in turn inquired after their health. They replied: "It is by good fortune that under your protection and blessing we, too, are all very well and have not suffered from sickness or loss of life. Our livestock also thrives. We, on our side, are very glad to learn that you have successfully made the pilgrimage to Di Se without having met with any difficulties on your way. Please be kind enough to sing us a song of your well-being." Milarepa answered, "I am as happy as this — listen!" And he sang of the "Twelve Happinesses of Yoga":

> Like avoiding the pitfalls of evil,
> Happy is it to practice the Yoga of Renouncing-
> One's-Own-Land.

> Like a good horse freeing itself from the bridle,
> Happy is it to practice the Yoga Free-from-Subject-
> and-Object!

> Like wild beasts creeping on low ground,
> Happy is it to practice Yoga in solitude!

> Like the eagle flying freely in the heavens,
> Happy is it to practice the Yoga of Conviction!

Like vultures gliding freely through the sky,
Happy is it to practice Yoga without hindrances.

Like a shepherd restfully watching his sheep,
Happy it is, in Yoga practice,
To experience the Illuminating Void.

Like the huge Mount Sumeru standing firm
On the ground at the world's center,
Happy it is to practice the steadfast Yoga without
        disturbance.

Like the wide rivers flowing freely,
Happy is the continual sensation of the Yoga
        Experience.

Like a corpse lying quiet in the cemetery
Doing nothing and having no worries,
Happy is the Yoga of Non-action.

Like a stone thrown in the ocean, that never returns,
Happy is the Yoga of No-returning.[1]

Like the sun shining in the sky,
All other lights o'ershadowing,
Happy it is to practice the Yoga
Brighter than all lights.

Like leaves falling from the Dali tree,
That can never grow again,
Happy it is to practice the Yoga of No-birth.

This is the song of the "Twelve Happinesses of Yoga."
I now present it to you, my patrons, as a gift of
        Dharma.

After listening to this song, the patrons all returned home with
deep faith in their hearts.

· · ·   · · ·   · · ·

To test the accomplishment and experience of Rechungpa, and also
to find out how strong was his spirit of renunciation, one day Milarepa
casually sang for him the song of the "Twelve Deceptions":

Worldly affairs are all deceptive;
So I seek the Truth Divine.

Excitements and distractions are illusion;
So I meditate on the Non-dual Truth.

Companions and servants are deceptive;
So I remain in solitude.

Money and possessions are also deceptive;
So if I have them, I give them away.

Things in the outer world are all illusion;
The Inner Mind is that which I observe.

Wandering thoughts are all deceptive
So I only tread the Path of Wisdom.

Deceptive are the teachings of Expedient Truth;[2]
The Final Truth is that on which I meditate.

Books written in black ink are all misleading;
I only meditate on the Pith-Instructions of the
    Whispered Lineage.

Words and sayings, too, are but illusion;
At ease, I rest my mind in the effortless state.

Birth and death are both illusions;
I observe but the truth of No-Arising.

The common mind is in every way misleading;
And so I practice how to animate Awareness.

The Mind-holding Practice[3] is misleading and
    deceptive;
And so I rest in the realm of Reality.

Rechungpa thought to himself: "My Guru is Buddha Himself; there is no illusory idea in his mind. But because of my incapacity for devotion, as well as that of others, he has sung me this song." And Rechungpa sang in answer to explain to his Guru his understanding on the teaching of View, Practice, and Action.

Hearken to me, please, my Father Guru,
My darkened mind is full of ignorance.
Hold me fast with the rope of your compassion.

At the crossroad where Realism and Nihilism meet
I have lost my way in seeking the View of
          Non-Extremes;
So no assurance have I in the knowledge of the Truth.

Drowsy and distracted all the while,
Bliss and Illumination are not yet my lot.
And so I have not conquered all attachment.

I cannot free myself from taking and abandoning,
And needlessly I continue my impulsive acts;
So I have not yet destroyed all delusions.

I was unable to shun all deeds of fraud
And observe the Tantric Precepts without flaw;
So I have yet to conquer all temptations.

The illusory distinction between Saṃsāra
          and Nirvāṇa
I have not realized as the Self-Mind Buddha;
So I have yet to find my way to Dharmakāya!

I was not able to equate hope with fear
And my own face behold;
So I have yet to win the Four Bodies of Buddha.

I have been protected by your compassion in
     the past;
Now, putting my whole being in your hands,
Pray, still grant me more of your blessings.

Thereupon, Milarepa [sent his compassionate grace-wave to bless Rechungpa, and] said to him, pretendingly, "Oh, Rechungpa, you have had more understandings and experiences than those you have just told me. You should not hide anything from me. Be frank and candid." *As Milarepa said this, Rechungpa suddenly became enlightened.* At once he sang "The Seven Discoveries":

Through the grace of my Father Guru, the holy Jetsun,

I now have realized the Truth in Seven Discoveries.

In manifestations have I found the Void;
Now, I have no thought that anything exists.

In the Voidness have I found the Dharmakāya;
Now, I have no thought of action.

In myriad manifestations the Non-Dual have I found;
Now, I have no thought of gathering or dispersing.

In the Elements of Red and White,[4]
Have I found the essence of equality;
Now, I have no thought of accepting or rejecting.

In the Body of Illusion[5] I have found great bliss;
Now, in my mind, there is no suffering.

I have found the Transcendental in the world;
Now, delusion has no hold upon my mind.

In the Self-Mind I have found the Buddha;
Now, in my mind Saṃsāra no more exists.

Milarepa then said to Rechungpa, "Your experience and understanding is close to real Enlightenment, but it is still not quite the same. Real Experience and true understanding should be like this." And he sang "The Eight [Supreme] Realms":

He who sees the world and Voidness as the same,
Has reached the realm of the True View.

He who feels no difference between dream
    and waking,
Has reached the realm of True Practice.

He who feels no difference between Bliss
    and Voidness,
Has reached the realm of True Action.

He who feels no difference between "now"
    and "then,"
Has reached the realm of Reality.

He who sees that Mind and Voidness are the same,
Has reached the realm of Dharmakāya.

He who feels no difference between pain and pleasure,
Has reached the realm of the True Teaching.

He who sees human wishes and Buddha's Wisdom as
        the same,
Has reached the realm of supreme Enlightenment.

He who sees that Self-Mind and Buddha are alike,
Has reached the realm of True Accomplishment.

Thereafter, through the mercy and blessing of his Guru, Rechungpa gradually improved in understanding and Realization. He then composed "The Song of the Six Bardos,"[6] in which he presented to Milarepa his insight and final understanding:

I bow before the holy Gurus.

In the Bardo where the great Void manifests
There is no realisitic or nihilistic view;
I do not share the thoughts of human sectaries.

Beyond all apprehension is Non-existence now;
Of the View this is my firm conviction.

In the Bardo of Voidness and Bliss there is
No object on which the mind can meditate,
And so I have no need to practice concentration.
I rest my mind without distraction in the natural
        state.
This is my understanding of the Practice,
I no longer feel ashamed before enlightened friends.

In the Bardo with lust and without lust
I see no Saṃsāric bliss;
And so, no more a hypocrite, I meet no bad companions.
Whate'er I see before me I take as my companion.
This is my conviction of the Action,
No longer feel I shame before a gathering of great
        yogis.

Between vice and virtue I no more discriminate;
The pure and impure are now to me the same.
Thus, never shall I be untruthful or pretentious.
Now have I wholly mastered the Self-Mind.
This is my understanding of Morality,
No longer feel I shame before the Saints' assembly.

In the [new-found] realm of Samsāra and Nirvāna
Sentient beings and the Buddha are to me the same;
And so I neither hope nor yearn for Buddhahood.
At this moment, all my sufferings have become a
        pleasure.
This is my understanding of Enlightenment,
No longer feel I shame before enlightened beings.

Having freed myself from words and meanings
I speak no more the language of all scholars.
I have no more doubts in my mind.
The universe and all its forms
Now appear but as the Dharmakāya.
This is the conviction I have realized.
No longer feel I shame before a gathering of great
        scholars.

Milarepa was highly delighted, and said, "Rechungpa, this is indeed the real Experience and knowledge. You can truly be called a well-gifted disciple. Now there are three ways in which one may please one's Guru: First, the disciple should employ his faith and intelligence to gratify his Guru; then, through unmistakable learning and contemplation, he should enter the gate of Mahāyāna and Vajrayāna, and practice them diligently with great determination; then finally, he can please his Guru with his real experiences of Enlightenment, which are produced step by step through his devotion. I do not like the disciple who talks much; the actual practice is far more important. Until the full Realization of Truth is gained, he should shut his mouth and work at his meditation. My Guru, Marpa, said to me: 'It does not matter much whether one knows a great deal about Sūtras and Tantras. One should not merely follow the words and books, but should shut his mouth, unmistakably follow his Guru's verbal instructions, and meditate.' Therefore, you should also follow this admonishment, forgetting it not, and putting it into practice. If you can leave all Samsāric affairs behind you, the great merits and accomplishments will all become yours."

Rechungpa replied, "Dear Jetsun, please be kind enough to tell what Marpa said." Milarepa then sang "The Thirty Admonishments of my Guru":

Dear son, these are the words He said to me:

> "Of all refuges, the Buddha's is the best;
> Of all friends, faith is most important;
> Of all evils, Nhamdog is the worst;
> Of all devils, pride;
> Of all vices, slander."

He said:

> "He who does not purify his sins with the Four
>   Powers[7]
> Is bound to wander in Saṃsāra.
> He who with diligence stores not merit,
> Will never gain the bliss of Liberation.
> He who refrains not from committing the Ten Evils,
> Is bound to suffer pains along the Path.
> He who does not meditate on Voidness and
>   Compassion,
> Will never reach the state of Buddhahood."

He said:

> "If in this life you want Buddhahood,
> Observe your mind without diversion
> And practice the Six Yogas,
> The essence and final teaching of all Tantras.
> Practice, too, the Skillful Path of Tantra,
> The essence, the final teaching of the Pith-
>   Instruction.
> If you look for fame, goods, and recognition,
> You throw yourself into the mouth of devils.
> If others you revile, and praise yourself,
> You will fall into the abyss.
> If you tame not your elephantine mind,
> The teachings and Pith-Instruction will be useless.
> The greatest merit is to raise the Heart-for-
>   Bodhi;
> To understand the Non-arising is the highest View.

Profound meditation is the teaching of the
Skillful Path.
The Nāḍī and breathing exercises should be prac-
ticed too."

He said:

"Behold and recognize the face of the Innate-Born!
Put yourself in the hands of holy beings!
Do not dissipate your life by doing worthless
things."

He said:

"Behold and watch your unborn mind,
Look not for pleasures in Saṃsāra,
Think not that all sufferings are ill."

He also said:

"When you realize your mind, you become a Buddha.
It is unnecessary to talk and do a lot!
There is no other teaching more profound than
this.
Follow and practice, then, all these
instructions!"

After hearing this song, Rechungpa, improved greatly in Realization
and Understanding.

. . .   .

Later when Milarepa and his disciples were living ascetically during
their retreat, many Ḍākinīs came and offered them a sacramental
feast. They addressed Milarepa thus: "It is good for you during your
devotions to accept food and clothing from human beings, and also
to receive a little heavenly nourishment from the Ḍākinīs. We will
always bring provisions for you." Milarepa replied, "The possessions,
facilities, and food of the common people can never match the merits
of Enlightenment and the power of Realization. Therefore, worldly
needs are dispensible. Now, hearken to my song":

I bow down to all Gurus.

From the realm of Absolute Reality
I, the Yogi Milarepa, sing this song;
From the realm of Universal Non-existence
I, Milarepa, chant this hymn.
Please listen, Mothers and Ḍākinīs.

The Law of Cause and Effect is e'er supreme —
The convincing Buddhist doctrine.
How can common faiths e'er match it?

Supreme it is to live and meditate alone;
How can trance compare with this?

Samādhi is supreme, free from "this" and "that";
How can common knowledge e'er attain it?

"Essence" is supreme in the state of "After-
    Meditation";
How can common practices ever equal it?

Mindfulness beyond all words also is supreme;
How can common actions e'er attain it?

The unison of Love and Voidness is supreme;
How can common accomplishment e'er reach it?

Supreme, too, is my cotton robe that's never cold;
How can the gaudy clothes of common people match it?

Supreme is my Samādhi that's never hungry;
How can meat and wine compare with it?

This drink of mine comes from the stream of Bodhi;
How can common drinks compare with it?

Within, my heart is brimming with contentment;
How can food and wealth o'ershadow it?

My Guru, the Translator Marpa, is supreme;
How can other yogis equal Him?

Seeing the Buddha-face of the Self-Mind is supreme;

How can the common "patron Buddha" meditation
  match it?

I, the Yogi Milarepa, am supreme;
How can other yogis match me?

My body is immune from pain and illness;
How can drugs or doctors so insure it?

Please listen and give judgement, oh Ḍākinīs,
Where there is no light, I see but brightness;
The light itself is very radiant too.
Where there is no warmth, I feel well-heated;
This single cotton robe has warmth in plenty.
Where'er discomfort is, I rest in ease;
This body of illusion is most comfortable.
Where there is no joy, I feel most joyful;
This life of dreams is itself delightful!
I, the Yogi, feel but happiness and joy!

Is not the Drajadorje Mountain high enough?
If not, why would vultures float above it?

If the cold December wind is not severe enough,
How can it freeze the waterfalls and rivers?

If my cotton clothing is not warmed by Inner-Heat,
How can a single robe shut out the coldness?

If Samādhi food does not sustain me,
How can I e'er endure insatiate hunger?

If there is no Stream-of-Bodhi for my drinking,
How can I live without water and not thirst?

If my Guru's Pith-Instructions are not profound enough,
How can I conquer hindrances and devils?

If a yogi has no Realization and Experience
[To make him confident and full of joy]
How can he ever meditate in solitude?

These accomplishments are gained through the grace
      of my Guru.
Thus should one concentrate on meditation practice.

Having heard this song, the Ḍākinīs exclaimed, "What you have said
is indeed wonderful! Tomorrow, a well-destined disciple will come here.
Please take care of him." With these words, they all disappeared like the
rainbow.

The next day, a few patrons came on a visit from Gu Tang. They
asked Milarepa to preach the Dharma for them. Whereupon, the Jetsun imparted to them the Prayer of Taking Refuge, together with explanations on the benefits of practicing the Dharma. The patrons asked,
"Do you also practice this Prayer of Taking Refuge?" Milarepa replied,
"Yes. This prayer is my sole shelter, and I depend upon it alone in my
devotion and practice. You should also pray earnestly to your Guru and
the Three Precious Ones, not merely by words but by sincerely taking
them as your true Refuge. The benefit of this is very great as I have
told you before. All of you should therefore be very happy and satisfied
with this prayer." Milarepa then sang a song in which he described the
different frames of reference in which the Refuges are set, and urged
them to practice the Dharma.

Obeisance to all Gurus.

The Buddha, the Dharma, and the Saṅgha
Are the three outer Refuges;
Even I take them as my shelter.
By putting all my trust in them,
I have gained joy and satisfaction.
Fortune will come, if in them you take your refuge.

The Guru, the Patron Buddha, and the Ḍākinīs
Are the three inner Refuges.
Even I take them as my shelter.
By putting all my trust in them,
I have gained joy and satisfaction.
Fortune will come, if in them you take your refuge.

The Nāḍīs, Prāṇa, and Bindu are the three secret
      Refuges;
Even I take them as my shelter.
By putting all my trust in them,
I have gained joy and satisfaction.

Fortune will come, if in them you take your refuge.

Form, Voidness, and Non-distinction
Are the three real Refuges;
By putting all my trust in them,
I have gained joy and satisfaction.
Fortune will come, if in them you take your refuge.

If you look not to the Refuges,
Who will protect you from eternal suffering?

Day and night the rotting house of your body
Is invaded by the [Four] Elements.
Through months and years,
Rain brings it to dissolution.

To the dying these eroding drops
Bring neither joy nor pleasure.

'Tis like the shadow of the setting sun;
You may try to fly away from it
But never can you escape.

Observation of death is a Buddhist's "teacher,"
From whom one learns to practice worthy deeds.
One should always think, and remember,
That joy is absent at the time of dying.

If a sinner sees the nature of death,
He learns a good lesson of truth.
He will then ponder on the thought,
"How regretful I will be when that moment comes!"

If a man of wealth sees death around him,
He has learned a good lesson of truth —
That goods and money are his great foes.
Let him then ponder on the thought,
"I should try always to be generous!"

If an old man feels that death is near him,
He has learned a good lesson of truth —
That life is short and transient.
Let him then ponder on the thought,

"Life is, after all, a sad dream."

If a young man sees death around him,
He has learned a good lesson of truth —
That life is short and fades soon to oblivion.
Let him then practice his devotions!

Our parents bear the burdens of our worries,
But orphans must endure them by themselves.

A smooth, fine leather coat is indeed a comfort —
But, beyond imagination, for him who never wore one.

Crops on the farm are the cure for poverty,
But those who do not work can ne'er enjoy them.

[A couplet is omitted here as the text is corrupt. Tr.]

He who practices the Dharma will be joyful;
But those who practice not, can never share it.

Give more away in gifts, and you will ne'er be hungry.
If you want to conquer drowsiness and sleep,
Practice more good deeds.[8]

Remembering the miseries of the lower Realms
Helps one and all to practice Buddhism.

After hearing this song, many patrons became devoted Buddhists.
Among the group, there was one young man who had confirmed within
him an immutable faith towards Milarepa. He asked permission to follow him in order to give him service. Milarepa thought, "This is the
man whom the Ḍākinīs predicted. I should take him as my disciple."
And he imparted the Initiation and instructions to him. After practicing these teachings, the young man attained Accomplishment and
Liberation. He was known as Ron Chon Repa, one of the close sons
of Milarepa.

This is the story of Milarepa meeting Ron Chon Repa on his later
trip to Drajadorje Tson.

NOTES

1 Yoga of No-returning (T.T.: Phyir.Mi.lDog.Pahi.rNal.hByor.): implying an advanced stage on the Path. When a yogi reaches it he will never regress in his spiritual development or fall back again into Saṃsāra.

2 The Expedient Truth, or the Expedient Teachings: There are two very important terms in Mahāyāna Buddhism which explicitly reflect the Mahāyāna Buddhist view and its evaluation into the various conflicting doctrines as upheld by different Schools of Buddhism, and by other religions. One is known as the "Expedient Teaching" (T.T.: Draṅ.Don.), and the other, as the "Ultimate," or "Final Teaching" (T.T.: Ñes.Don.). The "Expedient Teachings" are those doctrines arranged and preached for the unevolved or not-yet-ripened devotees who are not ready to receive the higher form of teaching. The "Final Teachings" are those which may be described as supreme and ultimate.

The myriads of Buddhas see only one final Reality in the realm of Supreme Enlightenment. However, to enable all sentient beings to realize this Reality, various approaches, teachings, or steps appropriate to different groups and individuals are necessary because all sentient beings do not share the same dispositions, capacities, and Karmas. A teaching that is beneficial to one group or to one individual may not be helpful to another; hence, a variety of approaches is needed to ripen these innumerable types of people. For the Hīnayāna-bent, Hīnayāna Buddhism is taught; for the Mahāyāna-bent, Mahāyāna Buddhism. This approach is also true for Christians, Hindus, and other religionists — an appropriate teaching, even in the guise of a different faith, is wisely given to all and sundry who may require it.

Because of this all-embracing attitude, Mahāyāna Buddhism is impregnated with an extremely inclusive and tolerant spirit, which has been unmistakably demonstrated throughout Buddhist history. This recognition of the value and usefulness of all religions is typically reflected in the popular Buddhist proverb, "Since sentient beings suffer many different sicknesses, Buddha, the King of Physicians, has to prescribe for them various treatments and medicines; hence all the teachings of the different Schools and religions are merely the differing remedies prescribed by Him for the benefit of each case."

Although the Expedient Teachings are necessary for those who have not evolved to a level advanced enough to accept the highest teachings (the Final Truth), they do lay a foundation for approaching it; without these Expedient Teachings, it would not be possible for many who, for the time being, do not yet possess the capacity, to appreciate and practice the higher teachings.

3 Mind-holding Practice: Most of the meditation practices are devised for the development of mental concentration, i.e., to hold onto an object in one's mind's-eye. In other words, a mental effort is required in all of them. But the meditation of Mahāmudrā is of a quite different nature. It is effortless and natural; in its practice no object whatsoever is held in the yogi's mind. In comparison with the teaching of Mahāmudrā, all others are temporal and expedient.

4 The White Element is the positive, and the Red Element the negative force of the body.

5 Body of Illusion: Any body possessing form and attributes is illusory; this applies to both Saṃsāric and Nirvāṇic bodies, including the Reward Body and Transformation Body of Buddha.

6 Bardo here does not mean the state after death, it means "in-between" states of all kinds.

7 The Four Powers through which one's sins can be purified are:

(1) The Power of sincere repentance.

(2) The Power of determination not to commit the same sin again.

(3) The Power of undertaking good deeds to compensate for the wrong deeds previously committed.

(4) The Power of contemplating on the void nature of being.

8 To lessen one's drowsiness by practicing good deeds: Some people constantly feel drowsy while they are practicing meditation. As soon as they cease meditating, drowsiness disappears. If all methods of curing drowsiness are tried without success, it is due, according to many Gurus, to sins committed in the past. The remedy for this is to practice confession-prayers and perform diligently various meritorious deeds.

24

THE CONVERSION OF
A DYING BONIST

Obeisance to all Gurus

E ARLY one morning on the eighth day of a lunar month, when Jetsun Milarepa was meditating at Drajadorje Tson and observing
silence, a number of Ḍākinīs dressed as earthly ladies came to him
and prophesied:

> Oh, silent yogi with great power of will
> Who practices austerity,
> The sole lion in the midst of all this snow,
> Who sees, alone, Saṃsāra in Nirvāṇa,
> Listen to us — the four Ḍākinī sisters
> Who come to prophesy.
>
> Tomorrow, in the early morning,
> Go to the eastern shore of Baltang Lake,
> Where people sin and sport in wanton pleasures.
> You, the Lion of the snow mountain,
> Should help them back into the path of virtue,
> Guiding those who have lost their way to the
>   right Path.

After conveying this message to the Jetsun, the Ḍākinīs vanished.

Accordingly the next day Milarepa journeyed eastward. On the way,
he met a shepherd. When the shepherd saw him walking above the
ground — his feet never touching the earth — an unshakable faith toward Milarepa arose within him. He offered the Jetsun his own food,
and asked for the teachings of Dharma. Whereupon Milarepa preached

241

on the Law of Kharma; on the errors of Saṃsāra; on the difficulties of obtaining favorable human birth, body, and environment; and lastly, on the unpredictableness and inevitability of death. Convinced by these teachings, the shepherd said, "Dear Lama, your preaching has been a reminder of the great sufferings of Saṃsāra. On thinking it over, [I find] I have no more desire for any gain or loss, happiness or misery in this life. The sufferings which you have mentioned, distress me so much that I feel I cannot bear them any longer. Please give me some instruction that can help me." "Very well," said Milarepa, "I shall teach you." The shepherd then confided to him, "I — and I alone — know of a secret cave called Mamo Tson. Please, let us go there."

When they arrived at the cave, the shepherd offered food and gave service to the Jetsun, and then asked for the teachings that would release him from Saṃsāric suffering. Milarepa then taught him how to meditate. [Not long after], the shepherd confided, "When I am concentrating, I feel very peaceful and there is no suffering whatsoever. But when my mind begins to wander, pictures of the miseries in Saṃsāra all appear before me; I can hardly bear the distressing experience of seeing them. With your great compassion, please bring me to the state of eternal happiness." Milarepa replied, "If you want to be always happy, you must ever avoid sinful deeds and follow my example by practicing all the virtues." The shepherd answered, "I am willing to do so for the sake of attaining the longed for perpetual happiness. I would like to become your servant. Please take me with you."

Milarepa recognized that this shepherd was a destined disciple, so he took him in and granted him the Initiation and Pith-Instructions. Later on, the shepherd was known as Tsiwo Repa, the most oustanding student among those "Disciples-with-Realization."

On the morning of the day that the Jetsun met Tsiwo Repa, the Ḍākinīs said to him, "There is a place called Lapu; you should go there." And so Milarepa went to Lapu where lived a very rich old man, a pious follower of Bon, who had many sons. Recently he had contracted a very serious disease. On the day of Milarepa's visit, one of this man's sons had just returned home from consulting a diviner, who had said that the remedy was to kill one hundred yaks, one hundred goats, and one hundred sheep, and with the meat to hold a great festival and sacrifice for the Bon monks. Following this instruction, the rich man's sons had made all the arrangements for the feast and were just about to slaughter the animals when the Jetsun arrived.

Milarepa, on first reaching Lapu, had met a girl on her way to fetch water and had asked alms from her. She informed him of the great Bon festival to be held for the sick rich man, saying that she was sure he would find alms if he went there. As Milarepa approached the rich man's house he saw all kinds of people entering it. It seemed that anyone could walk in, even the dogs. Nevertheless, the hosts said, "Dear Lama, our father is very sick. Please leave us." Milarepa replied, "All I want is something to eat. Please give me food." The sons then prepared a little food for him, and were about to send him away, when the sick man's relatives and doctors began to gather round to observe his illness. Milarepa went to them asking for charity.

When the rich man beheld Milarepa's face, a great faith arose in him, and somehow a change took place in his mind. He clutched Milarepa's robe and besought him, saying, "Dear Lama, I am a [living] man for only today or tomorrow. Look on me with your compassion!" Thus he implored, while tears streamed down his face. Milarepa said, "It is a good omen that you have such faith in me. If I cure your illness, will you renounce the world and practice Dharma?" The rich man replied, "If I'm relieved of this illness, I shall do whatever you say. Not only will I practice Dharma, but I will also cause my sons to become Buddhists." The Jetsun thought to himself, "The Ḍākinīs prophesied that I should convert certain evil and pleasure-loving men and thus accomplish benevolent deeds and give blessings to all. This must be the opportunity [they] meant, so I shall act accordingly." Whereupon he said to the rich man, "You may slaughter all the yaks and goats you wish, but that will not cure your illness. In fact, it will only make your situation worse. Rather, you should set all those cattle free. On the other hand, I know a method that will definitely cure you; but first — what religion do you profess?" The sick man answered, "While I do not disbelieve in Buddhism, I have always loved and placed my faith in Bon." "In that case," said Milarepa, "You should now dismiss all these Bon monks and doctors. I will perform a 'Bon' ceremony for you which will certainly help your recovery." To which the eldest son of the rich man added, "I propose that both the Bon monks and this Lama perform their ceremonies together. Cannot this be done?" "Your suggestion is apt," the Jetsun replied, "but there are already too many doctors and too much hocus-pocus here. All this does not help. It would be better to dismiss them all." The sick man supported him by adding, "We should do what the Lama says." Accordingly, both the ritualists and the physicians were dismissed. Learning of this, the people began to murmur, "Are not the ceremony-makers and doctors capable? Surely, this foreign yogi can neither diagnose nor help. The sick man will probably die soon." After voicing such thoughts, they became all the more worried and distressed.

The sick man asked Milarepa, "What animal, then, should we slaughter for an offering?" The Jetsun said, "In the performance of my ceremony, no sacrifice is necessary. I have a 'Bon'[1] prayer of my own. Listen attentively!" Thereupon, Milarepa, chanting a Bon melody after the Bon manner, sang for the sick man "The Parable of the Twenty-two Family Members":

"Sou, yon yon, yon, yon, yon yon ngo . . . . ."[2]
In the beginning of time, arose a manifestation.
At that moment, as the first of all happenings,
The outer objects appeared as something with
      attributes.

The assembling of elements, the Aggregations,
[Formed] the great city, the Three Realms of Saṃsāra
The inner mind, which discerns, was comprehended
      as one with qualities;
In the Illuminating-Void Awareness,
Thereby sprang up a myriad ideas and perceptions.
This is the source of all Karma and Kleśas!

All dwellings in this distressed world are illusory,
For they are built upon forms of delusion.
Because of clinging to the god and father image,
One fashions his active mind as the ego.
Because of clinging to the mother and goddess image,
One's mind pursues a myriad things.

When the mother and father united,
Then were born the twelve Nidāna sons[3]
And the eight Consciousness daughters.
These brothers and sisters, with their parents,
Totaled twenty-two.

From the arising of this family
Came the four-and-eighty thousand Kleśas
And the three hundred and sixty Distractions.
Thus arose the eighty thousand Evils and Hindrances,
 And the four hundred and four kinds of disease.

This is the first chapter of my song,
The Chapter of the Members of the Family.

All the two-and-twenty members are beset with illness,
They are wrapped in the sickness of a blinded mind
And they suffer from a myriad afflictions.

Fever inflames their upper parts,
The fire of anger ever burns within them,
While like yaks distraught they deeply groan.
Chills plague their lower parts
And churning pools of lust
Drive them to lechery.

Skran-blindness⁴ afflicts their middle parts;
The dropsy of ego-clinging swells and distends them.
Troubled are they by sub-Prāṇa sickness
And choked by swollen pride;
Diseased in heart,
They denounce others while they praise themselves.
They make their bed among the Five Poisonous
    [Desires].

Surrendering their minds
To the nonsense of "this" and "that,"
They lose all appetite for being virtuous.
For the waters of sin they thirst
And vomit virtue's medicine.

To the Ten Directions they spit the saliva of
    worthless talk;
They take the Eight Worldly Claims for clothing,
Relatives of the Ten Evils surround their beds.
Minds clouded, they wander in the realms
Of distraction, longing for food and wealth.
Dark and hopeless are these diseases.

This is the second chapter of my song,
The Chapter Describing Sicknesses.

For diseases such as these what is the cure?
"Bon" will help, and divination too;
Thus, I, the Yogi, will divine for you.

A messenger, the transiency of all lives,
Was sent to ask a divination.
An expert diviner was then called,
And a cushion of faith unshakable provided.
The beverage of trust was mixed
And a barley-heap for augury arranged

In veneration of the Dharma.
The question, the inquiry into the profound teaching
      of Dharma,
Was presented to the soothsayer.

The augur, a proficient Guru, charts
A horoscope of the Four Elements.
He counts the rounds of years, the Twelve Nidānas,
And also numbers the Eight Trigrams — or
      Consciousnesses.
The diagrams of the Nine Vehicles[5] are drawn.
A prediction of good or evil is thus made.

This is the third chapter of my song,
The Chapter of Divining by the Stars.

Reading the chart, the soothsayer prophesies:
For these two-and-twenty people,
The omen is bad indeed.
From the time of no-beginning,
On the foundation of Saṃsāra and Nirvāṇa
Was set up a stove of mental blindness.

The host, pure manifestation, was singed by words.
The burners, hate and lust, left behind a burning-spot.
Because of stove, fire, and burning-spot,
The Wisdom-Father god left the house and went to
      Heaven;
The local god of the Great Bliss withdrew and
      disappeared;
The conquering god of Self-Awareness also went away.

Because these three great gods withdrew,
The demons could send forth afflictions.
Hence arose the Eight Dharmas of the world,
And the pain of life came into being in Saṃsāra.
Burning anger — the most dreadful demon;
Stirring lust — that pernicious demoness;
Blind ignorance — the fierce dragon demon;
Stinging jealousy — the demon called Tsan Rigs;[6]
Egotism and prejudice — another, named Rtor Legs,[7]
Self-praise and self-inflation — the demon styled
      Mamo;[8]

Evil deeds and habitual-thinking — the dread demon
    called Shen Dre[9] —
My host, these are the demons which afflict you.

According to the divination,
Your life is in great danger,
For whoe'er is born, will die.
According to the divination,
Your family affairs are not auspicious;
At the end of a gathering there must be departure.
According to the divination,
Your monetary affairs do not prosper,
For the end of gain is loss.
According to the divination,
Your dealings with your foes are not lucky,
For no longer can you take the upper hand.
To reverse these evil omens,
Let us hold a "Bon" service.

This is the fourth chapter of my song,
The Ominous Divination of your Life.

Now I, the Yogi, will chant a "Bon" prayer for you.
"Bon," in its deeper teaching, says:
"In the morning of the first day was laid
The foundation of Heaven's Tripiṭaka;[10]
The ransom was given of hearing, practice, and
    contemplation."
The sacramental offerings of pure precept are now
    prepared,
And the hymns of the four Tantras now are chanted.
The initiatory gift which frees from craving is
    presented.

For the disappearance of the Father into Heaven,
The recognition of basic blindness
Is the remedy I offer.
For the withdrawal of the local gods of the Great
    Bliss,
Victory over the Four Demons is the remedy I offer.
For the absence of the conquering god of Self-
    Awareness,
The ransom of Self-Renunciation is my offer.

The evil thoughts of the Eight Worldly Affairs,
I amputate with the Awareness-knife that is free
        from craving.
To cure the lives of pain in this distressing world,
I offer the balm of Universal Bliss.
The fire-like, angry demon
I poison with the Wisdom of the Void;
The lust-stirring demoness
I conquer with Mind-Essence.

To quell the dragon demon of blind ignorance,
I summon the eight dragons, Self-liberating Forms.
To the king of demons, suffocating pride,
I give the hart's horn of the Wisdom of the Void.
To conquer the Tsan demon, stinging jealousy,
I raise the arrow-scarf, the Wisdom of Accomplishment.
To the bragging, self-praising demon called Mamo,
I recite the prayer of the Non-existence-of-Self-and-
        Others.
To cleanse clinging to self and egotisms,
I make altruistic offerings.
To nullify the evil of habitual-thinking, the
        Shen Dre demon,
I perform the conquering demon dance, the Voidness
        of Mental Functions.

If there be harmful demons,
These remedies will dispel them.
If there be ghosts of prosperity,
These acts will capture them.
If you make sacramental offerings,
Do so in this way.

Mind-Nature has nor birth nor death;
Through this "Bon" understanding
Threats to life are overcome.

The companion of Self-Manifestation
Gathers not nor separates,
But overcomes all threats of family strife.

Transcendental property cannot be exhausted;
By knowing this is the fear of poverty dispelled.

Through the teaching of this "Bon" doctrine,
Ill omens and divination are reversed.
If one understands [the Dharma] truly,
Even the sufferings he undergoes
Will appear to him as Divine Instructions.
Through this "Bon" teaching,
All evil encounters are transformed.

This is the fifth chapter of my song,
The Chapter of Subduing Devil-demons.

Oh, family of two-and-twenty members!
The ill of your mind-blindness has been cured,
The painful groaning of self-clinging ended.
Oh sick man! Upon your face appears
A fair complexion — the Illuminating-Void;
Food and drink — the illuminating and blissful Samādhi —
Become delicious and appetizing to you!

The sick man is now grateful for his cure;
With heartfelt sincerity, he renders thanks
And makes propitiation.
He sends his son, Self-Awareness,
To the mountain of the Great Perfection.[11]
The shepherd boy, Constant-Mindfulness,
Then takes a yak — the Nine Successive Vehicles,
A sheep — the Four Tantras, and a goat — the Three
     Canons.

Thence, upon the plain of Universal Equality
Guests are summoned to a feast of Myriad Wisdoms.
The oblation with butter is anointed,
Together with the food of Sūnyatā.
The arrow-scarf of Learning and Contemplation is
     spread out.
Appreciation is expressed to all the company.

Before the Guru, the soothsayer of skill,
Is hung the human skull of Faith, Veneration, and
     Sincerity,
For, with the holy teaching of "Bon" he rides
The horse of Skillful-Wisdom.
To the all-perfect "Bon" Body

He offers a yak of the Nine Successive Vehicles.
To the conquering gods, the Five Nirmāṇakāyas,
He offers a sheep of the Four Tantras.
To the Life-god, the Transformation Body of Tathāgata,
He offers a Tripiṭaka goat.
To the Goddess of Medicine who cures all diseases,
He offers a sacrificial meal of the Four Immeasurables.[12]
Such are the sacrifices and propitiations.

This is the sixth chapter of my song,
The Chapter of Propitiation and Sacrificial Offering.

In the wide courtyard of the "Bon,"
Are tethered yak and sheep and goat.
The butcher, All-Knowing Wisdom,
Sharpens the sword of Knowledge
And opens the life hole of Two Preparations.[13]
The butcher then severs the liferoot [spine] of
        the Two Hindrances[14]
And flays the skin of all-disturbing thoughts.
Understanding the meaning of the Sūtras and Tantras,
The butcher, knowingly, cleaves the limbs.
Relying on the holy sayings and sound judgment,
He divides the various parts
With the cleaver of the Pith-Instructions,
Chopping into pieces all the flesh.
The various portions of the meat, the "Bon" form,
Are piled into a cauldron, the "Bon" essence.
The three firestones of Primordial Trikāya are laid,
And the fire of Four Infinites is lit.
He boils well the meat 'til it is sweet and tender —
The consummation of Experience and Enlightenment.
Then he takes out the meat, the unison of Meditation
        and Activity.

In the great mansion of "Bon" essence,
In the illusory city of Six Realms,
To the feast throng crowds of guests.

The banquet is arranged by skillful hands —
Those of the Five Great Wisdoms.
The food and drinks — many yet one —
Are offered to all guests without discrimination.

To the wise Succession Gurus who have the power to
    bless,
The upper-body is offered in complete perfection.

To the Guru who illustrates the holy words and
    Pith-Instructions,
The liferoot [spine] of Bodhi, the Skillful Path,
    is served.

To the Guru who frees all beings from Saṃsāra
The pure eyeballs are given.

To the Guru who knows the words and meanings
    [of the Buddhist teaching],
The tongue that tastes all flavors then is given.

To the virtuous, precept-observing monks,
Are served the pleasant parts, pure and pacified.

To the men of "Bon" who know the Law of Karma,
Are given the meat and wine of "benevolent deeds."

To the yogi who knows the truth of Non-existence,
The fat of the Great Bliss is presented.

To the firm protector of the Buddhist doctrine,
Is given the gullet which brings benefits to all.

To the meditator of the Skillful Tantric Path,
The upper breast of greatest rapture is presented.

To the great yogi who meditates on the transiency
    of being,
The lower breast of the Skillful Bodhi-Path, is
    served.

To the yogi without sectarian ideas,
Is offered the castrated ram of all delight.

To the yogi with compassion that embraces all,
The knuckles and joints of the Four Infinities are
    given.

To the man who is disgusted with this world,
Is presented the breastbone, free from acts and craving.

To the one who practices the main teaching of "Bon,"
The four limbs, indispensible to life, are served.

To the physician, the nourishing Bodhi-Mind,
The backbone of this life and that beyond, is offered.

To all followers who are faithful and sincere
The heart, the essence of instruction, is presented.

To the steadfast one who ne'er forsakes the Path of
     Virtue,
Is given the liver — Cause-and-Effect that never fails.

To the industrious follower, are presented
The kidneys, Skill and Wisdom.

To beginners in the Dharma are presented
The feet, the well-designed Expedient Truths.

To the yogi, who always heeds his meditation practice,
Is given the herdsman's meat, the essential
     Pith-Instruction.

This is the seventh chapter of my song,
The Chapter that invites Superior Beings to a Feast.

Such was the feast that Milarepa served,
And then, the worthy guests went home.

                . . .   .

Though the universal foundation [Alaya] of all men
     is one,
Their conduct and dispositions vary greatly.
Therefore, to arrogant and pretentious monks,
Is given the penis that e'er clings to form.

To the teacher who follows nought but words,
The skinless and decayed part of the legs is served.

To proud, pompous, and evil priests
The meatless nape is offered.

To proud black magicians, who practice sorcery,
The neck grease, maker of black-bitterness, is given.

To bigoted and sectarian monks
Is given the spinal marrow of disputation.

To greedy and contemptible solicitors,
The barren nose-tip of vanity is given.

To the yogi who strolls about the village,
The rumor-hungry ears are presented.

To disciples of small faith but with gross heresies,
The ill-rewarding spleen is served.

To the person who upsets and subverts the Brotherhood,
The bitter gall is given.

To the "grand" teachers, who have not realized
    Mind-Essence,
The midriff, the ostentatious but vain Maṇḍala, is
    offered.

To the yogi whose meditation practice is merely of
    the mouth,
The lung, so tasteless yet so large in size, is
    served.

To the yogi who knows little but boasts much,
The skin of the stomach is presented.

To town-dwellers, "Bon" monks who eat up life,
The gullet, which fosters lust and hate, is given.

To fraudulent forecasters who throw lots,
The water-holding bladders are presented.

To the presumptuous man who claims there is no Karma,
Is served the tail, symbol of erroneous views.

To those who lack both modesty and scruple
Is served the anus, which ruins them and others.

To yogis, who cling to mind in meditation,
The brain, the source of blindness and folly, is
     offered.

To charlatans who claim that they have special
     teachings,
Are served the intestines, rounded like Saṃsāra.

To those who lust and crave, is given
The goiter, with which all are sore afflicted.

To those indifferent to the truth of Voidness
The cartilage,[15] which is neither meat nor fat, is
     served.

To people with small merit but great ambition
The tasteless and useless throat is given.

To persons who know little but want to
     teach
Are served the entrails from the lower parts.

To foolish yogis who blindly dwell in caves,
Tripe, smooth outside but coarse within, is given.

To him whose chief desire is to gather riches,
Is served the lower portion of the gullet.

To mean and brawling women
The head, with all its holes, is given.

To mean but wealthy men,
The round and storing belly is presented.

To people who see nothing but this life,
The testicles are served, fair on the surface but
     all foul within.

To the patron with sweet words but sullied heart,
The worthless, black intestines are presented.

To women who confuse themselves while still
    reviling others,
The teeth, of stony hardness, are served up.

To parents who at home have many mouths to feed,
Skin, both tough and meatless, is presented.

To the person who has nothing whatsoever,
But toils and struggles for his family,
The useless bowels are given.

Incapable disciples who rebel
Are served with thin and meatless soup.

To those who e'er postpone their Dharma practice,
Are given the remnants, symbol of their laziness.

To the countless sentient beings in the plane of
    Bardo
Are thrown the final scraps of meat.

The Four Initiations[16] of self-liberation from the
    Five Gates[17]
Are given by the butcher of All-Knowing Wisdom;
And with the jug of Wisdom that is immutable,
Sweet wine is offered to all guests without
    discrimination.

I, the rich man, have now prepared a feast for you,
So eat and drink, dear guests, just as you please.

This is the eighth chapter of my song,
The Chapter of Dining at the Feast with Guests.

      . . .   .

Now is the time to speak a few propitious words;
Words, surely to be heard by all the Buddhas.
The Precious Ones do not appear on earth but stay
    in Dharmadhātu,
While my Guru adorns me by sitting on my head
And my brothers in the Dharma sit in rows [before me].

The first thing one should remember is the
    transiency of life;
Then he should read the lives of holy Saints.
Next, he should study the simple or comprehensive
    Sūtras,
Choosing them to meet his own requirements.
Then he should contemplate on the Instructions.

If in this song I have hidden anything from you,
If my preaching has been unsound or incomplete,
If I have transgressed or misrepresented anything,
I beg forgiveness from the Holy Ones.

[Milarepa then continued]:

Now, it is time for me, your host, to sing a
    song of pride.

At first, when I had contracted this disease,
I sent for a diviner, a yogi of devotion.
As he revealed the divination,
Unsparingly I offered the sacrificial ransom.

When he performed the ritual of offering,
    I realized
He was indeed a free-handed yogi
For his riches were truly inexhaustible.
Then he served the feast and entertained
His guests with all propriety.
I became aware he was an experienced yogi;
When he spoke, after the dinner,
He proved that he could teach us all.

When the feast was over, he gracefully gave thanks.
Lastly, he wished for final liberation of all men.
Oh, who is this "Bon"? Of whose "Bon" is he?
He is the "Bon" whose family numbers two-and-twenty,
He calms the fears of those who are besieged,
He is the "Bon" who removes malignant pressures.

This is my little after-dinner song.
Oh guests, drink ye and be drunk with the wine
    of Reality!

In a happy mood, let us sing and sport and play!

It is happy to be blessed, and a joy to meditate!
Cheerful, cheerful, are these after-dinner words.
May all rejoice, be gay and full of mirth.
Happy it is to vomit when drunk with devotion,
Happy to shout and cry under the blessing.
Ever, then, be joyful under the grace of your Gurus!

This is the ninth chapter of my song,
The Chapter of the Sermon After Feasting.

So Milarepa sang, mimicking the Bon way of chanting. Hearing it, the sick man was blessed and cured. Sons, daughters, servants, and friends, including some learned Lamas, were so delighted that one could hardly describe their joy. The villagers declared, "It is indeed miraculous to revive a dying man. The blessing of Dharma is surely greater than that of the Bons!" An unalterable faith in the Jetsun arose in them all. The rich man then addressed the Jetsun, saying, "Dear Lama, your preachings were all Buddhist; they were not of Bon. I have always been a follower of Bon and believed its teachings, but now I will become a Buddhist and put my whole faith in Buddhism — I, and my sons, and all my family and household." The Jetsun gave assent, and thus the whole family, including the father with his eight sons, became Buddhists.

Among the sons was one who had been an expert in Bon, which he had mastered to a perfect degree and in which he thoroughly believed. But after his father's cure, an immutable faith toward the Jetsun and Dharma awoke in him. He said to Milarepa, "Outwardly, the practice and words used by Bon and Dharma appear alike, but the compassion and grace are different and so are the achievements. Bon practices are greedy and covetous. In whatever ceremony is held, at least one living being will be slaughtered as an offering. The gods we worship are all worldly. When a follower is about to die, he has no real assurance within himself. His heart is filled with fear and confusion. From now on, I will renounce Bon and become a Buddhist. Please accept me as your servant-disciple and allow me to go with you." It occurred to Milarepa that this man was a well-destined person. He, therefore, took him for a disciple and granted him the Initiations and Pith-Instructions. Eventually, this young man attained Liberation and all the Accomplishments. He became known as Shen Gom Repa, one of the close disciples of Milarepa. His father and his brothers all gave their best service and offerings to the Jetsun while he dwelt at Langgo Ludu Tson, Bepu Mamo Tson, and Barkon Gi Tson. They entered the Gate of Liberation and followed the

Path of the All-Knowing Ones, thus preventing themselves from falling into the miserable realms of Saṃsāra.

This is the story of Milarepa meeting Tsiwo Repa, the outstanding enlightened Yogi, and Shen Gom Repa, the close son-disciple of Milarepa, at Bepu Mamo Tson and Lapu Paima Tson.

NOTES

1 Milarepa did not, of course, perform a Bon ritual; he merely mimicked the Bon cult in fun.

2 This is the first line of a chant in which the Bon monks intone their hymns. Milarepa derisively mimicked the Bon way of singing in this song.

3 The Twelve Nidānas: The general twelve successive stages that characterize Saṃsāric becomings are: (1) ignorance, (2) action, (3) consciousness, (4) name and form, (5) the six sense organs, (6) contact, (7) sensation, (8) craving, (9) grasping, (10) existing, (11) birth, (12) old age and death.

4 The name of a disease.

5 The Nine Vehicles (T.T.: Theg.Pa.Rim.Pa.dGu.): The Ningmaba (T.T.: rÑiñ.Ma.Pa.) School of Tibetan Buddhism classifies all Buddhist doctrines into nine different approaches or Vehicles. They are : (1) the Sravākayāna, (2) the Pratyekayāna, (3) the Bodhisattvayāna, (4) the Kriyātantra, (5) the Caryātantra, (6) the Yogatantra, (7) the Mahāyoga, (8) the Anuyoga, and (9) the Ādiyoga. The first three belong to the exoteric (Sūtra) doctrine, and the last six to the esoteric (Tantric) doctrine. (The 7th, 8th, and 9th are subdivisions of the Anuttara Tantra.) The new schools of Tibetan Buddhism, i.e., Ghagyuba, Sajyaba, and Geluba do not follow these classifications. It is interesting to note that Milarepa, a founder and follower of Ghagyuba tradition, used the Ningmaba terminology on this occasion.

6, 7, 8, 9 The four main types of demons found in Tibetan legends.

10 Tripiṭaka: the Buddhist Canon, which consists of three main bodies: Sūtra, Sāstra, and Vināya.

11 Great Perfection (T.T.: rDsogs.Pa.Chin.Po.): the Ningmaba version of the teaching of Mahāmudrā.

12 The Four Immeasurables, or the Four Infinite Thoughts: friendliness, compassion, sympathetic joy, and evenmindedness.

13 Two Preparations (T.T.: Tsogs.Lam.gÑis.): This refers to the preliminary and advanced stages of preparation in the Bodhisattva's spiritual development.

14 The Two Hindrances: the Hindrance of Passions and the Hindrance of Knowledge. Perfect Buddhahood is achieved through the complete annihilation of these two hindrances.

15 T.T.: Krab-Krab, a term probably denoting cartilage.

16 The Four Initiations: See Story 1, Note 7, and Story 17, Note 37.

17 The Five Gates: the five senses and sense organs.

ༀ༅༎

25

CHALLENGE FROM
A CLEVER MAIDEN

Obeisance to all Gurus

WHEN Milarepa and his heart-son-disciple Rechungpa were begging
alms and helping sentient beings at the place of the Five Small
Lakes in the Dritsam region, their reputation ran high. People said,
"Look! The Jetsun Milarepa and his son Rechungpa are now meditating
at Di Se Snow Mountain and Ma Päm Lake!" Influenced by their great
fame, all the people of Joro Dritsam were convinced that Milarepa and
Rechungpa were truly marvelous and unusual yogis. As their respect
and admiration grew, they said, "Let us go to visit these two acom-
plished yogis!"

So one day, a number of patrons came to see the Jetsun, and brought
with them provisions and oblations. Among them was a young girl called
Rechungma, who was intelligent, compassionate, and had great faith in
the Dharma. Actually, she was a Ḍākinī who had incarnated in human
form. Having heard the life-story of Milarepa, the faith of this well-gifted
girl was confirmed, and she came today with four young girl friends to
visit him. But in order to test, and thus verify the reputation of the Jetsun and his son, she and her friends challenged Milarepa by singing this
song:

> We take refuge in the Three Precious Ones;
> Pray, bless us with your great compassion.
>
> Oh, you two exalted Repa Yogis,
> You have a great reputation from afar!
> Oh, ye faithful here assembled,
> Please be silent now and listen to our song.
>
> We five young girls from good families,

259

Now sing for you our offering;
Please judge our words and ponder on our parables.
For you two Repas, this our song is sung!

The fame of Di Se Snow Mountain is great
When one sees it not, but hears much of it.
People say, "Look, the snow of Di Se
Is like a crystal stūpa."
But when one comes near and sees it clearly,
Nothing great or wonderful is found.

The top of Di Se is wrapped in drifts
Of snow, its body is snow-clad.
In this we see nothing great or wonderful,
Except that these mountains round about
Are rather nice and charming.

The fame of Lake Ma Päm is great
When one sees it not, but hears much of it.
People say, "Look! Lake Ma Päm
Is like a Maṇḍala of greenish gems!"
But when one nears it and sees it clearly,
Nothing great or wonderful can be seen.

'Tis but a lake filled by the rain,
A place where water trickles.
Encircling it are rocks and meadows.
In this we see nothing great or wonderful.

Great is the fame of the height of Red-Rock
When one hears about it from far away.
People say, "This rock is like a precious jewel!"
But when one comes near and sees it clearly,
It is but a great stone jutting out.

Upon it bushes and trees are growing,
And round it brooks and small streams flow;
In it there is nothing great or wonderful.

You, the elder and the younger Repa,
Have a fame that spreads to far-off places;
From far away we have heard much of you.
People say, "They are indeed accomplished beings!"

But when one comes near and scans you closely,
One sees an old man and a callow youth
Who chant, and hum, and sing together,
Exhibiting their bodies, nude and shameless.

He sees two common people wearing cotton,
Two beggars who eat the food of alms;
He sees two unscrupulous rascals
Who roam unrestrained at large.

There is nothing wonderful or good about you;
There is nothing great that we can find.

To us sisters who have wandered everywhere,
Our morning's pilgrimage has wasted time.
To us sisters who have traveled the world over,
Our morning's journey is meaningless;
The trip was never worth sore feet.

To us sisters who in this world have seen everything,
To see an old and young man like you two, is a
           waste of time.
To us sisters who have heard all things in this world,
The claims of your good name are but empty clamor.
You two, either a pair of Buddhist puppets,
Or devil-possessed agents,
Will cause but evil hindrances.

If you understand what we are singing,
You may answer us with verses.
If you cannot understand, you may
Get up and go, for we do not want you!

Thus they sang. The Jetsun said, "Oh Rechungpa, the three lakes of the Snow Mountain were prophesied by the Buddha Himself to be a superb place for devotion. If we do not answer those who disparage them, not only will these slanderers be damned, but also the merits of such holy places will be misconstrued. We yogis who act candidly with our bodies, mouths, and minds, should also answer the slanders made against us. Thus, not only will the merits and rightness of yogic action be illustrated, but the slanderers will also be corrected. Now, Rechungpa, sing in chorus with your father for these young women!"

Oh, faithful patrons here assembled,
And you young people who love to chant and sing,
Especially you five loquacious maidens,
Listen to this reply, the song that I shall sing.

Know ye who we are?
We are the older and younger Repas.
I, the old man on the right side singing,
Am the Yogi Milarepa;
He, the young man chanting on the left,
Is Dor Draug Rechung.

With a good tune and words of meaning,
I sing to you my patrons here assembled,
The song which flows from my enlightened spirit.
Think, as you hear it, and listen mindfully.

The fame of Di Se Snow Mountain is far-spreading;
People say of it in distant places,
"Di Se is a crystal-like pagoda!"
When one approaches closer,
One sees the summit is snow-covered.

The prophecy of Buddha says [most truly],
That this snow mountain is the navel of the world,
A place where the snow leopards dance.
The mountain top, the crystal-like pagoda,
Is the [white and glistening] palace of Dem-Chog.

The great snow mountains which Di Se encircle,
Are the dwelling places of five-hundred Arhats.[1]
Here all deities of the Eight Divisions pay their
        homage!
Surrounding it are hills and marshes.
The region abounds with "incense" plants,
The source of nectar-producing drugs.
This is the great place of accomplished yogis;
Here one attains transcendental Samādhis.
There is no place more wonderful than this,
There is no place more marvelous than here.

The fame of Ma Päm Lake is indeed far-spreading;
People say of it in distant places,

"Ma Päm Lake is like a green-gemmed Maṇḍala!"
When one approaches closer,
One sees there waters [cold and] plentiful.
As prophesied by the Buddha in past ages,
This lake is called "The Lake-That's-Never-
    Warm,"[2]
The fountainhead of four great rivers,
A place where fish and otters swim.

Because it is the Eight Nāgas' dwelling,
It appears to be a Maṇḍala made of gems.
The water falling in it from the heavens
Is like a stream of milk, a rain of nectar;
It is the Hundred Devas' bathing place,
The water with eight merits.

The lovely plains and rocks this lake encircling,
Are treasuries of the lesser Nāgas.
Here grows superb Tsanbudrisha wood.
The Southern Continent, Tsanbu,
For this reason has its name.
There is no place more wonderful than this,
There is no place more marvelous than here.

The fame of the height of Red-Rock is far-spreading;
People say of it in distant places,
"That huge rock is like a heap of jewels!"
When one approaches closer,
One sees a great rock towering above a meadow.
As prophesied by Buddha in past ages,
It is the Black Hill, the rock of Bije Mountain Range.
It is the central place, north of the woodlands
On the border between Tibet and India,
Where Indian tigers freely roam.

The medicine trees, Tsandan and Zundru,
Are found here growing wild.
The rock looks like a heap of glistening jewels;
It is the palace where live the heavenly saints;
It is a seat of hermits, blessed by the Ḍākinīs,
And where accomplished yogis live.

Here the river all the hill encircles,

Making [a solitary] place, forbidden.
There is no place more wonderful than this;
There is no place more truly marvelous!

The fame of the elder and younger Repas is far-
    spreading;
People say of us in distant places,
"They are truly the accomplished beings!"
When one approaches closer,
One sees only an old man and a younger fellow,
With nothing wonderful about them!
The plain looks of these two
Show the complete exhaustion
Of form-clinging and discriminating thoughts!

Lying with our bodies naked, shows
That we need not clothes of the Two Clingings.
Heedlessly exposing our male organs proves
That we have no self-made shameful feelings.

These little verses flowing from our mouths
Come from our inner Experience.
The cotton clothes we wear
Show blissful inner heat a'burning.

That we eat left-over food as beggars
Proves our abnegation of desires and pleasures,
Shows our spirit, unconcerned and fearless.
Thus we live with our six senses in a
Way most natural and ingenuous!

I am the Guru of the faithful and well-gifted,
The source whence their Pith-Instructions came.
I am the symbol to which patrons pay their homage,
The exemplar of all the saints and sages.

To me, great yogis tell their understandings;
Through me, wrong views may be eliminated.
I am the source from which Truth is illumined —
The one who has realized the Law of Non-existence.

I am the one whose mind remains [in peace],
Who leads others on the Path's Experiences.

I am the one who realized himself as Dharmakāya,
Who with compassion works for others.
There is nothing else more wonderful than this;
There is no one else more marvelous than I.
Young lady visitors,
You have pilgrimaged to every land,
But your journeys were but toil and drudgery.
If you want to make a pilgrimage of value,
Travel to the holy Shrine of Paugba Wadi.[3]

It may be true that you have journeyed everywhere,
But all of this was waste of time,
And made you feel footsore and weary.
If you want to make a [worthwhile] journey
Visit holy Bodhgaya!

There may be no place that you have not visited,
But they are all of little meaning.
If you want to make a [real] pilgrimage,
Visit Lhasa Chrunon Temple![4]

There may be nothing of which you have not heard,
Yet all that has been without significance.
If you want something truly meaningful
Listen to the Pith-Instructions of the Oral
        Lineage.
You may have relied on many people,
Yet they were but your kinsfolk.
If you seek a person on whom you can rely,
Find a capable Guru!

You may have done all things, everywhere,
But most of them were deeds of Karma.
If you want your deeds to be truly worthy,
You should practice the teaching of the holy Dharma.

This is the old man's answer to you maidens;
If you can understand it, these are the real teachings.
Otherwise you may regard it as a common song.
The time has now come for you to leave.
We are the yogis who do whate'er we will —
You visitors may go and do the same!

Rechungma, who was the leader of the girls, and who stood in the center, was thereupon confirmed in her great faith. As tears rolled down her cheeks, she untied the jade from her belt and took off the jeweled ornaments from her head. Prostrating herself before Milarepa she cried: "We five girls all sincerely ask you to grant us the teaching of Dharma. Also we beg that you give us the profound Pith-Instructions, for we have now made up our minds to meditate in a hermitage." And she sang prayerfully:

> As one light is kindled from another,
> The teaching has been transmitted down
> From Dharmakāya, the great Dorje-Chang.
>
> The [holders] of this great Succession
> Are compassionate and enlightened;
> Are they not the great Tilopa and Nāropa?
> He who journeyed to India with such hardship,
> Was he not great Marpa the Translator?
> He who underwent such trials for his teacher, Marpa,
> Is he not the great and faithful Milarepa?
> His naked body is full of splendor,
> His speech rich and melodious,
> His loving mind shines forth with radiant light.
> I bow down to the body, speech, and mind of my
>   Father Repa.
>
> We five girls who have come to this meeting,
> Must have had small merit in our previous lives.
> We have attained human bodies, but are lowly born;
> We have no self-control in practicing the Dharma.
> To-day, because of your blessing, most precious Jetsun,
> Deep faith from our hearts up-wells.
>
> This precious jade upon my belt,
> And the jeweled headdress,
> I now untie, and offer to you.
> Pray grant us Buddha's teaching,
> Pray tell us your life-story!

Milarepa replied, "I have no use for your gems and ornaments. If you sincerely intend to practice Dharma, there are many better and wiser Gurus than I. Go and ask the Dharma from them. I am a person who pays no heed to clothes and food, and always dwells in no-man's land.

You could not follow my way of living, and it is doubtful whether you would be able to endure want of food and clothing. Please, then, listen to my song":

> The Marvelous One, who underwent
> Such hardships for Nāropa,
> The one blessed by the great Tilopa and Dorje-Chang,
> Is he not the Father Translator who speaks two tongues,
> The Father Translator, Guru Marpa?

> I am Milarepa blessed by His mercy.
> My father was Mila Shirab Jhantsan,
> My mother Nyantsa Karjan,
> And I was called Tubhaga ["Delightful-to-Hear"].

> Because our merits and virtues were of small account,
> And the Cause-Effect Karma of the past spares no one,
> My father Mila passed away [too early in his life].
> The deceiving goods and belongings of our household
> Were plundered by my aunt and uncle,
> Whom I and my mother had to serve.
> They gave us food fit only for dogs;
> The cold wind pierced our ragged clothing;
> Our skin froze and our bodies were benumbed.
> Often was I beaten by my uncle,
> And endured his cruel punishment.
> Hard was it to avoid my aunt's ill temper.
> I lived as best I could, a lowly servant,
> And shrugged my shoulders [in bitter resignation].
> Misfortunes descended one after the other;
> We suffered so our hearts despaired.

> In desperation, I went to Lamas Yundun and Rondunlaga,
> From whom I mastered the magic arts of Tu, Ser,
>   and Ded.[5]
> Witnessed by my aunt and uncle, I brought
> Great disaster on their villagers and kinsmen.
> For which, later, I suffered deep remorse.

> Then I heard the fame of Marpa, the renowned Translator,
> Who, blessed by the saints Nāropa and Medripa,[6]
> Was living in the upper village of South River.

After a hard journey I arrived there.
For six years and eight months[7] [I stayed]
With him, my gracious Father Guru, Marpa.
For him I built many houses,
One with courtyards and nine stories;
Only after this did he accept me.

From him I received the Pointing-out Instruction.
Thus I truly understood Mahāmudrā,
The view of the profound Absolute.

He also taught me the Six Yogas of Nāropa,
The final teaching of the Path of Means.[8]
I was ripened through the Four Initiations,
And obtained a true, decisive understanding
Of the great Guru Nāropa's teaching.

Having received the Pith-Instructions from Marpa,
I renounced all the affairs of this life;
And, no longer lazy, devoted myself to Dharma.
Thus have I reached the State of Eternal Bliss.
Such is the story of my life.

I wish you five young ladies
All good fortune and great joy.
Leave us now and go home.

Hearing the Jetsun's life story, all the maidens' faith was strengthened anew. They begged Milarepa to accept them as his servants. He said, "You are spoiled girls from rich families, and if you come with me, you will never be able to endure the hardships of my life. If you want to practice the Dharma, you should live ascetically, as I do. But I doubt if you can." Then he sang a song called "The Self-Examination":

I bow down at the feet of Marpa, the Translator.

If you, the five young sisters,
Really want to practice Dharma
And insist on coming with me,
Think this song over carefully
And obtain the answer for yourselves.

You should ask yourselves: "Have I

The persistence to endure the hardships
Of the ascetic life?
Have I a will strong and dominant enough
To renounce all Saṃsāric desires,
And follow the instructions of my Guru?"

Though you leave your native land,
The prison of all evils,
Can you persevere alone in rugged places?

Though you renounce your kinsmen, the noose of devils,
And realize their detriments,
Can you depend upon a qualified Guru?

Though you realize that properties and goods
Are poisonous, the enticing bait of demons,
Can you live in destitution and endure hardship?

Though you forsake soft woolen clothes from Weu,
Can you produce the warm and blissful Dumo
       [Inner-Heat]?

If you renounce a city life
And forsake your friends and lovers,
Can you live alone in no-man's land?

Though you disavow the Eight Desires,
Can you live in a humble and lowly way?

Though you understand the transiency of this life,
Do you realize the precariousness of [all] life?

This is the tradition of the Ghagya Lama,
The way of Practice in our Lineage.
You may come with me if you can answer "Yea."
I shall then give you the Tantric teaching
And the Pith-Instruction of the Skillful Path.
Then shall I bless you and grant you the Initiations.

Having heard this song, the girls all became very happy. Their leader, Rechungma, said, "Though we were born in a female form, which is considered to be inferior, nevertheless, so far as the Alaya [Store]Consciousness is concerned, there is no discrimination between man and

woman. We are convinced of the faults of Saṃsāra, and shall try to follow our Guru's instructions. But, in view of our inability to practice the
Dharma in a perfect way, we beg you to accept us as your servants. No
matter whether we have, or have not, the ability to practice the Dharma,
please do not forsake us!" Then in song she expressed her confidence in
being able to practice the Jetsun's teachings, and besought him to accept
her as his servant:

> Father, Qualified Guru, Precious One,
> Your naked body is full of splendor!
> I bow down at your feet, Jetsun Repa,
> Through ascetic practice you help all sentient beings!
>
> We five sisters who come to this assembly,
> May have a lower body-form as women,
> But in the Bodhi-Mind, there is neither man nor woman!
> Thinking of the defects of Saṃsāra, please allow
> Us to practice austerities and follow your instruction!
> Let us leave our country, the prison of demons,
> And remain forever in a hermitage!
> Let us leave for good our relatives, the trouble-
>   makers,
> And rely solely upon our Guru!
>
> Property and possessions are the lure of devils.
> Let us fore'er renounce them and practice austerity!
> Let us give up fine woolen clothes from Weu,
> And kindle the blissful, wondrous Inner Heat!
> Let us leave our native land and lovers
> And remain in no-man's land.
>
> Let us each act humbly with our body, speech, and mind;
> Let us depart from the Eight Worldly Claims and realize
> That all is transitory.
>
> Let us remember the uncertainty of coming death!
> Let us follow the instructions of our Lama.
> Oh, most perfect Guru, most precious one!
> Please be kind and grant to us the Dharma,
> Please accept us, the five sisters, as your servants!

Milarepa realized that they were well-destined disciples, and so accepted them.

At that time, Milarepa and his son-disciples were still dwelling at the Five Small Lakes. There he imparted the Initiations and Pith-Instructions to the five girls, and set them to meditating. Rechungma attained the warm and blissful experiences and other merits of Dumo within three days.

Later Rechungma became ill. In order to test her perseverance in remaining in solitude, Milarepa told her that she might go wherever she liked. But the girl replied, "Although I am ill, I will stay in the hermitage," thus proving that she had the persistence to endure misfortunes.

One day, Rechungma went to see Milarepa when he was sojourning elsewhere, and met him in a great assembly. In order to test her faith and see whether she had full confidence in him, he sang before the assembly a song with two meanings:

> I pray to all the holy Gurus,
> I take refuge in the Patron Buddha.
>
> Listen, faithful patrons,
> If you cannot renounce the Eighty Worldly Desires,
> Never say that you are men with faith;
> Your faith may so be lost when adverse conditions come.
>
> If you do not avoid the Ten Evil Deeds,
> Never call yourselves men of discipline,
> Lest you should fall down to the lower paths.
>
> If distracted thoughts still haunt your mind,
> Never claim that you observe the Tantric Precepts,
> Lest you should fall into the Vajra Hell.[9]
>
> Never criticize the teachings of other Schools
> If you have not made impartial and wide studies,
> Else you will violate the principle of Dharma
> And scorch your own mind badly.
>
> If you have not realized the illusory nature of
>   all beings,
> Never neglect virtuous deeds, and avoid all sinning,
> Lest you should fall into the Three Lower Realms!
>
> If you do not understand the minds of others,
> Never slander others or condemn their views,

Lest you be misled by self-conceit and egotism.

If you have not unified your mind with Dharma-Essence,
Do not boast of your meditation experiences,
Lest devils interrupt your progress.

If you have not reached the state of beyond-talking,
Do not boast of your great understanding,
Lest you be left in a pitiable position —
Longing for, but ne'er obtaining the tantalizing Fruit.

If you have not reached the realm of spontaneous
        action,
Do not do what you will or neglect your self-control,
Lest the sling-stone that you throw rebound upon
        your head.

Through my mouth the Dharma has been preached;
It should be treasured in your hearts.
Comprehend it clearly, and bear it in your minds!

Among the audience [only] Rechungma fully understood the meaning of this song. She rose from the crowd and said to Milarepa: "Regarding the accomplishments of my Guru, his acts and deeds, I have never
had a single moment of doubt nor the slightest skepticism. Please listen
to my song," Whereupon, she chanted "The Fifteen Realizations":

I bow down to all holy Gurus!
Toward the Jetsun, my Father Guru,
I have steadfast reverence and faith immutable!

The Three Precious Ones are but one Entity;
Amongst [the deities] I cannot discriminate.
In the Pith-Instructions of the Whispered Lineage
        given by my Guru   ·
There are no playwords or vain babblings.
In the practice of the Yidham Yoga,
Whose essence is the Jetsun,
There are no periods of time or intervals.
Things as they manifest are by nature magic-like;
I do not deem them to be substantial,
Nor do I cling to them with habitual thoughts!

In the Mind-Essence, the quintessential "light,"
There is no adulteration by distracting thoughts.
In the real nature of beings, the realm of Mind,
There is no subject-object difilement.
In the natural state of the Mind-Essence
There is no ground from which habitual thought may
  rise.

The nature of the mind is Dharmakāya;
It is not defiled by forms
And from attributes is free.

Our bodies are the meeting-place of the Four Diseases,
And so we should not quarrel with our friends.

Devils and misfortunes should be used to help in
  our devotions;
There is no need to seek imaginary divinations.

Dreams are delusory emanations of habitual thoughts;
One should not deem them to be true or cling to them.

Forgive the foe, who is your real teacher,
For you should never cherish vengeful thoughts.
Toward the behavior of an accomplished being
Do not raise doubts and criticism.
Self-manifestation is the Buddha, the One originally
  existing;
So do not seek the Accomplished One in other places.

My holy Guru, gracious teacher,
Pray always bless all capable disciples,
[Bathing them ever] in the stream of love and grace!

Pray, always remember me, this ignorant disciple!
Pray embrace me ever with your great compassion!

Milarepa was very pleased; he decided that Rechungma was a qualified female yogi, fitted to be a companion in [Tantric devotion]. And so
he imparted to her all the Pith-Instructions without reservation.

Then he said to Rechungpa, "You are very good at teaching the disciples. You should take care of this girl." And he handed her over to Rechungpa, who for a time took her as a companion in devotion. Thereafter,

she went to meditate at Semodo of Namtsoshumo in the North, observing absolute silence for eight years. Eventually she gained the Ten Experiences and Eight Merits, and perfected all spiritual Purifications and Realizations of the Path; and in this life she went to the Pure Land of the Dākinīs.

This is the story of Milarepa meeting Rechungma, one of his four [foremost] female disciples, at Five Small Lakes of Joro Dritsam.

NOTES

1 Arhat: an (enlightened) being who has forever annihilated all desires and passions; the name for the enlightened being of the Hīnayāna Path.

2 The Lake-That's-Never-Warm (T.T.: mTso.Ma.Dros.Pa.): "The Lake of Ma Päm, in Nari. The Hindus describe it as something like the northern ocean, inhabited by Nāgas, and Tibetans in good faith repeat such legends, at least in their literature, although they know better. This lake has a reputation of being extremely cold all the year round." (Quoted from Jaschke's Dictionary.)

3 Paugba Wadi: a sanctuary in Nepal containing the image of a Buddha called Wadi-zunpo, the good or holy Wadi.

4 Lhasa Chrunon: a famous temple built by King Sron.bTsan.sGam.Po.

5 Tu, Ser, and Ded (T.T.: mThu., Ser., [and] gTad.): three different arts of black magic.

6 Medripa (Skt.: Maitrpa).

7 According to the general belief among Tibetan Lamas, Milarepa apparently stayed with Marpa, his Guru, for much longer than six years and eight months as this text suggests. It is possible that some mistake has slipped in here.

8 Path of Means: See the translator's comments in the Appendix; see also Story 7, Note 7, and Story 5, Notes 18 and 19.

9 Vajra Hell: the horrible hell to which the precept-violator of Tantrism goes.

26

THE HUNTSMAN
AND THE DEER

Obeisance to all Gurus

HAVING directed his disciple to remain at different hermitages for their devotions, Jetsun Milarepa went to a secluded place at Nyi Shang Gur Da Mountain on the border between Nepal and Tibet. The upper slopes were very rugged, cloudy, foggy, and continuously deluged with rain. To the right of the mountain towered a precipitous hill where one could always hear the cries of wild animals and watch vultures hovering above. To its left stood a hill clothed with soft, luxuriant meadows, where deer and antelopes played. Below there was a luxurious forest with all kinds of trees and flowers and within which lived many monkeys, peacocks, turkeys, and other beautiful birds. The monkeys amused themselves by swinging and leaping among the trees, the birds darted here and there with a great display of wing, while warblers chirped and sang. In front of the hermitage flowed a stream, fed by melting snow and filled with rocks and boulders. A fresh, clear, bubbling sound could always be heard as one passed by.

This hermitage was called Ghadaya. It was a very quiet and delightful place with every favorable condition for devotees. And so it was here that Jetsun Milarepa indulged in the River-Flow Samādhi, while all the benevolent local deities rendered him services and oblations.

One day, Milarepa heard a dog barking [in the distance], after that a great noise arose. He thought, "Hitherto, this place has been very favorable for meditation. Is some disturbance on the way?" So he left the cave, came to a huge rock, and sat upon it absorbed in the Compassion of Non-discrimination.[1] Before long, a black, many-spotted deer ran up, badly frightened. Seeing this, an unbearable compassion arose within the Jetsun. He thought, "It is because of the evil Karmas this deer has acquired in the past that he was born in such a pitiable form. Though he has not committed any sinful deeds in this life, he must still undergo great suffering. What a pity! I shall preach to him the Dharma of Mahāyāna, and lead him to eternal bliss." Thinking thus, he sang to the deer:

> I bow down at the feet of Marpa;
> Pray, relieve the sufferings of all beings!
>
> Listen to me, you deer with sharp antlers!
> Because you want to escape
> From something in the outer world,
> You have no chance to free yourself
> From inner blindness and delusions.
>
> With no regret or sadness
> Forget your mind and outer body —
> The time has come for you
> To renounce all blindness and delusion.
>
> The Ripening Karma is fearful and compelling,
> But how can you escape from it
> By fleeing with your delusory body?
>
> If escape is what you want,
> Hide within Mind-Essence;
> If you want to run away,
> Flee to the place of Bodhi.
> There is no other place of safe refuge.
>
> Uprooting all confusion from your mind,
> Stay with me here in rest and quiet.
> At this very moment the fear of death is full upon you;
> You are thinking, "Safety lies on the far side
>   of the hill;
> If I stay here I shall be caught!"
> This fear and hope is why you wander in Saṃsāra.
>
> I shall now teach you the Six Yogas of Nāropa,
> And set you to practicing the Mahāmudrā.

Thus he sang in a tuneful voice like that of the God Brahmā. Had there been anyone to hear, he could not have helped feeling charmed and delighted.

Affected by the Jetsun's compassion, the deer was relieved from its painful fear of capture. With tears streaming from its eyes, it came near to Milarepa, licked his clothes, and then lay down at his left side. He thought, "This deer must be hunted by a ferocious dog, the one whose barking I heard just now."

As Milarepa was wondering what kind of a dog it could be, a red bitch with a black tail and a collar round her neck, ran toward him. She was a hunting dog — such a savage and fearful creature that her tongue was hanging out like a blazing ribbon, while the sharp claws on her feet could rend any prey, and her threatening growl was like thunder. Milarepa thought, "It must be this bitch that has been chasing the deer. She is indeed ferocious. Full of anger she regards whatever she sees as her enemy. It would be good if I could calm her and quench her hatred." Great pity for the bitch rose in him and he sang with great compassion:

> I bow down at the feet of Marpa;
> I pray you, pacify the hate of all beings.
>
> Oh you bitch with a wolf's face,
> Listen to this song of Milarepa!
>
> Whatever you see, you deem it to be your foe;
> Your heart is full of hatred and ill thoughts.
> Because of your bad Karma you were born a bitch,
> Ever suffering from hunger, and agonized by passion.
>
> If you do not try to catch the Self-mind within,
> What good is it to catch prey outside?
> The time has come for you to capture your Self-mind;
> Now is the time to renounce your fury,
> And with me sit here restfully.
>
> Your mind is full of greed and anger,
> Thinking, "If I go that way, I shall lose him,
> But I will catch him if I go forward on this side."
> This hope and fear is why you wander in Saṃsāra!
>
> I shall now teach you the Six Yogas of Nāropa,
> And set you to practicing the Mahāmudrā.

Hearing this song of Dharma, sung in a heavenly voice and with immense compassion, the bitch was greatly moved and her fury subsided. She then made signs to the Jetsun by whining, wagging her tail, and licking his clothes. Then she put her muzzle under her two front paws and prostrated herself before him. Tears fell from her eyes, and she lay down peacefully with the deer.

Milarepa thought, "There must be a sinful person who is following these two animals. He will probably be here any moment." Before long a man appeared looking very proud and violent; from under his lashes his eyes glared fiercely, his hair was knotted on the top of his head, and his long sleeves flapped from side to side as he ran toward the Jetsun. In one hand he held a bow and arrow, and in the other a long lasso for catching game. As he dashed up, one could hear his breath coming in suffocating gasps and see streams of sweat pouring down his face and almost choking him to death. When he saw the Jetsun with the bitch and deer lying beside him, like a mother with her sons, he thought, "Are the deer and my bitch both bewitched by this yogi?" He then cried angrily to Milarepa, "You fat, greasy repas and yogis! I see you here, there, and everywhere! High in the mountain snows you come to kill game; low on lake-shores you come to hook fish; on the plains you visit towns to trade in dogs and fight with people. It does not matter if one or two like you die. You may have the power of keeping my bitch and my deer, but now see whether your clothes can also keep out my arrow." So saying, the hunter drew his long bow, aimed at Milarepa, and shot. But the arrow went high and missed. The Jetsun thought, "If even ignorant animals understand my preaching, he should be able to understand it too, for after all he is a man."

So he said: "You need not hurry to shoot me, as you will have plenty of time to do so later. Take your time, and listen to my song." Whereupon, in a tuneful voice like that of the God Brahmā, the Jetsun sang to the hunter, whose name was Chirawa Gwunbo Dorje:

> I pray to all accomplished beings;
> I pray you to extinguish the Five Poisonous Kleśas.

> You man with a human body but a demon's face,
> Listen to me. Listen to the song of Milarepa!

> Men say the human body is most precious, like a gem;
> There is nothing that is precious about you.
> You sinful man with a demon's look,
> Though you desire the pleasures of this life,
> Because of your sins, you will never gain them.
> But if you renounce desires within,
> You will win the Great Accomplishment.

It is difficult to conquer oneself
While vanquishing the outer world;
Conquer now your own Self-mind.
To slay this deer will never please you,
But if you kill the Five Poisons within,
All your wishes will be fulfilled.

If one tries to vanquish foes in the outer world,
They increase in greater measure.
If one conquers his Self-mind within,
All his foes soon disappear.

Do not spend your life committing sinful deeds;
It is good for you to practice holy Dharma.
I shall now teach you the Six Yogas of Nāropa,
And set you to practicing the Mahāmudrā.

While the Jetsun was singing this, the hunter waited and listened. He thought, "There is nothing to prove that what this yogi has just said is true. Usually, a deer is very frightened, and my bitch very wild and savage. Today, however, they lie peacefully together, one on his left and the other on his right, like a mother with her sons. Hitherto I have never missed a shot during my winter hunting in the snow mountains, but today I could not hit him. He must be a black magician, or a very great and unusual Lama. I will find out how he lives."

Thinking thus, the hunter entered the cave, where he found nothing but some inedible herbs; [seeing such evidence of austerity], a great faith suddenly arose within him. He said, "Revered Lama, who is your Guru and what teachings do you practice? Where did you come from? Who is your companion, and what do you own? If I am acceptable to you, I should like to be your servant; also I will offer you the life of this deer."

Milarepa replied, "I shall tell you of my companion, from whence I come, and how I live. If you can follow my way of life, you may come with me." And he sang to Chirawa Gwunbo Dorje:

The Lamas, Tilopa, Nāropa, and Marpa —
These three are my Gurus;
If you they satisfy,
You may come with me.

The Guru, the Yidham,[2] and the Ḍākinī —
To these three Mila pays his homage;

If you they satisfy,
You may come with me.

The Buddha, the Dharma, and the Saṅgha —
These three are Mila's refuge;
If you they satisfy,
You may come with me.

The View, the Practice, and the Action
These three are the Dharmas Mila practices;
If you can absorb these teachings,
You may come with me.

The snow, the rocks, and the clay mountains —
These three are where Mila meditates;
If you they satisfy,
You may come with me.

The deer, the argali, and the antelope —
These three are Mila's cattle;
If you they satisfy,
You may come with me.

The lynx, the wild dog, and the wolf —
These three are Mila's watchdogs;
If you they satisfy,
You may come with me.

The grouse, the vulture, and the singing Jolmo —
These three are Mila's poultry;
If you they satisfy,
You may come with me.

The sun, the moon, and the stars —
These three are Mila's pictures;
If you they satisfy,
You may come with me.

The gods, the ghosts, and the sages —
These three are Mila's neighbors;
If you they satisfy,
You may come with me.

The hyena, the ape, and the monkey —
These three are Mila's playmates;
If you they satisfy,
You may come with me.

Bliss, Illumination, and Non-thought —
These three are my companions;
If you they satisfy,
You may come with me.

Porridge, roots, and nettles —
These three are Mila's food;
If you they satisfy,
You may come with me.

Water from snow, and spring, and brook —
These three are Mila's drink;
If you they satisfy,
You may come with me.

The Nāḍīs, Breaths, and Bindus —
These three are Mila's clothing:
If you they satisfy,
You may come with me.

The hunter thought, "IIis words, thoughts, and actions are truly consistent." The uttermost faith thus arose within him. He shed many tears and bowed down at Mila's feet, crying, "Oh precious Jetsun! I now offer you my deer, my bitch, my bow and arrows, and my lasso. I and my bitch have committed many sins. I pray you to free my bitch, Red Lightning Lady, thus delivering her to the higher Realms; and [I pray you] to bring this black deer to the Path of Great Happiness. I pray you grant me, the huntsman Chirawa Gwunbo Dorje, the teaching of the Dharma and lead me to the Path of Liberation." Then he sang:

Sitting on my right side is the deer
With horns as white as snow.
The markings round his mouth are his adornment.
If I slay him, my ravenous appetite
For seven days might be satisfied.
Now I do not need him and offer him to you.
Pray deliver this black deer to the Path of
　　Great Happiness,

Pray lead Red Lightning Lady to the Path of Bodhi,
Pray bring me, Gwunbo Dorje, to the Land of Liberation.

This black rope with its metal ring
Is fit to bind wild yaks on Great North Plain;
Now I do not need it and offer it to you.
Pray deliver this black deer to the Path of Great
      Happiness,
Pray lead Red Lightning Lady to the Path of Bodhi,
Pray bring me, Gwunbo Dorje, to the Land of Liberation.

To wear this goat-skin with spotted pattern
Will keep one warm, however high the mountain;
Now I do not need it and offer it to you.
Pray deliver this black deer to the Path of
      Great Happiness,
Pray lead Red Lighning Lady to the Path of Bodhi,
Pray bring me, Gwunbo Dorje, to the Land of Liberation.

In my right hand I hold arrows,
Each shaft adorned with feathers four;
When I shoot them with a "Phei!",
They always hit the target;
Now I do not need them and offer them to you.
Pray deliver this black deer to the Path of
      Great Happiness,
Pray lead Red Lightning Lady to the Path of Bodhi,
Pray bring me, Gwunbo Dorje, to the Land of Liberation.

This superb white bow in my left hand
With white bark [of birch] is decked;
When you bend it, e'en the dragon
In the sky will roar [with fear];
Now I do not need it and offer it to you.
Pray deliver this black deer to the Path of
      Great Happiness,
Pray lead Red Lightning Lady to the Path of Bodhi,
Pray bring me, Gwunbo Dorje, to the Land of Liberation.

In this manner Chirawa Gwunbo Dorje, the huntsman, offered the
deer, his bitch, and all his belongings to Milarepa. He then said, "Oh
Lama! Please accept me as your servant. I will go home to get provisions
from my children and then return. Do you intend to remain here? Please

tell me clearly, where are you going to stay?" The Jetsun, very pleased with his offering of the deer and with his change of heart towards the Dharma, then said, "Huntsman, it is very wonderful that you have determined to renounce your sinful activities and perform virtuous deeds. But it will be difficult for you to rely on me completely. Though you may have confidence in me, it will be difficult for you to find me, because I have no permanent residence. Nevertheless, if you want to practice the Dharma, you should cut off all attachment to your family and follow my example at once. I will tell you why I have no definite dwelling place, so listen to my song":

> I, the strange Repa in my hermitage,
> For three months in the summer
> Meditate on the Snow Mountain.
> That refreshes body, mind, and inspiration.
> For three months in the autumn I go out for alms —
> Begging grain for sustenance.
> For three months in the winter
> I meditate in forests,
> And so am free from bad and untamed Prāṇas.
> For three months in the spring
> I haunt meadows, hills, and brooks,
> Keeping in good health my lungs and gall.
> In all seasons of the year,
> I meditate without distraction.
>
> Our bodies, formed from the Four Elements,
> Are subject to affliction and decay.
> Ever must one watch and meditate;
> This is the only way to conquer the Five Kleśas!
>
> I eat whatever food is there;
> This is the way to be content,
> To quench desires and their consequences.
> The sign of the great diligence of yogis
> Is their constant practice of the Dharma.

The huntsman then said: "A Lama like you is indeed marvelous and unique. From the bottom of my heart I want to practice the Dharma. I am going home to say a few words to my family and also to get some provisions with which to sustain my devotion. I will soon be back. Please remain here until then."

The Jetsun replied, "If you really want to practice the Dharma, there is no need to see your family. Following the ascetic way of practice, one does not have to look for provisions for his devotion, because he can live on fruits and vegetables. No one can be sure when death will come. Besides, your present meritorious thought and earnestness may change, so it is better to stay here. Listen to me before you talk with your family." And Milarepa sang:

> Hearken, hearken, huntsman!
> Though the thunder crashes,
> It is but empty sound;
> Though the rainbow is richly colored,
> It soon will fade away.
> The pleasures of this world are like dream-visions;
> Though one enjoy them, they are the source of sin.
> Though all we see may seem to be eternal,
> It soon will fall to pieces and will disappear.
>
> Yesterday perhaps one had enough or more,
> Today it is all gone and nothing's left;
> Last year one was alive, this year one dies.
> Good food turns out to be poisonous,
> And the beloved companion turns into a foe.
>
> Harsh words and complaints requite
> Good will and gratitude.
> Your sins hurt no one but yourself.
> Among one hundred heads, you value most your own.
> In all ten fingers, if one's cut, you feel the pain.
> Among all things you value, yourself is valued most.
> The time has come for you to help yourself.
>
> Life flees fast. Soon death
> Will knock upon your door.
> It is foolish, therefore, one's devotion to postpone.
> What else can loving kinsmen do
> But throw one into Saṃsāra?
> To strive for happiness hereafter
> Is more important than to seek it now.
> The time has come for you to rely on a Guru,
> The time has come to practice Dharma.

Hearing this song, Chirawa Gwunbo Dorje was completely converted to the Dharma. He then remained with Milarepa and did not return home. After meditating for some time, he had several experiences, which he told Milarepa, and then asked for further instruction. Milarepa was very pleased, and said, "You have already begun to produce merits [within you], so you should follow these instructions":

> To rely on a Guru,
> One should pray to him often and sincerely.
> When one practices the devotion of the Yidham and
>   Ḍākinī,
> Clearly and often should he meditate on the Arising
>   Yoga.
> When one meditates on transiency and the approach
>   of death,
> He should e'er remember
> That death cannot be predicted or avoided.
>
> When one practices Mahāmudrā,
> He should cultivate it step by step.
> When one meditates on parent-like sentient beings[3]
> He should e'er remember to repay his gratitude to them.
> When one meditates on the deep teaching of the
>   Whispered Lineage,
> He should persevere with great determination.
>
> When one reaches the consummation of Dharma,
> He should avoid ups-and-downs and make it stable.
> When one examines his devotions
> To see if they agree with Dharma,
> He should not waver nor be fickle,
> But should bring them to one-pointedness.
> When one cultivates the holy Dharma,
> He should renounce the world.
>
> When food is offered by the deities,
> One does not need to find food for himself.
> If like a miser one is ever hoarding goods,
> He never can succeed in gaining more;
> This is witnessed in the oath of all Ḍākinīs,
> Hence you should abandon worldly play.

Thereupon, the Jetsun gave to Chirawa Gwunbo Dorje the complete Initation and Pith-Instructions. Through practicing them, the huntsman eventually became one of the heart-sons of Milarepa and was known as

Chira Repa — The Cotton-clad Huntsman. The deer and the bitch were also forever removed from the Paths of Sorrow. It is said that the bow and the arrows which the huntsman offered to the Jetsun are still in that cave.

This is the story of Milarepa meeting his heart-son, Chira Repa, at Nyi Shang Gur Da.

NOTES

1 Compassion of Non-discrimination or Non-discernment (T.T.: dMigs.Pa. Mei.Pahi.sÑyiñ.rJe.), is a spontaneous, non-discriminating, and infinite love embodied in the Uncreated Voidness — the exclusive Compassion of Buddhahood. From the human point of view, compassion cannot arise without an object about which it is concerned. Compassion or love seems necessarily to be involved in a dualistic or subject-object mode. But according to Mahāyāna Buddhism, the highest compassion is one that transcends both subject and object, and is brought forth through the realization of Voidness. It is, in essence, identical with the intuitive Wisdom-of-Voidness. This is one of the most inscrutible mysteries of Buddhahood.

2 Yidham: the Patron Buddha of a Tantric Yogi. See Story 7, Note 29.

3 As sentient beings have been wandering in Saṃsāra throughout beginning-less, infinite time, they must all have had parental relationships with one another in one or more of their innumerable past incarnations.

27

THE INVITATION FROM
THE KING OF NEPAL

Obeisance to all Gurus

W HEN the Jetsun Milarepa was practicing the River-Flow Samādhi and observing silence in the Riga Daya Cave of Nyi Shang of Mon, a few local huntsmen came that way. Seeing the Jetsun sitting motionless, they were all struck with wonder and doubt. After staring at him for a while, they suddenly became frightened and ran away. After a time they crept back one by one. Drawing their bows, they asked the motionless Jetsun: "Are you a human or a ghost? If you are a man, answer us." But the Jetsun still sat motionless without uttering a word. The huntsmen then shot many poisonous arrows at Milarepa, but none of them could hit him. They tried to throw him into the river, but they could not lift his body. Then they lit a fire, but even this could not burn him. Finally, they moved his body [by lifting the seat and ground he sat on] and heaved it over a steep cliff into the great turbulent river below. Yet, still in a serene lotus posture, the Jetsun's body did not touch the water, but floated above the river. Then it started moving upward and finally came back to rest in its original place, all this without Milarepa having uttered a single word.

All the huntsmen were amazed and hastily departed. On their way home, talking loudly about the incident, they approached the foot of a hill. Chira Repa, being nearby, heard their talk and appeared before them, saying, "That was my Guru, the supreme Yogi of Tibet. These miracles have proved him to be an accomplished being; even animals understand his preaching!" Then he told them the story of Milarepa and the deer and bitch, also how he had been practicing the Dharma through the Jetsun's influence. At this, great faith and reverence toward the Jetsun arose within the huntsmen, and from then on the name of Milarepa was heard throughout Nepal.

At that time, the reputation of, and the tales about, Milarepa reached the ear of the King of Ye Rang and Ko Kom, who also became filled with great faith and reverence toward him. One day, the All-Merciful Mother Tārā revealed Herself to the King and said, "The cloth of Ka Shi Ka and the supreme Ahrura [myrobalan — a universal medicine] which are now stored in your treasury should be offered to the great Tibetan Yogi, a Bodhisattva of the tenth [and final] stage, who is now at the mountain cave of Nyi Shang Gadaya north of Nepal. This will have great significance for the future." Thus She prophesied. The King then sent a man who spoke Tibetan to visit Milarepa. When the man saw the ascetic way in which the Jetsun was living, and how he had renounced all the necessities and affairs of this life, he was greatly impressed and struck with wonder. A great faith arose within him. Thinking, "This yogi is undoubtedly Milarepa himself, however I must make sure," he said to the Jetsun, "Oh Guru! What is your name? Don't you find it hard to live thus without taking nourishing food? What does this mean? Why is it necessary to abandon all belongings and material possessions?" Milarepa then answered the envoy, "I am the Tibetan Yogi, Milarepa. 'Without belongings' means 'without sufferings.' Now, listen to my song":

I bow down to all holy Gurus.

I am the man called Milarepa.
For possessions I have no desire.
Since I never strive to make money,
First I do not suffer
Because of making it;
Then I do not suffer
Because of keeping it;
In the end, I do not suffer
Because of hoarding it.
Better far and happier is it
Not to have possessions.

Without attachment to kinsmen and companions,
I do not seek affection in companionship.
First I do not suffer
Because of heart-clinging;
Then I do not suffer
From any quarreling;
In the end I do not suffer
Because of separation.

It is far better to have no affectionate companions.

Since I have no pride and egotism,
I do not look for fame and glory.
First I do not suffer
Because of seeking them;
Then I do not suffer
In trying to preserve them;
In the end I do not suffer
For fear of losing them.
It is far better to have no fame nor glory.

Since I have no desire for any place,
I crave not to be here, or there.
First I do not worry
About my home's protection;
Then I do not suffer
From a fervent passion for it;
In the end I am not anxious to defend it.
It is far better to have no home nor land.

With great faith in Milarepa, the envoy went back to the King of Ye Rang and Ko Kom and informed him in detail about the Jetsun. Then the King's faith and reverence were also confirmed. He said to the envoy, "Go and see whether you can persuade him to come here. If he does not accept the invitation, you may offer him this cloth of Ka Shi Ka and also this supreme drug, Ahrura."

Accordingly, the envoy went back to Milarepa and said, "I was sent by the King of Ye Rang and Ko Kom, a ruler with great faith in the Dharma, to invite you, the Tibetan Yogi, to come to his country." Milarepa replied, "In general, I do not look up to people and do not stay in cities; in particular, I do not know how to entertain kings, nor do I need good food or worldly pleasures. It is not mere words or a myth that a man practicing the Dharma should be indifferent to hunger and cold, and should hold the knife-of-starving to his death. You, envoy of the King, may return to your country. I will follow the order of my Guru, Marpa, to meditate in solitude." The envoy then said to the Jetsun, "So be it, if you insist. But would it not be a sorry case indeed that a great king, having sent a special envoy to fetch a common yogi, got nothing back but the return of his own envoy's empty hands and thorn-pricked feet?" To this the Jetsun replied, "I am the great Universal Emperor. There is no other emperor who is happier, richer, and more powerful than I." The envoy retorted, "If you claim that you are the great Universal Emperor himself, then you must have the Seven Precious Articles of Royalty.[1] Please show me one of them." The Jetsun replied, "If you worldly kings and officers will follow my Royal Way, each of you may also become the Supreme Emperor, and thus be rich and noble." Whereupon he sang:

> If you kings and courtiers who seek pleasures,
> Follow the Royal Succession of Milarepa,
> Eventually you will obtain them.
> This is the Royal Succession of Milarepa:
>
> My faith is the Royal Precious Wheel
> Revolving around the Virtues day and night.
> My wisdom is the Royal Precious Gem
> Fulfilling all the wishes of the self and others.
>
> The observance of discipline is my Royal Precious
>   Queen;
> She is my adornment, one most beautiful.
> Meditation is my Royal Precious Minister;
> With him I accumulate the Two Provisions![2]
> Self-respect is my Royal Precious Elephant,
> Which takes responsibility for the Buddhist Dharma.
>
> Diligence is my Royal Precious Horse,
> Which bears the Kleśas to Non-ego Land.
> Study-and-contemplation is my Royal Precious General,
> Who destroys the enemy of vicious thoughts.
>
> If you have these Royal Precious Trappings,
> You will gain a king's fame and prosperity,
> And conquer all your foes.
> You then may spread the Ten Virtues in your dominion,
> And urge all mother-like sentient beings
> To follow my noble teachings.

"This is indeed the tradition of Dharma," cried the envoy. "It is truly wonderful. If you insist upon not coming with me, I have here two precious things to offer you. They are sent by my King; one is the cloth of Ka Shi Ka, and the other is the supreme drug, Ahrura."

The Jetsun accepted these two gifts and then duly offered good wishes and dedications for the King.

About this time, Rechungpa and Shen Gom Repa set out to find the Jetsun in order to invite him [to return to Tibet]. While on their journey, they encountered a band of brigands from Nyi Shang and Nepal. When the bandits were about to rob them, they cried out that they were yogis, and asked to be spared. But the bandits replied, "Only the San Chia Yogi [Milarepa] can be considered as a real yogi. He is one whom poisoned arrows cannot harm, fire cannot burn, and water cannot drown. When one throws him over a cliff, he flies up again. He even refused the invitation of the King of Ko Kom."

Rechungpa then told the bandits that it was just for the sake of finding the Jetsun that they had come to this place. The bandits then directed them to Milarepa's abode.[3]

When the two Repas finally found the Jetsun, they saw that he was dressed in the cloth of Ka Shi Ka and that upon a stone plate [before him] was laid the supreme drug, Ahrura. They bowed down to him and asked, "How have you fared, dear Guru? How is your health?" The Jetsun replied, "I am very well indeed. Let me tell you how well I am! Now, hearken to my song":

> This is a place where flowers bloom,
> And many kinds of trees dance and sway;
> The birds here sing their tuneful melodies,
> And monkeys gambol in the woods.
> It is pleasant and delightful to stay here alone.
> Truly this is a quiet and peaceful place.
>
> With my Guru above my head, it is joyful here to
>   meditate;
> It is pleasant here to enjoy the Inner Heat;
> It is happy here to practice the Illusory Body,
> The spontaneous liberation from all worldly desires.
>
> Happy is the melting away of the dream of confusion;
> Joyous is absorption in the Great Illumination;
> Happy is the sight of the dark Blindness leaving;
> Joyful it is to become Buddha Himself
> Without practicing Transformation Yoga.
>
> It is happy to realize completely
> The true nature of Bardo and to remain
> In the transcendental realm of the Great Bliss.
>
> Your Father finds so much happiness and pleasure

In enjoying his invaluable blessings —
The joy of eating luscious fruits grown on the mountain,
And drinking sweet cool water from the springs.
Reflect upon my words, and you will understand my
        meaning.

Were you robbed, my sons, by bandits on your way here?
If so, credit it to your previous Karma.
You should realize that no money means no foe.
Never, oh my sons, hoard or pile up wealth.

If you can tame your mind,
You will have no foe!
Never, oh my children, hold hate in your hearts.

If you can tame your mind
You will have no foe!
Look up to the face of Buddha!
If your compassion ever grows,
You will have no enemy!

My sons, you should regard others as dearer than
        yourself.

Shen Gom Repa then said, "It is just because a yogi like you, dear
Jetsun, can have such happiness and tolerance toward his enemies, that
we have come here to invite you [to return to our own country]. We
see no need for you to remain in the solitude of a hermitage. Please
come to Tibet to help sentient beings there." The Jetsun replied, "To
stay in a hermitage is, in itself, to help all sentient beings. I may come
to Tibet; however, even there I will still remain alone in a hermitage.
You must not think that this is an ill practice; I am merely observing
my Guru's orders. Besides, the merits of all stages in the Path are acquired in the hermitage. Even if you have very advanced Experiences
and Realization, it is better to stay in the land of no-man, because this
is the glory and tradition of a yogi. Therefore you, also, should seek
lonely places and practice strict meditation. Now, hearken to my song":

Thanks to my Guru must still be paid,
And sentient beings still liberated.
I meditate in gratitude to Him,
Not because He, the Jetsun, is in need;

This is the oath and act of accomplished beings.

The wild ass, with white mouth, in the North,
Never bends low his head, even at threat of death.
It is not because he desires to die;
This is but his act and way —
The natural function of this wild beast!

The flesh-eating tigress, in the South,
Never eats her own breed's flesh, even when she starves,
Not because there is a principle to follow;
This is but her act and way —
The natural function of this great beast!

The white lioness, in the West,
Never leaves the snow mountain, even when she freezes,
Not because she cannot go elsewhere;
This is but her act and way —
The natural function of this queen of beasts!

The great eagle, in the East,
Strains his wings whenever he is flying;
But never in his mind is there the fear of falling.
To hover in the sky,
Is the natural way and action
For this king of birds!

When in meditation Milarepa perseveres
And renounces all wordly things,
He is not a prey to base ambition;
To abjure craving is his natural function.

Liberated yogis remain in seclusion,
Not because they fear disturbance and distraction;
It is the way and the tradition
Of all accomplished beings.

When monks and lay disciples
Discipline themselves in meditation,
It is not to gain in precedence o'er others;
It is the way and the tradition
Of all liberation-seekers.

For you, faithful and well-gifted disciples,
I sing these Pith-Instructions;
This is not for sport or pleasure —
It is the tradition of my Lineage.

Rechungpa then said, "I will keep these admonitions in my heart. You, dear Jetsun, are indeed different from other people. By the way, who offered this fine cloth and superb Ahrura to you?"

Milarepa then replied in this song, "The Gift from Man and Deity":

In the country of Ye Rang and Ko Kom
Lives a pious king, a Bodhisattva,
Victorious in the Dharma.
A prophecy from the Mother of All Mercy
To him was given in revelation.

Said the Mother of All Mercy,
"Invite Milarepa to see you.
He is now meditating
In the cave Gadaya of Nepal."

Knowing the uncertainty of death,
I refused the invitation.
I was then offered this cloth of Ka Shi Ka,
Made from fine bark of the Bal Dkar,
Now a sweet companion for my Dumo⁴ meditation!

I was also offered the superb drug, Ahrura,
Which cures all ills of the Four Elements.
Because of this worthy gift,
I foresee that in the next seven years
All people in this King's country
Will be immune from sickness and disease.

Both Repas said to the Jetsun, "We will not indulge in the Eight Worldly Desires and will sincerely practice our devotions. Now for the welfare of sentient beings, please come to Tibet." Because of their earnest and repeated requests, the Jetsun finally agreed and went to the Nyan Yuan Cave of Chu Mdo on Lashi Snow Mountain, and resided there.

. . .   .

One day Tserinma, a local goddess, came to molest Milarepa while he was enjoying the company of some low-born fairies in the forest of Sen Ding, but in a silver mirror he saw and recognized Tserinma [in her true form]. Thereupon she vanished into the sky.

The next year, when the Jetsun was staying at Chon Lun, Tserinma again tried to intrude. She saw Milarepa riding on a lion, painted with cinnabar, dressed in sun and moon clothes, and holding a canopy and a victorious banner in his hands — then vanishing into the sky. Having failed again to trap Milarepa she withdrew.

This is the story of Milarepa receiving offerings from the King of Ko Kom in Mon, together with a brief account of the intrusion of [the goddess] Tserinma.

NOTES

1 Seven Precious Articles of Royalty: These are the wheel, gem, queen, minister, elephant, spirited horse, and commander-in-chief — the symbols, or necessary possessions, of a king.

2 The Two Provisions (T.T.: Tshogs.gÑis.): Journeying along the Path toward Buddhahood, one needs a supply of two "spiritual provisions." One is the Provision of Wisdom and the other is the Provision of Merits. The former is the study, understanding, and practice of the Prajñāpāramitā, the latter is the study and practice of all meritorious deeds, including charity, discipline, diligence, tolerance, and meditation.

3 The meaning of the passage here is very obscure. This is only a approximate translation.

4 Dumo (T.T.: gTum.Mo): the mystic heat produced by the practice of Heat Yoga.

28

THE GODDESS TSERINMA'S ATTACK

Obeisance to all Gurus

> He, who is born in the Snow Country,
> Free from all worldly taints,
> Blessed by the Succession of Nāropa —
> The wondrous one who has conquered pain
>   and trials —
> The cure, the supreme remedy
> For the ills of sentient beings,
> Revered by all like sun and moon,
> He is the Holy One, the famous Mila.
> I bow to Him, the Father Repa, with great veneration.

. . .　　. . .　　. . .

In the snow country to the North, on the border between Tibet and Nepal, where the people speak different languages, there was once a magnificent and prosperous trading center where one could find all kinds of merchandise. There stood the palace of the King of the Nāgas, and there the sound of the conch-trumpet could be heard. It was a place where wealth and fortunes spontaneously increased. On the east side of the gem rock rising like a leaping lion, at the left corner where the Heavenly Nun, the Propitious Goddess of Long Life [Tserinma] lives, there was a quiet spot where dwelt the great Repa Yogi, Milarepa. It was a place encircled by the deities of the snow mountains, and abounding in pastures and meadows where many healing herbs could be found. It was a place of blessing, situated near the bank of the Lohida [Loda-han?] River — the quiet hermitage of Medicine Valley.

In the year of the Water Dragon, while Jetsun Milarepa was practicing the Flowing-River Yoga, just past midnight of the eighth day of the first month of the summer season, the eighteen Great Demons, leading all the ghosts and spirits in the whole Universe, came to attack him in order to hinder his devotion. By their great power they shook the earth, changed [the appearance of] the sky, and made their magic. Among them there were five extremely dreadful, wild-looking, flesh-eating female demons who displayed themselves in a number of ugly and ferocious forms conjured up to distract the Jetsun from his meditation. Whereupon, Milarepa sang a song, "Calling the Buddhas and Ḍākinīs for [my] Army":

> I pray to you, precious Guru,
> The famous Lho Draug Wa with Three Perfections.
> I, the destined disciple, sincerely pray to you.
>
> Father from the Realm of No-form
> You see all that happens.
>
> In this quiet place on the way to Drin River,
> I, the Tibetan Repa Yogi, have been deep in meditation.
> The visions, produced by concentrating Prāṇa
>   [in my body][1]
> Amuse and fascinate me
> Like a fantastic play!
>
> The ghosts and Devas in the Realms of Form
> Are all assembled here; none is left out.
> Most eminent among them are the five female demons
> Who into dread and hideous shapes have turned.
> They have come to hinder my devotion,
> And seek occasion [to distract me].
> I see a demoness grin like a skeleton,
> And lift up Mount Sumeru;
> I see a red one put out her tongue which drips with
>   blood
> And swallow the ocean waters.
> The most dreadful one appears as Yamāntaka,[2]
> Clashing a pair of sun-and-moon-like cymbals.
> I see an ash-smeared demoness dancing
> On the stars and planets, while she loudly laughs.
> I see a beautiful coquettish goddess,
> Whose looks incite one's ardor to extremes.
> With her enticing smile and captivating features,

She is most attractive and alluring.

There are also other vicious demons,
Stretching out huge arms, without their bodies showing,
They bend the forest trees,
Toss rocks, and shake the earth.
I see them digging trenches in the Four Directions
          [to surround me];
I see the four borders guarded by four giants;
I see fires aflame throughout the heavens,
And floods all the Four Continents submerging.
The sky is crowded with Non-men demons
With loud and piercing voices.
They shout, "Out! Out! Get out of here!"
Sending down a rain of dread diseases,
They laugh: "Ha, ha! The foundation of his
          wisdom is collapsing!"

When such hindrances descend upon me
I pray you, oh my gracious Gurus
And Patron Buddha, bestowers of accomplishment,
I pray you, holy Bha Wo and Bha Mo³
Who dwell in the Region of Reality —
I pray you, guards of Dharma, protectors from all
          hindrances,
Who have great magic power and mighty armies —
Protect, support, and help me;
Bless me and consecrate my mouth and body;
Display your anger, bare your canine teeth,
          and show your fearful faces;
Pray manifest in your most dreadful forms.
Oh Father and Mother deities,
Display the ghostly form of Yamāntaka —
He who is most prideful and most insolent.
I pray you, Wrathful Deities in the heavens,
Let from your mouths the lightning flash;
With thunder growl, "Hūm! Pai!" midst sheets of rain.
Arrogantly laughing in twelve different ways,
Destroy the nets and snares of all these demons!

That which hinders body is thus destroyed without;
That which hinders mind is thus destroyed within;
The unfavorable conditions are thus transmuted

Into the practices and teachings of the Bodhi-Path.
Pray drown these vicious demons in your floods.
Do you not hear me, holy, supreme Yidham and Ḍākinīs?

Thus the Jetsun sang and prayed fervently to the Gurus and Patron Buddhas [Yidham]. In the meantime, the eighteen Devas and demons, the main party among the adversaries, thought: "Judging by the words he has just spoken, he appears to have lost his peace of mind and to have been disturbed by us. We will soon have a chance [to destroy him.]." This thought pleased them, but they were still uncertain about [the extent of] Milarepa's inner Realization and Enlightenment. With hesitation and misgivings, they decided to attack him with many insulting and threatening words in order to test his achievement in Yoga. Whereupon, the Devas and demons sang together a song called "Proclamation of the Hindrances":

> Oh you, the deep-voiced singer,
> Who chants loudly and lyrically
> Like the humming of Vedic sages!

> You, the Yogi, who remains alone in the hermitage,
> You, who have sent for Deva and Ḍākinī armies,
> Are you not the great Repa ascetic?
> But when your body is deprived of all assistance,
> You will be shaken and alarmed.

> Though you are in a state of panic now,
> Listen to our song while we show our lenient faces.

> The gem-dragon with a pair of golden wings
> Is called the Ruler of Nam Lo.
> When he flies up in the sky he sees beneath his wings
> A propitious forest growing on the cliff.
> Embraced by ranges of snow mountains,
> Lies Medicine Valley on the high plateau.
> Upon this auspicious eighth day in the lunar month,
> Eighty-thousand trouble-makers are here assembled.
> The sky is overshadowed by this demon army.

> From the great Devas and mighty spirits of the Cosmos,
> Down to the small and low earth-crawling serpent
>   spirits,
> All have appeared in their conjured wrathful forms.

With miraculous power and insatiable yearning
We have come to confuse you and to hurt you.

The Eighteen Great Demons are the leaders;
The guards in the Ten Directions are the Ten
        Retinue Demons;
We have with us the fifteen great Child Demons,
And the five unique Flesh-eating Demonesses.
We have with us the Bha Mo Demoness;
She eats the flesh of humans and drinks blood.
She lives on [sacrificial] odors and eats stones.
We have with us the Srinmo Demoness,
Who can demonstrate all actions in the world.
We, all the Devas and spirits here assembled,
Cast dice for lots before we came.   .
The divination said, "Now it is your turn
To be slaughtered, Yogi."

There is no way of your escaping!
You have no power, no freedom.
We have come to take your life, your soul, and spirit;
To stop your breath and take consciousness from
        your body,
To drink your blood and eat your flesh and Skandhas.[4]
Now your life has come to its final ending —
Your Karma and all your merits are exhausted.
Now the Lord of Death will eat you,
And the black rope of Karma bind you fast.
Tonight you leave this world.

Do you regret your deeds done in this lifetime?
When the army of the Lord of Death arrests you,
Will you be certain of escaping,
Or prepared without fear to die?
Are you confident of not falling
Into the Three Miserable Realms?
This we ask you.

Tonight you shall follow in our footsteps;
A guide sent by the Lord of Death will lead you.
Most dreadful are the dark realms of the Bardo —
To these new places, unfamiliar,
You now must go.

For your body, have you a protector?
For your mouth, have you the Horse of Wishing?
For your mind, are you ready to go to other realms?

Alas, poor Yogi, you have neither friends nor kinsmen,
This remote place is dark and perilous,
This lonely path is difficult and hazardous,
For you must proceed alone without companions.
Here you should not stay —
You should depart at once.

Thus sang the Devas and ghosts. The Jetsun then thought, "You demons and all the manifestations in the cosmos are merely conjurations of one's own mind; this is explicitly taught in all the holy Sūtras and Śāstras. According to the nectar-like teaching, clearly pointed out by my holy Guru, the nature of mind is the Illuminating Essence, beyond all extremes of playwords. It is never born and it never dies. Even though the myriad armies of the Lord of Death encircle it, and rain weapons upon it, they cannot harm, destroy, or sully it. Even though all the Buddhas in the Ten Directions and the Three Times should gather all their merits, and ray their infinite beams of light upon it, they could not make it better; nor could they color it or form it into substance. It will remain as it is, and can never be destroyed. This fetter-like body of mine was made out of subject-object clingings, and is destined to die. If these Devas and demons want it, I will give it to them. All life is transient and changeable. Now I have the opportunity to give my body away; if I do so, I shall make a worthy offering. It is owing to wrong subject-object thoughts that I see the shadows of Devas and ghosts as they now appear before me; the perception of the afflicter and the afflicted is as delusory as clouds, mist, and flickering mirages seen through impaired eyes. These delusory visions are like 'veils' created by wavering thoughts, which themselves have been produced by habitual-thinking derived from Original Blindness since beginningless time in Saṃsāra. In these phantom visions there is nothing to be afraid of." With this thought in mind Milarepa began to absorb himself into the Realm of Reality. Fearlessly, and with unshakable confidence, he sang a song:

This is the well-known place called Dinma Drin —
A town to which both Hindus and Tibetans come,
A market-place where many traders gather.
Here you live, Queen of Heaven.
Oh cruel Lady Tserinma of the Snow Lakes,
Your hair is decked with the mountain snow;

Embroidered on your skirt in all their beauty,
Are the verdant fields of Medicine Valley.
In this place, encircled by the river,
Have now assembled eighty thousand trouble-makers.

From the Heaven of Conjuration[5] above,
To the Realm of Hungry Ghosts below —
All the Devas and spirits here are gathered,
Singing their stupid songs [to hurt and confuse me].

Floating in the sky above are the fragrance-eating,
The rotten, the man-like, the hungry,
The vampire-ghoulish, the cannibalistic, the harmful,
The corpse-raising, and the Jung Po demons . . . .
Oh these unthinkable myriad demons!
Hardly can I recall their names!
Especially fierce among them
Are the five cannibal demonesses
Who, with abusive language, curse me,
And shout, "Die you shall, you must!"

Because of my [human] fear of death
I meditate on Immortal Mind,
Absorbed in the Uncreated Realm.
The keystone of the principle I practice
Is self-liberation from Saṃsāra.
With this quintessence of all teachings,
I clearly see Awareness, naked and unsubstantial.

My confidence in the View is the transparency of flux;
Since I know the Illuminating Void,
I fear not life or death.

Due to my [human] fear of the Eight Non-freedoms
I meditate on flux and on Saṃsāra's faults,
And train myself to watch the Law of Karma.
Then I take refuge in the [Three] Precious Ones.

Through constant meditation on the Bodhi-Mind
I eradicate forever the obscuring
Shadows of habitual thoughts.
Whatever may appear before me,
I see as false illusions;

Thus I fear not the Three Miserable Paths.

Fearful of life's uncertainty,
I have developed skill in Nāḍī-Prāṇa practice.
Through practicing the Key-instruction
Of the Three Identifying Exercises,[6]
I have checked my understanding of the Six Groups
    [of sense].
Thus, am I sure to see the Dharmakāya,
And lead myself to the Path Divine.

Since my mind has been totally absorbed
In the uncreated Dharmadhātu,
I have no regret nor fear of dying even now.

You, the worldly Devas and foolish demons
Who steal the lives of sentient men and women,
Listen closely to my words.
This human body, composed of Skandhas,
Is transient, mortal, and delusory.
Since in time I must discard it,
He who would, may take it now.

May the offering of my body serve as ransom
For all mankind and sentient beings.
May this offering serve as dedication
For the benefit and blessing of my parents.[7]

Since I have offered this, my body,
With sincerest dedication,
May you all be satisfied and happy.
I hope, through this one virtuous deed,
That the debts and Karmas I have owed
From time-without-beginning in Saṃsāra
May all be cleared and settled finally.

The running mind is void and unsubstantial —
I see this more clearly than you demons.
You thought that I would easily be frightened
When you raised the hosts of demon armies
From the Eighteen Hells and Lokas to attack me.
But I am a yogi of the Void,
Who clearly sees the nature of Ignorance.

I do not fear you demons —
Fictions conjured up by mind,
Manifest yet non-existent.
Oh, how fascinating is the play,
How fantastic are the dramas of Saṃsāra!

Thus, without the slightest fear in his mind, the Jetsun sang. Then he cried out to the demons in these truthful words: "From beginningless time in the past until now, we all have taken myriads of bodily forms in our past incarnations, comparable only to the total sum of grains of sand in the great Universe. Nevertheless, we have seldom utilized these bodies for a worthwhile purpose. Instead, we have wasted them by doing meaningless things [over and over again], thus accumulating more and more Skandhas and pains. If you Devas and demons are interested in taking my body, which is made of the Four Elements and worldly Skandhas and filled with thirty-two kinds of filthy things, I can give it to you right now. Why not? Furthermore, all the sentient beings in the Six Realms are either my mother or my father. For the sake of clearing the debts I owe them, I now give my body away, from the top of my head to the toes on my feet — the twelve limbs, including the head, the five organs, the five essentials, the six internal contents, the flesh and bones, the feet and fat, the brain and cortex, the grease and blood, the hair and nails, the skin and dirt, the breathing, the life, the semen, and the vital energy — I now offer all of them to you. Whatever part you may desire, take it with you and enjoy it. I hope, through this merit of offering my own body, that from now on all demons and malignant spirits will be relieved of the hatred and ill-will in their hearts. Let this Merit become the very seed of their great compassion, and may it grow forever in their hearts! May the seed of this compassion, combining with the nourishment of Innate-Born Wisdom, free all demons forever from malignance and bitterness. May you all become very merciful, lenient, and kind. I now dedicate this Merit as a boon to all sentient beings, for their perfect happiness, goodness, and contentment."

Upon hearing the Jetsun's words and sincere wish, all the Devas and demons [felt great remorse], and became very respectful to him. They ceased their hostile conjurations and remained there peacefully. The five extremely fierce flesh-eating Ḍākinīs, who had displayed such dreadful forms, exclaimed, "The fact that you have no attachment or concern for your body is truly marvelous! We did not come here with so much hatred and determination really to harm you. We came only to test your Realization and understanding. Generally speaking, all the outer hindrances created by demons depend on one's inner clinging-thoughts.

When we first arrived, we saw you displaying a certain amount of apprehension, and heard you calling to the deities and Ḍākinīs for help. Seeing this, we thought you might still have fears and desires in your mind. Consequently, we have been threatening you and ridiculing you with outrageous words. But, since we have heard your sincere and truthful replies, we regret our wrongdoing. Hereafter, whenever you run into danger or find your mind running wild, you should meditate on the Mind-Essence in an effortless manner. You will then surely conquer all hindrances. By so doing, even if all the Cosmos, from the [Heaven of] Brahmā to the earth, should be shaken and overturned, you will not be frightened or overwhelmed." Having given this good advice to the Jetsun, the five intemperate demonesses sang together from the upper sky:

Oh great Yogi Repa,
Because of your accumulated merits
You were born in a human body.
You are well-gifted, endowed
With leisure and favorable conditions.
As the glad time ripens for fulfilling
The wishes made in your past lives,
You have found the teaching of holy Dharma,
Thus enabling you to practice its devotion.
You are a good man, a superior being,
While we are only low and worldly creatures.
Our intelligence is small, and great our ignorance;
Our births are in the lowly forms of women.
Having little merit,
We ever nurse malignant thoughts;
Because of our sinful deeds, we in the sky must travel.
As you may not understand what we have realized
Through these obscure words,
They will be explained in parables.

Your mind is profound and deep
Yet, in the Mudrā posture listen,
And reason on what we sing.

In the East, in the auspicious gate of China,
A Chinese woman weaves a silken web;
If she makes no mistakes
Through chattering with her sisters,
The wind without will not harm her work.

Therefore, to weave with care
Is of great importance.

In the North, lies the country of the Mongols;
Their brave and powerful troops are quick to fight.
If no revolt takes place inside the country,
They fear not even the men of King Gesar.[8]
Therefore, to rule the people well and wisely
Is of great importance.

In the West, at the steep gate of King Tazee [Persia]
Stands the gate of the secret-sign,
In shape resembling a fleshy shell;
If the forged iron bolts within it do not break,
No cannon-ball from outside can shatter it.
Therefore to fasten tight the inner portal
Is of great importance

In the South lies Nepal, the land of rocks and thunder.
If the natives with their axes
Cut not the healing tree of sandalwood,
The Mon intruder will not harm them.
To preserve the woods among compatriots
Is of great importance.

In this quiet place near the Drin River
You, Milarepa, meditate correctly.
If the thought of demons
Never rises in your mind,
You need not fear the demon hosts around you.
It is most important to tame your mind within;
Do not cherish any doubt there,
Oh ascetic Yogi.

Upon the hills of the Void Dharma-Essence
You should guard the castle of firm Samādhi.
If you wear the clothes of Bodhi-Mind
And hold the sword of Wisdom-and-Compassion,
The army of Four Demons cannot hurt you.
If you harbor not subject-object thinking,
No demons can e'er harm you.
Even if you are surrounded by the hosts
Of Yama, they cannot defeat you!

The attractions and inducements
In the world outside are great;
The drowsiness and distractions
Within are powerful;
Passions and attachments ever follow you like shadows.
E'en though you may absorb yourself in transcendental
     Wisdom,
It is still hard for you to conquer
The illusions of the demons and ghosts within —
For extremely quick and clever are these Nhamdog.[9]
On the steep path of fear and hope
They lie in ambush
With their ropes and snares,
Waiting for a chance to trap you.
The sentinel of vigilance
Should therefore be posted
To guard your inner citadel!

This melodious song with four
Parables and five meanings,
Is precious as a pearl.
A mirror of illumination,
It lights up the mind.
Please think of it with all attention,
Oh well-gifted Yogi!

Milarepa then replied, "As a rule, all trouble-making demons and Devas in the outer world are creations of the delusory thoughts of the
clinging [mind], which grasps forms and deems them to be real. What
you have said may all be very true. Nevertheless, we yogis do not consider obstacles as entirely evil and pernicious. Whatever forms and visions the demons may conjure we accept as helpful conditions and gra-
·cious gifts. Like the crack of a horsewhip, these demonic obstacles are
very good stimulants for indolent beginners. An unexpected shock will
undoubtedly sharpen one's awareness. Also, these demonic obstacles are
the very causes that will aid one's body and mind in devotion, and quick-
en the arising of Samādhi; to those advanced yogis who have already
reached stability on the Path, these obstacles become the nourishment
of Wisdom. Such hindrances will also deepen the clarity of the Light-
of-Awareness and improve one's inner Samādhis. Through them supreme
Bodhi-Mind will arise, thus enabling the yogi to better his devotion in
a rapidly progressive way. Today I have witnessed the fact that all the
Devas and demons have become Guardians of the Dharma. By the

merit of seeing these Guardians as the Transformation Body of Buddha, I shall achieve many more accomplishments. I have thus trans-muted the obstacles into aids for spiritual growth and turned the evils into virtues. Now, all the Nhamdog — those distracting, illusory, and confusing thoughts — appear as the Dharmakāya itself. Thus you have actually given me all the assistance [necessary] for devotion on the Path. Insofar as the Ultimate, or the true nature of being is concerned, there are neither Buddhas nor demons. He who frees himself from fear and hope, evil and virtue, will realize the unsubstantial and groundless nature [of thoughts].[10] Saṃsāra will then appear to be the Mahāmudrā itself; all turbulent, distracting thoughts will vanish into the Dharmadātu — the so-called non-gathering and non-separating Dharmakāya."

The Jetsun again expounded these points as follows:

Upon this earth, the land of the Victorious Ones,
Once lived a Saint, known as the second Buddha;
His fame was heard in all the Ten Directions.
To Him, the Jewel a'top the eternal Banner [of Dharma]
I pay homage and give offerings.
Is He not the holy Master, the great Medripa?

Upon the Lotus-seat of Medripa
[My Father Guru] places his reliance;
He drinks heavenly nectar
With the supreme view of Mahāmudrā;
He has realized the innate Truth in utter freedom.
He is the supreme one, the Jetsun Marpa.
Undefiled by faults or vices,
He is the Transformation Body of Buddha.

He says: "Before Enlightenment,
All things in the outer world
Are deceptive and confusing;
Clinging to outer forms,
One is ever thus entangled.
After Enlightenment, one sees all things and objects
As but magic shadow-plays,
And all objective things
Become his helpful friends.
In the uncreated Dharmakāya all are pure;
Nothing has even manifested
In the Realm of Ultimate Truth."

He says: "Before Enlightenment,
The ever-running Mind-consciousness[11] within
Is shut in a confusing blindness
Which is the source of passions, actions, and desires.
After Enlightenment, it becomes the
    Self-illuminating Wisdom —
All merits and virtues spring from it.
In Ultimate Truth there is not even Wisdom;
Here one enters the Realm where Dharma is exhausted."

This corporeal form
Is built of the Four Elements;
Before one attains Enlightenment,
All illness and all suffering come from it.
After Enlightenment, it becomes the two-in-one Body
Of Buddha clear as the cloudless firmament!
Thus rooted out are the base [Saṃsāric] clingings.
In Absolute Truth there is no body.

The malignant male and female demons
Who create myriad troubles and obstructions,
Seem real before one has Enlightenment;
But when one realizes their nature truly,
They become Protectors of the Dharma,
And by their help and [freely-given] assistance
One attains to numerous accomplishments.

In Ultimate Truth there are no Buddhas and no demons;
One enters here the Realm where Dharma is exhausted.
Among all Vehicles, this ultimate teaching
Is found only in the Tantras.
It says in the Highest Division of the Tantra:
"When the various elements gather in the Nāḍīs,
One sees the demon-forms appear.
If one knows not that they are but mind-created
Visions, and deems them to be real,
One is indeed most foolish and most stupid."

In time past, wrapped up in clinging-blindness,
I lingered in the den of confusion,
Deeming benevolent deities and malignant
Demons to be real and subsistent.
Now, through the Holy One's grace and blessing

I realize that both Saṃsāra and Nirvāṇa
Are neither existent nor non-existent;
And I see all forms as Mahāmudrā.

Realizing the groundless nature of ignorance,
My former awareness, clouded and unstable
Like reflections of the moon in rippling water,
Becomes transparent, clear as shining crystal.
Its sun-like brilliance is free from obscuring
     clouds,
Its light transcends all forms of blindness,
Ignorance and confusion thus vanish without trace.
This is the truth I have experienced within.

Again, the foolish concept "demons" itself
Is groundless, void, and yet illuminating!
Oh, this indeed is marvelous and wonderful!

In this manner Milarepa showed his faithful obedience to his Guru's instructions and his decisive understanding of the Dharma. Whereupon the eighteen Great Demons and the other Devas and ghosts all addressed him with deep respect: "You are a yogi who has reached the stage of stability. Unaware of this, we came to insult you and make many troubles for you. Now we feel very sorry and regretful. Henceforth, we shall follow all your commands and serve you." Having taken this oath, the innumerable demons and ghosts prostrated themselves before him like mud splashing and falling in heavy rain. Then the Devas and demons all returned to their own abodes.

This is the story of how the great Repa, the indescribable Laughing Vajra, met the five worldly Ḍākinīs, and replied [to their attacks upon him] in song. This story is told by Bodhi Radsa, the Master of Ngan Tson, from his indelible memory of the original account. It is written in a poetic style called "The Rosary of Pearls."

NOTES

1 According to Tantrism, most of the visions that a yogi sees in his meditation are brought about by the "concentrating" of a particular Prāṇa, either the Prāṇa of earth, water, fire, or air, in a specific "psychic" center of the body.

2 Yamāntaka (T.T.: gÇin.rJe.): one of the most wrathful deities in Tantrism, a sublimation of Yama, the King of Death.

3 Bha Wo and Bha Mo (T.T.: dPah. Wo, dPah.Mo.). The latter appears in the Tibetan text here as "Dakima." Bha Wo and Bha Mo are male and female deities, especially those associated with the teaching and practice of Tantrism.

4 Skandhas, or the Five Skandhas: the five constituents that made up a man, i.e., form, feeling, perception, impulses, and consciousness.

5 The Heaven of Conjuration (T.T.: lHa.dWañ.Phyug.): the Heaven of Iśvara.

6 The Three Identifying Exercises: to identify one's mind with the manifestation, with the body, and with the Dharmakāya.

7 Since one has been reincarnating for innumerable ages on every plane, and must have had two parents in each incarnation, he has thus inevitably built a parental relationship with all sentient beings. It is out of this conviction of the kindred relationship of all beings that the Bodhi-Mind and the great Compassion of the Bodhisattva were brought forth.

8 Gesar (T.T.: Ge.Sar.): The name of a legendary king of ancient Tibet whose romantic and literary adventures, as well as his military and religious achievements, have been the fountainhead of inspiration and imagination to Tibetan minds. The *Book of Gesar* (T.T.: rGyan.Druñ.) is a great Tibetan epic comparable to the Mahābhārata and the Iliad. It has been one of the most beloved and widely read books in Tibet. The exact number of volumes composing this book is almost indeterminable because of its many complex versions and editions, but it is generally believed to contain about 15 large volumes, totaling more than a million words. The professional Tibetan troubadours, whose knowledge is confined almost entirely to this one great book, are called by the Tibetans the "wandering story-tellers of King Gesar."

9 Nhamdog here implies the volatile and capricious aspects of the mind. See also Story 4, Note 4, and Story 1, Note 12.

10 The literal translation of this phase should be: "The confusion has no ground or substance" (T.T.: hKhrul.Pa.gShi.Med.).

11 The phrase "Yid.Gyi.rNam.Çcs.", appearing in the original text, is tautological. It has therefore been translated here as "Mind-consciousness."

THE CONVERSION OF
THE GODDESS TSERINMA

Obeisance to all Gurus

> Crowned with the adornment of the
> Transformation Body of Tathāgata
> Is the Supreme One, the translator Marpa.
> From His face flows
> The nectar stream;
> From His Whispered Lineage
> Comes to birth the Innate-Born.
> Grown out of this pure Wisdom
> Is He, the famous Yogi, Mila.
> To you is paid sincerest homage
> Father Repa.

· · ·   · · ·   · · ·

On the border between Nepal and Tibet, at the left shoulder of the misty snow mountain, Queen of the Azure Heights, under floating golden clouds lay the blessed place, the Valley of Medicine. Close to the bank of the celebrated Lodahan [Lohida?] River, it was encircled by a crystal range of snow hills. There dwelt the renowned great Repa Yogi Mila, who kept his unbounded mind absorbed in the teaching of the Supreme Vehicle, and perfectly consolidated in the limitless Bodhi-Mind. When the "Up-going Bliss"[1] reached the Throat-center of Enjoyment, the Song of Vajra flowed spontaneously from him. Blessed by an uninterrupted wave of grace, he had transformed his base consciousness into Wisdom, and, through Tantric Madness[2] had conquered all the demons and evil spirits. He was a yogi of great power and might.

Tranquilly absorbing his mind in the original state of Dharma-Essence, he occasionally demonstrated, with great compassion, the Samādhi resulting from the conquering of the Elements,[3] now concealing and now manifesting his powers to subdue evil spirits. While residing there, for the benefit of faithful human beings as well as devoted spirits and Devas, he also performed numerous and wondrous miracles.

On the eleventh night of the summer month in the year of the Water Snake, five bewitchingly lovable maidens came to [visit] him. They greeted him and circumambulated him many times. Then they said, "We have brought you some yogurt made from wild ox [Ba Men][4] milk." Saying this, they offered Milarepa a [big] blue-gem spoon filled with yogurt. Then they sat one by one on his left and said, "We five girls beg you to take us to your heart and permit us to make our Vow-for-Bodhi before you." The Jetsun thought, "I have never seen such a precious and unique spoon, nor is there in the world any food comparable to this wonderful yogurt! [As to these girls], their manner of prostration, their reverse way of circumambulation, and their other unusual behavior prove that they are heavenly beings." But in order to find out whether they would speak the truth, the Jetsun pretended to be ignorant. He looked at them and asked, "Who are you? Where did you come from?" And then he sang tunefully:

> For the sake of several well-destined disciples,
> The Holy Dorje-Chang, the essence of Four Bodies,
> At a time of dispute and corruption,
> Incarnated as Marpa, the Translator,
> In the mountainous Country of Snow, Bar Dha Na,[5]
> In the northern part of Tsamlin.
>
> With the voice of a roaring lion,
> He, the Supreme Being, rode the Supreme Vehicle.
> By merely hearing His Voice one will
> Be saved from falling into the Lower Paths.
>
> I pray to you great Marpa, for those who seek me —
> Pray grant them your blessing and accomplishment.
> Oh Father, with the power of your compassion,
> I pray that their minds with ease may be converted,
> That within them the buds of Enlightenment may sprout.
>
> In the Pure Land of the Void
> Abide the Buddhas and their Sons.
> With your sunlit compassion,

Pray send forth your rays of light
To shine o'er the Wisdom-lotus
In the hearts of your disciples,
And make them blossom.
Pray make the anthers
Of the Four Infinities grow today.

I have something to ask you
Lovely maidens sitting on my left.
There is nothing special I want to know —
Just tell me, are you human beings,
Or heavenly angels?
For this is the first time I have seen you.

Oh you five attractive damsels
With such fine and charming bodies,
In the dazzling light of magic
Your enchanting elegance
Glorifies the splendor of your beauty!

Oh you radiant maids from Heaven,
He who sees you at a distance seems
As in a dim evening fog to see five
Young maidens shopping in the town.
But when he looks more carefully,
He sees no tangible or steady image,
Only a hazy, flickering silhouette.
Thus am I much bewildered and perplexed.

When I venture on the road,
I see you run like rolling pearls,
Chatting gaily with much laughter.
But behind your coquettish charms and glamor,
Like the morning star shining in the east
You slowly fade away.

Seeing that you disperse and assemble e'er in groups,
I suspect that you are Devas or else fairies.
When one looks at your eyes a'twinkle,
One cannot help but smile!
I wonder to myself, "are you magic Ḍākinīs?"

The Buddhist way of circling in obeisance

Is from left to right,
But yours from right to left,
So you must Devas be, or fairies.

The usual way to render "Eye Obeisance"[6]
Is from left to right,
But yours from right to left,
So you must fairies be, or Devas.

You shake the upper body when you bow;
In every nine prostrations you ask of my welfare thrice;
You nod and shake your heads
When you make the "Eye Obeisance" once;
Only heavenly ladies prostrate in such a way,
But though you imitate, you are not really like them!

In every eight prostrations you ask of my welfare twice
After the fashion of all Devas;
You bend your knees to earth —
The form of your obeisance is unusual.

This spoon that's made with gems of blue
With various jewel ornaments that you gave me,
From Heaven came: it is not of this world.

I come from a distant country,
And have traveled in many different lands.
I have eaten many sorts of food
And many wondrous things have I seen and heard.
Compared to others, my experience should be not less,
    but more;
But in all my life I have never tasted
Such delicious yogurt made from wild ox milk,
Nor have I ever seen such wondrous things.
This is food from Heaven,
It is not of this world.

What you have said, oh happy fairies,
Is indeed a cause for wonder,
Especially your request to know the Bodhi-Mind.
Judging by your faith and fondness for the Dharma,
In past lives you must have had
Deep affiliation with the Doctrine.

I cannot but be pleased and most delighted.

Listen to me, my good young women.
I have more questions still to ask.
I shall make no false remark,
But only utter sincere words.

From whence did you come this morning,
And whither will you go this afternoon?
Where is your home and what your family?
What do you do with your magic powers?
What magic power can you bestow?
How came you to know of me?
Was it through hearsay, or have we met before?
Let no hesitation block your speech.
Please answer me with honest words.

The fairies replied, "You are the Jetsun, the supreme being. In your
past lives you must have accumuulated many merits. Thus you were able
to meet a unique and accomplished Guru. With a heart full of the nectar-like Dharma, you have fully realized the fallacy and illusiveness of
worldly pleasures and desires. Thus, great compassion and benevolence
arose in the depths of your heart, and a determination to cross the perilous, rolling river of Saṃsāra was established. Through great hardships
and austerities you have devoted yourself to the practice of Dharma.
Having perfectly mastered the illuminating Samādhi within, you also
attained great miraculous powers by means of which you are able to see
people's private affairs and thoughts [clearly and vividly] like images reflected in a mirror. Although you are perfectly aware of our families,
lineages, and other things, still you pretend [not to know], and ask us
about them. Surely, we shall be glad to tell you the full truth. Great Jetsun, please give us your attention for a moment, and listen to our song."
And they sang melodiously together:

At this sad time of Five-defilements
Near Pakshu in Tibet, the home
Of the red-faced demoness, was born
A rare man in Snow Valley,
Surrounded by evil, icy hills.
Is he not the great Yogi, Mila?

Because of your worthy deeds in previous lives
You have met an accomplished Guru,

And are blessed by the divine Lineage.

Bathed in the Nectar Stream of Grace,
You have transformed your mind.
Thus you see all pleasures and glories
As phantom-like delusions.

Having left this world so hard to leave,
Diligently you persist in your devotions
Allowing nothing to distract you.
So you have become a heavenly yogi
Forever dwelling in the Realm of Dharmakāya.

Staying on the plane that is "Away-from-Playwords,"
You can use the power of that Samādhi, transforming
Into many forms —
A reward for conquering all the elements.
Yet even without it, all evils have you conquered.
Seeing the miracles that you have wrought,
Your faithful disciples were inspired and heartened;
Filled with wonder, and with joyful hearts,
Their hair stood up and their tears ran down.

Oh, you are the Jetsun, the Pearl of the Crown.
To you, all homage and offerings should be made.
You are the Jetsun Yed Pa,[7] Buddha's son,
The refuge of all sentient beings.

We, the five sky-going maidens
From a non-human tribe,
Who now sit beside you,
Are low in birth and lesser still in merit.
Pray, take pity on us with your great compassion!

From the clouds of your grace,
We pray the rain of nectar soon will fall
Whereby the obstinate passions — the cause of all evils
[In the world] — will be appeased,
And the precious bud — the supreme Bodhi-Mind — will
    flower.

You are the master of Yoga,
The majestic Yogi of Forbidden-Acts.

Through cultivation of awareness in Samādhi,
You know well the minds and the capacities,
The lineages, and Dharma-relationships of all men.
Though you know them clearly without error,
You pretended ignorance, and asked about us.

We are Nu Yin, worldly demonesses,
Ahdsidharata is our family line.
We are ghosts who wander in graveyards,
Worldly Dākinīs,[8] who magic make.
Many powers and accomplishments
Can we bestow and grant.

This morning in the house of Heaven,
We opened the cloud gate,
Rode the sun's rays, and came.
This evening we are bound for India
To attend the sacramental feast
In Cool Garden Cemetery.

On the right side of this valley,
Fashioned like a triangle,
Stands a high snow mountain.
On the summit of the central peak we dwell.
The crowning ornament of our house
Is a crystal-like ice-mirror
Reflecting rays of sun and moon.
Half way up the mountain
Lies a vase-shaped lake;
The hovering clouds above it roof
Our house, below lies the base,
Forever wreathed in fog.
This is Blue Queen Snow Mountain,
The famous place, our home.

First we saw you in the summer
When we came to harm and to insult you.
But you harbored neither anger nor resentment.
In return, you bestowed on us the rain of Dharma.
Thus for our evil-doing we all repented.
Having tasted the nectar of your Dharma,
We felt yet more thirsty and yearned for more to drink.
So to-day we come to visit you,

The supreme Being who gives refuge.

We pray you, the perfect man,
To let us quench our thirst and satisfy
Our yearnings at your nectar-stream.

Milarepa then said, "Formerly, you were very malicious and resent-
ful. You have repeatedly threatened me in wrathful shapes, and tried to
harm and revile me. But I have fully realized that all manifestations are
plays of the mind, and that the Mind-Essence is illuminating yet void.
Therefore, I have never had the slightest fear or concern about delusory
hindrances caused by demons. Observing this, you should sincerely repent of the damage and harm you have inflicted upon people and devoted yogis. With deep remorse you should confess all your sinful deeds
and should not commit any more, or harm other beings. You must first
take an oath on this. If you do so, I can then admit you and grant you
the prayer of Taking-the-Three-Refuges, and initiate you into the Raising of Bodhi Mind. Otherwise, if you have not made yourselves hand-
maidens of the profound Teachings and of the Supreme Precepts, it will
be like 'throwing a yak cow into the abyss,' or like 'dragging the nose of
a corpse to the place of lament.' Now, pay the strictest attention and
listen to the song of this old man":

On this auspicious evening when midnight is
    drawing nigh,
A silvery light gleams brightly in the East
Chasing the darkness back across the sky.
Is that not the lucid, crystal-pure moonlight?

Riding on the glittering rays — your horses,
You five maidens came
Clad in shrouds of light.
Are you not the five earth-bound Dākinīs?

Near the bank of Lodahan River
Is a delightful and quiet cell,
Where lives a mad ascetic
Who knows not disgrace and shame.
Naked, he knows not bashfulness
And feels nor heat nor cold.

Absorbed in the mind-transcending Essence,
Undistracted for even a single moment,

He contemplates the nature of the Void.
Is he not Mila, the great meditator?

You five maids of magic have sung a song to me;
I, the cotton-clad Yogi, sing in return for you.
We have shared some vows and Karma in the past;
'Til now you have of this been unaware.
How happy must you be to know it now!

In the late spring of last year
You caused all ghosts and Devas
To come here and afflict me.
As the flags unfurled
And the demon-soldiers drew up in array,
All four armies showered missiles down
And tried to harm me in all sorts of ways.
But since I had already realized
That all form is of the mind,
While the mind itself is void,
I was never frightened
By these demonic shadow-shows.

By merely seeing you poor sinful beings,
An unbearable compassion, quite beyond control,
Rose of itself within me.
In return I showered on you
The mercy-rain of Dharma.
You were thus converted
To faithful be, and pious.

To-night as five lovely maids you came;
Once more with your dazzling beauty
You circled and bowed many times before me,
Folding your hands upon your breasts
To show sincere respect.
With your melodious song
You asked me for the Dharma, saying:
"Pray, gather and precipitate the clouds of Bodhi-Mind,
And shower down on us the Dharma-nectar."
Since you have such earnest faith
[I will give you the teaching
And so fulfill your wish].

Upon the lotus-seat a'top my head[9]
Sits my precious Guru —
The great Translator, matchless Marpa!
Like the immaculate Sambhogakāya,
He sits gracefully upon my head.

From the radiant moon of His sweet compassion,
Cloudless and resplendent,
Emanates bright light,
Shining upon the hearts of His disciples;
It freshens the awakening anthers
And brings quick to blossom
The water-lily of their minds.
You bewitching sorceresses,
Have you ever seen these things?
If not, the reason is your sins.
You should thus confess, without reserve
All that you have e'er done wrong
Since time without beginning;
Else you can ne'er receive my teaching
And may fall into the wretched Realms once more.

Before, you were malignant and were bitter,
Accustoming yourselves to vice;
For you to take an oath meant nothing,
Nor would it have helped the Doctrine.
He who does not respect the Law of Karma,
[Will fall] into the dread Realms of Misery.
You should, therefore, take heed
Of even the smallest sin.

He who knows not the faults of wordly pleasures,
And from his depth of heart does not renounce them,
From the prison of Saṃsāra can ne'er escape.
He should know that the world is but illusion,
And work hard to subdue his desires [Kleśas].

If for the wrongdoings
Of all sentient beings
In the Six Lokas
One has great pity,
He will avoid the Hīnayāna path;
With a great compassion

He should strive hard to emulate a Bodhisattva!

Oh Ḍākinīs of the Mahāyāna Path,
If you can accept this beneficial preaching
Which I have just imparted to you,
Brothers and sisters, then, we may tread the Path
    together,
Entering at last the Pure Land of Happiness.
There we will consummate all merits and good works,
There without doubt we will meet once more.

Milarepa continued: "We are living in a time of defilement. Corruption and vice abound everywhere, people are voracious and harbor strong desires and passions [Kleśas]. This is a very difficult time for one to subdue all his desires at once; therefore one should examine himself, and see what precepts he may take and live up to."

The Ḍākinīs then said to Milarepa, "Yes, indeed, Lord. It is only because you are so compassionate that you have preached for us the truth of Karma and called our attention to morality and virtue. This is all very wonderful, but we have heard this kind of preaching before. In the great cemetery of Sinhala, the Wisdom Ḍākinī, the outstanding Earth-Protecting Goddesses, such as the Lion-faced one, Damala Richroma, the Dumo Ngosungma, and the accomplished yogini, Bhina Betsar, have already preached to us the merits and glory of the Bodhi-Mind. We have heard many sermons on morality and discipline. Therefore, please do not merely preach to us these [fundamental and preliminary] teachings. As to our demonstration of malignant and wrathful forms before you a while ago,[10] it was to make a crucial test of your Realization. Since we are protectors of Dharma, we would not do anything truly harmful to people. But now we pray you to give us the [Precept] for raising the Bodhi-Mind."

The Jetsun replied, "Why not, since you ask with such sincerity and earnestness? Of course I will give the Precept to you. Now, prepare your offerings and Maṇḍala for the ceremony. I would like to tell you this, however: I am not a person who cares for worldly goods and pleasures, but each of you may now offer your special worldly accomplishments[11] to me, and also tell me your true names."

Whereupon, with great enthusiasm and respect, the Ḍākinīs sat in a row with folded hands to make their offerings. The first said, "I am the leader in this group. My name is Auspicious Fair Lady of Long Life [Drashi Tserinma]. I now offer you the accomplishment of protecting and increasing one's progeny." The Ḍākinī who sat on the right side of the leader said, "My name is Fair Lady of the Blue Face [Tingeyalzun-

ma]. I now offer you the accomplishment of divining with a mirror."
The Ḍākinī who sat to the right of Tingeyalzunma said, "My name is
Crowned Lady of Good Voice [Jupan Drinzonma]. I now offer you the
accomplishment of refilling a storehouse with jewels." The Ḍākinī who
sat to the left of the leader said, "My name is Immutable Fair Lady of
Heaven [Miyo Lonzonma]. I now offer you the accomplishment of
winning food and prosperity." The remaining Ḍākinī, who sat to the
left of Miyo Lonzonma said, "My name is Fair Lady of Virtue and Action [Degar Drozonma]. I now offer the accomplishment of increasing
livestock."

Thereupon, the Jetsun imparted to them one by one the teaching of
Taking Refuge, the Code of Morals, and the raising of the Bodhi-Mind
of Wish and of Action, explaining them in general terms as well as in
detail. Whereupon, the magical Ḍākinīs were very much pleased and
fascinated. They said to Milarepa, "Although we will not be able to
practice these teachings in as perfect a manner as you have so edify-
ingly instructed us, we will try not to violate these principles and will
never forget the gratitude that we owe you." They then expressed their
sincere thanks to the Jetsun by bending their bodies towards him,
laying their foreheads upon his feet, circling round him, and prostrating before him many times. Then they all flew into the sky and
vanished in the far distance in a blaze of light.

One evening, later in the month, the hostile and insolent demons of
the Eight Divisions who had come before, returned to Milarepa with
their servants and sons. From the low regions also came many lovely and
coquettish worldly Ḍākinīs [including the five who had come before],
wearing splendid silk garments which fluttered lightly in the breeze, and
adorned with jeweled bracelets, necklaces, and various other ornaments
of precious stones. Together with their retinues and associates, these
Non-men spirits all came to Milarepa, filling the sky before him. They
then began to rain flowers upon him, to play all kinds of musical instruments, to burn fragrant incense, and to offer abundant food and drink.
They said, "Pray relate to us your experience of Final Enlightenment —
the utmost understanding of all Buddhas in the Three Times, and the
absolute consummation of the Path. Pray preach for us the Final Truth
of Dharma." In response to their request Milarepa sang a song called
"The Understanding of Reality," in which he illucidated the essence of
the Final Truth and the Ultimate Reality:

> On the border of Tibet and Nepal
> Lies Dinma Drin, a wonder town.

There lives the Medicine Deva, protectress of the
    natives.
On the splendid Snow Queen Mountain, the beauty
    of this land,
Dwells the great Auspicious Lady of Long Life —
She is the lady with the braided hair,
Her life is lasting as a diamond.

At the left side of the mountain,
Covered by clouds throughout the year,
Are pasture lands and ranges of snow hills
Where gently flows a winding river;
Close by is Medicine Valley.

With great earnestness, I,
The Yogi Milarepa,
Meditate alone in this quiet place.
You, proud worldly demons —
Thieves who steal yogis' lives —
Who came here once before to insult and scorn me,
Have returned today.
Are you not the same group
Who afflicted me before?
Late last evening, close to midnight,
Five lovely maids came here.
They vowed to raise the Bodhi-Mind,
Offering wish-fulfilling accomplishments,
And then they disappeared.

Tonight, while the clear moon
Shines o'er the earth serene,
You five charming maidens, gay and skittish,
Come once more.
The silk scarfs round your lovely bodies
Sway and flutter, your jewels
Sparkle in the light.
You have been conjured to perfection,
Enchanting and most beautiful.
At the Goddess Leader's call, the proud
Devas and spirits of the Eight Divisions
Have come with you, filling all the sky.
They all offer me delicious food,
And play such charming tunes.

Since you have asked for the utmost Truth and Final
    Teachings,
You should heed most carefully, and give your
    full attention.

Sentient beings in the Three Kingdoms
Possess different Passion-Bodhis.[12]
Among them there are many kinds of egoism
And many types of behavior;
They have a myriad ways of ego-clinging.
To suit the minds of ignorant men,
The Buddha said, "All things are existent."

But in [the realm of] Absolute Truth
Buddha Himself does not exist;[13]
There are no practices nor practisers,
No Path, no Realization, and no Stages,
No Buddha's Bodies and no Wisdom.
There is then no Nirvāna,
For these are merely names and thoughts.
Matter and beings in the Universe
Are non-existent from the start;
They have never come to be.
There is no Truth, no Innate-Born Wisdom,
No Karma, and no effect therefrom;
Samsāra even has no name.
Such is Absolute Truth.

Yet, if there are no sentient beings, how
Could Buddha in the Three Times come to be?
For if there is no cause, there will be no effect.
Therefore Buddha says, "In Mundane Truth,
All Samsāric and Nirvānic things exist."
In Ultimate Truth, manifestation and the Void,
Existence and non-existence,
Are the same, being one in "taste"![14]
There is no difference, such as "this" and "that."
All Dharmas are two-in-one in the Greatness.
This is understood by those enlightened ones
Who see no consciousness but Wisdom,
Who see but Buddhas, and no sentient beings.
Who see no Dharma-forms, but Dharma-Essence.
Spontaneously a great compassion

Flows out from their hearts.
Their powers and virtues ne'er decline.
They possess all merits and wish-granting powers.
They have realized all virtues and the Truth.

Oh, you ghosts and Devas here assembled,
[When you approach the preachers]
You hear not the profound Dharma
But hark to pagan ranting;
When you reach the country of Ahbhira,
You do not visit wise men,
But go to mad instructors.

Wolves and foxes wandering in graveyards
Are frightened when they hear a lion's roar.
Should there be a gifted one in this assembly,
Through hearing this, my preaching,
He will in time be liberated.
Most joyful now am I;
May you also be gay and happy.

After singing this song, he said to the visitors, "The Buddha has preached numerous Dharmas, commonly known as 'The Eight Thousand Groups.' All these various teachings are given to different people, in accordance with their needs and capacities. However, the [utmost Truth is One] and the final destination [to which all paths lead] is One. This sole, absolute Foundation [of all] is the unaltered [unacted-upon and untouched] real nature of being. *By merely understanding this Truth, one will not be able to liberate himself. He must proceed on the Path. Only thus can he actually realize what he has understood.* The essence of the Path is the Two-in-One Voidness-Compassion, and though there are myriads of different paths or doctrines, they all lead to the Two-in-One Realm of Wisdom and Means, or the realization of the non-distinction of the Two Truths."[15]

Then the five Ḍākinīs who had come to Milarepa the night before to take the oath of Bodhi-Mind, rose from the assembly and, standing to the left of the Jetsun, sang together a song of praise, "We See His Merits":

Beneath the bright light in the sky
Stand snow mountains to the North.
Nigh these are auspicious pasture lands,
And fertile Medicine Valley.

Like a golden divan is the narrow basin,
Round it winds the river, earth's great blessing.

At this time of defilement and corruption
Came you, the ascetic Yogi, full of wonders.
The food you eat is nectar of Non-thought,
The drinks you quaff are natural secretions.
In your mind, there is no disgrace or shame;
In your mind there is nothing clean or filthy.
You act like a madman leading an ascetic life.

For the sake of testing your ability,
We came last summer to this river bank —
To the left of Lashi Mountain —
And found you in Sendentsema Wood
With your naked body indifferent to shame,
Amusing yourself with the lesser fairies.

We saw you in the mirror silvered thick,
We saw your meditation powers and your wondrous feats,
We saw your body vanish in the sky.
By these wonders we were so amazed
That in midautumn we returned.
You were then meditating in the Tsonlung Cave,
Absorbed in deep Samādhi. We crept in
And saw you wearing clothes of sun and moon
With a precious garland on your head.
Your body was besmeared with ash of cinnabar,
And in your hands, the canopy and victorious banner.

We saw you riding a fierce animal, flying
Through the firmament to vanish in the sky.
Thus we had no chance to harm you.

We came again last summer to put you to the test,
Intending to disturb your meditation.
But your mind was like the ocean,
While your body burned with fire.
Poisonous snakes were writhing round your head
As an adorning diadem.

Leaning on the blade of a sharp knife,
You sat in the lotus posture on a spear.

We saw you play a'top a wish-granting
Ball, and swallow a whole mountain.
Thus were we fascinated and bewildered too!

You are a yogi who has mastered Mind-awareness,
And like Indra, you can conjure and dissolve
Your body and perform countless miracles.
In your mind there is no pride, no thought.
You are free of doubt, of hope and fear.

You are a yogi like unto a lion,
For you fear not and have no misgiving.
You are a yogi like a great elephant,
 For you will ne'er be frightened by any obstacle.
 When one sees you, his heart is full of joy
And the hairs of his body stand on end.
By merely touching and beholding you,
All obstacles are cleared away,
All altruistic deeds accomplished.

You are the Wish-fulfilling Gem,
You are the Yogi, as the heavens great.
Since you have realized what "beyond-words" means
And never would be swayed by thoughts,
Demons can ne'er disturb you!

When we found we could not harm you,
It seemed it was ourselves whom we were mocking.
Thus we have changed our hostile stand,
Conjuring wondrous and delightful visions for you.
You also preached to us the Dharma,
And led us to the harmonious Path and Peace!

On that auspicious night last month
You sowed in us the Buddha-Seed.
The priceless buds in our hearts have grown.
You are the supreme teacher for the Path that no
        one can mistake,
You are the shelter and refuge of all beings.

Later, when you go to the Pure Land of Joy[16]
Where stands the palace of Mijurpa Buddha,
All the great Bodhisattvas will come to greet you.

The Ḍākinīs above, on, and beneath the earth,
Together with the meritorious Devas
Will also come to greet you. They will bring
Victorious banners and great canopies
And play melodious music for your welcome.
They will make you splendid offerings,
Showing you the way to the Pure Land.
Let us, who have seen you and heard you preach,
Both human beings and Non-men,
All become your servants
And follow you to the Pure Land!

Thus they sang, offering their sincere wishes and expressing their admiration.

Milarepa thought, "These worldly Ḍākinīs are very arrogant and incorrigible. They still have to be subdued and disciplined." So he said, "Fair ladies, it is indeed wonderful that you have such faith and respect for me and have expressed your sincere, pure wishes for the future. I have shown you the Path leading towards Buddhahood, and granted you the Precepts of the Bodhisattva. Now I am going to give you the Instructions and Precepts of the Diamond Vehicle, which abounds with skills and means; it is the easiest, fastest, and most versatile Path leading towards Buddhahood. Now you should prepare the offerings, and also surrender to me the quintessence of your lives."

The Ḍākinīs were thrilled with great joy. Immediately they arranged oblations on a grand scale, prostrated themselves before the Jetsun, and circumambulated him many times; and finally they offered him their lives. They then sat round him, as before. Thereupon, Milarepa vouchsafed them the Initiation called "Demonstrating the Awareness of Drol Ma," and the Initiation of the Goddess Kurukullā, together with the teaching of the Reciting-the-[words-of-] Essence. He admonished them to observe the discipline strictly, and instructed them to visualize their Guru sitting on their heads at all times. He taught them that whatever the crisis they might encounter, good or bad, they should look only to the Three Precious Ones for guidance and help. Never should they put their trust in pagan gods. The Jetsun then said, "You should know that the outer world is, in essence, identical with the Beyond-measure Palace of the Buddhas; all sentient beings are, in essence, identical with the Patron [Yidham] Buddhas. Whoever you meet, you should respect him and love him. Not even for a single moment should you have any malignant and hostile thoughts towards anyone, nor should you revile or hurt him in any manner. In all circumstances and at all times you should not forget the Self-Buddha Pride." [17]

The five goddesses then said to Milarepa, "Oh Jetsun, the teaching of Tantra is indeed the fastest, easiest, and most resourceful of all teachings. We are very grateful that you bestowed it and its precepts upon us. We impure sentient beings have been driven by deep-rooted habitual thinking since beginningless time in Saṃsara. We women, especially, are low of birth and inferior in intelligence. Though we cannot really understand that which you have imparted to us, we shall try our best to learn and practice it. Though we may not be able to perceive that all sentient beings are Buddhas, we shall not harm them in any manner. We will give assistance and service to the followers of Dharma, and will try our utmost to give special protection and help to the followers of your Lineage. We will provide them with all they need for their devotions and assist them to obtain all the favorable conditions they require. We will serve them as their servants." Swearing thus, they bowed down to Milarepa and circumambulated him many times. Then they all disappeared into the sky.

This is the story of how the indescribable great Yogi Milarepa, the Laughing Vajra, met with the five worldly Ḍākinīs, including their leader, the Auspicious Lady of Long Life. Also found in this story is the song which answered the Ḍākinīs' inquiry about the principle of raising the Bodhi-Mind. This event was recorded by the well-gifted, virtuous Repa Shiwa Aui on the peak of the Auspicious Mountain of Tuntin, by the left side of Dinma Drin market. In recording this story, Shiwa Aui has carefully and repeatedly inquired, and discussed [the matter] with the Auspicious Lady of Long Life in person. Afterwards, he met the Jetsun himself three times, the Jetsun also giving him, with approbation, some needed information. In that quiet, delightful, and accomplishment-granting place, the Meritorious Forest of Ahom Chun, Shiwa Aui and Ngan Tson Dunba Bodhiradza, in consideration of benefiting some destined persons in the future, have faithfully put the Jetsun's words down without adding to or abridging the original narrations and events. Their rhetorical and well-arranged writing [deserves to be called] the Illuminating and Nectar-like Rosary of Words.

NOTES

1 "Up-going Bliss": According to the supreme Bliss-Void Yoga, a great bliss will arise if a yogi can lift his life-energy from the lower part of the Central Channel

to a higher position. The consummation of this bliss is achieved when the life-energy reaches the Cakra at the top of the head.

2 It is said that when a Tantric yogi reaches a very advanced stage of Enlightenment, he should practice the Tantric Madness or Act-of-Insanity by behaving like a lunatic, to completely emancipate himself from all conventional thoughts and habits and thus reach final and perfect Enlightenment.

3 Lit.: The Samādhi of "Elements-Exhaustion" (T.T.: Zad.Pa.hByuñ.Bahi.Tiñ. Ñe.hDsin.): Having completely mastered the art of Dhyāna, the yogi is said to be capable of working miracles by manipulating the Prāṇa in various ways within his mind-body complex. He is thus able to conceal or bring into manifestation the power of each Element for a specific performance or purpose.

4 Ba Men, the wild ox of Tibet: Some say this is another name for the Tibetan yak.

5 T.T.: Bar.dHa.Na.: This seems to be another geographical name for Tibet.

6 The Tibetan word, "sPyan.Phyag," means literally "eye obeisance." The translator presumes that this term refers to a certain eye-gesture (mudrā) performed for the purpose of veneration. This may still be used in India, but is no longer extant in Tibet.

7 Yed Pa (T.T.: bShad.Pa.): Milarepa was given the name of Yed Pa Dorje (the Laughing Vajra) by his Guru, Marpa, when he was first initiated.

8 Worldly Ḍākinīs (T.T.: hJin.rTen.mKha.hGro.Ma.): Khandroma, or Ḍākinīs, the sky travelers, are not all more holy than, or spiritually superior to, ordinary sentient beings. According to traditional Tibetan beliefs, there are two kinds of Ḍākinīs: one is the holy, or transcendental type, and the other is the worldly kind. Tārā, Dorje Paumo, etc., belong to the former category, for they are fully enlightened Buddhas manifesting in female form. The worldly Ḍākinīs, such as Tserinma, are still bound by Saṃsāric desires and ignorance despite their superhuman powers.

9 Lit.: "... at the upper end of my three Nāḍis."

10 A while ago: See Story 28.

11 Worldly, or mundane accomplishments: miraculous performances and superhuman powers which are still of a Saṃsāric nature.

12 Passion-Bodhis (T.T.: hDod.Bahi.Byañ.Chub.): This is a very rare term seldom seen in the general Buddhist scriptures. Literally it means the "Bodhi of Kleśas." Although, according to the principle of Tantrism, it is permissible to say that human passions and desires (Kleśas) are *in essence* identical with the merits and wisdom of Buddhahood, it is incorrect to say that the two are absolutely identical in every aspect. Passion-Bodhis, or the Bodhi of Kleśas, should therefore be treated as an exceptional term reflecting a certain special Tantric thought outside the general framework of Buddhist orthodoxy.

13 This sentence as it appeared in the Tibetan text (Folio 151a, line 6) is as follows: "bGegs.Pas.Sañs.rGyas.Ñid.Kyañ.Med." The translator believes that "bGegs. Pas.," meaning "because of hindrances," is a misprint, otherwise it would be very difficult to explain, and to fit into this context.

14 T.T.: Ro.gCid., lit.: "one-taste." A freer translation is "at-one-ment," or "the great one identity." "Ro.gCid." is a very widely used term in Tantric literature, denoting the all-identical or non-differentiated nature of beings.

15 Two Truths: They are, first, the Mundane Truth (T.T.: Kun.rDsob.bDen. Pa.), and second, the Transcendental Truth (T.T.: Don.Dam.bDen.Pa.). The former can also be rendered as the "conditional, dependent, or expedient Truth," and the latter as the "absolute or final Truth."

16 The Pure Land of Joy (T.T.: mÑon.dGha.): the land of Buddha Mijurpa (T.T.: Mi.hGyur.Pa.; Skt.: Akṣobhyā): His position among the five Dhyāna Buddhas is in the East.

17 Self-Buddha Pride (T.T.: lHahi.Ña.rGyal.): A Tantric yogi should, in all daily activities, always remember his Patron-Buddha-Identification "feeling" which he has gained during his Arising Yoga practice. This Patron-Buddha-Identification Yoga is designed for the transformation of all worldly, empirical experiences into a higher order that may be described as corresponding to that of perfect Buddha-hood. Thus, in the practice of this Yoga, the yogi is taught to think and to visualize his body as becoming the Buddha's body, his words as the Buddha's preaching, and his thoughts as the Buddha's all-manifesting Wisdom. The meditation exercise of "Identification-with-Buddha" is also called the "Arising of Self-Buddha Pride."

30

ॐ॥

GUIDING INSTRUCTIONS
ON THE BARDO

Obeisance to all Gurus

The God of gods,
Lord of Ḍākinīs,
Marpa the great Translator —
Blessed is he by the Transmission Gurus.

A pearl radiates waves of grace
From the crown he ever wears —
Blessed is he, the great Repa Mila.

Delivered and matured is he
Who has completed his devotion.
To him, the Laughing Vajra, the gifted Repa Jetsun,
I pay sincerest homage!

To help the ignorant
I now relate this story
Of Mila's answer to the fairies,
Wherein is given the pith of the instructions
On guidance through the perilous Bardo.

When Marpa the Translator was imparting the Initiation to Milarepa, the Buddha Saṃvara and other deities of the Maṇḍala, together with the thirty-two Guards of Dharma and Ḍākinīs, and the sixteen Heavenly-Ladies-of-Offering, all revealed themselves in the upper sky. Milarepa saw this vision clearly for a moment. He was then given the name, "Laughing Vajra," by his Guru and the Ḍākinīs.

Urged by Marpa, Milarepa devoted his life to meditation. Because of

333

his extreme asceticism, he had gained the Tantric Accomplishments and Merits by [mastering] the [inner and outer] causations. Through his physical body he had attained the rainbow-like Body-of-the-Mind[1] and so became the great Jetsun — one who had achieved the Ultimate Realization of Mahāmudrā.

Now, Milarepa was residing [in a green valley] to the east of the wondrous [market] town of Dinma Drin, bordering on the Mon region west of the lower Khum Bu. Beneath dark clouds, above the gate to the passage of the black planet Rāhu and to the left of a snow mountain perpetually wreathed in clouds, lay this pasture land, Medicine Valley, where flourished emerald-like meadows, jasmine flowers, and various kinds of herbs. Gently flowing by were two rivers — the Auspicious Milk, and the Nectar and Power. [Milarepa's hut] was in a quiet and blessed spot known as the "Virtuous Palace Hermitage of Chu Bar." He was then completely absorbed in the Universal Realm of the Absolute Essence — the realm of departing-from-all-playwords, the illuminating realm of no-arising and no-extinction.

It was in the autumn of the year of the Wooden Horse, while the 24th Constellation was declining, that the inhabitants of Dinma Drin were afflicted with the white and black smallpox, [and with] vomiting of blood, dizziness, fever, and many other severe and contagious diseases.[2] Many livestock and human beings had died.

In the late afternoon of the eleventh day of the second month of that autumn, when the declining sun looked like a fireball, a young girl [whom Milarepa recognized as a Ḍākinī] came to see him. Beautiful, charming, and radiant, she was dressed in a white silk robe of magnificent design, edged with jewel-like lace, and having an apron of exquisite silk with gorgeous tassels. She bowed down at Milarepa's feet, circled him seven times, and made nine more prostrations. She then said, "Oh Jetsun, our people are very, very sick. Please be kind enough to come with me to the other side of this snow mountain [to help us]." Milarepa replied, "It is better that we go tomorrow. You may stay here tonight." The girl said, "If we go by the Road of Miraculous Light, through Manta Tsari [?] there will be no hardship. Oh please, please come! You must come today!" "This old man has never seen such a road before," replied Milarepa, "nor do I know where it is. But because of your earnest request, I shall go with you. It is better if you go ahead and show me the way." The girl then produced a woolen blanket, and lifting it up toward the sky, said to the Jetsun, "Let us ride on this blanket — it will carry us there at once." As soon as Milarepa stood upon the blanket, it rose in the air, and quick as lightning, they reached their destination on the other side of Queen of the Azure Heights Snow Mountain.

On the left slope stood a white silk tent with a golden covering. The ropes and pegs were inlaid with precious stones of magnificent quality. In this tent lay another beautiful girl, wrapped in many bedcoverings, and with a long tassel, which almost reached the ground, in her hair. Her eyes were flame-colored [as if she had a fever]. As the Jetsun entered, she made an effort to lift her head up a little, crying, "I am very sick. Please help me!" Milarepa asked, "How did you catch this disease? How long have you been ill? What are your symptoms?" The girl answered, "Last summer some shepherds came and lit a big fire near here. I was caught in the flaming smoke, which made me very sick at the time. Since last autumn I have not been feeling at all well, and today I feel extremely ill.³ Therefore I had to send for you. The vapors from our mouths have caused many people in this area to contract many diseases." Milarepa thought, "That's why so many people here have caught the pestilence. I cannot consent to cure her right away; first I must admonish her." Then he said, "Fair lady, not long ago you came to me and took the Bodhisattva's Vow, and also received the teachings of the Patron Buddha. I preached to you at length on the virtues and Karma, but instead of following my instructions, you have violated them all. You have never given the slightest consideration to your moral obligations and the precepts! You could not even endure such a slight discomfort as that caused by the shepherds, and in revenge you have spread the worst kind of pestilence among innocent people, causing them great suffering and misfortune. Since you have violated the precepts, you well deserve such punishment. In view of what you have done, I can no longer trust you. If you will immediately heal all the people in this area, I shall then see whether or not I can help you. If you do not promise to do so, I shall leave at once. Since you, the She-ghost, have broken your own oaths and violated the precepts, you will surely be damned!"

Hearing this warning from the Jetsun, the Dākinī was very frightened and immediately clutched Milarepa's feet and said, "We are blind and wicked beings. Because of our ignorance we have spread illness in this region. But please do not talk to us like this! As a rule, if the pure Devas and spirits from the higher ranks do not afflict us, we will never attack them first. Expecially, in consideration of your [former] admonishment, I have not harmed any people or sent others to afflict them. In the last month of this summer the river here overflowed, and all the narrow and precipitous places were flooded. [Taking advantage of this], some of our retainers, associates, and kinsmen, together with many flesh-eating and blood-drinking servants of ours, went about afflicting people. I will stop all the contagious diseases as soon as I get better. Therefore, please look after me and have pity on me." Thus she earnestly besought the Jetsun.

Milarepa then performed for her the Hundred-Words Cleansing Ritual[4] and prayed for her to the Gurus and the Precious Ones many times. He also increased her longevity by performing the ritual of the Victorious Mother of the Crown.[5] The next morning she was able to get up from her bed and make obeisance to him.

During the next seven days the Jetsun continuously blessed her with the power of Illuminating-Awareness, and the girl was then completely cured. She became even more healthy and vigorous than before. After this Milarepa said to her, "Fair lady, as you have completely recovered, now is the time for you to go to the villages and help the people. Tell me what offerings you would like them to make to you? What rituals should be performed to cure the sick?" She replied, "According to the reciprocal-relation principle of the Law-of-Causation, when we recover from a disease, so will the people. It is the common oath of all wordly Ḍākinīs[6] that if one of us has been made unwell or unhappy, we are all offended and the Devas and spirits support us, throwing the world into confusion. Therefore, if one wants to convalesce quickly, he should recite the quintessential Mantra of Buddha Tsudor many times, read the profound Mahāyāna Sūtras, perform the Ritual of Cleansing with Vase-Water, mark a circle round the village and confine people in it, offer white and red oblations and huge Dormas,[7] deck the altars, dedicate the merits to all, and then make his wish. He who does all these things will soon be cured."

Milarepa then went to Drin and said to the villagers, "I have had indications from a dream that the pestilence now prevailing in this area was caused by the local goddesses who are angry with you because you offended and injured them by the fires you kindled. In revenge they have spread the diseases. You should now perform suitable rituals and make various offerings."

Thereupon, the villagers all prayed to the Gurus, the Buddhas, and the Guards of Dharma, offering them many oblations and huge Dormas, and dedicating these merits to the Devas and spirits. Through the infallible power of these prayers and blessings, the pestilence completely disappeared within a short time.

On the 29th day of that month, the five Auspicious Ladies of Long Life, together with many of their followers and local deities, came to visit the Jetsun. They brought delicious food and excellent wine in jeweled beakers and offered them to Milarepa. After they had made obeisances to him and circled him many times, they stood in a row and said, "It is you, the Jetsun, who have saved our lives and cured our illnesses. You have been most gracious to us." Whereupon, with sweet voices they sang:

He who can foretell the fall of rain
Knows how to observe the sky.
When one sees that dark clouds gather,
And the dragon thunders,
He knows that the Dragon King will soon give rain
To nourish all sentient beings.
When slowly the rain drizzles,
It shows that moisture and heat
Are in balance on the earth.
When the deafening thunder peals,
It indicates the clashing conflict
Between heat and cold.

Under the flying clouds
Stands a great snow mountain with three peaks —
The central one is highest.
A crown of crystal
Is her head ornament;
Starlight, soft and glimmering,
Surrounds her in the serene night;
The rays of sun and moon gleam upon her.
Beauteous and resplendent was she fashioned.
There our noble castle stands!

By the left slope of the snow mountain
Are the wondrous pastures of Medicine Valley.
A canopy of rainbows ever hangs above it,
Reflecting beams of glowing light.
Lovely are the herbs grown in the valley,
Here dance and play the local gods,
Here lies the land of crops and fruit —
A garden full of lovely flowers.

Your hut stands by the river bank,
A place of great blessing,
Where the great Yogi Mila dwells.

Through the merits of your previous lives
You receive a precious human body.
By sloth unhindered
You meditate without diversion.
Thus, you have realized Mind-nature, the Unborn,
And mastered the magic gestures.

No obstacles and distractions can frighten you.
Unshakeable as a mountain,
You are a yogi of stability.
Having mastered Prāṇa to perfection,
You have no need of clothing,
Exposing your body freely.
By your grace and your devotions
Many beings have been saved.
At a time of defilement and distress
You came to the red-faced country [of Tibet]!
You are the glory of the world,
Our shelter and our pride!

[The leader of the four Ḍākinīs continued to sing]:

On the eleventh of this month
I was hurt and sullied by smoke and fire.
With great pain was my body wracked —
The unbearable torment tore at me.
So I became most angry and malignant.
Then I asked your help, and graciously you
          blessed me,
Performing the Ritual of Cleansing.
Also, you enlightened me
On the Mind-Essence which is beyond both life
          and death.
Of a sudden, I came to realize the Truth.
Like clouds that vanish in the sky
All my hurt was cleared away,
My mind became fresh and alert,
My body light as wool,
So comfortable and well.
The fevers left, health was restored,
And my failing breath regained its strength.
Thus the peril of death was overcome!

Failing to complete their missions
The agents of Death went back with shame.
A great debt of gratitude I owe you, oh great Yogi!
Though my birth is low and great my ignorance,
My compassion small and inferior my mind,
How can I forget he who saved my life?
Till the end of it,

I shall ne'er forget this boon!

Showing my deepest thanks
I now offer you my magic powers.
With loyalty confirmed
I shall obey your teaching.
From now until I win perfect Buddhahood
I will consort with you;
By the power of this sincere wish
May I never leave you even for a second.
As a shadow, may I follow in your steps.
Like the five first disciples of Gautama Buddha,
May we be the first disciples in your Pure Land,
When you reach perfect Buddhahood.
May we be the first to drink your nectar
And become the children of Dharma.
May we gather the clouds of the Four Actions[8]
And rain down heavenly waters
To nourish ignorant beings!

Thus, in making their pure wishes, the Auspicious Fair Lady of Long
Life led her four Ḍākinī-sisters in singing this song. The Jetsun thought,
"Now these malicious goddesses have shown their gratitude to me for
healing their sickness. If I give them the preliminary Instructions of the
Arising and Perfecting Yoga, they may be able to practice them." Then
he said, "Fair ladies, with great sincerity you have now shown me your
deep gratitude for the recovery of your health. Your words and attitude
seem to have met the requirements for Tantric teaching. I intend to
give you an Instruction, through which you may forever free yourselves
from sufferings on the perilous path of Saṃsāra. But will you be able to
practice it?" Milarepa then sang them a song, "The Growth of Joyfulness":

Under the canopy of sunlight in the East
Towers the propitious peak of Mount Menlha;[9]
Like the head of a crystal eagle
It reflects the glowing golden beams.
The floating clouds are like a roof,
And arched above it shines the rainbow.
On the mountain's waist
The gem-like rocks are girdled in dense fog.
Is this not the great snow mountain, Queen of
    the Azure Heights?

Residing on it are there not five wondrous ladies?
In an enchanting voice
One has just sung divinely.
Is she not the Fair Lady of Long Life,
Most sparkling and most glamorous?

This time you are really frightened,
For you have lost your pride!
Your body was torn with agonizing pain,
And your mind was full of grievances!
Your breath was failing like a thinning mist,
And your life was nearly at an end.

All this was due to your past sinful deeds —
A bitter retribution of the Ripening Karma.
If from these sinful deeds you do not refrain,
Into the great Hell you may fall perchance.
That is more dreadful than any sickness!

That you did not die is fortunate,
Praiseworthy that your seed of faith has grown.
With great compassion have I blessed you.
Through the great power of Tantra
Have I saved you from the hand of Death.

All despair and misfortune
Has turned to good and boon.
In joy you thanked me with deep gratitude,
Which in many others would be lacking.
In a charming voice
You have sung sweetly with good meaning.
Hearing it, I too feel glad and joyful.

If you would follow my instruction
Please listen and remember well:
Painful is the path of Saṃsāra,
Perilous and hard to cross
Are the Four Rivers.[10]
Dismal is the "forest" of Eight Strivings,
Hard to escape are the triple Bardo's dangers.
To live under the constant threat
Of Four Devils[11] is distressing.
But here is a path of no-fear —

An escape from all miseries,
Leading to the Land of Bliss Eternal.

I may not be superb,
But my Lineage is supreme.
From the great Dorje-Chang, the Sixth Buddha,[12]
To my teacher, the Translator Marpa,
All the Transmission Gurus are Nirmāṇakāyas.
Never has a commoner corrupted the Lineage.
Cherish then and value all my teachings!

The stories of Medripa and Nāropa are well known;
You also must have heard their names before,
As their fame is known all over India.
Blessed by these two accomplished beings
Is my father Guru, Marpa.
Like a shadow to its body,
I stayed close to him for six years and eight
    months.
By following his orders faithfully,
Joy and aspiration filled my heart.

The profound Tantra Hevajra, the gracious Dem-Chog,
The quintessential Tantra of Mahāmāya,
The lofty Tantra of Sungdue,
The concealed Tantra of Den Yi,
And the Nirmāṇakāya of the Skull —
All these vital Tantras
And their commentaries, deep as the ocean,
Were bestowed on me,
A gift of precious gems.

The Key-Instructions, essential and most pithy,
Must be taught intimately, face to face.
To master them one also needs to practice;
Like an apprentice to a master goldsmith,
One must learn the art of melting and alloying
Gold, and how to stoke the fire.
The vital teachings of Tantra
Are also taught by word of mouth.

Witnessed by Ḍākinīs, I was given
The Pith-Instructions of the Lineage.

To my father Guru, I am forever grateful!
To repay him, I practice meditation.
By hard and steady work
I have mastered the Five Prāṇas;
With confidence I can perform the Action of
        Equality.[13]
No longer do I fear the pains of sickness.
Oh my daughter-disciples,
If you also want to attain such joy
Follow my words and footsteps.
Enter now the Path,
And you will soon be happy!

The human body is beset with sickness,
And trying to free one's mind from grief
Often leads to more distress.
By the force of Karma and the senses
All self-made confusions are created.
They are but dreams passing in a flash;
Even Hell with all its torture through the aeons,
Does not exist.
From evil and habitual thoughts [within]
Arise the pains without.
This is the Final Truth
Buddha Gautama preached to Dorje Ninpo.
The whole Universe is but "imagination,"
All in all, it is but a shadow-show
Of one's own mind.
If one knows not this truth
He may possess the world of Brahmā
But never can he win true happiness.

The Four Dhyānas[14] that for kalpas last
Are on the lower path;
Never can they bring one to Omniscient Buddhahood.
Only through cultivating Bodhi-Mind
And contemplating on the Void
Can Karmas, troubles, hindrances, and habitual
        thoughts be killed.

Oh well-endowed fair ladies,
It is our lot to meet here today.
Wear the armor of zeal

And abjure distraction!
Your wishes for good soon will be fulfilled.

Milarepa then said to the Ḍākinīs, "Please think carefully about this song and its meanings and practice Dharma at once. You may think that the Four Bodies of Buddha are something beyond yourself, an exterior object or goal that you should strive to reach. But, in fact, there is no Buddha to be found outside of one's own mind. The Light-of-Death [or, the Light that shines at the moment of death] is the Dharmakāya; the [pure manifestation of] Bardo is the Sambhogakāya; the different births one takes are the Nirmāṇakāyas; and the inseparable unity of the Trikāya is called the Body-of-Essence.[15] They are with us all the time, yet we are unaware of them. To unfold them, one must rely on the profound Pith-Instructions from an accomplished Guru of an uninterrupted Lineage."

The Fair Lady of Long Life then said, "When our Guru Padmasambhava first came to Tibet from India, we all went to afflict him, but we were subdued by his powers and mighty gestures. Then we obeyed his orders and offered him our lives and service. We also besought him for the essential teachings of Tantra. From him we received instructions on the truth of Karma and other Dharmas and Sūtras. At the Dark Noisy Cemetery[16] in India we received great Initiations and Vajrayāna teachings from Guru Shojigocha,[17] and the Black Performer.[18] Therefore, perhaps we may consider ourselves to be qualified to receive esoteric instructions. This time we have suffered greatly from illness. This painful lesson was so real and so frightening that we are convinced once and for all that never would we be able to endure the torment of Hell for a moment. The warnings in your song also impressed us deeply. So, pray protect us from these fears, cleanse us from all sins, and show us the way to Buddhahood." Whereupon, they sang:

Floating in the bright firmament,
The golden clouds by magic and wonder are created
To adorn the Nagas' crowns.
Under them, the lesser Devas, the Non-men,
And the Fragrance-eating She-ghosts
Dance and gaily sing, enjoying
Sensuous pleasures with much laughter.

Beneath those flying clouds
Lies the lucky valley of Dinma.
Its upper region is circled by snow ranges,

Its lower part abounds in springs and brooks.
In the center of this valley
Grows a luxuriant meadow
Where Devas sport and play.
This brilliant Medicine Valley
Is the Nagas' treasure house,
Filled with fruit and honey.
This is where four-footed creatures thrive —
A land of pastures, quiet and delightful.

Near the river bank is a hut
Wherein a wondrous yogi dwells.
By merely hearing of his name,
Or seeing his splendrous body,
One's hindrances and sins are cleared.
He works all miracles and Mudrās.
Having realized the Omniscient Mind,
With mastership of Dharma-Essence,
He preaches Voidness with compassionate voice.
To him all Devas and spirits
Should pray and give homage.
Trust and reliance should one place in him.
He is the son of Buddha,
Who grants us all our wishes.

Driven by deep-rooted ignorance,
We worldly, magical Ḍākinīs
Wander in Saṃsāra from time without beginning.
First, we must take an earthly birth —
We have no other choice.
Then we think we can live for long,
But suddenly we hear the call of Death
And our hands are tied —
We cannot escape.
Dizzy are our heads and dark our thoughts.

Without freedom from death, we must fade,
And with us all our beauty and our splendor.

When the living organs cease to function
The awesome play of Bardo must begin.
Along the fearful Bardo path
Wanderers, confused and desolate,

Are chased by merciless demons.
They are torn apart
By anxiety and fear;
By sinful acts and habitual thoughts
They are driven away.
Then, regardless of their wishes,
They are reborn in a strange and foreign land.

In the rolling ocean of Saṃsāra we repeat
The round of birth, old-age, sickness, and of death;
No one yet has rescued us from drowning.
Today you have given us the raft of Bodhi-Mind
On which we shall escape the witch-land of desires,
And elude the dreadful monster of the deep.
Riding the gale of wrong thoughts
We shall arrive safely
In the Happy Land.
From despair and weariness
We shall revive;
With hope and guidance,
Will our wishes be fulfilled.

In Saṃsāra's dark and fearful woods
Roam ghostly beasts, our passions.
Seeing them, in panic do we tremble.
In this dark and thorny forest
We have lost our way;
Pray show us the path
And deliver us in safety.
As the bright autumn moon
Illumines the great earth,
Enlighten, pray, our ignorance
And grant us your guidance.
In the dread Bardo path,
Perilous and inescapable,
Point out the dangerous traps.

We have been enslaved by the Devil's band,
And fettered in a dungeon by our acts;
From this dread imprisonment
We could not escape.
But today we have met you,
The Savior Guru whom none dare dispute.

With your guidance and protection
We will surely cross the road.

Pray show us the way to Dharmakāya
Through recognizing the Death Light.[19]
Pray show us the way to Samboghagakāya
Through recognizing Bardo's phantom forms.
Pray show us the way to Nirmāṇakāya,
Thus letting us incarnate at our will!

Beyond the fearful realm of the Three Bardos[20]
Lies the Pure Land of No-regression.[21]
Much have we heard of it
But we have never been there.
Oh compassionate Guru, savior merciful,
Pray guide us to it now!
Pray answer the cry for help
From those in despair and grief.
Pray now reveal to them
The Fourfold Body of Buddhahood!

Then they offered the Jetsun a silver mirror Maṇḍala decorated with a golden lotus and various gems. The Jetsun said, "Since you have petitioned me so earnestly, I shall now bless you in the tradition of my Lineage. Please prepare a sacramental feast for the occasion."

That evening the five Ḍākinīs offered a Maṇḍala filled with sixty different kinds of food to the Jetsun. He blessed and initiated them into the order of the Inborn Mother[22] of the Whispered Lineage, and then sang a song in which he gave them the instruction for identifying the perilous Bardo with the Trikāya, by means of which one delivers himself [forever from Saṃsāra] to the Pure Land of Great Bliss:

In the land of India,
In the center of this earth,
There is a great monastery, Bidrama[23] called.
A university is found therein
Whence springs the fountain of all learning.
There the professor of the Northern School
Is the peerless Paṇḍita, lion of men,
A mighty champion who has
Defeated every heretic.
Is he not the great Nāropa,
Master of the four Tantras,

Master of both the mundane and the ultimate
  Accomplishment?

The foremost son of this great Paṇḍita
Is my Father Guru, the Translator Marpa,
A man with strong will and perseverance,
A man of great fame, thunder-like.

He said, "At the time of defilement,
When declines the Buddha's teaching,
Lives will be short and merits poor.
Evils and hindrances, in myriad forms,
Will o'ershadow all the world;
Leisure and long life will become most rare;
Knowledge will [expand] to a point
Too stupendous to comprehend;
Proofs and conclusions will be hard to reach.
To understand the truth of Tantra will be
  most difficult.
Therefore, my son, try nothing else,
But work hard at the practice!"

Following this injunction,
I abjure indolence, and meditate
With perseverance in my hermitage.
Thus I have gained a few Experiences.

Destined fair ladies, now listen with attention!
Along the Path of the Three Existences[24]
There is no end of wandering in Saṃsāra!
Know then that the Six Dharmas of Bardo
Are the root of all.
[The following parables,
Will explain the teaching of Bardo.]

Three traveling [merchants], on a long journey,
When in a perilous place sent out for help.

When they saw their guides return with
  native welcomers
They were o'erwhelmed with joy.
Without reliable guides they would have lost
Their way and fallen into the hands of enemies.

If merchants go abroad without these three good
        guides[25]
Fear and misgiving fill their minds;
By false prophesies and revelations
Three Devils lead them
To a bandits' ambush.

Thus wanderers in the dark Sidpa Bardo
Will freeze and burn for nine and forty days,
Driven by the force of Karma
To Saṃsāra's prison to return.
If from this prison you would escape
You should contemplate the Oneness
Of the Saṃsāra-Nirvāṇa Bardo,
And meditate on the Root-principle,
Truth Absolute, the Mahāmudrā.

The Bardo of Birth-and-Death
Is a good ground on which to drill the illuminating
        mind.
Upon it one should practice the Arising and
        Perfecting Yogas.

The essence of the Bardo-of-the-Path
Is that of Innate Wisdom.
The Whispered Lineage practice will unfold it.

The Bardo of Dream-and-Sleep is best
To convert habitual thinking into Wisdom;
Within it one should practice the Yogas
Of Light and of the Phantom Body.
At the end of the Sidpa Bardo
The Three Bodies of Buddha will appear.
This is the time to enter the Three Pure Lands.[26]

If in Bardo one fails to realize Trikāya
And time elapses till the Incarnation-Bardo[27]
        comes,
By his faith and purity
He can still be born in a land of fortune,
His body well endowed with leisure.
Because the Law of Causation never fails to bring
        what one deserves,

By waking from past Karma
And perfecting meditation,
He will gain Liberation soon!

To you five wondrous maidens
Who asked with sincerity and faith
Is given this important Bardo teaching.
Even if the Jetsun Marpa should Himself come here,
He could give you no instruction more profound
        than this!

The five Ḍākinīs then prostrated themselves before the Jetsun and circumambulated him seven times. They offered him a Maṇḍala made of precious stones; praised his body, word, mind, and merits; and finally made him the supreme-bliss-void offering of the Wisdom-of-Four-Blisses produced through the ecstasy of union. Then they said, "Your instructions on the Bardo are clear and comprehensive. Now please give us the pith of this teaching to make it easier for us to practice," and they sang:

We pay homage to you, gracious Guru,
The refuge of all sentient beings.
With the teaching of the Whispered Lineage
You have transformed our pains to joy,
As by [a magician] iron is turned to gold.
Pray, most holy Buddha,
Always pity and protect us.

Above the immaculate lotus
Untarnished by Saṃsāric soil,
Your throne, oh Jetsun Guru,
Illuminates the Void!
A myriad Ḍākinīs cloud around you;
The sun and moon shine down on you,
Illumining the absence of wavering thoughts!

For your handsome face and radiant
Body we feel insatiable,
And desire to look once more.
Beautiful, with well-proportioned features,
You are like the son of the Victorious Ones.
Seeing you, one feels joy and happiness.
To the tune of Dri Za[28] we sing
A song of praise to you.

Your voice is like the roaring
Of a lion, great and mighty,
Like the Dharma, clear yet void.
Your voice frightens the devils and pagans
And fulfills the wishes of the gifted ones.
In the Ten Directions your fame will spread afar.

Like a diamond, your mind cannot be broken;
Like space it embraces all.
From the sky of No-conception
Shines the light of your Bodhi-Mind
Emancipating disciples from darkness.

Your body, word, and mind are like those of Buddhas —
From them spring all Accomplishments.
If one thinks of you, the Wish-fulfilling Gem,
All one's wishes will be fulfilled.
If one worships you with earnestness,
As the adorning crown-of-grace
Upon his head, all his hopes will be fulfilled.
If one prays to you wholeheartedly night and day
Like a mighty king, you will grant
All his requests.
To you, the precious Jetsun,
We pay homage and give praise.

From the clouds of your compassion
Falls the nectar rain of blessing;
When the destined disciple drinks it
He will conquer all his desires
In this very life, and the seed
Of Enlightenment will sprout within him.
Reaching the Thirteenth Stage,[29]
He will become the great Dorje-Chang.

With your teachings, wisdom, and performance
May all beings become filled and happy!
May the flower of perfection bloom in joy!
May we serve you as escorts on the Path,
Till we reach the Ultimate Enlightenment.
May we attain final Samādhi
Through normal worldly rapture.
By the Wisdom-of-Four-Blisses

May we stabilize the bliss-void Samādhi.

As women of intelligence we are convinced
Of the truth of the Middle Way.
With joy we shall obey your orders,
Pray grant us permission to serve you.

At the close of this song we ask
You for concise teaching on the Bardo.
Pray grant us the instruction for realizing
    Buddha's Four Bodies
At the time when death calls us.

Nourished and fostered by your grace,
May we win merits like yours.
In this very life
May we all attain perfect Enlightenment.

The Jetsun continued: "Fair ladies! Driven by the three desires and flowing thoughts, sentient beings have been wandering down the endless road in the Three Realms, forever subjected to the Eight Deprivations. This journey is so long and hazardous that one feels very weary and exhausted. There are three different kinds of travelers on this road. The first have received, followed, and practiced the Instructions; the second have also received but have not practiced them; while the third have not even the Instructions. The first kind do not fear or worry about the dangers of the road nor about the traps of demons, because by practicing the Dharma they are able to vanquish all these fears. The third kind are ordinary people who spontaneously enter the perilous path, and are automatically seized by the devils-of-Karma. They will undergo all the pains of birth and death, and wander in the Three Realms of Saṃsāra forever. The second kind have the same fears and hazards as the third. But they have received the Instructions and have learned to recognize and fight against evil influences; and so, if they have an unshakeable faith towards [Buddha] and an understanding and aspiration for the Dharma together with the armor of unyielding diligence, they may slowly and gradually recognize the Trikāya of Buddha by observing carefully how the senses and elements subside [at the time. of death]. You ask me about the teaching of realizing the Trikāya. You should know that at the time of death, when the outer and inner elements successively subside, the [consciousness] of the dying man will be [temporarily] set free from the string of Kleśas. The absolute Reality, the essence of the voidness of Dharmadhātu beyond all thought, will unfold itself, shining bright as the sun and moon in the sky. This is the Light-of-Death, or the Dharmakāya itself. One should recognize it as it is. But to do so at the time of death, a man must first understand the nature of Mind in the way his Guru pointed out during his lifetime, and also practice the Illuminating Light-of-the-Path.[30] In the perilous path of the Sidpa Bardo, the wanderer will be pursued and attacked by 'executioners' who are, in fact, created by his own previous Karmas and thoughts. These 'mind-created body-forms' are luminous, their organs are complete, and they possess the miraculous powers of a mundane karmic nature, which include the ability to pass through material objects, [telepathy,] and so forth. The Bardo body of this stage is, in fact, identical with the Sambhogakāya. At this time one should invoke the magic-like two-in-one Buddha Body [to replace and purify] the karmic Bardo body created by habitual thoughts, and thus recognize the Sambhogakāya as it is. To recognize this Sambhogakāya in the Bardo stage, one should practice the Arising Yoga and clearly visualize the Patron Buddha's Body during his lifetime, and also practice the Dream Yoga, to master the [manifestation] of the Phantom Body. At the final stage of Bardo, driven by the winds of Karma and Blindness and having no choice whatsoever, he searches for somewhere to incarnate. When he watches sex intercourse between [his future] mother and father, hate [towards one] and lust [toward the other] rises in him. But if at this time he can remember the Pith-Instructions, and enter the void-bliss experience [of Samādhi] and remain there, then karmic and worldly thoughts will not arise again. When he intends to incarnate he should think and observe that all he sees are manifestations of the Nirmāṇakāya Buddha, and recognize the Nirmāṇakāya as it is.

"In order to be able to recognize the Nirmāṇakāya, one should, in his present life, endeavor to arouse [transcendental] Wisdom through practising the Heat Yoga of the Liberation Path and the Karma Mudrā of the Path-of-Love. Only then will he be able to realize the full meaning of the Third Initiation[31] and thus vanquish [instinctive] jealousy. In brief, one must know well the different stages and times [in the Bardo state] in order to realize the fruit of the Trikāya. Even the ultimate Pointing-out Instruction of the Whispered Lineage — the core of the Skillful Path, the most cherished prize in Marpa's heart — can give you no profounder instructions than this. I have no better and no more convincing teaching than this to rely on and confide. So, fair ladies, appreciate what I say, follow, and practice it."

The Fair Lady of Long Life, the leader of the [Four] Ḍākinīs, was greatly inspired by these profound Instructions of the Skillful Path, and her faith was confirmed. She bowed down at the feet of Milarepa and said, "Oh Jetsun! From now on I will follow you and practice Karma Mudrā with you until I have consummated my Experience and Realization of this quintessential Bardo instruction. Please always remember and look after me." Praying to him with great sincerity and earnestness, the Ḍākinī again made obeisances and circumumbulated him many times. Then she returned to her own abode.

This is the story of the Great Repa Mila, the Laughing Vajra, and his meeting with the five worldly, magical Ḍākinīs, including the songs of inquiry and answer known as the "Golden Rosary," in which are found the instructions for emancipation from the perilous Bardo.

. . .   .

This is the story of the gracious Guru,
The accomplished, Gem-like Repa,
His meeting with five worldly Ḍākinīs of low birth,
And their songs of inquiry and his answers.
It is written with garlanded words
As a song containing
The profound hidden teaching of the Toagal.[32]

I have not added to this story
For fear of losing and forgetting it;
But for the benefit of disciples in the future
And to inspire their joy,
I have written this tale
In my Guru's words.

Three times did I seek my Guru's permission
To write this book.
He smiled at me, [but] did not grant it
Until the third time.
I dare not violate the rules
Because the Ḍākinīs are most severe and strict.

My Guru says this story should be told
Only to great yogis in the future
As a reference for their devotions;
But from others it must be secret kept.

Lest I violate the Ḍākinīs' rules and wishes
I now sincerely pray to them

To conceal this story from those
[Who cannot profit by it],
And never let it widely spread.

When Buddha Sākyamuni won Enlightenment,
In the latter part of the [month)
In which he worked miracles,
I, Auijee Thajan, and the Guru Bodhi Radsa,
In a tamarisk grove where wild beasts roam,
Asked our Elder Brother, perfect in the Tantric
        precepts,
In detail about this story,
And wrote it down in words.
It is "The Song of the Golden Rosary"
On how to free oneself from the perilous Bardo.
I now dedicate the merit of writing it
To the emancipation of all beings
From fear and danger in the Bardo.

At the request of the five Shajhamas,[33] the Fair Lady of Long Life
and her sisters, the instruction for freeing one from the perilous path
of Bardo was given by the peerless Yogi, the great Milarepa. After
careful discussions, the two Repas put it down in words as a service
and offering to the Dharma.

NOTES

1 Rainbow-like Body of the Mind (T.T.: hJah.Tshon.lTa.Buhi.Yi.Kyi.sKu.):
This term is not an established or often-used term in Tibetan Tantrism. It was
perhaps created by the author to denote the illuminated "mental body" of an accomplished yogi, usually known as hJah.Lus. — the Rainbow Body.

2 These are free translations of the diseases' names. Because of their obscuri-
ty, it is difficult to identify the equivalent medical terms.

3 The Tibetans believe that smoke caused by a forest or mountain fire will
usually injure or afflict the local deities. Thus, in revenge these deities will spread
germs of disease in the region.

4 The Hundred-Words Cleansing Ritual (T.T.: Yi.Ge.brGya.Pahi.Khrus.Chog.):
This is the cleansing ritual of the Vajrasattva whose main Mantra consists of one
hundred words.

5 The Victorious Mother of the Crown (T.T.: gTsug.Tor.Nam.Par.rGyal.
Ma.): a Tantric goddess who can bestow great powers of attraction.

6 Worldly Ḍākinīs (T.T.: hJig.rTen.mKhah.hGro.Ma.): Ḍākinīs are not necessarily all enlightened and benevolent beings. Worldly Ḍākinīs are local goddesses, or fairies who, like ordinary human beings, are still bound by desires and passions. They are by no means holy or divine. See Story 29, Note 8.

7 Dormas (T.T.: gTor.Ma.): In making the various oblations for Tantric rituals, Tibetan lamas have developed a highly sophisticated art of making these oblation objects from baked flour dough. Using this material as the main ingredient, together with additional decorative articles and figurines, Tibetan lamas can make up a great variety of oblations called Dormas.

8 Four Actions (T.T.: bsDus.Wa.rNam.bShi.; Literal translation: "Four Cooperative Acts"): These are the four Bodhisattva's virtues (Skt.: Catuh-saṁgrahavastu). They are (1) to give the things that others like to receive; (2) to say the pleasant words that others like to hear; (3) to do profitable deeds for sentient beings; and (4) to adapt oneself under all circumstances for the benefit of sentient beings.

9 Menlha (T.T.: sMan.lHa.): a holy place in Tibet.

10 Four Rivers: a symbolic term denoting the pains of birth, old-age, sickness, and death, that, like hazardous rivers, are difficult to cross.

11 Four Devils: the Devils of Illness, of Interruption, of Death, and of Desires.

12 Sixth Buddha: Counting clockwise, the first four Buddhas in a Maṇḍala, starting from the East, are (1) Buddha Vairocana, East; (2) Buddha Ratnasambhava, South; (3) Buddha Amitābha, West; and (4) Buddha Amoghasiddhi, North. The fifth Buddha, Vajrasattva, occupies the center place, and the sixth, Vajradhara (Tib.: Dorje-Chang) sits in the center above Vajrasattva. Dorje-Chang is the source and center of all the other five. Chronologically He is the First Buddha. The so-called Sixth Buddha is, therefore, a very misleading term created because of the Oriental habit of counting in the direction starting from the East.

13 Action of Equality (T.T.: Ro.sNoms.Kyi.sPyod.Pa.): When a yogi reaches the advanced stage he is able to "equalize" fear and hope, joy and pain, evil and virtue, etc. He is then no more affected by polarity, and begins to equalize and unify the opposing forces as manifested in dualism.

14 The Four Dhyānas: These denote the Four Formless Dhyānas, i.e., the Dhyānas of Infinite Space, of Infinite Consciousness, of Nothingness, and of Neither Consciousness nor Non-Consciousness.

15 Body-of-Essence (T.T.: Ño.Wo.Ñid.Kyi.sKu.): The complete name for this term should be "Body of the Universal Essence" (T.T.: Chos.dWyiñ.Ño.Wo.Ñid. Kyi.sKu.), which is the unity, or the indivisible aspect of the Trikāya. This term seems to be found only in the Tantric literature, and is criticized by some Buddhist scholars as senseless and redundant, since its characteristics have been well covered by the tenets of the Dharmakāya.

16 Dark Noisy Cemetery (T.T.: Mun.Pa.sGra.sGrogs.).

17. Guru Shojigocha (T.T.: sLob.dPon.Phyogs.Kyi.Go.Cha.).

18 Black Performer (T.T.: sPyod.Pa.Nag.Po.).

19 Death Light (T.T.: hChi.Bahi.Hod.Zer.): the light of the Dharmakāya that shines forth at the time of death.

20 The Three Bardos: (1) Chikhai Bardo (the Bardo at the moment of death); (2) Chönyid Bardo (the Bardo of Reality); (3) Sidpa Bardo (the Bardo of Rebirth). See "The Tibetan Book of the Dead," 3rd ed., edited by W. Y. Evans-Wentz, Oxford University Press, 1957.

21 The Pure Land of No-Regression: Buddha's Pure Land is said to be immune from all adverse conditions that may pull one back from his progress on the spiritual Path, therefore it is also known as the Pure Land of No-Regression.

22 Inborn Mother (T.T.: lHan.Cig.sKyes.Ma.): another name for Dorje Pagmo, who symbolizes the Inborn Wisdom of Buddhahood.

23 Bidrama (T.T.: Bi.Kra.Ma.): This is probably a corruption of the word Vikramasila (Monastery).

24 Three Existences: These are the Existences of Life, of Death, and of Bardo.

25 The names of the so-called "three guides" are not mentioned in the text, and the translator is not certain about them.

26 The Three Pure Lands: Judging from the context, the Three Pure Lands in question seem to be the Pure Lands of the Dharmakāya, of the Sambogakāya, and of the Nirmānakāya. But this locution is rather unusual, and lacks sufficient reason. It is acceptable in Mahāyāna Buddhism to say that there is a Pure Land of the Sambhogakāya or a Land of the Nirmānakāya, but it would be difficult to accept the idea of a Land of the Dharmakāya, which is formless and void. The translator presumes that this locution is merely an embarrassing sacrifice to style, caused by the Procrustean approach of the trisymmetrical form adopted in this song.

27 The Incarnation-Bardo (T.T.: sKye.gNas.brGyud.Pahi.Bar.Do.): commonly known as the Srid.Pa. Bardo.

28 Dri.Za.: the Smell Eater. It is said that most of the spirits, or metamorphosis-born beings, are fed on odors. This is true of Devas, Asuras, and ghosts.

29 The Thirteenth Stage: Generally, Mahāyānists accept only ten progressive enlightenment stages of a Bodhisattva, known as the Ten Bhūmis; passing the tenth stage, Buddhahood is then reached. Therefore, Buddhahood is considered as the eleventh stage. But according to some Tantrists, the Supreme Vajra-Buddhahood is still two steps beyond the general eleventh stage. Thus, the stage of Dorje-Chang is considered as the Thirteenth Stage — a very controversial topic in Tantric Buddhism.

30 The Illuminating Light-of-the-Path (T.T.: Lam.Gyi.Hod.Zer.): This is the Wisdom-Light a yogi sees on the Path (or during his meditation practice). Altogether there are three kinds of "Lights": (1) The Light of Origin, or the Mother Light (T.T.: Mahi.Hod.Zer.); (2) The Light of the Path, or the Light of the Son (T.T.: Lam.Gyi.Hod.Zer.); and (3) The Light of Fruit, or the Light of Union (T.T.: hBras.Buhi.Hod.Zer.).

31 The Third Initiation: Third Initiation is also called the Wisdom Initiation (T.T.: Ye.Çes.Kyi.dWan.) During this initiation the disciple is shown the truth of the unity of bliss and voidness by the symbol of sexual union.

32 Toagal (T.T.: Thod.rGal.): This is the advanced teaching of the Great Perfection of the Ningmaba School, which is quite different and unique in comparison with the Yogic teachings of the New Schools of Tibetan Tantrism. This is a type of "Light Yoga," stressing the functional or manifestating aspect of the "Innate Light." Literature of this Yoga has so far never been translated into any Western language.

33 Shajhama (T.T.: Phyag.rGyag.Ma.): the female yogi who helps one in the practice of the Third Initiation Yoga.

31

TSERINMA AND THE
MUDRĀ PRACTICE

Obeisance to all Gurus

LATE on the night of the eighth day of the Month of the Fire
Chicken, a great light shone upon Milarepa's quiet hermitage in
Chu Bar.[1] Milarepa then sensed a fragrant odor he had never smelled
before and heard the sound of approaching voices. While he was wondering about them, the Auspicious Lady of Long Life [Tserinma], well-
dressed and wearing beautiful ornaments, appeared with her sisters —
one bringing various kinds of incense; one, many delicious foods and
drinks; one, musical instruments; another, fine and pretty clothes; and
still another, beautiful flowers. They all bowed down before the Jetsun, circumambulated him many times, and offered him desirable oblations conjured by their miraculous powers. Then they sang in chorus:

> Oh perfect, precious, destined and well-endowed
>   Guru,
> Is "Laughing Vajra" the name that Buddhas and
>   Gurus call you?
> Did not your parents name you "Toubagha,"[2]
> While people call you "The Great Accomplished
>   Repa"?
> Are you not the one with three wondrous names?
>
> To the left of the mountain, Lhaman Jalmo,
> Stands your hut by the bank of Lodahan River.
> The King of the Nagas sounded
> His magic conch-shell trumpet,
> And into a wish-fulfilling Palace
> Was this hut transformed.

357

On this river-bank in Medicine Valley,
You, a wondrous yogi,
Industriously practice the Pinnacle Teachings.
Renouncing the Eight Worldly Desires,
From Saṃsāric temples you are freed.
Through our wondrous powers
We five girls have come
To praise and sing for you
With sweet words and tuneful voices.
We represent the four known types of womanhood
Called Lotus, Conch, Mark, and the Elephant.[3]
Pray practice Karma Mudrā with us.
Will you grant our prayer?
Do you know well
The four techniques of Karma Mudrā
Called falling, holding, turning back, and
        spreading —
If so, you may apply them now,
For your servants are prepared.

It is said in the Supreme Tantra,
[That the qualified yogi] should attract the
        maids of Heaven,
Of Nāgas, of Asuras, or of human kind.
It also says that of all services
The best is Karma Mudrā.
Thus we come here this evening.
Pray witness this, oh great Yogi,
Whose naked body is full of splendor
        and radiance.

The Jetsun answered:

At this late hour
I hear your tuneful voices raised,
And your thoughts expressed in song.
[From whence come you, fair ladies?]
Does not your abode
Stand on the shining summit,
The Snow Mountain's crystal peak?
Towers not a palace
Under the canopy of clouds
'Midst the flower-galaxy of stars?

Long are your lives and great your powers —
This of your mercy is the meed.
Your fortune rivals that of the God of Wealth —
This of your bounty is the meed.
Your servants are faithful and obedient —
This of your patience is the meed.

In practicing meritorious deeds
You are full of aspiration —
This is the sign of your diligence.
The fact that you have met me in this life
Proves your good wishes in past lives.
I sing this song for you
To reveal the deep relationship.

I am a follower of Nāropa's Lineage,
Who has mastered Prāṇa and Bindu.
'Tis true that of all offerings
A qualified Mudrā is the best.
Most wondrous indeed are the four perfected
        Mudrās.

The radiant Face and Lotus promote bliss;
The shell-shaped Nāḍī speeds the ecstasy;
The Mark in the deep recess prevents all waste;
While through the "Elephant" Reality is realized.

You are the auspicious, noble, and fault-free
        Lady of Long Life.
In your secret Wisdom Lotus
Lies the bīja,[4] "Bham" shaped like the sign "ĕ";
The male gem is likened to the blue bīja "Hum";
And, when combined with "Pad," fixes
        Tig Le well.
When Wisdom and Skill together join
The Bliss of Two-in-One is offered best.

The Four Blisses and Four Moments are
The essence of the Four Bodies of Buddha.
Like the crawling of a tortoise
[Slowly Tig Le] should drip down.
Then hold it in the Central Channel,
And like a coursing beast,

Reverse it [to the head].
Later when you spread it,
Use the Liberating Mudrā.
"Tig" is Nirvāna Path!
"Le" the Bliss of Equality;
"Las"⁵ means the various actions and plays,
"Kyi" the intercourse 'twixt Bliss and Voidness;
"Phyag" is this and that to hold;
And "rGya," to embrace Nirvāna and Samsāra.

"Las" is to contact this and act on that,
"Kyi" to do this and that for the associate;
"Phyag" is the Union of the Bliss and Void;
While "rGya" is not to go beyond.
This is the speed-path of Union,
A path full of retained-bliss,
A path to consummate the accomplishment
Of the Illuminating-Void,
Leading toward undiscriminating Dharmakāya,
Directing one to the perfect Sambhogakāya,
And leading to the Manifesting-Void of the
      Nirmānakāyas.
This is a path of bliss — of voidness, of no
      thoughts, and of two-in-one,
A path of quick assistance by a goddess.
Following this inspiring way
You, fair ladies, will reach Liberation,
And, in the Realm of No-arising will remain.
Oh gifted fairies, you are indeed well qualified!

The Karma Mudrā was then performed, during which the five goddesses offered Milarepa their bodies, words, and minds — also many foods and drinks to please him.

Among the five Ḍākinīs — the Auspicious Lady of Long Life, the Drogmanzulema of Lashi Snow Mountain, the Mannmo of Linpa Draug, the Tsomanma of Nepal, and the Yidagmo of Yolmo Snow Mountain⁶ — the Auspicious Lady of Long Life was the one who gained the best Karma Mudrā inspiration from the Jetsun.

This is the story of how the Repa, "Laughing Vajra," the great Yogi who was capable of attracting and using goddesses for his Mudrā practice, met with the Lady of Long Life; and in which the songs of inquiry and the answers, named "The Rosary of Bliss-Void Wisdom," are found.

After sincere prayers and offerings to the Deities, the two brother yogis — the compilers of this story — received a delightful revelation of permission, upon which the story was written.

Samaya Ja Ja Ja! [Warning: Secret! Secret! Secret!]

The story of the Lady of Long Life and Milarepa, including several preachings of Mila and the requests of the five Ḍākinīs, was compiled and preserved by Ahtsarya Bodhi Radsa and Repa Shiwa Aui.

This is the end of this wondrous account, composed of three successive stories.

NOTES

1 Lit.: " . . . . in the quiet dwelling, the Palace of the Nirmāṇakāya of Chu Bar."

2 Toubagha (T.T.: Thos.Pa.dGah.): Milarepa's first name, given him by his father. See W. Y. Evans-Wentz' "Tibet's Great Yogi Milarepa."

3 The four different types of Shajhama, or women qualified to serve as "Mudrās." "Shell," "Mark," "Lotus," and "Elephant," are all figurative terms designating the various patterns of physical make-up of the Shajhamas.

4 Bija means the seed, core, or Essence of a Mantra.

5 Karma Mudrā is translated in Tibetan as "Las.Kyi.Phyag.rGya." "Las" is equivalent to the Sanskrit word "Karma," meaning Action; "Kyi" is a preposition meaning "of," and "Phyag.rGya." is the equivalent of "Mudrā," meaning symbol or gesture. "Las.Kyi.Phyag.rGya." can thus be translated literally as "Action of Symbolic Teachings Practiced Through Concrete Actions." It is customary in Tibetan poetry, to break down a phrase and use its every component word to begin a line, thus making the poem more illustrative.

6 Compared with Story 29, the names do not correspond. However, the translator presumes these are different names for the same Ḍākinis — one series being their formal names and the other, designations given according to the places from which they came.

32

ADMONISHMENT TO REPA DORJE WONSHU

Obeisance to all Gurus

A T ONE time when the Jetsun Milarepa was living in the Regba Dhujen Cave of Dinma Drin, he gave instructions to his disciples and patrons and set them to meditating; as a result they all gained good Experiences.

Among the disciples there was a very industrious young man, a descendant of the Tiger Tribe.[1] His deep faith in the Jetsun was confirmed when Realization had dawned upon him. In an assembly he said, "Dear Jetsun, when I think of the miseries of Saṃsāra and the happiness of Liberation, I cannot sit in idleness for a single moment. Please accept me as your servant and I will meditate day and night with you. Also, when I think of your merits and the noble deeds of the Gurus in our Linage, all worldly merits and virtues become trifling and worthless. Pray, therefore, grant me the quintessential teachings of the Dharma."

In reply Milarepa sang:

> My Lineage is the Lineage of Dorje-Chang,
> My great-grandfather was the noble Tilopa,
> My grandfather was the great Paṇḍita Nāropa,
> My father is Marpa the Translator,
> I am the Yogi Milarepa.
> These, with the fountainhead of profound Instructions,
> Make the six mainstays of my background.
>
> Now I shall tell you of the "Six Deceptions":
> Monasteries are like collecting-stations
> For hollow driftwood —

Though they claim
That the priestly life is divine and pure,
It is deceptive and illusory to me;
Of such companions I have no need!

I am a man who cherishes peace of mind
And abhors all gossip and accusations!

When the Dumo-heat is kindled within,
All woolen clothes are useless;
Of burdensome robes I have no need,
And for disheartening housework I have no desire.

When detestation arises within,
All things and possessions lose their worth;
For business I have no appetite;
For accumulating wealth I have no desire.

When perseverance and industry grow within,
Sons and disciples cease to be important;
I have no need for meetings and visitors
For they would merely interrupt devotion.

When the Pith-Instructions are practiced,
Dharma preachings lose significance;
Since they only incite one's pride,
I have no need for books and learning!

This is the Song of the Six Deceptions
In which the Pith-Instructions may be found.
Think on it, and bear it well in mind.

"This is indeed wonderful," said the young disciple. "Now, for the sake of ignorant sentient beings like us, I pray you to sing a song relating to your own Six Merits and Greatnesses." Milarepa then sang:

Seldom in my life have I boasted of "greatness,"
But for praising the greatness of the Lineage
I now sing the Song of the "Six Greatnesses": [2]

Great is the benevolence of Gurus and Buddhas!
Great is the grace of Yidhams and Deities!
Great is the power and might of the Protectors!

Great are the oral instructions of the Whispered
        Lineage
Great is Mila's perseverance,
And great the faith of his disciples!

Now I shall sing the Song of the "Six Joys":
Joy it is to stay in the land of no-man;
Joy it is to think of my Guru's instruction;
Joy it is to sit on the hard cushion beneath me;
Joy it is to remain in the solitary cave;
Joy it is to meet hunger and cold with
        indifference;
Joy it is to practice the Krunkol Exercises.[3]

Now I shall sing of the "Six Gatherings":
In the daytime people gather here
And at night the Ḍākinīs come.
Morning and evening, food and clothes are
        brought.
The Wheels-of-Bodhi gather in my living soul,
The outer world and my mind gather into one.

Now I shall sing of my "Six Keeps":
In Ragma I have a keep called "Bodhi-Practice,"
In the Red Rock Gem Valley I own the "Eagle
        Keep,"
On the summit of Red Rock is my "Sky Keep,"
In the Mon region there's the "Tiger Cave
        and Lion Keep."
Also I have the "Plantain Keep" of Kadaya Crystal
        Cave,
And at White Horse-Tooth Rock I have the
        "Central Keep."

Now I shall sing of the "Six Goodnesses of
        Mila":
Good is the view of Mahāmudrā,
Good is the practice of the Six Yogas of Nāropa,
Good is the profound practice of the Skillful
        Path,
Good is the inborn fruit of the Trikāya,
Good is the grace of the Ghagyuba Sages,
Good are the Pith-Instructions of Milarepa.

Oh faithful patrons and disciples,
Evildoers are many, but virtue-practicers are
few.
All sufferings are of sins the retribution,
All joys of virtues are the meed,
Yet both are due to all that one has done.

Let us now make a vow to meet
Again and again in future times!

Hearing this song, all the disciples and patrons were very much impressed and pleased. They then left for their homes. The young man, however, was taken as a servant-disciple by the Jetsun. Later he became one of the close-sons of Milarepa, and was known as **Daugom Repa Dorje Wonshu**.

This is the story of Repa Dorje Wonshu.

NOTES

1 Tiger Tribe (T.T.: Rus.sTag.).

2 The Tibetan text, on folio 172, mentions only five Greatnesses. This could be a "copygraphical" error. The translation is based on the corrected version of the fifth Greatness.

3 Krunkol Exercises (T.T.: hKhrul.hKhol.): Various specially designed physical exercises to further a yogi's meditation progress, and to overcome the hindrances that he may encounter in his Yoga practice.

33

MILAREPA'S MEETING
WITH DHARMA BODHI

Obeisance to all Gurus

A T THE time when Milarepa was setting in motion the Wheel of Dharma at the Belly Cave of Nya Non with Rechungpa and his other son-disciples, there were five contemporary, great accomplished yogis. They were the Gurus Tsem Chin of La Dud, Dhampa Sangje of Dinrin,[1] Shilabharo of Nepal, Dharma Bodhi of India, and Milarepa of Nya Non.

Once Dharma Bodhi was invited by Shilabharo to Bhalbo Dson to preach the Dharma. Many Tibetans as well as Nepalese went to pay homage to him. A number of Milarepa's disciples also wanted to go. Rechungpa gave many reasons to Milarepa, urging him to visit Dharma Bodhi. In answer to his request, Milarepa sang:

> By the Gurus' grace
> Many accomplished Sages come.
> The wondrous Dharma thus spreads far,
> And with joy are blessed all living beings.
> Many pilgrims paying homage to the Sages
> Show that a few destined persons will emerge.
>
> The Dhampa Sangje of Dinri,
> The Guru Tsem Chin of La Dud,
> The Shilabharo of Nepal,
> The Dharma Bodhi of India,
> And the Milarepa of Gung Tang —
> All have attained the Wisdom.
> Each has succeeded in meditation,
> Each knows the Illuminating Mind-Essence.

They all are capable of working miracles,
They all possess the overflowing Void-Compassion,
They all work wonders and produce amusing marvels.
As to the spontaneous making of songs,
I am the best of all the five;
My perseverence and austerity are also greater;
Nothing special or superb have they.
I see no need to go;
But you, my sons and disciples,
Should do so by all means!
It is not because I think ill of them
[That I remain behind]
But merely that I am too old to journey [there].
I now make a sincere wish that I may meet
Them in the Pure Land of Oujen.
Oh my son, do not be bewildered,
But have confidence [in me].

Rechungpa said, "If you do not go, people will think that you are proud and jealous, and they will so accuse you with much reviling. By all means, please go!" In reply, Milarepa sang:

I pray you, ye accomplished Beings
To cleanse all sins and evil-doing.

He who cares what people say
Will only make himself confused.
Journeying to many places
Merely hinders one's devotion.
Meddling in too many things
When visiting a holy Guru
Will confuse and irritate the consorting Deities.
Treading the Path of the deep Tantra,
Should one's mind divided be,
Never can he attain accomplishment.
Great is the blessing of the Accomplished Ones,
But too many visitors produce ill will.
However, Rechungpa, do go to see
Him with your brothers [if you so wish].

Rechungpa replied, "[Your unwillingness to go will directly cause] people to commit sinful deeds. And so please go! We will also be great-ly benefited if you will grant our request." After such persistent entreaties, Milarepa finally gave in, saying, "All right. In that case let us go to greet Dharma Bodhi." Upon the Jetsun's consent, Rechungpa and the other disciples all cried for joy. They said, "Indians all like gold; therefore we should obtain some for him as a token of our welcome." In commenting on their suggestion, Milarepa then sang:

> I pray you, ye accomplished Beings,
> To remove the cravings of this poor mendicant;
> I pray that all my deeds may accord with the
>   Dharma!
> Why practice the Bodhi-Mind
> If one's acts are in conflict with the Dharma?
> He who has attained Samādhi
> Ne'er needs a companion!
> He who has experienced self-liberation
> Ne'er needs a consort!
> Else what would be the use and meaning
> Of his long work in meditation?
> If I, Milarepa, pursue gold,
> My renunciation will be pointless.
> Dharma Bodhi wants no gold,
> Else his accomplishment would be valueless.
> Dordrag Rechungpa wants no profit,
> Else his apprenticeship would be meaningless.

The Jetsun continued, "You go first — I shall follow you." Thus he dispatched them. On their way, in doubt, they all thought, "Will the Jetsun really come?" With this misgiving, as they approached Bhalbo Dson, lo and behold! Milarepa, who had transformed his body into a pagoda, [suddenly] descended in the midst of them like a shooting-star falling from the sky. Seeing this miracle, Dharma Bodhi was very much impressed, and all Milarepa's disciples were struck with great surprise and joy. The whole party then approached Dharma Bodhi, who was surrounded by crowds of people. Seeing Milarepa and his disciples coming, Dharma Bodhi of India at once descended from his seat and prostrated himself before Milarepa of Tibet. Thereupon, people all thought that Milarepa must be even greater than Dharma Bodhi; but they were also confirmed with a faith that both men were no different from the perfect Buddha. The two accomplished beings then sat together on one seat and conversed joyfully with each other. Dharma Bodhi said to Milarepa, "I am very pleased that you always remain in solitude. This is indeed remarkable." In reply to this praise, the Jetsun sang:

I pray you, ye Nirmāṇakāya Gurus,
For blessings from the Accomplished Ones
    of the Whispered Lineage!

To Dharma Bodhi of India and the gifted
Tibetans and Nepalese assembled here,
I, Milarepa, the Yogi of Tibet
Sing a song of Wisdom Experiences,
Lest people fail to recognize an accomplished
    being.

The Five Twisted Nāḍīs are straightened by
    Prāṇa-Practice,
The Five Winding Prāṇas are straightened by
    the Taming Practice,
The Five Sullied Elements are burned out,
And all Five trunks of the poisonous Passion-
    Mind are overthrown.
In the Central Channel the savage
Karmic wind of errant thoughts is pacified.
Now there is no need for me
To entangle myself with evil companions.

Dharma Bodhi then said, "The way you have conquered the 'adversaries' is indeed wonderful. Now please tell me of some good methods to this end." In response, Milarepa sang:

I pray to all accomplished Beings,
I pray that, through your blessing,
A companion may be found within me.

When the Mother of the Five Pure Nāḍīs
Meets the Father of the Five Pure Prāṇas,
The Five Sons of the Pure Elements are born,
And the face of Self-Mind, the Five Purities,
    is seen.
In the Beyond-Measure-Palace of the Central
    Channel,
The proclaimer of Buddha achievement
Shouts to the Four Rainbow Cakras.[2]
To the armies of the Web of Myriad Forms[3]
For discipline [I] give the order of non-
    clinging.

By realizing that all forms are self-awareness,
I have beheld my consort's face — the true
    Mind Within.
So none of the sentient beings in the Three
    Great Worlds
Eludes the embrace of this great Thatness.
This is my companion, the wonderful Bodhi-Mind.
Happy it is to consort with her always,
For never will she take leave of me!

Upon hearing this song, Dharma Bodhi was very much pleased. He said, "Truly the inner experiences of a yogi are beyond description. Nevertheless, please tell us briefly about [your understanding] of the View, Practice, and Action." In response Milarepa sang:

He who can watch his mind without distraction
Needs no talk or chat;
He who can absorb himself in self-awareness,
Need not sit stiffly like a corpse;
If one knows the nature of all forms,
The Eight Worldly Desires will vanish of
    themselves.
If no desire or hatred is within his heart,
He needs no pretense or show.
The great Wisdom and Trikāya
That transcend Saṃsāra and Nirvāṇa both,
Can never be achieved by search and aspiration;
Never can one attain them
Without first receiving blessing from the Lineage.

Dharma Bodhi then said, "Your View, Practice, and Action are truly marvelous." Milarepa replied, "Now please tell us your understanding on the profound Key-Instructions gained in your practice." Dharma Bodhi then sang:

For the gifted ones in this assembly
I pray to the wondrous Succession of the
    Practice —
Through this propitious Karma
Soon may we all behold [your holy faces].

If one cannot subdue habitual thinking and
    wandering thoughts,

What will be the use of observing the mind?
If one cannot conquer ego-clinging and
       pleasure-craving,
What will be the use of meditating for an age?
He who does not strive for altruistic deeds,
Will be o'ertaken by his pride
And gain no progress.
If one follows not the Guru's guidance,
What benefit can he gain
By being with pleasant friends?

Pretense and vanity directly cause disgrace,
Quarrels and discord bring misfortunes.
If one always tells the truth,
It often smites another's heart.
If one practices not altruism
How can he attain Buddahood?
*The instructions one has learned will
       become profounder*
If restfully he remains alone.
Oh you great Yogi of Tibet,
You are proficient in poetry and song —
I am not good at chanting or at singing,
But now, exhilarated, excited, and inspired
I can sing this song for you.
May we soon, in the Pure Land of Great Happiness
All sing the holy hymns [together].

Dharma Bodhi and Milarepa continued their delightful conversation for some time, then both took their leave.

When Milarepa and his disciples returned to Nya Non, people in the village brought wine to welcome them, and asked about the meeting with Dharma Bodhi. In answer, Milarepa sang:

When rises the sun or moon,
All Four Continents are bright;
When moisture and warmth abound,
Fruits will ripen on the trees;
When mother and son together meet,
The pain of longing ceases;
When an accomplished one appears
The world is gay and prosperous!

When Dharma Bodhi came to the wood of Bhalbo
    Dson,
I, Milarepa of Tibet, went there to see him.
He rose from his seat
And made obeisance to me.
Thus people were caught in surprise and doubt.
Folding his two hands and bending both his
    knees
He bowed down before me.
This symbolized the Truth of Two-in-One.
He asked about my health and welfare —
This symbolized the all-embracing Whole.
In answer to his kind inquiry
I showed him the [signless] Mahāmudrā.
In the Temple of Non-dual Purity
We had an illuminating talk of no-words,
    with joy.
A pure wish in our past lives
Had brought about this meeting.
I must have had a Karma-link with him before,
When Buddha descended to this world.

This meeting with my brother-friend
Was delightful and auspicious.
It will be heard and asked about
In far-distant lands.

Hearing this song, the patrons of Nya Non were all very much pleased and excited. It is said that because of Dharma Bodhi's obeisance, the Jetsun's fame and fortune became even greater than before.

This is the story of Milarepa meeting with Dharma Bodhi.

NOTES

1 Dinrin: This name also appears as Dinri.

2 The Four Rainbow Cakras: The literal translation of this phrase should be "The Rainbow Place or State of the Four Cakras." It actually denotes the state of thorough liberation and ultimate Enlightenment. The mind of one who has reached this state becomes the All-knowing Wisdom, and his body, the radiant and

magic-like Rainbow Body (T.T.: hJah.Lus.). The Tantric expression of "attaining the Rainbow Body," or "reaching the Rainbow State," thus signifies the achievement of Buddhahood.

3 Web of Myriad Forms (T.T.: sGyu.hPhrul.Dra.Wa.): This may also be translated as "The Magic Manifestation Web, or Net." This is an important term, reflecting the basic Tantric view on the Realm of Totality, which is strikingly similar to the philosophy of Hwa Yen. To explain it very briefly, all manifestations are unsubstantial, delusory, dream-like and magic-like, devoid of any self-nature. Because of this very unsubstantial or void nature, all manifestations can arise simultaneously in the same place without hindering one another — in fact each and every manifestation can arise in another's place simultaneously in an interpenetrating manner. Thus, using a graphic expression to describe this awesome, interpenetrating state, "Manifestation Web," or "Web of Myriad Forms" is used in the Buddhist Scriptures. See "The Essence of Buddhism," by D. T. Suzuki, The Buddhist Society, London. See also the translator's forthcoming book, "The Philosophy of Hwa Yen Buddhism."

34

THE CHALLENGE
FROM THE LOGICIANS

Obeisance to all Gurus

HAVING fully mastered the Mind-realms of himself and others, Jetsun Milarepa was able to cause Dharma Bodhi of India to make obeisance to him. His fame thus spread afar. The people of Nya Non, at that time, all made offerings to him for the benefit of both the living and the dead. With ever-increasing fortune he remained happily in the Belly Cave of Nya Non to help sentient beings.

Now there were some scholar-monks [logicians and theologians] in the Nya Non Monastery, who were very jealous of Milarepa. They vilified him by calling him a heretic, and heaped many abuses upon him.

At one time, a mild famine broke out at Nya Non, and many villagers went to the scholar-monks for loans [in order to buy seeds for] sowing. The monks said to them, "Since we do not practice or know anything about heretic teachings, we have never received any offerings from you people for performing the rites for the dead. Our largess is used for the single purpose of providing provisions for studying and practice of the immaculate Dharma, which of course is of no help to you. Now if you want a loan you should go to your heretic teacher to whom you gave all your belongings when you had them." Thus the peoples' request was rejected. One among the borrowers commented, "Well, to some extent what the monks have said is quite true. We may regard the Jetsun as our refuge in this life and the lives after. But we have needs in this life too. We should, therefore, also make offerings to the scholar-monks." Then the villagers made an agreement and compromised with the monastery.

Not long after this incident the scholar-monks held a conference under the leadership of Lodun Gedunbum and Radun Dharma Lhodre.

One conferee said, "Milarepa must be chased out of this place, otherwise we can never attract more people or spread our teachings. Besides, Milarepa's teaching is heretical and evil, he surely deserves to be ousted." But the elders replied, "It would not look well if we drove him out, people would criticize us. The best way is to send three of our most learned scholars who are well-versed in Sanskrit, logic, philosophy, and the Sūtras to challenge him in debate on Buddhist doctrines. Since he is so ignorant, possessing nothing but a tongue, he will not be able to answer our challenges and arguments. Out of one hundred questions, at best he may answer but one or two; then we can scorn and abuse him. Mortified by such a disgrace, he will run away of his own accord." Three most learned scholars were then sent to the Jetsun. When Rechungpa saw them coming he was not pleased. He went in and asked Milarepa, "There are three scholar-monks here who want to see you — should I let them in?" The Jetsun replied, "My Guru Marpa said to me, 'You should devote your body, mouth, and mind to benefit sentient beings in all possible ways; even in your daily conversation you should try to serve them.' By all means let them in. I will see them." Then they were led in and given water to refresh them. Milarepa said, "The power of one's faith can split rocks, crack the earth, and divide the water. Now, please preach for me the teaching of the Sūtras." The leader of the scholars then rose from his seat snapping his fingers, and said proudly, "Yes, we are teachers who have mastered the Three Learnings[1] and their disciplines and possess the three robes of the Dharma — the symbol and source of all merits. I may or may not preach for you the teaching of the Sūtras, but now let me ask you first: What merit do you possess that you, a layman, have been receiving and enjoying people's offerings and gifts without the slightest qualm and with so much confidence?" In answer to his question, the Jetsun sang "My Realizations from Meditation":

> Embodied in my Guru's nectar-like instruction
> Is the pinnacle Dharma of the Ultimate Truth —
> The essence of all teachings from Scriptures
>   and from Reason,
> To which all scholars and priests aspire in
>   veneration.
> Pray may He not depart from me
> But ever sit above me
> As my glorious adornment.
>
> [To you learned scholars]
> I now relate my devotion-practices

By dividing them into three groups.
The first group that I practice,
Is the Arising Yoga of my Patron Buddha,
The second is the Nāḍīs, Prāṇas, and Bindus,
The third is the Mahāmudrā.

In the four periods of each day
I practise the Yoga of Bodhi-Mind.
In accumulating the true Bread of Faith
I contemplate the Voidness;
In accumulating the Karmic Bread of Faith
I offer the Dorma;[2]
In accumulating the Bread of Self-faith
I give oblations to the deities.
To the ghosts I give away the Dorma remnants.
I am a yogi who turns the Wheel of Nourishment.
Having realized the Voidness of all things
I am qualified to receive and enjoy offerings.

One of the scholars said, "As a person with maimed hands can never climb mountains, so one without knowledge of Buddhist studies can never attain Liberation. As a blind man sees nothing in the chapel, so one without experience of meditation will never see Reality. To practise the Arising Yoga one must first know *how* to practice it. Now you said that you have done so, but tell us how?"

The Jetsun then sang:

When I practise the Arising Yoga of the Patron
      Buddha
I see my body, vivid like a rainbow yet void,
Of which no substance whatsoever can be found.
So have I freed myself from all desires.

All talk is like an echo in a deserted valley.
For it I have neither fancy nor aversion.
So have I exhausted all likes and dislikes.

The Illuminating-Void of Mind
Is like the radiance of the sun and moon,
Without limitation or attribute.
Dissolved into it, my ego-clinging becomes
      nought.

The common human body, word, and mind
Are themselves the Body, Speech, and Wisdom of
      the Self-Buddha.
Being free from all that's vulgar,
I always feel great happiness and joy.

I am happy because my deeds are in accord
      with Dharma,
I am inspired because I follow
The right Dharma Path.

"What you have said may be correct," commented the scholar. "Now
tell me how you practise the Nāḍīs, Prāṇas, and Bindus?" In reply the
Jetsun sang:

In practising the Nāḍīs, Prāṇas, and Bindus
I meditate on the Three Channels and
      Four Centers.
As the attachment to body is exhausted
The ego into nought dissolves itself.
The Key-words of the [Five] Elements[3] are
      purified,
So they vanish not, but become illumined.
I behold the self-face of Reality,
So there is no chance for me to make mistakes.
The Prāṇas all are gathered in the Central
      Channel,
And thus they hit the vital point.
The White and Red Forces unite within me,
The experiences of bliss, illumination, and
      non-thought spontaneously arise,
And so the knots of doubt and ignorance are
      untied.
I practice the Dharma by heart and not by mouth,
I conjoin together the Mother-and-Son-Light
And exterminate the complex of desires.
As form and Void into one are merged,
My mind is at ease and full of joy.
I am every happy
For I never fall into the trap
Of mere conceptualization of the Void.
As all confusions have vanished into Dharmadhātu
I feel but joyful and gay!

The scholar then said, "The marmots who live underground can sleep [hibernate] for four months during one flow of the Prāṇa-current without even slightly shaking their bodies. Remaining under the water for any length of time, the fishes can still survive. They can do so merely because of their [inherited] Prāṇa powers, yet these animals cannot be conceived of as possessing any merit, as their minds are completely blind! You should know that all merits consist in one's understanding. Now tell me, how do you practice your so-called 'Mahāmudrā'?"

The Jetsun sang:

> When I practice Mahāmudrā,
> I rest myself in the intrinsic state,
> Relaxingly without distraction or effort.
> In the realm of Voidness,
> I rest myself with Illumination.
> In the realm of Blissfulness,
> I rest myself in Awareness.
> In the realm of Non-thought,
> I rest myself with a naked mind.
> In manifestations and activities,
> I rest myself in Samādhi.
> Meditating on the Mind-Essence in such a manner
> Numerous understandings and convictions arise.
> By Self-illumination all is accomplished without
>   effort.
> Looking no more for Enlightenment,
> I am extremely happy.
> Free from both hope and fear,
> I feel very joyful.
> Oh, what a pleasure it is to enjoy
> Confusion when as Wisdom it appears!

"It is true that from your mouth no [meaningful] thing can come out but your tongue," remarked the scholar. "What you have just said seems not so bad, but it is like an imitation of the original thing. Now tell us who is your Guru?" The Jetsun replied, "I attain all my knowledge through studying my mind within, thus all my thoughts become the teachings of Dharma. So long as I do not become separated from my own mind, I am always accompanied by sūtras. I have realized that all manifestations are Mind, and the mind itself is the illumination. These are my Gurus." Whereupon he sang:

I shall now tell you who my Gurus are.
My Gurus are the Jetsuns,
Whose immaculate Bodies manifest as the Buddha's
    Pure Land.
The purified Five Prāṇas are their thrones,
The purified Five Nāḍīs are their lotus seats,
The purified Five Elements are their Sun-and-
    Moon cushions.
The void Mind-Essence is my Guru's body;
My Guru is Dorje-Chang, with the Wisdom-Body;
My Guru is Tilopa, with the Six Miraculous
    Powers;
My Guru is Nāropa, with the Net of Myriad
    Spells;[4]
My Guru is Marpa, to whom I owe the
    greatest debt.
They sit e'er upon my head as my glory.
If you have a pair of clear and sincere eyes
You will see them as real Buddhas.
If with sincerely and faith you pray to them,
The rain of grace will ever fall upon you.
If you offer practice and devotion,
The treasury of Accomplishments will be opened
    to you.

Having heard this song, faith in the Jetsun was aroused in the three scholars. They all bowed down to him and said, " 'Ignorance, blindness, and confusion — these three evils have created all misfortune in the world!' How true this is! How true this is! With our blind minds we thought that you were an ignorant man who took people's offerings by [deceiving them] with your crazy Dharmas. But you have answered our challenging questions with ease and without the slightest hesitation. We now regret very much the quarrel we have imposed upon you. Please forgive us. Since we do not have the opportunity or merits to meet your Gurus, we shall look up to you and pray to you with sincerity and veneration, for you are even greater than the 'Treasury-of-Accomplishments.' Pray now vouchsafe us the Initiations and instructions." So they besought Milarepa in a very humble and respectful manner. The Jetsun was greatly pleased. He then gave them the Initiations and Pith-Instructions, and set them to meditating. Later, they all gained Experiences and Realizations, and became the three enlightened snow-lion-like yogi-scholars.

Now, at this time the people of Nya Non held a great festival in the village and invited the Jetsun and all his disciples, including these three scholar-priests, to attend. A throne was prepared for the scholar-priests Lodun[5] and Dhar Lho[6] — and also a row of seats for the other scholar-monks. A throne and more seats were made ready for the Jetsun and his Repa disciples.

The three scholar-priests who were sent to dispute with the Jetsun came. Dressed like yogis, they appeared as Repas sitting on the lower seats, and drank wine from the Kapāla [skull-cup], draught by draught. When Lodun and Dhar Lho saw this they were convulsed with rage, and said to themselves, "You scoundrels, dirty lice, betrayers! As long as you stay here, our doctrine will be disparaged and confounded! We will talk to these dirty traitors and get rid of them in an appropriate manner." Lodun then got up from his seat and said to the Jetsun, "You are an extraordinary yogi, so you must have a sound knowledge of logic. Otherwise, acting like this, you will degrade the Dharma, ruin yourself and others, and disqualify yourself as a Dharma-practicer. Therefore, please give us a simple proposition in accordance with the rules of logic." The Jetsun replied, "My dear scholar, you should try to rest yourself in the inborn Dharma-Essence instead of in words and talk. In daily life you should always attempt to subdue your desires. Correct understanding and merit can only grow from within, otherwise you will be driven into the Miserable Realms by jealousy and the Five Kleśas. So please do not ruin yourself! I do not understand the logic of your School. My own 'logic' is that of the Guru, of the Pith-Instructions, of diligence and perseverance, of remaining in solitude, of meditating in the hermitage, of producing the Realizations and true understanding within, of the sincere patrons with true faith, and of being a genuine and worthwhile receiver of patronage. Being bound by the 'logic' of jealousy and evil cravings, one is liable to experience the 'logic' of Hell and suffer the 'logic' of pain. I do not know any 'logic' other than this. In order fully to describe my 'logic,' I shall sing you a song, so listen to me":

I bow down to my Kleśa-free Gurus.

Alas, at this time of defilement,
Great is people's jealousy!
Please listen to me, Lodun and Dhar Lho.
If from my mother's womb I did not come,
How could I have drunk her milk?
If she fed me not on her sweet milk,
How could I have eaten the three kinds of grain?

If I did not eat the grain,
How could I have grown up?
If I did not grow up,
How could I have crossed the door?
If I did not cross the door,
How could I have wandered in all countries?
If I did not visit all countries,
How could I have found my gracious Guru?
If I did not meet my Guru,
How could I have received the Pith-Instructions?
Without instructions how could I meditate in
    solitude?
Without meditating in solitude,
How could the inner Experience and Realization
    arise?
Without the Realizations and the inner-heat,
How could I keep warm
In a garment of sheer cotton cloth?
If I cannot live in a cotton robe
How can the patrons have faith in me?
If my patrons have no faith in me
How can you, oh teacher-scholar, be jealous
    of me?
If jealousy and hatred had ne'er arisen in you,
How could you, oh teacher-scholar, go to Hell?

On the high plateau yonder
The wild beasts run and play,
Making the hounds keen and jealous;
Is not this the very reason
For the hounds becoming angry?

In the Belly Cave of Nya Non
I, the worthy Milarepa, stay.
This makes you, the teacher-of-words, painfully
    envious.
Is not this the very reason you are so distraught?
Seeing the alms offered by my patrons,
You, the learned priest, became jealous.
Is not this why you were angry and confused?
Oh great teachers and scholars,
Cling not to meaningless words and empty talk
Deeming them to be the Truth!

Even heretics can play with them.
One can waste two-and-thirty lives and gain
    nought,
If his mind but follows words.
It would be much better, therefore,
To conquer the devil of egotism.
I have no time to waste in words, words, and
    still more words!
Nor do I know logic or how to pose a proposition.
Therefore, you are the one
Who wins the argument to-day!

Dhar Lho then said, "I asked you in the language of Dharma, but you did not answer my question in Buddhist terms. Instead, you have sung a deceptive song to cheat gullible folk. Who cannot sing this kind of trash? Your song may deceive fools, but never me. If you cannot answer my questions today with scholastic language in Buddhist terms of academic tradition, but [shamelessly] still intend to receive alms from people with your deceiving songs, you well deserve to be trampled down." Saying this he seized a handful of earth and threw it in the Jetsun's face. The Jetsun brushed it off, smiled at him, and said, "How can you, the scholar who adheres to words and books merely for the sake of the pleasures of this life, act in accordance with the Dharma? Driven by your powerful Karmas and sins, all your learning and priestly disciplines will only bring you more unhappiness. As I understand them, all Dharmas are remedies for human passions and desires; but the way in which you practice them will only *increase* your passions and desires. Therefore, my Dharma and yours are completely different and contradictory. Since we do not speak the same language nor believe the same principle, how can we find a common base from which to discuss the Dharma?"

Now seeing all these things, Rechungpa thought to himself, "Although I am not worthy even to match a single hair of my Guru's head, if I do not beat this sinner who is now trying to hurt the Jetsun, I shall then violate the Samaya Commandment [Tantric Precept]; but if I punish him I will create great merits." He then picked up a stick and rushing towards the priest, was about to strike him. At once the Jetsun caught his arm, saying, "Rechungpa, my son! The wealth that cannot be used when one is in want, the kinsmen who do not assist when one is in need, and the Dharma that cannot help when one is under [adverse] conditions, will only make one more miserable. You should control yourself and try hard to think of the Admonishments. I shall now sing a song to awaken your good thoughts and Awareness."

I bow down to Marpa, my gracious Guru and
    my glory,
The great Jetsun, the shelter of all beings!
I pray you save us from doing evil deeds!

Oh Rechungpa, my son,
Calm yourself and listen to me!
Those hypocritical Buddhists who "talk big"
Become commoners at once
When they meet with adverse conditions.
Because their intentions are evil
From wrong-doings they will always suffer.
If you ever fight with people,
You violate the precepts through and through!
Calm yourself my son
And listen to your Guru!

In the vast firmament of the peerless Dharma,
My eagle-child of Awareness learns to fly;
But never should he pride himself on his flying
        power,
Lest he fall into the sectarian abyss.

Rechungpa, listen to your Guru's words!
In the great ocean of the Dharma Practice
My fish-child of Awareness learns to swim;
But never should he pride himself on his power
        of swimming,
Lest he fall into the net of confusion.

Rechungpa, listen to your Guru's words!
On the Snow Mountain of Dharma Actions,
My lion-child of Awareness learns to fight;
But he should never pride himself on his
        fighting power,
Lest he be lost in the snowstorm of desires.

Rechungpa, listen to your Guru's words!
In the Precious Land of Dharma-Accomplishment
My child of Awareness learns to trade;
But never should he trade with shrewdness,
Lest he lose the great pearl of Dharma-Essence.

Rechungpa, listen to your Guru's words
And try to keep your temper,
Lest you be scorched by anger!
Rechungpa, discipline yourself
And quench your passions!

Hearing the Jetsun's song, Rechungpa calmed down. The patrons
in the assembly all blamed the scholar-priests. Rechungpa was also
slightly criticized [for his outburst]. After this incident, the patrons
were all confirmed with a deeper faith than ever in Milarepa. It was
the scholar-priests who first had the intention of slandering the Jetsun,
but in doing so they had only disgraced and discredited themselves.

Being frustrated and humiliated, Dhar Lho, Lodun, and some other
monks again went to the Jetsun [on the following day] to seek revenge. They brought much meat and many books with them. When
they arrived, they asked permission to see the Jetsun in order to apol-
ogize for their conduct of the day before. Rechungpa said, "There is
no need for apology, nor for further debate, and there is no necessity for you to meet the Jetsun." While Rechungpa was trying to stop
them, some other disciples [slipped into] the Jetsun's room and besought him to see the priests. He said very kindly, "The best thing
is not to do any wrong, but if you have, and can repent of it with
sincerity afterwards, this is also very good. Now, let the scholar-priests
come in and talk to me." Thus he accepted the interview. The priests
then offered the meat and said, "Yesterday, you were in the right. We
regret what we did. In apology, we offer you this meat. Using these
books as frames of reference for judgment, let us now discuss the
Buddhist teachings in a friendly manner." The Jetsun replied, "Dear
teachers, the proverb says, 'Judging from the complexion of his face,
one knows whether the man has eaten or not.' In the same light, the
fact that one knows or knows not the Dharma, can easily be detected
by whether or not he can conquer his own ego-clinging desires. If he
can, that proves he knows and also practices the Buddhist teachings.
One may be very eloquent in talking about the Dharma, and win all
the debates, but if he cannot subdue even a fraction of his own ego-
clinging and desires, but merely indulges himself in words and talk,
his victories in debates will never bring him any profit but will only
increase his egotism and pride. This is the cause of wandering forever
in Saṃsāra and falling to the bottom of Hell. Therefore, as I can see,
all this argumentation is harmful and destructive. Your apology for
[your misconduct yesterday] is very good indeed. Now we have finished our discussion and you may return to your home."

Dhar Lho then said, "Only Buddha can say whether one has conquered his ego-clinging and desires. One may not be able to subdue his ego-clinging, but that does not mean his knowledge about Buddhism and eloquence in debate condemns him to fall into Hell and wander in Saṃsāra forever; to say that is to say knowledge and learning are sinful. One may claim that scholarship itself is a great sin, but this will not absolve him from his [conceit] of being virtuous, nor protect him from doing the wrong thing even with a right intention. This perhaps will cause his direct fall to the bottom of Hell. Therefore, it is of great importance to learn well and to distinguish what is right and what is wrong. For these reasons we must discuss the Buddhist teachings. Since I am familiar with the rules and manners of conducting a debate, I suggest that you choose a topic in which you are well-versed, and propound a proposition in its light. We will then evaluate it and give you our opinion. On the other hand, if you think that we are not well-learned scholars, you may ask us any question you like and we will try to answer it." The Jetsun replied, "If you must insist, I have no other choice. Both of us are known to the people here. They have heard of us, see us, and know us well. I shall now take up a topic beyond both erudition and ignorance. I will ask you some questions; also I will propound my proposition [on Buddhist teachings]. Now, please answer me, Is space obstructing or non-obstructing?" The scholar replied, "No one would ever ask this kind of question. But since I have given my word just now, I must give you my answer: Of course space is non-obstructing — what else could it be?"

"But *I* think space is obstructing," said the Jetsun.

"What is your reason for daring to make such a presumptuous assertion?"

In the meantime, Milarepa had entered the "Samādhi-of-Solidifying-Space" and replied, "Let us see whether space is obstructing or non-obstructing! Now, will you please stand up and move around, or stretch your limbs?"

The scholar then tried to move but found he could not do so. He had to remain in his original posture, unable even to open his mouth, and sat stiffly there [like a dead image]. Whereupon the Jetsun [levitated] and walked, stood, lay down, and sat in the lotus posture, right out in space. Then he emerged from Samādhi and said to the scholar, "You have maintained that space is non-obstructing, but why cannot you move your body?"

"This is because you have learned evil spells and black magic from your Gurus. What happened to me was simply due to your evil mantras and sorceries; it is a well-known fact, recognized by all sentient beings, that space is non-obstructing."

Milarepa then asked, "Is it true that without conceptualization and rationalization, space is regarded by all as non-obstructing? Do the animals also consider space to be so? You and your teachers, who deem that it is, are now refuted by your own experiment. All of this may be due to my 'black magic,' but the fact that the obstructing nature of space has been proved to you is quite sufficient. Now, I shall give you my proposition: I declare that the rock in front of us is non-obstructing. What is your reaction to *this* statement?"

The scholar replied, "Unless you apply your evil mantras and sorceries [again], the rock cannot be otherwise than obstructing."

To this the Jetsun said, "In accordance with what you suggested in the beginning [(that each party may test the other in any subject), I now want to test your magic powers], for I do not think that you are well-versed in this subject. Now, please perform some magic to make the rock in front of us become non-obstructing."

"To be able to make magic, and to be willing to do so, are two quite different things," replied the scholar. " 'Capable of making' does not mean being allowed to make. Only you evildoers play these black-magic tricks to cheat others."

"Just now you gave me the impression that you seem to know and can do everything," said the Jetsun. "What you called 'forbidden magic,' is now being performed like rainfall by infinite Buddhas throughout the universe."

Lodun then said, "Just as space became obstructing a while ago, now please demonstrate a spell for making the rock non-obstructing."

Whereupon, the Jetsun entered the Samādhi-of-Space-Exhaustion, making the rock permeable, and then passed through it from the top to the bottom and from one side to the other; also, he kept half of his body in the rock and half outside of it. Then, he threw the rock up and let it fall. Finally he lifted up the rock with his hand, and cried to Rechungpa, "Bring a pillar!" Rechungpa brought a pillar-shaped stone and set it up. [Milarepa then placed the huge rock upon it] leaving his hand-prints indented on the rock. These marks can be seen to this very day.

The scholar Lodun then said, "It seems that you have made the rock non-obstructing. If this is not delusive magic, *we too* should be able to pass through the rock. Now tell us, can we also do it?"

The Jetsun replied, "Of course! If the rock were *obstructing*, should I not then have been killed when it fell?"

The scholar, Dhar Lho, then said, "The rock never touched *me*. If there was no rock in the first place, what is the use of talking about its non-obstructiveness?"

"The fact [that you did not feel the rock come down and crush you] is the very proof that it is non-obstructing," replied the Jetsun. "That you fail to feel a thing does not imply the non-existence of that thing."

Now Dhar Lho became even more angry than before, but Lodun began to be uncertain, and to waver. He thought, "All this seems to be genuine. We skeptical and incredulous scholars are always very difficult to convince. If these performances are not created by magic but are proofs of his accomplishment in the Path, I should acquire from him the teaching of the Six Pāramitās." He then asked, "Will you please tell us how to practise the Six Pāramitās?" In answer Milarepa sang:

Oh Three Great, Precious Refuges,
Sitting on my head as my joy and glory,
I pray with sincerest heart
That you may never leave me.
I pray you to fold me in your compassion,
I pray that you attend me with kind thoughts,
I pray you to grant Ultimate Truth to all
    sentient beings.

The Mahāyāna Yogi hears not the Dharma of
    mere words;
In the truth of Voidness, [he knows] there is
    no practice.
So he renounces of himself the Ten Vices.

If from parsimony one cannot free oneself,
What is the use of discussing charity?
If one does not forswear hypocrisy and pretence,
What is the use of keeping discipline?
If one abjures not malicious revilings,
What is the use of exercising pretentious
    "patience"?
If one abandons not indifference and inertness,
What is the use of swearing to be moral?
If one conquers not the errant thoughts within,
What is the use of toiling in meditation?
If one does not see all forms as helpful,
What is the use of practicing the Wisdom?
If one knows not the profound teaching
Of forbidding and allowing,
What is the use of learning?
If one knows not the art of taking and rejecting,
What is the use of speaking on Karma-causation?
If one's mind does not accord with Dharma,

What is the use of joining the Order?
If the poisonous snake of Klesa is not killed,
The yearning for wisdom only leads to fallacy.
If venomous jealousy is not overcome,
One's yearning for Bodhi-Mind will be an illusion.
If one refrains not from hurting people,
His longing for respect and honor
Is merely wishful thinking.
If one cannot conquer ego-clinging and prejudice,
His craving for the Equality-of-Dharma
Only brings wrong views.
If one cannot subdue the demon, clinging-ego,
His Kleśas will be great and his Yoga bound
　　to fail.
If one's actions conform not with the Dharma,
He will always hinder the good deeds of others.
If one has not yet absorbed his mind in Dharma,
His babbling and prattling will only disturb
　　others' minds.
Therefore, do not waste your life in words and
　　chatter
But try to gain the assurance of no-regret
And the confidence of facing death!

"Well, I admit that you have heard of the Six Pāramitās," commented Dhar Lho. "Now tell me how should one practise the Ten Pāramitās?" In answer to his challenge, Milarepa sang:

Oh gracious Jetsun, Marpa the Translator!
I pray you to quench the "dharmas of jealousy,"
I pray you to protect us in these evil times.

Now, listen to me Dhar Lho, you evil-minded scholar!
Without remembering or thinking of death
You have indulged in words and arguments.
For the past two-and-thirty years
You have failed to realize this fact.
But you can gain far more
If you devote yourself to actual practice.
Alas, in this time of defilement,
Great are people's passions and desires,
And unbearably glib are sinful people's tongues.

On the Other Shore[7] of Non-ego which I have reached,
There is no distinct Pāramitā of Charity.
On the Straightforward Other Shore on which I live
There is no distinct Pāramitā of Discipline.
On the Other Shore of No-Separation-from-Devotion,
There is no distinct Pāramitā of Diligence.
On the Other Shore of the Immediate-Presence
    where I dwell,
There is no distinct Pāramitā of Concentration.
On the Other Shore of Realizing-the-Absolute,
There is no distinct Pāramitā of Wisdom.
On the Other Shore of All-Perfections where I live,
There is no distinct Pāramitā of Means.
On the Other Shore of Conquering-Four-Demons,
There is no distinct practice called
    "Pāramitā of Power."
On the Other Shore of Two-Benefits[8] where I dwell,
There is no distinct practice called "Pāramitā
    of Vow."
Since the faulty Kleśas are themselves Illumination,
There is no thing outstanding
To be known as "Wisdom."
This is the right way of practicing the Dharma;[9]
Empty words are useless and help little!

"Your practices and understanding are indeed right!" exclaimed Lodun. On the other hand, Dhar Lho remarked, "Your words are like
third-hand imitations; they cannot stand close examination. As to the
magic and sorcery, even pagans can perform them perfectly. The Ten
Pāramitās you have just talked about are merely nominal, they are not
at all in accordance with these books. Now, we should discuss the sub-
jects indicated in *them*." [He pointed to the books in front of him,
and continued]: "All human knowledge should be examined and eval-
uated through logic.[10] Logic is the most important science of all learning. If one knows logic, all other studies become secondary. Therefore, I shall first discuss logic with you. If you can answer my questions I shall then acknowledge you. Generally speaking, logic is the
study of judgment and definitions, of which the most important sub-
jects are the studies of direct experience, of inference and deduction,
of 'sufficient reasoning' and 'false-reasoning,' of 'non-decisive proofs,'
and of the patterns for constructing propositions. Now, tell me about
all these things!"

The Jetsun replied, "Teacher, your body and mind are both possessed by devils. Since you have neither faith in yourself and in your Yidham, nor any veneration toward Buddha Himself, how can I expect you to agree with me? When I drink the soup of your favorite Dharma-of-no-Compassion, my tongue and palate are burned. When I eat the food of your beloved Dharma-of-no-Renunciation — which tastes like [a dish of] vegetable greens cooked with dust and ashes but without any salt or seasoning — my stomach is filled with arrogance and egotism! Then from the upper part of my body I belch with self-conceit and vomit the waste of jealousy; from the lower part I break the wind of slandering and discharge the feces and urine of vanity. I am then caught by the deadly sickness of injuring-all. Therefore, I know nothing about your teachings, which, if used as an antidote, would only worsen the sickness, and as a Dharma would only lead people to sin. What I understand is that all manifestations [consist in] Mind, and Mind is the Illuminating-Voidness without any shadow or impediment. Of this truth I have a decisive understanding; therefore not a single trace of inference or deduction can be found in my mind. If you want me to give some examples of 'false-reasoning,' your own knowledge is a 'good' one, because it is against the Dharma; and since this 'false reasoning' only enhances your cravings and makes them 'sufficient,' it is a good example of 'sufficient reasoning.' Your hypocritical and pretentious priestly manner contains the elements of both 'false' and 'sufficient' reasoning, which in turn stand as a good example of 'non-decisive proof.' "

Hearing the Jetsun's remarks, Lodun covered his head with his shawl and laughed; Dhar Lho shook his head, burst out laughing, and cried, "Thank you for correcting my 'spelling'! You are the one who can hardly imagine the difference between the head and the tail of my feces, but yet takes himself as the Holy Buddha. How amusing! How ridiculous! You said that both my body and mind are possessed by devils, but who is the witness of that? If it is because of scholarship and knowledge of logic that I praise myself and denounce others, you are just like me: for you even talk as if you were Buddha Himself, and humiliate me even to *this* extent! By the same token, you also have your own 'logic.' In brief, you have no merits or fortune to [learn the right doctrine]. Besides, instead of answering my question correctly, you have puffed out a lot of nonsense and big words — bigger than the penis of an ass! I think you had better hide it, sit quietly, and shut your mouth."

The Jetsun replied, "I wanted to sit quietly, but you would not let me! Naturally you have no need for my 'logic,' but my 'logic' has brought me happiness and peace. Therefore it is very helpful and important. Since I was talking to you from the viewpoint of the innate

Truth which just hit you on the spot, it appeared as if I were praising myself. The minds of all sentient beings are void yet illuminating. They can neither be affected by the defilements of Saṃsāra nor by the glories of Nirvāna. This very mind is called the Buddha of Universal Origin, or the Treasury of Buddhahood.[11] It is only because we do not understand ourselves that our minds are veiled by temporal blindness; we, as a result, begin to wander in Saṃsāra and become miserable sentient beings-of-desire. He who [fully] realizes his own mind, is called the Enlightened One, the Pure One, or the Buddha, and he attains Nirvāna. Lord Buddha said:

> 'The Matrix of Buddhahood permeats all sentient
>   beings.
> All beings are therefore Buddhas in themselves.'

"Also He said:

> 'Sentient beings are Buddhas in themselves,
> Yet are they veiled by temporal defilements;[12]
> Once the defilements are cleansed,
> Then will they be Buddhas.'

"[Buddha also said]: 'He who realizes his own mind, knows that the mind itself is the Wisdom, and no longer searches for Buddha from other sources. This is the highest teaching one can practice.'

"[As I understand] it, whoever realizes the inborn Illuminating-Void Mind becomes Buddha. I consider that the Ultimate Truth is no other than the realization of one's own mind, but you scholars have no faith in this. As to your body and mind being in the hands of devils, evidence can be shown, and all people here may witness it. However, this would hurt and damage you too much, therefore it is better that I do not talk about it."

The scholar replied, "How wonderful is this! You say that my mind and body are in the hands of devils; if you have any convincing proof why don't you bring it out now? I think I am much better than those fakers who cheat people through deceptive sorcery and gloomy songs."

The Jetsun smiled at him and said, "Well, if you insist, I have no choice but to convince you. Now, pay attention and try to understand what I am going to say! A thing that you cherished with great affection is now in someone else's hands. Is not this very action [of giving a cherished thing to another] itself a sufficient proof that your body and mind are possessed by devils?"

Hearing this, Dhar Lho was nonplused. His face first turned green and then black. Although the Jetsun now tried to stop Rechungpa from [further] exposing Dhar Lho's scandals, Rechungpa would not listen and went forward to a girl (among the visitors), who had little faith towards the Jetsun but great faith in Rechungpa, and took a bracelet off her wrist. Dhar Lho was so ashamed that he became utterly speechless. Then, [recovering himself], he turned on the Jetsun and Rechungpa, attacked them outrageously in abusive language, and walked out. Rechungpa was so delighted that he showed the bracelet to everybody. Afterwards Rechungpa went again to the girl's home and obtained a rosary [that the scholar had given her], brought it back, and showed it to all. People were thus convinced of Dhar Lho's infamy.

Meanwhile, the scholar Lodun thought, "If the information was not given to Milarepa by others, he must be a genuine and great [accomplished being]. I must think of a way to test him." Then remarking, "We have had enough discussions and debates today," he returned home. On that same evening he poured blood into his begging-bowl but filled his skull-cup with milk,[13] and inverted the images of Gautama Buddha and his attendants. He said to himself, "If he knows what I have done, then he is really an accomplished being and has genuine miraculous powers."

The next day Lodun went to the Jetsun again. Upon his arrival, he first met Rechungpa, who said to him, "Well, my dear scholar, have you come to disgrace yourself and the Dharma again?" Lodun replied, "No, this time I have come to pay homage to the Jetsun, for I now have great faith in him." Saying this he slipped into Milarepa's room. The Jetsun smiled at him and commented, "My dear teacher, you don't have to test me like this. I see all the secrets hidden in your heart as vividly [as if they were in my own hand]. You have poured the Essence of the Five Poisons[14] into the monks' utensil [the bowl] and poured the juice supposed to fill the begging bowl, into the skull-cup. Also you purposely inverted the Buddha's and Bodhisattva's images. Now please do not do such reactionary things, things that no Dharma-follower would dream of doing. Please pour the right drinks into the right vessels, and put the images back in their correct positions." When Lodun heard this remark he was nonplused and frightened half to death. His faith in the Jetsun then rose high. "Pray preach me the Dharma that you practice yourself," he implored, "for I am now fully convinced!" Milarepa replied, "It is very good that you now consider yourself convinced. But my teachings cannot be given to the wrong person, one who is not capable of receiving them. Listen to my reasons":

I bow down to Marpa, the Translator;
I pray you to enable me, the mendicant,
To observe the Secret Precepts.

The divine teachings of the Secret Doctrine
Are precious yet formidable!
Should I give them to you, the bigoted scholar
Who knows nothing but words and argument,
It would be a sheer waste!

If one absorbed in meditation talks nonsense,
His meditation will be ruined and interrupted.
The teachings of Tantra should be practised secretly;
They will be lost if demonstrated in the marketplace.
Accomplishment is attained by practicing
        the Bodhi-Mind;
A great Yogi will go astray
If he follows priestly rules.
The Pith-Instructions are meant for good Vessels;
They will but wasted be,
If given to the incapable.
If one adheres first to seclusion
But later abandons it,
His efforts will all be wasted.
The songs of yogic experience are profound,
But if one sings them to all people,
It will only lead to waste and pride.
There are too many ways in which
To lose oneself and squander life!
In answer to your question
I have said enough today.

The scholar said again, "You may not like to tell me your inner Experiences, but apparently you seem to have brought forth the Wisdom through your meditations. Now please tell me briefly about your understanding of the Initiations, Path, Stages, View, Practice, and Action." The Jetsun replied, "I know nothing of your teaching concerning these topics, but mine is as follows":

I bow down at the feet of Marpa.

I sing in answer to your question.
Please listen and think carefully,

And for a time forget your criticism!

The best scenery is nought-to-see —
That is the Mind-Essence of Illumination.
The best gain is nought-to-get —
That is the priceless treasure of Mind-Essence.
The best food for satiation is nought-to-eat —
That is the food of beyond-form Samādhi.
The best drink is nought-to-quaff —
That is the nectar of the Bodhi-Mind.
Wisdom is but Self-awareness,
Beyond all words and talk!
This is not the Hīnayānist's world,
This is no realm for fools.
The highest Initiation is that of "This."
He who realizes the truth of "nor-high nor-low,"
Has reached the highest Stage.
He who realizes the truth of no-action,
Is following the Supreme Path.
He who realizes the truth of no-birth, no-death,
Obtains the best that he can hope for.
He who realizes the truth of no-inference,
Has mastered the best logic.
He who realizes the truth of no-great, no-small,
Understands the teaching of the Supreme Vehicle.
He who realizes the truth of no-virtue and no-evil,
Has acquired the Supreme Means.
He who realizes the truth of not-two,
Has attained the Supreme View.
He who realizes the truth of no-observations,
Knows the supreme way to meditate.
He who realizes the truth of no-accepting and
        no-abandoning,
Knows the supreme way to practice.
He who realizes the truth of non-effort,
Approaches the highest Accomplishment.

This truth cannot be understood by
Arrogant and self-conceited teachers —
The prideful scholars of mere words,
And the "great yogis" who prejudge.
For they are those who aspire to Liberation
But only find enslavement.

They are caught by the "two-clingings."
They want emancipation but only find confinement;
They want release, but are bound instead.
They sink down, down to the bottom of Saṃsāra;
They wander, wander in the Three Gloomy Realms.

After this, the scholar Lodun's pride and arrogance were completely broken down. He prostrated himself before the Jetsun and asked him for the Dharma, but he was not able to get the Instructions from the Jetsun at that time. Confirmed with great faith, he said to Milarepa, "The debates we have had are indeed 'true debates,' I admit that you have won."

He then returned home and said to Dhar Lho, "I am convinced that what Milarepa has said is true, and that we logicians have little sincerity, faith, or devotion; nor do we have the pure thoughts and spirit of renunciation. I am now really skeptical about the usefulness of our knowledge. Truly, I do not know whether this knowledge is helpful or obstructive to the course of Liberation. I also regret very much that I thought his genuine superpowers were morbid sorceries." Dhar Lho replied, "The change in your attitude merely shows that you have no confidence in the Dharma; what you have said is like childish babbling. I think he is possessed by a great devil, and his magic powers and telepathy are merely devil-inspired. He does not know one iota of Buddhist teaching. Nor did I have an affair with that woman; his slanderous accusation was absolutely untrue!" Saying this he died, full of hatred and vicious thoughts. Because of his hate and cravings, he became a fearful demon after death. Later, the Jetsun told his disciples, "Because of Dhar Lho's ill-omened attack on me, he has now fallen to the far edge of Saṃsāra!" Thus, those scholars who slandered the Jetsun all incurred loss for themselves.

Later the scholar Lodun put himself in the Jetsun's care. After meditating for some time he eventually became the foremost of the five scholar-yogis in the ranks of the close-sons of Milarepa. His story will be related in the pages to follow.

This is the story of Milarepa overcoming the ill-intentioned challenge [of the scholars] through his miraculous powers and wonder-performances.

NOTES

1 The Three Learnings (T.T.: Slob.gSum.): the learnings of Precept, of Meditation, and of Wisdom.

2 Dorma: See Story 30, Note 7.

3 Key-words of the Five Elements: Each of the Five Elements that constitute the physical body is symbolized by a specific key-word (bija), i.e., the Fire Element bija, "Rūṁ," the Space Element bija, "Ā" and so forth.

4 See Story 33, Note 3.

5 Lodun: His full name was Lodun Gedunbum (T.T.: Lo.sTon.dGe.hDun. hBum.).

6 Dhar Lho: His full name was Radun Dharma Lhodre (T.T.: Ra.sTon. Dar.Ma.bLo.Gros.).

7 Other Shore: "Pāramitā" is translated by both Chinese and Tibetan scholars as "Reaching-the-Other-Shore," meaning reaching the Nirvāṇa beyond Saṃsāra. Some Western scholars also translate this term as "Perfection."

8 The Two Benefits: deeds that lead to the benefit of oneself and that of others.

9 In addition to the Six Pāramitās practiced by Bodhisattvas, four more are given for the advanced stages. They are: the Pāramitās of Means, of Power, of Vow, and of Dharma Clouds, subsequently assigned for the practice of Enlightened Bodhisattvas of the 7th, 8th, 9th, and 10th stages.

10 Logic (T.T.: Tshad.Ma.), meaning measurement, standard, correct thinking, and so forth. "Tshad.Ma." is derived from the Sanskrit word "Pramāna," signifying [that which is] prior to opinion or thinking; the means of acquiring right knowledge.

11 The Treasury of Buddhahood (T.T.: bDe.gÇeg.sÑiñ.Po.; Skt.: Tathāgatagarbha). This term may also be translated as "the seed or cause of Buddhahood," without which the attainment of Buddhahood is not possible no matter what spiritual efforts may be made.

12 Temporal defilements: All "defilements" (T.T.:. Dri.Ma.), such as passions, desires, ignorance, etc., are in their deepest sense, rootless, delusory, and temporal. To regard them as something concrete or permanent is erroneous and misleading.

13 Skull-cup, or Kapāla (T.T.: Thod.Pa.): the human skull used as an essential utensil in Tantric practice. It is employed by Tantric yogis as a cup to fill with wine as an offering to the deities. In rare cases, in the performance of certain rituals of the Fierce Deities (T.T.: Khro.Wo.), blood, semen, urine, feces, and saliva — the so-called "impurities" and "filthy things," as men regard them — are offered to the deities. The main purpose of this curious rite is to eliminate discriminative thoughts and to transcend both the realms of purity and impurity. This is strictly Tantric. No Hīnayāna or other Mahāyāna School practices it.

Here the scholar Lodun reversed the customary way of offering in Hīnayāna, and in the Tantra, to test Milarepa.

14 The Essence of the Five Poisons: The Five Nectars (T.T.: bDud.rTsi.lŃa.) of Tantrism are the five major "filthy" discharges, i.e., urine, feces, semen, blood, and spittle. Milarepa refers to blood here as the Essence of the Five Poisons. See Note 13.

35

RECHUNGPA'S THIRD
JOURNEY TO INDIA

Obeisance to all Gurus

THROUGH his miraculous powers the Jetsun Milarepa had conquered the scholar-priests in their ill-intentioned debate and had won the argument. However, his heart-son, Rechungpa, was not satisfied with this victory, for he thought that the Jetsun had not answered the monk's questions in a scholarly manner. "The only way," Rechungpa thought to himself, "to conquer these scholars, who cannot even be convinced by the evidence of miracles, is through logic and argument, or by black magic and curses. I might ask the Jetsun to teach me black magic, but it is not likely that he would. Oh, confound it! These damned scholars who belittle genuine miracles as sorceries! They certainly deserve to be dealt with! But the Jetsun will never do it. Well, it is true that my Guru is well-versed in the Pith-Instructions for attaining Buddhahood in one life, but in order to beat these scholars, I shall go to India to learn logic and science." He then went to Milarepa and told him of his intention. The Jetsun said, "Rechungpa, if we had been defeated in the debate, how could the scholars have credited us with pure [thoughts]? If you go to India merely for the purpose of learning the art of debate, you are then doing something wrong and worthless. [That also means that you will] forsake meditation practice. In learning 'semantics,' you may acquire some knowledge about words, but still you will not be able to win all the debates, nor can you master the whole study of letters. Only Buddha can answer all questions and challenges, but to achieve Buddhahood one must practice. Therefore, the best way is to abjure the world, renounce all thoughts and wishes of this life, and devote oneself to meditation. One may slay people by black magic, but if he cannot deliver the victims [from Samsāra], both he and the victims will be damned. Formerly

I used black magic to curse my enemies, but because of this sinful deed I had to go through many painful trials under Marpa. Life is very short, no one can tell when death will fall upon him. Therefore please forget everything else, and concentrate on your meditation."

[In spite of his Guru's advice], Rechungpa pressed the Jetsun to grant him permission to go to India. Milarepa then said, "If you insist upon ignoring my advice, you may go to India; but I am not sending you there to study logic and science. When I was with Marpa, I received from him only four of the nine complete teachings of the Formless Ḍākinī Dharma Series. He said that the other five were still available in India, and also prophesied that a disciple in our Lineage would later secure them from [a teacher of] Nāropa's Transmission. Thereby many sentient beings will be benefited. Since I have been devoting myself to meditation, I have not yet attended to this matter. These teachings, therefore, are still to be obtained. I am now old and sick, also I have fully realized my own mind — there is no need for me to go. I think it fitting that you go to India to procure them. You will, however, need some gold for your journey."

Thereupon, the Jetsun and Rechungpa collected all the gold that people had offered them, which totaled quite a large sum. Then Shindormo and Lesebum, together with many patrons, prepared a sacred banquet as a farewell party for Rechungpa. In the assembly, the Jetsun presented his disciple with all the gold, and said, "Rechungpa, my son! Listen to my song and think about it. You should try to secure the teachings in India in this manner:

I bow down to Marpa, the Translator.
Pray bless us that we keep to your Tradition.

This uninformed son of mine, the loser of debate
And full of doubts, has stopped his meditation
And is about to wander far away to study.
This is the very thing a yogi should avoid!

Rechungpa, when you arrive in India,
Try to secure the Formless Ḍākinī Dharmas
Of the great Paṇḍita Nāropa's Succession;
But, never give yourself to studying words!

In the beginning I met the right person,
I put myself in the hands of Marpa.
In the middle, I practiced the right teaching,
Meditating on the White Rock Mountain.[1]

At the end, I asked for alms in the right places
    for alms;
I beg here and there without friends or kinsmen.
Since I have disposed of Saṃsāra and Nirvāṇa
And have nor hope nor fear in my mind,
I shall ne'er regress in my meditation.

When with my Guru Marpa on that steep hill
He once said to me:

> "The King of the Mighty Wheel holds
>   [It as] the Jewel,
> And the Bird with Five Families
> Flies in [It's] expanse of Dharma-Essence.[2]
> Five special teachings in India still survive:
> First, the Lamp of Illuminating Wisdom,
> Second, the Wheel Net of Nāḍī and Prāṇa,
> Third, the Great Bliss of Precious Words,
> Fourth, the Universal Mirror of Equality,
> And Fifth, the Self-liberation Mahāmudrā.
> These five teachings are still taught
>   in India."

I am now too old to go,
But you, child of Marpa's Lineage,
Should go to India to learn them!

Rechungpa was delighted. He picked up the best piece of gold, tossed it to the Jetsun as [his farewell offering], and sang:

> Bless me, my teacher,
> Let me risk my life
> To fulfill the Gurus' will.
> Pray help me get the Ḍākinīs' Teachings as prophesied.
> With your great Wisdom-Compassion
> Pray e'er protect, and ne'er part from me.
> Pray, at all times look after this, your son,
> Who has no kinsmen and no friend.
> Pray conquer all his hindrances
> And save him from going astray!
> Pray safeguard him where'er he goes in India —
> A land of danger, and full of bandits!
> Pray lead him to the right teacher,

As he wanders on alone in that foreign land!

In response, the Jetsun sang:

My son Rechungpa, on your way to India
Remember these seven Trinities of counsel:

The Skillful-Path of Tantra,
The Guru's Pith-Instruction,
And one's own judgment,
Are three important things for your remembrance!

Respect and serve the learned,
Have faith in your Guru,
Be determined and perservering.
These are three things you should remember.

Rightly to direct the Life-stream [Prāṇa],
To enter the Dharma-Essence,
And to master all the teachings,
Are three techniques you should remember.

The views of the Bliss-Void,
Of the myriad forms,
Of reasoning and following the scriptures,
Are three essentials you should remember.

A partner qualified in Mudrā,
Experience of the bliss therein,
And the "Elephantine Work,"[3]
These are the three delights you should
        remember.

To instruct an idler brings misfortune,
To speak of one's experience leads to loss,
In towns to wander damages one's Yoga.
These are three dangers to remember.

To join the assembly of the Brethren,
To attend the meeting of Ḍākinīs,
And be present at the [secret] feasts,
Are the three occasions not to miss.

> Think of the meanings of this song,
> And put them into practice!

Rechungpa made many obeisances to the Jetsun and then set out for India. Accompanying him were fifteen monks, their leader being a Ningmaba Lama⁴ called Jidun. In Nepal, both Rechungpa and Jidun had some success [in spreading the Dharma]. They also met Dipupa's disciple, Bharima.

[When they asked the King of Ko Kom in Nepal] for a "Travel-Permit," the King said, "It is wonderful that you, the heart-disciple of the great Yogi who refused my invitation before, have now come to me." He was delighted and granted all Rechungpa's requests. Arriving in India, Rechungpa met Dipupa and obtained all the teachings he wanted. Dipupa also had great faith in Milarepa. He entrusted Rechungpa with his gift — an aloewood staff — to present to the Jetsun upon his return to Tibet.

On this journey Rechungpa also met the accomplished Yoginī, Magi,⁵ and he received from her the teaching of the Buddha of Long Life. He also learned much black magic and many deadly spells from pagan Indians.

On his way home, Rechungpa again met Bharima in Nepal. As to the story of Bharima correcting the jealous translator-scholars, and Rechungpa's other adventures in Nepal and India, the reader may refer to Rechungpa's Biography, in which all is told in full.

In his illuminating [Samādhi] Milarepa foresaw Rechungpa's return. He then went to Balkhu plain to welcome him. Thus, the father and the son met again.

This is the story of Rechungpa and Dipupa.

NOTES

1 White Rock Mountain (T.T.: Brag.dKar.rTa.So.): Literally "White Rock Horse Tooth [Mountain]."

2 The meaning of these two statements is very enigmatic. The translator presumes that the first statement, "The King of the Mighty Wheel [Cakravarti] holds [It as] the jewel," is an expression of praise for the Teaching of the Dakinī. "It," in the brackets, in both the first and second statments implies the total teaching of the Dakinī.

3 The "Elephantine Work" (T.T.: sPyod.Pa.Glañ.Chen.): The advanced yogi acts fearlessly, with great inspiration, for his own need in various unusual acts, that common people may judge him as "crazy" or "immoral."

4 Ningmaba Lama (a free translation): literally, "a Lama who follows the teaching of the Great Perfection (T.T.: rDsogs.Chen.Pa.)." rDsogs.Chen. is the Ningmaba version of Mahāmudrā.

5 Magi: an outstanding woman philosopher and yogini of Tibet. She was the founder of the gGod. School.

36

THE REALIZATION OF MEGOM REPA

Obeisance to all Gurus

WHEN the Jetsun Milarepa was living in the Belly Cave of Nya Non, a merchant of the Mes tribe[1] came to see him and became filled with an unshakeable faith toward him. He offered Milarepa and his sons all that he had. [He was then given the name of Megom, and became a disciple.] Having received the instructions, he set out to meditate and gained outstanding Experiences and Realizations. Thereupon Milarepa initiated him with the Two-in-One-Pointing-out-Demonstration of the View, Practice, and Action. Immediately, with infinite joy and delight, he beheld the self-face of the Immanent Realty.

After the ceremony, while Megom was preparing a sacred feast in honor of the occasion, he was asked by Drigom Repa, "Do you really understand the Dharma and the instructions? How have your inner Experiences developed?"

Megom replied, "By the mercy of my chief Guru[2] and the Gurus in the Lineage, I am now fully convinced by these teachings. Nothing either good or bad can alter my conviction. For the rest of my life all I need is my Guru's instructions. I have made up my mind, and sworn, to remain in hermitages all my life."

Hearing this, the Jetsun was very pleased and said, "Quite right, Megom. For him who has faith in his Guru and in the instructions, the Experiences and Realizations are bound to develop. They may not arise quickly, but one must have the determination to mediate alone [until they do]. Now listen to my song:"

I bow down at the feet of Marpa.

Oh Megom, and all my disciples here,

403

Please listen, think, and practice what I sing —
The song of an old man
Who is an expert in these things.

Because confusion is uprooted in me,
I realize that Self-awareness is my Guru.
He who has not realized this truth,
Ne'er should leave an accomplished teacher.

All thoughts and forms are but the Holy Truth.
If one has not realized this truth,
He should ne'er neglect the Holy Scriptures.

Try to renounce all desires and craving!
If aversion toward worldly things
Has not arisen in one's mind,
He should watch and discipline himself!

Try to realize the sole truth of Non-being.
If one has not yet experienced this truth,
He should closely watch his Karma.

Try to understand that Nirvāṇa and Saṃsāra
        are not two.
If one has not reached this understanding,
He should practice the equality of the Two Truths.[3]

Try to realize the oneness of self and others.
He who has not yet done this,
E'er should hold to Bodhi-Mind.

Try to let Realization of itself arise.
If of itself it has not done so,
Never forsake the rules and rites.

Try to transcend the Chief and Ensuing Samādhis.[4]
He who has not passed through both realms
Should follow the Skillful Path in solitude.

Try to let the Experience perpetually arise.
He who cannot yet do this
Should continue with the Three-Points practice.[5]

Try to realize the self-nature of Trikāya.
Until this has been realized,
Practice the Arising and Perfecting Yoga.

Try to make yourself
Always relaxed and free.
If you cannot do so,
Keep your vows and precepts!

In great joy, Megom cried, "Jetsun, you are most kind to instruct me in the two-in-one nature of the View, Practice, and Action by combining them into one teaching!" Whereupon he sang:

I pay homage to the gracious Jetsun.

Joyful it is to see the Two-in-One,
Cheerful it is to meditate thereon,
Delightful it is on it to act,
Oh, marvelous are these three "Two-in-Ones"!

If one knows not the View of Two-in-One,
How can he understand that all things
Are but the Dharmakāya?
If one knows not how to practice the Two-in-One,
How can he realize that all pains are glories?
If one knows not the Action of Two-in-One,
How can he spontaneously relinquish worldly wants?

All sentient beings in the Six Realms
Are but the Wisdom of Nirvāna.
This is the View of Two-in-One.
All positives and negatives
And the Wisdom of the Whole
Are but the Dharmakāya.
This is the Practice of Two-in-One!

Like the moon reflected everywhere in water,
Like a rainbow that by no one can be held,
Like lamplight shining brightly [in the dark],
Such is the Action of Two-in-One.

The core of the View
Lies in non-duality,

The Essence of the Practice
Lies in non-distraction,
The "pivot" of the Action is
To embrace and absorb.
That is Enlightenment!

This is the understanding
Your son gained in his devotion!

All the disciples profited greatly from this song. Then on the eve of his departure to meditate in solitude, Megom asked the Jetsun to give him a teaching, effective yet easy to practice. The Jetsun replied, "Great merits have grown in me since I practiced these instructions. You should also follow them. Now listen to my song":

I, the Yogi Milarepa, see the Essence
By gazing nakedly upon It!
I see Beyond-playwords, clear as the sky!
By letting go, I see Reality;
By resting at my ease, I realize
The voidness of all and everything.
I relax, relax, and come to the Self-Realm;
I let go, let go, and in the flow of Awareness
The pure and impure become one!

Because I search for nothing,
Thoughts and ideas are all cut off;
The perils of Saṃsāra are thus forever crushed!
Since I realize that Buddha and my mind are one,
I no longer wish for accomplishment!
As the sun disperses darkness,
When Realization dawns upon one
Kleśas and Nhamdogs vanish by themselves!

Hearing this song, Megom was filled with joy. As instructed by his Guru, he then went to a hermitage and meditated there alone. Later he gained many merits on the Path, attained superb Experiences and Realizations, and became one of the close sons of the Jetsun, known as Megom Repa, who [in his lifetime] helped many well-endowed men.

NOTES

1 The text reads, "Rus.Mes.Yin.Pahi.Tshon.Pa.Shig.". "Rus.Mes." literally means "ancestral lineage," but here the translator presumes "Mes" is the name of a tribe, and not to be understood as "ancestral" in the original meaning of the word.

2 Chief Guru: A Buddhist yogi may have many Gurus. However, the most important Guru is he who brings the yogi to the initial Enlightenment; this Guru is considered as one's *Chief Guru*. Not only is he more important than the others insofar as he has actually opened one's mind to the Prajñā Truth, but also he is the main reliance of the yogi in his progress on the Path. The first priority should be given to him in service, worship, and prayer, as shown by the relationship between Milarepa and Marpa.

3 Two Truths (T.T.: bDen.Pa.gÑis.): These are the Mundane and the Transcendental Truths. The former deals with the basic principles of the phenomenal world, and the latter with the Ultimate. See also Story 29, Note 11.

4 Chief and Ensuing Samādhis (T.T.: mÑam.bShag. [and] rJes.Thob.): The Chief, or Main Samādhi is the real Samādhi stage; the Ensuing Samādhi is the after-Samādhi stage, i.e., the daily activities in which the Samādhi experience still prevails to some degree.

5 The Three-Points practice: The translator presumes that this refers to the practice of observing the nature of the three successive stages of any passing event, i.e., the beginning, the middle, and the final phases. By observing them, one's inner Experience can be widened.

SAHLE AUI AND
HER UNDERSTANDING

Obeisance to all Gurus

THE Jetsun Milarepa went for alms to Ngogang from the Belly Cave of Nya Non. He stayed at La Shin for half a day, and then proceeded to Nagchar. On his way there he met a pretty young girl about sixteen years of age, with dark eyebrows and gleaming hair, well-dressed and well adorned. She was on her way home from fetching water. The Jetsun said, "Dear lady, will you offer me a meal this evening?" The girl replied, "If we who live by the road gave food to every alms-beggar we would be preparing meals for them all the time." Saying this she entered the house and left Milarepa outside.

That night the girl had an auspicious dream. The next morning, recalling her dream, she thought, "Generally, sentient beings are veiled by blindness. They cannot recognize the Buddha nor the Jetsun Milarepa, who is the Buddha too. Without his grace and blessing, I would not have had that dream last night. Can that yogi be Milarepa himself? I will go and find out."

She then prepared some food and took it to the Jetsun. "My dear Yogi, who are you?", she asked.

"I am an alms-beggar who lives in your neighborhood."

"Are you not the Jetsun Milarepa from the Belly Cave of Nya Non?"

"Yes, you may say so."

Hearing this, a faith that was strong enough to dissolve her entire body at once arose within her, and her hair stood on end. She bowed down before Milarepa and cried, "Yes, yes — now I understand! This is why I had such a wonderful dream last night!" The Jetsun then asked her, "What was the dream?"

"I dreamed that a sun and a moon were in my house, but they did not shine. Then another sun and moon appeared in the East, bright and radiant. They lit up the dark sun and moon in my house, and made them shining bright. Then they (the dark ones) rose up and united with the sun and the moon in the East. The whole universe was thus illuminated. Will you please accept me as your servant, so that I can develop myself in the Dharma?"

The Jetsun replied, "I believe you can." Then he blessed her with his Samādhi power and returned to the Belly Cave.

Soon after, the girl visited the Jetsun, bringing a friend with her. She gave Milarepa a nugget of gold, and sang:

> Please listen to me,
> Great Repa Yogi, the accomplished One.
> When I look at human lives
> They remind me of dew on grass.
> Thinking thus, my heart is full of grief.
>
> When I see my friends and relatives,
> They are as merchants passing in the street.
> Thinking thus, my heart is grieved and sad.
>
> When I see goods hard to earn
> They remind me of the honey
> Of hard-working bees.
> Thinking thus, my heart is filled with grief.
>
> When I see my native land,
> It suggests a den of vice.
> Thinking thus, my heart is sad.
>
> By day, I contemplate this truth,
> At night, I think about it without sleep.
>
> Because of my good deeds in former lives,
> I was born this time a human being.
> My past life drives me from behind,
> Cooking and household duties pull me on.
> I draw closer to death every minute.
> This decaying body
> At any time may fall.
> My breath, like morning-fog,
> At any time may disappear.
> Thinking thus, I cannot sleep.
> Thinking thus, my heart is sad.

Oh, my Father Jetsun,
For the sake of Dharma I visit you.
Pray bless, protect, and pity me,
And grant me the holy Teachings!

To test whether the girl could really devote herself to the Dharma,
or whether she might still be interested in worldly things, the Jetsun
said, "I do not want your gold. It is very seldom that the rich can
practice the Dharma, though they may have great ability in other things.
Since you are still very young, I think it is better for you not to renounce the world completely. Now, hearken to my song":

I bow down to the gracious Marpa,
The incarnation of the wheel-turning King!

In the luxuriant garden of the Joyous Heaven[1]
The flowers are sweet-smelling and exquisite,
But common bees can never find them,
Though a hundred flowers they may touch!

On the Tsanglin Continent,[2] south of Mount Sumeru,
There is a bathing pool with Water-of-Eight-Merits
Which common birds can never find,
Though they may locate all other places.

To the north of Bodhgaya
Grow Tsandan, trees of healing,
Which cure all congestions.
But not all sick men can find them,
Though they gather other herbs.

On the border between Nepal and Tibet
Is found the Refuge of the grieved,
He is the immanent Buddha, the good Wadi.[3]
Men without merit cannot see Him.
They may see other images of Buddha,
Yet no faith will grow in them.

In the endless ocean of Samsāra
Wander lonely crowds,
Oft falling to the Lesser Realms.
If once born as human beings,
Few can make provision

For their "souls."
Vain and deluded, they will lose
Once more what they have gained!

To be born a human being
Is rarer than a star that shines by day.
If blessed enough to win a human body,
Many will waste it by running after pleasures,
But few can tread the Path of Dharma.
Though hundreds the gate may enter,
Few can keep the disciplines.

By the grace of my Father Guru
I have realized that all forms are golden;
I have no need for your precious gold.
This is my reply, my faithful patroness,
A song with five parables and six meanings.
The enthusiasm that you now have
Is transient and can be changed;
A will that is not shaken is ever hard to come by;
And so, dear lady, I suggest that you go home.
Trust in the Dharma, is the advice I give.
Take care of your dear husband
As though you served a god.
Maintain your house and fields
And give your children love.

Worship Gurus and Buddhas above;
Protect and help the poor below;
In between look after your in-laws
And keep on good terms with your neighbors.
Now you have been blessed by this old man
Who wishes you prosperity, long life, and success.
May you always have the boon of finding holy
        Dharma.

She bowed down before the Jetsun and said, "I am not interested
in worldly pleasures, but utterly disgusted with everything in Saṃsāra.
Please allow me to give my reasons." Whereupon she sang:

I bow down to the gracious Jetsun.
Pray fulfill my wishes with your blessing,
Pray judge my words and my sincerity.

Pray, great Repa, listen to this girl's request.

With ignorant and bewildered mind
I have thought and searched.
In the depths of my heart
I have reflected on the transiency of life.
I have seen death strike down both young and old
Since first I saw the light of day.

Life is precarious and fleeting
Like dew upon the grass.
Time flies unnoticed, and then life is o'er.
I have never seen or heard of an immortal man.
I am certain beyond doubt
That I shall die one day.
I have no freedom or choice
Of where to go when I am dead.
I am sad and fearful
When I think of the pains that I
In Lower Realms might bear.

This world is but a play —
The endless toil of housework,
The struggle for a living,
Leaving one's gracious parents,
Giving up one's life to one's betrothed —
If into the Lower Realms one falls,
Progress and Liberation will be lost.

Sometimes to myself I thought,
How does it make sense —
Freely to give yourself with your parents' goods
To someone who for life enslaves you as a servant?

At first a lover is an angel,
Next a demon, frightening and outrageous,
In the end a fierce elephant,
Who threatens to destroy you.
Thinking thus, I feel sad and weary.
Now, this maid shall devote herself to the Dharma,
Now, she will join her Vajra-brothers![4]

Most men are but credit-collectors;

Seldom does a gifted one appear.
First they steal your youthful beauty,
Next they snatch your food away,
Then they pull jewels from your hands.
Thinking thus, I feel sick at heart.
Now, I shall devote myself to practicing the Dharma.
Hereafter I shall foster the children of Wisdom.

Houses and temples are like prisons;
At first, they break your heart,
Then they give you an aching back,
In the end, they leave you in despair.
Thinking thus, I feel sick at heart.
This maid will now devote herself
To building a chapel for the immortal Dhyāna.

'Tis meaningless to worship symbols and the Sūtras
Except for those who have real faith and sincerity.

I see people fighting over land,
Then they quarrel over water,
In the end, blows are exchanged.
Thinking thus, I feel sick at heart.
Now I shall farm the land of self-discipline,
Now I shall devote myself to practicing the Dharma.

If one adheres to the Bodhi-Mind
His merits will surely grow.
Yet should he crave for wealth
He will commit much sin in his endeavors.

In the beginning, burning desire consumes one,
Then is he possessed by pride and jealousy,
In the end he fights his foes in desperation.
Thinking thus, my heart is filled with grief.
Now I shall devote myself to the Dharma,
Now I shall cultivate goodwill to all men.

Clearly we see others' faults
But seldom see our own.
How, then, can harmony exist among us?
Even the immaculate Buddha,
All-knowing and all-perfect,

Was found with faults by sinners.
How, then, can peace exist among us?
Thinking thus, I feel sad and weary.
Now I shall devote myself to the Dharma,
Now I shall look at the self-face of my mind.

All things appear like gold to you,
The Nirmāṇakāya of the Buddha!
One may not have experienced this,
Yet [in reality] there is neither existence
          nor non-existence.
To conquer my greed and clinging
I now offer you my most cherished thing.

As the Lord Buddha said,
"One should renounce belongings
That increase one's craving.
All possessions, like magic, are delusive —
One should give them away
For good purposes and charity."
Following this injunction of the Enlightened Ones
I now offer you this gold.
Accept, please, this small token of my faith
And grant me your instructions.

Whereupon the Jetsun Milarepa accepted the gold from the girl and then returned it to her, saying, "If you have determined to practice the Dharma, disregarding life and death, you have already entered the gate of Dharma. Now you should prepare offerings for the Gurus and the Patron Buddha."

A sacramental offering was then made on a grand scale. The Jetsun ordained her as a Geninma[5] in accordance with the general Buddhist Rules,[6] initiated her into the esoteric Tantric Order, and gave her many verbal instructions. He then named her "Sahle Aui," and ordered her to meditate. In a very short time she gained good Experiences and merits, and learned to meditate alone. The Jetsun then said to her, "I am very pleased with your faith and perseverance; the Experiences and Realizations that you have now gained will enable you to meditate independently in solitude. You should go now into the mountains and meditate by yourself. Until we meet again, remember these words from my heart." Whereupon he sang:

Great is the blessing of qualified Gurus!

Safe is the shelter of the Three Jewels!
Mighty is the merciful power of the Guards
    and Ḍākinīs!
To you all I pay sincerest homage!

My voice and melody may not be good,
But this song will surely carry
The blessing of the Lineage,
And illustrate the gist of Buddha's teaching.

Listen, faithful Sahle Aui, the woman devotee!
If you want to cleanse the rust from the mirror
    of your mind,
Look into the depth of the pure sky!
And meditate in quiet mountains
Blessed by accomplished beings!

To stay alone in a hermitage
One should know how to observe
The deep Essence of the wavering mind.
Listen carefully, Sahle Aui,
As I tell you how to meditate.

To have faith unshaken
While a Novitiate of Dharma is wonderful;
Like a mountain standing firm,
Meditate with steadfastness.
To win the merits of the Buddha,
Disregard both pain and pleasure!

Like a river flowing on and on,
Meditate without interruption.
To receive the blessing from your Guru,
You should have incessant faith.

Like the firmament, devoid of edge or center,
Meditate on vastness and Infinity.
To understand the innate Truth,
Unite Skill and Wisdom.

Like sun and moon in all their glory,
Meditate clearly without darkness.
Knowing that all beings are your parents,

Love and show compassion to them.

Use the ocean as a parable.
Meditate without drowsiness or distraction.
To see directly the Self-mind,
You should follow straight the Guru's words.
Like this great earth,
Meditate with unshaken firmness.
To make yourself a vessel of the Dharma
Meditate beyond all words.
To realize that all things are holy Dharmas,
Watch your mind.

At all times and in all you do
Provide for yourself with care.
Deck yourself with the ornament of discipline,
Wear the clothes of patience, made of sheepskin,
Ride on the wonder horse of diligence,
And enter the holy City of Dhyāna.
With the Jem of Wisdom you will be enriched.
Forget not to repay the bounty of your Guru,
But give him the best offering —
All you have experienced and realized.
Do you, my faithful daughter, understand what
        I have said?

With an even greater faith in the Jetsun than before, Sahle Aui gave a great feast in his honor. Then, obediently, she renounced all worldly affairs and went to meditate on the mountain of Nonyul in the Nya Non area, while Milarepa left for the Red Rock of Drin.

Some time later the Jetsun saw in his so compassionate mind a beam of glittering light shoot from a crystal stūpa, [a sign that Rechungpa was having trouble in his devotions]. The fact was that Rechungpa was having difficulty with his breath-control as a result of the black-magic practices that he had learned from the heretics. Seeing this, the Jetsun thought, "What hindrance is my son Rechungpa having now?" He then flew from the summit of the Red Rock Mountain toward Lashi. Half way there he landed at Rechin Meditation Cave leaving his footprints on the rock. Again absorbing himself in the illuminating Samādhi, he observed the fortunes of Rechungpa and saw that neither Rechungpa's body nor life would be affected, but that some unorthodox thought was hindering his mind.

Milarepa then set out for Nya Non to learn the whereabouts of his female disciple, Sahle Aui. On the way he met some monks who told him that Sahle Aui was still meditating in the cave to which she had first gone. They said that she never spoke or moved her body, but sat still like a dead corpse all the time. They believed that she must have gone astray in her meditation. Milarepa thought, "To absorb oneself in Samādhi like that is a good thing and not a hindrance." He then went toward the girl's abode. Meanwhile, in an illumination, Sahle Aui also saw the Jetsun coming, so she went to the edge of the valley to welcome him.

After making obeisances and inquiring after his health, Sahle Aui sat down to one side quietly, without uttering a word. In order to examine her meditation experience, Milarepa sang:

> Oh, Sahle Aui, the hermit
> Who took the Dharma to her heart,
> With faith and veneration
> You first relied on your Guru;
> And through his blessings
> Your mind has ripened.
> Sipping the heavenly nectar of the Skillful Path
> A real knowledge of Dharma has grown in you.
> Without sloth and laziness in your devotion
> The Warm-Experience that all saints have had
> Has now grown within you.
>
> Since no hindrance has arisen,
> You may as well keep silent now.
> As hunger is not killed by poisonous food,
> Nor Liberation reached by a wrong path,
> Efforts so made will be wasted.
>
> Deer stay in the mountains,
> What is the use of that?
> The black-bird Dorge can sing,
> What is the sense of that?
> The white-bellied Gyuar Mo[7] can hold Life-Prāṇa
>   well,
> What is the benefit of that?
> The Dombu Tukar[8] is skilled in mixing elixirs,
> All pagan yogis practice the Samādhi of No-thought,
> The Brāhmans are ascetic all their lives,
> What is the good of that?
> Parrots can talk with eloquence,

But he who follows not
The Path of Liberation,
For all his passionate striving
Hardly can emancipate himself.

The human mind is like a whirling vortex.
Through the power of Samādhi
One may suppress desires and wandering thoughts,
But this alone will never ferry one
Across the ocean of Saṃsāra!

To practice the Tsandali Yoga of Forms,⁹
One needs Wisdom beyond form.
To practice the Tsandali at the Heart-Center,
One must recognize the Bardo Illumination.
To practice the Ultimate Tsandali of Immanence,
One must realize the State beyond birth and death.
To practice the Tsandali Yoga of Bindu and Nāḍī
One must cease clinging to all forms.
The Central Channel, Dhuti,¹⁰ is beyond
      all efforts and acts;
It is non-acting, self-existent, originally pure.
[Seeing it], the knots of the two clingings
Will spontaneously unravel.
This is the foremost truth of Mahāmudrā.
Dear Sahle Aui, have you realized it yet?

Presenting her inner Experience to the Jetsun, Sahle Aui sang:

The holder of the Lineage of Dorje-Chang,
The one who was prophesied by all Ḍākinīs,
By the grace of Tilopa and Nāropa
Mastered the Four Tantras, the knowledge profound.
He was Marpa, of the Whispered Succession!
By his grace in the Ten Directions,
You have raised many crops;
By his grace, you have borne immaculate fruits
One after the other!
With your blessings, I have gained the great
      Freedom.
To you, the glory upon my head,
I ever pay my homage.

You are the compassionate one,

The great Repa from Gung Tang
Whose fame has spread afar to all lands.
To you, the crowning gem upon my head,
I pray with great sincerity and faith.
Oh, my Father Guru, it is through your grace,
That we, confused wrong-doers, were converted
      to the Dharma.
It is you who led us to the right path.

You ripened the unripened,
You emancipated those who were not free.
You made me realize that all
Manifestations in the outer world
Are unreal and magic-like.
I have thus seen the Mother of the Illuminating
      Dharmata,[11]
I have thus realized that flowing thoughts
Are phantom-like projections;
As waves rise from the sea
They will vanish into it again.
All doubts, errors, and
Temptations in the world
Are thus wiped out!
Following the clear Path
I have gained true knowledge,
Understanding what the Tantras mean.
Truth of the lesser path should not
Be taken for the higher.
By craving it one cannot reach Buddhahood.
I now sincerely ask you, my Guru,
To instruct me in the Tantra.

Comparing my experience with my Dharma-brother
      Ngan Tson's,
I cannot help but feel a deep respect for him.
Like food, my conceit and wrong ideas
      are swallowed;
Thus my long, leaden slumber has been shortened.
I have now renounced all men,
And given myself to meditation.
For many years I have avoided soft cushions,
And contemplated on Mahāmudrā without distraction.
I am a woman aspiring to Nirvāṇa,
Who, from Voidness and Compassion would n'er depart.

Free from conceit and arrogance,
I shall e'er be glad to learn the Doctrine.
Ever in you I trust as in the Buddha.
With all Ḍākinīs caroling with me,
This is my song to you, my gracious Guru.

The Jetsun, very much pleased, said, "You have gained good understanding and Experiences from your meditation. It is indeed difficult to win Realization like this. Although you have now entered the Path of the Omniscient Ones, you should still remain and meditate in solitude."

Obeying this injunction Sahle Aui again meditated in the hermitage. Later on she became one of the four foremost yoginī disciples of the Jetsun. During her lifetime she performed a great service to the Dharma and benefited many sentient beings. The story of her life may be found in a book written by Ngan Tson Dunba Shun Chub Jhalbo.

This is the story of Sahle Aui.

NOTES

1 Joyous Heaven (T.T.: dGah.lDan.).

2 Tsanglin Continent (T.T.: 'hDsam.Glin): the Southern Continent. (See Story 2, Note 16.)

3 Wadi (T.T.: Ran.Byan.Wa.Ti.; lit.: the self-born Wadi): a famous Buddha image legendarily believed to have descended from Heaven.

4 Vajra Brothers, or Brothers-of-Vajra (T.T.: rDo.rJe.sPun.): Those who are initiated by the same Guru are Vajra brothers.

5 Geninma (T.T.: dGe.bsÑen.Ma.): the laywoman Buddhist who has taken a vow to observe the five basic virtuous rules.

6 General Buddhist Rules (T.T.: mDo.Lugs.; lit.: Sūtra Traditions): This implies the Rules and traditions that one finds in the general Mahāyāna Schools whose doctrines are based on Sūtras but not on Tantras.

7 White-bellied Gyuar-Mo (T.T.: Gyur.Mo.lTo.dKar.): According to the text, Gyuar-Mo seems to be a hibernating animal, presumably a porcupine.

8 Dombu Tukar (T.T.: Dom.Bu.Thugs.dKar.).

9 Tsandali Yoga (Skt.: Caṇḍālī Yoga) is called in Tibetan the "gTum.Mo." (Heat) Yoga. See W. Y. Evans-Wentz' "Tibetan Yoga and Secret Doctrines," 2nd ed., 1958, pp. 171-210. See also the translator's volume, "Teachings of Tibetan Yoga."

10 Dhuti: This is the abbreviation of Avadhūti, the Central Channel.

11 Mother of the Illuminating Dharmata: The illuminating Dharma-Essence is here referred to as "Mother," a symbol of "origin" or foundation, upon which all dharmas depend.

THE STORY OF
THE YAK-HORN

Obeisance to all Gurus

Having helped Sahle Aui, the outstanding Yoginī, to further her devotion, Jetsun Milarepa went toward Balkhu to welcome his heart-son Rechungpa [upon his return from India. On the way there] he stayed at Betze Duyundzon [the Land of Pleasure] for some time. As Rechungpa was approaching from Gung Tang, the Jetsun saw in a vision that he was suffering from pride. [With this knowledge in mind] he went to welcome Rechungpa.

When the father and son met in the center of the Balkhu plain, Rechungpa thought, "I have now gone twice to study in India. Heretofore, I have been following my Guru's instructions to serve the Dharma and sentient beings. My Jetsun Guru's compassion and grace are indeed great, but I am much more learned in Buddhist philosophy and logic than he. Now he has come to welcome me, I wonder if he will return the obeisance to me when I bow down to him." With this thought in mind Rechungpa prostrated himself before Milarepa and presented him with the Ahkaru staff that Dipupa had given him to offer to the Jetsun. But Milarepa gave not the slightest sign that he would even consider returning the courtesy. Rechungpa was very displeased. However, he said, "Dear Guru, where did you stay while I was in India? How is your health? How are my Repa brothers? Where shall we go now?"

The Jetsun thought, "How is it that Rechungpa has become so proud? He must either have been possessed by demons or affected by the evil influence of pagans. No matter what the cause, I must rescue him from this hindrance of pride!" So he smiled and answered Rechungpa's questions in this song:

I am a yogi who lives on a snow-mountain peak.
With a healthy body I glorify the Maṇḍala of
    the Whole.
Cleansed of vanity from the Five Poisons,
I am not unhappy;
I feel nought but joy!
Renouncing all turmoil
And fondness for diversion,
I reside alone in perfect ease.
Forswearing the bustle of this world,
Joyfully I stay in no-man's land.
Since I have left embittered family life,
I no longer have to earn and save;
Since I want no books,
I do not intend to be a learned man;
I practice virtuous deeds,
I feel no shame of heart.
Since I have no pride or vanity,
I renounce with joy the saliva-splashing debate!
Hyprocisy I have not, nor pretension.
Happy and natural I live
Without forethought or adjustment.
Since I want nor fame nor glory,
Rumors and accusations disappear.
Where'er I go, I feel happy,
Whate'er I wear, I feel joyful,
Whatever food I eat, I am satisfied.
I am always happy.
Through Marpa's grace,
I, your old father Milarepa,
Have realized Saṃsāra and Nirvāṇa.
The Yoga of Joy ever fills my hermitage.

Your Repa brothers are well;
On hills remote they make progress in their
    meditations.
Oh, my son Rechung Dorje Draugpa,
Have you returned from India?
Did you feel tired and weary on the journey?
Has your mind been sharpened and refreshed?
Has your voice been good for singing?
Did you practice and follow your Guru's
    instructions?

Did you secure the teachings that you wanted?
Did you obtain all the various instructions?
Have you gained much knowledge and much learning?
Have you noticed your pride and egotism?
Are you altruistic in your thoughts and actions?
This is my song of welcoming for you,
On your return.

In reply, Rechungpa sang:

Obeying my Guru, I went to India.
My journey was hazardous and full of fear,
I underwent great pain and toil —
But the trip was well worthwhile.
I saw Dipupa, the great Tantric Master,
And met Magi, the great Yoginī.
Also I saw the wondrous Patron Buddha
And witnessed fulfillment of the Ḍākinīs'
      prophecy.
I have unmistakably attained
The longed-for Pith-Instructions —
Those of the Illuminating Wisdom Lamp,
The Wheel Net of Prāṇa and the Nāḍīs,
The Universal Mirror of Equality,
The Lantern of the Great Bliss Injunctions,
The True Words on the Mirror of Self-Mind,
The Supreme Form of the Sun-like Realization,
And the Self-liberation Mahāmudrā.

I drank Nectar — the Essence of Immortality,
I received teaching on the Bardo,
The Pith-Instructions on Dhyāna practice,
On the Five Gems and Symbols Three.
I was told how to practice the Six Yogas,
And how to win what I wanted in the world.
The Mothers and Ḍākinīs gathered for me
All these wonderful instructions.
The Deities and Gurus were all well pleased,
And my mind united well with theirs.
Like a rain of flowers,
Accomplishments fell upon me.
Heavenly food was fed into my mouth,
The Pith-Instructions were put into my hand.

In farewell, the Deities wished me good luck.
My desires were met and success was won.
Like the rising sun
My heart is bright with joy.
Now I am back, my Jetsun Guru!
Now I give you the Ḍākinīs' teachings!
Please observe them,
Praise and serve them —
The holy Dharmas that have brought me my achievement.

Then Rechungpa gave the books [that he had acquired in India]
to the Jetsun. In order to clear up Rechungpa's pride and arrogance,
Milarepa sang:

Do not be proud and pompous,
My little child, Rechungpa,
Whom I have nurtured from your teens.

In a tuneful voice I sing for you
A golden-rosary of song with meanings deep.
Keep it in your mind, if you agree with it.

Goddesses cherish the Formless Ḍākinī Dharmas,
[But] he who strives to become too big
Is liable to be slain by villains.
The hoarded goods of wealthy men
Provide enjoyment for their enemies;
To indulge in luxury and pleasure
Is the cause of poverty and death.
He who does not know his limit
And acts above his station,
Is stupid as a fool.
If an officer ill-treats his servants,
He harms his country.
If a servant respects not his master,
He will lose his mind
And bring misfortune on himself.
If a Doctrine-holder cannot behave,
He will destroy the Dharma.
He who does not keep the Ḍākinīs' teaching secret,
Disturbs and offends them.

Oh, my son, your pride in what you learned

Will lead you well astray!

To preach a lot, with empty words,
Ruins your good Experience and meditation.
To be swollen with pride and arrogance
Proves you have betrayed the Guru's precepts.
Nothing gives cause for more regret
Than disobedience of the Guru.
No one is more distracted and confused
Than he who ceases to meditate in solitude!
Nothing is more fruitless
Than a Buddhist who renounces not his kin!
Nothing is more shameful
Than a learned Buddhist who neglects his meditation.
Nothing is more disgraceful
Than for a monk to violate the rules.

My son Rechungpa, if you agree with what I say
You should hold it in your heart;
If you disagree, do whate'er you please.
I am an old man fearing death,
And with no time for chat and gossip.
You are young and self-conceited,
Whoever remonstrates with you, you will condemn
      him in return.

Oh, my gracious Guru, Marpa the Translator,
Pray help me, the poor beggar
Who forever abjures all wordly desires!

Picking up the books and the Ahkaru staff, Milarepa ran ahead with great speed by means of his miraculous power. Rechungpa could not catch up with him. He ran, gasping and panting, after his Guru as he sang this song:

Oh, please listen to me, my Father Jetsun!
How could a son ever disrespect his father?
I only pray you to accept the teachings I have
      attained.
I was given, beyond any doubt or possible error,
The instructions on the Formless Ḍākinī Dharmas.
From the profound, and the profoundest, doctrines
I have gained conviction!

I pray you to understand this, my dear Guru!

In addition, I also attained the Yoga of Longevity,
The Ḍākinīs' Symbolic Secret Words,
The principles of the Vajra Body,
And the instructions of the Mother Buddha.[1]
I now offer them all to you, my Jetsun Guru!
Also I have attained
The profound Tiger Protection, the Cures of Diseases,
And the Teaching of Dispersing Demons.
All these golden instructions I now offer to you.

Upon my shoulder I have brought back
The Medicine of Six Merits,
And the elixirs of gods and goddesses;
Now I offer them to you, my gracious Guru.
This marvellous staff made of the supreme Ahkaru
      plant
Was used by Ḍākinīs to rest upon.
It is a priceless and wondrous thing,
Symbolizing the Tantric teachings of Dipupa;
I now offer it to you, my Jetsun Guru.
Please appreciate these wonderful teachings
And have pity on me, the weary Rechungpa!
Please commiserate me, and give me
A chance to stop running and panting!
If you would please, please do so,
It would be the best charity.
If one can satisfy the hunger and thirst of others,
It is of the greatest merit.
To console people in distress is the best giving;
To serve people with kindness and show them the
      right path
Is the obligation of all Dharma-followers,
As taught by Buddha, our Lord.

The Jetsun heard Rechungpa singing this song while he was running after him. When the song was finished, the Jetsun stopped. He
then sat down on the ground and replied to Rechungpa, singing:

It is fine that father and son are in harmony —
Maintaining harmony with people is a great merit;

But the best merit is to keep harmony with one's
    father.
If one is discordant with all the people he knows
He must be a person ominious and obnoxious.
Yet even more ominious is discord between father
    and son.

Good it is to maintain harmony with one's father
    by right deeds,
Good it is to repay one's mother's kindness and
    bounties,
Good it is to act in concord with all.

One's wish can be fulfilled
If he is on good terms with his brothers;
To please one's Guru
Is to gain his blessings;
To be humble is to succeed.
A good Buddhist is one who conquers all bad
    dispositions.

Kindness is toleration of slanders;
To be modest is to gain fame and popularity;
To maintain pure discipline
Is to do away with pretense and concealment;
To live with a sage is to gain improvement;
To be indifferent is to stop all gossip;
To be good and compassionate is to advance one's
    Bodhi-Mind.
These are the things a wise man should do,
But a fool can never distinguish friend from foe.

Where the [actual practice of the] Path is
    concerned,
The Formless Ḍākinī Dharmas do not mean too
    much.
My relationship with you
Is much deeper and more important
Than the Tantric staff of Dipupa.
Of the accomplished Mother Magi
There is no better disciple than I.
If Ḍākinīs keep their secret teachings from me,
To whom will they impart them?

In the golden Maṇḍala
I have enjoyed many sacramental festivals.
With the Patron Buddha, Dorje Paumo,
I have had much longer acquaintance than you.
There is not a land of Ḍākinīs and Bha Wos[2]
That is unfamiliar to me.
Much more than yourself,
I am concerned about the things you are doing.
Oh, Rechungpa, do not be proud and go astray!
Let us go into the mountains and meditate in
          solitude!

Thereupon, the Jetsun and Rechungpa set out together on their journey. This is the first chapter of Rechungpa's meeting with the Jetsun at Yaug Ru.

As the Jetsun and Rechungpa proceeded along the road, Rechungpa again thought, "Had this been another Guru, I would have had a good reception and been most hospitably treated upon my return from India. But my Guru lives under such poor conditions himself, naturally it would be impossible for me to expect any comforts or pleasures from him! I have been in India and have learned so many of the Tantric teachings! A man like me should not practice his devotion as an ascetic, but should practice it with pleasure and enjoyment." With these arrogant and evil ideas in his mind, strong thoughts, full of infidelity toward the Jetsun, arose within him.

At once, Milarepa read Rechungpa's mind. He then pointed to a yak's horn lying along the side of the road, saying, "Pick up this yak-horn and bring it with you." Rechungpa thought, "Sometimes my Guru wants nothing as he always claimed, but at others 'his hatred is much stronger than that of an old dog, and his greediness is greater than that of an old miser,' as the proverb says. After all, what is the use of this torn-out yak-horn?" He then said to the Jetsun, "What good can this piece of waste do us — leave it alone!" The Jetsun replied, "To take a small thing like this will not increase one's greediness, and sometimes these discarded things are very useful." Saying this he picked up the yak-horn and carried it himself.

When they reached the central part of Balmo Baltang Plain where no hiding-place could be found for even a small mouse, the heretofore clear sky suddenly became darkened by gathering clouds. Then a great storm, accompanied by violent hail, arose. In the midst of this onslaught Rechungpa covered his head in such haste and confusion that he completely forgot even to look at his Guru. After awhile, when the hail began to abate, Rechungpa started to search for Milarepa, but could not find him. For a time he sat upon the ground and waited. Then he seemed to hear the Jetsun's voice coming from the yak-horn which had been left beside the road. He walked toward the place and saw it was undoubtdly the same yak-horn which the Jetsun had taken a few moments before. Rechungpa then tried to pick it up, but it was so heavy that he could not move it, even an inch. Then he bent down and looked into it, and saw Milarepa seated comfortably within with ample room to spare; his body was no smaller, and the horn no larger than before, just as the reflection of a large image may be seen in a small mirror. He heard the Jetsun sing:

> The grace of my Guru enters into my body.
> If one's body remains like a commoner's
> He is not a great yogi.
> Rechungpa you should pay homage to my miraculous body.

> The grace of my Guru enters into my mouth.
> If one makes nonsensical remarks
> He is not a great yogi.
> All Pith-Instructions are found in my song.
> Rechungpa, you should bear them in your heart.

> The grace of my Guru enters into my mind.
> If any unfaithful thought ever arises in one's mind
> He is not a great yogi.
> Rechungpa, you should pay homage to my power of telepathy.

> Oh, son Rechungpa, your mind is like a nimble bird;
> Now it flies high, and now it swoops low.
> You should observe this unstable change,
> Stop thinking so much,
> And devote yourself to the Repa's practice!

> If you think you can match your Guru,
> Now you may come into this horn.
> Come in right now —
> Here is a spacious and comfortable house!

> Rechungpa, your Enlightenment is like the sun and moon;

Sometimes they shine bright, but sometimes they are
     darkened by clouds.
You should observe this unstable change,
Stop thinking so much,
And devote yourself to the Repa's practice!

If you think you can match your Guru,
You may come into this horn.
Come in right now —
Here is a spacious and comfortable house!

Son Rechungpa! Your behavior is like the mountain
     wind;
Now it blows fast and violent,
And now it blows gentle and slow.
You should observe this unstable change,
Stop thinking so much,
And devote yourself to the Repa's practice!

If you think you can match your Guru,
You may come into this horn.
Come in right now —
Here is a spacious and comfortable house!

Son Rechungpa, your accomplishments
Are like the crops in the field.
Sometimes they grow badly, and sometimes well.
You should observe this unstable change,
Stop thinking so much,
And devote yourself to the Repa's practice!

If you think you can match your Guru,
You may come into this horn.
Come in right now —
Here is a spacious and comfotable house!

If one's mind can master the domain of space
He can enter this horn and enjoy it.
Come in right now, my son, your father is calling!

It wouldn't be nice
If a son refuses to enter his father's house.
I am a sick and worn-out old man

Who has never been in India in all his life;
His insignificant body is frightened
By the dangerous road outside,
Therefore inside this horn he stays!
Son Rechungpa, you are young, and have been in
    India.
Also, you have studied under many learned and ac-
    complished Gurus.
You should now step into this horn
With your splendid and prominent body.
Of little value is this rotten yak-horn;
Surely it will not inflate one's egotism and desire.
Come in, Rechungpa, come and join your father in-
    side!

Rechungpa thought, "There seems to be plenty of room there; can
I also get in?" Thinking this, he tried to enter the horn, but he could
not even get his hand and head in, [let alone his whole body]. Then
he thought, "The Jetsun's miraculous power may, or may not be genuine, but he can surely produce hail." Putting his mouth close to the
horn, Rechungpa sang in a quavering voice:

Oh, my father Jetsun Guru, please listen to me!
Whether the View, Practice, Action, and Accomplish-
    ment
Of your servant and son, Rechung Dor Draug,
Be high or low, bright or dim, great or small,
Better or worse, it makes no difference;
He shall continue to pray to you.
Whether his cotton robe be dry or wet,
He shall continue to pray to you.
He may or may not match his father,
But he shall continue to pray to him!

Milarepa came out of the horn. He gestured toward the sky, and
at once the storm began to abate, the clouds to disperse, and the
sun to break through. Immediately the air became very warm, and
before long, Rechungpa's clothes were dried.

After resting a while, the Jetsun said, "Rechungpa, I knew from the
beginning that your trip to India was unnecessary. Being quite satisfied with the teaching of Mahāmudrā and the Six Yogas, I did not
go to India. I am very glad that you have now returned with the
teaching you wanted."

"Dear Lama, I am very hungry and cold," said Rechungpa, "let us go to the tents over there and beg some food."

"But this is not the time to beg alms," replied Milarepa.

"I do not know whether it is the time to beg alms or not, but I know that I am starving to death right now. By all means let us go."

"Very well, we shall go. I think perhaps it would be better to go to the first tent."

"But in begging alms one must not look only for rich people, and neglect the poor," said Rechungpa. "Therefore let us go to that small brownish tent near the lower end [of the terrace]."

So they went toward the small tent. When they reached its entrance to ask the host for alms, a fearful old woman came out and said, "A yogi should stick to poverty all the time. Good yogis always refuse our offerings, even when brought to them. But greedy people like you, never content with what they already have, always come after others' belongings. All the things that I had to spare for charity, I already gave to some beggars this morning. Nothing is left now. You had better go somewhere else to beg." Upon hearing these malicious remarks, the Jetsun said, "The sun is about to set; it makes no difference whether we get food or not this evening, so let us find a place to sleep."

That night the Jetsun and Rechungpa slept nearby. About midnight, they heard a noise in the tent. Then it subsided and all became quiet again. The next morning when the sun arose, the Jetsun said to Rechungpa, "Go over to the tent and take a look inside." Rechungpa did so, but he found nothing left in the tent except the corpse of the old woman who had refused to give them alms the evening before. Rechungpa then informed Milarepa of what he had seen. The Jetsun said, "The food and other things must be hidden somewhere underground," and they went over to the tent together.

The fact was, that regardless of her malicious talk, the hour had come for the old woman — the land was full of epidemics at the time. [They found that] her jewelry had all been stolen by the nomads. Left behind on the ground was nothing but a small bag of butter, some cheese and barley flour, and a pail of yogurt. The Jetsun said to Rechungpa, "Son, all things are like this. Last evening this old woman was full of stinginess and worry, but now she is dead. Oh, in sooth one should give alms to those in need." Thereupon, Milarepa and Rechungpa prepared a sacramental offering for the dead woman with the things that were left. Rechungpa then packed up the remnants of the edible food and was about to carry it away with him, when the Jetsun said, "It is not good for one to eat the food of a corpse without benefiting it. The proverb says, 'The old men should eat the food and the young men should produce it.' Now, carry the corpse upon your shoulder and I'll go ahead to lead the way!"

With misgivings that he might be contaminated by the filth of the corpse, Rechungpa unhappily carried it upon his shoulder while the Jetsun went ahead to guide them on the road. When they reached a marsh, the Jetsun said, "Now put the corpse down." He then placed the point of his staff at the heart of the corpse, and said, "Rechungpa, like this woman, every sentient being is destined to die, but seldom do people think of this fact. So they lose many opportunities to practice the Dharma. Both you and I should remember this incident and learn a lesson from it." Whereupon, he sang the "Song of Transiency and Delusion," having six parables:

> Oh, the grace of the Gurus is beyond our compre-
> hension!
>
> When the transiency of life strikes deeply into
> one's heart
> His thoughts and deeds will naturally accord
> with Dharma.
> If repeatedly and continuously one thinks about
> death,
> He can easily conquer the demon of laziness.
> No one knows when death will descend upon him —
> Just as this woman last night!
>
> Rechungpa, do not be harsh, and listen to your Guru!
> Behold, all manifestations in the outer world
> Are ephemeral like the dream last night!
> One feels utterly lost in sadness
> When he thinks of this passing dream.
> Rechungpa, have you completely wakened
> From this great puzzlement?
> Oh, the more I think of this,
> The more I aspire to Buddha and the Dharma.
>
> The pleasure-yearning human body is an ungrateful
> creditor.
> Whatever good you do to it,
> It always plants the seeds of pain.
> This human body is a bag of filth and dirt;
> Never be proud of it, Rechungpa,
> But listen to my song!

When I look back at my body,
I see it as a mirage-city;
Though I may sustain it for a while,
It is doomed to extinction.
When I think of this,
My heart is filled with grief!
Rechungpa, would you not cut off Saṃsāra?
Oh, the more I think of this,
The more I think of Buddha and the Dharma!

A vicious person can never attain happiness.
Errant thoughts are the cause of all regrets,
Bad dispositions are the cause of all miseries.
Never be voracious, oh Rechungpa,
But listen to my song!

When I look back at my clinging mind,
It appears like a short-lived sparrow in the woods —
Homeless, and with nowhere to sleep;
When I think of this, my heart is filled with grief.
Rechungpa will you let yourself
Indulge in ill-will?
Oh, the more I think of this
The more I aspire to Buddha and the Dharma!

Human life is as precarious
As a single slim hair of a horse's tail
Hanging on the verge of breaking;
It may be snuffed out at any time
Like this old woman was last night!
Do not cling to this life, Rechungpa,
But listen to my song!

When I observe inwardly my breathings
I see they are transient, like the fog;
They may vanish any moment into nought.
When I think of this, my heart is filled with grief.
Rechungpa, do you not want to conquer
That insecurity now?
Oh, the more I think of this
The more I aspire to Buddha and the Dharma.

To be close to wicked kinsmen only causes hatred.

The case of this old woman is a very good lesson.
Rechungpa, stop your wishful-thinking
And listen to my song!

When I look at friends and consorts
They appear as passers-by in the bazaar;
Meeting with them is only temporary,
But separation is forever!
When I think of this, my heart is filled with grief.
Rechungpa, do you not want to cast aside
All worldly associations?
Oh, the more I think of this,
The more I think of Buddha and the Dharma.

A rich man seldom enjoys
The wealth that he has earned;
This is the mockery of Karma and Saṃsāra.
Money and jewels gained through stinginess and toil
Are like this old woman's bag of food.
Do not be covetous, Rechungpa,
But listen to my song!

When I look at the fortunes of the rich,
They appear to me like honey to the bees —
Hard work, serving only for others' enjoyment,
Is the fruit of their labor.
When I think of this, my heart is filled with grief.
Rechungpa, do you not want to open
The treasury within your mind?
Oh, the more I think of this
The more I aspire to Buddha and His teachings.

The corpse of the old woman was buried [in the swamp], and her soul was delivered to the Dharmadhātu. Thereupon the Jetsun and Rechungpa took the edible food with them and set out for Betze Duyundzon.

This is the second chapter, the story of the yak-horn.

Later, while the father Jetsun and the son Rechungpa were residing at Betze, Rechungpa gained great improvement in his meditation. In an Experience of great joy, numerous thoughts appeared in his mind. Being aware of this, the Jetsun said, "Rechungpa, what have you experienced in your meditation lately?" In relating his Experiences, Rechungpa sang:

> Living with my Guru, I had
> An Experience powerful like a sharp knife;
> With it I have cut inner and outer deceptions.
> Because of this I am happy and gay!
>
> In the midst of many manifestations,
> I felt as if I were a radiant lamp;
> All instructions thus became clearer than ever
>   before.
> Because of this, I am happy and gay!
>
> When I sat on the peak of a snow mountain,
> I felt like a white lioness,
> Predominating and surpassing all others in the world.
> Because of this, I feel happy and gay!
>
> When I dwelt on the hillside of Red Rock,
> I felt as if I were a majestic eagle;
> Forever have I conquered
> The fearful expanse of the sea.
> Because of this, I am happy and gay!
>
> When I roamed from country to country
> I felt as if I were a tiger cub, or a bee —
> Non-attached to all and utterly free.
> Because of this, I am happy and gay!
>
> When I mingled with people in the street,
> I felt as if I were an immaculate lotus
> Standing above all filth and mud.
> Because of this, I am happy and gay!
>
> When I sat among crowds in the town,
> I felt as if I were like rolling mercury —
> It touches all but adheres to nought.
> Because of this, I feel happy and gay!
>
> When I sat among faithful disciples,
> I felt as if I were the Jetsun Mila;

With cheer and ease I gave instructions through
    songs!
It is the blessing of my Guru
That brings me this joy.
It is through resting one's mind at ease
That Buddhahood is realized.

The Jetsun commented, "If not brought out by pride, these Experiences are fine; and you have truly received your Guru's blessings. Toward such Experiences, however, one needs certain understandings, in which you still seem to be lacking. Now listen to my song":

From the depths of my heart, when the great
    Compassion arose,
I felt that all beings in the Three Realms
Were enslaved in a prison of fire.

When the Instructions of the Lineage
Were imbibed in my heart,
As the dissolving of salt into water,
I experienced thorough absorption.

When the Wisdom shone bright from within,
I felt as if awakened from a great dream —
I was awakened from both the main and ensuing
    Samādhis;
I was awakened from both "yes" and "no" ideas.

When one secures the great bliss through Viewing,
He feels all Dharmas spontaneously freed
As mists of rain vanish into air.

When one comes to the Essence of Being,
The shining Wisdom of Reality
Illumines all like the cloudless sky.

When both pure and impure thoughts are cleared,
As in a silver mirror,
The immanent bright Wisdom shines forth.

When the Ālaya consciousness dissolves into the
    Dharmakāya,
I feel my body and soul break forth

Like the crushing of an egg when stamped upon.

When the rope-of-clinging is cut loose,
I feel the existence of Bardo disappear
Like the uncoiling of a snake.

When I act without taking or leaving,
My mind is always at ease and non-doing.
I feel as if I were a lion,
With the power of the Three Perfections.

The Illuminating Voidness, the Illuminating Wisdom,
And the Illuminating Manifestations
Are my three inseparable friends;
Like the sun shining from a cloudless sky,
I am always in the Great Illumination.
Like dividing the horses from the yaks,
The [outer] world and the senses are clearly
       distinct [from the inner].
The string of mind and Skandhas is forever cut!
Having fully utilized this human form,
I have now completed all Yoga matters.
Rechungpa, do you also have these Experiences?
Oh, my son, do not be proud and presumptuous!

Hearing this song, Rechungpa's mind was straightened out. Then Milarepa said, "Now let us, father and son, go to Di Se or Lashi, those remote mountains, to meditate." Rechungpa replied, "I am very tired — my physical strength has reached the point of exhaustion. I think it best that I go to a near-by monastery to recover [my strength], otherwise I will not be able to meditate or travel at all."

"If a determination is made from the bottom of one's heart, one can practice his devotion under any circumstances, at any time," countered the Jetsun. Thereupon, he sang a song called "The Six Sufficiencies":

Oh Son, one's own body suffices as a good temple,
For the vital points within are Heavenly Paradise.
One's own mind suffices as the Guru,
For all true understanding comes from it.
The outer phenomena suffice as one's Sūtras,
For they are all symbols of the Liberation Path.
The Food-of-Samādhi is sufficient to sustain one,

For the Father Buddhas will come and bless him.
The Dumo-heat suffices for one's clothing —
The warm and blissful dress of the Ḍākinīs.
To cut off all ties is the best companion;
To live alone is to become a friend of deities;
To regard all enemies as passers-by on the road
Is to avoid hatred.
The best remedy for all obstacles
Is to meditate on Voidness,
For they are all magic-like plays of the mind.
This is the right way for you to follow —
Against it, you will go astray!

I am an old man close to death,
Who has no time for chatting.
You are young, vigorous, and healthy
And would not listen my helpful advice.
To talk with honesty and straightforwardness
To prideful and greedy persons would be a sheer waste.
If you want to meditate, you may come along with me;
If you do not, you may do whatever you please.

The Jetsun was about to set out on his way, when Rechungpa grasped his clothing in time [to stop him], and sang this song called "The Eight Needs":

Though the best temple is one's own body,
We need a place for cover and sleep;
Without mercy, the rain and wind attack all.
Because of this, we always need a temple.

Though the best Guru is one's own mind,
We need a teacher to illustrate our Mind-Essence —
We cannot neglect for a moment to pray to him.
Because of this, we always need a Guru!

Though outer phenomena may substitute for the
        Sūtras,
Hindrances and doubts in any case will arise.
To clear them up,
A lucid reference to the Sūtras is necessary.
Because of this, we always need the Sūtras!

Though the food of Samādhi may be sufficient,
Provisions for nourishment are necessary;
On food this delusory body must live.
Because of this, we always need food!

Though the best clothing is the Dumo-heat,
Something to cover the body is necessary,
For who is not afraid of shame and disgrace?
Because of this, we always need clothing.

Though the best thing is to cut off relationships
       with all,
To get support and aid is ever necessary;
Good or bad, who has not some friends?
Because of this, we always need friends.

Though to avoid one's enemies is sufficient,
Sometimes one meets them on the road —
For who can be immune from hostility?
Because of this, we always need protection.

Though the best remedy is to view all hindrances
       as void,
The demons and ghosts are malignant and powerful;
To conquer the demon of ego
Is even more difficult.
Because of this, we always need safeguards.

To stay with my Guru, brings happiness;
To return to you brings joy.
Wherever you go, I will go.
But I beseech you, by all means,
To stay in the valley for a short time.

Milarepa replied, "If you have confidence, to follow my way will
be quite sufficient; otherwise, there will always be a need for something. Well, if by all means you are unwilling to go to no-man's mountain now, let us go to Bouto to preach the Dharma." Thereupon, the
Jetsun and Rechungpa went to Bouto of Red Rock.

This is the last chapter of the yak-horn story.

NOTES

1 Mother Buddha (T.T.: Grub.Pahi.rGyal.Mo.), a free translation.

2 Bha Wo (T.T.: dPah.Wo.; Skt.: Vira): the Brave One. This term refers to the male deities of Tantra. All male Tantric deities, except the chief Buddha in the Maṇḍala, can be considered as Bha Wos — the Brave Ones who can destroy evils and hindrances. Bha Wo is the counterpart of Ḍākinī, or a "male Ḍākinī." Ḍākinī, the female deity, is also called Bha Mo — the Brave Woman.

39

RECHUNGPA'S
REPENTANCE

Obeisance to all Gurus

Whenthe Jetsun Milarepa and his son Rechungpa were approaching Drin on their way to Bouto, Rechungpa said, "I would like to stay in Drin tonight and meet the patrons." But Milarepa replied, "My son, let us first go to Bouto without the knowledge of our patrons, disciples, or the monks." In a displeased mood Rechungpa obeyed, and continued with Milarepa to Jipu Nimadson at Bouto of Red Rock. Upon their arrival, the Jetsun said, "Rechungpa, fetch some water and I will make a fire."

On his way back to the hermitage with the water, Rechungpa reached [a slope, from where he could see below him] the great, delightful plateau between Bouto and Jipu. He saw in the center, a mountain she-goat giving birth to a kid. Then the mother and daughter each gave birth to another kid; they, in turn, bore more kids, until eventually there were two hundred of them. These wild mountain goats frisked about so happily, with such innocence and spontaneity, that Rechungpa was amazed. He thought, "These mountain goats are even livelier and in many ways better than those of Baltang." With great interest, he watched them play for some time.

Meanwhile Milarepa, who had lit the fire, opened the books that Rechungpa had brought back from India, and said with great compassion: "I sincerely pray to all Ḍākinīs. I pray you to save and keep the Formless Ḍākinī's Dharma for which I sent from India — the teachings that will benefit the Doctrine and all sentient beings! I sincerely pray to all Guards of Dharma to destroy all heretical books of vicious Mantras that will certainly bring great harm to the Doctrine and to sentient beings!" After this prayer, Milarepa meditated for a short time; and then he burned most of the books until only a few incomplete folios were left.

Now while Rechungpa was watching the mountain goats at play, he saw a masterful goat take the part of a wolf and drive the flock across the ridge to the other side of the mountain. At this point Rechungpa thought, "Goodness! I have been dallying too long. I must go back at once, or the Jetsun will reprimand me."

He immediately started to return. When he reached a bridge leading to the cave, he saw smoke rising from it and smelled burning paper. He thought, "Are my books being burned?" When he entered the cave, he saw there was almost nothing left except the empty wooden covers! He felt as if his heart had been torn asunder. "Where are my books?" he cried to the Jetsun in great resentment. Milarepa replied, "You have been away for so long fetching water, that I thought you were dead and so I have burned all the unimportant books. As far as I am concerned, they were useless, and are merely temptations to distract one's mind and hinder one's devotion. By the way, what made you linger so long?"

In his pride, Rechungpa thought, "My Guru has now become very bitter and egoistic. He has affronted me sorely. Should I return to Dipupa and stay with him again or should I go elsewhere?" Thinking thus, Rechungpa lost all faith in the Jetsun. He sat there deadly quiet for some time. Then he said, "I was watching the wild goats at play, that's why I was late. Now the gold you gave me and the hardship I underwent in India have all become meaningless and wasted. I am leaving for another country now." Saying this, Rechungpa became hostile and disdainful to the Jetsun out of his bad faith toward him. Milarepa then said, "My son Rechungpa, you do not have to lose all your faith in me. All this should be blamed on your dalliance. If you want to be amused, I can entertain you. Now watch!"

Instantaneously, this wondrous vision took form: Upon Milarepa's head the Translator Marpa appeared clearly as Dorje-Chang, sitting upon the sun and moon Lotus Seat of Gems. Encircling him were the Gurus of the Transmission. To the right and left of Milarepa's eyes and ears, shone two suns and moons. From his nostrils streamed rays of light of five different colors like silk threads, from his eyebrows shone a radiant light. His tongue became a small eight-petaled lotus-seat with a sun and moon orb above it, from which sparkled brilliant and extremely fine letters — vowels and consonants — as if written by a single, split hair. From his heart rayed forth other beams of light, which then turned into numerous small birds. Whereupon, Milarepa sang:

Hearken to me, my son Rechungpa!

Above my head,
Upon the sun-moon orb of the Lion Seat
Sits my Gracious Guru Marpa —
The divine embodiment of Buddha Dorje-Chang!

Round him like a string of jewels
Are the Gurus of the Lineage.
If you behold them with faithful eyes
You will be blessed by the rain of grace,
And fulfilled will be your wishes.
Interesting it may be to watch the play of goats,
But how can it compare to *this* wondrous game?

Rechungpa, listen to me for a moment!
On the tips of my ears
A sun and moon shine, glowing as a radiant rainbow.
This reveals the Union of Wisdom and Skill,
This proves my steadfast Illumination.
Amazing it may be to watch the play of goats,
But how can it compare to *this* wondrous game?

Rechungpa, listen to me for a moment!
The five-colored rays from my nostrils,
Streaming like jewelled threads,
Are the essence of sound, a marvel.
This shows my mastery of Prāṇa
Through the Vajra-reciting Yoga.[1]
This proves that I have entered
The Central Channel of my Life-Force.
Amazing it may be to watch the play of goats,
But how can it compare to *this* wondrous game?

Rechungpa, listen to me for a moment!
At the mid-point between my eyes,
Appears the auspicious sign of the radiant
        Dsudbhu;[2]
This shows the essence of pure form,
This proves the blessed radiance of Buddha's
        compassion!
Amazing it may be to watch the play of goats,
But how can it compare to *this* wondrous game?

Rechungpa, listen to me for a moment!

A red lotus with eight petals opens in my mouth,
Adorned with a garland of consonants and vowels.
They are the symbols of all Vajra teachings —
That which is without end or limitation.
Beholding them with reverent eyes,
You will realize all Dharmas are your speech.
Amazing it may be to watch the play of goats,
But how can it compare to *this* wondrous game?

Rechungpa, listen to me for a moment.
From the center of my heart stream
Glowing beams of light.
This shows the Trikāya's immutability,
This shows the unity of mercy and the Void.
Amazing it may be to watch the play of goats,
But how can it compare to *this* wondrous game?

Rechungpa, however, paid no attention to the Jetsun's advice, but sat there silently and in deep resentment. He looked askance at the miraculous scene, but showed not the slightest sign of interest in it. Then he said, "There is nothing surprising in all this; it is more amusing to watch the play of goats!" Although the Jetsun had worked such a great miracle, Rechungpa showed neither interest nor admiration, but continued to demand that the Jetsun give back his books. For a while he merely sat there in persistent indignation and silence. Then he [got up], stamped heavily, and sat down again. Putting his elbows on his knees, and resting his chin on his hands, he began to hum [meaninglessly].

In the meantime, the Jetsun's body had become radiantly transparent; on his Secret Center appeared Buddha Dorje Danyi, on his Navel Center appeared Buddha Dem Chog, on his Heart Center, Buddha Jeba Dorje, on his Throat Center, Buddha Mahāmāya, between his eyebrows, Buddha Śākyamuni, and upon his head, Buddha Sungwong Duba, all encircled by many deities and their retinues. These divine bodies, vivid, yet devoid of any self-nature, were all distinctly visible under a great five-colored canopy of light. Whereupon, Milarepa sang:

My body is the Infinite Palace of Goddesses,
Wherein dwell all Buddhas [in the Universe].
In my Secret Center, where Bliss is preserved,
Dwells the Buddha Dorje Danyi and his retinue,
Glorifying my sealed Cakra of Bliss.
He embodies Buddha's Innate Wisdom.

In the Conjuration Cakra at my navel
Dwells the Buddha Dem Chog and his retinue;
This is the Cakra and two-and-sixty gods,
Where in essence dwells the Vajra Body.

In the Dharma Cakra in my heart
Dwells Buddha Jedor and nine deities;
They are the Essence of the Three Sattvas [?].
This is the Cakra of the Vajra Mind.

In the Enjoyment Cakra in my throat
Dwells the Buddha Mahāmāya and his retinue,
Symbolizing the enjoyment of all forms.
This is the Cakra where the Vajra is expressed.

In the White Conch Cakra between my eyebrows
Dwells Buddha Śākyamuni and many deities;
He is the symbol of Wisdom and Merits.
This is the Cakra of Unity!

In the Great Bliss Cakra in my head
Dwells Buddha Sungwong Duba and many gods;
This is the Cakra of Great Bliss,
Where the Nāḍīs and Bindus both unite.
Son, if you can identify your self with the Buddha,
The Divine Body will vividly appear;
Your flesh and blood will be transformed into
     the Rainbow Body.
Of all marvels, this is most marvellous.
Son, do not lose your faith
But increase your veneration!

Rechungpa said, "Your miracles are indeed wonderful, but my mind
will not be at ease if I cannot have my books back, so please return
them to me." The Jetsun then passed through rocks and other obstacles, flew by on a rock, walked and sat on water, poured fire and
water from his body, flew through and sat in the sky, and transformed
his body from one to many and from many to one. While doing so
he sang:

Rechungpa, listen to me for a moment.
Look, nothing can impede me!
This proves my mind with all forms has merged.

> That I can ride upon a rock, flying through the air,
> Proves I have mastered outer objects.
> Walking on water as on earth
> Proves I have unified the Four Elements.
> The flow of fire and water from my body
> Proves I have mastered all the Elements.
> Transforming one body into many
> And many into one,
> Proves I can benefit all beings
> By miracles.
> Sitting, walking, and lying in the sky
> Proves my Prāṇa rests in the Central Channel.
> Amazing it may be to watch the play of goats,
> But how can it compare to *this* wondrous game?
> Son, if you lose not your faith,
> Your prayers will be fulfilled.

Rechungpa said, "Your miracles are like child's play, you have demonstrated them so much that instead of being interesting, they are dull and tiring. If you are really compassionate, please return me my books."

Milarepa replied, "My son, do not lose faith in your Father! If you pray sincerely, you will realize that all manifestations are holy books. Now try to pray to me for this realization!"

Then Milarepa went to a narrow path used by merchants on their way to Drin. There he picked up a huge rock [that blocked the path], cut [a part of it] into pieces [with his hands] as if slicing a cake, threw the bits into the sky as if spraying water, and stamped on the [remaining] rock as though trampling on soft clay. Finally, with one hand, he threw this huge rock into the river in the valley below, and sang:

> Rechungpa, listen to me for a moment!
> On this narrow [mountain] path
> Stood an iron rock with eight edges.
> Its right edge was brushed when travellers mounted,
> Its left when they the path descended.
> One hundred blacksmiths with their hammers
> Could not have split this gigantic stone;
> A fire heated by one hundred bellows
> Could not have melted it.
> But behold,
> I sliced it as I would cut a cake,
> I threw the bits as I would sprinkle water,

I stamped upon it as I would trample mud,
And flung it like an arrow from a bow.
If with faith you look upon your father,
Wish-fulfilling rain will fall upon you;
The treasury of wish-fulfillment will be realized.
Interesting it may be to watch the play of goats,
But how can it compare to *this* wondrous game?
Try, my son, to change your mind at once!

Still without faith in the Jetsun, Rechungpa said, "If you can perform the miracle of restoring my books I shall then have faith in
you, otherwise I shall not be happy or satisfied." Whereupon, as though
spreading wings, Milarepa held out his robe and flew straight into the
sky above the precipice of the Red Rock. He fluttered and hovered
there like a hawk, and then darted to the ground like a flash of
lightning. While performing these miracles he sang:

Rechungpa, listen to me for a moment!
Here, on the peak of Red Rock stands
Sky Castle. Flying over it,
A huge hawk flaps its wings,
While small birds shake in fright.
No human being has flown here before,
None will fly here again.
Now look at this old man in flight,
Look at him soaring
Like a vulture in the sky.
See, he hovers like a hawk,
Darts to the ground like lightning,
And floats cloud-like in the air!
If you have faith in miracles
Through mastering the body,
Practice that mastery;
Then you can conquer and unite Saṃsāra and Nirvāṇa.
Amazing it may be to watch the play of goats,
But how can it compare with *this* wondrous game?
Try, my son Rechungpa, to straighten out your
    mind!

Milarepa's miracles, however, did not overly impress Rechungpa. He
only glanced at them indifferently and still had no faith in the Jetsun.
Then, once more, Milarepa held out his robe like a bird spreading
its wings, and flew into the sky. There he sang:

Rechungpa, listen to me for a moment!
On the peak of Red Rock in the Mon Mountains
Suddenly appeared a flock of goats
Without any reason,
A spontaneous play
Of non-arising Reality.

One goat played the wolf,
Chasing the flock o'er the ridge.
This symbolized the awareness
And the conquest of one's foibles;
This indicated the crossing
O'er the mount of dualism;
This was Milarepa's conjuration
To show Rechungpa the essential teachings!

To the miracles of your Father
You showed indifference,
But in the play of goats
You showed great interest;
This is indeed the sign
That you have lost your mind.
I have showed you such great miracles
Yet you have no faith in me.
When I think of men like you,
Faithless disciples all,
At this time of defilement
I feel sad, and sick at heart.

Rechungpa, listen to me for a moment!
Hard horn, and solid wood,
Can be bent if one tries;
But a harsh mind is hard to "bend."
Rechungpa, try to subdue your mind within!

Fierce tigers in the South,
And wild yaks in the North
Can be tamed if one tries;
But pride and egotism are hard to tame.
Rechungpa, try to subdue conceit within!

Mice under the ground,
And birds in the sky

Can be caught if one tries;
But a lost mind is hard to catch.
Rechungpa, try your own faults to see!

The Dharma of words
And speculation
Can be learned if one tries;
But the void Self-mind is hard to learn.
Rechungpa, try to meditate on the uncreated mind!

A son may leave his father
And his loving mother too,
But a bad temperament is hard to leave behind.
Rechungpa, try to change your temper and conceit!

Jewels, house, and land
One renounces if one tries;
But to renounce pleasure-craving is hard.
Rechungpa, try to give up your desire for pleasure!

Good jewels and a lovely sweetheart
If need be can be left,
But to leave a soft, warm bed is hard indeed.
Rechungpa, try to give up the "blind" sleep
        of a corpse!

Here and there hills and rocks
May meet face to face,
But to see the Self-face of your mind is hard.

The queen's and king's decrees
Can be evaded if one tries;
But no one can evade
Yama, the Lord of Death.
Rechungpa, make use of death for your devotion!

My son, try to correct your wrong ideas,
Abandon your bad actions,
Discipline your unruly mind,
Your impious thoughts restrain,
Avoid the demon of egotism.
When I come to die this shall I will for you;
No profounder teaching can I give you in my life.

Rechungpa, my son, bear my words in mind!

As Milarepa sang, he flew higher and higher into the sky until he disappeared. [Then, of a sudden,] Rechungpa was filled with remorse, and an unusual faith toward the Jetsun burst forth within him. He thought, "Because I could not control my temper and give away those worthless books, I have lost my Jetsun Guru. I have paid too great a price for those worthless books. The Jetsun has performed such great miracles for me, yet I still had no faith in him. Now he has forsaken me as though shedding a heavy burden, and has gone to the Ḍākinī's Pure Land. An unbeliever such as I can never be born there. What is the use of books without a Guru? I shall throw myself over this cliff and meet my death. I now make my last wish: In all my future incarnations may I always meet the Jetsun, and may my mind ever be at-one with his!" Having made this wish, Rechungpa plunged into the abyss below with every determination [to die]. He crashed on a great rock, from where he saw the shadow of the Jetsun. Crying with all his strength, he called to Milarepa in a most pitiful voice, and tried to fly after him, but could not do so. Nevertheless, he managed to walk [in the air] after Milarepa's shadow until he reached the waist of Red Rock cliff. He could not go a step farther but could see the Jetsun and hear his voice.

He saw Milarepa sitting in a cavity hollowed out from the side of the cliff with his other two transformed bodies sitting beside him, all singing together in response to Rechungpa's call of repentance:

> Rechungpa, listen to me for a moment.
> Look, from one Father Jetsun emanate two others!
> To them you should confess your sins,
> Of them you should ask of their well-being,
> From them you should receive the Tantric Precepts,
> And ask for Initiations and Instructions.
> Of them you should beg the profound Demonstration,
> In them should you take refuge,
> And place your confidence.
>
> If you have faith in my miracles,
> Your pride will be curtailed.
> Ill deeds indicate the victory of Yama;
> If of him you are afraid
> You should abstain from vices.
> Bad thoughts hinder one's devotion,
> So of them repent.

As the tears poured down his face, Rechungpa sang:

Listen to me, Father Guru,
Embodiment of wisdom and of blessings.
Listen to Rechungpa, your blind and impious son,
Who had no faith in your miracles.
Listen, Jetsun Guru in the center,
To you I make obeisance, and offerings.
Of you I ask of your well-being and confess my sins.
Oh, my Father Guru, it was you
Who gave me the Precepts, Initiations, and
    Instructions,
It was you who enlightened me
And gave me a lasting refuge.
Save me, I pray, from stumbling,
Protect me with your mercy,
Safeguard this poor and impious mendicant.

Rechungpa managed to reach the place where Milarepa sat, and then hugged him with such great and overpowering emotion that he fainted. When he came to, Milarepa brought him back to the hermitage.

The Jetsun then said to Rechungpa, "If you wish to attain Buddhahood, you must practice the Pith-Instructions. Those books of polemics and the evil Mantras of the heretics had no value for us. The Formless Teachings of the Ḍākinīs are good and sound — these I did not burn, but I burned all the rest because they would only have caused one to fall into the Lower Realms, in spite of one's original intention to attain Buddhahood. Now hearken to my song:

Rechungpa, my son,
Whom from childhood I have cherished,
You went to India for the Pith-Instructions
But have brought back books full of arguments.
You were thus exposed to the danger
Of becoming a debater.
You wanted to be a yogi,
But books like those and their ideas
Could make you a pompous preacher!
To know both one and all, that was your wish;
But if you are caught up in endless words,
You will wreck the most important *one*.
Your intention was to understand the Dharma,
But if you are caught up in endless acts,

Greedy and arrogant will you become.
The immaculate Dharma for which I sent you
Has flown into the crevice of a rock
And is preserved by the Ḍākinīs;
You may recover it if you pray sincerely.
I have burned the magic books and evil Mantras
As an offering to the God of Fire;
Many will be helped by this.
Do not lose your temper,
Lest you be scorched by anger;
Do not distress yourself or grieve,
For that will hurt your mind and body.
Do not bestir yourself with many things,
But relax, and sit at ease,
Remembering your Guru
And his grace and bounties!

Rechungpa thought, "My Guru's words are absolutely true and do not differ from the Buddha's. I will now pray the Ḍākinīs to give me back my books." He sat and prayed, and in a short while the Formless Ḍākinī Teachings, together with other books that were beneficial to the Dharma and to sentient beings, all miraculously returned to Rechungpa's hand. He was delighted beyond all measure. He confirmed and imprinted on his mind a faith that Milarepa was Buddha Himself. He thought, "So far, I have served the Jetsun in many ways. Hereafter, I will serve him even better than before." This vow he kept, and lived up to it all his life.

Now, the disciples and patrons gathered to welcome Rechungpa. From the assembly Sevan Repa arose and said, "You must have learned and brought back from India both the Pith-Instructions, as prophesied by the Jetsun, and the science of logic. Now please tell us, how can we win a dispute should we ever become involved in one?" Milarepa said, "Rechungpa, you may tell them how to 'win' a dispute in the light of the Ḍākinīs' [teachings]." In response, Rechungpa sang:

The great Transmission Buddha, Dorje-Chang,
Will quench all disputes in the Lineage.
Our Guru, Buddha-Repa, will end
The disputes of craving teachers.
The Pith-Instructions and the Transmission's
        Skillful Path
Will quench all evil argument

Derived from constant thinking.
The omnipresent Mirror of Equality
Will reveal all concealed vices.
The precious teachings of the Great Bliss
Will burn all wandering thoughts in its Wisdom
        flame.
The Nāḍīs and Prāṇas in the Cakras
Will dispel at once all drowsiness and distractions.
The Teaching of the self-liberating Mahāmudrā
Will conquer the demon of ego-clinging to the
        Five Consciousnesses.
The Teaching of the radiant Wisdom Lamp
Will dispel darkness and ignorance.
The Act of Chu La³ Swordsmanship
Will cut, with ease, the ties of worldly desire.

Milarepa commented, "What you have said is very good. But in addition, we need the Instructions on the View and Practice. Now listen to my song:

The View is the wisdom of the Void,
The Practice is the illumination of non-clinging,
The Action is the everlasting play without desire,
The Fruit is great immaculate Nakedness.

Concerning the view of Void-Wisdom,
The danger is to miss it
Through words and thoughts.
If absolute knowledge
Has not been gained within,
Words alone can never free one from ego-clinging.
Thus, you should strive for true understanding.

Concerning the practice of Illumination free
        from clinging,
The danger is to miss it
By adhering to mere concentration.
If Wisdom has not shone within,
Steady and deep concentration by itself
Will never lead to Liberation.
Wisdom never comes
With distractions and drowsiness;
You should thus work hard on mindfulness.

Concerning perpetual Action without desires,
The danger is to miss it
By indulging in idle talk.
Before all appearances have become
Aids in one's meditation practice,
"Tantric Acts" will be
Worldly desires disguised.
You should thus strive for purity and non-clinging!

Concerning the immaculate Fruit of Nakedness,
The danger is to miss it through your thought.
If ignorances are not purged within,
Hard effort will bring but small results.
You should thus strive to wipe out ignorance.

All present at the meeting were convinced by the truth of this song, and all were inspired with joy.

This is the story of the wild goats.

NOTES

1 Vajra-reciting Yoga (T.T.: rDo.rJe.bZlas.Pa.): A very important breathing exercise almost indispensible to all Tantric Yoga practices, it is also called the "Three Vajra Words Recitation." Describing this exercise briefly, the yogi recites the "Om" upon inhaling, "Ah" at the pause, and "Hum" upon exhaling, thus coordinating a complete breathing process with the recitation of three essential Vajra words.

2 Dsudbhu (T.T.: mDsod.sPu.): a circle of hair between the eyebrows in the middle of the forehead, one of the thirty-two superb marks of a Buddha, from which he sends forth divine rays of light.

3 The text reads: "sPyod.Pa.Chu.La.Ral.Gri.Yis.". The meaning of "Chu.La." is very obscure. "Chu" originally means water; it could therefore be interpreted as Act-of-fluidity — denoting the non-clinging and all-free attitude of an enlightened mind.

40

THE SONG OF "HOW TO GAIN HAPPINESS AND AVOID SUFFERING"

Obeisance to all Gurus

A T THE feast held for Rechungpa on his return from India by the patrons and disciples of Red Rock and Bouto, Jetsun Milarepa prophesied the coming of the peerless Gambopa. Then he was invited by the patrons to remain in Chu Bar. [While Milarepa was there], a great yogi [mediator] of the Lan tribe, having heard of his reputation and filled with enthusiasm and aspiration, arrived from Dagbo. As soon as he saw the Jetsun a Samādhi of bliss, illumination and non-thought arose within him. His faith confirmed, he said to Milarepa, "I am a yogi from Dagbo. I have learned many teachings, including the Great Perfection, from several Gurus; I have also practiced the Meditation-of-Distinctive-Observations,[1] and the [Tantric] Action-of-Equality.[2] I am not satisfied with the shallow experiences of mere understanding and have been greatly inspired by your reputation, therefore I now come to you for the Dharma. Please be kind enough to grant me the Instructions." The Jetsun asked, "Have you yet had these Experiences during your devotion? Now listen to my song":

> Have you missed the holy Guru's Pith-Instructions,
> Because of mere verbal knowledge?
> Have you missed the profound Distinct Wisdom
> Because of your Two Clingings?
> Have you lost the view of profound insight
> Because of the hindrance of dualism?
> In practicing the Meditation-of-No-Perception

456

Have you fallen into the pitfall of forms?
In practicing the Action-of-Equality
Have you gone astray through indulgence and
    skepticism?
Have you failed to understand that Nirvāṇa's fruit
Is found within yourself?
Have you thought the false experiences,
Contrary to the sayings of the Tantras,
To be genuine and sound?
Have you missed the intrinsically void Mind-Essence
By obstructing it with artificial thought?
When you practiced Yoga in solitude
Were you misled by demons in disguise?
As a potter turns his wheel,
The forces of ignorance
Turn one ever in Saṃsāra.

The yogi replied, "It is true that I have been like that. Now please initiate and instruct me in order to correct these faults." Milarepa granted his request and set him to meditate. After some time, the yogi, now called Lan Gom Repa, was still unable to get rid of his attachment to virtues, still thinking them to be concrete and with definite form. Many wandering thoughts rose in his mind, so that he could not free it; he had an urge to visit the town, and so forth. Milarepa was fully aware of this, so when Lan Gom Repa came to report his Experience and progress he said, "Lan Gom, you should not cling to the formality of virtuous deeds, but try to subdue your wandering thoughts about going to the town, and concentrate on your meditation; otherwise you can never free yourself from the Three Realms of Saṃsāra. Take heed of these things." Then Milarepa sang:

For him who keeps the tradition of the Lineage
All errors vanish in the Ultimate,
All things come with ease at the right time.
He who acts like this is a true yogi.

In the practice of Mahāmudrā
There is no room for thinking with a clinging mind.
When Realization of the State-Beyond-Playwords
    arises
There is no need to chant or keep the rules.

Yogis wandering in towns

Always yield themselves
To the will and favor
Of relatives and friends.
Their actions become pretentious,
Their talk nonsensical.
The light of the Void by hypocrisy is dimmed.
If in town one pays no attention to what people
        feel,
Troubles and worries will rain upon him.

To avoid fear and regret at the time of dying,
To escape the fatal chasm of Saṃsāra,
One should conquer the enemy — desire.
Remember always transiency and death,
And ever meditate in solitude.

He who observes not his mind *nakedly*,
Becomes apathetic and indifferent.
He who prays not with earnestness,
Is prone to be misled by false experiences.
If with great diligence and perseverance
He does not practice the profound teaching of
        the Skillful-Path,
He is prone to be vanquished by desires.
If he remains in a hermitage,
Merits will surely grow within him.

Lan Gom Repa thought, "The Jetsun's words have hit the crux of the matter: he is right about my faults." So he meditated in a hermitage without distraction until he gained superb Realizations. Then he came to report this progress to the Jetsun. Greatly pleased, Milarepa said, "That is very good; but you should still continue to practice like this until you attain Buddhahood. These are the important things you should always remember:

A son, a wife, and fame
Are three fetters for a yogi;
A Dharma-practicer should abandon them!

Goods, enjoyments, and prestige
Are three hindrances to a yogi;
A Dharma-practicer should abjure them!

Relatives, patrons, and disciples
Are three obstacles to a yogi;
A Dharma-practicer should forsake them!

Wine, fatigue, and sleep
Are three robbers of a yogi;
A Dharma-practicer should avoid them!

Chatting, joking, and entertainment
Are three distractions to a yogi;
A Dharma-practicer should abjure them!

The Guru, the Instruction, and diligence
Are three refuges for a yogi;
A Dharma-practicer should e'er rely on them!

Solitude, merits, and good companions
Are three staffs for a yogi;
A Dharma-practicer should ever use them.

Non-distraction, non-thought, and bliss
Are three good friends to a yogi;
A Dharma-practicer should e'er consort with them!

Relaxation, spontaneity, and naturalness
Are the three attributes of a yogi;
A Dharma-practicer should ever keep them!

Non-desire, non-hate, and supernormal powers
Are three signs of a yogi's success;
A Dharma-practicer should e'er achieve them!

Lan Gom Repa said, "Because of your blessing I have now relinquished all that should be relinquished, and can practice the right Dharma spontaneously and with ease. I feel happy and cheerful all the time." The Jetsun replied, "Yes, my son, this is correct. A yogi who has completely abandoned all the faults and acquired all the merits is always happy. If he does the opposite he will suffer all the time. Therefore, he should always discriminate between right and wrong for his own happiness and safety. Whereupon, he sang a song, "How to Gain Happiness and Avoid Suffering":

He who knows his own nature

And the immanent Truth,
Is ever joyful.
He who wrongly acts
Is ever sad.

He who rests in the state of nature
And is ever spontaneously pure,
Is ever joyful.
He who surrenders to impulses and environments,
Being subject to hatred and to cravings,
Is ever sad.

He who realizes that all things are the Dharmakāya,
Freed from all fears, hopes, and doubts,
Is ever joyful.
He who is impatient, talkative, and rash,
Being overpowered by worldly desires,
Is ever sad.

He who knows that all things are his mind,
That all with which he meets are friendly,
Is ever joyful.
He who squanders his life away,
Carrying remorse to his grave,
Is ever sad.

He who has a thorough Realization,
At ease in the self-sustaining Reality,
Is ever joyful.
He who is enslaved by his desires,
Insatiable and always longing,
Is ever sad.

He who is freed from all forms without effort,
Always immersed in the Experience,
Is ever joyful.
He who merely follows words,
Unseeing of the mind,
Is ever sad.

He who renounces all worldly things,
Free from worry and consideration,
Is ever joyful.

A Buddhist who measures and stores up grain,
Cherishing the women and relatives he loves,
Is ever sad.

A yogi who discards all worldly ties,
Realizing all is magic and illusion,
Is ever joyful.
He who diverts himself, taxing
His body and mind with sensuality,
Is ever sad.

A yogi who rides the horse of diligence
Towards the Land of Liberation,
Is ever joyful.
He who is weighted with a stone
That pulls him to the bottom of Saṃsāra
Is ever sad.

He who avoids misunderstandings,
Amused at the play of his own mind,
Is ever joyful.
He who has sworn to practice Dharma
But indulges in sinful deeds,
Is ever sad.

He who has done away with fears, and hopes, and
        doubts,
Perpetually absorbed in the State of Origin,
Is ever joyful.
He who submits to the will of others —
Obsequious, artificial, and ingratiating,
Is ever sad.

He who leaves all "this and that" behind,
Always practicing pure Dharma,
Is ever joyful.

Lan Gom Repa and the other disciples were all greatly inspired
[and filled with] joy. With the power of absorbing themselves in the
unwavering Samādhi of Mahāmudrā, they were able to further their
spiritual progress in this magic-like world of forms. The Jetsun was

very pleased with Lan Gom Repa, who later became the patron, the disciple, and the Dharma brother of the Dagpo Rinpoche [Gambopa].

This is the story of Milarepa's intimate son, Lan Gom Repa.

NOTES

1 Meditation-of-Distinctive-Observations, or Meditation and Observation of the Distinctive Wisdom (T.T.: So.So.rTog.Pahi.Shes.Rab.Kyi.rTog.dPyod.).

2 Action-of-Equality (T.T.: Ro.sÑoms.): To set one free from fear and hope, likes and dislikes, Tantrism provides a practice for advanced yogis, known as the "Action of Equality." In the execution of this practice, the yogi is urged to do things against the standard of conventional values.

41

THE HOLY GAMBOPA—MILAREPA'S FOREMOST DISCIPLE

Obeisance to all Gurus

MARPA, in his interpretation of Milarepa's significant Dream of the Four Pillars,[1] foretold that the supremely exalted Gambopa, the heart-son of the great Yogi, Mila the Laughing Vajra, would appear as the Peerless Sage. The Patron Buddha, Vajra Ḍākinī, also told Milarepa that he would have one disciple like the sun, another like the moon, and twenty-five accomplished disciples like stars, and that Gambopa would be the foremost of all, like the sun.

The all-perfect Buddha, Sāykamuni Himself, also prophesied the coming of Gambopa in the Royal Samādhi Sūtra and elsewhere. For instance, in the Great Compassion Lotus Sūtra,[2] Buddha says: "Ananda! In the future, after my Nirvāṇa, a monk called the Physician [T.T.: hTso.Byad.] will appear in the North. He rendered outstanding services to the previous Buddha after having served hundreds of thousands of Buddhas in his former lives. He is well grounded in virtues and supreme thoughts and has entered the immaculate Path of Mahāyāna for the benefit and happiness of many sentient beings. He will appear as a well-informed man, highly versed in the Scriptures of the Bodhisattva's Doctrine, who speaks the words of the Great Vehicle and demonstrates faultlessly and perfectly the Mahāyāna teaching." And so at this time of five defilements, appeared in Tibet, the Snow Country of the North, Dagbo Lhaje [the Physician from Dagbo] whose fame was heard in all lands. He was a great Bodhisattva who had reached the Tenth (Final) Stage of the Path, and realized its direct insight. The Jetsun Milarepa foresaw him in his illuminating Samādhi. He blessed Gambopa with the grace of Samādhi, and attracted him with his mind power. It was he, the great Gambopa, who dawned upon the Buddhist religion and brought many sentient beings to the great Bodhi-Path. His life story is vast like the mighty ocean, of which this epitome of his biography is [but] a single drop.

The Lord Gambopa was born in the Seba Valley of Nyal in Tibet. His family was the Nyi Wa. His father, a physician called Wutso Gabar Jalbo, had two wives, Yunlaza and Sangdan Dranma, each of whom gave birth to a son. Gambopa was the eldest, and was called Dunba Dharmadraug. His father, being an excellent consultant in worldly affairs, trained him well so that he became proficient in speech and in consultation. When Gambopa was fifteen he had already learned many Tantric teachings of the Ningmaba, such as the Basic Tantra of Sungwa Nyinbo, Heruka Galbo, the Tantras of the Wrathful and Peaceful Buddhas and of the Great Merciful Net-Holder, and many other teachings of the Old School. He had also mastered the eight branches of medical science taught by his father.

At twenty-two he married the sister of the powerful [local] chieftain, Dharma Aui. She had all the admirable qualities of a lady. They had a son and daughter, but [a pestilence broke out in that area, and] the son died. Gambopa accompanied the corpse to the cemetery, and when he returned home, found that his daughter had also died. A few days later his wife caught the same disease. Every kind of medical treatment was tried, and prayers were repeated and sacraments held, but in vain.

After suffering great pain for a long time, she was still trying desperately to hold on to life. [Sitting beside her pillow] Gambopa recited the holy Sūtras to her. He thought, "She has been trying so hard to cling to life under such an ordeal, and will not let herself die peacefully. This must be due to her extreme attachment to something."

He then said to her, "Those who do not understand the true nature of Saṃsāra are toilworn and overburdened; those who are compelled to linger in Saṃsāra are miserable and pitiful. I am indeed sorry for those unenlightened people who are subject to intense attachment to their dream-like consorts and relatives. You will not let yourself die peacefully after enduring such a prolonged, unbearable ordeal. This must be due to your clinging to something or someone. If it is the house and land that you cannot abandon, I will offer them to the monks. If it is the jewels that you cannot give up, I will give them to the priests and the poor. What else is there that you cannot bear to leave? We met in this life because of our mutual vows in previous lives. But because of your bad Karma you have now caught this disease. I have tried everything to help, but have only made you suffer more. [This painful lesson has taught me] to decide that no matter whether you live or die, I shall devote my whole life to the Dharma."

His wife said, "I am now about to die. I am not attached to the land, the house, my jewels, or anything else. It is you that I cannot give up. I shall send for my brother [Dharma Aui] to prevent your being seduced by women. Besides, [as you have said], family life in Saṃsāra is without true happiness. I hope, my dear husband and physician, that you will now devote your body and soul to the Dharma."

Gambopa replied, "Even if you recover from this disease, we cannot stay together forever. If you die, I will devote my life to practicing the Dharma and will not marry again. Do you want me to swear to it before you?"

His wife said, "I know you are a man who will never go back on your word, but in order to set my mind at rest I would like you to take an oath before me. Please fetch a witness."

Gambopa then called in his uncle, Balsud, to be the witness, put the holy Sūtra, written with golden words, upon his head and took the oath. His wife said, "My dear physician, I shall see from a crack in my grave whether or not you dedicate your life to the Dharma!" Saying this, she took her husband's hand, gazed into his face with her eyes full of tears, and died.

Gambopa then divided his property into three parts, using one to pay for his wife's funeral and offerings, another for meritorious charities, and the third to provide for learning and practicing the Dharma. He then cremated his wife's corpse, built a stūpa, and made a number of Tsa Tsa[3] Buddha images with her ashes and bones. Later this stūpa became very famous, and people called it Jomo Chod Dan (the Stūpa of the Hostess). It can still be seen in the region of Nyal.

After the funeral and winding up his affairs, Gambopa felt very much at ease. He thought, "It is now time for me to practice the Dharma." He then went alone to Nyi Tong and meditated there.

Gambopa's uncle, Balsud, thought, "My poor nephew must be heartbroken after the loss of his dear wife. I must go to console him." So he went to see Gambopa, taking with him much wine and meat.

During their talk Gambopa said to his uncle, "Since my wife passed away I have been feeling very much at ease and happy." This remark made Balsud exceedingly angry. "Where could you find as good a woman as your [late] wife?", he cried indignantly. "Had Dharma Aui heard of this, he would have said that you were breaking the oath!" With this, he threw a handful of dust in Gambopa's face. Gambopa merely replied, "My dear Uncle, have you forgotten the oath I made before my wife with you as a witness? Am I not practicing the Dharma as I promised?"

"Nephew, you are quite right," said Balsud. "Though I have grown old like this, I seldom think of the Dharma. I really feel very much ashamed of myself! Prosper, my nephew, in your Dharma practice; I will take good care of your land and property."

After some time, without his relatives' knowledge, Gambopa went to the Bodor Monastery in the Pan region. There he saw Lama Bodorwa Rinchinsal, to whom he said, "Precious Lama, I am a native of Nyal, and I have come here for the Dharma. Please guide me through its gate and keep me for a time."

Bodorwa replied, "I have no charity to give you. You must provide your own food and clothing if you want to learn the Dharma." Gambopa thought, "If I had the means, I would not ask. According to the Tantra of Sungwa Nyinpo, to benefit sentient beings a Guru should have four kinds of compassion — the constant compassion, the spontaneous compassion, the compassion of granting benediction and prayers, and the compassion of guiding the disciples according to their needs. Only thus can a Guru help sentient beings. This Guru seems to be lacking in compassion. I doubt whether my Karma is linked with his, and I cannot venerate him."

He soon returned to his native land and prepared sixteen ounces of gold as a means for studying the Dharma. Then he went to the Jhajogri Monastery at Pan, received ordination from Lama Jhachil as a Bhikṣu [a fully ordained monk] and was given the name of Sudnam Rinchin, the Precious Meritorious One.

Then under Professors Shapa Linpa and Shadulwa Tsinpa, Gambopa studied the Śāstras of Dodejan (Mahāyāna Sūtrālaṅkāra), Ngundojan (Abhismayālaṅkāra), Ngunbatso (Abhidharma Kośa), and others. In Mon, he studied the Tantras of Jedor, Sungdu, and others under Guru Lodan Sherab, and received the Initiations and Pith-Instructions from him. From Professors Nyurumpa and Jhajogripa, Gambopa learned numerous teachings of the Ghadamba School. Thinking, "Now I must practice these teachings," he meditated in Jhajogri.

The Jetsun Gambopa was a man whose intelligence and compassion were great, whose clingings and desires were small, whose industriousness and faith toward the Dharma were prodigious, and whose apathy and indolence were negligible. By day he studied Buddhism diligently, and at night he meditated strictly; or he circumambulated, and performed other meritorious acts. [Because of his compassion and purity], no insect ever grew on his body.[4] He could live comfortably without food for five or six days, and his body always felt blissful. He could absorb himself in Samādhi for many days, and all crude forms of lust, anger, and blindness dwindled away within him. As prophesied in the Golden Light Sūtra[5] all the signs preceding achievement of the Tenth Bhumi [the final and ultimate stage of Enlightenment of a Bodhisattva] had appeared unmistakably in his dreams.

Some time afterwards, Gambopa had a vision in which he saw a green yogi dressed in rags, who put a hand upon his head, and, wetting a finger with spittle, flicked it in his face. He [at once] felt his Dhyāna growing better and deeper. In addition, he gained a decisive [and immediate] understanding of Reality. In an Experience fraught with joy, his mind became clearer, lighter, and more alert than ever before. He told some monks in the town about this Experience, and they commented, "You were ordained a Bhikṣu, and have been observing the immaculate precepts flawlessly. A monk like you, who dreams of yogis and the like, will come up against difficulties, for these premonitory dreams are conjured up by the [demon] Beghar. You should therefore go to your teacher, ask him to give you a holy recitation,[6] and invite a large group of monks to bless you with the rite of One Hundred Dorma Offerings." This Gambopa did, yet the vision of the yogi appeared more often than before.

At that time, in the Sunlight Happy Cave of Draugmar Bouto, the Jetsun Milarepa was setting in motion the wheel of Dharma, both of the Expedient and of the Ultimate Truth, for his heart-sons Rechung Dorje Dragpa, Shiwa Aui, Sevan Repa, and Ngan Tson Dunba; for his patrons Tsese of Drin, and Ku Ju, and for others. One day, the elders among the Repas said to Milarepa, "Jetsun, you are now very old. If one day you go to the Pure Land, we Repas will need someone who can act for you to help us in our difficulties and to further our progress on the Path. Our patrons also need a spiritual leader to increase their merits. Whom do you think can assume this responsibility? Whoever you have in mind should be given all the Pith-Instructions without reservation, and should be invested with power and status. Without such a man, neither our teachings nor our Lineage can spread widely, nor can our disciples be properly guided." Hearing their request, the Jetsun at first appeared slightly displeased. Then he replied, "Yes, indeed I shall have a good disciple, who will develop my teachings immensely. I shall, this evening, observe where he is and [will tell you] if you return early tomorrow morning."

The next morning, Milarepa arose earlier than usual, summoned all his disciples and patrons, and said:

"Like a Dharma-replenished vessel, the man who will receive my Pith-Instructions in full will soon come. He is a fully ordained monk, who bears the title of 'Physician,' and will hold my doctrine and spread it in all the Ten Directions. Last night I dreamed of his coming

with a empty crystal vase, which I filled with nectar from my silver
vase. This old father now has a son who will benefit numerous sentient beings and will illumine the doctrine of Buddha as the rising
sun lights [the earth]. Oh, I am overflowing with joy and happiness!"
In great delight Milarepa sang:

I bow down to all Gurus,
I pray to the Gracious Ones!

In the East is found the White Lion's milk,
The source of supreme strength;
One will, unless one taste it,
Never understand its power.
Only after drinking can
Its strength be felt most deeply,
Yet only the Deva Indra can imbibe it.

In the South, the great tiger
Leaps with all his might;
Great and majestic as this is,
One can never understand it
Without an actual contest.
Only by vying with a tiger
Can one fully appreciate its leap,
But only the great Dombhi Heruka rides it.

In the West, the Jurmo Fish has a bitter gall;
Nothing in this world can taste more bitter,
Yet, without directly sampling it,
None can imagine how it feels.
Only after tasting it
Can one fully understand its bitterness;
But only the Dragon Gawojobo has experienced it.

In the North, great is the power of the Blue
        Gem Dragon,
Yet, without a formal contest,
Its strength is never felt.
Only after wrestling with this monster
Can one fully understand its might,
But only the athlete Deva Galugha matches it.

The milk of the White Lioness in the East

Must be poured into a golden bowl,
Not into any common vessel
Lest the vessel break and the milk be lost.

The holy teaching of Nāropa and Medripa
Is deep and most profound,
Yet if one does not practice it,
One sees nothing deep therein.
Only after one has practiced can
One fully understand its depth.
This is the teaching my Father Marpa had!
This is the teaching Milarepa practiced.

Milarepa's Experience, insight, and instructions
Are always most effective and precise,
Yet those of little weight cannot receive them.
They are only given to the able student,
Yet they all will be imparted
To the monk, my coming heir.

One day Gambopa went out for a walk of circumambulation. At the gate [of the monastery] he overheard three paupers talking about their urgent need, as a great famine had broken out that year. One of them remarked, "At a time like this, our kind monks of Jhajogri give timely preaching to all Buddhists; they also invite everyone, without discrimination, to share their food. After we have eaten there, we can also beg a measure of the porridge left over and go to some pleasant place nearby to eat it together." Another suggested, "I have a better idea. Let us gather one full measure of half-ripened grain, make dough, and season it with pepper; then we can enjoy it together quietly in some abandoned house." The eldest said, "A cunning man always laughs and smiles, even if he is desperately hungry, while a good bird always flies like a vulture, even if it is starving. Let us, therefore, not say anything that might betray our yearning for food. Look! A Lama is coming this way! We had better not let him hear our conversation. It would shame us to be overheard. Besides, if you want to make a vow, you had better make a big one! Vow, therefore, to become the immaculate Son of Heaven —the great Emperor — protecting and spreading the holy Dharma and governing all Tibet here and now; or vow to become a yogi like Milarepa, the king of all yogis, who lives an ascetic life in the snow mountains to the West, sustained mainly by the food of Samādhi, dressed only in a thin cotton garment, and keeping his body warm by means of the blissful

Dumo. He is a yogi who practices the illuminating Mahāmudrā day and night. When he goes from one place to another, he flies. If you can renounce the world and practice the Dharma as *he* does, that would be the best of all; but if you cannot do this, you should vow to see his face at least once in this life." Saying this, the old man shed many tears.

When the Jetsun Gambopa heard the name of Milarepa, he could not stop the spontaneous arising of great faith toward him. The emotion that struck him was so great that he fell into a faint for half a day. When he came to, he shed many tears and made many prostrations in the direction of Milarepa's abode. Then he prayed with great sincerity, calling repeatedly, "Oh, Jetsun, Jetsun, please have pity on me! Please take care of me!" He then performed the ritual of the Seven Main Oblations as an offering to Milarepa. In a great and incessant inspiration, Gambopa gained extraordinary, hitherto unattained, Experiences in his Samādhi. Engrossed as he was with the thought of visiting Milarepa, the night [rapidly] passed.

The next morning Gambopa called the three paupers in and served them with meat and food far exceeding their expectations, making them completely satisfied and happy. He then said, "I wish to visit the Lama whom you mentioned yesterday. It seems that you know a great deal about him. I shall appreciate it very much if you will guide me to his place. I have sixteen ounces of gold and will give you half for studying the Dharma."

The two younger men replied, "We know very little about this Lama," but the older one said, "All right, I will guide you to him."

That evening Gambopa made offerings and said prayers to the Three Precious Ones. That night he blew a long, huge brass trumpet, the mighty voice of which reached to every corner of the earth. Even today, there is no trumpet anywhere in all Tibet, [in Weu and Tsang][7] with a greater or more far-reaching sound.

Gambopa then hung a drum in the air and beat a rhythm upon it, producing a solemn, pleasant, and overwhelming boom heard by numerous men and animals. On the same night, he had a vision: A girl, looking like a native of Mon, came to him and said, "You beat a drum for human beings, but many animals have [also] been blessed by the sound." She then handed him a skull-cup full of milk, saying, "Having blessed even the animals to such an extent, please drink this cup of milk. [Before long] not only all the animals here, but all living beings in the Six Lokas will come to you. I am now going to the West." She then disappeared.

Afterwards, Gambopa made this comment: "The human beings who heard the sound of my drum that night are those men of lesser capacity who must go through the successive stages of the Path in a gradual manner. Great, indeed, are the bounties given to us by the [Ghadamba] Lamas.[8] The animals who heard my drum are my great yogi disciples who pracice meditation in caves. This vision also indicated that I shall go to my Guru Milarepa and rely solely on his instructions in the Skillful Path and Mahāmudrā."

Gambopa and the old man then set out to find Milarepa. In the course of the journey Gambopa now murmured, now spoke, and now cried aloud, "Oh, when can I see my Guru?" His yearning to see the Jetsun was so great that tears never left his eyes, and the thought of obtaining rest and comfort never entered his mind.

When they arrived at New Place, in Upper Nyang, the old man fell sick. He said to Gambopa, "I do not know much about the way from here on. There is, however, a monastery called Sajya [nearby]; you can inquire there." He then left Gambopa to go on alone.

Gambopa walked on like a blind beggar wandering in no-man's land. When night fell, he covered his face with his hands, bent down to the ground, and wept bitterly. [Suddenly] the old man [appeared again] and said, "Do not weep so bitterly! I will show you the way." Later [Gambopa] realized that all three paupers were Milarepa's transformations.

Gambopa continued his journey, asking for directions along the way. When he reached Dronso Charwa, he met a number of tradesmen from the highlands and asked them about Milarepa. A merchant from Nya Non called Dawazungpo said, "The master of Yoga, the great Milarepa, the accomplished Guru whose fame is known all over Tibet, is now residing at Chu Bar of Drin." Hearing this, Gambopa became so excited that he thought the merchant was Milarepa Himself. In wild confusion he hugged the man and burst into tears.

With the newly acquired information, Gambopa now went towards Din Ri. When he reached the center of a big plain he became exhausted, and sat down to rest on a rock. But due to extreme hunger and fatigue his entire Prāṇa-system had become so unbalanced and disordered that he fell from the rock and fainted, lying unconscious for half a day. When he came to, there was not even a single hair of his entire body from his head down to his feet, which did not feel painful. He was desperately thirsty, but there was no one to bring him water. He remained there without food and water for two days and nights. Then he made this vow: "If I cannot see the Jetsun in this life, I swear that in the next life I will be born near him, and that my mind will be united and become one with his. In the Three Bardos after my death I will look only to him as my sole refuge." With the greatest sincerity, and in tears, he made this vow.

Before long, a Ghadamba monk from Sha Yul came by, and asked Gambopa, "Where are you going?"

"I am going to Drin to visit Jetsun Milarepa."

"I too am going in that direction. But aren't you very sick?"

"Yes, indeed, and I am also very thirsty. Could you give me a drink of water?" The monk gave him a bowl of water and after drinking it Gambopa was completely refreshed. Then, accompanied by the monk, he resumed his journey.

Meanwhile, the Jetsun, in a very happy mood, was preaching the Dharma at Fortune Hill. During the discourse, he would sometimes remain silent for a time and then laugh heartily. A very well-gifted lady patron from Drin, called Tsese, asked him, "Why, dear Jetsun, do you now laugh heartily and now remain silent? Do you laugh because you see the progress made by some well-gifted disciple, and sit in silence when you see the wrong thoughts of an incapable one?"

"I am thinking of neither the demerits of the bad disciples, nor of the merits of the good ones," replied Milarepa.

"Why, then, did you smile and laugh today?"

"This is because my son, the Monk from Weu, has now arrived at Din Ri. He fell fainting and in pain beside a rock. With tears pouring down his face and in great faith and earnestness, he called to me for help. Feeling pity for him, I blessed him in Samādhi; then I became very joyful and burst into laughter." As he said this, his eyes filled with tears.

Tsese asked again, "When will he arrive?"

"He will get here sometime between tomorrow and the day after."

"Do we have the Karma of seeing this man?"

"Yes. Whoever has the opportunity of preparing his seat upon his arrival will be sustained by the nourishment of Samādhi. Whoever has the opportunity of first seeing him will be guided to the happy Pure Land of Liberation."

When Gambopa and the Ghadamba Lama arrived at the center of the marketplace they saw a woman weaving. "Do you know where the great Yogi Milarepa lives?" asked Gambopa. "Where do you come from?", she asked.

"From the great sun-like province of Weu, to visit the Jetsun Milarepa."

"In that case please come to my house — I would like to offer you some food."

Tea, cakes, and other refreshments were served them. Then the lady patron said, "The Jetsun knew, yesterday morning, that you were coming. He also made a prophecy about your future. Knowing that you were tired and sick in Din Ri, he blessed you in Samādhi. I obtained permission from him to welcome you first."

Gambopa thought, "It was the grace of the Jetsun that saved my life. Judging from his predictions about me, I must be a well-gifted person." Thinking thus, Gambopa became a little proud of himself. Knowing of this self-conceit, Milarepa refused to see him for a fortnight in order to subdue his pride. During this time Gambopa was told to live alone in a rocky cave, and Sevan Dunba provided him with fuel and utensils for cooking.

[A fortnight having passed], the lady patron brought Gambopa to see the Jetsun. With his power of working miracles, Milarepa transformed both Rechungpa and Shiwa Aui into the appearance of his own form. As a result, Gambopa was unable to identify the real Jetsun. Then Rechungpa pointed to the central figure and said, "*This* is the real Jetsun."

Whereupon Gambopa, the Precious One, offered Milarepa sixteen ounces of gold as a Maṇḍala, together with a brick of tea, introduced himself, and related the story of his journey from Wcu. Then he earnestly besought the Jetsun to recount his life story.

Milarepa looked straight ahead for a while, solemnly, and with his eyes fixed picked up a piece of gold from the Maṇḍala, tossed it into the sky, and said, "I offer this to Marpa Lho Draugwa." As he said this, heavenly music and light appeared [all around them], in magnificence beyond description. Milarepa took a full skull-cup of wine and drank half of it. Then he handed the remainder to Gambopa, and said, "Drink it up!"

Gambopa hesitated, thinking, "This is against the priestly rule, particularly in front of so many people."

"Do not think so much, drink it!" said Milarepa.

Being afraid of spoiling the good omen, Gambopa at once drained the skull-cup, proving [by this behavior] that he was a good vessel, capable of receiving the Pith-Instructions, and would become the holder of the Lineage.

"What is your name?" asked Milarepa.

"My name is Sudnam Rinchin [the Precious Meritorious One]."

The Jetsun then repeated thrice: "His merits were gained by accumulating a store of Virtues; he is truly Precious to all sentient beings!"

Milarepa thought to himself, "Whoever hears the name of this son of mine will be liberated from Saṃsāra, but I had better not speak of it now." [After a while] he said to Gambopa, "It is very wonderful that you have faith in me and come here to see me. I do not

need your gold or tea. As to my life story, I shall sing you a song."
Then, accompanied by Rechungpa and Shiwa Aui, Milarepa sang:

In the sky of Dharmakāya, beyond playwords,
Gathering the clouds of ever-flowing Compassion,
I bow down at the feet of gracious Marpa,
The shelter and refuge of all beings!

On my right sits my son Rechungpa,
On my left, sits Shiwa Aui;
Both join me in chorus, singing
A song for you, dear Physician!

In the holy land of India,
Though many teachers boasted much,
The two most famous Gurus were
The great Nāropa and Medripa [Maitṛpa],
Who like sun and moon lit up the world.
Their heart-son was Marpa, the Translator,
Who mastered Buddha's teachings,
Was the host to all Maṇḍalas, and
Attracted well-endowed disciples.
Hearing of the great Master, praised
By all Ḍākinīs, I yearned to see him.

I sought him with all my strength.
On seeing him I swooned in ecstasy,
Bowed at his feet, and sought profound Instruction
That in this life would lead to Buddhahood.
My father Buddha said,
"By the mercy of Nāropa
I have this knife-like teaching,
Sharp enough to cut Saṃsāra's chain."

Exerting my body, mouth, and mind,
A pauper, I worked hard to please him.
Looking at my fervor and devotion
With omniscient eyes, he said kindly:
"The Instructions of the Four Series[9]
Are not perfect today;
Some are deficient, some are overdue.
Though one may risk a headache
Imparting them to one's disciples,

Little profit can they bring.
In days of defilement such as these
People have little time for leisure,
While their activities are great.
Waste not your time in studies,
But practice the Essential Teachings."

To repay the bounty of my Guru
And conquer the fear of death,
I meditated hard and resolutely,
Converting into blessings my wrong thoughts.
Realizing what the Three Kleśas are,
I saw the Trikāya Omnipresent.
To my capable disciples will I transmit
The inner Experience and blessings; to you
Will I impart the profoundest Pith-Instructions;
With their practice, you will spread the Buddhist
      faith.
Bear this in mind, my dear Physician;
You soon will reach the State-of-Relaxation.
This in brief is my life story;
The details can wait until some other time.

I, the old man, do not want your gold,
I have no stove on which to brew your tea.
If you want the doctrine of the Whispered Lineage,
Follow my way and practice as I do.
Venerable Sir, in answer,
I have sung this song.

Milarepa then commented, "This is my reception of our revered Physician Priest." Then Gambopa brewed the tea and brought it to the Jetsun, saying, "Please accept this offering, this symbol of my veneration for you."

Milarepa accepted it with delight. He said to Rechungpa, "We should offer this monk some tea in return. Now go and collect a little from every Repa here." Accordingly Rechungpa [did so, and] prepared the tea. Milarepa continued, "Now we need some seasoning." Saying this, he made water into the pot, making the tea extraordinarily delicious.

The Ghadamba Lama then asked the Jetsun to bless him, and, for the sake of establishing a Dharmic relationship, to give him some instruction.

The Jetsun asked. "What do you have to offer me in return for receiving my blessing?"

The Lama replied, "I having nothing to offer."

"It is shameful to say that you have nothing to offer when I see that you have plenty of gold with you. After all, what is the use of blessing the faithless or giving the Pith-Instructions to the irresolute? I think it might be better for you to resume your business trip to Nepal without interruption."

"One cannot deceive the Jetsun," thought Gambopa, "One must be careful about what one thinks in front of him." Henceforth Gambopa was convinced that the Jetsun was identical with the perfect Buddha.

"Have you received any initiations before?" Milarepa asked Gambopa. "Yes," he replied, and then described in detail the initiations and instructions he had been given by his other Gurus, together with his Experiences and attainment of Samādhi.

The Jetsun laughed, saying, "One cannot extract oil from sand, for it is produced from seeds. First practice my Heat Yoga to see the Mind-Essence. By this I do not mean that your previous initiations are not good enough, I merely want to stress the importance of a correct Karmic relationship, and the absolute need for you to receive the blessing from my Lineage."

Thereupon Milarepa blessed Gambopa and initiated him into the Pagmo practice of the Whispered Lineage, in the Maṇḍala painted in cinnabar, and then he was given the Pith-Instructions. After practicing them for some time, Gambopa gained good Experiences. He compared Milarepa's teachings with those he had received before from other Gurus, and as a result many doubts arose in his mind. In order to uproot them, Gambopa went to Milarepa for the essentials of the View, Practice, and Action. Then, having cleared up all Gambopa's doubts, Milarepa sang a song relating the teaching of Tantra in accordance with the Ghagyuba traditions:

> My dear Physician Priest,
> The Ultimate View is to observe one's mind
> Steadfastly and with determination.
> If one searches for the View outside one's mind,
> 'Tis like a [blind] monster
> Seeking in vain for gold.
>
> My dear Physician Priest,
> The Ultimate Practice is not to consider
> Distractions and drowsiness as faults.

Doing so to stave them off is like
Kindling a lamp in bright daylight.

My dear Physician Priest,
The Ultimate Action is to cease
    taking and abandoning.
To take and to abandon is to be
Like a bee trapped in a net.

My dear Physician Priest,
The Ultimate Discipline is to rest
At ease in the View.
If one seeks the Discipline-Without-Rules
Outside [of one's own mind], it is like
Lifting the flood-gates of a dam.

My dear Physician Priest,
The Ultimate Accomplishment is the full conviction
    of one's mind.
If one seeks elsewhere the Accomplishment of
    Non-being,
It is like a turtle trying
To leap into the sky.

My dear Physician Priest,
The Ultimate Guru is one's mind.
If one seeks elsewhere a Guru,
It is like trying [in vain]
To get rid of one's own mind.
In short, my good Physician Priest,
You should know that all forms
Are nothing but the mind!

Gambopa thought, "What the Jetsun has just said is very true," so
with great diligence he persisted in his meditation. The first night he
practiced naked in a cave, but warmness and ecstasy arose within him
spontaneously. Before dawn he fell asleep, but his body still remained
upright, as firmly as a rock.

He continued to meditate thus for seven successive days, the heat
and blissfulness arising effortlessly. Then he saw the Five Buddhas in
the Five Directions. In commenting on this Milarepa said, "This experience is like a man pressing his eyes and seeing two moons in front

of him. What you have experienced is only due to your having controlled the five Prāṇas. It is neither good nor bad."

Although the Jetsun had told him that this experience was of no [significance or] merit, Gambopa was full of enthusiasm, and in a delighted mood continued the meditation for another three months. Then one morning at daybreak, he was [suddenly] overcome by a feeling that all the vast Three Thousand Great Millenary Worlds in the Universe were spinning round like a turning wheel. He vomited many times, and fell to the ground in a faint which lasted for a long time. He reported this to the Jetsun, who commented, "This was because the Tig Le [Bindu] in the Great Bliss Cakra [of your Head Center] is increasing. It is neither good nor bad. Just continue wtih your meditation."

Again, one evening, Gambopa saw the Black Spot Hell.[10] Because of this vision, his upper chest[11] became congested, and a strong current of Heart-Prāṇa arose [and stirred his entire body]. He reported this to the Jetsun, who said, "This was because your meditation-belt[12] is too short and binds the Nāḍīs too tightly, so loosen it. This experience was caused by a constriction of the upgoing Prāṇas. It is neither good nor bad. Keep on with your meditation."

One day Gambopa saw clearly the Deva-of-Desire[13] and all the other Devas of the Six Lokas; he saw that those in the higher Realms rained down nectar to feed those in the lower Realms, satisfying them all — [but Gambopa himself] was unable to drink the nectar-rain, and died under the blade of a knife [?]. Asking Milarepa about this vision, he was told, "The raining-down of the nectar was due to the Tig Le [Bindu] increasing in the Right and Left Channels [Roma and Jhunma] at the Throat Center. Your inability to drink the nectar was because your Central Channel has not yet opened. You should practice certain vigorous bodily exercises." Saying which, the Jetsun taught Gambopa a few forceful exercises [including those of leaping and tumbling].

Gambopa practiced for another month, then one day his body began shivering, trembling, and shaking incessantly. He thought, "What has happened? Am I possessed by demons?" He informed the Jetsun who said, "This was due to the Tig Le increasing in the Dharma Cakra at the Heart Center. It is neither good nor bad. You should now concentrate on your exercises, and do not stop them."

From then on, Gambopa needed little food. One day he saw both the moon and the sun, covered by the [dragon] Rāhu which had two thin tails. The Jetsun commented, "This was because the Prāṇas in Roma [Iḍā] and Jhunma [Piṇgalā] are now entering the Central Channel [Avadhūtī]; it is neither good nor bad." Then Milarepa repeated thrice: "He is a mighty vulture, now is the time, now is the time."

Gambopa practiced most industriously for another month, and then he saw a red Maṇḍala of the Hevajra before him. He thought, "Last time, the Jetsun said, 'Now is the time, now is the time.' That must have presaged this Maṇḍala of my Patron Buddha." He asked the Jetsun about this vision, who replied, "This is because the Red Tig Le[14] at the Dharma Cakra of the Heart Center, which was coming up from below, is now stabilized. It is neither good nor bad. You should now meditate in a relaxed and spontaneous manner."

Gambopa continued practicing for some time longer, and then one day he saw a skeleton-like Maṇḍala of Dem Chog Luyipa.[15] "This," the Jetsun explained, "was because of the increase of Tig Le in the Transformation Cakra at the Navel Center. It is neither good nor bad."

Gambopa again practiced diligently for fourteen days, then one night he felt that his body had become as vast as the sky. From the top of his head down to the tips of his toes, his whole body, including all the limbs, was full of sentient beings, most of them drinking milk. Some were drawing the milk from the stars, and drinking it. He also heard a roaring noise like that of a great storm, but knew not from whence it came. At dawn he loosened his meditation-belt, and the noise then stopped. Gambopa reported this experience to the Jetsun, who explained, "This was because the Karmic Prāṇas have driven all the Tig Le into the hundreds of thousands of Nāḍīs throughout your entire body. Now these Karmic Prāṇas have become transformed into the Wisdom Prāṇas." Whereupon Milarepa imparted to him the Superb Dumo Instruction[16] and set him to practicing.

One day the whole valley appeared to Gambopa to be full of smoke, so that in the afternoon all became dark to him. Like a blind man, he crawled and groped his way to the Jetsun's abode. The Jetsun said, "This does not matter at all. Just sit at ease and meditate." Then he taught Gambopa the method of clearing the hindrances in the upper part of the body; as a result, the smoke dispersed like [darkness at] the dawning of day.

Then one evening Gambopa's whole body appeared to contain neither flesh nor blood, but only bones linked together by numerous Nāḍīs. He asked the Jetsun about this experience, who said, "This is because you have worked too hard: your Prāṇa has become too rough, so practice more gently." Thereupon Gambopa practiced the Yoga of the Patron Buddha in the evening, and the Guru Yoga, with many prayers, at midnight. Before dawn he practiced with the Life Prāṇa, and at dawn he slept for a short while.

[After a time] twenty-four signs, which bore no relationship at all to his previous habitual thinking, appeared in his dreams. Upon awakening he thought, "Were these dreams good or bad signs?" He became doubtful, and hesitant. Then he thought, "My Guru is actually the omiscient Buddha Himself; why don't I ask *him*?" Thinking thus, he immediately arose and went directly to Milarepa, even forgetting to put on his robe.

At that time the Jetsun was sleeping in a cave at Chu Bar with his clothes bundled up for a pillow. Gambopa bowed down before him and said, "Dear Jetsun, I have a very important matter to report to you. Please do not sleep! Please get up!"

"It came to me this morning that some distracting thoughts had arisen in your mind," said Milarepa. "Now tell me, what disturbs you so?"

Gambopa replied, "Oh my precious Guru! I had certain dreams last night. I wonder whether they are good or bad omens. Please interpret them for me." Whereupon he sang:

Oh wondrous Jetsun Yogi,
The Cotton-clad, practicing ascetic deeds!
To all beings you, the famous Mila,
Are the glory, veneration, and adornment.

The first time I heard your name
I was filled with joy and inspiration.
With great earnestness, and disregarding
Hardships, I set out to seek you —
As did the Ever-Crying Bodhisattva.[17]

Throughout my rugged journey
I cried with yearning heart:
"When can I see my Jetsun Guru?"
'Twas like the Ever-Crying One.

When I reached a place from here
One-and-a-half days' journey,
I came close to death — lying
In the road like a discarded stone.

Due to my unyielding will
And indomitable faith,
I was able to complete my journey
To meet you, my Father Jetsun,
In this wondrous place, Auspicious Hill.
[This experience reminds me of]

The Story of Meeting the Holy Chupoa[18]
At the Fragrant Palace in the East.

When I saw you, my hair rose in delight.
Beyond description was my joy
As my longing was fulfilled at seeing you.

Little have I to offer you;
I am disgusted with Saṃsāra,
Frightened by the toil of life and death,
And abhor all worldly things.
From the bottom of my heart
This echo sounds:
"Go to practice! Go to meditate."

Pray, my Jetsun Guru, always remember me
And embrace me with your compassion!
Please listen to your servant,
Who has something to report this morning.

Last night I recited the Yidham's Mantra,
At midnight I prayed to you, my Jetsun Guru,
Then I practiced the Life Prāṇa.
Before dawn I fell asleep
And had these wondrous dreams,
Apparently not caused by my habitual thoughts.

I dreamt I wore a hat with silken brim
Beautified by fur along its edge;
Above it was the image of an eagle.

I dreamt I wore a pair of greenish boots
Well cut, embossed with brass
And fastened by silver buckles.

I dreamt I wore a white silk robe,
Red-spotted and adorned
With pearls and golden threads.

I dreamt of a belt around my waist
Made of cloth from Mon
And embroidered with fine flowers,
Silk tassels, and [many] pearls.

I dreamt of wearing round my neck
A white, uncut felt scarf
With jasmines made of silver.

I dreamt I held a Tsandar staff,
With seven precious stones adorned
And golden lattice-work design.

I dreamt that in my left hand lay
A skull brimful of golden nectar.
Then said I: "Let me use
This as my drinking bowl."

I dreamt of a many-colored sack
Filled with two loads of rice.
Then said I: "Let me use
This for my Dharma food."
And then I shouldered it.

I dreamt of a wild beast's pelt,
With head and claws attached.
Then said I: "Let me use it
As the cushion for my seat."
And then I shouldered it.

Looking to my right I saw
A fertile mead of golden flowers,
Where many sheep and cattle grazed.
I watched them closely like a shepherd.

Looking to my left I saw
A jade-green meadow full
Of many kinds of flowers,
Where many women bowed to me.

In the center of the meadow on a mound
Of golden flowers, a Bodhisattva sat
Crosslegged upon a Lotus Seat,
Golden and many-hued.

I dreamt that before the Bodhisattva
A fountain played, and from his back
A brilliant aura radiated

Surrounding him with blazing fire,
While sun and moon were shining from his heart.

These were the wondrous things of which I dreamt.
I know not if as omens they were good or bad.
Oh great Yogi, who sees the past, the present,
And the future, pray interpret them clearly for me.

The Jetsun replied, "Dear Physician-monk, my son, do not feel uneasy, but relax and set your mind at rest. Do not let distracted thoughts mislead you into the trap of ego-clinging. Let the knots of skepticism untie themselves, cut the string of dual clinging at its most subtle length, and pierce through the most delicate and subtle 'frame' of habitual thinking. Do not bestir yourself and think too much, but, putting your mind at ease in a state of naturalness, make no effort whatsoever. I am a yogi who has fully mastered this illusory body. With a full knowledge and direct realization of the very essence of all dreams as such, I can, of course, interpret as well as transform them. Today I, your old father, will explain their meanings to you. Now give me your full attention, and listen carefully to my song":

This, my dear Physician,
Is my answer. Hearken
Carefully to what I say!

My son, you have learned the teaching
Of Dem Chog in the tradition of Zung Ghar;
Also the teaching of Ghadamba, in Upper Weu.
You have mastered and stabilized
The good Samādhi. I have always thought
That you were wondrous and outstanding.

But now, in your great enthusiasm,
By your dreams you have been caught.
Is this due to lack of understanding,
Or merely a pretense? Have you
Not read Sūtras and many Tantras?
Dreams are unreal and deceptive, as was taught
By Buddha Himself, in the Final Truth of Pāramitā.
To collect, supply, and study them
Will bring little profit.
So Buddha used dream as one of the Eight Parables
To show the illusory nature of all beings.

Surely you remember these injunctions?
And yet, your dreams were marvelous —
Wondrous omens foretelling things to come.
I, the Yogi, have mastered the art of dreams,
And will explain their magic to you.

The white hat on your head indicates
That your View will go beyond the "high" and "low."
The fair trimming on the brim is a sign
That you will demonstrate the Dharma
Essence, subtle yet profound.
The lovely colors of the fur imply
That you will explain the various teachings
Of the Schools without mixing them.
The flying eagle on the top means that you
Will gain Mahāmudrā, the foremost View —
And will see the Essence of the Unborn.

The Mongol boots that you dreamt of wearing
Portray your climbing from the lower to the higher
        Vehicles.
Their green color and adorning bosses
Mean that you will attain Buddha's Four Bodies.
The "pair" shows increase of the Two Provisions.
The silver ring-strap on the boots
Is the absence of wrong practices;
Also it foretells that you
Will be like a son of Buddha —
Humble and self-restraining,
The exemplar of all Buddhist acts.

The silk robe you dreamt of wearing
Indicates that you will not be sullied
By any vice. The threads of gold
Symbolize a worthy and stable
Mind. The red spots foretell
Compassion and altruism.

The decorated belt you dreamt of wearing
Means that you will "fasten" the Three Realms.[19]
The jewels, white flowers, and silk ornaments
Show your adornment by Three Learnings[20]
And guidance over virtuous disciples.

The Tsandar staff you dreamt of holding
Proves that you have a perfect Guru;
The seven jewels on the staff
Symbolize the greatness of His merits.
The finery of golden lattice work
Foretells that you will nurture your disciples
With the Pith-Instructions of the Whispered-Lineage.
Holding the staff in your right hand
And striding forward with delight
Proves that you will dwell in the Pure Land.

The magnificent Vajra skull you dreamt of holding
Shows that you will illustrate the truth of Voidness.
The nectar, filling full the skull,
Means your enjoyment of great blissfulness.
The nectar's brilliant, golden light
Indicates you will brighten forms.
The thought of the skull as your drinking bowl
Signifies the merging of the three previous delights.
Holding the skull in your left hand shows that
The inner Experience will never leave you.

The varicolored bag of which you dreamt
Proves that you will bring all forms
        into the Path.
The two loads borne upon your shoulder
Foretell your march along the Mahāyāna Path
Through the practice of Wisdom and of Skill.
The rice therein — the thought
Of using it for sustenance —
Means that you will enjoy good health,
Long life, and Samādhi's food.

Your dream of the pelt on your left shoulder
Proves mindfulness, immune from wandering thoughts.
The head and four claws symbolize
Your ever-increasing Bodhi-Mind
And the Four Good Thoughts[21] with which
You will relieve the people's pain.
The thought of using the skin for cushion
Means you will realize the solidarity
Of Void-Compassion in your mind.

Your dream of golden flowers on your right
Shows the growth of your outer and inner merits.
The sheep and cattle grazing in the fields
Symbolize that refuge in the Dharma
Will fulfill the wishes of all beings.
The thought of herding them implies
That you will always be compassionate
To helpless and suffering men.

Your dream of a jade-green meadow on your left
Indicates that you will know Bliss-Wisdom
Through constant practice of Transcendental Samādhi.[22]
The blooming flowers of many kinds show how
The various experiences of different stages
Will grow step by step within you.
Many women bowing down before you
Presage that you will master all Dākinīs
Residing in all the Nāḍis [Channels] and Tig Les.

The mound of golden flowers in the center
Indicates that with Realization, Samādhi,
And immaculate observation of the discipline,
You will attract around you many monks
Like clouds that gather in the sky.

The luxuriant golden leaves
Upon the lotus seat imply
That your mind will n'er be sullied by Saṃsāra,
Keeping like a lotus its head above the mud.
The Bodhisattva in the Lotus Posture
Signifies that you, the young Bodhisattva,
Will abide not in Nirvāṇa,
But with great compassion
Will transform your body into many forms to help
The mother-like sentient beings in Saṃsāra.

The fountain playing before you shows
That your fountain of Dharma will ever spout.
The aura radiating from behind you
Means that your virtues will purify Tibet.
The fire blazing from your body symbolizes
That the warm and blissful wisdom of Dumo-heat
Will melt the ice of wandering thoughts.

The sun and moon shining from your heart
Presage your e'er remaining in
The never-coming, never-going Realm of Great Light.

My dear son, your dream
Was very good, not bad.

To prophesy by judging signs correctly
Is a virtue allowed by the Dharma;
But 'tis harmful to be attached
And fond of dream interpretation,
Thereby incurring ills and hindrances.
Knowing that "dreams" are but illusions,
You can bring them to the Path.

How can you explain them
Without thorough knowledge?
Some evil dreams appear as good —
[But only an expert] sees they presage ill;
Only a master of the art
Can recognize good dreams
When they take on ominous forms.
Do not, good priest, attach yourself
To either good or evil signs!
Bear, dear monk, these words in mind!

Milarepa continued, "Physician-priest, my dear son, all your dreams predicted that the Dharma would grow to full bloom within you. I, your old father, with infinite knowledge and confidence, have explained to you in detail the symbolic meanings of your dreams. Do not forget my predictions, and see if they come to pass. When the time comes, and they are verified, a supreme faith toward me, unlike that which you have now, will arise in you. You will then realize the effortless Mind-Essence in an extraordinary way. Here and now you will gain liberation from both life and death.

Again, my son, if you want to be a devoted yogi you should never cling to dreams because, by doing so, you will eventually expose yourself to the influence of devils. If one disobeys the instructions of one's Guru, disregards the good advice of others, and clings to self-conceit, one will in the long run lose one's mind. Dear son, you should not look at the faults of your friends, nor raise vicious thoughts and bestir yourself in many activities. Failure is always a result of the ignorance of others' minds. Furthermore, you should know that this life is merely a part of the *Bardo of Birth-Death*; its experiences are unreal and illusory, a form of reinforced dreaming. Mental activity in the daytime [creates a latent form of] habitual thought which again transforms itself at night into various delusory visions sensed by the [semi-] consciousness. This is called the deceptive and magic-like *Bardo of Dream*.

"When habitual thoughts become deeply rooted, they drive one into good and bad activities, thus creating the *Bardo of Samsāra* and compelling one to experience pleasures and miseries. To purify this [vicious circle of Saṃsāra], one should practice the Dream Yoga and the Illusory-Body Yoga. He who can master these Yogas, can then realize the Sambhogakāya in the Bardo State. You should, therefore, practice them diligently until you reach perfection."

Gambopa then besought the Jetsun for an easy and practical teaching on these different Bardos. In reply, Milarepa sang:

> I bow down to all Jetsun Gurus!
> Especially I take refuge in Him
> Who bestowed upon me many bounties.
> In answer to your request, my son,
> I sing this song of Bardo for you.
>
> Sentient beings in Saṃsāra
> And all Buddhas in Nirvāṇa
> Are in nature equal, and the same in essence.
> Son, this is the *Bardo of View!*
>
> The all-manifesting Red and White [Forces][23]
> And Mind-Essence indescribable
> Are but the true non-differentiated state.
> Son, this is the *Bardo of Practice!*
>
> The myriad forms of illusion
> And the non-arising Self-mind
> Are one, not two, in the Innate-Born.
> Son, this is the *Bardo of Action!*
>
> The dreams that arose last night through habitual
>   thoughts,
> And the knowledge of their non-entity this morning,
> In the light of Maya are the same.
> Son, this is the *Bardo of Dream!*

The five impure Skandhas and the pure
Buddhas in the Five Directions
Are one in the Perfecting Yoga —
The state of non-discrimination.
Son, this is the Bardo of Arising
And Perfecting Yoga, the *Bardo of Path!*

The Father Tantras that come from Skillfulness
And the Mother Tantras that arise from Wisdom
Are one in the Third Initiation of the Innate-Born.
Son, this is the *Bardo of Quintessence!*

Self-benefit is reflected in the changeless
    Dharmakāya,
Altruistic deeds are done by the ever-manifesting
    Body-of-Form,[24]
Yet, in the primordial state, they are but one.
Son, this is the *Bardo of Trikāya.*

The impure illusory body of the womb-gate
And the pure form of Buddha's Body
Are one in the great light of Bardo.
Son, this is the *Bardo of Accomplishment!*

The Jetsun then said to Gambopa, Rechungpa, and Shiwa Aui, "Remember your dreams tonight and report to me tomorrow. I will then interpret them for you."

The next morning Shiwa Aui came [to the Jetsun] first, and said, "Jetsun! Last night I had a very good dream. I dreamt that a warm sun shone forth in the East, and then it entered into my heart." Rechungpa followed, and said, "I dreamt that I arrived at three big valleys and shouted in a loud voice." Then Gambopa came in remorseful tears, saying, "I had a very bad dream." Milarepa replied, "We do not know whether it was good or bad; do not come to a conclusion about it too hastily. Now tell us about it."

"I dreamt that I slaughtered many people of different races, and stopped their breath. Oh, I must be a sinful person with bad Karmas!" Milarepa said kindly, "My dear son, do not cry so bitterly — give me your hand." Saying this, he held Gambopa's hand and continued: "Son! You will accomplish what you have longed for. Many sentient beings will put their hopes in you for their deliverance from Samsāra, and their wishes will be fulfilled. My son is born! Now the old father has done his share of serving the Dharma!" [Then, turning to the others,] he said, "Oh Shiwa Aui, your dream was only a fair one. Because your vow [to serve the Dharma] was not great enough, you cannot benefit many sentient beings. Nevertheless, you will be able to go to Buddha's Pure Land. Rechungpa, because you have violated my injunctions three times under evil influence, you will reincarnate thrice more, in three different valleys, as Buddhist scholars whose fame will be heard afar."

The Jetsun Gambopa, the Physician from Nyal, then meditated for another month with great diligence. At first he saw the Seven Healing Buddhas.[25] He needed to take no more than one breath in a whole day. After one exhalation the Prāṇa dissolved itself automatically. One afternoon he held his breath and saw the Sambhogakāya Buddha's Pure Land, with the infinite View of Wonders. Distracted and amazed by these marvelous scenes, he [had to] let out his breath —[and suddenly] he found it was already evening. He thought of telling his Guru, but being afraid of disturbing the Jetsun's meditation, he did not go to him that evening. In the meditation period at dawn he again held his breath, and saw Buddha Sākyamuni appear as the Chief among a thousand Buddhas.

At daybreak he went to the Jetsun and made obeisance to him. The Jetsun said, "There is no need for you to tell me your visions. I know them already. Now you have seen both the Nirmāṇakāya and the Sambhogakāya of your Patron Buddha. But you still have not seen the Dharmakāya. My son, although you would like to stay with me, because of your vows in past [lives], you must now go to Central Tibet. So go, and meditate there. The dangers that you have so far met [in your meditation] have been countered by me. Hereafter you will face another danger, that of miraculous power. [That is to say], when you attain these wonder-powers, the Devil of the Son of Heaven will come to you; and that is the time you should be extremely cautious, [and careful] in keeping these powers most secret. Generally speaking, the Secret Word Doctrine[26] [Tantrism] is an esoteric teaching. The Accomplishment is also brought about through secrecy. An extremely gifted person with highly developed capacity will not be affected by evil influences. You are one of this kind; therefore no devil can ever influence you. For the sake of benefiting all sentient beings you should gather disciples and teach them.

"You can start to teach and spread the Dharma when you behold and stablize the realization of Mind-Essence. In time you will see it more clearly, which will be quite a different experience from those you are having now. Then you will see me as the perfect Buddha Himself. This deep and unshakable conviction will grow in you. Then you may start to teach. He who can bring his Prāṇas to the tips of his fingers can then overcome all the Prāna-hindrances. Try and see whether you can do so now."

Gambopa then laid a heap of ashes on a slab of stone. Charging his fingers with the Prānas, he pointed at the heap. When midnight came,[27] the ashes began to disperse.

The next morning Gambopa informed the Jetsun of this happening, who said, "You have not yet mastered the Prānas, but have only partially controlled them. However, you will soon attain both the Common and Special Miraculous Powers, and perform transformations. As now you need no longer stay with me, go to Mount Gambo Dar, in the East. There you will find a hill resembling a king sitting on his throne, its top looking like an ornamental helmet similar to the one I am now wearing; its woods resemble a golden Maṇḍala. In front of this hill lie seven others shaped like heaps of jewels; they appear like seven ministers prostrated before the king. On the neck of this hill you will find your disciples. Go there now and benefit them." Whereupon Milarepa sang:

> Oh Venerable Monk, my son!
> Will you go to Central Tibet?
> If so, you may think of delicious meals.
> Whenever such yearning arises,
> Eat the food of divine Samādhi
> And realize that food is but delusion.
> Bring, therefore, all experiences
> To the Realm of Dharmakāya!
>
> At times you may think of your native land.
> Whenever such yearning arises,
> Realize that your true home
> Is in the Dharma-Essence,
> And know that all countries are delusive.
> Bring, therefore, all experiences
> To the Realm of Dharmakāya!
>
> At times you may think of gems and money.
> Whenever such yearning arises,
> Consider the Seven Heavenly Jewels
> And realize that gems and wealth are but illusions.
> Bring, therefore, all experiences
> To the Realm of Dharmakāya!
>
> At times you may think of companionship.

Whenever such yearning arises,
Think of Self-born Wisdom as your consort.
Remind yourself that all companions
Are temporal and deceptive.
Bring, therefore, your experiences
To the Realm of Dharmakāya!

At times you will think of your Guru.
Whenever such yearning arises,
Visualize Him upon your head
And for His blessing pray.
Visualize Him sitting
In the center of your heart,
And forget Him never.
But you should know that even your Guru
Is delusory and dream-like,
That all things are unreal and magical.

The Gambo Dar Mount in the East
Is like a king upon his throne,
The hill behind is like a floating scarf,
The hill before's a heap of gems,
Its top a jeweled helmet.
Surrounding it are seven small hills
Bowing like ministers before the king,
While the woods are like a golden Maṇḍala.

On the neck of this mountain
You will find disciples.
Go there — you will help sentient beings!
Go there — you will accomplish altruistic deeds!

Milarepa continued, "I now give you the name of World Glory
Vajra-Holder Bhikṣu." Whereupon he initiated Gambopa, giving him
all the Instructions, and blessed him. Then the Jetsun bestowed upon
him a golden Ahrura[28] and blessed it with his tongue and saliva. A
tinder-pouch was also given as a farewell gift. Then Milarepa said,
"Now you may go to your destination and meditate there."

Upon Gambopa's departure for Central Tibet [Weu], Milarepa escorted him as far as Shamboche. When they came to a stone bridge
the Jetsun said, "Venerable Monk from Weu, as a good omen, let us
not cross the river [together]. Now put down your load, and let us,
father and son, talk for a while. Oh Monk from Weu, renounce pride

and egotism, cut the strings of affection and attachment, and abandon all worldly desires of this life as a good Buddhist should do. Merge all the teachings into one practice. Always pray to me; never associate with wicked persons, those whose avarice, hatred, and ignorance are great, lest you be contaminated by their shadows of sin. There are people who see nothing but others' faults and take all to be their enemies. They vilify others, criticize the Dharma, and bring bad influences to all, for in the depths of their hearts the fires of hatred are always burning. To give an example, the snake has neither wings, legs, nor hands — logically it should be a feeble, meek creature; but as soon as one sees it, one is seized by abhorrence. This reflects the great hatred existing within the snake. He who cherishes hatred within, will see all men as his enemies. Again, some people are very mean — they grasp and store up everything, even if it be a piece of wood or a basket of stones. They say, 'When we become old we will need a means of livelihood; when we die, we will need food for sacrifice in the cemetery.' They say that one cannot practice the Dharma without money, that even a Bodhisattva needs money to accumulate his Spiritual Provisions. Then they indulge in usury and all forms of profit-seeking. Their blood is always boiling with greed. Again, some people will say, 'Now is not the time for us to practice the transcendental teachings. He who does not cultivate his compassion, will fall into the path of Hīnayāna. One should never stick to one teaching, otherwise he will be possessed by bigotry and narrow-mindedness.' These people are veiled with great ignorance — you should never associate with them or pay attention to their babblings. If you talk to them, they will ask you who your teacher is and what kind of Dharma you practice. But your answers will eventually lead them to anger. Because of their narrow-mindedness, good advice will never do them any good, but only incur their vituperation. As a result they will lose their refuges and be damned. In other words, one's good advice causes other people to sin. This is why you should not associate with men who are dominated by the ever-increasing Three Poisonous Desires. [The Holy Tantra says]:

'To stay seven days in a Hīnayāna temple
[Brings a Tantric yogi harm, not benefit.]
Like a tiny, cautious sparrow, watch
Your conduct with the greatest care!'

"My son, do not take pride in your continence and discipline. Be in harmony with all; be patient, persevering, virtuous, and noble; and bridle your wandering thoughts. Always talk less and restrain yourself from distractions. Constantly dwell in hermitages and spend all your time in furthering your Three Learnings. You may have realized that your Self-mind is Buddha Himself, yet you should never abandon your Guru. You may have known that all deeds are intrinsically pure, yet you should never abandon even the smallest virtue. You may have realized that all causes and Karmas are void, yet you should abstain from committing even the smallest transgression. You may have realized that self and others are one in the Great Equality, yet you should not denounce the Dharma and forsake sentient beings. Son, in the Year of the Rabbit, the Month of the Horse, and on the fourteenth day of that month, you should come to see me. Now listen to my song:

My son, when the Realm that is beyond
Playwords in your mind appears,
Do not let yourself indulge in talk
Lest you become proud and garrulous,
Carried away by worldly claims.
It is important to be humble and modest.
Do you understand, Venerable Monk from Weu?

When Self-liberation appears within,
Engage not in logic and speculation
Lest meaningless activities involve you.
Son, rest yourself without wandering thoughts.
Do you understand, Venerable Monk from Weu?

When you behold the void nature of Mind,
Analyze it not as one or many
Lest you fall into the void-of-annihilation!
Son, rest at ease in the sphere beyond all words.
Do you understand, Venerable Monk from Weu?

When you practice Mahāmudrā,
Practice not virtuous deeds with mouth or body
Lest your Wisdom of Non-distinction vanish.
Son, rest at ease in the non-doing state.
Do you understand, Venerable Monk from Weu?

When revelations and prophesies are disclosed,
Be not conceited or overjoyed
Lest you be deceived by devilish presages.
Son, rest at ease in the non-clinging state.
Do you understand, Venerable Monk from Weu?

When you observe your mind with penetration,
Stir not ardent passion or attachment
Lest the devil of desire possess you.
Son, rest at ease and without hope.
Do you understand, Venerable Monk from Weu?

Then Milarepa placed his feet upon Gambopa's head and said, "Venerable Monk from Weu! I have just imparted to you all the Four Initiations. Now be happy and joyful." Thus [in this one act], the Jetsun gave Gambopa, [first,] the Initiation of the Divine Body, blessing his body to become Buddha's Maṇḍala; [second,] the Initiation of Divine Speech, blessing his words to become Mantras; [third,] the Initiation of Dharma, enlightening his mind to the Dharmakāya. The very act of putting his feet upon Gambopa's head symbolized that Milarepa had given his disciple the Initiation of Vajra-Guru, ordaining him as a full-fledged Teacher of Tantra. Again the Jetsun gave Gambopa the Initiation of Expression-Samādhi and said, "I have an unusually profound pith-instruction, but it is too precious to give away. Now you may go!"

Milarepa then sent Gambopa on his journey, himself remaining where he was. When Gambopa had crossed the river and reached a distance from whence he could barely hear the Jetsun's voice, Milarepa called him back, saying, "Who else but you would deserve to receive this most precious pith-instruction, even though it is of too great a value to be given away? Now come here, and I will impart it to you." In great joy Gambopa asked, "Should I now offer you a Maṇḍala?" "No, it is not necessary to offer me one. I only hope that you will cherish this teaching and never waste it. Now look!" *Saying this, Milarepa pulled up his robe, exposing his naked body covered with lumps of callus.* "There is no profounder teaching than this. See what hardships I have undergone. The most profound teaching in Buddhism is 'to practice.' It has simply been due to this persistent effort that I have earned the Merits and Accomplishment. You should also exert yourself perseveringly in meditation."

[This unforgettable sight] made an indelible impression upon Gambopa, who, in obedience to his Guru's instruction, began his journey to the East.

As for the account of Gambopa's life-story, and his great achievements in spreading the Dharma and benefiting sentient beings, the reader is advised to refer to Gambopa's own Biography in which detailed information may be found.

Then the Jetsun Milarepa went to Chu Bar, gathered all his disciples together, and said, "This physician-monk will benefit a great many sentient beings. Last night I dreamt that an eagle flew from here to Weu and alighted on the top of a precious gem. Then many geese flocked round it. After a short while, they dispersed in different directions, each goose again gathering about five hundred more companions. Thus all the plains and valleys became full of geese. This dream indicates that although I am a [lay] yogi, numerous followers in my Lineage will be monks. I am happy beyond words that I have now completed my service to the Dharma!" Milarepa spoke with deep feeling and great joy.

This is the story of Milarepa's foremost heart-son — His Holiness, Gambopa.

NOTES

1 In order to predict the future growth of the Ghagyuba, Marpa one day told his disciples to remember their dreams that night and report to him the next morning. Milarepa dreamt of four huge pillars in the Four Directions, upon which four animals performed different acts. Marpa gave this dream a detailed interpretation in which he predicted the various accomplishments of his four great disciples and the coming of Gambopa. See W. Y. Evans-Wentz' "Tibet's Great Yogi, Milarepa," 2nd ed., 1951, pp. 149-155.

2 The Great Compassion Lotus Sūtra: T.T.: sÑin.rJe.Chen.Po.Padma.dKar. Pohi.mDo.; Skt.: Mahākaruṇāpuṇḍarīkasūtra.

3 Tsa Tsa: See Story 45, Note 10.

4 It is believed that a truly compassionate Bodhisattva is immune from the attacks of insects or beasts. Tibetan lamas even use this as a yardstick to judge and measure the compassion of their fellow lamas.

5 The Golden Light Sūtra: T.T.: gSer.Ḥod.Dam.Pahi.mDo; Skt.: Suvarṇaprabhāsottamasūtra.

6 This is a free translation. Literally, " ... ask him to impart to you a recitation (T.T.: Luñ.) of the [Mantra] of the Immovable White [Goddess]." The Immovable White Goddess seems to be the Goddess gDugs.dKar.

7 Weu (T.T.: dWus.): Central Tibet; Tsang (T.T.: gTsañ.) Southwestern Tibet.

8 The translator suspects that some printing errors may have crept into the text here. It seems more appropriate in this instance for Gambopa to remind himself of the bounties he received from the Ghadamba (T.T.: bKah.gDams.Pa.) Lamas, though the text reads " ... bKah.sDom.Gyi.bLa.Ma. ... ," meaning the Lamas who are bound by Injunctions. Ghadamba is an independent School of Tibetan Buddhism, founded by Atisha and his disciples, and Gambopa was formerly associated with this School before he met Milarepa.

9 Lit.: "The Instructions of the Four Directives" (T.T.: bKah.Babs.bShi.). The translator presumes this implies the Four Tantras.

10 Black Spot Hell: T.T.: dMyal.Wa.Thig.Nag.

11 Upper Chest, literally, the upper portion of the heart (T.T.: sÑiñ.sTod. Du.).

12 Meditation belt: a soft cloth belt fastened about the yogi's body in order to help him keep his posture erect and balanced during meditation.

13 Deva-of-Desire (T.T.: hDod.lHa.): This refers to the Devas or heavenly beings in the Realm of Desire (hDod.Khams.).

14 Red Tig Le (T.T.: Thig.Le.dMar.Po.): the Essence of the female, or negative, force.

15 Dem Chog Luyipa (T.T.: bDe.mChog.Lu.Yi.Pa.): a form of the Tantric deity Samvara.

16 The Superb Dumo Instruction (T.T.: mChog.Ge.gTum.Mo.): This seems to be a special instruction imparted only to the most advanced yogis, not included in the over-all Dumo practice.

17 The Ever-Crying Bodhisattva (T.T.: rTag.Du.Ñu.): a Bodhisattva who longed for the teaching of Prajñāpāramitā but could not obtain it. In his long search for the teaching he traveled through many lands and underwent many trials. The repeated extraordinary distresses and disappointments that he encountered during his journey made him cry all the time. The full story is related in the Mahāprajñāparamitāsūtra.

18 The Holy Chupoa: T.T.: Chu.nPhags.

19 The Three Realms, or the Three Kingdoms (T.T.: Khams.gSums.), i.e., the Realms of Desire, of Form, and of Non-form, which include all realms in the cosmos. See Story 5, Note 21.

20 The Three Learnings: The Learnings of Precepts, of Dhyāna, and of Wisdom.

21 The Four Good Thoughts, or the Four Immeasurable Good Wills (T.T.: Tsad.Med.bShi.): They are (1) to wish that all sentient beings may gain happiness and cultivate the "seeds" of happiness, (2) to wish that all sentient beings may be separated from all sufferings and their causes, (3) to wish that all sentient beings may attain pure happiness — that which involves no sufferings of any kind, and (4) to wish that all sentient beings may be freed from gain and loss, desire and hatred, hope and fear, and may abide in the Realm of Equality.

22 Transcendental Samādhi, literally, Leakless Samādhi (T.T.: Zag.Med.Tiñ. hDsin.). "Zag.Pa.," though literally signifying "leak," here means desires or Klesas. "Zag.Med.," therefore, means the desire-free, or, transcendental Samādhi.

23 Red and White (T.T.: dKar.dMar.) here imply the positive and negative forces.

24 Body-of-Form (T.T.: gZugs.sKu.): This implies both the Nirmānakāya and the Sambhogakāya.

25 Seven Healing Buddhas: T.T.: sMan.bLa.mChed.bDun.

26 The Secret Word Doctrine (T.T.: gSuñ.sÑags.), or the teaching of Vajrayāna.

27 This is a rather important account of the sign of a yogi's mastery of Prāṇa, but unfortunately the text does not specifically mention the time when Gambopa first started the test. Here the text reads, " ... Nam.Phyed.Tsam.Na.Thal.Wa. Bun.Bun.hDug." "Nam.Phyed" usually means midnight; however, in this case it could possibly be interpreted as "a half day." Thus, it could mean that it took Gambopa half a day to disperse the ashes.

28 Ahrura (T.T.: A.Ru.Ra.): a universal medicine which supposedly can cure all illnesses, probably myrobalan. See Story 27.

THE CONVERSION
OF THE SCHOLAR, LODUN

Obeisance to all Gurus

WHEN the Jetsun Milarepa was staying in the Small Tamarisk Forest,[1] he was visited by a monk named Lodun Gedun, a follower
of Rechungpa and Sevan Repa, but formerly an associate of Monk
Dhar Lho, who once disputed with the Jetsun.[2] After making many
obeisances to Milarepa, he said, "Most precious Jetsun, when I first
saw you I admired you greatly and I witnessed how my friend [Dhar
Lho] died; yet, I could not then decide whether the Dharma that we
practiced was right or wrong. Nevertheless, when I left I greatly respected you. I now come to you for instruction. Pray be kind enough
to teach me."

The Jetsun replied, "The Dharma practice of a man who indulges
in diversions but not in remembering death, will be of little use, because he can neither reduce his wrongdoings nor increase his virtues.
Now listen to my song":

Our Lord Buddha preached the Dharma
To conquer worldly wishes,
Yet those conceited scholars
Are slaves to their desires.

The Buddha instituted priestly rules
So that the world could be renounced,
Yet those restrained and "virgin" monks
With the world are fully occupied.

Buddha praised the recluse's way of living
So that worldly ties should be renounced,

Yet many "hermits" of today
Are more attached to worldly ties.

If you forget that death will come, your Dharma
Practice means little and helps nothing.

"To my regret, I have always been like that," said Lodun. "From now on I shall ever remind myself of the coming of death. Now pray give me some instructions to practice." The Jetsun, thinking "I shall see whether he can really devote himself to meditation," replied, "Whoever has little desire for this life, can reach Buddhahood by practicing scholastic Buddhism, although it may take a longer time." He sang in elaboration:

I bow down to all Gurus.

Listen to me, Venerable Monk!
The basic Priestly Rules are the
Great pillars of the Buddhist Hall.
One should rect them straight,
Keeping them from leaning.

Study in logic and the Sūtras is
A precious cleanser of Buddhist teaching,
Removing the rust of wrong ideas.

The disciplines of the Three Learnings[3]
Are of Buddhism the friends;
They should not as foes be treated.

The logic and views of Mahāyāna
Conquer the disputes of fools,
Enlightening those in darkness.

But Lodun said, "Hitherto I have only practiced verbal Dharma. Pray grant me the quintessential Teachings." Thus, with great earnestness, he continued to petition the Jetsun.

Knowing that Lodun's time for initiation had come, Milarepa at first sat quietly and pretended to frown. Whereupon Lodun besought Rechungpa, Sevan Repa, and the other disciples to intercede for him. Milarepa, very pleased by their sincere petitions, finally gave his consent, saying, "The persuasion of two Repas is too strong for me to resist. Our venerable monk is also a gifted man capable of genuine practice." [Then, turning to Lodun Gedun, he continued], "Under these circumstances, I will give you the instructions, and I sincerely hope you will practice them diligently! If one only knows but does not practice the Dharma, the results will be like this": Whereupon he sang,

I pay homage to all Gurus!

Both you, the priest, and you yogis, have pled
    with me.
The peititioner is our venerable monk,
A learned man, renowned in three valleys.
He asks for instructions to enter the Path;
Of good will are he and his assistants.

I am the Yogi Milarepa,
Beloved son of Buddha Marpa.
I speak not from hearsay, nor with pomp,
My words are sensible and from the heart,
They will stand criticism and analysis.
So with care listen to what this old man says:

He who practices not the Dharma with devotion,
Can at most become a sky-going Preta.[4]
These sky-going creatures are
Well-versed in rhetoric and logic.
Knowing much of Tantra, they possess
Magic powers and work wonders.
Living in comfort, they enjoy all pleasures.
But since they do not truly practice Dharma
Nor take heed of their minor faults,
They can never free themselves
From worldly desires and self-conceit.
Thus the Compassion-Voidness will ne'er arise
    in them,
Nor will the buds of pain within them wither.
In Samsāra's sea they will forever flounder.

Much knowledge, sharp intelligence, and mighty magic —
These powers are like fire and wood, scorching one's mind.
One can be sure that unhappiness
Will result from his own sinful deeds. Practice
Of the Dharma is the unmistaken way.

The Death-reviving Drug[5] is a life-saver,
But 'tis useless of not taken.
If a sick man wants to be cured
He should take the right medicine.

The heavenly nectar of long life
Is at hand for the Asuras. If they fail
To drink it, they suffer from untimely death.
What good can the elixir do them?
To protect yourself from untimely death, pour
The nectar in your mouth and drink it.

In Yama's treasury much food
Is stored of a hundred flavors.
But many Yamas fail to eat it,
And from starvation die.
What does this food benefit them?
He who would relieve his hunger should
Put the food in his mouth and eat it.

With great faith Lodun said, "Each word of yours impresses me with deep conviction. Your preaching is indeed most profound. Now please be kind enough to instruct me in the essence of the Six Pāramitās." In response, the Jetsun sang:

I am not well-versed in words,
Being no scholar-preacher,
Yet this petitioner is sincere and good.

The Six Pāramitās contain all Buddhist teachings.
To those who practice Dharma,
Wealth is but a cause of diversion.
He who gives his all away,
Will be born a prince of Heaven.
Noble is it charity to practice!

Moral Discipline is a ladder to Liberation
Which neither monks or laymen can discard.
All Buddhist followers should practice it.

Buddhist Patience, by Drang Sung[6] exemplified,
Is the virtue which the Buddha cherished most.
It is a garment difficult to wear,

Yet all merits grow when it is worn.

Diligence is the short path to freedom
And a necessity for Dharma practice.
Without it nothing can be done.
Ride then the horse of diligence.

These four Dharmas bring merit to men,
Being indispensible for all.
Now I will speak of Wisdom.

Meditation is a teaching between these two,
As it applies to both Wisdom and Merit practice.
By it all distractions are overcome,
For all Buddhist practice it is most important.

Wisdom-Pāramitā is the teaching of Final Truth,
The dearest treasure of all Buddhas.
Enjoy it then without exhaustion;
It is the wish-fulfilling gem of Heaven,
Fulfilling the hopes of all sentient beings.
To those who can renounce activities,
Wisdom-Pāramitā will bring final rest.
This Provision of Wisdom is most precious;
By it one will reach perfection step by step.

This is my reply, Venerable Monk.
Remember and practice it with joy!

Having heard this song, many of the disciples gained great progress. The Jetsun then said to Rechungpa and Sevan Repa, "Prepare the offerings; I am going to initiate our venerable monk." The Initiation and Pith-Instructions were thus given to Lodun.

After meditating for some time, Lodun had many Experiences. One day he came to Milarepa while a number of disciples were also assembled there, and said, "[During my meditations] too many wandering thoughts and wild visions came to me. No matter how hard I tried, I could not keep my mind quiet and restful. I do not know whether this is good or bad; if it is bad, please teach me how to overcome it; if it is good, please show me the way to further it."

"He has really been practicing hard," thought Milarepa, who then remarked, "You may have had many wandering thoughts and wild visions, but [in essence] they are all one. It matters not whether they are good or bad. What you should do is to concentrate your effort on practicing the *View*. Now hearken":

Obeisance to all Gurus!

Listen to me, Lodun and you others.
Know you what mind-projection is?
It creates and manifests all things.
Those who do not understand,
Ever wander in Saṃsāra.
To those who realize, all appears as the Dharmakāya.
They need search no more for another View.

Know you, Venerable Monk,
How to set your mind at rest?
The secret lies in letting go —
Making no effort and doing nothing,
Letting the mind rest in comfort
Like a child asleep at ease,
Or like the calm ocean without waves . . . .
Rest, then, in Illumination
Like a bright and brilliant lamp.

You should rest your mind in peace,
Corpse-like without pride.
Rest your mind in steadfastness;
Like a mountain, do not waver.
For the Mind-Essence is
Free from all false assertions.

Know you, Venerable Monk,
How all thoughts arise?
Like dreams without substance,
Like the vast rimless firmament,
The moon reflected in water,
The rainbow of illusion — like all these they arise.
Never consciously deny them,
For when the light of Wisdom shines
They disappear without a trace
Like darkness in the sun.

Know you, Venerable Monk,
How to cope with wavering thoughts?

Versatile are flying clouds,
Yet from the sky they're not apart.
Mighty are the ocean's waves,
Yet they are not separate from the sea.
Heavy and thick are banks of fog,
Yet from the air they're not apart.
Frantic runs the mind in voidness,
Yet from the Void it never separates.
He who can "weigh" Awareness
Will understand the teaching
Of Mind-Riding-on-the-Breath.[7]
He who sees wandering
Thoughts sneaking in like thieves,
Will understand the instruction
Of watching these intruding thoughts.
He who experiences his mind wandering *outside*,
Will realize the allegory
Of the Pigeon and the Boat at Sea.[8]

Know you, Venerable Monk, how to act?
Like a daring lion, a drunken elephant,
A clear mirror, and an immaculate
Lotus springing from the mud, thus should you act.

Know you, Venerable Monk,
How to achieve the Accomplishments?
The Dharmakāya is achieved through Non-discrimination,
The Sambhogakāya through Blissfulness,
The Nirmanakāya through Illumination,
The Svābhāvikakāya[9] through Innateness.
I am he who has attained all these four Kāyas,
Yet there is no flux or change in the Dharmadhātu.

The View, Practice, Experience,
Remedy, Act, and Accomplishment,
Are the six essential things
A yogi faces in his devotion;
Learn and apply them in your practice!

Following his Guru's instructions, Lodun continued to meditate with
great diligence and perseverence. As a result, he gained superb Experiences, which he presented to the Jetsun in this song:

I pay homage to all Father Gurus!

Beyond creation and extinction
Is this illuminating Self-mind!
Riding on the moving Prāṇas it runs
In all directions to all places.
Since the mighty animation of the mind
Is in itself beyond all knowing,
Everything that I desire is found
In the mind-treasury within.

Devoid of form and color,
Excelling the sense realms,
Is this wondrous mind
Out-reaching words and phrases.

By practicing the profound Instruction,
Heat and bliss spring forth without;
As a result, deep understanding grows within;
Then one is forever freed from all adulteration.

Accomplishment can never be attained
When off the Path of Skillfulness;
Wondrous are these instructions
Of the Whispered Lineage.
By following this profound Path of Skill,
Realization have I, the Yogi, gained.
These wondrous teachings are good indeed to practice!

Milarepa advised Lodun: "Venerable Monk, do not fasten your mind to any 'ground,' do not close it to any contact, do not fall into bigotry or extremes. Your mind is something that can never be described, explained, or designated, yet you may call it anything you like, when you have fully realized this truth."

Lodun then continued to meditate in the mountains and gained [further] Realization. By study he cleared away all outer doubts, and through actual practice he wiped out all inner misconceptions until, a yogi monk, he became the snow-lion-like intimate son of Milarepa.

This is the story of the monk, Lodun.

NOTES

1 The Small Tamarisk Forest (T.T.: Hom.Chuñ.dPal.Gyi.Nags.): literally, the Small Tamarisk Meritorious Forest.

2 See Story 34.

3 The Three Learnings (T.T.: Slobs.gSum.): The Learnings of Precepts, of Meditation, and of Wisdom, are the three main topics of Buddhist studies.

4 Sky-going Preta: Here, the word "Preta," (T.T.: Yi.Dags.), does not imply the Preta or Hungry Ghost generally known as a denizen of one of the three lower miserable Realms. It is used here in a very loose sense to denote certain sky-going spirits.

5 Death-reviving Drug (T.T.: Çi.Sos.sMan.Gyi.bDud.rTsi.): literally, the Death-reviving Drug Nectar.

6 T.T.: Drañ.Sroñ.; Skt.: ṛṣi: This refers to the story of Kṣāntyṛṣi who patiently endured insult and injury, i.e., Sākyamuni in a former life suffering mutilation to convert Kalirāja.

7 The teaching of Mind-Riding-on-the-Breath: According to the central teaching of Tantrism, namely, the theory of the Identicalness-of-Mind-and-Prāṇa (T.T.: Rluñ.Sems.dWyer.Med.), mind cannot function without relying on, or "riding upon" the breath or Prāṇas. It is the Prāṇa that makes the mind move. See the translator's Foreword to "Tibetan Yoga and Secret Doctrines," W. Y. Evans-Wentz, Ed., 2nd ed., Oxford University Press, London, 1958.

8 Flying off from a boat in the sea, a pigeon cannot fly very far before it is forced to return to the boat because no landing-place is in sight. This metaphor alludes to the fact that wandering thoughts, no matter how wild and uncontrollable they are, will eventually return to the Mind-Essence, as there is nowhere else to go.

9 The Svābhāvikakāya, known as the "Fourth Body" of Buddha. Actually it is the unification aspect of the Trikāya.

SONG OF THE
EIGHT WONDROUS JOYS

Obeisance to all Gurus

WHEN the Jetsun Milarepa was staying at the Red Rock Height of Drin, a monk of the Dre Tribe, who had never seen the Jetsun before but was greatly impressed by his fame, came in great faith to visit him. Reaching Milarepa's abode, he saw only a cooking pot in the cave and thought, "There is nothing here — not a single page of Buddhist scripture, not a Buddha-image, not even a small symbol of the Dharma, let alone the necessary supplies for amusement and livelihood! [Since there is no holy symbol] such as a Sūtra or image of Buddha on which he can put his whole reliance,[1] I wonder what will happen to him when he dies?"

The Jetsun knew his thought at once and said, "Venerable Monk, you need not worry about that. I do have my Holy Scriptures, images, and reliance on the Dharma. I shall have no regret, but shall rejoice when I die. Now listen to my song":

> I bow down to all Father Gurus!
>
> My body is the Holy Maṇḍala itself,
> Wherein reside the Buddhas of all Times.
> With their blessings I am freed
> From all needs and attachments.
> By day and night I offer to them;
> Happy am I to do without material things.
>
> Knowing that all beings in the Six Lokas
> Are latent Buddhas, and all Three Realms
> The Self-creating Beyond-measure Palace,

Whate'er I do is a play of Dharmadhātu;
Whoe'er I am with is the Patron Deity;
Where'er I stay is the Buddha's abode.
With my great wisdom I clearly see them all.
Happy am I to forego outside help and symbols!

On the "paper" of the Red and White
Forces I use the "ink" of Wisdom,
Writing the words of the Five Senses.
All forms then becomes the Dharmakāya.
Happy am I without those foolish books.

All sentient beings in Saṃsāra
Have "Thatness," but realize it not.
Applying the Profound Instructions, I absorb myself
In the Samādhi of the Three-in-One Trikāya.

Oh, whenever death may come
I shall feel nought but joy!

The monk thought, "It is indeed correct that he has telepathic power; this also proves that the other claims concerning him must be true." His faith irrevocably confirmed, he besought Milarepa with great earnestness to accept him as a disciple.

Recognizing that this monk was well-endowed, Milarepa gave him the Initiation and verbal instructions, and then sent him to meditate. [After a time] he gained excellent experience of blissfulness. One day he came to the Jetsun while many disciples were also gathered there and said, "In the past I had no experience of joy within, therefore my craving for wealth and material things was very great. But you, the Jetsun who has no attachments whatever, have a great joy within you all the time. From now on I shall follow your way, meditating for the rest of my life in a hermitage so that I may always be joyful too."

Milarepa was exceedingly pleased. He replied, "This is very true. He who keeps to the hermitage will always be happy and can eventually become a good guide [on the Path of Dharma]." Whereupon Milarepa sang of "The Eight Wondrous Joys":

I bow down to you, the King of Kings,
The Buddha's wish-fulfilling Nirmāṇakāya,
The glowing torch that dispels the darkness
    of ignorance,

To you, Translator Marpa, I pay sincerest homage.

The sky keep of Red Rock Heights
Is where Ḍākinīs meet,
A place of delight that brings
Much inspiration to me.
Oh wise and persevering disciples,
Pay attention to the song
This old man sings in joy.

In this quiet hermitage
Where no sectaries are found
Resides a guide ever in Samādhi.
He knows the Path, a happy man
Realizing his own body as the Holy Temple.
Oh, how marvelous it is to know
That Mind-nature like the sky is pure!

A firm and steady faith is the guide
That can lead you from Saṃsāra.
Is there one here who has this guide?
Oh, happy it is to see that both
Saṃsāra and Nirvāṇa are self-liberating;
Oh, marvelous it is to realize
That the Four Bodies of Buddha
Ever exist in one's own mind.

The [non-clinging] contact with objects
By the Six Senses, is the guide
That turns all hindrance into help.
Is there one here who has this guide?
Happy it is to reach the shore of No-desire,
And wondrous to be freed from all duality.

An upright Guru with a [genuine] Transmission is
The guide who clears away your doubts and ignorance.
Is there one here who has this guide?
Oh, happy it is to be the man
Who serves his Guru as a Buddha.
'Tis wondrous to behold the Self-face of the mind!

This cotton clothing is the guide
That protects me in snow mountains

From both cold and heat.
Is there one here who has this guide?
Oh, wonderful it is to lie naked in the
      mountain snow,
Happy it is to fear neither heat nor cold!

The instruction of Identifying,
Transforming, and Uniting[2] is the guide
That can crush all fears of Bardo.
Is there one here who has this guide?
Oh, marvelous it is to reach the home of Reality,
Happy it is to be a man with nor life nor death.

The Skillful Path of the Whispered Lineage
      is the guide
That can distinguish the pure and the adulterated
      mind.
Is there one here who has this guide?
Oh, marvelous it is to feel the Life-Prāṇa
Coursing through the Central Channel!
Happy it is to have a mind and body
Always at ease and in Bliss!

The yogi who practices Voidness and Compassion
Is the guide who cuts off jargon and playwords.
Is there one here who has this guide?
Oh, happy it is to be surrounded by enlightened
      beings
And marvelous to win disciples through transformations!

This is the Song of the Eight Joys,
Sung for you with delight by this old man.
To clear the minds of my disciples,
I chant these words with cheer; forget
Them not, but hold them in your hearts!

Hearing this song, Dre Dun and the other disciples were all greatly
cheered and inspired. Drc Dun then said to the Jetsun, "All you have
said is most marvelous. Now please grant me an instruction on the
View, Practice, Action, and Accomplishment that is easy to understand, to practice, and to 'carry.' "
In reply Milarepa sang:

I pay homage to all Father Gurus.

When you deepen the View through thought profound,
Be not misled by verbal knowledge.

Before you have realized Awareness in itself,
Chatter not about the View of Voidness!

All that which manifests
Is unreal as an echo,
Yet it never fails to produce
An effect that corresponds.
Karmas and virtues therefore
Should never be neglected.

Revile not others with
Your bigotry and egotism,
Cling not to self-fixed ideas without
An understanding of the Supreme Truth.
First, fully realize Self-nature
And root up all errors from within!

Before the great Illumination
Shines forth in your mind, cling not
To sweet ecstasy and Voidness.
Though all things are Void-manifesting,
Never wallow in pleasures, nor expect
Your troubles to vanish without effort.

Things in themselves are void,
So never cling to Voidness
Lest you stray in formalism.

When, in the tide of mundane bliss
One's crude, wandering thoughts subside,
An ecstasy will then arise. But he
Who is attached to it, will go astray.

Before Realization shines forth within,
Or one can bless all objects and appearances,
Before all five sense-experiences turn into
    great bliss,
Or all delusory thoughts come to an end,

Engage not in anomalous acts at will,
Lest you go astray in practicing the Equal Acts.[8]

In bringing into being the last Accomplishment,
One should not seek Buddhahood elsewhere.
Before the essence of Self-mind is clearly seen
Beware of falling into hopes and fears.

Should you disciples think your body to be Buddha's,
Never deem it to be the real Nirmāṇakāya.
Should your wavering thoughts vanish in the Dharmakāya,
Never think of them as real entities
Now extinguished into nought.

The great Merits, Acts, and Pure Lands
Are natural manifestations of pure Wisdom;
Never should one regard them
As real things in the outer world.

Having heard this song, Dre Dun gained a decisive understanding.
For a long time he meditated in a hermitage and eventually gained
superior Experiences and merits. He was then known as Dre Dun Drashi
Bar, and became one of the intimate sons of the Jetsun among the
ranks of those senior Repas, such as Dungom Repa.

This is the story of Dre Dun.

NOTES

1 Reliance (T.T.: rTan.): any Dharmic Symbol upon which one puts his
trust. This can be a Sūtra, a Buddha-image, or the relics of a Buddhist saint.

2 This refers to the teaching of identifying all manifestations as Māyā, transforming all manifestations into pure forms, and uniting all manifestations with
the Dharmakāya. If one can do this, he will be able to overcome all fears in the
Bardo.

3 Equal Acts (T.T.: sPyod.Pa.Ro.sÑoms.): In the advanced stage, Tantric
yogis practice many anomalous actions in order to eradicate all their conventional
thoughts and habits, thus equalizing all their antithetical and dualistic ideas.

MILAREPA CONVERTS
THE UNBELIEVERS
THROUGH MIRACLES

Obeisance to all Gurus

ONE DAY Jetsun Milarepa made up his mind to visit a temple where the monks were extremely hostile to him, accusing him of being a nihilistic heretic. All his disciples implored him not to go, but he paid no heed. As he was approaching the gate of the congregation hall, all the monks saw him coming. They rushed at him, beat him savagely, dragged him into the hall, and tied him to a pillar. But after awhile Milarepa appeared again outside the temple! The monks gathered round once more, beating him severely, dragging him into the temple again, and smiting and chastising him in every manner possible. But strangely enough, no matter how fiercely they struck him or how forcefully they tugged and pulled at him, Milarepa remained still as an image, and they could not move him an inch.

More monks were then called, and every way of shifting him was tried, but in vain. Finally they bound his body with ropes — attempting to drag it from before and push it from behind. Yet it stood firm like a great, heavy rock. The monks, thoroughly exhausted by all this, gave up in bewilderment and frustration.

Some of them began to implore Milarepa to go away, while others asked him, "When we detained you inside the temple you suddenly appeared outside; when we tried to force you out, you stubbornly remained within. How could this happen?" Milarepa replied, "I am a nihilistic heretic, so if I am killed, I keep nothing; if I am beaten, I suffer nothing. When I was detained in the temple or chased out of it, I still retained nothing. Since I have annihilated clinging to both Saṃsāra and Nirvāṇa, I can, of course, do all these things!"

The elders among the monks then said, "Because of our ignorance we failed to recognize you as an accomplished yogi. Please forgive our misconduct, and leave us." The Jetsun replied, "I do not know whether or not I am an accomplished yogi. Nor do I know where such a yogi may be found, or what he would do now. But you monks should not be so proud of yourselves and wrong others to such an extent. You should know that to revile and wrong the innocent is even worse than to commit the Ten Vices, while to indulge in self-conceit is the very sign of ego-clinging and the cause of falling into Saṃsāra."

"We are fully convinced that you are an accomplished being," replied the monks. "Please tell us why you came here today and spoke as you did."

In answer, Milarepa sang:

> Like the transparent, crystal mind of Bardo,
> Nothing can wreck or hinder me,
> Catch me, or release me.
>
> Striking like a shooting star,
> I, Milarepa, have today worked wonders
> To convert all unbelievers.
> I shall work no more miracles,
> For I am sure that all impieties
> And misconceptions are destroyed.

Some monks then asked, "This is indeed wonderful, but why do you say that you will not work any more miracles?"

"There are only three occasions when miracles should be performed," replied the Jetsun, and sang:

> To convert the impious, to better
> Meditation Experiences, and to
> Identify the Three Accomplishments
> Should miracles and wonders be performed.
> At other times they should be concealed.
> This was what my Jetsun Guru decreed.

A monk said, "With such a [profound] understanding of the Manifestation-Void, one can surely study the Buddhist teachings with ease and delight." Milarepa replied, "When I studied these teachings, I never held my head high. Well, I may have studied much, but now I have forgotten it all! I think it is perfectly right for me to have done so. Now listen":

Forgetfulness of kinsmen comes
To him who realizes Equality.
Fitting is it then for him
To forget desires and attachment.

Forgetfulness of this and that will come
To him who realizes Wisdom beyond thought.
Fitting is it then for him
To neglect all pains and joys.

Forgetfulness of meditation practice comes
To him who realizes non-thought and non-consciousness.
Fitting is it then for him
To disregard all gain and loss.

Forgetfulness of the Gods of Arising Yoga[1] comes
To him who realizes the self-nature of Trikāya.
Fitting is it then for him
To ignore all conceptual teachings.

Forgetfulness of striving for accomplishment comes
To him who realizes the Fruit inherited within.
Fitting is it then for him
To forget all lesser dharmas.[2]

Forgetfulness of all words and talk comes
To him who practices the instructions of the
       Whispered Lineage.
Fitting is it then for him
To forget prideful studies.

Forgetfulness of black-printed books comes
       of itself
To him who realizes that all things are holy
       scriptures.
Fitting is it then for him
To forget Buddhist books.

Another monk then said, "Before one reaches Buddhahood, one is expected to encounter many hindrances, deviations, and doubts. It is not advisable then to forget the [regular] Buddhist teachings!" In reply Milarepa sang:

He who understands that all confusions
Are mind-made and is convinced about
Non-being, will stop making efforts,
Happily enjoying Truth immutable.

He who realizes Ultimate Reality,
Discriminates no more between the dharmas;
In joy he then experiences
The overthrow of ignorance!

When one realizes the truth of Non-extinction,
Hope and fear will in his mind arise no more;
In joy he then experiences
The departure of confusion!

Through ignorance one wanders in Saṃsāra,
But through the Pith-Instructions of an accomplished
        Guru
One can be freed from attachment and desires.
This is the supreme glory of the Saṅgha!

Philosophies are made by mind
And speculative words mean little,
For of no use are they
In conquering the passions.
Try to subdue your self-conceit,
My dear priests and scholars.

In Enlightenment one sees that the essence
Of perceiving and confusing is the same.
Oh followers of Dharma,
Abandon not Saṃsāra,
But rest your mind
Effortless, at ease.
Then with the vast Void you will
Identify yourself.
This is the teaching of all Buddhas!

Thereupon all the monks were filled with new faith toward Milarepa, and ceased cherishing impious and pernicious thoughts about
him.

Among the priests, there was a distinguished monk called Ligor

Sharu whom Milarepa accepted as a servant-disciple and initiated with the Pith-Instructions. After meditating for some time, Ligor Sharu gained good Experiences. Then he thought, "If the Jetsun, with such great power and blessing, could adapt himself slightly to people and conventions, many more outstanding scholars in Weu and Tsang [Central and Western Tibet] would come to him. As his fame and prestige increased he would be able to benefit more people and to serve the Dharma on a greater scale." So thinking, he came to Milarepa and told him of his ideas. But the Jetsun replied, "I will only act in accordance with my Guru's injunctions; other than that, I will do nothing in this life. Those who take heed of worldly affairs may do what they like, but I am not interested in their plans. Now listen":

I bow down to Marpa, the Translator.

Realizing that fame is unreal as an echo,
I abandon not the ascetic way of life,
Throwing away all cares and preparations.
Whatever reputation I may have,
I shall always be happy and contented.

Realizing that all things are illusion,
I cast away possessions;
For wealth obtained by strife
I have not the least desire!
Whatever my means and prestige,
I shall always be happy and contented.

Realizing that all followers are phantoms,
I have no concern for human relationship
And travel where I please —
Unlike those artificial scholar-priests
Who act with discretion and restraint.
Whatever the status I may have,
I shall always be happy and contented.

Realizing that desires and sufferings
Are themselves the great Equality,
I cut the rope of passion and of hatred.
With or without associates,
I shall always be happy and contented.

The nature of being is beyond playwords;

Attachment to any doctrine or concept
Is merely a matter of self-confusion.
Unshackling the fetter of the knower-and-the-known,
Whatever I become and wherever I remain,
I shall always be happy and contented.

In the great Illuminating Mind itself,
I see no pollution by wandering thoughts.
Throwing away all reasonings and observations,
Whatever words I hear or say,
I shall always be happy and contented.

Ligor Sharu, the monk-disciple, then said, "Dear Jetsun, for you, of course, this is quite enough. But I asked for the sake of benefiting inferior sentient beings and propagating the teaching of the Ghagyu-ba." Milarepa replied, "In the beginning I made a solemn vow to live in this way; I have done so up till now, and I will do so in the future. I am quite sure that by living thus I can benefit many sentient beings and serve the Dharma well."

"What vow did you make?" asked the monk. "This," replied Mila-repa, "and I hope that you, my disciples, will also make another like it." Whereupon he sang:

Because of my fear of Saṃsāra, and the grace of
          my Guru,
I vowed that I would never pursue things in
          the outer world
Before I had enjoyed the supreme taste of the
          Holy Dharma.

I vowed that I would never seek food for myself
Before I had carried out my Guru's injunctions.

I vowed that I would ne'er display the Tantric Acts
Before I had mastered fully the Skillful Path.

I vowed that I would never shoulder the Ghagyuba Doctrine
In defiance of Nāropa's admonishments.

I vowed I would never practice Dharma for
          self-benefit;
This was the oath I took when first I stirred
          the Bodhi-Mind.

I vowed that I would never try to spread Marpa's
     teachings
[In an artificial way], for He would act in
     secret
To spread the teaching throughout Tibet.

To please my Guru is to practice and meditate
     right now!
Other than this, I know of no way to please him!

Through the blessing of the Jetsun, Ligor Sharu changed his views
and, following the example of his Guru, also made the same vow.
With great determination he meditated continuously in the hermitage,
and as a result, he gained the extraordinary Merits of the Path and
Bhūmi.[3] Eventually he became one of the intimate sons of the Jetsun among the priest-yogi disciples, and was known as Ligor Sharuwa.

This is the story of Ligor Sharu.

*The foregoing [collection of] stories are those concerning Mila-
repa and his well-endowed disciples, those who became the Jetsun's
great intimate sons.*

NOTES

1 In the practice of Arising Yoga the yogi strives to remember and sustain
the vision of the Self-Buddha at all times. But since this is done with a conscious effort through the mundane mind, this Yoga practice is not of a transcendental
nature, being designed merely as a preparatory practice for higher Yogas.

2 Lit.: "To forget the mundane dharmas."

3 Bhūmi (T.T.: Sa.), literally means the earth, but this term is used in most
Mahāyāna scriptures to denote the advanced stages of the Path. Generally ten
major stages, or Bhūmis, are given. See Story 54, Note 2.

PART THREE
MISCELLANEOUS
STORIES

45

VARIOUS SHORT TALES

Obeisance to all Gurus

W HEN Jetsun Milarepa was living in the solitary place called Ku Ju, Rechungpa besought him for a teaching through which he could practice his devotion with body, mouth, and mind. In response Milarepa sang:

> To practice devotion with your body
> Is to observe the discipline of Non-distinction;
> To practice devotion with your mouth
> Is to keep it shut like the dumb buffalo;
> To practice devotion with your mind
> Is to see the nature of Non-existence.

Rechungpa asked again:

> Because of my ignorance,
> I still do not understand
> How to observe the discipline of body,
> How to control my mouth,
> And how observe Mind-Essence.

The Jetsun replied:

> To observe the discipline of body
> Is to keep the Rules of the Three Learnings,[1]
> To observe discipline with the mouth
> Is to keep it silent and at ease,
> To behold Mind-Essence is to observe
> It in a way that's free from clinging.

In expounding his Guru's instruction, Rechungpa sang:

In the innate-born Dharmakāya, free in itself,
Is the concept of the Sambhogakāya.
[Thus] can the Nirmāṇakāya serve innumerable beings.
The Foundation is the spirit of Renunciation,
The Path is the Bodhi-Mind and Bodhi-Acts,
The Fruit is the observance of Samaya rules.

Renounce the Eight Desires of the world,
Abandon all this life's affairs,
Forswear pleasures and wealth, abjure
Dishonesty and evil living.
Like a madman, pay no attention to your body;
Like a mute, keep your mouth shut at all times;
Like a child, free your mind without clinging;
These are the ways to practice one's devotion.

The Jetsun then commented, "But he who knows not the vital points is liable to err like this":

He who strives for Liberation with
The thought of "I" will ne'er attain it.
He who tries to loosen his mind-knots
When his spirit is neither great nor free,
Will but become more tense.
He who has no Realization
Wanders in the dark like a blind man.
He who cannot keep the discipline
Has no true spirit of renunciation.
Without a Bodhi-Mind,
Others one cannot help.
If there is no Tantra, there
Will be no Teachings that guide.
The Eight Dharmas are the temptations of this world.
Desires and passions cause one to destroy the
        virtues;
By cunning and clinging, in Saṃsāra one is confined.
If thoughts arise, so does the "dual." Words
By talking cannot be transcended.
A teaching without Lineage is broken. Failure
To observe the discipline brings Yama.
If you become entangled with relatives
And foes you fall into confusion.
With the thought of "being," comes

The idea of taking and rejecting.
From the conception of "existence,"
Follows clinging. Without
Genuine Enlightenment, one's
Mind is obsessed by wishful-thinking.
All talking will become sheer nonsense
If one cannot elucidate the Truth!

. . .   .

At another time, Jetsun Milarepa covered his head and face while sitting on his meditation seat. A junior Repa came to him and asked, "Father Jetsun, how is it that you appear to be falling asleep?" In answer, Milarepa sang:

When I cover my head and face
I can see places far away,
But worldly beings nothing see
With their eyes wide open.
When I sleep with my body naked
I carry out the Dharma.

The Eight Worldly Desires
Are causes of distraction.
All acts are completed
Within one's mind. How
Wonderful is this experience
Of unceasing ecstasy!

I, the Yogi who has completed his devotion,
Ever feel joyful in whate'er I do!

. . .   .

On another occasion, when Jetsun Milarepa was staying at Tsiba Gonti Tson, Rechungpa asked him, "If a yogi's power, Experiences, and Realization are great enough, must he also make a secret of his accomplishments, or may he demonstrate them if he wishes?" In response the Jetsun sang:

The lion on the snow mountain,
The tiger in the forest,
And the whale in the ocean —

These are the three leading animals.
If they could conceal themselves
It would be wonderful for them,
For they would then avoid their foes.
These are my three outer parables.
Now listen to the inner ones:

The physical body of the yogi,
The Skillful Path of Tantra,
And the Accomplishment through Devotion,
[These are three precious things].
If a yogi could conceal them
It would be wonderful for him,
For he would then meet fewer foes.
Alas, few yogis in Tibet
Can now conceal these things.
Therefore, few accomplished
Beings can here be found.

. . .   .

At another time, Shangon Repa came and told the Jetsun that he
had many doubts in his mind. The Jetsun answered him in detail, and
sang in conclusion:

Without realizing the truth of Many-Being-One,
Even though you meditate on the Great Light,
You practice but the View-of-Clinging.
Without realizing the unity of Bliss and Void,
Even though on the Void you meditate,
You practice only Nihilism.
If you cannot meditate
At any time and anywhere,
Your non-thought meditation is merely a delusion.
If you do not realize your plain-mind,[2]
Your practice on the Not-two
Cannot transcend effort and exertion.
If you do not realize self-mind as non-existent,
Your practice of Non-distinction
Cannot transcend strife and effort.
If a deep renunciation has
Not yet arisen in your heart,
Your actionless actions are

Still bound by hopes and fears.
Virtuous deeds turn into vices if
You know not [what is] beyond rejection and
    acceptance.
All you do will enmesh
You in the toils of Saṃsāra
If you know not [what is] beyond life and
    death.

. . .   .

Later, a serious drought occurred while the Jetsun Milarepa was staying at the Water Wood Crystal Cave[3] beside the River of Benevolence, known as the Neck of the Goddess of Long Life. Because of the scarcity of water some patrons of Drin quarreled, and fought one another over the water-rights. Finally, they all came to the Jetsun for arbitration. He said to them, "I know nothing about worldly affairs. The rain will come — you do not have to fight among yourselves." Rechungpa, however, still urged the Jetsun to reconcile them, to which Milarepa replied, "We yogis have nothing to do with worldly arbitration. Now hearken to my song":

You are the treasure of perfect virtues,
A source fulfilling all desires;
To you, the great Translator Marpa,
I bow down with deepest reverence.

The advisor, the mediator, and the go-between —
These three cause discord and pain.
He who wants to be free and neutral should remain
Silent like a mute and take no sides.

Properly, kinsmen, and one's native land —
These three imprison one in Saṃsāra's realms.
He who would cross the river of wretchedness
Should cut relentlessly attachment's chain.

Self-conceit, trickery, and pretense —
These three drag one down to lower Realms.
He who would reach a higher plane and the Path
    of Liberation,
Should keep his mind upright and straightforward.

Talking, discussion, and scholarship —
These three cause jealousy and pride.
He who would practice holy Dharma,
Should humble and modest be.

The kitchen, [household] work, and cares —
These three spoil a yogi's meditation.
He who would uphold his innate Wisdom,
Should strengthen his self-respect.

The Master, the disciple, and the learning —
These three burden and distract the mind.
He who would meditate in solitude,
Should avoid them all.

Sorcery, magic, and To Tse[4], these three
Doom a yogi to evil influence.
He who would consummate the Dharma practice,
Should remember the singing bird of Jolmo,[5]

I have now sung of the seven
Demerits against the Dharma
And their seven antidotes,
Acquired through my own experience.
With this merit I hope that soon
You will attain Buddhahood.

Then Milarepa prayed to the Precious Ones; whereupon heavy rain
fell, and all disputes were calmed. The son-disciples and monks there
assembled then besought a blessing from the Jetsun, asking him to
vouchsafe them the essential teaching of Mahāmudrā and of the Six
Yogas. He replied, "If you can practice without fail, I will teach you.
These are extremely important points which you should all bear in
mind":

Though, Father Guru, you appear
To have entered into Nirvāṇa,
In truth you dwell in the Pure Land of the
        Sambhogakāya,
Doing benevolent deeds for all
Sentient beings in the Three Realms.

To you, Translator Marpa, I pay
Sincerest veneration.

Dewashun, Shiwa Aui, Ngan Tson Dunba,
And my well-endowed disciples here assembled
Who are dear to me as my own sons,
Have asked me for instructions on meditation.
In reply I sing of the Ten Essentials.

It is important to know
That the rainbow Buddha-Body
Is void yet manifesting.

It is important to know
That devils and ghosts are non-existent;
Their magic forms are merely
Conjurations of one's mind.

It is important at all times to have
The greatest veneration
For the gracious Jetsun Guru.

It is important to know
That one should renounce
Endless worldly affairs.

It is important to work hard without distraction
For the warm and blissful Experiences
Of the Prāṇa and Nāḍī practices.

It is important to have a strong will to unite
The combining practice of Dream Yoga
And the Yoga of Illusory Body.

It is important to work on the Beyond-symbol
     meditation
For the naked, illuminating Essence.

It is important to note the Cutting-through
     instruction[6]
For the All-manifesting Voidness.

It is important to have pity and kindness

Toward unenlightened sentient beings.

It is important to have a free-from-fear-and-hope
    conviction
Of the non-arising Dharmakāya of Self-mind.

My dear sons, these are
The important things that you
Should bear in mind and practice.

All the disciples were greatly inspired. Rechungpa then besought
the Jetsun to elaborate on the teaching called "Pointing-out the Wisdom of the Four Blisses." This request was granted, and in conclusion Milarepa sang:

In a solitary place, like a forest,
The yogi should practice all Four Actions[7]
And balance the Four Inner Elements.
Thus, the Wisdom of Four Blisses
Will in his mind appear.

. . .   .

On another occasion Jetsun Milarepa went to Phuyagzha of Drin
for alms. A patron said to him, "Near the temple called Lhaze there
is a very delightful cave. If you would like to live there I will serve
you, but I do not know whether the local she-devil will be friendly
to you." Milarepa asked, "What sort of a cave is it, and who is this
devil?" The man replied, "The cave is very cozy and delightful but
the trouble is, that she-devil will just gulp down whoever stays there.
You may, if you think you can, stay in the cave and keep her company."
Milarepa then went to the cave and remained there. At midnight
a woman appeared and thundered in a threatening voice, "Who is
staying in my home?" Milarepa paid no attention, but remained in a
mood of compassion. The she-devil then cried, "Damnation! It looks
as if he intends to stay here for good!" So she called a great army
of demons to throw rocks and hailstones at the Jetsun and conjured
many fearful visions to frighten him. But they could not even scratch
his skin because he was in Samādhi. The demons then all cried, "We
want to have our place and our beds for sleeping. Whatever reason
may have brought you here, go away now, go back where you belong! If you do not go, we shall call many more armies to come here

to drink your blood and eat your flesh!" But with great compassion the Jetsun sang in reply:

Listen carefully, you demon army,
You malignant and vicious Hungry Ghosts,
Do you know that you are being
Punished by your own Karma,
That the greater the malignant thoughts
The greater the sufferings one undergoes?
Do you know that fortune
Will vanish with ill-will,
That the greater your greed,
The harder is your food to find?
You are by pressing hunger
Deprived of opportunities,
Through too great love of moving
You have lost your home and beds.
Because you try too hard
You cannot finish what you do.
Because of your evil Karma
You can hardly accomplish anything.
Because you talk too much,
Your foes you cannot conquer.
The malicious visions that you conjured
Are to me most welcome and amusing.
To your sordid, delusive sorcery
I, the Yogi, have much to say.
You should beseech me with compliments
If you would have back your home and beds.
If you have any argument to make
Consult together and present it.

This is the stumbling place of many yogis;
I now come here solely to discipline you!
This is where I and you foregather.
But I am the one whose wishes are fulfilled.
You ghosts assembled here,
Depart not, but remain
And call your friends to join you!

The she-devil, leader of the specters, then said to Milarepa, "Because you wear the armor of Void-Compassion, you cannot be harmed in any way that we have tried!" Saying this, she and all the demons prostrated themselves before the Jetsun, offering him their lives and hearts, together with a solemn pledge [to reform]. Milarepa then preached the truth of Karma and the law of virtue to them.

Upon the Jetsun's return, the patron asked him, "Was the she-demon subdued?" Milarepa replied, "Yes indeed; now please listen to my song":

> In the Lhaze Temple at Drin
> I sat with this phantom body,
> Crossed-legged, absorbed in Non-dual Dhyāna. Without
> Distraction I contemplated on the truth of
>   non-being,
> Converting the vicious she-devil to Bodhi.
> Renouncing malice, my disciple she became.
> From now on, whoever meditates
> Will meet no trouble there,
> Whoever stays there will progress.
>
> That place has become an auspicious Cave of
>   Goddesses;
> The hostess there is now a lay-Buddhist —
> One of my faithful followers,
> A helpful friend to all.
> Whoever stays there is assured
> Of health, long life, and Accomplishment.

Hearing this song, the patrons were all delighted. With sincere faith they served the Jetsun with great hospitality during his half-day sojourn there. A faithful shepherd [among them] besought Milarepa to give him some Buddhist teachings that would be helpful to his mind. Milarepa said, "It is easy for me to preach the Buddhist teachings, but it is difficult to find people who can really practice them."

> Though grief in the Ocean of Saṃsāra
> Is preached, and its renunciation urged,
> Few people are really convinced
> And renounce it with determination.
> Though knowing life will ever turn to death,
> Few feel uneasy or think that it will end.
> Though their life is blessed with good prospects,
> Few can practice abstention for a day.
> Though the bliss of Liberation is expounded
> And Saṃsāra's pains are stressed,

Few can really enter the Dharma Gate.
Though the profound Pith-Instructions
Of the Whispered Lineage are given without stint, few
Without fail can practice them.
Though the teaching of Mahāmudrā is expounded
And the Pointing-out demonstration exercised,
Few can really understand the Essence of Mind.
To the hermit's life and Guru's wish
One may always aspire, but few
Can put them into practice.
The profound Skillful Path of Nāropa
May be shown without concealment,
But those who can really follow it
Are very, very few. My dear lad,
You should follow in my footsteps
If in this life you want to do
Something that is worthwhile.

His faith toward Milarepa firmly established, the shepherd followed him as a servant and was initiated with the Pith-Instructions. After meditating for some time, he eventually became a yogi with good Realizations.

. . .　　. . .　　. . .

At another time, for the benefit of sentient beings, Jetsun Milarepa went out for alms. Coming to a village in the center of a plain, he saw many people enjoying themselves. Some were playing dice, chess, and different games, while others were throwing stones and shooting arrows, and some women were weaving wool. Milarepa approached them and asked for alms. A young girl said, "My dear Lama, have you any kinsmen — father, mother, brother, or sister? Have you a house or land?" The Jetsun replied, "Yes, I have them all, and mine are better than most."

"In that case, they will provide you with all things needed for devotion," replied the girl. "But tell me something about your kinsmen." In answer, Milarepa sang:

My home is the Perfection Paradise,
My farm good will for all,
My house the great Compassion,
And my father's lineage the Tathāgata.
My uncles are missionaries

Who spread the Dharma everywhere.
My forefathers are Tilopa and Nāropa,
My father is the King of Skills,
My mother, the Fair Lady of Wisdom;
My elder brother is pure discipline,
My younger brother, stern diligence,
My sister is firm faith, and I myself
Am the offspring of spontaneity.
My body's elements are Merits,
And I meditate on Reality.
My sole visitors are deities.
As for my planting, I plow
Nothing but the Dharmakāya.

All the players in the party swarmed round Milarepa while he was singing. The girl then said, "Dear Lama, what you have sung is very wonderful. Since you are very rich, I would like to invite you to stay here as my spiritual teacher, one in whom I can confide my trust during misfortune and place my hope for present and future happiness. I will provide you with all things needed for the service of the deities and their holy symbols. You look, indeed, like a man with great blessing powers."

Some young men then said, "Dear Yogi, our delightful games and the pleasant work of the girls are signs of our joy and happiness. Do the heavenly beings have the same pleasures? You seem to have a very good voice. Please sing a song of comment for us on these things." The Jetsun replied, "Your joys are not the same as those of the heavenly beings. I shall tell you the differences in my song":

In the houses of you evil persons, gods
And holy symbols are like the roots of sins.
The oil lamps that flame in your stingy hearts
Are like bonfires before greedy tax-men.
The owners of much livestock
Are like meat-eaters' teeth.
The parents of many children
Are like pieces of boiled meat
In the grasp of a hungry man.
The worn-out elders, the forsaken
Housecleaners, resembles lonesome flies
Scenting scum amidst the ruins.
The owner of a great fortune
Is like the demon guard, Gordag.[8]

The games of throwing stones and shooting arrows
Are like fierce battles between gods and Asuras.
The games of chess resemble
Sordid intrigues between kings.
Those who play at shooting dice and throwing water
Are like demons grasping sacrificial food.
The burdens and tangles of your business
Resemble cobwebs on the trees.
Your singing and your dancing
Are the foolish play of gnomes.
The spectators of your games
Are ignorant animals
Gazing attentively at mirages.
The commentators on your games
Are writhing snakes without a head.
Those who crave for games and diversions
Are like hungry ghosts, the Fragrance-eaters,
Greedily sniffing at their hunted food!

Hearing this song, the listeners all prostrated themselves before the Jetsun with faith and veneration. Then the young girl invited Milarepa into her house and served him hospitably. Later, she practiced the instructions received from him and was able to enter the Path at the time of her death.

· · ·   · · ·   · · ·

On another occasion, when Jetsun Milarepa went out [again] for alms, he reached the middle of a great plain and saw many people working on a house. He then lay down on the ground [near by as if nothing were going on there]. The hostess said to him, "My dear Yogi, you seem to be unoccupied — here are some tools, please use them to work for us a little and I will bring you some hot food." After a while she returned, and seeing that Milarepa was still lying there, said, "No wonder they say that some people deserve to be treated as good-for-nothing trash! You have plenty of time on your hands, yet you won't do *anything*, not even a little patching work. You are useless!" Saying which, she went off and left Milarepa alone.

Then Milarepa followed her into the house where the workers were having their dinner, and begged for some food. The hostess said, "One who does not work with his lazy body should not bother to eat with his lazy mouth." The Jetsun replied, "I did not help you to patch the walls because I was occupied on other business much more important than yours." The patrons then asked him what this important business was that had drawn away his attention. In answer, Milarepa sang:

> I bow down to all Gurus. Above all,
> I take refuge in the Gracious One!
>
> You see me as though I were doing nothing,
> But I see myself doing something all the time.
>
> On the plain of the uncreated Beyond-Extremes,
> I was building busily the Dhyāna Wall;
> I had no time to patch clay walls.
> On the Northern Plain[9] of Voidness,
> I was taming the wild goats of my desires;
> I had no time to plough my father's land.
> In the realm of Not-two and the Word-beyond,
> I was subduing the demon Ego;
> I had no time to fight with bitter foes.
> In the Palace of Beyond-measure —
> The Non-dual Mind-Essence —
> I was busily attending my affairs;
> I had no time to do household work.
> In the Buddha's Maṇḍala of my own body
> I was feeding my little child, "Awareness";
> I had no time to feed others and wipe their noses.
> In the courtyard of Great Bliss,
> I was gathering the Dharma wealth;
> I had no time to make money in this world.
> On the mountain of the immutable Dharmakāya,
> I was herding the steeds of Self-awareness;
> I had no time to tend other sheep and cattle.
> With the clay of my flesh and bones,
> I was building the Stūpa of Immanence;
> I had no time to make the Tsa Tsas.[10]
> On the triangular Heart Center,
> I was kindling the lamp of Illumination;
> I had no time to offer butter lamps[11] to deities.
> In the chapel of the Bliss-Void,
> I was offering Immortality
> To the Buddha of Dhyāna-Mind;
> I had no time to make material offerings.
> Upon paper of Immaculate Mind

I wrote the words of conquering desires;
I had no time to bother with worldly script.
In the Drinking-Skull of Sūnyatā
I was mixing the Three and Five Poisons;[12]
I had no time for priestly rules.
Filled with love and pity,
I was guarding all in the Six Realms;
I had no time to attend my kinsmen.
Before my Father Gurus,
I was brooding over their instructions;
I had no time for worldly actions.
In a quiet hermitage in the remote mountains,
I was practicing the Bodhi teachings;
I had no time to indulge in sleep.
With my triangular, shell-like mouth,
I was singing the song of Dharma;
I had no time for idle talk.

Hearing this song, all the attendants were converted. Then they asked, "Are you, by any chance, the Jetsun Milarepa?" "Yes," replied the Jetsun. "We are indeed fortunate!" they all cried. Whereupon they bowed down to him, circumambulated him many times, praised him, and served him with perfect offerings. The hostess also acknowledged her repentence.

A young man then said to Milarepa, "We would like to come to you for instructions; please tell us where your temple is and who provides your sustenance." In answer Milarepa sang:

I bow down to all Father Gurus.

My temple is an unnamed hermitage,
My patrons are men and women everywhere,
No one can tell where I go or stay.
In the caves where no man comes
I, the Yogi, am lost to view.
[When I travel] I carry
Only my Guru's instructions — lighter
Than feathers, I shoulder them with ease;
More handy than gold, I conceal them where I please;
Stronger than a solid castle,
In all perils they stand firm.
In the Three Winters I dwell happily in forests;

In the Three Summers I stay cheerfully on snow
    mountains;
In the Three Springs I live with pleasure in
    the marshes;
In the Three Autumns I wander joyfully for alms.
In the teaching of my Guru, my mind is always happy;
Singing songs of inspiration, my mouth is always happy;
Wearing cotton from Nepal, my body's always happy.
In delight I accomplish all and every thing —
To me there is but cheer and joy.

Milarepa accepted this young man as his servant, and later on he
become a yogi with good Realizations. Everyone in the assembly also
vowed to do a specific virtuous deed.

         . . .   .

[Yet again] the Jetsun Milarepa went out for alms and came to a
place where men and women were having a beer-drinking party. They
were all followers of the Dharma in either the Tantra or Sūtra schools.
Milarepa asked them for food, but was derided and ridiculed, especially
by those who sat in the upper row. The leader of the group then said,
"Dear Yogi, where did you come from and where are you going?"

"I am just a person who never mingles with the crowd, but spends
his life in no-men's mountains," replied the Jetsun.

"You talk as if you were Milarepa; are you?"

"Yes, but since I know nothing about the Eight Worldly Dharmas,
I never mingle with any Buddhist group."

"This may be very true," replied the leader, "But if you are really
he, you should be able to preach the Dharma through songs. As we all
know, the Jetsun Milarepa is a yogi who has completely opened the
Nāḍīs of the Throat Center, and is thus capable of preaching any Dharma without the slightest hesitation or difficulty. To inspire those attending this meeting, therefore, please now sing for us."

In response, Milarepa sang a song, "The Ocean of Saṃsāra":

The peerless Guru always sits upon my head.

Alas, is not Saṃsāra like the sea?
Drawing as much water as one pleases,
It remains the same without abating.
Are not the Three Precious Ones like Mount Sumeru,
That never can be shaken by anyone?

Is not Samaya like a feather
That's been shed and for which no one cares?
Are not the pure priestly rules
Like a leper's corpse abandoned
By the roadside, which none will touch?
Are not badgers' skins laid over seats
Full of thorns that prick the buttocks
Of eminent priests?
It is not true that many people think
It meaningless to keep the priestly rules?
Is it not true that many monks ignore their
      disciplines?

Are there Mongol bandits invading yogis' cells?
Why, then, do great yogis stay in towns and villages?
Are not people craving for rebirth and Bardo?
Why, then, do they cling so much to their disciples?
Are woolen clothes in the next life more expensive?
Why, then, do women make so much of them here?
Do people fear that Saṃsāra may be emptied?
Why, then, do priests and laymen hanker after
      children?
Are you reserving food and drink for your next life?
Why, then, do men and women not give to charity?
Is there any misery in Heaven above?
Why, then, do so few plan to go there?
Is there any joy below in Hell?
Why, then, do so many prepare to visit there?
Do you not know that all sufferings
And lower realms are the result of sins?
Surely you know that if you now practice virtue,
When death comes you will have peace of mind and
      no regrets.

By this time the whole party had become aware that the singer was the real Jetsun Milarepa. Imbued with deep faith and veneration, they served him with great hospitality. Milarepa then preached the Dharma for them. By practicing these teachings, some of the group were able to enter the Path at the time of their death. If these cases were all recounted, it would make many more stories.

. . .   .

In this story [which actually contains a number of tales], Milarepa answered various questions asked by his close disciples as well as by his general patrons, in different places and at different times. Therefore, it cannot be ascribed to any one specific group.

NOTES

1 Three Learnings: See Story 42, Note 3.

2 The plain-mind (T.T.: Thal.Ma.Çes.Pa.): This term, which one very often sees in the literature of Mahāmudrā, is surprisingly similar to, or rather identical with, the Zen phrase, "P'ing Ch'ang Hsin" (the plain, or ordinary mind) which is the natural, spontaneous, straightforward, and naked mind. A monk asked Zen Master Chao Chou, "What is Tao?" Chao Chou replied, "The ordinary mind is Tao." Reading the literature of Zen and Mahāmudrā one finds many similiar expressions, but this phrase, "the plain-mind," is perhaps the most outstanding one.

3 Water Wood Crystal Cave: T.T.: Çel.Phug.Chu.Çiñ.rDsoñ.

4 To Tse (T.T.: Tho.Tshe.): the magic of producing hail and storms.

5 The singing bird of Jolmo (T.T.: hJol.Mo.): This refers to a Tibetan legend, but as the source is not available to the translator at this time, he is unable to give it.

6 Cutting-through Instruction (T.T.: gShi.rTsa.Chod.Pahi.gDams.Ñag.): A more literal translation of this phrase would be: "The clear-cut instruction that clarifies the basis, or the core, of the issue."

7 The Four Actions: walking, sitting, standing, and lying.

8 Gordag (T.T.: dKor-bDag.): "The owner of property. It generally signifies the spirit of a demigod who is supposed to be the custodian of the images of all Buddhist deities, scriptures, symbols; in short, of all church and sacerdotal properties." (Quoted from Chandra Dass' "Tibetan-English Dictionary.")

9 Northern Plain (T.T.: Byañ.Thañ.): the vast, grassy land of Northern Tibet.

10 Tsa Tsa (T.T.: Tsha.Tsha.): a miniature Stūpa-shaped oblation, made out of clay in a specially designed mold. It is widely used in Tibet.

11 Butter is the only oil supply available for lamps in Tibet.

12 The Three Poisons are lust, hatred, and ignorance; the Five Poisons are lust, hatred, ignorance, pride, and jealousy.

46

THE PREACHING
ON MOUNT BONBO

Obeisance to all Gurus

W HEN the Jetsun Milarepa was dwelling in the Nirmāṇakāya Castle at Chu Bar, he cleared up the peerless Gambopa's doubts and misgivings concerning the Pith-Instructions. Then he proceeded toward the East, but heavy rain fell for many days and nights, and Milarepa's disciples were much wearied by it.

One day the sky began to clear, and the sun shone pleasantly warm upon the hills. Milarepa and his seven disciples went for a walk to refresh their bodies and minds. They all felt very comfortable and happy at such a beautiful day.

As they walked to the mountain peak of Bonbo, some of the Repas who were not familiar with the region saw the Snow Mountain of the Lady of Long Life, and asked the Jetsun, "What is the name of this snow mountain?" He replied, "It is called the 'Blue Heights of the Fair Goddess'." Whereupon he sang:

> To the neck of the Mountain of Blue Heights,
> To the peak of the rocky Bonbo Hill,
> Come we, eight visitors at leisure.

> Do you not feel happy, my dear sons?
> I, your father, feel wonderful today.
> Here in this joyful gathering of Master and
>   disciples,
> I, the old man, cheerfully sing this song
> Of joy and pleasure, that will bring
> Auspicious luck and fortune.

Come, Dewashun and Shiwa Aui!
Come and join me in the singing;
You other Repas sit and listen.
Know you which this mountain is?
This is the Mount of the Auspicious Goddess
        of Long Life.
The triangular, sharp-edged peak looming above
        its waist
Is like a dumpling on a shell;
Flowing round its neck are silver-netted streams.

The high crystal peak that mirrors the first
        beams
Of sunlight in the morning is the crown,
Beautified by white hanging clouds.

Clinging to the lower Mount
Is perpetual mist and fog;
All day long the drizzle gently falls,
While rainbows brightly shine.
Here autumn flowers bloom
In different colors,
And thrive potent herbs
In great varieties.
This is the paradise of cattle,
This homeland of animals!
This is the Snow Mountain
The gods talk most about,
This is where I often meditate.
In answer to you Repas' questions
I sing this song, describing
This mountain vividly.

The Repa disciples were all pleased by this song. With great interest
they asked, "How powerful is this goddess? Does she follow the holy
Dharma, or evil?" In reply, the Jetsun sang:

The Lady of Long Life,
The five good sisters,
Lead the Twelve Goddesses.
They are worldly Ḍākinīs
With power to conjure.
Hostesses of the River Drin,

They speak Tibetan and Nepalese;
They assist all Buddhists
And protect their worshippers.
In chief they execute my orders,
And help you, my son-disciples.
Through my efforts and theirs Tibet
Will be led to the virtuous path,
And great Accomplishments will follow
In our Ghagyu Lineage.

The Repas all said, "It is wonderful that these goddesses have been converted as your disciple-servants. Please tell us what Dharma you preached for them and how they have served you?" In answer Mila-repa sang:

Upon the neck of this Snow Mountain
I, Milarepa, once preached the Dharma
To the benevolent local deities.

I taught them how to distinguish good from evil,
I preached for them the Sūtra's Expedient Truth
Of the Law of Cause and Effect.
The savage beasts and Nāgas of
The Four Divisions came to listen.

The five revengeful Ḍākinīs were the hostesses
Who invited the preacher.
The five formidable sisters were the hostesses
Who attended on the guests.
Many noble visitors gathered round,
While Devas and ghosts enjoyed the feast.

All who were there, I guided to the Dharma
And converted them, not by great power
But by compassion and by love.
With skill I converted those formless ghosts
        and Devas,
With sincerity I preached to them the Dharma of
        peace.

I have no regrets for my past deeds.
Now I am old why should I be regretful?
When I die I shall have no fear, but only joy.

Dear Repas, who stay here to renounce the world,
You should practice with determination,
With a happy-to-die feeling when you meditate.

They again asked, "Between human beings and Asuras, which are
better endowed to practice the Dharma, and which serve sentient beings better?" The Jetsun replied, "Human beings are superior in practicing the Dharma, and more powerful in helping others than the
Asuras. But the Lady of Long Life is a semihuman goddess.[1] She
will devote herself with great power to serving my Doctrine. I have
resigned from public life and renounced the Eight Worldly Claims for
devotion. I have now forgotten many gods and deities and lost contact with them. Following my steps, you should also renounce the
Eight Worldly Desires and devote yourselves to undistracted meditation. Listen to my song":

My Guru's power of blessing
Descended from above,
Assuring me of freedom
From the bonds of Dualism.

As a vagabond I wandered in all lands
Until fate brought me to the Gracious One.
I renounced the world as he bade me,
Meditating without diversion.
All evils and misfortunes
Are now Paths for me.

In humbleness, I have practiced in solitude;
Near death, I have exerted myself in devotion.
I have been meditating all my life
Till this old age.
Bliss and warmness thus grow within me.

I am a yogi who disregards good fortune,
I am a yogi who abjures worldly happiness —
One who remembers the pains of lower Realms.
I am a yogi who never ingratiates his patrons —
One who clings to the hermitage for meditations.
By the blessing of my Guru
I was "blown to the top" by a wind of love.
Sitting near the edge, I arrived at the center;
Adhering to humbleness, I cam to nobility.

In departing from men, one meets Buddha;
In undergoing sufferings, one attains happiness;
By exerting oneself in devotion, compassion
    grows within.
By remaining in solitude, one acquires more
    followers and disciples;
By practicing the Ghagyuba teaching,
The transmission of the Dharma spreads afar.

With my gracious Guru Marpa
Sitting e'er upon my head,
Like an old tiger, without fear of death,
I am well advanced in age.
With good cheer I sing this happy song!
My Repa sons, fritter not your lives away,
But determined and persevering,
Strive on in your devotions!

Milarepa and his disciples remained there for half a day and performed an offering ritual with the provisions they had brought. Then some of the disciples expressed their intention to enter different hermitages, others to go for alms to various places, and yet others asked the Jetsun for permission to stay with him. On their behalf, Rechungpa [and Gambopa] asked him to give some admonishments for all. In response, Milarepa sang a song for Rechungpa and the other disciples called "The Six Essentials":

On behalf of all Repas here,
My son Gambopa, the learned scholar,
And son Rechungpa, the unswerving yogi,
Have asked me to sing to you.
If you are wise, you will now listen
To this old man's song.

A bird knows when and where
To spread and close its wings;
The true rich man is e'er content;
A good agnostic e'er plays safe.
These are my metaphors.

After this Holy Offering on the tenth day,
Some of you say they will visit different
    countries,

Some that they will stay in various hermitages,
Others that they will follow and stop with me.
But as for me, if a great yogi
Aspires to fame and profit,
He will soon be trapped by devils.

It is therefore wise, my sons,
To seek protection from your Father
And listen to advice and criticism.

Do not hear my song as a sweet melody,
But listen carefully to its instructions;
Forget them not, inscribe
Them deeply in your heart.

He who has mastered his Tig Le
And gained the Power of Attraction,
Without relying on a qualified Rig Ma,[2]
Should never practice Karma Mudrā.
It is as dangerous to do so
As to climb a steep, rugged mountain.

Unless with a great, flowing compassion
One practices the vivid Yidham Samādhi
For the sole purpose of furthering
The Dharma and the welfare of all men,
One should never use the malicious Mantra
Or practice the Cursing Yoga,
Lest by Karma he will be
Reborn a malignant ghost.

Even if one has mastered his Prāṇa-Mind,
Unless he can work miracles through his bodily
     power,
And transform himself into beasts and snakes
With full realization of Māyā and of Voidness,
He should never bring corpses from cemeteries,
Lest he provoke the hatred
Of flesh-eating Ḍākinīs.

Except to one's own Vajra Brothers
And to Gurus thrice qualified,[3]
One should ne'er reveal his meditational Experience —

Even to men who deeply understand the Dharma —
Nor to devotees of other Lineages
Of different Practices and Views,
Let he lose the Power of Blessing
From the Practice-Succession.

Give not the Instruction of the Whispered Lineage
To him whose talent you have not observed;
Give it not without permission from
Ḍākinīs, nor for the sake of wealth
Or expediency to those who ask,
Lest by sins and transgressions you be shadowed.

Before one has the power of crushing others'
    doubts
Or can convert fault-finding unbelievers,
One should not perform the profound Secret Festival,
Or demonstrate Tantric Acts in villages
And towns, lest one be slandered;
These should only be performed
In hermitages and in solitude.

This little song of Six Guides to Devotion
Is a precious gem for Dharma followers;
Bear them, my Son-disciples,
Deeply in your hearts.

These words were imprinted profoundly on the minds of the heart-son disciples. Those junior Repas who wanted to stay with the Jetsun then said to him, "We are now in an age of defilement. For the sake of inferior and slow-witted persons like us, please preach something appropriate to our needs." In response, Milarepa sang:

Hearken further, my Son-disciples!

At this time of defilement
That shadows the Dharma of Śākyamuni,
One should strive with perseverance,
And carve upon his mind-stone
The word, "Diligence."

When you feel sleepy during meditation, try

To pray hard with your awakened body, mouth,
    and mind.
When the fire-spark of Wisdom dims, try
To inflame it with the wind of mindfulness.
If you want to be freed from Saṃsāra's prison,
Practice hard without diversion.
If to Nirvāṇa you aspire,
Abandon then this world.
If from the depths of your heart
You want to practice Dharma,
Listen to my words and follow in my footsteps.
If you want to consummate the [Supreme]
    Accomplishment,
Never forget that death will come.
If hard and long you meditate, all Buddhas
In the past, the present, and the future
Will be well pleased. If you are ever
Straightforward and upright in the Dharma,
You will receive the grace of your Guru.
If without error you understand these words,
You can be sure that more happiness
And joy will come your way,
For such is my experience.

With gratitude and delight, the disciples made up their minds to
renounce all things of this life, and to strive for their devotions.

This is the story of Mount Bonbo.

NOTES

1 Semihuman goddess (T.T.: Mi.Ci.Rigs.Cig.): This is a free translation — a
literal translation of this term is difficult. It seems to imply a goddess who has a portion of human inheritance.

2 Rig Ma: well-gifted and qualified females who aspire to the Tantric
practice.

3 Lit.: "with three qualifications." Presumably the three capabilities of a
Guru: (1) giving proper instructions to the individual disciple, (2) guiding him
in his devotion, and (3) dispelling hindrances that he may encounter on the Path.

THE MIRACLE
OF THE VASE INITIATION

Obeisance to all Gurus

O NCE when the Jetsun Milarepa was staying at the Belly Cave of Nya Non, the Holy Vajra Ḍākinī revealed herself in person and explained to him the hidden meaning of some abstruse passages in certain Pith-Instructions in the Tantra of the Whispered Lineage of the Ḍākinīs.[1] Then she told him that this teaching could be imparted to a few well-endowed disciples.

[Before long] Milarepa gave Rechungpa, Ngan Dson Dunpa, and other heart-like son-disciples the Vase Initiation[2] of the Whispered Succession. [During the ceremony] Milarepa said to the vase, "I am now too old, please initiate them yourself." Thereupon, the vase flew up into the sky, and initiated all the disciples one by one.

During this, [they all] heard heavenly music in the sky and smelled a fragrance they had never smelled before; also, they beheld flowers falling down from the firmament, and many other wondrous, auspicious signs. All the disciples came to a full realization of the wise meanings of the Initiation.

Seeing that they were all amazed by these wonders, the Jetsun sang:

> In the immaculate Maṇḍala of the Whispered
>   Lineage,
> The oblation of Non-desire is made.
> During the precious Vase Initiation —
> A pointer to the Buddha's Wisdom —
> We heard [heavenly] music
> And saw deities in the Maṇḍala
> Receiving the celestial offerings.
> The vase flew up to give initiation,

549

And wondrous Wisdom rose within you all.
The reason for all this was through
The grace of the Ghagyu Gurus.

Milarepa then told the disciples that they should keep this teaching very secret for some time.

. . .   .

One day Rechungpa completed his painting of the Vajra Yoginī. Bringing it to the Jetsun, he asked him to sanctify it. Milarepa replied, "This old man does not know how to perform an elaborate ritual of sanctification. But I will try to pray the Wisdom-Sattva [the Divine Power][3] to descend and sanctify your picture of the Samaya-Sattva [the object to be sanctified]."[4] So saying, he threw a flower into the picture [as if bringing the true Wisdom-Sattva to dissolve in it]. Whereupon the picture shook and vibrated [as a sign of receiving the blessing power of the Wisdom-Sattva]. Meanwhile, the symbols of Buddha's Body, Word, and Mind — the brilliant light of rainbows — shone from the sky and entered and dissolved into the picture. Heavenly flowers also fell down like rain. Milarepa received them on his head, as if using a blessing-skull [in a Tantric initiation], and all the flowers then dissolved into his body and united with him. As the disciples stood wonder-struck, Milarepa sang:

The pictorial form of the Samaya-Sattva
Is blessed by the holy light of Body, Word,
      and Mind;
This is the embodiment of the Wisdom-Sattva,
The Body of the Real.
When the light [of Wisdom] enters the picture
And dissolves, it completes the blessing.

Though Mila is old and did not rise,
The Wisdom Ḍākinīs have brought divine
Flowers from the Land of Dharmakāya,
Which merged into the Patron Buddha's [picture].
When I performed this sanctifying rite
These wondrous flowers adorned my head and body;
Then the Patron Buddha entered and united with me.
You who have witnessed this great miracle
Are indeed well-gifted and well-destined.

Thus, Rechungpa and the other disciples all witnessed the fact that the Jetsun was no different from the Vajra Yoginī Herself.

This is the story of the [Vase] Initiation and of the sanctification of [Rechungpa's picture of the Vajra Yoginī].

NOTES

1 Whispered Lineage of the Dākinī (T.T.: mKhah.hGro.sÑan.brGyud.).

2 Vase Initiation (T.T.: Bum.dWañ.): This is the first initiation among the four Anuttara Tantra Initiations. The disciple is given the instruction of the Arising Yoga, which includes all Mantra and Maṇḍala practices.

3, 4 Wisdom-Sattva (T.T.: Ye.Çes. Sems.Pa.), and Samaya-Sattva (T.T.: Dam. Tshig.Sems.Pa.): In sanctifying an object or symbol, such as a Buddha's image, figure, or Stūpa, a consecration rite called Rab.gNas. is held. The sanctified object is called Dam.Tshig.Sems.Pa. or Dam.Tshig.Pa., and the divine consecrating power, embodied in a form identical with the object, is called Ye.Çes.Sems.Pa., or Ye. Çes.Pa.

THE STORY OF
SHINDORMO AND LESEBUM

Obeisance to all Gurus

SHINDORMO and Lese were a [married] couple who had had great
faith in the Jetsun from early days. At one time they invited him
to Tsar Ma. As soon as Shindormo saw him coming, she [went to
him] at once and held his hands, saying, "Now that we are growing
old and death is approaching, we are afraid, and sorry that we have
not been able to practice the Dharma with you." Saying this, she cried
mournfully for a long time. Milarepa said to her, "My dear patroness,
except for advanced Dharma practitioners, the pains of birth, decay,
illness, and death descend upon everyone. It is good to think about
and fear them, because this enables one to practice the Dharma when
death is approaching." Whereupon he sang:

> In the river of birth, decay, illness,
> And death we worldly beings are submerged;
> Who can escape these pains on earth?
> We drift on with the tide. Amidst
> Waves of misery and darkness
> We flow on and on. Seldom in
> Saṃsāra can one find joy.
>
> More miseries come by trying to avoid them;
> Through pursuing pleasures one's sins increase.
> To be free from pain, wrong
> Deeds should be shunned.
>
> When death draws near, the wise
> Always practice Dharma.

"I do not know how to observe the suffering of birth," said Shindormo, "Please instruct me how to meditate upon it." In answer, the Jetsun sang:

> My faithful patroness, I will
> Explain the suffering of birth.
>
> The wanderer in the Bardo plane
> Is the Alaya Consciousness.
> Driven by lust and hatred
> It enters a mother's womb.
>
> Therein it feels like a fish
> In a rock's crevice caught.
> Sleeping in blood and yellow fluid,
> It is pillowed in discharges;
> Crammed in filth, it suffers pain.
> A bad body from bad Karma's born.
>
> Though remembering past lives,
> It cannot say a single word.
> Now scorched by heat,
> Now frozen by the cold,
> In nine months it emerges
> From the womb in pain
> Excruciating, as if
> Pulled out gripped by pliers.
> When from the womb its head is squeezed, the pain
> Is like being thrown into a bramble pit.
> The tiny body on the mother's lap,
> Feels like a sparrow grappled by a hawk.
> When from the baby's tender body
> The blood and filth are being cleansed,
> The pain is like being flayed alive.
> When the umbilical cord is cut,
> It feels as though the spine were severed.
> When wrapped in the cradle it feels bound
> By chains, imprisoned in a dungeon.
>
> He who realizes not the truth of No-arising,
> Never can escape from the dread pangs of birth.
>
> There is no time to postpone devotion:

When one dies one's greatest need
Is the divine Dharma.
You should then exert yourself
To practice Buddha's teaching.

Shindormo asked again, "Please preach for us the sufferings of old age." In response, the Jetsun sang:

Listen, my good patrons, listen
To the sufferings of old age.

Painful is it to see one's body
Becoming frail and quite worn out.
Who can help but feel dismayed
At the threat of growing old?

When old age descends upon one,
His straight body becomes bent;
When he tries to step firmly,
He staggers against his will;
His black hairs turn white,
His clear eyes grow dim;
His head shakes with dizziness,
And his keen ears turn deaf;
His ruddy cheeks grow pale,
And his blood dries up.

His nose — the pillar of his face — sinks in;
His teeth — the essence of his bones — protrude.
Losing control of tongue, he stammers.
On the approach of death, his anguish and debts
    grow.
He gathers food and friends,
But he cannot keep them;
Trying not to suffer,
He only suffers more;
When he tells the truth to people,
Seldom is he believed;
The sons and nephews he has raised
And cherished, oft become his foes.
He gives away his savings,
But wins no gratitude.

Unless you realize the truth of Non-decay,
You will suffer misery in old age.
He who when old neglects the Dharma,
Should know that he is bound by Karma.
It is good to practice the Divine
Dharma while you still can breathe.

Shindormo then said, "What you have just told us is very true; I have experienced these things myself. Now please preach for us the sufferings of sickness." In reply, Milarepa sang:

Dear patrons, you who know grief and sorrow,
Listen to the miseries of sickness.

This frail body is subject e'er to sickness,
So that one suffers excruciating pain.
The illnesses of Prāna, mind, gall, and phlegm[1]
Constantly invade this frail human body,
Causing its blood and matter to be heated;
The organs are thus gripped by pain.
In a safe and easy bed
The sick man feels no comfort,
But turns and tosses, groaning in lament.
Through the Karma of [past] meanness,
Though with best of food you feed him,
He vomits all that he can take.
When you lay him in the cool,
He stills feels hot and burning;
When you wrap him in warm cloth,
He feels cold as though soaked in sleet.
Though friends and kinsmen gather round,
None can relieve or share his pains.
Though warlocks and physicians are proficient,
They cannot help cases caused by Ripening Karma.
He who has not realized the truth of No-illness,
Much suffering must undergo.

Since we know not when sicknesses will strike,
It is wise to practice Holy Dharma —
The sure conqueror of illness!

"I hope to practice [more] Dharma when death draws near," said

Shindormo, "Now please preach for me the suffering of death." In answer, Milarepa sang:

> Listen, my disheartened patroness:
> Like the pain of repaying compound debts,
> One must undergo the suffering of death.
> Yama's guards catch and carry one
> When the time of death arrives.
> The rich man cannot buy it off with money,
> With his sword the hero cannot conquer it,
> Nor can the clever woman outwit it by a trick.
> Even the learned scholar cannot
> Postpone it with his eloquence.
> Here, no coward like a fox can sneak away;
> Here, the unlucky cannot make appeal,
> Nor can a brave man here display his valor.
>
> When all the Nāḍīs converge in the body,
> One is crushed as if between two mountains —
> All vision and sensation become dim.
> When Bon priests and diviners become useless,
> The trusted physician yields to his despair.
> None can communicate with the dying man,
> Protecting guards and Devas vanish into nought.
> Though the breath has not completely stopped,
> One can all but smell the stale odor of dead flesh.
> Like a lump of coal in chilly ashes
> One approaches to the brink of death.
>
> When dying, some still count the dates and stars;
> Others cry and shout and groan;
> Some think of worldly goods;
> Some that their hard-earned wealth
> Will be enjoyed by others.
>
> However deep one's love or great one's sympathy,
> He can but depart and journey on alone.
> His good friend and consort
> Can only leave him there;
> In a bundle his beloved body
> Will be folded and carried off,
> Then thrown in water, burned in fire,
> Or simply cast off in a desolate land.

Faithful patrons, what in the end can we retain?
Must we sit idly by and let all things go?
When your breath stops tomorrow
No wealth on earth can help you.
Why, then, should one be mean?

Kind kinsmen circle round
The bed of the dying,
But none can help him for a moment.
Knowing that all must be left behind,
One realizes that all great love
And attachment must be futile.
When that final moment comes,
Only Holy Dharma helps.

You should strive, dear patroness,
For a readiness to die!
Be certain and ready; when the time
Comes, you will have no fear and no regret.

Whereupon, Shindormo besought the Jetsun for instructions. Practicing them [for some time, she gained such great progress that] at the time of her death she entered the initial stage of the Path.

. . .   .

About the same time [another patroness], Lesebum, invited Milarepa to stay with her. She said, "Although you, Jetsun Father and Sons, cannot stay with us long, remain at least for a few days." Upon this earnest request, Milarepa and his disciples stayed with her for seven days.

During this period, the people of Nya Non gathered in large numbers to make Tsa Tsa [miniature images of Buddha]. All the villagers helped with the work. Lesebum then asked Milarepa, "Would you, Jetsun Father and Sons, care to come to this meeting to enjoy yourselves?" "No," replied Milarepa, "I do not care to go." "Then," said Lesebum, "since this is a day-for-merit, I hope your Reverence will be kind enough to make offerings in my prayer room, and mold some Tsa Tsa for me. For the sake of sentient beings, please also look after my baby son, my sheep, and my household during my absence."

Well-dressed and adorned, she then went to the gathering. But Milarepa and his disciples let the time pass by and did nothing she had requested. As a consequence, the sheep trampled the field and ate up all the crops [and, worst of all,] when Lesebum entered the house on her return, her baby was crying at the top of his lungs. She thus became aware that the Jetsun had done nothing she had asked.

She then said, "It is understandable that you did not do the other things I asked you, but a Buddhist should have great compassion; is it not then a fault, and a great shame, that you disregarded the child and the sheep when they were in need?" In reply, the Jetsun sang:

On the pasture of the Great Bliss,
I was herding Immortal Sheep;
I had no time to watch
Those of blood and flesh.
I leave them, Lesebum, for you!

As a mother of Love and Great Compassion,
I was tending Illumination's child;
So I had no appetite
To tend the nose-wiping boy.
I leave him, Lesebum, to you!

On the firm mountain of No-change
I was making Tsa Tsa of Mindfulness;
I had no time to mold clay images.
I leave them, Lesebum, for you!

In the prayer-room of my upper body
I was lighting Illumination's lamp;
I could not erect the pole
For hanging prayer-flags.[2]
I leave that, Lesebum, to you!

In this shabby house of my phantom body,
I was cleansing the dirt of normal thoughts;
I had no time to clean your house.
I leave it, Lesebum, to you!

Among the many forms of life,
I was watching Māyā's play;
I could not wash the cups and dishes.
I leave them, Lesebum, for you!

Lesebum replied, "Oh Jetsun, please do not look down upon the good deeds that we worldly beings try our best to do. I have also served many other Lamas [besides you]." In answer, Milarepa sang:

To serve a Lama without compassion
Is like worshipping a one-eyed demon;
He and patron will misfortune meet.

Practicing the Dharma without Bodhi-Mind
Is the self-delusion of a fool;
It but intensifies desire and greed.

To give alms with partiality
Is like paying back a feast;
It will only fortify more hopes.

· To make offerings to the wrong person
Is like giving an imposter money;
It only brings more trouble and confusion.

To give charity without compassion
Is like tying oneself to a pillar
With a strong leather strap;
It only binds one tighter [in Saṃsāra's prison].

Bearing a high view without taming the mind,
Is like a swaggerer bragging about
Nonsense through a worn-out throat;
One only violates the virtues.

To meditate without knowing the way
Is like a juggler conjuring a magic
House. Its falsehood will soon be exposed.

To engage in various [Tantric] acts
Without a real sign of Karma, is like
A madman from a hot spring drinking;
The more he drinks, the thirstier he gets.

If, from wordly desires,
One has lead a solemn life,
It is like wrapping filth
In a pretty dress of silk —
Beautiful and grand without,
Within stinking and rotten.

"Accomplishment" that is joined
With desires and self-conceit,
Is like a doll of clay.
It will soon break in pieces
When tested by striking.

Hearing this song, Lesebum became very remorseful. Taking a fine jewel from among her ornaments she offered it to the Jetsun, and besought him for the Instructions. Milarepa then sang, "The Words of the Gem":

Hearken, my rich Lesebum
With sparkling intelligence!
When you turn back and look into your body,
Meditate without craving for pleasures.
When you turn back and look into your mouth,
Meditate in silence and in quiet.
When you turn back and look into your mind,
Meditate without wavering thoughts.
Keep body, mouth, and mind from distractions,
And try to practice *without* practicing.

Following these instructions in her meditation, Lesebum gained some experience. She then sang a song to the Jetsun as her Seven Offerings:[3]

To you, the wondrous [yogi] clad in cotton,
Who has indomitable courage,
A man assured of freedom,
Beyond both greed and fear,
To you, ascetic Repa, I pay homage,
To you, great Repa, I present my offerings.

I now repent all my wrongdoings before you
And take sympathetic joy in all your deeds.
I pray you to turn the Wheel of Dharma,
I beg you, Nirvāṇa ne'er to enter.
To all beings I now dedicate my merits.

When I watch my body, and try
To stop craving for pleasure,
The craving oft arises.

When I observe my mouth, and try
To subdue the wish for talking,
Alas, the longing still prevails.

When I watch my mind, and try without
Wandering thoughts to meditate,
Wandering thoughts always arise.

When I concentrate my body, mouth,
And mind to practice the Non-practice,
The effort-making practice is still there.

To overcome these difficulties
And to further my progress,
Pray grant me more instructions.

In response to her request, the Jetsun sang:

Listen, listen, Lesebum, with care.
If you are harassed by craving for pleasure,
Leave all your associates,
Giving all away in alms;
Rest yourself at ease without
Yearning or attachment.

When you feel like talking, try
To abjure worldly desires.
Beware of your pride and egotism,
And rest yourself at ease in humbleness.

If wavering thoughts keep on arising,
Catch hold of your Self-mind with alertness.
Be attached not to Saṃsāra nor Nirvāṇa,
But rest yourself at ease in full Equality.
Let what arises rise,
Take care not to follow.

If in meditation you still tend to strive,
Try to arouse for all a great compassion,
Be identified with the All-Merciful.

Always think of your Guru as sitting on your head,
And meditate with perseverance on the Void.

Then dedicate to all your merit.

On my words ponder, Lesebum,
And practice with zeal the Dharma.

In accordance with Milarepa's instructions, Lesebum continued her meditation. Eventually she became a yoginī, and reached the initial stage of the Path.

This is the story of Shindormo and Lesebum.

NOTES

1 The Prāṇa, gall, and phlegm illnesses: According to Tibetan pathology, these are the three major sicknesses of man, i.e., the sickness of Prāṇa (T.T.: rLuñ.), of gall (T.T.: mKhris.Pa.), and of phlegm (T.T.: Bad.Kan.).

2 Prayer-flags: Certain Mantras and prayers are printed on specially designed flags made of thin cloth, which are then hung on high poles as a symbol of blessing and good will.

3 Seven Offerings (T.T.: Yan.Lag.bDun.Pa.): This is the famous and widely practiced "Seven Offerings" exemplified by Bodhisattva Samantabhadra as described in the Av ataṃsaka Sūtra. The prayer of the Seven Offerings is included in almost every ritual and ceremony of Tibetan Buddhism; they are: (1) to pay homage to all the Buddhas and sages in the infinite universes; (2) to make offerings to them; (3) to confess one's sins; (4) to delight in all virtues of others, or to feel sympathtic joy over others' merits; (5) to beseech Buddhas and sages to preach the Dharma; (6) to implore Buddhas and sages not to enter Nirvāṇa; and (7) to dedicate all merits that one has accumulated to the attainment of Buddhahood.

The original Samantabhadra's Vows — the exemplars of "the Bodhisattva's Act," are not seven as stated in the Avataṃsaka Sūtra, but ten; three are omitted in the so-called Seven Offerings.

MILAREPA AND
THE DYING SHEEP

Obeisance to all Gurus

A T ONE time when the Jetsun Milarepa and his heart-son Rechung-pa were living in the Belly Cave of Nya Non, Rechungpa was still harboring a slight craving for worldly pleasures, which the Jetsun had often admonished him to give up. But Rechungpa thought, "I have already renounced my native land and the Eight Worldly Desires, yet the Jetsun considers this insufficient — merely halfway in the practice of the Dharma. Can this really be true?" Full of doubt, he questioned Milarepa, who answered, "In a general sense what you have said may be true, but by itself it is not enough. Now listen to my song":

> He who sits upon my head
> In the Palace of Great Bliss,
> Is the Immaculate One —
> The glory of all merits.
> He [Marpa], is the essence of the Lineage Gurus,
> The source of my perpetual inspiration.
> To Him I pay sincerest homage,
> To Him I send my heart-felt praise!
>
> Though you renounce your native land
> Living far away alone,
> You must still observe the precepts.
> He who cares for his good name,
> Will fail into the world once more.
>
> Though you renounce good food and care,

Be careful in receiving alms.
He who still yearns for tasty food,
Will fall into the world again.

Though an elegant garment is far superior to
        a plain dress,
It must be made according to the principle of
        tailoring.
Yogis who cling to fine, soft clothes
Will fall into the world once more.

If you've forsaken home and land,
Modest be and persevering.
He who aspires to fame and eminence,
Will fall into the world again.

When you forsake the "big" estate
And till your own small land [of self],
You must obey the rules of farming.
Should you expect big harvests quickly,
You will fall into the world once more.

Saṃsāra in itself is groundless and unreal;
When you look you find it hard
To define, ungraspable.
Yet when you realize it,
It is Nirvāṇa itself.
All things in themselves are void;
A yogi is attached to nothing.

Rechungpa asked, "Since I am following the Path of Tantric Skill, may I take some comfort and enjoyment to increase my devotion?" The Jetsun answered, "If you can really advance your devotion by means of enjoyments and pleasures, you may use them, but not if they only increase your [worldly] desires. I was enjoined by my Guru, Marpa, to renounce all worldly desires for an ascetic life of devotion. As a result of following his words throughout my life, a little merit has now grown within me. You, also, should renounce all Eight Worldly Desires and meditate hard while you still have the chance. Now hearken to my song":

Remember how your Guru lived
And bear in mind his honeyed words.

He who wastes a chance for Dharma,
Will never have another.
Bear, then, in mind the Buddha's teaching
And practice it with perseverance.
By clinging to things of this life,
In the next, one suffers more.
If you crave for pleasures
Your troubles but increase.

One is indeed most foolish
To miss a chance for Dharma.
Practice hard in fear of death!
Committing sins will draw
You to the Lower Realms.
By pretending and deceiving,
You cheat and mislead yourself.
Merits diminish with
The growth of evil thoughts.
If you are concerned with future life,
Diligently practice your devotions.
A yogi longing for good clothes
Will soon lose his mind;
A yogi yearning for good food
Will soon do bad deeds;
A yogi loving pleasant words
Will not gain, but lose.
Renounce worldly pursuits, Rechungpa,
Devote yourself to meditation.

If you try to get a patron
Who is rich, you will meet a foe.
He who likes to be surrounded
By crowds, will soon be disappointed.
He who hoards much wealth and money,
Is soon filled with vicious thoughts.
Meditate, my son Rechungpa,
And put your mind into the Dharma.

Realization will be won
At last by he who practices;
He who cannot practice
But only talks and brags,
Is always telling lies.

> Alas, how hard it is to find
> The chance and time to practice long.
> Rechungpa, try to meditate without diversions!
>
> If you merge your mind with the Dharma,
> You will e'er be gay and joyful;
> You will always find it better
> If you dwell oft in solitude.
> Son Rechungpa, may the precious
> Illuminating-Void Samādhi
> Remain forever in your mind!

Milarepa then thought, "Because of my urging, Rechungpa's desires for worldly pleasures may have lessened to a certain extent, yet he still cannot overcome [all of] his wrong inclinations. I shall try to further his spirit of renunciation." So he took him to the market of Nya Non for alms.

Many butchers had gathered there. The meat was piled up like walls, animals' heads were stacked in huge heaps, skins were scattered over the ground, and blood ran together like water in a pond. In addition, rows of livestock were fastened to stakes for slaughtering. An old man from Mon with a crippled arm was butchering a big black sheep, pulling out its entrails while it was still alive. Fatally wounded, it managed to escape and staggered moaning toward the Jetsun for help. Watching this pitiful scene, Milarepa shed many tears. He immediately performed the Transformation Yoga for the sheep and delivered its soul [consciousness] to the Bodhi-Path. Whereupon, with overwhelming compassion, Milarepa sang:

> How pitiful are sentient beings in Saṃsāra!
> Looking upward to the Path of Liberation,
> How can one but feel sorrow for these sinful men.
> How foolish and sad it is to indulge in killing,
> When by good luck and Karma one has a human form.
> How sad it is to do an act
> That in the end will hurt oneself.
> How sad it is to build a sinful wall
> Of meat made of one's dying parents' flesh.
> How sad it is to see meat
> Eaten and blood flowing.
> How sad it is to know confusions
> And delusions fill the minds of men.
> How sad it is to find but vice,

Not love, in people's hearts.
How sad it is to see
That blindness veils all men
Who cherish sinful deeds.

Craving causes misery,
While worldly deeds bring pain.
With this in mind one feels sorrowful,
Thinking thus, one searches for a cure.

When I think of those who never
Take heed to their future lives,
But indulge in evil deeds,
I feel most disturbed and sad,
And deeply fearful for them.

Rechungpa, seeing all these things,
Don't you remember Holy Dharma? Don't
You in Saṃsāra lose all heart?
Rouse the spirit of renunciation, go,
Rechungpa, to the cave to meditate!

Heed the bounty of your Guru
And avoid all sinful deeds;
Casting worldly things aside
Stay firm in your practice.
Keep your good vows and devote
Your life to meditation.

Rechungpa was filled with sadness, and a fervent desire for renunciation arose from the depth of his heart. Shedding many tears, he vowed, "Dear Jetsun, from now on I shall renounce all worldly desires and pleasures, and devote myself to meditation. Let us, Master and servant, go to the remote mountains; but tell me where." In answer, Milarepa sang:

Alas, trapped by evil Karmas, in the dark
Sentient beings wander in Saṃsāra.
The robber, wandering thoughts,
Drives them wild, thus depriving them
Of the chance for cultivation.
Wake up, meditate now, everyone!
Let us two Repas go to the Snow Lashi mountain.

Long and hazardous is Saṃsāra's road, pressing
And pernicious is the bandit of Five Poisons,
But Son Rechungpa, hold tight your Child-
Of-Awareness, seek Wisdom's Escort.
Sinful men seldom think that death will come;
To Snow Lashi we two Repas
Will go now for meditation!

High is the Mountain-of-Faults,
Fearful the hounds and hunters.
The "Dyāna-beast" is e'er exposed
To the danger of being captured.
Be wise, then, escape to the Land of Peace.
Sinful men seldom think that death will come;
To Snow Lashi we two Repas
Will go now for meditation!

This house of the human body
Is falling down and, weathered
By seepage of food and drink, is
Decaying with the months and years;
'Tis dangerous to live in it.
Escape then to safety,
Ready to die with joy.
Sinful men seldom think that death will come;
To Snow Lashi we two Repas
Will go now for meditation!

Deep and full of perils is Saṃsāra's sea;
It is wise to cross it now
In the boat of Awareness.
Fearful is confusion's rolling tide;
Escape from it now,
To the "Not-Two Land."
Sinful men seldom think that death will come;
To Snow Lashi we two Repas
Will go now for meditation!

Wide is the marshy bog of lust,
Harassing the muddy swamp of family life;
Be wise, escape from it, riding
Renunciation's Elephant.
Be wise and escape to safety,

In the dry land of Liberation!
Sinful men seldom think that death will come;
To Snow Lashi we two Repas
Will go now for meditation!

Great is the danger now of falling
Into Hīnayāna's views and deeds;
Only the ignorant make
About nothing much ado.
Sinful men seldom think that death will come;
To Snow Lashi we two Repas
Will go now for meditation!

On this occasion, many people in the bazaar were spontaneously confirmed with great faith in the Jetsun and his son. They all wanted to offer them much food and service, but Milarepa told them that their food was the food of sin [directly produced] through the Eight Worldly Desires, and refused to accept it. He and Rechungpa then set out on their journey to the Snow Mountain of Lashi.

This is the story of Milarepa's admonishments on the importance of being ready to die.

THE BEER-DRINKING SONG

Obeisance to all Gurus

A T ONE time when the Jetsun Milarepa and his son Rechungpa
were living in the Great Conquering Demon Cave[1] on Lashi Snow
Mountain, the frightful conjurations created by the Asuras became
so great that Rechungpa [had to] hide in the back of the cave and
absorb himself in Samādhi.

One day a great number of Devas and specters arrived, and displaying many dreadful forms, threw numerous weapons at Milarepa to
frighten him. With threatening voices, they shouted, "Let us grab him,
eat his flesh and drink his blood!" But [undaunted] Milarepa sang:

> I pray all Gurus to subdue
> All hatred and malignance!
>
> Pitiable are you ghosts and demons.
> Accustomed to evil thoughts and deeds,
> With joy you afflict sentient beings.
> Addicted to flesh-eating,
> You crave to kill and strangle!
> Born as hungry ghosts
> Ugly and repulsive,
> You commit more sinful deeds.
> You are doomed to go to Hell.
> Since you forget the seed of Liberation,
> You find the door to freedom ever shut.
> Alas, how pitiable and sad this is!
>
> Sitting on Compassion-Voidness' seat,
> I can perform all miracles.
> If you ghosts can grab and eat me,

I shall be most pleased and happy.
With compassion's Bodhi-Mind
I rejoice to see you here!

Whereupon Milarepa entered the Water-Samādhi.[2] Before long more demon and Deva armies arrived. Among them was an extremely fearful demoness who said, "Who is this man?" A demon replied, "Let us first move to [the safe side] near the water, and see." In doing so he kicked loose a few pebbles [with a clatter], and at that very moment Milarepa suddenly appeared, saying, "I am here!" He also showed his naked body to the demons who, surprised and panic-stricken, all ran away.

After a while they returned and once more vainly attacked Milarepa with their magic. Finally they gave up, crying, "Let us all be reconciled!"

In a state of great compassion Milarepa then sang:

Listen carefully, you Non-men,
You army of ill-Karm'd demons.
Your evil deeds will harm none but yourselves!

Since to me all forms are but the Dharmakāya,
Even a demon army is my glory.
Hearken, Devas and demons all. If you
Will take refuge in the Triple Gem,[3]
You will be reborn in a good place.
If you stop eating flesh and drinking blood,
You will attain high birth and freedom.
If you stop harming others, then
You will soon enter Bodhi's Path;
If you withdraw from sinful deeds,
You can embrace the Buddhist Doctrine.

Only by practicing Ten Merits
Can you understand the meaning
Of your Guru's [firm] instructions!
Only when you have removed
Confusions of body, word, and
Mind can you join the order of
Illumination-holders. Only when
You vow to keep the disciplines can we

Agree as friends. Only when you keep
Samaya's precepts can you be my disciples.

In repentence, the demons were all converted. They said, "From now on we will obey your orders. Please teach us the Dharma." Milarepa then preached for them the truth of Karma, the teaching of Taking-in-Refuge, and the Growth of the Bodhi-Mind. Confirmed with faith, the demons all offered their lives to Milarepa as a pledge of their solemn vows and departed.

The next morning Milarepa went to Rechungpa and asked, "Did anything happen to you last night?" "I was in the [Samādhi of] Illumination," said Rechungpa, "and had an amusing vision: someone came and threw a pebble at you while you were lying on your bed. Did it hit you?" Milarepa replied, "In great joyfulness, my body turned into water last night.[4] I am not sure whether that pebble hit me or not, but my chest feels a little uncomfortable. You may check on it for me." So saying, he again transformed his body into water, wherein Rechungpa found a small pebble and removed it. After that the Jetsun felt comfortable once more.

At that time many disciples came to visit Milarepa. One day he suggested that they all take a walk to the [top of the] high mountain in front of Lashi. But the disciples said, "It will be too strenuous for you because of your age. We advise you not to go." The Jetsun replied, "I think I can manage it easily." Whereupon he sang:

I bow down to all Gurus!

Milarepa wants to climb that
Mountain peak, but he is now too old;
His body is worn out and frail.
Shall he lie still and restful
Like you, my brother Mountain?

Milarepa had hardly finished singing when he suddenly appeared on the top of a cliff — his feet set firmly on the rock. Then he ascended higher until he reached the top, sitting there comfortably for some time [clothed] in a rainbow-shroud. He then flew back to the cave and said to the disciples "I need someone to pour beer for me when I am up there." "But please tell us how do we get there and how we can serve you beer?" they asked. "If you want to reach the mountain peak," replied, Milarepa, "you should practice like this":

Hearken, my sons! If you want

To climb the mountain peak
To enjoy the view,
You should hold the Self-mind's light,
Tie [it] with a great "Knot,"
And catch it with a firm "Hook."
If you practice thus
You can climb the mountain peak
To enjoy the view.

Come, you gifted men and women,
Drink the brew of Experience!
Come "inside" to enjoy the scene —
See it and enjoy it to the full!
The incapable remain outside;
Those who cannot drink pure
Beer may quaff small-beer.
He who cannot strive for Bodhi,
Should strive for superior birth.

Rechungpa said, "I can practice the Dharma and aspire to drink the beer. But please show me how." The Jetsun replied, "The best way to drink the 'beer' is to follow the good advice of Marpa." Then he sang:

I bow down to the Translator Marpa
Who in primordial Reality
Abides, Master of the essential truths.
It is not easy to describe him.
Like the sky, he is bright and clean,
Omnipresent as the sun and moon;
He never discriminates between
"High" and "low," like bushes in a swamp.
He is my Lord Buddha,
Sitting upon my head,
My glory and adornment.

In the Six Realms the chief
Actors are human beings
Who use their poorer crops to brew
Beer in the autumn and the spring.
But to brew for ourselves,
The Dharma's followers,
Build a fireplace with Three Gates, prepare

A cauldron of Śūnyatā, and then fill it
With grain of the pure White Element[5]
And the water of Compassion.
Then light the fire of Wisdom
And boil well the mash.

In the Central Plain where all is equal,
The flag of the Great Bliss is raised.
When the yeast of instruction has been added
[To the cauldron] one then may sleep at ease
On the bed of the Four Infinities.

The fermented barley of One-in-Many
Is taken out and put into a jar.
Strengthened by non-dual Wisdom-Skill,
The beer of Five Prajñās is matured;
At the entrance of the Wish-fulfilling
House, the beer of pure nectar is purified.
The Pure Heruka[6] causes it, by the
Heruka of Totality is it conditioned
And by the Lotus Heruka colored.
Its smell is the Heruka of Variety;
Its taste, of Vajra; and its touch, of Gaiety.

I am a yogi who drinks beer, because
It illumines the Dharma Body,
Completes the Body of Sambhoga,
And gives form to all Nirmāṇakāyas.
From Non-cessation's pulp
Only men with hardened heads
Can drink this nectar beer.

Here is another parable:

From the brew of Dharma-Essence
Comes precious and stimulating beer;
To Gurus and Buddhas of the Three Perfections
It is a superb oblation!
Along the middle way of Skillful-Wisdom
The rules of Samaya are observed;
Thus the Maṇḍala's deities are pleased.

With the brew of common and special instructions

[Mystical] sensations are obtained;
One thus fulfills one's wishes
And those of other men.

Whoever in the cup of Six Adornments[7]
Drinks the pure beer of the Whispered Lineage,
In him will the Great Bliss flame up.
Of this Bliss a single sip
Dispells all griefs and sorrows.
This is the beer a yogi drinks —
A special Dharma shared by few,
An act most wonderful and splendid,
An act superb and marvelous.

Hearing this song, the disciples all gained firm understandings.

This is the story of Milarepa conquering demons in the Great Cave and singing a Drinking Song while strolling [with his disciples].

NOTES

1 Great Conquering Demon Cave (T.T.: bDud.hDul.Phug.Mo.Che.).

2 Water-Samādhi: Literally this should be, "Exhaustion-of-the-Elements Water-Samādhi" (T.T.: Zad.Par.hByun.Wa.Chuhi.Tin.ne.hDsin.). This rather enigmatic term denotes a Samādhi in which the yogi manipulates his power to "exhaust" or subdue all the other four elements — Earth, Fire, Wind, and Space — thus preventing their manifestation and activity, and bringing the Water Element alone into manifestation. It is said that a spectator will not see the yogi's physical body, but a vision of water when he is engaged in this Samādhi. Likewise, the proficient yogi can also apply his power to manipulate the other four elements; thus we have the Exhaustion-of-the-Elements: Earth-, Fire-, Wind-, and Space-Samādhis.

3 The Triple Gem: the Three Precious Ones, i.e., Buddha, Dharma, and Saṅgha.

4 See Note 2.

5 The Pure White Element (T.T.: dKar.Po.Dan.Wa.): This seems to imply the white Tig Le — the Essence of male semen, a symbol of positive energy.

6 Heruka: the general name for Tantric deities, usually of a fierce form.

7 The Six Adornments: (1) the tiara of human skulls, (2) the necklace of human heads, (3) the bone armlets and wristlets, (4) the anklets, (5) the breastplate Mirror-of-Karma, and (6) the cemetery-dust ointment.

HEARTFELT ADVICE
TO RECHUNGPA

Obeisance to all Gurus

AT ONE time the Jetsun Milarepa was staying at Ramdin Nampu with his son-disciples, Rechungpa, Drigom Repa, and others. One day, while Rechungpa and Drigom Repa were having a long debate about the teachings of Nāropa and Medripa, the Jetsun commented, "First listen to my song, then continue your discussion."

My gracious Guru always sits upon my head,
The Realization is always in my mind.
Oh how can one describe this joyful feeling!

Listen you two, one Repa and one priest,
Who still linger in the realm of action.

If you do not understand *within*,
Your noisy bark will but inflate
Your pride and egotism.

Is not the clearance of misunderstandings
Within called the "Endless View" — a yogi's glory
Confirming reasons and the Scriptures?

Is not Nhamdog dissolving in the Dharmakāya
Called spontaneous practice — a yogi's glory
Confirming meditation principles?

Is not self-purity of the Six Senses
Called the Action-of-One-Taste — a yogi's glory

Responding freely to times and changes?

Is not the Experience of the Bliss-Void
Called the fruition of the Whispered Lineage —
A yogi's glory conforming with
The *Four Initiations?*

Is not the art of brightening Śūnyatā
Called the Stages and Bhūmis of the Path —
A yogi's glory witnessing
The sign-posts on the Way?

Is not the consummation of Self-mind[1]
Called the attainment of Buddhahood
In one life — a yogi's glory
Confirming the Four Bodies?

Is not a possessor of the Pith-Instructions
Of Reason and the Scriptures called
A Guru with Lineage — a yogi's glory,
Embodiment of Love and of Compassion?

Is not one with compassion and great faith
Called a disciple-with-capacity —
A yogi's glory embodying
The merit of veneration?

One must observe the mind to gain a decisive
View. To win progress one must meditate;
One must act to reach the consummation.

Perfection of Mind is the Accomplishment;
The Fourfold Body of Buddha is
A presence and Realization.
He who knows one, knows all.

Hearing this song, their misunderstandings were all cleared. Then
the Jetsun told Rechungpa that if one determines to practice the
Dharma, he should practice like this; whereupon he sang:

Listen, my son, the Illumination-Holder.
To practice the Dharma you should know these things:
That your Guru who produces merit,

The embodiment of all the Buddhas,
Is the Dharmakāya in Itself.
Rechungpa, are you thus convinced?

You should know his instructions
Are superb, nectar-like antidotes
That cure the Five Poisonous Desires.
Rechungpa, are you thus convinced?

His deeds and acts are those
Of the Nirmāṇakāya.
Son, are you thus convinced?

The mind's ever-flowing thoughts are
Void, intrinsically groundless;
[They seem] to rise, and yet they n'er exist.
In unwavering mindfulness
You should have a firm belief.
Rechungpa, are you thus convinced?

The pleasures that heavenly beings love
Are subject to change and transience.
Firmly believe that in Saṃsāra
True happiness can ne'er be found.
Rechungpa, are you thus convinced?

All things with form are momentary and fleeting,
Like flowing water and incense smoke, like lightning
In the sky. Know that leisure in this life is rare.
Rechungpa, are you thus convinced?

That all on earth will die is certain —
There's no escape: for Beyond-death strive.
Rechungpa, are you thus convinced?

Hearing this song, all the son-disciples gained further understanding.

One day some patrons of Nya Non arrived. They invited Rechungpa to accept hospitality in their village for a time, and the Jetsun gave
him permission to sojourn there for a fortnight. Other Repas also
went to the village for alms.

In the meantime Tsese, Ku Ju, and other patrons from Drin came
to visit Milarepa. When they saw him sitting there with his penis

freely exposed, they were shamed and horrified, and feared to go near him. Finally Tsese approached and offered him a covering-cloth. Whereupon all the visitors gathered round him and said, "Oh Jetsun, the manner in which you expose your naked body and organ makes us worldly men feel very embarrassed and ashamed. For our sake, please be compassionate and considerate enough to cover it."

When he heard this request, Milarepa suddenly stood up naked and sang:

> Through wandering long in many places,
> I have forgotten my native land.
> Staying long with my Holy Jetsun,
> I have forgotten all my kinsmen.
> Keeping for long the Buddha's teaching,
> I have forgotten worldly things.
> Staying for long in hermitages,
> I have forgotten all diversions.
> Through long watching of monkeys' play,
> I have forgotten sheep and cattle.
> Long accustomed to a tinder-box,
> I have forgotten all household chores.
> Long used to solitude without servant or master,
> I have forgotten courteous manners.
> Long accustomed to be carefree,
> I have forgotten worldly shame.
> Long accustomed to the mind coming and going
> By itself, I have forgotten how to hide things.
> Long used to burning Dumo-heat,
> I have forgotten clothing.
> Long accustomed to practice non-discriminating Wisdom,
> I have forgotten all distracting thoughts. Long used
> To practicing the Two-in-One Illumination,
> I have forgotten all nonsensical ideas.
> These twelve "oblivions" are the teachings of this Yogi.
> Why, dear patrons, do you not also follow them?
> I have untied the knot of dualism;
> What need have I to follow your customs?
> To me, Bodhi is spontaneity itself!
>
> The Dharma of you worldly people
> Is too difficult to practice.
> Caring for nought, I live the way I please.
> Your so-called "shame" only brings deceit

And fraud. How to pretend I know not.

The patrons then made fine, bountiful offerings to Milarepa, and left. Meanwhile, Rechungpa remained in the village, and though he only stayed one day in each patron's house, it was many days before he could return to the hermitage. When he finally came back, he found that the door was shut. Rechungpa thought, "Was it because I stayed too long in the village that the Jetsun became displeased?" And he sang:

> In the immanence of Dharma
> There's no need to read the stars;
> Those who consult the stars
> Are far from Immanence.
>
> The Great Perfection[2] has no dogmas;
> If an obstinate creed arises,
> It is not the Great Perfection.
>
> In the Mahāmudrā there is no
> Acceptance or rejection. If there
> Be, it is not the Great Symbol.
>
> In the Experience of Great Bliss
> There is neither light nor shade.
> If either of the two arises,
> It is not Great Bliss.
>
> The great Middle Way cannot be described;
> Nor can it be defined, for if it could,
> It would not be the Middle Way.
>
> I, Rechungpa, have just returned;
> Are you, my Father well today?

From over the top of the door Milarepa sang in reply this song:

> There is no Buddha other than one's mind; there is
> No faster Way than Prāna and Nādī practice;
> There is no cruelty or vengeance in the Three
>   Refuges;
> There is no experience greater than that of the
>   Bliss-Void;

No grace is higher than the Jetsun Guru's —
The refuge and glory of all men.

By practicing the correct instructions
Conviction will grow in one's mind.
With complete Realization,
Those instructions are fulfilled.
Once a firm resolution has been made,
Experience and conviction blossom.
When in one's heart kindness grows,
One through love can help all others.
He who sees his Guru as the Buddha,
Will then receive the great blessing power.

Rechungpa, the quotations
You have made are excellent.
If you understand them,
You will find the Dharma
There. If not, your remarks
Are babble and jabber.

How have you been, my son Rechungpa?
Your old father is well and healthy.

The Jetsun then opened the door and Rechungpa went in. Mila-repa said, "We will take a rest today, and have a talk. I see now that you still have great desires for worldly things. You should renounce them and meditate alone in the mountains. Now listen":

Through my Guru's grace I have been
Able to stay in the mountains.
Pray enable me e'er to remain in solitude.

Listen attentively, well-gifted Rechungpa.
When you dwell in solitude,
Think not of whispered accusations
Lest you stir your mind with anger.
When you meditate with your Guru,
Think not of religious affairs
Lest you fall into confusion.
When you give Dormas[3] to spirits,
Expect not assistance from them
Lest you, yourself, become a demon!

When engrossed in meditation,
Meet no friend or companion
Lest they interfere with your devotions.
When ascetically you persevere,
Think not of meat and wine lest
You be born a hungry ghost.
When you practice the Whispered Successions'
Skillful Path, yearn not for learning
Lest to the wrong path you stray.
When in the hills you dwell alone,
Think not of leaving lest
Evil thoughts arise.

My son, it is through perseverance
That the Holy Dharma is attained.
It is through hard work that the pains
Of Saṃsāra are relieved.
My son, my vowed disciple,
Let your father help you to bring
Forth the true Enlightenment!
Let me help you to the Last Realization
That the Dharmakāya and all forms are one!

His song struck [to the root of] Rechungpa's hidden faults. Whereupon Rechungpa prostrated himself before the Jetsun and sang:

I have through your blessing
The chance to practice Dharma.
When for good I left my parents,
Your grace was written in my heart.
Though long ago I left my home,
I still long for companionship,
Thinking of food, and dress, and wealth.

An ascetic, I have lived and dwelt in caves,
Far from temptations in the world.
Yet the thought of gathering
And gaining still rises in my mind.

What I now see is the accomplished being,
What I possess are the Whispered Pith-
Instructions. I have meditated long and hard,
Yet I still think of seeing other Gurus

To learn more teachings from them.

I have tried to serve my Guru,
I have strived to reach
Buddhahood in this life,
I have stayed in lonely places,
Yet I still think of doing this and that.

My Jetsun Guru, the Immutable Essence,
Dorje-Chang, pray help, bless, and convert your son!

Milarepa then gave Rechungpa many verbal instructions, and as a result he made great progress. After this incident, the patrons of Nya Non invited Milarepa and his son to dwell in the Belly Cave.

This is the story of Ramdin Nampu.

NOTES

1 The text reads: "Rañ.Sems.Zad.Sar.sKyol.Wa.La." More literally, "Is not the exhaustion of Self-mind called the attainment of Buddhahood . . .?" Mahāyāna Buddhism holds that the phenomena of exhaustion and of consummation seem to be always inseparable; exhaustion of something, such as the desires and ignorance, implies the simultaneous consummation of something else, such as transcendental Wisdom and Compassion. The "exhaustion of Self-mind" here seems to be used in a more positive, rather than in a negative sense.

2 The Great Perfection (T.T.: rDsogs.Pa.Chen.Po.; Skt.: Mahāsampanna): This is the "teaching-on-the-mind" of the Ningmaba School, or the Ningmaba's version of the Mahāmudrā teaching. Mahāmudrā, Mahāsampanna, and Ch'an Buddhism are all one teaching under different names.

3 Dormas: See Story 30 Note 7.

52

RECHUNGPA'S JOURNEY TO WEU

Obeisance to all Gurus

B Y THE invitation of his patrons in Nya Non, who provided perfect food and service, Jetsun Milarepa dwelt in the Belly Cave, while Rechungpa stayed in another cave above it. At one time the Gurus, patron Buddhas, and Ḍākinīs all revealed themselves to Rechungpa in his dreams, persuading him to ask the Jetsun to relate his life story. After Milarepa had done so, Rechungpa yearned to go to Central Tibet [Weu].

At that time some patrons said, "Compare the father [Milarepa] with the son [Rechungpa]; the son seems to be far superior because he has been in India." Then the younger people all went to Rechungpa, while the older ones came to the Jetsun. One day many patrons arrived. They brought Rechungpa fine and bountiful food, but gave Milarepa only meager offerings. [Not knowing this], Rechungpa thought, "Since they have brought me such good food, they must have made even better offerings to the Jetsun." He went to Milarepa and said, "Dear Jetsun, haven't we received fine offerings today? With all this food we can hold a sacramental feast with all the Repas. Shall we do so?"

"Very well," replied Milarepa, "you will find my share under that slab of stone. Take and use it." But Rechungpa found only a portion of rotten meat, a bottle of sour beer, and a small quantity of barley flour. On his way back, Rechungpa thought, "Is this fitting of those patrons? Compared with my Buddha-like Guru, I am nothing. I cannot match a single hair of his head, even with my whole body. But now these ignorant patrons are doing this foolish thing. Hitherto I have been living with my Guru and receiving all the Instructions from him. My intention was to go on living with him so that I could serve and please him. But as things stand now, if I stay with him too long

I will only become a hindrance and stand in his way. Thus, instead of being a helper I will become a competitor. I ought to ask his permission to leave."

Very early next morning, Rechungpa went to see the Jetsun. He noticed that Milarepa was sleeping with his head hidden [under his arms, like a bird]. Megom Repa was also asleep in his bed. Rechungpa thought, "Concerning self-achievement, my Guru has completely realized the Dharmakāya. And as to altruism, does he not at times practice it like a bird?" Knowing what Rechungpa was thinking, the Jetsun sang a song called "The Four Activities":

> Listen with care, my son Rechungpa!
> Your old father, Mila, sometimes sleeps,
> But in sleeping he also practices,
> For he knows how to illumine Blindness;
> But not all men know this Instruction.
> I shall be happy if all can share this teaching.
>
> Your old father, Mila, sometimes eats,
> But in eating he also practices,
> For he knows how to identify
> His food and drink with the Holy Feast;
> But not all men know this Instruction.
> I shall be happy if all can share this teaching.
>
> Sometimes your old father, Mila, walks,
> But in marching he also practices,
> For he knows that walking
> Is to circle round the Buddhas;
> But not all men know this Instruction.
> I shall be happy if all can share this teaching.
>
> Rechungpa, you should also practice in this way.
> Get up, Megom, it is time to make some broth!

In asking the Jetsun's permission to leave, Rechungpa gave many reasons for going to Weu. At the end of his petition, he sang:

> To visit different places
> And journey to various lands,
> To circumambulate holy Lhasa,
> See the two divine faces of Jo Shag,[1]
> Visit the saintly Samye Temple,

Circle round the Yuru Kradrag,
Visit the seat of Marngo,
"Sightsee" at Nyal and Loro,
And to beg for alms,
I must go to Weu.

Milarepa replied, "My son, although you will have disciples in Weu, the time has not yet come for you to go there. Please do not go against your Guru's injunctions, but listen to this song":

Born for the Supreme and Skillful Path of Secret
    Words,[2]
He is the Jetsun Buddha disguised in human form,
Possessing the divine Four Bodies,
The embodiment of Blisses Four.
To Him, the great Marpa,
I pay sincerest homage.

On this early morning
Of the auspicious eighth,
The dawning sun, like a crystal ball of fire,
Radiates its warm and brilliant beams.
I, the Yogi, feel very well and happy.

Son Rechungpa, as people have well said,
You are the spear-holder
Of a hundred soldiers.
Please do not talk like this,
But control your mind.
Try to cleanse it as a mirror bright,
And lend your ear to this old man.

When you live in a quiet hermitage,
Why think about staying in other lands?
Since you meditate on your Buddha Guru,
Why need you circle Lhasa?
While you watch your mind at play,
Why need you see Samye Temple?
If you have annihilated doubts within,
Why need you visit Marngo?
Since you practice the Whispered Lineage teaching,
Why need you "sightsee" at Loro and Nyal?
If you observe with penetration your Self-mind,

Why need you circumambulate the Kradrag?

But Rechungpa still kept on pressing his request. Whereupon the Jetsun sang:

> It is good for you, the white lion on the mountain,
> To stay high, and never go deep into the valley,
> Lest your beautiful mane be sullied!
> To keep it in good order,
> You should remain on the high snow mountain.
> Rechungpa, hearken to my words today!
>
> It is good for you, the great
> Eagle on high rocks to perch,
> And never fall into a pit,
> Lest your mighty wings be damaged!
> To keep them in good order,
> You should remain in the high hills.
> Rechungpa, hearken to your Guru's words.
>
> It is good for you, the jungle tiger,
> To stay in the deep forest;
> If you rove about the plain
> You will lose your dignity.
> To keep your splendor in perfection,
> In the forest you should remain.
> Rechungpa, hearken to your Guru's words.
>
> It is good for you, the golden-eyed
> Fish to swim in the central sea;
> If you swim too close to shore,
> You will in a net be caught.
> You should remain in the deep waters.
> Rechungpa, hearken to your Guru's words.
>
> It is good, Rechungdordra of Gung Tang,
> For you to stay in hermitages;
> If you wander in different places,
> Your *Experience* and *Realization* will dim.
> To protect and cultivate devotion
> You should remain in the mountains.
> Rechungpa, hearken to your Guru's words!

"Dear Guru, if I stay too long with you, I shall become a hindrance rather than a help," countered Rechungpa. "It is also for the sake of *furthering* my Experience and Realization that I want to go to different countries!" And he sang:

> Hear me, my Father Jetsun!
> If I, the white lion on the snow
> Mountain, do not rise up and act,
> How can I glorify my splendid mane?
> Rechungpa wants not to remain, but to visit Weu.
> I beg your permission to depart today.
>
> If I, the great eagle, king of birds,
> Do not fly high into the firmament,
> How can I magnify my mighty wings?
> Rechungpa wants not to remain, but to visit Weu.
> I beg my Guru's permission to depart today!
>
> If I, the great tiger, the jungle lord,
> Do not rove in the deep forest,
> How can I better my grand smile?
> Rechungpa wants not to remain, but to visit Weu.
> I beg your permission to depart today!
>
> If I, the fish in the deep ocean,
> Swim not to the ocean's edge,
> I can never sharpen my golden eyes.
> Rechungpa wants not to remain, but to visit Weu.
> I beg my Guru's permission to depart today!
>
> If I, Rechungdordra of Gung Tang,
> Travel not to different countries,
> I can ne'er improve my Experience and Realization.
> Rechungpa wants not to remain, but to visit Weu.
> I beg your permission to depart today!

The Jetsun then said, "Rechungpa! Before you have reached the Ultimate Realization, it would be far better for you to stay with me and not go away. Now listen to this song":

> Listen, Rechung Dorjedrapa,
> The well-learned Buddhist scholar.
> Listen, and think with care on what I say.

Before faith and yearning arise for Dharma,
Beg not alms for mere enjoyment.
Before you have realized primordial
Truth, boast not of your sublime philosophy.
Before you have fully mastered the Awareness
Within, engage not in blind and foolish acts.
Before you can feed on the Instructions,
Involve not yourself in wicked occultism.
Before you can explain the profound Teaching,
Be not beguiled by partial knowledge.
Before you can increase your merits,
Dispute not over others' goods.
Before you can destroy your inner cravings,
Treat not charity as if it were your right.
Before you can stop projecting habitual thoughts,
Guess not when you make predictions.
Before you have gained Supreme Enlightenment,
Assume not that you are a venerable Lama.
Before you can master all virtues and practices,
Consider not leaving your Guru.
Son Rechungpa, it is better not to go, but stay!

[In spite of the Jetsun's attempted dissuasion], Rechungpa was still bent on going. Milarepa then said, "It seems that you will not take my advice, but have made up your mind to leave. Well, although once I promised our patrons not to let you go to Weu, and swore to it, all oaths are like phantoms and dreams. So I will now grant your request and let you go. You may make your preparations at once."

Rechungpa was so delighted that he almost cried. He then stayed with the Jetsun for a few more days to learn more Pith-Instructions and to copy some scriptures.

At the time of his departure, Rechungpa dressed very simply in a cotton robe. He put the Ahru [drug?] of Bhamen and the trident on his back, put the Scripture of the Whispered Succession under his arm, and came to the Jetsun for his farewell blessing.

Milarepa thought, "Rechungpa has lived with me for such a long time! After this separation we may never meet again." [With this thought in his mind] he escorted Rechungpa for a distance. When they came to the crest of a hill, he asked, "How will you walk on your way?" Rechungpa sang in answer:

Using the Dharma View as a simile,

I walk forward in the Manifestation-Void.
With no thought of Nihilism or Realism, I walk ahead;
Following the immutable Path, I walk straight on.
Though my understanding may be poor, I have no regret.

Using the Dharma Practice as a simile,
I march forward in the Bliss-Illumination.
Neither drowsy nor distracted, I march ahead;
Following the Path of Light, I march straight on.
Though my practice may be poor, I have no regret.

Using the Dharma Action as a simile,
I walk forward in the Discipline.
Without foolish talk, I walk ahead;
Following the Path of Non-clinging, I walk straight on.
Though my action may be poor, I have no regret.

Using the Dharma of Samaya as a simile,
I walk forward in Purity. Without
Hypocrisy and circumvention, I walk ahead;
In the Path of Straightforwardness, I walk straight on.
Though my discipline may be poor, I have no regret.

Using the Accomplishment of Dharma as a simile,
I march forward in Immanence.
Without fear and hope, I march ahead;
In the Path of the Four Bodies, I march straight on.
Though my accomplishment may be small, I have no regret.

Using the Jetsun Marpa as a simile,
I walk forward in the Whispered Lineage.
Without talk and words, I walk ahead; following
The Path of Pith-Instruction, I walk straight on.
Though my spiritual provision is meager, I have
       no regret.

Using my Guru Milarepa as a simile,
I march forward in Fortitude. Without
Laziness and sloth, I march ahead;
In the Path of Diligence, I march straight on.
Though my perseverance may be small, I have no regret.

Using myself, Rechungpa, as a simile,

I walk forward in the way of the Gifted Ones.
Without deviation and wrong thoughts, I walk ahead;
In the Path of Veneration, I walk straight on.
Though my prayer may be feeble, I have no regret.

"Your understanding is very good," Milarepa replied, "But you should know that a child grows better with its mother, an egg ripens quicker in a warm place, and a yogi will never go astray if he lives with his Guru. Now you will not listen to my advice but insist upon going away. With my pity and love I will never forsake you. You should also pray constantly to me."

When Rechungpa heard these words, he shed many tears. Then he said, "I shall never, at any time, lose the faith and conviction that my Jetsun is Buddha Himself; so far, I have had no other Guru but you; hereafter, before I attain perfect Buddhahood, I will look to no other Guru. In the state of Bardo after this life, please also protect and escort me." Whereupon he sang:

Pray, my Buddha Guru, the e'er compassionate one,
Pray escort your son, Rechungpa!

When I climb the mountain of the *View*,
I see the traps of Realism and Nihilism,
The bandits of bigotry in ambush,
And the "twin roads" steep and perilous.
Pray, my Father Guru, Buddha's Nirmāṇakāya,
Pray escort and protect me
Until I reach Perfection's Road.

When I climb the mountain of *Practice*, I see
The snares of drowsiness and distraction,
The perilous passage of constraint,[3]
And the danger of misleading, wandering thoughts.
Pray, my Father Guru, Buddha's Nirmāṇakāya,
Pray escort and protect me
Until I reach Non-being's Plain.

When I climb the mountain of *Action*,
I see my old companion, desire,
Debauchery's perilous path,
And the strong robber, frivolity.
Pray, my Father Guru, Buddha's Nirmāṇakāya,
Pray escort and protect me until I reach

The pass of Freedom and Spontaneity!

When I build the Castle of Samaya,
I see my knowledge is insufficient,
That my assistant is incompetent,
And that great are the dangers of discordance.
Pray, my Father Guru, the Buddha's Nirmāṇakāya,
Pray escort and protect me until I reach
The pure base of Non-existence!

When I reflect on the Accomplishment,
I can see the long road of Saṃsāra,
The perilous passage to Nirvāṇa,
And the savage bandits of hope and fear.
Pray, my Father Guru, the Buddha's Nirmāṇakāya,
Pray escort and protect me until
I reach the home of the Four Bodies.

Great is Rechungpa's wish for travel,
Great his desire for pleasure and for comfort.
People in Tibet are impious;
The thief of hypocrisy
Is ready now to act.
Pray, my Father Guru, Buddha's Nirmāṇakāya,
Pray escort and protect me until
I return home from my journey!

"For your auspicious and successful trip," said the Jetsun, "I shall sing you in farewell":

Do you know what my Transmission
Is? It is not bad, but good;
It is the Transmission of Dorje-Chang.
May it bring good fortune and success!
May my son Rechungpa be blessed with [good] luck.

Do you know who my Patron Buddha
Is? She is not bad, but good;
She is the holy Dorje Paumo.
May she bring good fortune and success!
May my son Rechungpa be blessed with [good] luck.

Do you know who are my Guards?

They are not bad, but good. They are
The Ma Goun Brothers and Sisters.
May they bring good fortune and success!
May my son Rechungpa be blessed with [good] luck.

May the View, the Practice, and the Action
All bless you, my son Rechungpa!
May the Principle, the Path, and the Accomplishment
All bless you, my son Rechungpa!
May the Tsa, the Lun, and the Tig Le[4]
All bless you, my son Rechungpa!
May the Bliss, the Illumination, and Non-thought
All bless you, my son Rechungpa!

Most true is the Buddha, most true
The Dharma and the Saṅgha.
May these three Gems bless you
Forever, my son Rechungpa!

Do you know who I am?
I am called Milarepa.
May all Mila's blessings fall upon his son,
May Rechungpa soon exceed his father.

The Jetsun continued, "In Central Tibet [Weu] a bitch will 'catch' your feet. At that time do not forget your Guru and your meditation."

Rechungpa circled and prostrated before the Jetsun many times, and then set out on his journey. In the meantime, Milarepa thought, "Rechungpa will probably look back at me. If I do not stay here, he will be very disappointed when he finds me gone. I had better remain for a while." So he sat down, but Rechungpa never turned his head. Milarepa wondered, "Why does he not look back? Does he have any wrong ideas about his Guru and his brothers? At any rate, he is a man who can keep the Dharma and the Succession secret wherever he goes." Then, holding his breath, Milarepa [flew ahead] and overtaking Rechungpa, transformed himself into seven identical Repas standing before a huge rock shaped like a rearing lion. In order to test Rechungpa's intention, the seven Repas all sang together:

Listen, Repa traveler! Who
Are you and who is your Guru?
Who are your forebears, what

Instructions do you know?
Which is your Transmission, what
Meditation do you practice?
Where's your temple, what's this mountain?
Can you name this rock?
Whither are you bound,
By who's order do you travel,
And in what way do you go?

Rechungpa thought, "No other Repa would say things like this to me; they must be the transformations of the Jetsun." He then prostrated himself before the Repas and sang:

Hear me, my great Jetsun Father!
You ask who I am. My name
Is Rechungpa from Gung Tang;
My Guru is Milarepa,
My forebears, Marpa and Ngopa,[5]
My great-grandfathers, Tilopa and Nāropa,
My Instructions are of the Ḍākinīs' Whispered
    Lineage,
My Transmission was founded by Dorje-Chang,
My hermitage is on Lashi Snow Mountain.
This hill is Biling Zurkha, this rock
Is known as the Great Rearing Lion,
The place to which I go is Weu,
My Jetsun Guru gave me leave.
This is the story of my journey.
I pray you, Jetsun, for instructions.

Milarepa then withdrew all the transformation bodies into the real one and said, "I did this to find out why you did not even look back at me after you left. Now I know that you have not violated the Samaya precepts. Since you have observed them properly, we will never separate from each other. You may now proceed to Weu."

Overjoyed at these words, Rechungpa bowed down at the Jetsun's feet and made many good wishes. Then he set out for Weu, and the Jetsun returned to the Belly Cave.

That day, some patrons came with food and offerings. But as soon as they learned that Rechungpa had left, they hid all the things they had brought for him in a brass basin in the recesses of a cave. Then they came to Milarepa's abode and found that he was already up.

They asked, "Revered Jetsun, usually you do not get up so early. What made you do so today?" Milarepa replied, "Rechungpa left for Weu this morning, and I went down to the plain to see him off. Upon my return I felt a little sad, and I have been sitting here ever since."

"Did you, Revered Jetsun, ever try to stop him from going to Weu?"

"Yes, I did." Whereupon Milarepa sang:

> Rechungpa, my beloved son, has left
> For Weu. He never follows the advice
> Of others but acts as he wishes.
>
> He said that he would visit Marpa
> And Ngopa's temple, see Loro,
> Nyal, and the Samye Chapel,
> And circle the holy Lhasa.
>
> I advised him thus:
> "When you put all your trust in your Guru,
> What is the need for Jowo Shagja?[6]
> When you meditate in a solitary retreat,
> Why go to see Marpa and Ngopa's temple?
> When you have learned the Whispered Lineage's
> Instruction, why visit Loro and Nyal?
> When you can amuse yourself by watching
> The play of your own Dharmakāya Mind,
> What need have you to see Samye Chapel?
> When you have destroyed all your wrong ideas,
> What need have you to circle Lhasa?
> I repeat, Rechungpa
> Our beloved, has gone to Weu.
> Had you, good patrons, then been here
> You might by circling round have stopped him.

"When a Guru grows old," said the patrons, "it is the primary duty of his disciple to attend him. Your Reverence has gone to every length to dissuade him, but still he would not listen. He is indeed shameless, with little consideration for other people." Milarepa replied pretendingly, "Yes, Rechungpa had no shame and no discipline." Then he sang:

> A son fostered, loved, and cherished
> Seldom cares for his old parents.

Out of a hundred men 'tis hard
To find an exception.

An undisciplined disciple seldom
Helps his Guru when he grows old.
Out of a hundred men 'tis hard
To find an exception.

A lion white, he went to Weu; I was left
Behind abandoned like an old dog.
Yes, my son has left me for Weu.
Like a young tiger who forsakes
The fox, he went to Weu.

Yes, he has left his old father and gone to Weu.
Like a great vulture who forsakes
A cock, he went to Weu.

As a superb steed of Dochin
Leaves the asses from Jungron,
My son has left his old father and gone to Weu!

Like a wild and blue-horned yak
Deserting an elephant,
My son has left his old father and gone to Weu.

With body handsomer than a Deva's,
He went to Weu.
With voice mellower than an angel's
He went to Weu.
With words sweeter than all music,
He went to Weu.
With mind brighter than embroidery,
He went to Weu.
Smelling more fragrant than [good] incense,
He went to Weu!

The patrons then said, "Revered Jetsun, you are indeed most compassionate toward him. On such a long, hard journey you must have
provided a companion for him and made all necessary preparations
for his trip. Please tell us all about it." In answer, Milarepa sang:

He was well escorted when he went.

In time friends are always separated,
But Rechungpa's friend will never leave him;
She is self-arising Wisdom. My son
Rechungpa left with a fine friend.

Even good horses sometimes stumble,
But Rechungpa's will ne'er miss a step.
Riding the steed of Prāna-Mind,
Riding on it, he set out for Weu.

Clothes at times are warm, at others cold,
But what Rechungpa wears is always warm,
For it is the blazing Dumo. Wearing
This superb dress, he left for Weu.

Food is sometimes good, and sometimes nasty,
But what Rechungpa eats is tasty at all times,
For it is the savory dish of Samādhi.
With this fine food, he has gone to Weu.

Jewels are the aim of thieves,
But Rechungpa's gems can ne'er be stolen,
For they are the wish-fulfilling Instructions of
　　　the Whispered Lineage.
With these precious jewels, he has left for Weu.

While singing this song, Milarepa appeared a little sad. The patrons said, "Since Rechungpa has left you without showing the slightest affection, you, Jetsun, should also forget about him. Besides, Shiwa Aui, Sevan Repa, and many other disciples are still here. They can attend you just as well." "Yes," replied the Jetsun, "there are many Repas, but one like Rechungpa is hard to find. There may be many patrons, but it is difficult to find one with true faith. Please listen to my song":

The Nyan Chung Repa of Gung Tang,
The Ngan Tson Dewa Shun of Jenlun,
The Sevan Jashi Bar of Dodra,
And the Drigom Linkawa of Dhamo —
These are the four sons
I cherish as my heart.
Of them Rechung, my long-time
Companion is most dear.[7]
I think of him and miss him much now he has gone.

The word-conditioned "View" is nominal.
Though people call it "View,"
'Tis but a word.
It is most hard to find a man who can
Cease to be distracted by Duality;
It is most hard to find a man who can
Absorb himself in the sole Realization!

The "Practice" that cannot widen
The mind is nominal.
Though people call it "Practice,"
'Tis but a form of Dhyāna.[8]
It is most hard to find a man
Who can merge both Dhyāna and "Insight";
It is most hard to find a man who knows
How to work on the vital point of mind.

When the mind's "Action" is now dark,
Now light, it is but nominal.
Though people call it "Action,"
'Tis a deed of involvement.
It is most hard to find a man
Who can conquer worldly desires;
It is very hard to find a man
Who can complete the Dharma practice.

Observance of discipline when feigned
And artificial is but nominal.
Though people call it "Discipline,"
'Tis nought but mockery.
It is most hard to find a man
Who never violates his oath;
It is very hard to find
An honest witness of his mind.

"Accomplishment" when longed for hard
Is a notion [cherished by fools].
Though people call it "Accomplishment,"
'Tis nothing but delusion.
It is most difficult to find a man
Who can plumb the abyss of Reality;
It is most hard to find a man
Who on the real Path can stay.

The Pith-Instructions may seem
Most profound on paper;
They are but written words.
It is difficult to find a man
With diligence and perseverance;
It is most hard to find a man
With direct teachings from a Lineage.

The Gurus who involve themselves
In worldly life are nominal;
They only bring entanglements.
Small are people's faith and veneration.
It is most difficult to find a man
Ever relying on an accomplished Guru.

The merits of ostentatious faith
And veneration are nominal,
For they change and are short-lived.
Where Karma's bad prejudice is strong,
It is hard to find a man
Who fears and cares for nothing.
It is most hard to find a man
With the Three Determinations.[9]

The small temple on the outskirts
Of a town is but nominal.
Though people call it "Temple,"
It is really part of "town."
Always there is great craving for
Amusement and distraction.
It is most hard to find a man
Staying long in hermitages.

The head of a restrained young monk
Is stiff and hard like stone.
Though people call him "disciplined,"
He is but acting in a play.
It is hard to find a man with perseverance,
It is hard to find another
Observing the strict priestly rules.

The handsome belles of Nya Non
As patrons are but nominal,

For they are deceivers and seducers.
Poor and low is woman's comprehension.
Hard indeed is it to find a patron
To serve one and make all the offerings.

The faiths of evil-doers are in their mouths;
The faiths of you patrons are in your private parts.
I, the Yogi, in my heart have faith.

When a rock grows old
Grime encrusts its face;
When a stream grows old
Wrinkles cover its bed.
When a tree grows old
Its leaves soon fall off.
When a hermitage grows old
Water and plantains disappear.
When a yogi ages, his Experience
And his Realization dimmer grow.
When patrons grow old
Their faith soon wears out.

Some patrons are like peacocks
Who pretend and swagger.
Some patrons are like parrots
Gossiping and gabbling.
Some patrons are like cows —
They think you a calf or goat.

My patrons, it is getting late,
It is time for you to go.
Besides, in the cave beneath,
The sack of flour in the bowl
By mice is being nibbled;
The cake of butter has been tossed
And is now rolling on the ground;
The vixen has upset the wine,
The crows have scattered all the meat,
So run fast and hurry [home].
Patrons I will vow to see you soon.
In a happy mood you may leave me now.

The visiting patrons were nonplused. They looked at one another timidly, and nudged each others' elbows. Too filled with shame to say a word, they all went home. As the Jetsun had unmistakably exposed the truth, they felt guilt and deep regret; but also, as a result, their faith in him was firmly established.

One day they came again and brought excessive offerings, saying, "Please sing for us to awaken our insight into the transiency of beings." Milarepa would not accept their offerings, but he sang this for them:

Hearken, you mean patrons!
For the sake of fame to do
Meritorious deeds —
For this life's sake to seek
The protection of Buddha —
To give alms for the sake
Of returns and dividends —
To serve and offer for the sake
Of vanity and pride —
These four ways will ne'er requite one.

For the sake of gluttony
To hold a sacramental feast —
For the sake of egotism
To strive for Sūtra learning —
For distraction and amusement
To indulge in foolish talk and song —
For vainglory's sake to give
The Initiations —
These four ways will never bring one Blessings!

If for love of preaching one expounds
Without the backing of Scripture;
If through self-conceit,
One accepts obeisance;
If like a bungling, fumbling fool one teaches,
Not knowing the disciple's capacity;
If to gather money one behaves
Like a Dharma practicer —
These four ways can never help the welfare of
        sentient beings!

To prefer diversions to solitude,
To love pleasures and hate hardship,

To crave for talk when urged to meditate,
To wallow arrogantly in the world —
These four ways will ne'er bring one to Liberation!

This is the song of Fourfold Warning.
Dear patrons, bear it in your minds!

Drigom Repa, who was present, besought the Jetsun to preach still more of the Dharma. In response, Milarepa sang:

The long-lived heavenly beings above
Are hostile to Awareness when arising.
They are ever eager for Dhyāna of No-thought.

The hungry ghosts beneath, not knowing
That they are hunted by the mind's projections,
Resent their pillagers with jealousy and avarice.
Because of their evil Karma,
They are pressed by thirst and hunger.

In between are we poor miserable humans.
Not knowing the golden treasure underground,
From our fellow men we steal and cheat.
The more we cheat and deceive,
The more suffering we have to bear.

The foolish and "enterprising" patrons
Of Nya Non acquire no merits through the Jetsun,
But make offerings to young, handsome Repas.
Yet remorse and shame are all their alms will bring.
Enterprises so wrong and meaningless should cease,
So give your services and offerings to the Buddhas!

Their faith confirmed, the patrons all bowed down to the Jetsun many times and shed many tears. "Oh Revered Jetsun!" they cried, "We beg you to remain here permanently. From now on we will give our offerings and services in accordance with the teaching of Dharma." Milarepa replied, "I cannot stay here long, but I will bestow the blessing of long life and good health upon all of you. Also I will make a wish that we meet again under auspicious circumstances conducive to the Dharma." Then he sang:

In the immense blue sky above

Roll on the sun and moon. Their
Courses mark the change of time.
Blue sky, I wish you health and fortune,
For I, the moon-and-sun, am leaving
To visit the Four Continents for pleasure.

On the mountain peak is a great Rock
Round which oft the vulture circles,
The king of birds. Their meeting
And their parting mark the change of time.
Dear rock, be well and healthy, for I,
The vulture, now will fly away
Into the vast space for pleasure.
May lightnings never strike you,
May I not be caught by snares.
Inspired by the Dharma,
May we soon meet again
In prosperity and boon.

Below in the Tsang River,
Swim fish with golden eyes;
Their meeting and their parting
Mark the change of time.
Dear stream, be well and healthy, for I, the fish
Am leaving for the Ganges for diversion.
May irrigators never drain you,
May fishermen ne'er net me.
Inspired by the Dharma,
May we soon meet again
In prosperity and boon.

In the fair garden blooms the flower, Halo;
Circling round it is the Persian bee.
Their meeting and their parting
Mark the change of time.
Dear flower, be well and healthy, for I
Will see the Ganges' blooms for pleasure.
May hail not beat down upon you,
May winds blow me not away.
Inspired by the Dharma,
May we soon meet again
In prosperity and boon.

> Circling round the Yogi Milarepa
> Are the faithful patrons from Nya Non;
> Their meeting and their parting
> Mark the change of time.
> Be well and healthy, dear patrons, as I
> Leave for the far mountains for diversion.
> May I, the Yogi, make good progress,
> And you, my patrons, all live long.
> Inspired by the Dharma,
> May we soon meet again
> In prosperity and boon!

Moved by this song, some patrons became devoted followers of the Jetsun, and the faith of all was greatly strengthened.

During his journey to Weu, Rechungpa came to the Buddhist Study Center at Sha, and was appointed a Mindrol Professor[10] there. Then he met, and formed an attachment to a certain noblewoman, but through the grace of the Jetsun became ashamed of his conduct and returned to Milarepa to live with him again. The details of this episode are clearly given in the Biography of Rechungpa.

This is the story of Rechungpa's journey to Weu.

NOTES

1 Jo Shag (T.T.: Jo.Çak., an abbreviation of Jo.Wo.Çakya.): the holy images to which many Tibetans make pilgrimages.

2 The Path of Tantra, which is full of ingenious instructions and Mantras or secret words.

3 This is a free translation. The text reads: "dMigs.gTad.Sa.hPhrañ.Dam.Pa. Dañ. . . . ." "dMigs.gTad." literally does not mean "constraint," but "[adherently] facing the object," i.e., the constant pursuing of objects in the outside world by the consciousness.

4 Tsa, Lun, Tig Le (T.T.: rTsa.rLuñ.Thig.Le.; Skt.: Nāḍi, Prāṇa, [and] Bindu), i.e., the nerves, the breathing, and the semen.

5 Ngopa: Milarepa's other Guru. See W. Y. Evans-Wentz' "Tibet's Great Yogi, Milarepa," Chapters 5 and 6.

6 Jowo Shagja (T.T: Jo.Wo.Çakya.): See Note 1.

7 Rechungpa was Milarepa's closest disciple, who had spent most of his lifetime living with the Jetsun. See Story 10.

8 Dhyāna is an equivalent of Samādhi. According to Buddhist tradition, it is but a state of mental concentration.

9 Presumably these Three Determinations are: (1) to determine to rest one's mind on the Dharma, (2) to rest Dharma on poverty, and (3) to rest poverty on death.

10 Mindrol Professor (T.T.: mKhan.Po.sMin.Grol.): "sMin.Grol." is the name of a monastery.

53

THE MEETING WITH
DHAMPA SANGJE

Obeisance to all Gurus

Early one morning when the Jetsun Milarepa was staying at the Belly Cave of Nya Non, he had a clear vision of a Ḍākinī with a lion face, who came to him and said, "Milarepa, the Dhampa Sangje of India is coming to Tong Lha. Are you not going to see him?" Milarepa thought, "There is no doubt or discomfort in my mind that needs dispelling. However, Dhampa Sangje is an accomplished being, and it would do no harm for me to see him." With this thought in mind, Milarepa held his breath for a [short] period and went to Tong Lha of Nya Non.

In the mountain pass he met a few merchants who had just come from the plain below. Milarepa asked them, "Has the Dhampa Sangje of India arrived yet?"

"We don't know who the Dhampa Sangje is," they replied, "but last night we saw an old Indian with a bluish-black face, who was sleeping at the inn." The Jetsun thought, "This must be he, but these merchants do not know." He then proceeded to the top of the mountain pass, from whence he saw Dhampa Sangje approaching.

While staying overnight in the Guest House of Compassion, Dhampa Sangje, also, had been persuaded by the Ḍākinī with the lion face to meet the Jetsun. As soon as Milarepa saw him, he thought, "People say that Dhampa Sangje has the Transcendental Miraculous Power. I shall now test him." He then transformed himself into a clump of flowers growing beside the road. Dhampa Sangje passed by the flowers with his eyes widely open as if he did not see them at all. Milarepa thought, "It seems that he does not have the Perfect Miraculous Power!" But just then Dhampa Sangje turned back. Approaching the flowers, he kicked them with his foot and said, "I ought not

606

do this — this is the transformation of Milarepa." Having spoken these words, he picked the flowers and addressed them: "You have been singing all the precious teachings that are cherished by Ḍākinīs as their very lives and hearts, and so they all became angry. The flesh-eating Ḍākinīs have thus taken your heart, breath, and spirit away from you. Last night I met them and saw that they had carried your bleeding heart away [in their hands]. We then ate it during our sacramental feast, so that you can only live until this evening. Now tell me, what confidence do you have in facing death?" In reply, the Jetsun suddenly arose from his transformation, and sang a song called "The Six Assurances on Facing Death":

> The great Liberation from Extremes
> Is like a gallant lion lying
> In the snow at ease, displaying
> Without fear its fangs.
> In this View do I, the Yogi, trust.
> Death leads to the Liberation Path!
> Death brings joy to he who holds this View!
>
> The stag calm and magnanimous
> Has horns of "One Taste" with many points.
> He sleeps in comfort on the plain of Bliss-Light.
> In this practice do I, the Yogi, trust.
> Death leads to the Liberation Path!
> Death brings joy to he who practices!
>
> The fish of Ten Virtues
> With rolling, golden eyes,
> Swims in the River of Perpetual Experience.
> In this action do I, the Yogi, trust.
> Death leads to the Liberation Path!
> Death brings joy to he who acts!
>
> The tigress of Self-mind Realization
> Is adorned with showy stripes.
> She is the glory of Altruism-without-
> Effort, walking firmly in the woods.
> In this discipline do I, the Yogi, trust.
> Death leads to the Liberation Path!
> Death brings joy to those with Discipline!
>
> On the paper of forms Postive-and-Negative

I wrote an essay with my "awaring" mind.
In the state of Non-duality
I watch and contemplate.
In this Dharma do I, the Yogi, trust.
Death leads to the Liberation Path!
Death brings joy to those with Dharma!

The purified quintessence of the Moving
Energy is like a great eagle flying
On wings of Skill and Wisdom
To the castle of Non-being.
In this Accomplishment do I, the Yogi, trust.
Death leads to the Liberation Path!
Death brings joy to the accomplished man!

Dhampa Sangje replied, "What you have said has no reason at all.
You cannot use things in the outer world as parables [or parallels]
to compare with the true Realization. If you were a real yogi you
would know this *immediate Awareness* in a decisive and unmistakable
manner." [In answer to his challenge] Milarepa sang a song called
"The Six Positive Joys of the Mind."

In the solitary retreat
Where Ḍākinīs always gather,
I contemplate the Dharma
In great ease and joy.

To the ego-killing Bha Wo,
I pay my sincere homage.
Absorbing in the Void my mind,
I reach the Realm of Immortality,
Where death and birth vanish of themselves.
Happy is my mind with a decisive View —
Happy and joyful as I gain supremacy!

Absorbing myself in the Practice-without-Practice,
I reach the Realm of No-distraction,
Where the Main and Ensuing Samādhis vanish of
    themselves.
Happy is my mind with the decisive Practice —
Happy and joyful as I gain supremacy!

Living in full spontaneity and naturalness,

I achieve the state of Unceasing, in which
All forms of discipline vanish of themselves.
Happy is my mind with the Ultimate Action —
Happy and joyful as I attain supremacy!

Absorbing myself in the Realm of No-initiation,
I achieve the state of No-attainment;
All forms of Buddha's Body vanish of themselves.
Happy is my mind with the Ultimate Initiation —
Happy and joyful as I attain supremacy!

Absorbing myself in the Realm of No-discipline,
I attain the state of No-transgression;
All forms of Precept vanish of themselves.
Happy is my mind with the Ultimate Discipline —
Happy and joyful as I gain supremacy!

Without hope for accomplishment
I achieve the state of No-fear;
Hopes and fears vanish of themselves.
Happy is my mind with the Ultimate Accomplishment —
Happy and joyful as I gain supremacy!

Dhampa Sangje commented, "I, also, have gone through all you have just said. A Buddhist who needs no more practice or improvement has now been found in Tibet! It is very difficult, even in India, to find one or two advanced Buddhists comparable to you. I do not need you, and you do not need me."

Having said these words in a pleasant manner, he turned and was about to go away. Milarepa immediately caught hold of his robe, saying, "It is said that you have a teaching called 'Relieving all Sorrows,' [1] and that in practicing it one reverses his mind inwardly, thus instantaneously realizing the Buddha's Mind. Now please explain it to me in a song." Dhampa Sangje replied, "So far, no one has ever heard me sing, and no one will." However, the Jetsun asked him so persistently that finally Dhampa Sangje sang:

This is the Dharma called "Relieving All Sorrows":

When demons come to harm you is the time
To apply your Occult Powers.
When pain and sickness strike you is the time
To merge them with your intrinsic Awareness.

Whenever subtle Nhamdogs rise
It is time to stir the passions
And transcend them.

When lying in a hidden place alone,
Is the time to rest one's naked Awareness.
When mingling with many people,
It is time to bring all to the
View. When comes drowsiness
It is time to use the bīja Pai.[2]
When distracting thoughts arise,
It is time to lead them to the Real.
When the mind runs after worldly things,
'Tis time to observe the truth of Suchness.

In short, this teaching of Relieving Sorrows
Turns all adversities into good fortune.
Whatever wild thoughts rise, you feel but joy.
Whenever illness comes, you use it as your aid;
Whatever you encounter, you feel but happiness.
Whene'er death comes, you utilize it for the Path.
This teaching of Relieving Sorrows is the Dharma
Of all Buddhas in the Three Times —
It is the instruction given by Dorje-Chang,
The life and heart of all Ḍākinīs in the Four
        Di isions;[3]
It is the pith of the Tantras Four,[4]
The quintessential Dharma of the Whispered Lineage,
The key of all Essential Teachings!
Such is the teaching of "Relieving All Sorrows"!

Milarepa listened to this song with great delight as he sat to one side with his penis freely exposed. Dhampa Sangje remarked, "You are like a lunatic who neglects to cover up the place that should be covered." In reply, the Jetsun sang "The Song of a Lunatic":

To all Gurus I pay my homage.
I take refuge in the Gracious One,
I pray you, dispel my hindrances;
Bring me to the right Path, I pray.

Men say, "Is not Milarepa mad?"

I also think it may be so.
Now listen to my madness.

The father and the son are mad,
And so are the Transmission
And Dorje-Chang's Succession.
Mad too were my Great-grandfather, the Fair Sage,
    Tilopa,[5]
And my Grandfather, Nāropa the great scholar.
Mad, too, was my Father, Marpa the Translator;
So too is Milarepa.

The demon of the intrinsic Bodies Four
Makes Dorje-Chang's Succession crazy;
The devil of the Mahāmudrā made
My Great-grandfather Tilopa crazy;
The demon of the secret Awareness
Made my Grandfather Nāropa crazy;
The devil of the Tantras Four
Made my Father Marpa mad;
The demons of Mind and Prāṇa
Have driven me, Milarepa, mad.

The impartial Understanding itself is crazy;
So are the free, self-liberating Actions,
The self-illuminating Practice of No-perception,
The Accomplishment-without-Hope-and-Fear,
And Discipline-without-Pretension.

Not only am I mad myself,
I madly afflict the demons.
With the Gurus' Pith-Instruction
I punish all male demons;
With the blessing of Ḍākinīs
I harrow female demons;
With the he-devil of Happy Mind
I enter the Ultimate;
With the she-devil of Instantaneous
Realization I perform all acts.

Not only do I punish demons,
I also suffer pains and sickness —
The Great Symbol hurts my back,

The Great Perfection afflicts my chest.
In practicing the Vase-breathing,
I catch all kinds of sickness —
The fever of Wisdom attacks me from above,
The cold of Samādhi invades me from below,
The cold-fever of the Bliss-Void assails me in
        the middle.
From my mouth I vomit the blood of Pith-Instructions;
Lazily I stretch, thrilled by the Dharma-Essence.

I have many sicknesses,
And many times have died.
Dead are my prejudices
In the [vast] sphere of the View.
All my distractions and drowsiness
Have died in the sphere of Practice.
My pretensions and hypocrisy
Have died in the sphere of Action.
Dead are all my fears and hopes
In the sphere of Accomplishment,
And my affectations and pretenses
In the sphere of Precepts. I, the Yogi,
Will die in Trikāya's Realm.

Tomorrow when this yogi dies
No fair shroud will he see,
But the subtle, divine Revelations.
His corpse will not be bound by hempen rope,
But by the cord of the Central Channel.
His corpse-bearers to the cemetery
Will not be nose-wiping sons,
But his blessed Son-of-Awareness.
Not by the gray, earthy road,
But along the Bodhi-Path
The [funeral parade] will go.

The Gurus of the Whispered Lineage will lead
        the way;
The Ḍākinīs of the Four Divisions will be the
        guides;
The corpse will not be brought
To the red and massive hill,
But to the Hill of Adi Buddha;

The corpse will not be carried
To the cemetery where foxes play,
But to the Park of Skill and Wisdom;
It will be buried only
In the Grave of Dorje-Chang.

Dhampa Sangje was greatly pleased by this song. He said, "Your kind of craziness is very good." The Jetsun replied, "Since we two yogis have now met, it would be appropriate for us to have a sacramental feast together."

"Well, since you are a Tibetan, you should play the part of host," commented Dhampa Sangje, "you be the first to prepare the feast." Milarepa then removed his skull with the brain inside, and, cutting off his forearms and neck, used them to build a hearth. Then he put the skull upon the hearth. From his navel he ejected the Dumo Fire to heat the skull, and then the brain began to emit five-colored rays in all directions. Dhampa Sangje transformed himself into seven bodies standing upon seven stalks of grass, and Milarepa also transformed his body into seven [Mandalas] of Dem Chog, complete with the Eight Gates, etc., upon the tips of seven stalks of grass. In each of the Mandalas Buddha Dem Chog was offered the sacramental feast with six wondrous enjoyments.[6]

The grasses upon which Milarepa's transformed bodies stood were slightly bent [as if by the weight of the load]. The Jetsun then said to Dhampa Sangje, "As to proficiency in the Vase-breathing Practice, there is no difference between you and me. Why, then, is the grass [upon which I stand] slightly bent?" Dhampa Sangje replied, "There is no difference between my Realization[7] and yours. This is simply due to the fact that you were born a Tibetan. Your Views and Actions are identical with mine, therefore both the disciples in your Lineage and in mine will see eye to eye in their practices and understandings."

By their magic powers Milarepa and Dhampa Sangje then returned to their own abodes.

This is the story of Tong Lha.

NOTES

1 The Instruction, or Dharma of Relieving All Sorrows (T.T.: Dam.Chos.sDug. bsÑal.Shi.Byed.).

2 Bija Pai: Bija is the seed-word of a Mantra. For Pai, see Story 14, Note 4.

3 These four divisions are probably the East, South, West, and North of the Maṇḍala.

4 The Four Tantras are: Kriya-tantra, Carya-tantra, Yoga-tantra and Anuttara-tantra.

5 The text reads: "Yañ.Mes.Te.Lo.Çer.bZañ.sMyo." "Çer.bZañ" is perhaps the abbreviation of dGe.Wahi.bÇes.gÑen.bZañ.Po., meaning the good sage or good teacher.

6 This probably refers to the six different tastes: sour, sweet, bitter, pungent, salty, and aromatic; it can also refer to the six sexual attractions arising from color, form, carriage, voice, smoothness, and features.

7 Lit.: "There is no difference between your accomplishments in Realization and Purification, and mine."

54

THE SALVATION
OF THE DEAD

Obeisance to all Gurus

W HEN the Jetsun Milarepa was dwelling at the Belly Cave of Nya Non, many followers of Bon were living nearby in a place called La Shin. In the vicinity of La Shin there also dwelt a very rich man who, [although born a Bon] was a devoted Buddhist and, being a patron of the Jetsun, never patronized any Bon monk. He had been initiated with the Pith-Instructions by Milarepa, and also practiced them.

One day this man caught a fatal illness, which brought him to the point of death. Planning to make his last will and testament, he summoned all his relatives and said to them, "For my salvation's sake, please offer all my properties and belongings to the Jetsun Milarepa and his disciples. You have all been followers of Bon, but I hope you will become Buddhists and practice the beneficial Dharma in your next lives."

But his relatives would not follow his instructions. Fearing that they would never invite the Jetsun to visit him, the man said to his daughter, "Why do you people stab a dying man in the heart? If you do not follow my wishes and instructions, I will kill myself. Then you will be condemned by all!"

Hearing these words, they gave in, and consented to do what he wished. The man then requested, "Do not perform any Bon rite-for-the-dead for me — it is nominal and useless. But please invite the Jetsun to come for my sake!" Thus saying, he died.

In accordance with the deceased's wish, the Jetsun and his disciples were invited to the house. They all stayed on the top floor,[1] while the Bon monks, who were also invited for the occasion, remained on the lower floor to perform their rites.

[While these rites were in progress, suddenly], on the base of the Bon Maṇḍala, there appeared the [unmistakable] form of the dead man. Greenish in color, with long hair, it stood there cheerfully drinking beer. Bedha [Milarepa's sister] passed by and saw it. The Bon monks said to her, "Milarepa and his followers always fight against us. But look, everyone here can witness that we Bonists have actually brought the deceased one back — Milarepa and his men could never do this!" Saying which, they jeered and laughed at the Jetsun.

Bedha then reported this incident to Milarepa, who replied, "This is not the apparition of the dead man. It is only a trick the Bonists have played to beguile people. Now, Shiwa Aui, go and grasp the apparition's ring-finger, and ask him for the name that was given him by the Jetsun Milarepa in the Belly Cave during his Initiation."

After a while Shiwa Aui returned and said, "The apparition could not withstand the Jetsun's glowing light-of-mercy. When I was just about to speak, it said, 'I am leaving now. I am the one who leads dead men's spirits for the Bonists — a ghost who comes to this world-of-appearance to make a big noise and eat human flesh. Since not the slightest benefit can be gained from the Bon teaching, I have just come here to get my wages from the Bon priests.'

"Then I chased it out," continued Shiwa Aui, "and, with its greenish face and long hair, it dashed away through the streets of the village and to the other side of the mountain, where it became a wolf."

Having witnessed this occurrence, all the people there were convinced that the apparition was not the real spirit of the dead man.

The Jetsun then said to the Bonists, "You are showing the way for a murderer, but I am showing the way for the dead man." The Bon relatives asked, "Then you, Jetsun, must be able to see him; otherwise, how could you show him the way?" Milarepa replied, "Yes, I see him. Because of some slight [bad] Karma in his former lives he was unable to complete his meritorious deeds, and has now been born as an insect. Under a lump of brownish yak dung you will find a long, slender insect — that is he. I am now going to send him to the Land of Liberation."

"To convince us, please show us how you liberate him," said the patrons.

"Very well, let us go there, and [you will] see."

All the people then went with the Jetsun [to the upper valley] where they soon came to a lump of brownish, dry dung. The Jetsun first called the man by his secret names a few times, and then said, "I am your Guru, Milarepa. Now, come out, and come here!"

From somewhere under the dung a small insect appeared, flew directly toward the Jetsun, and alighted on him. Milarepa then preached

the Dharma and performed the Transformation Yoga and the Rite
of Deliverance for it. [At once the insect died] and its corpse began
to give out a thin, bright light, which entered and dissolved into the
Jetsun's heart. Milarepa meditated for a short while, and then from
his heart the dead man's consciousness emerged, embodied in a white
"Ah" word glowing with brilliant light; and it ascended higher and
higher to the sky. Meanwhile the people all heard its voice saying,
"The precious Jetsun has now delivered me to the joy of Liberation.
Oh great is his blessing! Great is his bounty!"

Having witnessed these things, all the spectators were convinced
[and confirmed with] great faith. They bowed down to the Jetsun and
cried, "This is marvelous! This is wonderful!"

"I have many other things even more marvelous than this," replied
Milarepa. Whereupon he sang:

> I pray to my wondrous Guru, Marpa;
> I cherish his grace in my mind.
> Pray bless my disciples with your mercy.
>
> Of all marvels, the greatest is
> The first meeting with my Guru.
>
> Of all marvels, the greatest is to earn
> Instructions from the Whispered Lineage.
>
> Of all marvels, the greatest is
> To renounce all worldly things.
>
> Of all marvels the greatest is
> To stay in the hermitage.
>
> Of all marvels the greatest is the birth
> Of inner Experience and Realization.
>
> Of all marvels the greatest is
> To endure hardship in solitude.
>
> Of all marvels the greatest is
> Indifference to the Eight Worldly Gains.
>
> Of all marvels the greatest is
> To please my Guru through devotion.

Of all marvels the greatest is
The will left by the dead Bonist.

Of all marvels the greatest is
Observance of the dead man's will.

Of all marvels the greatest is
The liberation of the dead.

Of all marvels the greatest is
The growing faith in this assembly.

The relatives of the dead man all said, "Surely he did not make
any mistake in choosing his faith. In order to attain Buddhahood at
the time of death one should certainly do what he has done.'"

"We all need a savior like the Jetsun," said Shiwa Aui, "But it is
most difficult to meet such a one and to have faith in him."

Milarepa then replied, "If you, my disciples, want to guide dead
men's consciousnesses to the Path, you need these qualifications."
Whereupon he sang:

Good and sure is the grace of the Whispered Lineage,
Through which one may attain the Accomplishment
        of Ḍākinīs.
My son disciples, ne'er mistake
Your Dharmic Transmission.

To cleanse the Karma of ill-fated ones,
You yourself must keep pure discipline.
To receive offerings and worship from the patrons,
You must have compassion and the Bodhi-Mind.
To be honored as the Chief Lama in the group,
You require Realization and merits.

To please the accomplished Guru, you need
Unshakable faith and perseverance.
To take the oblation for the dead, you must
Have the merit of superb Enlightenment.[2]
To emancipate the dead,
You need miraculous Power
And genuine Accomplishment.
To convert faithless men you must
Be able to work miracles.

To perform the Maṇḍala Ritual on the seventh day,
You must truly deliver
The dead man to the Path.

My disciples and patrons of the Bon,
Hold doubt in your minds no more.

The Jetsun's sister Bedha said, "Brother, you have redeemed other people's 'souls' like this, but you have done nothing to save the 'souls' of our own parents! Why?" Saying this, she sobbed bitterly. Milarepa took her hand and said, "Bedha, do not feel sad like this. To repay the bounty of our parents I have done these things for them." Then he sang:

I pray to the Jetsun Gurus — pray
Help me to repay my parents' bounties.

In guiding my parents' "souls"
Out of their phantom bodies,
I merged them with my own mind,
And dissolved them in the Mind-Essence
Of the Victorious One.
By His mercy a rainbow light
Shone forth from the Pure Land;
And into the "appearing" yet void
Buddha Kāya their bodies vanished.
How wondrous is it thus to merge
In Immanent Buddhahood.

Their voices, unreal echoes,
Were merged with Buddha's speech.
How wondrous is it thus
To merge with the Self-sound.

Their minds, in Bardo wandering,
Were caught by my Samādhi's power.
Thus thy beheld the Self-face of
The Illuminating-void Awareness.

Holding the mind in its natural state
All confusions are dispelled.
How wondrous is this state immutable.

In my life-long devotion,
With love and with good will
I recite the Mantra day and night.
By this merit my parents' sins are cleansed;
In the Six Realms they will ne'er be born again.

With holy companions, they are living now in joy;
With pleasures and enjoyment, they now live happily.
In the Pure Land of Happiness they are
Surrounded by Bha Wos and Ḍākinīs.
Dear sister Bedha, worry not nor grieve for them!

Bedha said, "This is indeed wonderful. But please tell me, what ritual did you perform for them?" In answer, Milarepa sang:

I pray to the Refuge of all beings —
Pray help me to repay my parents' bounties.

In the Maṇḍala of Non-dual Bliss
I placed the Buddha images
Of illuminating Self-awareness.

In the vase of Holy Scriptures and Instructions
I placed for rinsing, water of the Six Pāramitās.
With it I cleansed the filth of the Five Poisons.

With the Ghagyu Guru's nectar
I conferred the Four Initiations
On their bodies, mouths, and minds.
I showed them the non-distinction of Great Bliss,
And the successive Realizations of the Path.

The unity of the Trikāya
Was the oblation I made for them;
The Emancipation-from-Desires
Was the ritual I performed for their deaths.
With perfect knowledge of timing I brought
For them the offering of spiritual assistance.
For them I dedicated the Mahāmudrā,
For them I vowed to serve all [sentient beings].

My wishes, and those of parent-like beings
Are all fulfilled and merged in one.

By thinking of my Guru's grace
I repaid their bounties.

Having heard this song, Bedha was firmly convinced. To persuade his
sister to practice the Dharma with determination, Milarepa sang again:

I bow down at the feet of Marpa.
Pray quench the passions of my kinsmen,
And with the Dharma fuse their minds.

Awake and listen, sister Bedha!
If when young you do not practice,
Why practice then when you grow old?
If you depend not on the Jetsun Guru,
Why rely on pleasant Gurus?
Without the Instruction of the Whispered Lineage,
What's the use of vain talk and arid words?

If you do not know your mind,
What's the use of learning?
If in the Void you cannot rest at ease,
Vain remarks will but increase your sins.

Self-conceited people
Who always make a show
Have no experience within.
Overweening and suspicious people
See not that appearances
Are but amusing plays.

The pretentious and over-critical
Are men without compassion, faith, or Bodhi-Mind.

He who never thinks of
Buddhahood, is angry,
And anxious over money,
Cannot a real Buddhist be.

Lacking compassion for all beings,
Filial piety causes Saṃsāra.
If one acts against the Dharma
Friends soon turn to enemies.
Those who only harm their friends

Are of the devil's kin,
However charming they may be!

He who claims to be a yogi
But cannot practice Immanence in depth,
Is only a bewildered man.
To those who cannot patiently help others
Friendship brings only quarrels and regret.

Dear sister Bedha, your sorrow for our mother's grief
Shows that you have yet to clear
Your obstacles and sins.

The Jetsun then sent her to meditate, and as a result, she attained extraordinary Experiences and Realizations. The Jetsun was very much pleased. To inspire and encourage her, he sang again:

Listen once more, sister Bedha!
If one ne'er loses faith in Dharma,
The ending of all pain will come.
If one ne'er accuses others,
People see one as an angel.
If one has no harmful thoughts,
Then one's merits will increase.

He who clings not now to things,
Will in his next life be joyful.
One who has little arrogance,
Will be loved by all.

Whoe'er intrinsic mind retains
Will soon win through to Buddhahood.
Whoe'er retreats in strict seclusion
And refrains from talking,
By Ḍākinīs will be blessed.

If you have no desire for pleasure,
Your Ripening Karma will be killed.
If till death you meditate,
You are the King of kings!

If mind be free of fraud and tangles,
Ḍākinīs and Bha Wos receive you.

If you pray [now and always] to your Jetsun Guru
Accomplishment and blessing will be yours.

Bear these words in mind, and meditate!
May joy and good fortune e'er be with you!

[Later], Bedha was able to meditate in solitude with great perseverance. As a result she gained exceptional Experiences and Realizations, and eventually she could match the merits of the four [foremost]
spiritual daughters of the Jetsun.

The Bonists who attended the ceremony on this occasion were all
confirmed with irrevocable faith toward Milarepa.

This is the story of the salvation of the dead man, and of Milarepa's
guiding his sister to the Bodhi [Path].

NOTES

1 Tibetan houses are usually constructed with three floors, the stable and
storeroom being located on the ground floor, and the living room, kitchen, etc., on
the middle floor. The prayer room, altar, and guest room usually occupy the top
floor.

2 The merit of superb Enlightenment: This is a free translation. Literally it
should read: "The merit of the [initial stage] of the Enlightment in the Path"
(mThon.Lam.Gyi.Yon.Tan.). The initial stage, or the First Bhūmi, is considered
the most important and critical stage in the Bodhisattva's Path. True Enlightenment is realized when one reaches this stage. See Story 44, Note 3.

FULFILLMENT OF THE
ḌĀKINĪS' PROPHECY

Obeisance to all Gurus

ONCE when the Jetsun Milarepa was dwelling in the upper valley of Tsar Ma at Nya Non, some of his patrons fought one another over the dowry of a new bride. When they came to the Jetsun for meditation he summoned all the participants, reconciled them with good advice, and preached much Dharma for them. Then he sang:

> Listen, you conceited men
> With rocks upon your heads!
> This is the sort of trouble that is caused by women
> Who for a long time have not had a man.
> Man-craving women are all trouble-makers
> Who foster only evil thoughts within.
> Wicked are the spreaders
> Of discord everywhere.
> This bride of an evil valley at an evil
> Time has become invaluable to the "blind";
> This filthy baggage has been the cause
> Of dispute among the men.
> Alas, these are unworthy, worldly acts;
> Elders, do not instigate them,
> Young men, be sane and sober.
> According to the Dharma's teaching
> Everyone here assembled
> Should try to change his mind!

Moved by this song, the disputants were all pacified. Then the lady patron Jham Mei, a very faithful follower of the Jetsun, made sumptuous offerings to him. Standing up from a row in the assembly, she asked, "Revered Jetsun, Precious One, please tell us, how have you accomplished your altruistic deeds? How many disciples do you have? And among them, how many have attained Enlightenment?" Milarepa replied, "It is very wonderful that these questions have arisen in your mind. As prophesied by the Dākinīs, I have done these things to benefit sentient beings":

> I pray to the Gurus and Dākinīs — pray
> Help me without effort to benefit all men.
>
> As Dākinīs foretold, like the sun
> Is the Nirmānakāya Dhagpo,
> Whose light will brighten all; like the moon
> Is Nirmānakāya Rechungpa;
> And Shiwa Aui, the elder brother,
> Is a tiger-like meditator.
> With Drigom and other Repas I have five-
> And-twenty leading disciples as foretold.
>
> Among my disciples, five-and-twenty are accomplished
>   beings;
> One hundred the Realization have attained;
> One hundred and eight, the Spontaneous Experience;
> Near one thousand, union with the Dharma; and more
> Than a hundred thousand have won Dharmic affiliations.
> A few disciples have
> Learned other arts from me.
> Your questions are most good,
> You are indeed well-endowed!

Hearing this, the disciples at the meeting all exclaimed, "Oh, many accomplished beings will come! How wonderful is this!" All were overwhelmed with joy and exaltation. Then they besought Milarepa to make good wishes for them. The Jetsun said, "Since this time both the receiver and the patrons are sincere, good wishes are automatically made. Nonetheless, I shall follow Buddha's example and say the dedication-wishes for you. You should now follow, and repeat this song after me":

> I pray to my Guru, Patron Buddha,
> And all gods — pray fulfill all my good wishes.
> Let all here now recite with me,

For I know the way to Buddhahood.
Pray remember me, ye Buddhas, Bodhisattvas, and
　　Saṅghas!

Since beginningless time in this great Saṃsāra,
I and all sentient beings have practiced
Charity, discipline, and other merits.
Thinking of them, my mind is full of joy!
To my parents and teachers I dedicate
All the merits that in this life I may have earned
In giving alms and service
To Buddhahood's attainment.
Before the [last] day comes, may I,
By the power of my merits,
Meet a Mahāyāna teacher
And observe the Precepts Three.
May all my good wishes be fulfilled,
And may I never commit sinful deeds.

By the power of my merits may I
Gain long life and prosperity.
Meeting good companions and favorable conditions,
May all hindrances to Liberation pass away from me.

While Milarepa was singing this song, an echo from Heaven was heard by all.

After some time, the people of Nya Non heard that the Jetsun was about to leave for other hermitages. They all came with good offerings, and besought him not to go. The Jetsun replied, "I have been staying here for quite a long time. My patrons may now have become wearied [of me]. I am going to another place to await the coming of my death. If I do not die soon, there will always be a chance for us to meet again. In the meantime, you should all try to practice these things":

Obeisance to my perfect Guru!

Property and possessions
Are like dew on the grass —
Give them without avarice away.

A human body that can practice Dharma is most
　　precious —

[To attain it again] you should keep the Precepts
    well
As if protecting your own eyes!

Anger brings one to the Lower
Realms, so never lose your temper,
Even though your life be forfeit.

Inertia and slackness never bring Accomplishment —
Exert yourself therefore in devotion.

Through distractions Mahāyāna can ne'er be under-
    stood —
Practice therefore concentration.

Since Buddhahood cannot be won without,
Watch the nature of your mind within.

Like fog is faith unstable —
When it starts to fade, you should
Strengthen it more than ever.

The patrons all cried, "Whatever you say, we won't let you go! By all means, please remain here!" Thus they besought him with the utmost earnestness. The Jetsun replied, "If I do not die, I shall try to come back to your village. If for some time we cannot see each other, try at times to remember and practice these things." Whereupon he sang:

Alas, how pitiful are worldly beings!
Like precious jade they cherish
Their bodies, yet like ancient trees
They are doomed in the end to fall.
Sometimes bridle your wild thoughts,
And pay heed to the Dharma.

Though you gather wealth as hard
As bees collect their honey,
The ills that on you may fall
Can never be foretold.
Sometimes bridle your wild thoughts
And pay heed to the Dharma.

One may offer to a Lama
Loads of silk for many years;
But when an ill-fortune descends,
Like a fading rainbow
One's faith at once dissolves.
Sometimes bridle your wild thoughts
And pay heed to the Dharma.

Like a pair of mated beasts,
Lovers live together,
But calamity by the wolf's attack
May fall on you at any time.
Sometimes bridle your wild thoughts,
And pay heed to the Dharma.

You may cherish your dear son,
Like a hen hatching her egg;
But a falling rock may crush it at any time.
Sometimes bridle your wild thoughts
And pay heed to the Dharma!

A face may be pretty as a flower,
Yet at any time it can be spoiled by violent hail.
Think at times of how this world
Is sorry, transient, and futile.

Though son and mother have affection
For each other, when discords arise,
Like foes they clash and quarrel.
Sometimes toward all sentient beings
You should feel compassion.

Basking in the warm sunlight
May be pleasant and a comfort,
But a storm of woe may rise
And choke you at any time.
Remember sometimes the deprived,
And give alms to those in need.

Oh, dear men and women patrons,
For he who cannot practice Dharma,
All his life will be meaningless,
All his acts wrongdoings!

"Yes, Revered Jetsun, we shall follow your instructions," said the patrons, "But we cannot bear to see you go away. Please, remain for our sake!" [But] Milarepa stayed in the Belly Cave for [only] a short time, and then went to the lower part of the valley. Standing on a rock, he left a pair of indented footprints on it as a token of memory to which the people of Nya Non might pay their homage and respect. Then, without the knowledge of the patrons, he went away.

This is the story of Milarepa giving his final admonishment to the patrons of Nya Non.

ADMONISHMENTS TO PHYSICIAN YANG NGE

Obeisance to all Gurus

THE Jetsun Milarepa and his five disciples now set out for Tong Lha. On the way they encountered five robbers, who searched them and found only some bowls and skulls. Then they asked, "Are you people called 'Milarepas'?" The Jetsun answered, "I am Milarepa." The robbers all bowed down to him and said, "We are indeed fortunate to meet you! Now please grant us some instructions." The Jetsun then preached for them the teaching of Karma, including such topics as the joy and merit of the higher realms, the miseries and vices of the three lower realms, and how good and bad deeds, respectively, would bring forth happiness and suffering. Then he added, "This is my advice: take it or not, it is entirely up to you. Listen to this song":

I bow down to the perfect Gurus.

High above, in the Heaven of Pleasures,
The Devas sow their rice,
And the crop is ripe
As the seeds are sown.
It is not that their method
Of farming is superior,
It is simply the Karmic reward
For their good deeds in former lives.
Men of endowment, give your alms!

Down below are wretched beings
In the great Eighteen Hells. When
Their bodies by the saw are cut

630

The wounds are healed at once;
'Tis not because their skin is healthy,
But is Karmic retribution
For those they killed in former lives.
Men of endowment, never kill!

In the dark realm yonder
Wander hungry ghosts.
As they finish eating
They feel hungry again;
The reason is not their stomachs' size,
It is Karmic retribution
For stinginess in former lives.
Men of endowment, never be parsimonious!

Near the Cleansing Pond
Is Duinjo's wondrous cow,
Ever ready to give milk.
But it is up to you
Whether or no you catch her.

Under the root of the Wish-fulfilling Tree
Is the drug that cures all five diseases.
Yet it is entirely up to you
Whether or no you dig for it.

In front of a good Guru
Is the Key of Pith-Instructions
To the door of the Two [Perfections],[1]
But it is entirely up to you
Whether or no you open it.

Hearing this song, great faith was aroused in all five robbers. Four of them swore that they would never kill or rob again. One decided to follow the Jetsun, and was accepted as a servant-disciple. Later he gained the Realization and became an advanced yogi.

After this incident, Milarepa and his disciples went down to Din Ri Namar. Meeting a shepherd on the way, Milarepa asked him, "Tell me, who is the outstanding patron in this place?" The shepherd answered, "There is a physician called Yang Nge — he is a rich and devoted Buddhist." They proceeded to the physician's house, and saw him standing among many people who were gathering there. Milarepa said, "Dear patron, we were told that you are the richest man here. We ask you to give us some food this morning." The physician replied, "On the other side of the mountain there is Milarepa, on this side, Dhampa Sangje. The stream of yogi pilgrims never stops flowing. How can I afford to give charity to every one of them? Now, I shall only give alms to Milarepa if he comes here himself. Of course, I know that I may not have the good Karma to see him at all." The Jetsun replied, "I can say that I am Milarepa himself. Now bring us the food."

"It is said that the Jetsun Milarepa can use anything at hand as a metaphor to preach. Now please use the bubbles of water in this ditch before us as a metaphor and give us a discourse," said the physician. In response, the Jetsun sang a song, "The Fleeting Bubbles":

> I pay homage to my gracious Guru —
> The Essence of all Buddhas at all times.
> Pray make everyone here think of the Dharma!
>
> As he said once, "Like bubbles is
> This life, transient and fleeting —
> In it no assurance can be found."
> A layman's life is like a thief
> Who sneaks into an empty house.
> Know you not the folly of it?
>
> Youth is like a summer flower —
> Suddenly it fades away.
> Old age is like a fire spreading through
> The fields — suddenly 'tis at your heels.
> The Buddha once said, "Birth and death are like
> Sunrise and sunset — now come, now go."
> Sickness is like a little bird
> Wounded by a sling.
> Know you not, health and strength
> Will in time desert you?
> Death is like an oil-dry lamp
> [After its last flicker].
> Nothing, I assure you,
> In this world is permanent.
> Evil Karma is like a waterfall,
> Which I have never seen flow upward.
> A sinful man is like a poisonous tree —
> If on it you lean you will be injured.

Transgressors are like frost-bitten peas —
Like spoiled fat, they ruin everything.
Dharma practicers are like peasants in the field —
With caution and vigor they will be successful.
The Guru is like medicine and nectar —
Relying on him, one will win success.
Discipline is like a watchman's tower —
Observing it, one will attain Accomplishment.

The Law of Karma is like Saṃsāra's wheel —
Whoever breaks it will suffer a great loss.
Saṃsāra is like a poisonous thorn
In the flesh — if not pulled out,
The poison will increase and spread.
The coming of death is like the shadow
Of a tree at sunset — it runs
Fast and none can halt it.
When that time arrives, what else
Can help but the holy Dharma?
Though Dharma is the fount of victory,
Those who aspire to it are rare.

Scores of men are tangled in
The miseries of Saṃsāra;
Into this misfortune born, they strive
By plunder and theft for gain.

He who talks on Dharma
With elation is inspired,
But when a task is set him,
He is wrecked and lost.

Dear patrons, do not talk too much,
But practice the holy Dharma.

"This is indeed very helpful to my mind," commented the physician, "but please preach still further for me on the truth of Karma and the suffering of birth, old age, illness, and death, thus enabling me to gain a deeper conviction on Buddhism." In response, the Jetsun sang:

In the realm of the Great Unborn
He shines with the Four Infinities —

To my wish-granting Jetsun Guru,
The Guide to the Path of Greatest Joy,
I pay my heart-felt praise.

Please listen to these words,
Dear friends here assembled.
When you are young and vigorous
You ne'er think of old age coming,
But it approaches slow and sure
Like a seed growing underground.

When you are strong and healthy
You ne'er think of sickness coming,
But it descends with sudden force
Like a stroke of lightning.

When involved in worldly things
You ne'er think of death's approach.
Quick it comes like thunder
Crashing round your head.

Sickness, old age, and death
Ever meet each other
As do hands and mouth.

Waiting for his prey in ambush,
Yama is ready for his victim
When disaster catches him.

Sparrows fly in single file. Like them, life
Death, and Bardo follow one another.
Never apart from you
Are these three "visitors."
Thus thinking, fear you
Not your sinful deeds?

Like strong arrows in ambush waiting,
Rebirth in Hell, as hungry ghost, or beast
Is [the destiny] waiting to catch you.
If once into their traps you fall,
Hard will you find it to escape.

Do you not fear the miseries

You experienced in the past?
Surely you will feel much pain
If misfortunes attack you?
The woes of life succeed one another
Like the sea's incessant waves —
One has barely passed, before
The next one takes its place.
Until you are liberated, pain
And pleasure come and go at random
Like passers-by encountered in the street.

Pleasures are precarious,
Like bathing in the sun;
Transient, too, as snow storms
Which come without warning.
Remembering these things,
Why practice not the Dharma?

Hearing this song, great faith in the Jetsun was aroused in all. They presented him with many good offerings, and asked him to stay there permanently. Milarepa did not accept their invitation, but only consented to remain overnight.

The physician besought the Jetsun to give them some instructions before he left. Then he summoned all the villagers, and added, "If, Revered Jetsun, you cannot stay here even for a few days, then please grant us some Dharma to practice." In response, Milarepa sang:

Listen with care, all you assembled here;
Do you truly want to practice Dharma?
If you do, you should try these things:
When lying down in bed, let not
Yourself go with ignorance;
At evening, recite the Patron Buddha
Mantra; at night, pray to the Holy Ones;
At midnight, meditate on Non-distinction. When
The day breaks, practice the Life-Prāṇa; in the morn,
Repent of your wrongdoings; when the sun
Rises, identify your mind with forms.

In practice, the main thing
Is the Self-mind to watch;
The pith of all instructions
Is received from your Guru.

You should, then, always pray
To your Patron Buddha;
Keep the Samaya Rules
With your Vajra brothers;
To the Three Precious Ones
Always offer service.

E'er on your head visualize Him who is All Merciful,
Reciting the holy Mantra of the Jewel Lotus.[2]
Always to the poor give charity, and help
Those in need; ever serve and give alms
To priests of learning and discipline;
At all times take care of your parents.
Were a hundred scholars and Gurus gathered
Here, they could not give you better instruction.
May prosperity and joy
Follow you through all your lives!
May good health and long life
Be with you at all times!

Moved by this song, the audience were all confirmed with an unshakable faith toward the Jetsun. Later, the physician entered the Path at the time of his death.

After this incident, Milarepa and his disciples set out for Chu Bar.

This is the story of the Physician, Yang Nge.

NOTES

1 Two Perfections: the Perfection of Merit, and the Perfection of Wisdom.
2 That is, the Mantra of Avalokiteśvara: Om.Ma.Ne.Padme.Hum.

RECHUNGPA'S DEPARTURE

Obeisance to all Gurus

RECHUNGPA, the heart-son disciple of the Jetsun Milarepa, had difficulty because of his affiliation with the [noblewoman], Lady
Dembu. In order to free him from this hindrance, Milarepa transformed himself into a beggar and came to Rechungpa for alms. Now
Rechungpa possessed [at that time] a very large piece of jade, obtained from a ravine in the valley of Yagder. This he gave to the
"beggar," saying, "Use this jade to buy your food." Milarepa thought,
"My son has no attachment to material wealth, but has great compassion."

As a consequence of this almsgiving, Rechungpa separated from the
Lady Dembu; disheartened and wearied of her, he left, and returned
to the Jetsun.

On his way back he came to the house of a rich man and was
given two portions of dried meat, which he preserved with great care
in order to bring them back to the Jetsun as a present. At that time
Milarepa was staying at Chu Bar with some of his disciples. He said
to them, "Rechungpa is coming, and is bringing us something so extremely large that a whole valley is not big enough to contain it."

Before long Rechungpa arrived. He offered a bag of the dried meat
to the Jetsun and asked after his health. In answer, Milarepa sang:

> A yogi, I roam the mountains;
> Like a great Maṇḍala,
> My body is full of bliss.
> Cleansed of desires and pride,
> I feel well and happy.
> With longing for diversions killed
> I feel joy in solitude.
> Since I have renounced all things,

Happy am I in no-man's land.
Since I have cut off ties of kinsfolk
Getting and saving are not worries —
Happy and joyous do I live.
Without desire for scholarship or study
Of more books, I have no inferior feelings —
With Mind-Essence I feel only happiness.

I am well and happy
Without "gab" and "babble,"
For I do not want proud talk.
I am well and happy
Without plans or schemes.
For my mind is free from fraud.
I am well and happy, for I never
Involve myself in slanderous gossip
And I desire no fame or glory.
Where'er I stay, whate'er I wear
Or eat, I feel truly happy.
At all times am I happy and well. Son
Rechungpa, you are in health on your return?

Whereupon Rechungpa offered the dried meat to all the Repas
without discrimination or stinginess. One of them asked Milarepa,
"Revered Jetsun, you have just told us that Rechungpa would bring
us a big present, larger than the whole valley can contain; but where
is it?" With a smile Milarepa replied, "The valley is your stomach,
and the meat is that big present — too big to be stuffed into it." Hearing this, the Repas all burst into hearty laughter.

The Jetsun then said, "I am going to give you all an Initiation, but
according to the Dharma an offering to the Guru is necessary; you
may bring anything you have, but Rechungpa is a special case — he
can do without one." Hearing this, Rechungpa unhappily joined in
the ceremony.

When he approached the Maṇḍala he saw the big jade which he had
given to the beggar standing right in its center. He was dumfound-
ed; then suddenly he realized that the beggar was his Guru's transformation, used to sever the bonds between himself and Lady Dembu.
[Reviewing the whole event in retrospect], Rechungpa now felt deeply grateful to the Jetsun.

"Rechungpa," said the Jetsun, "Had it not been for me, this jade
would have carried you to destruction. It is only because of your un-

ceasing faith and veneration toward me, and your great compassion
for all sentient beings, that you are freed from this hindrance. Now
you should be grateful and happy. Listen to my song":

> Great was the blessing of the Father Guru,
> Important was Milarepa's miracle,
> Vital were Rechungpa's charity and love!
> The jade you gave the beggar
> Is with us here; this evening
> We may offer it to Dem Chog
> At our Initiation rite.

> To give alms to the needy with compassion
> Is equal to serving Buddhas in the Three Times.
> To give with sympathy to beggars is
> To make offerings to Milarepa.
> Sentient beings are one's parents; to
> Discriminate between them is harmful and
> Ignorant. True sages and
> Scholars are always in accord;
> Clinging to one's School and condemning others
> Is the certain way to waste one's learning.
> Since all Dharmas equally are good,
> Those who cling to sectarianism
> Degrade Buddhism and sever
> Themselves from Liberation.
> All the happiness one has
> Is derived from others;
> All the help one gives to them
> In return brings happiness.
> One's pernicious deeds
> Only harm oneself.

> Enter this Maṇḍala with benevolent
> Mind; confess, repent you of your sins, observe
> All precepts with determination.

Rechungpa was deeply moved. In remorse, he confessed all his
transgressions before his Guru and his brothers-in-the-Dharma in this
song:

> Yearning for physical enjoyments,

In pursuit of pleasure I indulged.
Falling for tempations, I committed
Debasing deeds that lead to misery.
Before the *body* of my Father Guru
I now confess them fully.

Craving for talk leads to deceit
And lies, a glib tongue and clever
Words drag one right down to Hell.
Wine and meat that please the mouth
Turn one into a hungry ghost.
All my untrue and shameless talk,
I now confess in full before my Father Guru's *mouth*.

To crave for pleasure causes evil thoughts,
To yearn for fame creates most filthy acts.
All my sinful deeds, caused by desire and greed,
I now confess in full before
My Father Guru's *mind*.

Wandering in towns and hamlets,
My practices were interrupted;
Performing many exorcisms,
My Mantra power grew feeble;
Becoming far too active, my good
Samādhi experience faded.
To the Maṇḍala's Gods
I now confess these wrongs.

In a house where many people live
I distinguished between "mine" and "yours."
All my smallness and degradation
I confess to my Dharma-brothers.

Thereupon the Jetsun initiated the Repas with the "Pointing-out" exercise in an elaborate manner. After the ceremony, Repa Shiwa Aui arose from the assembly and asked, "Rechungpa is a yogi who has completely mastered the Prāṇa-Mind. Why should a man such as he still need the Jetsun's protection and care when he takes a lady for Tantric practice? And why should such a man still repent before you for this act?" The Jetsun replied, "This is because [in order to practice the secret action], one must know the right time and the right conditions." Whereupon he sang:

I bow down to my gracious Guru Marpa —
Pray lead me with your blessing to the Path,
Help me to understand the mind-state of my disciples!

Knowing not the right time to
Practice, one's Yoga will stray;
Knowing not the right time to
Speak, the elders will go astray;
Knowing not the right time to give
Food, the good housewife will go astray;
Knowing not the right time to perform
Their duties, the servants will go astray;
Knowing not the right time to meet
The foe, the fighters will go astray;
Knowing not the right time to meet
Conditions, noble monks will stray;
Knowing not the right time to help others,
Altruistic deeds will go astray.

Without perseverence and determination,
To stay in the mountains will be a waste of time.
If men consider not nor help each other,
Companionship and brotherhood are lost.
If a disciple does not keep his Guru's rules,
The relationship with him will soon be broken.
Boundless, alas, are errors and deviations,
How can one list them all?
Dear sons, you should practice
In accordance with my words!

Hearing this song, all the disciples gained a decisive understanding. Rechungpa then made a solemn vow before the Jetsun that he would observe and obey all his instructions. Thereafter he served Milarepa [even more] earnestly than before.

One night Rechungpa dreamt that he put a load of wool on [the back of] a dog, and shouted, "Write the words! Write the words!" Then they set out, and reached a mountain pass. From one side of the mountain came eighty-eight people to escort them, and from the other came another eighty-eight people to welcome them. Rechungpa asked the Jetsun to interpret this dream for him. In answer, Milarepa sang:

> The dog shows that you will have
> A friend, the wool that your mind
> Will be benign and gentle.
> "Write the words" means that
> You will be well-learned.
> The shouting shows you will sing
> From wonderful Experience.
> The two groups of eighty-eight
> Means that so many people
> Will escort and welcome you.

Another night Rechungpa dreamt that he threw off his clothes and washed his body with water, then became a bird that flew away and alighted on a tree. Then he saw a mirror and looked into it. In explaining this dream, Milarepa sang:

> Throwing off your clothes implies
> Relinquishment of all desires.
> Washing your body with clean water means
> Purification through the Instructions.
> [Transforming into] a bird implies
> Kindness and compassion. The bird's
> Two wings are the Two Provisions.
> Alighting on the branch reveals
> That in the Bodhi Tree you'll sit.
> The mirror you saw implies
> Revelations by Ḍākinīs.

Again one night Rechungpa dreamt that he rode backward on a donkey, and wore a robe called "Hope!" The Jetsun explained the dream in this song:

> Turning your back toward Saṃsāra
> You ride the Mahāyāna's ass.
> When Nirvāṇa's welcome comes
> You will fulfill the hopes of all.

Another night Rechungpa dreamt that he put a jewel upon his head and donned an immaculate robe. Then he looked into a bright mirror having no stain upon it. In the right hand he held a Vajra, in the left a human skull full of blood. He also dreamt that he sat cross-legged on a lotus seat; his back radiated beams of light and his body was ablaze with a great fire. He saw a fountain springing up be-

fore him, and the sun and moon shone from his heart. On his left
stood men and women in even number; on his right, a child was herding a kid, which then multiplied into many goats. Rechungpa went to
the Jetsun and asked him to interpret the dream. The Jetsun replied,
"The meaning of the dream is this":

> The jewel means that you should always
> Think of your Guru upon your head;
> The pure white robe implies the Whispered
> Lineage; looking into the mirror means
> The "Pointing-out" Performance; holding
> The Vajra in the right hand indicates
> The destruction of all wandering thoughts.
> The skull in your left hand is a symbol
> Of your Bliss-Void Experience; the lotus
> Seat implies your freedom from all faults;
> Your sitting cross-legged indicates
> You will be in Samādhi long;
> The light radiating from your back
> Means that you will realize aright.
> The fountain that gushes forth before you means
> That you will have Signs and Experiences;
> The fire that from your body flames
> Is the burning of Dumo heat;
> The sun and moon are proof
> Of your Illumination.
> The men and women standing on your left
> Means that Bha Wos and Mos will welcome you;
> On your right the kid and goats are proof
> That you will protect your disciples;
> The multiplying of the kids foretells·
> The spreading of the Whispered Lineage.

The Jetsun continued, "Since you have reached this state, it will not
be necessary for you to stay with me any longer. You should leave, now
that the right time has come for you to benefit sentient beings on a
grand scale." Then he sang:

> Hearken, my son Rechungpa! Knowing
> The dependent origination
> Of Saṃsāra and Nirvāṇa, if
> You can rely on a holy Guru,

To you will come the Pith-Instructions
Without effort and search.

Listen, my son Rechungpa! If you
Can conquer the desire for city
Life and remain in the hermitage,
The Accomplishment will come of itself
Without effort and striving.
If you can forego evil deeds and clinging
And can renounce all your wants and cravings,
Quietly will you tread the Path of Joy
Without attachment or desires.

Listen, oh my son, the root
Of Saṃsāra is *to bear*;
If you can cut off the clinging-love
For sons and live in solitude,
Quietly will you enter Buddha's Land.

Listen, my son, though through
Tibet the Dharma spreads, many
Adulterate it. People call
Themselves Gurus and disciples,
But with their clever tongues
They indulge in obscene talk.
Go, my son, go and teach them,
Show them the right teachings
Of the pure Lineage!

Listen, my son Rechungpa,
If from your heart you want
To practice holy Dharma,
Remember that Buddhism should
Make one conquer one's desires.
Try to renounce all greed,
Refrain from talking much.

Listen, son Rechungpa,
If you want Buddhahood
Forget all pleasures of this life, strive
For Realization stabilized within,
And never from the *base* of your Self-mind depart.

The Jetsun then said, "Rechungpa, in the past when you should have remained in one place, you wanted to go away. But now you should go to the Doh of Loro [near] Shar Bo forest [which is close to] Shambo Snow Mountain on the Tibetan border. There you can benefit sentient beings."

> Rechungpa, my elder son,
> You are going now to Weu.
> Of my four sons you are
> The most manly one.
> Dear son of various Successions,
> Think of your Guru on your head, and go.
>
> Keep the Samaya Rules with care, and go!
> Torch-bearer of the Whispered Lineage,
> Go and dispel the mists of ignorance!
> Go and ripen gifted disciples,
> Reveal nothing to the incapable.
>
> Go and plant the life-tree of Dharma,
> Looking with love after the gifted.
> Go south to the border regions,
> And meditate on Shambo Mountain.
>
> Son Rechungpa, you will have your temple
> On the border between Tibet and Doh.

Having made all preparations for the journey, Rechungpa came to the Jetsun, bowed down to him, and sang this song:

> Following your order, Father Guru,
> Your elder son is going now to Weu.
> Pray bless him with your Vajra Body,
> On his journey; pray, with your
> Immaculate Words, protect
> Him from all hindrances;
> With your mindless thought
> Lead him to the Path.
> Dear Father Jetsun, of yourself
> Take care and preserve your health.
>
> Your son is going now to Weu;
> Pray escort him on his journey.

Pray, Precious One — the shelter
Of all beings, who embodies
All Buddhas of all times —
Take care and keep in health.

Pray, Omniscient One, who works
Wonders with the Eyes of Dharma,
Pray keep well and of yourself take care.

Pray, Precious One, whose bounty
[I] hardly can repay —
Pray dispel all darkness,
And in good health remain.
Pray, mighty Guru, the Bodhi-
Path's benevolent guide,
Pray of yourself take care.

In sending Rechungpa upon his journey, the Jetsun sang a song
of the View, Practice, and Action:

Son, the View is to rid oneself of sectarianism,
The Practice is to remain in the hermitage,
The Action is to eschew bad companionship,
The Discipline is to harmonize all forms,
The Accomplishment is gained by thinking [e'er]
        of death.

The Jetsun continued, "In the year of the Hare, the month of the
Horse, and on the fourteenth day, you should return. This is very important." Then he gave Rechungpa a piece of gold and bestowed upon
him many of his most cherished Instructions. Rechungpa said, "Though
I cannot bear to depart from you, I have to obey your order. I must
now leave for Weu." As Rechungpa said this, tears rolled down his
face. To make the wish of seeing the Jetsun again, he sang:

The rivers of India and Nepal,
Divided by different valleys,
Flow in different directions.
Yet, as rivers, they are all alike —
In the great ocean they will meet again.

Divided by the Four Continents,
The sun rises in the East, the moon

Sets in the West; as light-bearers
They are both alike: on a cloudless
Autumn evening they sometimes see each other.

Veiled by ignorance,
The minds of man and Buddha
Appear to be different;
Yet in the realm of Mind-Essence
They both are of one taste. Some-
Time they will meet each other
In the great Dharmadhātu.

Because of Māyā's working,
The father Jetsun remains
On the hill, while Rechungpa,
The son, travels to far places;
Yet in the Dharmakāya
Never do they separate.
In the Og-Men Heaven
They will meet again.

Dear Father Jetsun, please keep well.
I, Rechungpa, am leaving now for Weu!

Rechungpa bowed down to the Jetsun, touching his feet with his
head, and once more made many wishes. Then he set out for Weu.

While Rechungpa was living at the Forest Temple of Shar Mo, his
lady came to him for forgiveness. At first he would not see her, but
later, because of his compassion and the earnest entreaties of Rin Chin
Drags, he relented and granted her an interview. She was destitute and
appeared to have undergone many physical and mental trials. Seeing
her in such a pitiful state, Rechungpa was deeply moved. He shed many
tears, gave her a nugget of gold, and sang this song:

I bow at the feet of Mila
The supreme. Pray in your pity
Make me remember your bounties.

You, the zealous talker,
Look not as you did before.
On my return to my Guru
I saw in the Maṇḍala that great lump

Of jade about which our dispute arose.
When I saw it, all the hairs
Of my body stood on end.

Formerly, my Guru said,
"Do not, do not go to Weu."
But later he said,
"Go now to Weu!"
Thinking of this, I can but feel amazed.

In the life of my Father Jetsun,
One finds that he treats gold like stones;
Giving me this gold, he said,
"Take it, take it with you now."
Thinking of this, I can but feel amazed.

With this piece of gold you can
Guild images of Buddha,
And cleanse your bodily sins.
With this piece of gold you can
Practice rituals and Mantras,
Cleansing thus your sins of speech.
With it you can also build
Many stūpas and Tsa Tsas,
Cleansing thus your sins of mind.

Referring all things to your Self-mind within,
Practice the teachings of the Whispered Lineage;
Pray and pray again to your Jetsun Guru,
Often rouse the thought of renunciation.
If you can do this you will
Attain great Accomplishment!

Feeling deep pity for her and her uncle, Rechungpa took them both under his care. He then imparted the Instructions to them and set them to meditating. The uncle was thus cured of leprosy, and the lady also gained good Experiences and Realizations. Later, it was said, she became a very good yoginī and benefited many sentient beings.

This is the latter part of the story of Rechungpa's journey to Weu.

ཨྠྃ

THE STORY OF DRASHI TSE

Obeisance to all Gurus

ONE time at Lha Dro of Drin, the Jetsun Milarepa was patronized by Drashi Tse, who, in an assembly attended by many patrons, stood up and said, "Revered Jetsun, when I hear people preaching the Dharma I always feel very happy. But I know that I cannot be a great yogi and a well-learned priest at the same time. Witnessing the fact that you, the Jetsun, have devoted yourself solely to the practice, I was confirmed with great faith. Do you think I should concentrate my effort on meditation alone, or not?" The Jetsun replied, "It is for the very sake of practice that the Dharma is preached and studied. If one does not practice or meditate, both studying and preaching will be meaningless. Now listen to my song":

> Without practice, the Dharma of preaching
> Leads only to pride. Without fostering,
> An adopted son always becomes a foe.
> Without instruction, a load
> Of books is but a burden;
> Except for lies and boasting
> What good can they ever do?
> Hearing the wily *Expedient*
> *Teachings*, people feel delighted,
> But very few would follow
> The Guru's *Final Teachings*.
>
> With faith practice holy Dharma,
> Dear patrons and disciples!
> Without deceit or boasting,
> Humble, honest, and straightforward,
> I now tell you the truth!

The Jetsun continued: "If one decides to practice the Dharma, he will learn a great deal; but if he could contemplate the Essential Truth for just a short time, it would help him more. If one talks much, the higher teaching will be overshadowed by his lower realizations. If one cannot stabilize his mind, all his seemingly good deeds will become self-deceiving. If one has a great attachment and desire for this world, any form of Dharma he may practice will be no more than a Dharma-of-the-mouth. Certain people study Buddhism for pleasure, then with great pride in their learning they begin to lose faith in the great teachers of the past. As a result, they will lose the blessings.

"Many people think they will have ample time to practice the Dharma, but without their notice or expectation, death suddenly descends upon them and they lose forever the chance to practice. What then can they do? One should turn all his Buddhist knowledge inside his mouth, and meditate. If one does not further his studies and meditation at the same time, but thinks that he should first learn a great deal before starting the actual practice [he will be completely lost], because knowledge is infinite, and there is no possibility of mastering it all.

"Again, if one talks to a revered priest who is rich in Buddhist learning he will be told that there is not a single thing in Buddhism that is not needed. He may then acquire many, many profound teachings; but he does not know which one to practice. He may choose one and practice it, but gain no Experience at all. Then doubts and skepticism creep into his mind and he begins to think, 'Should I try some *other* practice? Would not another Yoga suit me better than this one?' Thus he will never accomplish anything. This is comparable to a man who studies the Soma plant[1] but forgets the basic principles and his original intention, like a child holding a wild flower in its hand." Milarepa then continued his admonishment in this song:

> Hearken, my faithful patrons! Even sinful
> Persons, not knowing the great power of Karma,
> Dream of achieving Liberation.
> Life wears out as days and years go by,
> Yet in pursuing pleasures
> People spend their lives. They ask,
> "Will this month or year be good?"
> Blind to life's speedy passing,
> Fools cherish foolish questions.

He who truly wants to practice Dharma
Should make offerings to the Holy Ones,
Take refuge in the Triple Gem,
Give service to the Jetsun Guru,
Pay respect to his parents, give
Alms without hoping for reward.
He should offer help to those in need;
He should live and act up to
The Dharma's principles.
Not much is needed for Buddhist practice;
Too many vows lead to self-cheating.
Dear patrons, try to practice what I say.

"Your instructions are very helpful, and easy to understand," said
the patrons. "We shall try to follow them without fail. Now please
give us still more advice appropriate to our needs."

Milarepa replied, "I have many good teachings to give if you can
practice and follow them. Otherwise I see no point in doing so."

"We will practice them. Pray by all means teach us!"

"Well, then, these are the things you should do":

My dear patrons, if you decide to follow
My words and cultivate the Ultimate,
Remember that all will die,
And that to practice Dharma
Is the only good way of life.
Worldly wealth is a delusion —
Though much you may accumulate,
In the end you must abandon
All, so 'tis better to give alms.

Affection for one's loved ones may
Be very deep, yet one must
Eventually leave them.
Better 'tis to practice the Non-dual Truth.

However strong a house is built
Eventually it will fall.
'Tis better far to live in no-man's land.
Whatever food one may preserve,
In time will be consumed. Better far
Is it to store the food of Dharma.

Worldly affairs cannot be trusted;
It is better to renounce them all.

Since foolish talk is endless
'Tis better to shut one's mouth.

Instructions are like the art of oiling another's
        skin;
Better is it to rely on a proficient Guru.
[Spiritual] Experiences resemble
The moon's [brief] emergence from the clouds. 'Tis better
Unceasingly to practice,
Like an ever-flowing stream.

These are the ten essentials
That have risen in my mind.
May you, Drin's men and women patrons,
All gain good progress in the Dharma!

Then Milarepa taught them how to take the Three Refuges, how to rouse the Bodhi-Mind, to dedicate [themselves], and to take the [Bodhisattva's] Vow. These instructions greatly inspired them with good spiritual thoughts. Among those attending, many learned to practice meditation, and a few even gained good Experiences.

This is the story of Drashi Tse.

NOTES

1 Soma plant: "A climbing plant the juice of which was offered in libations to the gods; the Hindus also worshiped it on account of its intoxicating qualities." (Quoted from Sarat Chandra Dass' Dictionary, p. 1282.)

THE SONG OF
GOOD COMPANIONS

Obeisance to all Gurus

WHEN the Jetsun Milarepa was staying in the Stone House of Drin, Tsese, Ku Ju, and many other patrons came to him for the Dharma. Tsese said, "Please give us some Buddhist teaching that is easy to understand." Milarepa replied, "Very well, lend your ears and listen carefully to this song:"

> Pray, Father Guru, supreme Marpa,
> Pray bless us and bring the Dharma to our minds.
>
> Dear patrons, with care listen
> For a moment to my words.
>
> Superior men have need of Dharma;
> Without it, they are like eagles —
> Even though perched on high,
> They have but little meaning.
>
> Average men have need of Dharma;
> Without it, they are like tigers —
> Though possessing greatest strength,
> They are of little value.
>
> Inferior men have need of Dharma;
> Without it they are like a peddler's asses —
> Though they carry a big load,
> It does them but little good.

653

Superior women need the Dharma;
Without it, they are like pictures on a wall —
Though they look very pretty,
They have no use or meaning.

Average women need the Dharma;
Without it they are like little rats;
Though they are clever at getting food,
Their lives have but little meaning.

Inferior women need the Dhama;
Without it, they are just like vixens —
Though they be deft and cunning,
Their deeds have little value.

Old men need the Dharma; without
It, they are like decaying trees.
Growing youths the Dharma need;
Without it, they are like yoked bulls.
Young maidens need the Dharma; without
It, they are but decorated cows.
All young people need the Dharma; without it
They are like blossoms shut within a shell.
All children need the Dharma; without it
They are like robbers possessed by demons.

Without the Dharma, all one
Does lacks meaning and purpose.
Those who want to live with meaning
Should practice the Buddha's teaching.

The lady patron, Ku Ju, then said, "Revered Jetsun, you now have
many sons and disciples, yet you still like to live as a recluse. You
must find it a very happy life. Do you have good companions [un-
known to us] living with you?"

"Yes, I do. Now listen to this song":

I bow down to my Father Gurus.

Living as a yogi recluse,
I have one-and-twenty good companions:
The Gurus, Patron Buddhas, and Ḍākinīs
Are the three for prayer; the Buddhas, Dharmas,

And Sanghas are the three for refuge;
The Sūtras, Tantras, and Sāstras are
The three for learning; the Nerves, the Drops,
And Breathings are the three for practice
Of the Skillful Path; Bliss, No-thought,
And Illumination are the three
For meditation; piety, pure
Thought, and compassion are the three
For the Bodhi-Path; Bha Wo, Bha Mo,
And the Guards are the three escorts
Through whom to conquer hindrances.

"These things are wonderful," said Ku Ju, "but would you mind telling us more about them in similes?" In response, Milarepa sang:

Pray bless me, all Gurus in the Lineage.

Sitting upon the sun-moon seat[1] the Gurus
Of the Succession are on my head.
To describe them with a parable,
They are like a string of jewels —
Blessed and joyful is my mind.

The Three Precious Gems are my reliance —
Ever protected am I in their love.
To describe this feeling with a simile,
'Tis like a cherished baby
Fed on his mother's lap
Without fear or sorrow —
Blessed and joyful is my mind.

On my right are many Bha Wos
Whose blessing dispels all my hindrances.
To describe them with a parable,
They are like blades revolving o'er my head
Protecting me from all injuries —
Blessed and joyful is my mind.

On my left are many Ḍākinīs,
Blessing me with the gift of Two Accomplishments.
To describe them with a simile,
They are like kind mothers and sisters

Circling round me to fulfil my wishes —
Blessed and joyful is my mind.

Before me are the Guards of the Doctrine
Who carry out my orders.
To describe them with a parable,
They are like obedient servants
Fulfilling all my wishes —
Blessed and joyful is my mind.

My View on Reality is perfected in three aspects,[2]
With it I overwhelm the Hīnayāna teaching.
To describe this with a simile,
'Tis like a fearless lion strutting in the snow —
Blessed and joyful is my mind.

My Practice of Skill and Wisdom
Is like an eagle's mighty wings
With which I soar into the firmament.
I fly through the sky without fear of falling —
Blessed and joyful is my mind.

My Action is full of strength and valor,
Both distractions and drowsiness are destroyed.
To describe this with a parable,
'Tis like a tiger stalking through
The woods without fear or dread —
Blessed and joyful is my mind!

Having actualized the Trikāya,
With ease I benefit all beings
Through Bodies transformed.
To describe this with a simile,
'Tis like a golden fish that plays
With glee in water without effort —
Blessed and joyful is my mind.

Having mastered all manifestations,
I sing little songs
Opportune to the occasion.
To describe this with a simile,
'Tis like a dragon roaring in

The sky without fear or dread —
Blessed and joyful is my mind.

I am the Yogi Milarepa
Who wanders from one retreat to another.
To describe this with a simile,
'Tis like the wild beasts who live
In the mountains without fear —
Blessed and joyful is my mind.

I have sung for you, in cheerful mood,
A song with five parables and six meanings —
Listen carefully, men and Devas here assembled!
Do not be misled,
But observe your minds;
Try to reach the state
Of dying without regret.
In the light of Dharma
I wish you all good fortune!

All those attending were satisfied and pleased. Thereafter, they
made good efforts in virtuous deeds. Several of the young men present were accepted as servant-disciples by the Jetsun, who initiated
them with the Pith-Instructions and then sent them to meditate. A
few of them later became enlightened yogis.

This is the story of Tsese, Ku Ju, and the patrons of Drin.

NOTES

1 Sun-moon seat (T.T.: Ñi.Zlahi.gDan.): The Tantric deities are usually pic-
tured as sitting upon a seat containg three layers: the first layer is a lotus, the second
a sun, the third a moon symbolizing, respectively, the purity, the positive force
and the negative force.

2 The translator is not certain about these three aspects, or three functions
(T.T.: rTsal.gSum.). They probably denote the Foundation, the Path, and the Accomplishment.

THE EVIDENCE OF ACCOMPLISHMENT

Obeisance to all Gurus

A<small>T ONE</small> time when the Jetsun Milarepa was staying at the Sky Castle on Red Rock Mountain Peak, some sheep-owners came from Drin to visit him. They said, "Please give us some instructions that will help our minds." The Jetsun replied, "If you want to receive the Dharma you had better follow my example and first renounce the things that are against it."

"But what are they?" they asked.

In answer, Milarepa sang:

> Hearken to me, friends and patrons!
> An act that has no meaning,
> Unnatural pretense, and fearless empty talk,
> Are three things against the Dharma
> Which I have renounced. 'Tis good
> For you to do the same.
>
> The place that inflates one, the group
> That stirs up quarrels, the status
> By hypocrisy maintained,
> Are three things against the Dharma
> Which I have renounced. 'Tis good
> For you to do the same.
>
> The Guru with little knowledge,
> The disciple with small faith,
> The brother who keeps little discipline,
> Are three things against the Dharma

Which I have renounced. 'Tis good
For you to do the same.

The wife who always complains,
The sons who e'er need punishment,
The servant who ever swaggers,
Are three things against the Dharma
Which I have renounced. 'Tis good
For you to do the same.

After hearing this song, the patrons all went home filled with inspiration and faith.

At another time Milarepa was blown off a high cliff by a strong gale of wind. His body hit a tree in falling. Just as the disciples, filled with apprehension, were wondering [if he were badly hurt], Milarepa appeared and showed them that no injury had been done. Then he sang:

Blown off a cliff by a strong gale,
I was hit by a cruel tree
And gripped by pain unbearable,
But the Dākinīs healed me.

. . .   .

Again one day, Milarepa appeared to fall from the top of a cliff. [From below] the disciples saw this happen and immediately dashed to the spot to receive his falling body. But when they reached it, Milarepa was already seated there, bursting with laughter. They asked him what had happened. In answer, he sang:

Stretching eagle-wings of the Non-dual,
I flew to the top of Red Rock Cliff.
To fall, is to fall to the bottom of an abyss;
To play, is to play jokes on my disciples;
To liberate, is to liberate from Saṃsāra and Nirvāṇa;
To receive, is to receive the Bliss-Void of self.

. . .   .

Again one day, as Milarepa was sitting on the edge of a high cliff, a girl came by. Seeing him, she cried out, "Do not sit there, do not

sit there! That is too dangerous!" Ignoring her warning, he remained
where he was. Then the earth beneath him began to slip and trickle
down [the cliff]. As a huge lump of earth was about to fall, Milarepa made a Mudrā-of-Threat, and flew away. In the meantime the
disciples thought that he must have been seriously injured and rushed
to the scene. But [when they arrived] they found him sitting there
at his ease, singing this song:

> This body is like a flower.
> From the dangerous Red Rock
> The devils tried to grab it,
> But the Ḍākinīs bore it safely.
> No devil again will try.

The disciples then asked, "How, Revered Jetsun, can you fall from
a high cliff and hit a tree without being injured?" Milarepa replied,
"My body has become the Rainbow Body, and my Klesas, Wisdom;
having realized the truth of Non-being I shall never die. Since I
have conquered the Eight Worldly Desires, all the Four Demons have
been disgraced and frustrated by me." "Do you consider that you have
now completely conquered the Four Demons?" they asked. "Yes," he
replied, "You may say so. Hereafter, for the next thirteen generations,
followers of my Lineage will be immune from the intrusions of the
Four Demons."

                    . . .   .

One day a Tantric yogi from Weu came to visit the Jetsun. Sevan
Repa asked him, "What kind of accomplished beings are to be found
in Weu?" The yogi answered, "We have accomplished yogis whom
the Non-men serve and provide with food." "According to my standards," replied the Jetsun, "These cannot be considered as accomplished
beings." Sevan Repa then asked, "Do you, Revered Jetsun, also receive offerings from the Non-men?" "Yes, I receive them in this way":

> Inexhaustible as the Treasury
> Of Heaven, Samādhi is my servant;
> Ḍākinīs prepare my food and drink;
> But this is not evidence
> Of an accomplished being.

The yogi retorted, "But in Weu we do have yogis who can see
the Patron Buddhas." In reply, Milarepa sang:

To him who sees the mind's nature
And dispels the mists of ignorance,
The Ḍākinīs show their faces;
Yet, in the Real Realm,
There is nothing to be seen.
Without deliberate "non-observation" in one's mind,
All Dharmas rise and are illuminated by themselves.
This is preached by all Ḍākinīs.

The profoundest teaching can be had
Only from one's Guru, with whom all
Supreme and Worldly Accomplishments
Will be obtained and all good wishes
Fulfilled in this very life;
This is assured by all Ḍākinīs.
But even all this is not evidence
Of an accomplished being.

The yogi asked again, "With what simile would you describe the mind's nature?" In answer, Milarepa sang:

This non-arising Mind-Essence cannot
Be described by metaphors or signs;
This Mind-Essence that cannot
Be extinguished is oft described
By fools, but those who realize
It, explain it by itself.
Devoid of "symbolized" and "symbolizer,"
It is a realm beyond all words and thought.
How wondrous is the blessing of my Lineage!

Hearing this song, the yogi was awakened from his previous misconceptions, and was confirmed with an irrevocable faith toward the Jetsun, who accepted him as a servant-disciple and initiated him with the Instructions. Through practice he eventually became an outstanding and enlightened yogi.

This is the story of conquering the Four Demons, and of Milarepa's interview with the Tantric yogi.

THE MIRACLES AND THE LAST ADMONISHMENT

Obeisance to all Gurus

ONCE when the Jetsun Milarepa was staying at Chu Bar, his body became invisible to certain people. Others saw him [sitting still and] neither eating food nor engaging in any activity. But everyone noticed that at times he laughed, and at others he cried. Shiwa Aui then said to him, "Yesterday I could not see you. Some people could, but they saw you sitting still [as if] in Samādhi. What were you doing then, and why did you first laugh, and then cry, without any apparent reason?" The Jetsun replied, "Since yesterday many people have been attending my discourses. When I saw their happiness I laughed, when I saw their sufferings, I wept."

"Please tell us all about it."

"If you want to hear this story, you should now prepare a Maṇḍala offering."

This was done, and after the ceremony the Jetsun said, "Yesterday I went out to preach the Dharma to all sentient beings in the Six Realms. Seeing the joys of Devas and human beings and those who do good deeds, I laughed; but when I saw the miseries in the three lower Realms, and those who indulged in evil deeds, I wept." Shiwa Aui then asked, "Please tell us what are the joys and miseries that sentient beings in the Six Realms experience? Especially, please tell us, what are the pleasures that the Devas enjoy?" The Jetsun replied, "Do not be fascinated by the pleasures of heavenly beings; they also have miseries like these":

> I pray to the Gracious Ones. Pray embrace
> All sentient beings in your blessing!

The pleasures enjoyed by men and Devas
Are like the amusements of the Heavenly Yak[1]
It may low like thunder,
But what good can it do?

[Swooning in a state of trance],
The Devas in the Four Formless Heavens[2]
Cannot distinguish good from evil..
Because their minds are dull and callous,
Insensible, they have no feeling.
In unconscious stupefaction,
They live many kalpas in a second.
What a pity that know it not!

Alas, these Heavenly births
Have neither sense nor value.
When they think vicious thoughts
They start to fall again.
As to the reason for their fall
[Scholars], with empty words, have dried
Their mouths in explanations.

In the Heavens of Form,[3] the Devas of
The five higher and twelve lower Realms can
Only live until their merits are exhausted.
Their virtues are essentially conditional,
And their Karmas basically Saṃsāric.

Those Dharma practicers subject to worldly
Desires, and those "great yogis" wrapped in stillness,
Have yet to purify their minds;
Huge may be their claims and boasts,
But seeds of habitual thoughts
In their minds are deeply rooted.
After a long-dormant time,
Evil thoughts will rise again.
When their merits and fortunes are consumed,
They to the lower Realms will go once more!
If I explain the horrors of a Deva's
Death, you will be disheartened and perplexed.
Bear this in your mind and ever meditate!

In a sad mood, the disciples asked the Jetsun to preach for them the sufferings of the Asuras. In response, he sang:

> I pray to the Gurus and Ḍākinīs —
> Pray bless and enable all
> To rouse the Bodhi-Mind.
>
> Great are Asuras' sufferings.
> Misled by malignant thoughts,
> To all they bring misfortunes.
> Knowing not their true Self-mind,
> Their deeds are self-deceiving,
> Their feelings coarse, their senses crude.
> Deeming all to be their foes,
> Not even for moment
> Can they know the truth. Evil
> By nature, they can hardly bear a loss; harder
> Is benevolence for them to cherish. Blinded
> By the Karma-of-Belligerence,
> They can never take good counsel.
>
> Ill nature such as this is caused
> By seeking pleasures for oneself
> And bearing harmful thoughts toward others.
> Pride, favoritism, vanity, and hatred
> Are the evil Karmic forces
> That drag one to a lower birth,
> Making sinful deeds more easy.
>
> Ripening Karma brings
> An instinctive hatred;
> Failing to distinguish right from wrong,
> They hardly can be helped by any means.
> Bear this my disciples, in your minds,
> And meditate with perseverance all your lives!

Shiwa Aui said, "Now please tell us about the sufferings of human beings." In answer, Milarepa sang:

> I bow down at the feet of Jetsun Marpa —
> The Buddha as a man disguised.
>
> We human beings are endowed with power

To do good or evil deeds;
This is because our body
Is made of all Six Elements.[4]

You junior Repas who desire to be great scholars
Should know the "kernel and shell" of Buddhism,
Lest learning lead you only to confusion.

Knowing not the *root of mind*, useless
Is it to meditate for years.
Without sincerity and willingness,
Rich offerings have no real meaning.
Without giving impartial aid to all,
Patronage of one's favorite is wrong.
Knowing not the right counsel for each man,
Blunt talk will only bring trouble and discord.

He who knows the appropriate way
To help men of diverse dispositions,
Can use expedient words for kind and fruitful
Purposes. He who knows little about himself
Can harm many by his ignorance.
When good will arises in one's mind, stones,
Trees, and earth all become seeds of virtue.

Again, an over-punctilious person knows not how to
    relax;
A gluttonous dog knows not what is hunger;
A brazen Guru knows not what is fear.
Rich men are wretched creatures with money,
Poor men are wretched creatures without money.
Alas, with or without money, both are miserable!
Happiness will come, dear children,
If you can practice the Dharma. Remember,
Then, my words and practice with perseverance.

"It is very true that human beings suffer like this," agreed the disciples. "Now please tell us about the sufferings in the Three Miserable Realms, even though just to mention them may be distressing. Also, to spur our spiritual efforts, please preach for us the causes of Hell and its woe." In response, the Jetsun sang:

I pray to my Guru-protectors, pray

Dispel fear of the Miserable Realms.

Those who for meat and blood
Slaughter living beings,
Will in the Eight Hot Hells be burned.
But if they can remember the good Teachings,
They soon will be emancipated.

Ruthless robbers who strike and kill,
Wrongly eating others' food
While clinging to their own with greed,
Will fall into the Eight Cold Hells.
Yet, if they hold no wrong views against the Dharma
It is said that the time for deliverance will come.
[The Holy Scriptures] also say
Whene'er the denizens of Hell
Recall the name of Buddha,
At once they will be delivered.

Ever repeating sinful deeds means
Dominance by vice and evil Karma.
Fiends filled with the craving for pleasures,
Murder even their parents and Gurus,
Rob the Three Gems of their treasure,
Revile and accuse falsely the Precious
Ones, and condemn the Dharma as untrue;
In the Hell-that-Never-Ceases[5]
These evildoers will be burned;
Far from them, alas, is Liberation.
This, my sons, will certainly distress you,
So into the Dharma throw your hearts
And devote yourselves to meditation!

The Repas said, "Merely to hear these horrible things so frightens and distresses us that we wonder how anyone can actually undergo them! Nevertheless, for the benefit of sentient beings, please tell us now about the sufferings of the Hungry Ghosts." In reply, Milarepa sang:

I bow down to all Gurus. Pray
Protect the denizens of Hell
From fears with your compassion!

Filled with the urge to kill themselves
Those in Hell cannot escape from fear.

Hungry Ghosts, seeing all forms as foes,
Run from each successive terror. Wild beasts
Fight and eat each other.
Who of them is to blame?
The sufferings of Hungry
Ghosts grow from their stinginess.
Like a rat is he who fails
To give alms when he is rich,
Begrudges food when he has plenty,
Gives no goods to others, but checks
Them over, counts, and stores them —
Discontented day and night.
At the time of death he sees
That his hard-earned wealth will be
Enjoyed by others. Caught in
Bardo by the agony of loss,
He lives the life of a Hungry Ghost.
Due to his delusive thoughts
He suffers thirst and hunger.
When he sees his goods enjoyed by others
He is tormentated by avarice and hate.
Again and again will he thus fall down [to Hell].

I, the great Yogi of Strength,
Now sing for you the woes
Of Hungry Ghosts. Dear sons
And disciples here assembled, think on
My words and meditate with perseverance!

Shiwa Aui then requested, "Now please tell us of the sufferings of
animals." Whereupon Milarepa sang:

I bow down to all holy Gurus. Pray protect
All animals from fear with your compassion!

Animals, alas, are ignorant and benighted;
Most stupid men will incarnate among them.
Blind and enslaved by evil Karma,
The ignorant know not Dharma's Truth.
Blind both to evil and to virtue,

They quickly waste their lives away.
Unable to reason and use symbols,
They act like blind automatons;
Unable to distinguish wrong from right,
Like maniacs, they do much wrong.
Some people even say 'tis good
[To be an animal],
Since it does not regret or repent.
Alas, how foolish is this thought!

Then, all stupid life-takers
Will incarnate as beasts;
The fools who know not right from wrong,
And those who harbor vicious thoughts,
Will incarnate as common brutes.
It is hard for me to describe
Their Karmas, but think on my words
And cultivate your minds.

The Repas again asked, "Did you preach the Dharma for sentient beings in only one place, or did you go to different regions in the Six Realms to preach?"

"In accordance with the different capacities, Karmas, and needs of sentient beings," replied the Jetsun, "I manifested myself in different forms at different places to preach the appropriate Dharma for them."

The monks, disciples, patrons, and attendants in the assembly were all deeply impressed with a fear of the great sufferings of Saṃsāra and the lower Realms. With a greater aspiration toward the Dharma, they all exerted themselves in the renunciation of sins and the practice of good deeds.

. . .   .

At another time, Milarepa flew up into the sky, transforming his body from one to many, and then retracted them back into one. Also he preached various Dharmas in an invisible form, and performed many other miracles.

When Sevan Repa saw Milarepa flying he also held his breath and tried to fly; but all he could do was to walk above the ground. Commenting on this, Milarepa said, "If one has not yet practiced as I have, by venerating my Guru, respecting my brothers, renouncing Saṃsāra, pitying sentient beings, and practicing devotion with great diligence, he should never expect to perform these miracles easily and spontaneously. My son-disciples, if you have not yet completed these virtuous deeds to suffice the cause [of the Supreme Accomplishment], you should never expect to attain it too easily." Whereupon he sang:

> If there be neither Karma nor the required conditions,
> In this life one should not hope to attain Buddhahood.
> He who cannot put all his trust in his Guru
> Should not expect care and blessing in return.
> He who cannot satisfy disciples
> Should not expect to become a Guru.
> He who cannot master his own mind
> Should have no hope of leading others.
> He who cannot hold the Lineage tradition
> Should not aspire towards the Signs and Siddhis.
> He who cannot practice diligently
> Should not have wishful thoughts for Buddhahood.
> He who has not cut the bonds of dualism
> Should not expect an infinite Compassion.
> He who cannot sever the chain of clinging to
> An entity should not expect an all-free View.
> He who has not seen Self-mind in nakedness
> Should not expect to behold the True Essence.
> He who knows not how to cleanse impurities
> Should not expect unceasing Experience.
> He who cannot destroy attachment within
> [Himself], should not expect relaxed Six Senses.
> He who is not expert in Samādhi
> Should not expect the great Omnipresence.
> He who has yet to uproot subtle hopes and fears
> Should never expect the Trikāya to attain.
> He who cannot flawlessly observe moral rules
> Should never expect immediate happiness.
> He who has not completed the Two Provisions
> Should never expect to be a revered Buddha.
> He who cannot obey orders should not hope
> For popularity among his brothers.
> He who has yet to master Self-awareness
> Should not expect freedom from ghosts and Devas.
> He who has yet to master all appearances
> Should not expect to govern the Three Lokas.
> He who has yet to transcend the mundane level
> Should not cherish the thought of "no good and no evil."
> A yogi who heads a monastery

Should not neglect discipline and virtue.
He who does not understand the stages
Of the Experiences should not try
To prove and check those of gifted disciples.
He who has not fully practiced the Pith-Instructions
Should not expect in Bardo to gain Liberation.
He who cannot observe the precepts in perfect order
Should ne'er expect his wishes to be easily fulfilled.
He who cannot observe well the Samaya rules
Should n'er expect Ḍākinīs and Guards to like him.
He who has not obtained the Key Instructions
From logic and the Holy Scriptures
Should not neglect the words and symbols.
He who possesses not the Five Miraculous
Powers, should not make predictions from external signs.
He who has not stablized the Experience,
Should never neglect to cultivate his mind.

· · ·   · · ·   · · ·

On another occasion, the Jetsun's body became invisible to all who came before him. Some saw light, and some a glowing lamp shining on his bed; others beheld a rainbow, water, a bar of gold, or a whirlwind; and still others could not see anything. Then Repa Shiwa Aui asked the Jetsun what were the meanings and reasons behind all these phenomena. Milarepa answered him in this song:

I pray to all Gurus —
Pray enable me to change into many forms.

Listen Shiwa Aui, my dear son,
Who is as good as Rechungpa.
Since I have mastered Earth,
Earth of myself is now a part;
Since I have mastered Water,
Water of myself is now a part;
Since I have mastered Fire,
Fire of myself is now a part;
Since I have mastered Air,
Air of myself is now a part.
Since I have mastered the Void of space,
All manifestations in the Cosmos
Have merged and are identified with me.

Since I have mastered the projection of Prāṇa-Mind,
I can transform my body into any form.
Dear son, if you have faith
In the Accomplished Jetsuns,
You will indeed be blessed
And your wishes fulfilled.

. . .   .

Again one day the Jetsun transformed himself into a different body
before each of his disciples and faithful patrons, to preach the Dharma
to them. Also he conjured a child playing with clay beside each
preacher. In short, he performed many miracles in inconceivable varieties. The disciples asked him his reasons for doing so. He replied, "I
am a yogi who sees his own Self-mind, thus I can change and manipulate all manifestations in the outer world to any form and in any
manner I please. Also, I can project and multiply all objects from my
mind and bring them back to it again." Then he sang:

I bow down to all Gurus.

When my body has the Guru's blessing,
It can work many miracles
And many transformations.
When my mouth receives the Guru's
Blessing, it can sing lyric songs
And give Pith-Instructions.
When my mind receives the Guru's blessing
It realizes and is the Buddha.

Fire cannot burn nor water drown me;
Walking like an elephant, I act
And dance with great confidence.

With their different states of mind,
The faithful see my various forms
And hear my different preachings;
By this they will gain Liberation.
But impure men with evil Karmas
Cannot even see my body.
They must suffer for their sins —
Even Buddha cannot help them.

Dear sons, try with diligence to practice
The Dharma. I could talk on without end,
[But what better advice could I give you?]

Alas, pity all sinful men! Seeing them
Deprived of a chance for Liberation,
And bearing all sorrows, my heart is most
Distressed and troubled!
Oh friends, let us try
Firmly to practice our devotion.
Let us forget all worldly things,
For the next life preparing!

Hearing this song, all the son-disciples were inspired with great joy.

[Thus, and in this manner, the Jetsun Milarepa] caused the Buddhist religion to dawn in Tibet, and brought temporal and Ultimate happiness to sentient beings. Having unified forms and Mind, and consolidated the Main and the Ensuing Samādhis, the great Master Yogi, Milarepa, benefited sentient beings through his miraculous powers and melodious songs. These songs were cherished, remembered, and recorded in writing by his heart-son disciples. The major part of Milarepa's songs that are well known in the human world, is now compiled in this volume. It is befitting to state here that to collect all his innumerable songs would be a task quite beyond our reach.

This is the story of Milarepa performing miracles to inspire his disciples, and the end of the last series [of the *Mila Grubum*].
In the foregoing chapters three groups of stories,[6] serving as a good account of the Eight Deeds[7] of [the Jetsun Milarepa] through which he propagated the Practice Transmission in Tibet and bestowed blessing on sentient beings, are related with complete details.

(The End)

NOTES

1 Heavenly Yak: a legendary yak said to dwell in Heaven (T.T.: lHa.gYag.).
2 The Four Formless Heavens, or Realms (T.T.: gZugs.Med.sKye.mChed.

bShi.), are: (1) the Realm of Infinite Space; (2) the Realm of Infinite Consciousness; (3) the Realm of Nothingness; and (4) the Realm of Neither Consciousness nor Non-Consciousness. These Formless Heavens are considered to be the highest Heavens in Saṃsāra; only those who have attained very advanced Samādhis can be born in these Realms. However, according to Buddhism, a birth in these Heavens will not bring one to Liberation, hence it is only a waste of time.

3 Heavens of Form (T.T.: gZugs.Khms.Kyi.lHa.): In this Realm, it is said, there are 17 Heavens. They are:

> (1) Brahmaparisadya, (2) Brahmapurohita, (3) Mahābrahmā. (These three belong to the Heavens of the First Dhyāna.)
> (4) Parittābha, (5) Apramāṇābha, (6) Ābhāsvara. (These three belong to the Heavens of the Second Dhyāna.)
> (7) Parittaśubha, (8) Apramāṇaśubha, (9) Subhakṛtsna. (These three belong to the Heavens of the Third Dhyāna.)
> (10) Anabhraka, (11) Puṇyaprasava, (12) Bṛhatphala, (13) Avṛha, (14) Atapa, (15) Sudṛsa, (16) Sudarśana, and (17) Mahāmaheśvara. (These eight belong to the Heavens of the Fourth Dhyāna.)

4 Six Elements: the elements of earth, water, fire, air, space, and consciousness. In comparison with sentient beings in the Heavens, human beings are said to possess more elements. For example, in the Heaven of Form, sentient beings do not have the elements of earth, water, and fire; and in the Formless Heavens, sentient beings do not have the elements of earth, water, fire, air, and space, because they possess only the element of consciousness.

5 The-Hell-that-Never-Ceases (T.T.: mNar.Med.dMyal.Wa.): It is said that denizens of this Hell suffer unceasing torment, whereas in other hells, temporary relief of pain is possible.

6 According to the compiler, this book, the *Mila Grubum*, consists of three groups of stories. The first group of stories are those of Milarepa's conquering and conversion of the malignant demons — Stories 1 through 8; the second group are those of Milarepa and his well-endowed disciples — Stories 9 through 44; and the third group are those of various categories — Stories 45 through 61. See the last paragraphs of Story 8 and of Story 44.

7 The Eight Deeds (T.T.: mDsad.Pa.brGyad.): These are the well-known Eight Deeds of Buddha, performed in the eight phases of Buddha's life. They are: (1) descending from the Tuṣita Heaven; (2) entering His mother's womb; (3) birth; (4) renouncing the world; (5) conquering the demons; (6) attaining the Ultimate Enlightenment; (7) setting the Wheel-of-Dharma in motion (preaching); and (8) Nirvāṇa.

COLOPHON

ৡৡ৷|

On His two mighty wings
Of Wisdom and of Skill,
He flew to the sky of Supreme
Accomplishment, with a mind
Priceless and pure as Heaven's.

He was the Lord Jetsun Mila
Who danced, and sang with joy
In a drama of Totality.
With a mind firm as a diamond
He raised the flag of the Two Siddhis.
To Him, the changeless Vajra,
With a laughing voice that
Rolls the world and heaven,
I pay sincerest homage!

From reading His life story, one will profit;
From hearing His name, one will be freed from pain;
Bestowed will be the power of
Achieving Buddhahood this time.
To those Who remember and venerate Him,
He is the wish-granting jewel, the matchless
        treasure-opener,
The Great Sorcerer, a descendent from a brave Lineage.

Any man of sense who reads his stories
Will be inspired with a wish to follow him.
Those who read, hear, think, and touch
This book will all gain great profit.
With this in mind, to propagate the Dharma
The faithful Chueji Jangtse has arranged the wood-
        blocks
For publication of a late edition of this book.
By this merit may all living
Beings follow Milarepa,
Till they arrive at Buddhahood.
May all men who find this book, ever be born

In a Lineage of the Supreme Vehicle.
May they all meet a perfect Guru, rely
On him, and cherish him like their own eyes —
As Milarepa once did in his lifetime.
[By the merit of publishing this book],
May all Buddhist Schools, Sūtra or Tantra,
Scripture or Devotional, prosper and spread afar.
May all religious leaders everywhere live long.
May all preachers of all Sects agree
With each other in the light of Dharma.
May all Buddhist patrons gain prosperity
And power. May all men complete
Their preparatory work and soon
Enter the one supreme Path of Vajrayāna!
In the Two-in-One Palace of Ḍākinīs,
May they soon become Buddhas of the Ten Perfections!

By the earnest request of the benevolent practicer (sGrub. Pa.Po.),
I, Monk Jhambar Rolbi Lhodroe, have written these auspicious wishes.
May all of our good Vows, both temporal and eternal, soon be fulfilled.

APPENDIX

ༀ༔

THE "HUNDRED THOUSAND SONGS OF MILAREPA," ITS ORIGIN, BACKGROUND, FUNCTION, AND TRANSLATION

by GARMA C. C. CHANG

THE *Mila Grubum*,[1] or the "Hundred Thousand Songs of Milarepa," is perhaps the most outstanding masterpiece of Tibetan literature. Its rich contents, fascinating stories, and characteristic style, all revealed through a simple yet graphic expression, have capitvated the hearts and minds of Tibetans from all walks of life for the past eight centuries, providing them with solace and a source of inexhaustible joy and inspiration. It has been read as the biography of a saint, a guide book for devotions, a manual of Buddhist Yoga, a volume of songs and poems, and even a collection of Tibetan folklore and fairy tales.

In introducing this beloved, holy book of Tibet, I have naturally been concerned lest I do an injustice to it by possible misrepresentation — even profanation. I am inclined to believe that a proper introduction to a book of this kind should adhere as closely as possible to an "indigenous style," for none could know better or feel more intimate with the subject matter of the *Mila Grubum* than the owners of the book themselves — the Tibetan people who have inherited it and have lived with it for centuries. With this in mind I present this book to readers under three topics: (1) the life and contribution of Milarepa; (2) the central teaching of Tibetan Tantrism; and (3) the translation.

THE LIFE AND CONTRIBUTION OF MILAREPA

Milarepa, the great Buddhist saint and poet of Tibet, was born A.D. 1052[2] and died in 1135. His youth was full of misfortunes and sorrows. Following the early death of his father, his relatives treacherously and shamelessly seized his vast patrimony. After many years of hard labor, poverty, and humiliation, he was finally persuaded by his mother to take revenge upon the wrongdoers through magic, for they were much too powerful to be vanquished by ordinary means. He succeeded in obtaining, through his sincere devotion and service to a teacher of sorcery, a powerful spell, by means of which he assassinated many of his relatives and wrought great havoc on his native valley by destroying the harvest with hailstorms.

Not long after, he repented of his sinful deeds, and determined to seek salvation by devoting the rest of his life to the practice of the Dharma. Despite the fact that meanwhile he was initiated into the profound teachings of the "Great Perfection" (T.T.: rDsogs.Pa.Chen.Po.) by an enlightened lama, the shadows of sin and pride still made it impossible for him to make any spiritual progress. The lama then sent him to the famous Guru — Marpa the Translator — who had just returned from India after many years of study and practice there.

The day before Milarepa arrived, both Marpa and his wife dreamed of goddesses who prophesied the coming of a disciple who would one day become the greatest teacher of Tibet, bringing salvation to innumerable sentient beings, bestowing Enlightenment upon countless Dharma devotees, and glorifying the immaculate doctrine of Buddhism.

Perceiving Milarepa's past sins and his great potential capacities, and wishing to clear away all hindrances that might otherwise block his spiritual growth, Marpa relentlessly put him on trial by imposing upon him severe mental and physical penances. Milarepa was ordered to build, single-handed, one house after another on a desolate mountain, then to tear them down again for no apparent reason. In return for long years of service, devotion, and obedience to Marpa, Milarepa received only humiliation and unjustified harsh treatment. At last he was accepted as a disciple, and rewarded with the longed-for instructions. Then, for eleven continuous months, he meditated alone in a cave, where he finally attained direct Realization and an initial achievement on the Path to Bodhi.

By this time, Milarepa had been separated from his family for many years. One day, while meditating in the cave, he fell asleep and dreamed that he returned home and saw the bones of his mother lying in the ruins of his house. He then thought that she must have died during his long absence. He saw his only sister as a vagabond beggar, his house and fields deserted and overgrown with a tangle of rank weeds. He awoke weeping bitterly, calling the names of his mother and sister, his pillow wet with tears.

Stricken with grief and longing to see his mother, he left Marpa and went back to his home village, where all the premonitions of his dream were confirmed. Witnessing this painful human existence helplessly and futilely consumed in fleeting evanescence, an anguish of desire to renounce the world wrung his heart. He made a solemn vow that he would meditate on a remote mountain uninterruptedly until he reached the Ultimate Enlightenment.

This vow he kept. For twelve consecutive years he meditated alone in a cave, living on nothing but nettles, until his whole body became greenish in hue. As a consequence of this consistent effort, he finally earned his reward — the realization of Ultimate Enlightenement. After this, his fame gradually spread over the whole of Tibet and Nepal. In his later years he was called by all Tibetans, "Jetsun Milarepa" ("Holy Milarepa"), and is regarded to this day as indisputably the greatest poet, yogi, and saint in Tibetan history.

Milarepa had a fine voice, and loved to sing. Even when he was a boy, he was regarded by his countrymen as an excellent singer of folksongs. Sainthood and Enlightenment only made him sing more frequently and joyfully than before. When his patrons and disciples made a request, or put a question to him, or a dispute arose, he answered them not in dull prose but in freely flowing poems or lyric songs composed spontaneously. No one knows how many songs or "poems" he "composed" in his lifetime. Tibetans believe there were close to one hundred thousand. This claim may not be an exaggeration, if we consider that throughout almost half of his life Milarepa used songs to communicate his ideas in his teaching and conversation. Even if we discount this seemingly exaggerated claim, we must nevertheless admit that he was an extraordinarily prolific "composer" of songs. For him there was no difficulty in creating a new song at any moment, for, in the genius of his enlightened mind, the fountain of inspiration was inexhaustible.

In his songs, Milarepa has left us a treasury of valuable information on his personal yogic experience, and advice and instruction concerning the practical problems of meditation. To serious yogis and Dharma practitioners, they are indeed a most precious guide. Speculative and scholarly writings are abundant in Buddhist literature, but rarely can one find a volume having such life and vitality, and generating a magnetic force bright and powerful enough to dispel the darkness of grief and bring hope and joy to all.

Unlike many religious leaders, who exerted themselves in various tasks for the creation of their new Orders, Milarepa never tried to build a temple, form a group, or set up an organization of any sort, but faithfully followed his Guru's injunctions by leading the life of a true mendicant yogi in the remote mountains, the life of a saint-troubadour, wandering from place to place to preach the holy Dharma through his songs. Also, differing from those pedantic scholars and dogmatic Tantric yogis who either adhered to ideas and words or to rites and forms, Milarepa cast away all erudite Buddhist studies and cumbersome Tantric rituals, and marched directly toward Buddhahood by way of simple understanding and persistent practice. As a result, his teachings were also more precise, direct, and simple than those of conventional Tantrism, and well deserve being called the *quintessential teachings of practical Buddhism*. Though Milarepa was ridiculed by a number of jealous scholars of his time as being an ignorant hermit who knew nothing about Buddhism, history has proved that his teachings were far superior and more influential than those of any learned Buddhist scholar of his day.

Through the illustration of his own life, Milarepa set for all Buddhists an example of the perfect Bodhisattva, and a model of the incorruptible life of a genuine practitioner of Buddhist Tantrism. His life is an unmistakable testimony to the unity and interdependency of all Buddhist teachings — Theravāda, Mahāyāna, and Vajrayāna — for Buddahood is not attainable if any of the three are lacking. He made it clear to all that poverty is not a kind of deprivation, but rather a necessary way of emanicpating oneself from the tyranny of material possessions; that Tantric practice by no means implies indulgence and laxity, but hard labor, strict discipline, and steadfast perseverance; that without resolute renunciation and uncompromising discipline, as Guatama Buddha Himself stressed, all the sublime ideas and dazzling images depicted in Mahāyāna and Tantric Buddhism are no better than magnificent illusions.

Milarepa was one of the very few Buddhist saints whose transmitted teachings have given birth to more enlightened beings than have any of the Mahāyāna Buddhist Schools, except Ch'an Buddhism in China. Hui Neng, the founder of Ch'an, was perhaps the only figure in Buddhist history whose influence and contribution can, in various aspects, rival those of Milarepa.

These two great sages also had many other things in common. They both laid stress on actual practice and direct Realization, and in both instances their teachings were characterized by extreme simplicity and straightforwardness. But the teaching of Milarepa seems to be more thorough, complete, and "advanced" than that of Hui Neng because, unlike Hui Neng, who put all his emphasis on the Prajñāpāramitā, Milarepa accentuated *all* the essential teachings of Buddhism. In stressing the importance of the Dharmakāya, both are alike; but as to the teaching of the other two Kāyas — the manifestation, and the dynamic force of Buddhahood — Milarepa's seems to be the more thorough. Thus, through his life-example, Milarepa preached and demonstrated the unity and interdependency of all the essential teachings of Buddhism. Among his many important contributions, this is perhaps the greatest and the most unique one of all.

Those who have a serious interest in Milarepa's life and work should also read another important Tibetan work, "The Jetsun Milarepa Khabum," or "Namthar" — "The Biography of Milarepa," translated by the late Lama Kazi Dawa-Samdup and edited with an Introduction and annotations by Dr. W. Y. Evans-Wentz, under the title, "Tibet's Great Yogi, Milarepa," (Oxford University Press, 1951). A careful study of this celebrated book will not only broaden the reader's understanding of Milarepa's life and work, but will bring to him a broader comprehension of the spirit and teaching of Tibetan Buddhism.

THE CENTRAL TEACHING OF TIBETAN TANTRISM

A better understanding and deeper appreciation of the songs of Milarepa will be reached if a good knowledge of Buddhism in general, and a fair grasp of Tibetan Tantrism in particular, is acquired. In order to help those who may not have had such a background, a brief summary of the essential teachings of Tibetan Tantrism is given in the following pages. Information on general Buddhism is not included, since this may be obtained from sources easily available to all. It goes without saying that this brief summary is less than adequate to represent the vast and comprehensive contents of the Tibetan Tantra. One cannot expect, therefore, to glean from these brief lines more than a hint of the essential, underlying principles.

Tibetan Tantrism is a form of practical Buddhism abounding in methods and techniques for carrying out the practice of all the Mahāyāna teachings. In contrast to the "theoretical" forms of Buddhism, such as Sautrāntikā, Vaibhāṣika, Mādhayamika, Yogācāra, Hua Yen, Tien Tai, etc., Buddhist Tantrism lays most of its stress on *practice* and *Realization*, rather than on philosophical speculations. Its central principles and practices may be summarized as follows:

1. That all existence and manifestation can be found in one's experience, that this experience is within one's own mind, and that Mind is the source and creator of all things.

2. That Mind is an infinitely vast, unfathomably deep complex of marvels, its immensity and depth being inaccessible to the uninitiated.

3. That he who has come to a thorough realization and perfect mastership of his own mind is a Buddha, and that those who have not done so are unenlightened sentient beings.

4. That sentient beings and Buddhas are, in essence, identical. Buddhas are enlightened sentient beings, and sentient beings unenlightened Buddhas.

5. That this infinite, all-embracing Buddha-Mind is beyond comprehension and attributes. The best and closest definition might be:

"Buddha-Mind is a GREAT ILLUMINATING-VOID
AWARENESS."

6. That the consciousness of sentient beings is of limited awareness; the consciousness of an advanced yogi, of illuminating awareness; the consciousness of an enlightened Bodhisattva, of illuminating-void awareness; and the "consciousness" of Buddha, the GREAT ILLUMINATING-VOID AWARENESS.

7. That all Buddhist teachings are merely "exaltations," preparations, and directions leading one toward the unfoldment of this GREAT ILLUMINATING-VOID AWARENESS.

8. That infinite compassion, merit, and marvels will spontaneously come forth when this Buddha-Mind is fully unfolded.

9. That to unfold this Buddha-Mind, two major approaches or Paths are provided for differently disposed individuals: the Path of Means, and the Path of Liberation. The former stresses an approach to Buddhahood through the practice of taming the Prāṇa, and the latter an approach through the practice of taming the mind. Both approaches, however, are based on the truism of the IDENTICALITY OF MIND AND PRAṆA.[3] (T.T.: Rluñ.Sems.dWyer.Med.), which is the fundamental theorem of Tantrism.

The principle of the Identicality of Mind and Prāṇa may be briefly stated thus: The world encompasses and is made up of various contrasting forces in an "antithetical" form of relationship — positive and negative, noumenon and phenomenon, potentiality and manifestation, vitality and voidness, Mind and Prāṇa, and the like. Each of these dualities, though apparently antithetical, is an inseparable unity. The dual forces that we see about us are, in fact, one "entity" manifesting in two different forms or stages. Hence, if one's consciousness or mind is disciplined, tamed, transformed, extended, sharpened, illuminated, and sublimated, so will be his Prāṇas, and vice versa. The practice that stresses taming the Prāṇa is called the "Yoga with Form," or the "Path of Means." The practice that stresses taming the mind is called the "Yoga without Form," or the "Path of Liberation." The former is an exertive type of Yoga practice, and the latter a natural and effortless one, known as Mahāmudrā.[4]

(1) **The Path of Means:** The main practices of the Path of Means contain the following eight steps:

(A) The cultivation of altruistic thoughts, and basic training in the discipline of the Bodhisattva.

(B) The four fundamental preparatory practices, which contain:
(a) One hundred thousand obeisances to the Buddhas. This practice is for the purpose of cleansing all bodily sins and hindrances, thus enabling one to meditate without being handicapped by physical impediments.
(b) One hundred thousand recitations of repentance prayers. When properly performed, this cleanses mental obstructions and sins, clearing out all mental hindrances that may block spiritual growth.
(c) One hundred thousand repetitions of the prayer to one's Guru of the Guru Yoga Practice. This brings protection and blessings from one's Guru.
(d) Making one hundred thousand Special Offerings. This will create favorable conditions for one's devotions.

(C) The Patron Buddha Yoga, a training for identifying and unifying oneself with a divine Buddha as assigned to one by his Guru. This Yoga consists of mantra recitations, visualization, concentration, and breathing exercises.

(D) The advanced form of breathing exercises and their concomitant and subsidiary practices, including the Yogas of Dream, of Transformation, of Union, and of Light — generally known as the Perfecting Yogas.

(E) Guiding the subtle Prāṇa-Mind (T.T.: Rluñ.Sems.) into the Central Channel, thus successively opening the four main Cakras ("psychic" centers) and transforming the mundane consciousness into transcendal Wisdom.

(F) Applying the power of Prāṇa-Mind to bring about or to vanquish at will, one's death, Bardo, and reborn state, thus achieving emancipation from Saṃsāra.

(G) Applying the power of Prāṇa-Mind to master the mind-projection performances.

(H) Sublimating and perfecting the Prāṇa-Mind into the Three Bodies of Buddhahood.

(2) *The Path of Liberation*, or the Yoga without Form, is the simplest and most direct approach toward the Buddha-Mind. It is a natural and spontaneous practice, bypassing many preparations, strenuous exercises, and even successive stages as laid down in other types of Yoga. Its essence consists in the Guru's capability of bringing to his disciple a glimpse of the Innate Buddha-Mind in its primordial and natural state. With this initial and direct "glimpsing experience," the disciple gradually learns to sustain, expand, and deepen his realization of this Innate Mind. Eventually he will consummate this realization to its full blossoming in Perfect Enlightenment. This practice is called Mahāmudrā.

(A) The first glimps of the Innate Mind can be acquired either through practicing Mahāmudrā Yoga by oneself, or through receiving a "Pointing-out" demonstration from one's Guru. The former way is to follow the Guru's instructions and meditate alone; the latter consists of an effort by the Guru to open the disciple's mind instantaneously. Both approaches, however, require the continuous practice of Mahāmudrā Yoga to deepen and perfect one's experience.

(B) The central teaching of Mahāmudrā consists of two major points: relaxation, and effortlessness. All pains and desires are of a tense nature. But Liberation, in contrast, is another name for "perfect relaxation." Dominated by long-established habits, however, average men find it most difficult, if not entirely impossible, to reach a state of deep relaxation; so instructions and practices are needed to enable them to attain such a state. The primary concern of Mahāmudrā, therefore, is to instruct the yogi on how to relax the mind and thus induce in him the unfolding of his Primordial Mind. Paradoxically, effortlessness is even more difficult to achieve than relaxation. It requires long practice to become "effortless" at all times and under all circumstances. If one can keep his mind always relaxed, spontaneous, and free of clinging, the Innate Buddha-Mind will soon dawn upon him.

(3) *The Path of Means and The Path of Liberation*, exist only in the beginning stages. In the advanced stages these two Paths converge and become one. It is to the advantage of a yogi, in order to hasten

his spiritual progress, if he can either practice both teachings at the same time or use one to supplement the other. Most of the great yogis of Tibet practiced both Paths, as did Milarepa.

THE TRANSLATION OF THE BOOK

To the best knowledge of the translator, the *Mila Grubum*, or the "Hundred Thousand Songs of Milarepa," has never before been completely translated from Tibetan into any major foreign language. Translations of several sections, however, have been available for some time. Many thoughtful and interested readers may be curious as to why an important work such as this has never been fully translated. There are many reasons for this. In addition to the depth of the work itself, a number of technical difficulties are involved. Scholars of Tibetan Buddhism do not find it very difficult to translate the conventional type of Buddhist Sūtras and Śāstras, for they are all written with established terminologies, phraseologies, and styles. The enigmatic passages of a Tibetan text frequently can be deciphered by means of a comparative study of the equivalent text in the Chinese or Sanskrit language. But nothing of this kind is available in the case of the *Mila Grubum*; its language, style, and subject matter are in many ways different from those of conventional Buddhist texts. It was written not only in colloquial Tibetan, but in a form of ancient colloquialism strongly tinged with a flavor of the local dialect of Southwestern Tibet. The particular phrases with which Milarepa expressed his Tantric ideas and mystical experiences, present another formidable problem of translation. Moreover, the major part of the book is largely composed of verses and songs of an "uncommon" type, which further increases the difficulties.

Being fully aware of these difficulties, I have undertaken this formidable task not without apprehension and concern. I have always been of the opinion that a better translation of the Buddhist classics can be achieved only by pooling together the talents of many Buddhist scholars (in different fields) to make a joint effort in the task, as did King James of England with the translation of the Bible, and Emperors Tai Tsung and Khri.Sroñ.lDe.bTsan. of China and Tibet with the translations of Buddhist Sūtras in the Tang period. Individual efforts in this type of undertaking are always difficult. It is my hope, therefore, not to make a perfect translation, but rather to see that this important work of Tibetan Buddhism is soon made available to the world. As a Chinese proverb has said, "The purpose of my throw-

ing a brick is to induce people to cast their jade." My greatest desire
is to see that this pioneer translation, imperfect as it may be, rouses
a wider interest in the work itself, and thus serves as a prelude to more
and better translations of the *Mila Grubum* to follow.

Because no clear statement appears in the book, the author or compiler of the *Mila Grubum* is not clearly known. Except in Stories 29,
30, and 31, where the compilers' names — Shiwa.Hod. and Ñan.
rDson.sTon.Pa. — are given, the name of the compiler of the vast
majority of the stories — a total of 58 — is not clearly mentioned. It
is interesting to note, however, that these stories seem to have a uni-
form style, and, when compared with Stories 29, 30, and 31, they reveal an outstanding difference, flavor, and superior quality. Beyond
any doubt they were written by another author. I therefore assume
that this compiler or author is the same person as the author of the
Mila Khabum, or *Namthar* (Mi.La.bKah.hBum., or .rNam.Thar. —
the "Biography of Milarepa"), namely, the fabulous and mysterious
yogi, gTsañ.sMyoñ.Heruka. — "The Mad Yogi from gTsañ"[5] — who
was a disciple of Phag.Mo.Gru.Pa. (1110-1170), the celebrated pupil
of Gambopa (1079-1161), Milarepa's chief disciple. Another strong
piece of evidence seems also to support this opinion: in the *Mila
Khabum*, or *Namthar*, from Folio 109 to Folio 113, there is a detailed
account of Milarepa's life story which is identical with that of the
Grubum; even the sequence of the stories in the two books is in
perfect correspondence. There seems to be no other explanation than
the fact that both books were compiled by the same person, either in
the latter part of the 12th or in the beginning of the 13th century.

Professor Herbert V. Guenther, of the Sanskrit University, Varanasi,
India, was so kind as to do some research for me on this problem.
His findings are stated in a letter to me, as follows: " ... just to let
you know that your surmise that the biography of Mi.La.Ras.Pa. [the
Mila Khabum] is not by Ras.Chuñ.Pa. [Rechungpa] but by the "In-
sane Yogi" is correct. While I was studying my sÑan.r.Gyud., I came
across the following line: 'Dur.Khrod.Myul.Bahi.rNal.hByor.Pa.Sañs.
rGyas.rGyal.mTshan.gTsañ.Pa.He.Ru.Ka.Rus.Pahi.rGyan.Can.Sogs. Du.
Mahi.Miñ.Can.Gis.bKod.Pa.' The same names occur at the end of
Mi.La.Ras.Pa's rNam.Thar. It seems that the confusion with Ras.Chuñ.
Pa. is due to the fact that gTsan.Pa.Heruka is considered as an incarnation of Ras.Chuñ.Pa. and as one of the disciples of Phag.Mo.Gru.
Pa .... By this strong evidence the authorship of both the *Mila Khabum* and the *Mila Grubum* is thus established to be by Sañs.rGyas.
rGyal.mTshan, the 'Insane Yogi from gTsañ,' who bears many different names."

The sequence of stories appearing in the *Mila Grubum* seems to have been arranged, not in the strict chronological order of Milarepa's life, but rather into three groups according to the contents of the stories. Stories of Milarepa's encounters with malignant spirits are found in the first part of the book; stories of Milarepa and his human disciples, in the middle part; and stories of a more varied and general nature, at the end. This classification, of course, should not be treated too rigidly, for most of the stories contain, in some measure, all three elements.

The Tibetan text of the *Mila Grubum* has four major versions — those of Peking, of Narthang, of Dege, and of Lhasa. The Lhasa edition, containing 319 wood-printed folios and 61 stories, has been· used in this translation. I believe this edition to be the latest publication among the four, being more or less a reproduction of the Dege version.

Because of the complexity and particularity of Tibetan Buddhist terminology, explanatory notes for these terms are necessary. Nevertheless, I have tried to make these notes as simple as possible to avoid over-elaboration, lest they become a burden rather than a help to the general reader and thus impede the reading of the text itself.

The Tibetan names, both of places and persons, *are all rendered phonetically*[6] in order to avoid the cumbersome, confusing, and impractical transliteration of Tibetan words, e.g., instead of sNan.gYon., "Nyan Yuan"; Mi.La.Ras.Pa., "Milarepa"; gTsug.Tor.rNam.rGyal., "Tsudor Namjal"; Zla.Wa.bZan.Pu., "Dawazungpo," etc. This simplification is not only desirable and necessary from a practical viewpoint, but is also founded on the very fact that the Tibetans themselves have for several centuries abandoned pronouncing these cumbersome prefixes and suffixes in their everyday speech as well as in their reading. Nevertheless, to help scholars of Tibetanology in identifying these names, a list of important Tibetan names and terms is attached at the end of this book, wherein both the pronunciation and transliteration are given. The Romanization of Tibetan words in the book is based on the Sarat Chandra Das system.[7]

For the same reason Tibetan diacritical marks are omitted in the text, but included in the notes.

In the year 1950, when I was in retreat at Kalimpong, India, Lady Yutog, a devout Tibetan noblewoman, came to visit me. She was interested to hear that I, a young Chinese, who had spent a number of years studying Tibetan Buddhism in Eastern Tibet, was now practicing meditation at Kalimpong. After an exchange of information and ideas, she appeared to be delighted. The second morning she came to see me again, bringing with her a huge Tibetan book wrapped in an elegant yellow silk scarf, and said to me, "This is the *Mila Grubum*. I now offer it to you, for I understand how much this book would mean to a person in retreat. My greatest hope is, however, to see the message of Milarepa reach every corner of the globe. I hope you will translate this book into English some day, so that many people can read it and profit from it." Jubilantly I accepted this wonderful gift, for this was just the book I had been painstakingly seeking ever since I had lost all my Tibetan books during my escape into India from China.

In retrospect, now that the translation is completed, I feel more grateful than ever to Lady Yutog for this inspiring and deeply significant visit. Under divine wisdom and guidance she brought to me a precious gift, together with insight into an important mission and challenge — one which I accepted with joy and inspiration during a critical period in my life.

NOTES

1 *Mila Grubum* represents the Tibetan pronunciation of the title. The transliteration would be: Mi.La.Ras.Pahi.mGur.hBum.

2 According to "The Blue Annals," p. 427, Milarepa was born A.D. 1040 and died A.D. 1123. But according to the *Mila Khabum*, or *Namthar*, the dates should be 1052 and 1135.

3 Prāṇa: a Sanskrit term, equivalent to the Tibetan term Rluñ. and to the Chinese term Ch'i, conveying various meanings: air, energy, vital force, breathing, propensity, and so forth. An exact translation of this term into English is extremely difficult.

4 A renowned version of the Mahāmudrā system is set forth in English translation, along with Chang's "Yogic Commentary" thereon, in "Tibetan Yoga and Secret Doctrines," 2nd ed., edited by Dr. W. Y. Evans-Wentz (Oxford University Press, 1958).

5 Although the text of the *Mila Khabum* opens with Rechungpa's request to Milarepa to relate his life story in the very beginning of the book as well as in each of its successive chapters, this by no means suggests that Rechungpa was the author of the *Mila Khabum*, as some scholars are inclined to believe. On the contrary, this fact provides strong evidence that Rechungpa was an actor in the "drama of the *Mila Khabum*" as portrayed by the author, rather than the author himself. The fact that gTsañ.sMyon.Heruka was the author of the *Mila Khabum* is well known in Tibet.

6 In the case of personal names ending in ༤, *Pa* instead of *Ba* is used, e.g., Milare*pa*, not Milare*ba*, and Rechung*pa*, not Rechung*ba*, though phonetically "Pa" should be pronounced "Ba" in modern Tibetan. This compromise seems to be necessary since these names are now more or less established in the West.

7 In order to keep the transliteration as close to the "Tibetan way" as possible, the letter ༤ (Ba) is also transliterated as "Wa" after the prefix ད (Da), e.g., dWañ-bShi., not dBañ.bShi. This is because all Tibetans invariably pronounce it as "Wa." This, of course, should not be mistakenly identified with the other Wa (ཝ), the 20th consonant. This rule is also true in the case where the letter is used to form a noun, e.g., dGe.Wa., not dGe.Ba. The root of each Tibetan word is always capitalized to facilitate identification. In the case of ཕ , ཙ , ཚ , ཛ , and ཞ — Pha, Tsa, Tsha, Dsa, and Sha — only the first letter of the root is capitalized. Also note: "T.T." stands for Tibetan Transliteration.

GLOSSARY

Alaya Consciousness — the "Store" Consciousness. The function of this consciousness is to preserve the "seeds" of mental impressions. Memory and learning are made possible because of this consciousness. In a loose sense, it can also be regarded as the "Primordial Consciousness" or "Universal Consciousness."

Bardo — the intermediate stage between death and rebirth.

Bodhi — Buddhahood, or that which concerns Buddhahood.

Bodhi-Mind (Skt.: Bodhicitta) — the aspiration to Buddhahood; the determination to practice all the virtuous deeds that lead toward Buddhahood; the enlightened insight into immanent Reality; the great compassionate Vow to serve, benefit, and deliver all sentient beings.

Bodhisattva — a man who has taken a vow to strive for Enlightenment and save all sentient beings; a man who aspires to Buddhahood and altruistic deeds; an enlightened being; a follower of Mahāyāna Buddhism.

Bon Religion — the aboriginal religion of Tibet.

Ḍākinīs — goddesses, or female deities.

Deva — a general term for gods, angels, or heavenly beings.

Dharma — a term having two main usages: (1) to signify object, matter, or thing; (2) to mean the teaching and doctrine of Buddhism, hence, the religious truth and Law.

Dharmadhātu — Totality, or the realm of Ultimate Reality.

Dharmakāya — the "Body of Truth," or the real "Body" of Buddha, which is formless, omnipresent, ultimate, and yet void.

Dhyāna — an equivalent of Samādhi which, according to the Buddhist version, denotes a group of pure concentrative states.

Dumo's Fire — The "mystic" heat that is produced in the Navel Center through the practice of Heat Yoga.

Eight Worldly Winds, or Eight Worldly Dharmas — a metaphoric term denoting the "winds," or influences, which fan the desires and passions, i.e.: gain, loss; defamation, eulogy; praise, ridicule; sorrow, joy.

Experience and Realization (T.T.: Ñams.Dañ.rTog.Pa.) — The former term denotes the Yogi's experiences, understandings, and insights prior to Enlightenment; the latter denotes the real Enlightenment. The resemblance of the two often confuses a yogi into mistaking the former for the latter.

Foundation, Path, and Fruit — Foundation is the immanent Buddha-nature; Path is the action or practice that leads toward the unfoldment of the Buddha-nature; Fruit is its realization.

Jetsun — The Revered One (a title).

Kleśas — the worldly desires and impulses that cause one to wander in Saṃsāra.

692

Among them, three are most prominent: lust, hatred, and ignorance.

Mahāmudrā — the most important teaching of Tibetan Tantrism, by which one is led to the realization of the Dharmakāya; the practical verbal instruction on how to meditate on the Void.

Maṇḍala — meaning "circle" or "center." A maṇḍala is an extremely complex pictorial design that symbolizes the phenomenal world of Tantric Buddhas.

Nhamdog — the disturbing and wavering thoughts which one encounters in meditation; wrong or uncontrollable thoughts; misconception or misjudgment.

Nirmāṇakāya — the transformation or incarnation Body of a Buddha.

Pāramitās — the spiritual deeds of a Bodhisattva that bring him to Buddhahood.

Prajñā — Transcendental Wisdom, or the supramundane insight into Reality.

Prāṇa — Prāṇa conveys various meaning's such as air, breath, energy, wind, vitality, and so forth. Yogically speaking, Prāṇa is the vital force in the physical body to be tamed and mastered in order to achieve the total transformation of mind and energy.

Prāṇa-Mind (T.T.: Rluñ.Sems.) — According to Tibetan Tantrism, mind and Prāṇa are but two facets of one entity. They should never be treated as two separate things. If one's mind is disciplined, transformed, extended, sharpened, illuminated . . . so also is one's Prāṇa — the vital force that gives birth to all manifestations.

Samādhi — a pure concentrative state.

Saṃsāra — the wheel of life and death; the migration through many rebirths; the doctrine of reincarnation.

Śūnyatā — voidness or emptiness; that which denies the viewpoints based on existence or non-existence, being or non-being; the doctrine that holds that all becomings in the phenomenal world are devoid of self-nature, entity, or substance, that they are illusorily existent but not truly so; the all-inclusive Totality seen by an enlightened mind.

The Tantra — the holy scriptures of Tantrism.

Tantrism — the doctrine and teaching of Tantrayāna, or Vijrayāna; one School of Mahāyāna Buddhism; "esoteric" Mahāyāna Buddhism.

Three Main Channels, or Nāḍis — the three "mystical nerve channels" through which all supramundane knowledge and power are gained; through the Central Channel the Dharmakāya is realized, and through the right and left Channels, the Sambhogakāya and Nirmāṇakāya are realized.

Three Precious Ones, or the Three Gems (Skt.: Triratna) — the Buddha — the Enlightened One; the Dharma — His teachings; and the Saṅgha — the advanced or enlightened Sages.

Two Truths — the expedient truth and the final truth.

Whispered Transmission — the Ghagyuba School of Tibetan Buddhism, founded by Marpa and Milarepa.

TABLE OF TIBETAN WORDS

Dagbo	Dags.Po.
Dagbo Lhaje	Dags.Po.lHa.rJe.
Dagmema	bDag.Med.Ma.
Dagmo Ridra	sTag.Mo.Ri.bKra.
Damala Richroma	Ta.Ma.La.Ri.Khrod.Ma.
Darsen Gharmo	Dar.Señ.dKar.Mo.
Daugom Repa Dorje Wonshu	sTag.sGom.Ras.Pa.rDor.rJe.dWañ. Phyug.
Dawazungpo	Zla.Wa.bZañ.Po.
Degar Drozonma	gTad.dKar.hGro.bZañ.Ma.
Dembu [Lady]	lHa.lCam.lDem.Bu.
Dem Chog	bDe.mChog.
Den Yi	gDan.bShi.
Deut Jal	sTod.rGyal.
Dewashun	bDe.Wa.sKyoñ.
Dhamba Jhaupu	Dam.Ba.rGyags.Phu.
Dhamo	sTa.Mo.
Dhampa Sangje [of] Dinrin	Dam.Pa.Sañs.rGyas., Tiñ.Rin.
Dhar Lho	Dar.Blo.
Dharma Aui	Dar.Ma.Hod.
Dharma Bodhi [of India]	Dharma.Bodhi., rGya.Gar.
Dharma Wonshu	Dar.Ma.dWañ.Phyug.
Dhawa Norbu	Zla.Wa.Nor.Bu.
Dinma	Diñ.Ma.
Dinma Drin	Diñ.Ma.Brin.
Din Ri	Diñ.Ri.
Din Ri Namar	Diñ.Ri.sNa.dMar.
Di Se	Ti.Se.
Dodejan	mDo.sDe.rGyan.
Dodra	mDo.bKra.
Dogar Nya	lTo.dKar.Ña.
Doh	rDo.
Dor Draug Rechung	rDo.Grags.Ras.Chuñ.
Dorje-Chang	rDo.rJe.hChañ.
Dorje Danyi	rDo.rJe.gDan.bShi.
Dorje Paumo	rDo.rJe.Phag.Mo.
Dorje Semba	rDo.rJe.Sems.Pa.
Dorje Tson	rDo.rJe.rDsoñ.
Dormo	rDor.Mo.
Dochin	hDo.Chen.
Drajadorje	Brag.sKya.rDo.rJe
Drang Sung	Drañ.Sroñ.
Drashi Oma Chuwu	bKra.Çis.Ho.Mahi.Chu.Wo.
Drashi Tse	bKra.Çis.brTsegs.
Drashi Tserinma	bKra.Çis.Tshe.Riñ.Ma.
Draugmar Bouto	Brag.dMar.sPo.mTho.
Draug Srin Mo	Brag.Srin.Mo.
Dre	hBre.
Dre Dun	hBre.sTon.
Dre Dun Drashi Bar	hBre.sTon.bKra.Çis.hBar.
Dreloon Joomoo	hDre.Luñ.sKyog.Mo.
Dre Tze	hBre.rTse.

Drigom Linkawa	hBri.sGom.Gliñ.Kha.Wa.
Drigom Repa	hBri.sGom.Ras.Pa.
Drin	Brin.
Dritsam	hBrig.mTshams.
Drogmanzulema	hBrog.sMan.Zul.Le.Ma.
Drol Ma [Tārā]	sGrol.Ma.
Dronso Charwa	Grañ.So.Khra.Wa.
Dro Tang**	Gro.Thañ.
Drowazunmo	hGro.Wa.bZañ.Mo.
Dro Wo [Valley]	Gro.Wo.
Duinjo's [Wondrous Cow]	hDod.hJohi.Ba.Mo.
Dumo	gTum.Mo.
Dumo Ngosangma	gTum.Mo.sÑo.Sañs.Ma.
Dunba Dharmadraug	sTon.Pa.Dar.Ma.Grags.
Dungom Repa	sTon.sGom.Ras.Pa.
Gadaya [Cave]	Ka.Daya.
Galugha	dGah.Klu.dGah.
Gambo Dar	sGam.Po.gDar.
Gambopa	sGam.Po.Pa.
Garakhache [Guest House]	Ga.Ra.Kha.Che.
Gawojobo	dGah.Wo.hJog.Po.
Gebha Lesum	Gad.Pa.Gle.gSum.
Gelugpa	dGe.Lugs.Pa.
Ghadampa	bKah.sDom.Pa. [or] bKah.gDams.Pa.
Ghadaya	Ka.Ta.Ya.
Ghagyu	bKah.rGyud.
Ghagyuba	bKah.rGyud.Pa.
Gog Tang	lKog.Thañ.
Goh [Valley]	Go.Luñ.
Gung Tang	Guñ.Thañ.
Gungtuzunpo	Kuñ.Du.bZañ.Po.
Guru Tsems Chin [of] La Dud	Guru.Tsems.Chen., La.sTod.
Gu Tang	Ku.Thañ.
Halo [flower]	Ha.Lo.
Heruka Galbo	He.Ru.Ka.Gal.Po.
Jal	rGyal.
Jarbo Ton Drem [or] Jarbo Tang Drem	Gyal.Po.Thañ.hGrem.
Jaung Chub Tsong	Byañ.Chub.rDsoñ.
Jeba Dorje	dGyes.Pa.rDo.rJe.
Jen [Valley]	gCen.Luñ.
Jenlun Ngan Tson	gCen.Luñ.Ñan.rDsoñ.
Jetsun	rJe.bTsun.
Jhachil Lama	rGya.mChil.
Jhajogri [Monastery]	rGya.lCags.Ri.
Jhal Khrum	rGyal.Khrom.
Jhambar Rolbi Lhadroe	hJam.dPal.Rol.Pahi.bLo.Gros.
Jham Mei	lCam.Me.
Jhunma [and] Roma	rKyañ.Ma., Ro.Ma.
Ji Dron (Mang Yul Ji Dron)	sKyid.Groñ.

Jidun	Kyi.sTon.
Jipu Nimadson	sKyid.Phug.Ñi.Ma.rDsoñ.
Jolmo [Singing bird]	hJol.Mo.
Jomo	Jo.Mo.
Jomo Chod Dan	Jo.Mo.mChod.rTen.
Joro Dritsam	lCo.Ro.hBrig.mTshams.
Jo Shag	Jo.Çag.
Joupuva	rGyags.Phu.Wa.
Jowo Shakja	Jo.Wo.Shagja.
Jun Chub Tsong	Byañ.Chub.rDsoñ.
Jundhagho	Byañ.rTa.sGo.
Jung	gCuñ.
Jung Bo	hByuñ.Po.
Jungron	Coñ.Roñ.
Junpan Nanka Tsang	rKyañ.Phan.Nam.mKhah.rDsoñ.
Jupan Drinzonma	Cod.Pan.mGrin.bZañ.Ma.
Jurmo [fish]	Gyur.Mo.Ña.
Kar Chon Repa	mKhar.Chuñ.Ras.Pa.
Khum Bu	Khum.Bu.
Ko Kom	Ko.Kom.
Kollo Dompa	hKhor.Lo.sTom.Pa.
Ku Ju	Khu.Byug.
Labar Shawa	Lha.hBar.Bya.Wa.
Ladgu Lungu	La.dGu.Luñ.dGu.
Lan [tribe]	Rus.Glan.
Lan Gom Repa	Glan.sCom.Ras.Pa.
Langgo Ludu Tson	Glañ.sGo.Klu.bDud.rDsoñ.
Lapu	La.Phug.
Lapu Paima Tson	La.Phug.Padma.rDsoñ.
Lashi [Snow Mountain]	La.Phyi.
La Shin	La.Shiñ.
Lese	Legs.Se.
Lesebum	Legs.Se.hBum.
Lha Dro [of] Drin	Brin.lHa.Bro.
Lhaje Nu Chon	lHa.rJe.gNubs.Chuñ.
Lhaman Jalmo	lHa.sMan.rGyal.Mo.
Lhasa Chrunon	Lha.Sa.hPhrul.sNañ.
Lhaze [Temple]	La.Ze.
Lho Draug Wa	lHo.Brag.Wa.
Ligor Sharu	Li.sKor.Phya.Ru.
Linba	Liñ.Ba.
Linba Draug	Liñ.Ba.Brag.
Lodahan [River — see Lohida]	Lo.Ta.Han.
Lodan Sherab	bLo.lDan.Çes.Rab.
Lodun	Lo.sTon.
Londun Gedun	Lo.sTon.dGe.hDun.
Lodun Gedunbum	Lo.sTon.dGe.hDun.hBum.
Lohida [River — see Lodahan]	Lo.Hi.Ta.
Loro	Lo.Ro.
Lowo [Lake]	gLo.Wo.mTsho.

Ma Goun	Ma.mGon.
Mamo	Ma.Mo.
Mamo Tson	Ma.Mo.rDsoñ.
Man Chu [Manlun Chubar]	sMan.Chu.
Mang	Mañ.
Mang Yul	Mañ.Yul.
Mang Yul Ji Dron	Mañ.Yul.sKyid.Groñ.
Manlun Chubar	sMan.Luñ.Chu.Bar.
Mannmo	sMan.Mo.
Ma Päm	Ma.Pham.
Marngo	Mar.rÑog.
Marpa	Mar.Pa.
Medripa [Skt.: Maitṛpa]	Me.Dris.Pa.
Megom Repa	Mes.sGom.Ras.Pa.
Menlha [Mount]	sMan.lHa.Ri.
Mijurpa [Buddha]	Mi.hGyur.Pa.
Mila Shirab Jhantsan	Mi.La.Çes.Rab.rGyal.mTshan.
Miyo Lonzonma	Mi.gYo.Kloñ.bZañ.Ma.
Mon [Yul]	Mon.Yul.
Nagchar	sNag.Phrar.
Nam Lo	gNam.Lo.
Nam Men [Karma]	rNam.sMin.
Namtsoshumo	gNam.mTsho.Phyug.Mo.
Naro Bhun Chun	Na.Ro.Bon.Chuñ.
Naro Chu Dru	Naro.Chos.Drug.
Ngan Tson	Ñan.rDsoñ.
Ngan Tson Dewa Shun	Ñan.rDsoñ.bDe.Wa.sKyoñ.
Ngan Tson Dunba Shun Chub Jhalbo	Ñan.rDsoñ.sTon.Pa.Byañ.Chub.rGyal. Po.
Ngan Tson Dunba Bodhiradza	Ñan.rDsoñ.sTon.Pa.Bhodhi.Ra.Dsa.
Ngogang	sÑo.sKañ.
Ngogom Repa Dharma Wonshu Shawa	sÑo.sGom.Ras.Pa.Dar.Ma.dWañ. Phyug.Bya.Wa.
Ngomi	rÑog.Mis.
Ngunbatso	mÑon.Pa.mDsod.
Ngundojan	mÑon.rTog.rGyan.
Nhamdog	rNam.rTog.
Ningmaba	rÑiñ.Ma.Pa.
Nin Lung	rÑiñ.rLuñ.
Nonyul [Mountain]	sNañ.Yul.
Nu Yin	gNod.sByin.
Nya	gÑah.
Nya Chen Yor Mo	Ña.Chen.Yor.Mo.
Nyal	gÑal.
Nyan Chung Repa	gÑan.Chuñ.Ras.Pa.
Nyang [Upper]	Myañ.sTod.
Nyan Jue	sÑan.brGyud.
Nya Non	gÑah.Nañ.
Nya Non Tsar Ma	gÑah.Nañ.rTsar.Mar.
Nyantsa Karjan	Myañ.Tsha.dKar.rGyan.
Nyan Yuan [Cave]	sÑan.gYon.

Nyi Shang	sÑi.Çañs.
Nyi Shang Gur Da	sÑi.Çañs.Gur.rTa.
Nyi Shang Ka Daya	sÑi.Çabs.Ka.Taya.
Nyi Tong	Ñi.mThoñs.
Nyi Wa	sÑi.Wa.
Nyurumpa	sÑug.Rum.Pa.
Og Men	Ḥog.Min.
Oujen [Pure Land of]	Ao.rGyan.
Padru	Pha.Drug.
Pagmo	Phag.Mo.
Pakshu	Pakçu.
Pan [region]	hPhan.Yul.
Pat Ma Tod Tchin [Padma Saṃbhava]	Pat.Ma.Thod.Phreñ.
Paugba Wadi	hPhags.Pa.Wa.Ti.
Phuyagzha	Phu.Yag.Za.
[Queen of the Azure Height]	mThon.mThiñ.rGyal.Mo.
Radun Dharma Lhodre	Ra.sTon.Dar.Ma.Blo.Gros.
Ragma	Rag.Ma.
Ra La [Goat Hill]	Ra.La.
Ramdin Nampu	Ram.sDiñs.gNam.Phug.
Rechin [Meditation Cave]	sGrub.Phug.Ras.Chen.
Rechung Dor Draug Shawa	Ras.Chuñ.rDo.Grags.Bya.Ba.
Rechung Dorje Draugpa	Ras.Chuñ.rDo.rJe.Grags.Pa.
Regba Dhujen	Reg.Pa.Dug.Can.
Riga Daya [Cave]	Ri.Ka.Taya.Phug.
Rig Ma	Rig.Ma.
Rin Chin Drag	Rin.Chen.Grags.
Riwo Balnbar	Ri.Wo.dPal.hBar.
Roma	Ro.Ma.
Ron Chon Repa	Roñ.Chuñ.Ras.Pa.
Rondunlaga	Roñ.sTon.lHa.dGah.
Runpu	Ron.Phug.
Sahle Aui	Sa.Le.Ḥod.
Sajya [Monstery]	Sa.sKyar.
Samye [Temple]	bSam.Yas.
San Chia Yogi	San.Ca.Dso.Ki.
Sangdan Dranma	bSam.gDan.sGron.Ma.
Sangje Jhap	Sañs.rGyas.sKyabs.
Seba [Valley]	Se.Pa.Luñ.
Semodo	Se.Mo.Do.
Sendentsema	Señ.lDeñ.Tsher.Ma.
Sen Ding	Señ.lDeñ.
Sevan Dunchon Shawa	Se.Wan.sTon.Chuñ.Bya.Wa.
Sevan Jashi	Se.Wan.bKra.Çis.
Sevan Jashi Bar	Se.Wan.bKra.Çis.hBar.
Sevan Repa	Se.Wan.Ras.Pa.
Seyi Lhamo	bSehi.Lha.Mo.
Shadulwa Tsinpa	Bya.hDul.Wa.hDsin.Pa.

Shajaguna	Çakya.Gu.Na.
Shambo	Çam.Po.
Shamboche	Phyam.Po.Che.
Shangchub Bar	Byañ.Chub.hBar.
Shangon Repa	gÇen.bsGom.Ras.Pa.
Shapa Linpa	Ça.Pa.gLiñ.Pa.
Shar Bo	Byar.Po.
Shar Mo	Byar.Mo.
Sha Yul [region]	Bya.Yul.
Shin Dre	gÇin.hDre.
Shen Gom Repa	gÇen.bsGom.Ras.Pa.
Sherpug Chushin Dson	Çer.Phug.Chu.Çiñ.rDsoñ.
Shilabharo [of Nepal]	Çi.La.Bha.Ro., Bal.Po.
Shindormo	gÇen.rDor.Mo.
Shiwa Aui	Shi.Wa.Ḥod.
Shri Ri	Çri.Ri.
Shumo Semodo	Phyug.Mo.Se.Mo.Do.
Shun Chub Jarbo	Byañ.Chub.rGyal.Po.
Sidpa Bardo	Srid.Pa.Bar.Do.
Singalin	Siñ.Ga.Gliñ.
Sinhala	Señ.Ha.La.
Srinmo	Srin.Mo.
Sudnam Rinchin	bSod.Nams.Rin.Chen.
Sungdue	gSañ.hDus.
Sungwa Nyinbo	gSañ.Wa.sÑiñ.Po.
Sungwong Dueba	gSañ.Wa.hDus.Pa.
Tantra [of the Wrathful and Peaceful Buddhas]	Shi.Khrohi.rGyud.
Tārā [Drol Ma]	sGrol.Ma.
Ta Zig	rTa.Zig.
Tig Le	Thig.Le.
Tingeyalzunma	mThiñ.Gi.Shal.bZañ.Ma.
Tong Lha	Thoñ.La.
Tsamlin	hDsam.gLiñ.
Tsang	gTsañ.
Tsanbudrisha	hDsam.Bu.Tri.Ça.
Tsan Rigs	bTsan.Rigs.
Tsapu Repa	rTsa.Phu.Ras.Pa.
Tsar Ma	rTsar.Ma.
Tsem Chin Guru [of] La Dud	Tshems.Chen.Gu.Ru., La.sTod.
Tserinma	Tse.Riñ.Ma.
Tsese	mDses.Se.
Tsiba Gonti Tson	rTsig.Pa.rKoñ.mThil.rDsoñ
Tsiwo Repa	rDsi.Wo.Ras.Pa.
Tsomanma	mTso.sMan.Ma.
Tsonlung [Cave]	mTshoñ.Luñ.Brag.
Tsudor Namjhal	gTsug.Tor.rNam.rGyal.
Tubhaga	Thos.Pa.dGah.
Tuntin	mThon.mThiñ.
Wadi	Wa.Ti.

Wa Jal	Wa.rGyal.
Wala Tsandra	Wa.La.Tsandra.
Weu	dWus.
Weu [and] Tsang	dWus., gTsañ
Wurmo	Hur.Mo.
Wutso Gabar Jalbo	dWu.gTso.dGah.hBar.rGyal.Po.
Yagder	gYag.sDer.
Yagru	gYag.Ru.
Yang Nge	gYeñ.Ñe.
Yaugru Tangbha	gYag.Ru.Thañ.Pa.
Yei Ru Jang	gYas.Ru.Byañ.
Ye Rang [and] Ko Kom [King of]	Ye.Rañ., Kho.Khom.
Ye Shin Dsu Pud	Ye.gÇen.gTsug.Phud.
Yidagmo	gShi.bDag.Mo.
Yidham	Yi.Dam.
Yolmo	Yol.Mo.
Yaugra Tangbha	gYag.Ru.Thañ.Pa.
Yundun	gYuñ.sTon.
Yunlaza	Yañ.La.Za.
Yuru Kradrag	gYu.Ru.Khra.hBrug.
Zhaoo	Za.Hog.
Zung Ghar [Tradition]	Zañs.dKar.Lugs.

*The word-ending "ang" should be pronounced as "äng" throughout.
**"Tang" should be pronounced as "Ton," or "Täng."

INDEX

INDEX